Library of America, a nonprofit organization, champions our nation's cultural heritage by publishing America's greatest writing in authoritative new editions and providing resources for readers to explore this rich, living legacy.

JOAN DIDION

Joan Didion

MEMOIRS & LATER WRITINGS

Political Fictions
Fixed Ideas
Where I Was From
The Year of Magical Thinking
The Year of Magical Thinking: The Play
Blue Nights
South and West

David L. Ulin, *editor*

THE LIBRARY OF AMERICA

Published in the United States by Library of America.
Visit our website at www.loa.org.

This paper exceeds the requirements of
ANSI/NISO Z39.48–1992 (Permanence of Paper).

Distributed to the trade in the United States
by Penguin Random House Inc.
and in Canada by Penguin Random House Canada Ltd.

Library of Congress Control Number: 2024930267
ISBN 978–1–59853–787–1

First Printing
The Library of America—386

Manufactured in the United States of America

Joan Didion: Memoirs & Later Writings
is published with support from

THE FRAN & RAY STARK FOUNDATION

Contents

JOAN DIDION

POLITICAL FICTIONS

This book is for Robert Silvers.
It is also for John Gregory Dunne, who lived through my discovering what he already knew.

A Foreword

EARLY IN 1988, Robert Silvers of *The New York Review of Books* asked me if I would do some pieces or a piece about the presidential campaign just then getting underway in New Hampshire. He would arrange credentials. All I had to do was show up, see what there was to see, and write something. I was flattered (a presidential election was a "serious" story, and no one had before solicited my opinions on one), and yet I kept putting off the only essential moment, which was showing up, giving the thing the required focus. In January and February I was selling a house in California, an easy excuse. In March and April I was buying an apartment in New York, another easy excuse. I had packing to do, then unpacking, painting to arrange, many household negotiations and renegotiations. Clippings and books and campaign schedules kept arriving, and I would stack them on shelves unread. I kept getting new deadlines from *The New York Review*, but there remained about domestic politics something resistant, recondite, some occult irreconcilability that kept all news of it just below my attention level. The events of the campaign as reported seemed to have taken place in a language I did not recognize. The stakes of the election as presented seemed not to compute. At the very point when I had in my mind successfully abandoned this project to which I could clearly bring no access, no knowledge, no understanding, I got another, more urgent call from *The New York Review*. The California primary was only days away. The Democratic and Republican national conventions were only weeks away. The office could put me on a campaign charter the next day, Jesse Jackson was flying out of Newark to California, the office could connect me in Los Angeles with the other campaigns. It so happened that my husband was leaving that day to do some research in Ireland. It so happened that our daughter was leaving that day to spend the summer in Guatemala and Nicaragua. There seemed, finally, no real excuse for me not to watch the California primary (and even to vote in it, since I was still registered in Los Angeles County), and so I went to Newark, and got on the plane. From the notes I typed at three the next morning in a room at the Hyatt Wilshire in Los Angeles, after a rally in South Central and a fundraiser at the Hollywood Palace and a meet-and-greet at the housing project where the candidate was to spend what remained of the night ("Would you call this Watts," the reporters kept saying, and "Who knows about guns? Who makes an AK?"), my introduction to American politics:

> I was told the campaign would be leaving Newark at 11:30 and to be at the Butler Aviation terminal no later than 10:30. Delmarie Cobb was to be the contact. At Butler Aviation the man on the gate knew nothing about the Jackson campaign but agreed to make a phone call, and was told to send me to Hangar 14. Hangar 14, a United hangar, was locked up except for a corrugated fire door open about two feet off the ground. Some men who approached knew nothing about any Jackson plane, they were "just telephone," but they limboed under the fire door and I followed them.
>
> The empty hangar. I walked around Malcolm Forbes's green 727, "Capitalist Tool," looked around the tarmac, and found no one. Finally a mechanic walked through and told me to try the office upstairs. I did. The metal door to the stairs was locked. I ran after the mechanic. He said he would pick the lock for me, and did. Upstairs, I found someone who told me to go to "Post J."
>
> At "Post J," an unmarked gate to the tarmac, I found a van open in back and four young men waiting. They said they were Jackson campaign, they were waiting for the Secret Service and then the traveling campaign. I sat down on my bag and asked them to point out Delmarie Cobb when she came. Delmarie, one of them said, was already in California, but he was Delmarie's nephew, Stephen Gaines.
>
> "Who's she," the Secret Service agents kept saying after they arrived. "She hasn't been cleared by the campaign, what's she doing here." "All I know is, she's got the right names in Chicago," Stephen Gaines kept saying. In any case the agents were absorbed in sweeping the bags. Finally one said he might as well sweep mine. Once he had done this he seemed confused. It seemed he had no place to put me. I wasn't supposed to be on

the tarmac with the swept bags, but I wasn't supposed to be on the plane either. "Look," he said finally. "Just wait on the plane."

I waited, alone on the plane. Periodically an agent appeared and said, "You aren't supposed to be here, see, if there were someplace else to put you we'd put you there." The pilot appeared from the cockpit. "Give me a guesstimate how many people are flying," he said to me. I said I had no idea. "Fifty-five?" the pilot said. I shrugged. "Let's say fifty-five," the pilot said, "and get the fuel guys off the hook." None of this seemed promising.

The piece I finally did on the 1988 campaign, "Insider Baseball," was the first of a number of pieces I eventually did about various aspects of American politics, most of which had to do, I came to realize, with the ways in which the political process did not reflect but increasingly proceeded from a series of fables about American experience. As the pieces began to accumulate, I was asked with somewhat puzzling frequency about my own politics, what they "were," or "where they came from," as if they were eccentric, opaque, somehow unreadable. They are not. They are the logical product of a childhood largely spent among conservative California Republicans (this was before the meaning of "conservative" changed) in a postwar boom economy. The people with whom I grew up were interested in low taxes, a balanced budget, and a limited government. They believed above all that a limited government had no business tinkering with the private or cultural life of its citizens. In 1964, in accord with these interests and beliefs, I voted, ardently, for Barry Goldwater. Had Goldwater remained the same age and continued running, I would have voted for him in every election thereafter. Instead, shocked and to a curious extent personally offended by the enthusiasm with which California Republicans who had jettisoned an authentic conservative (Goldwater) were rushing to embrace Ronald Reagan, I registered as a Democrat, the first member of my family (and perhaps in my generation still the only member) to do so. That this did not involve taking a markedly different view on any issue was a novel discovery, and one that led me to view "America's two-party system" with—and this was my real introduction to American politics—a somewhat doubtful eye.

At a point quite soon during the dozen-some years that followed getting on that charter at Newark, it came to my attention that there was to writing about politics a certain Sisyphean aspect. Broad patterns could be defined, specific inconsistencies documented, but no amount of definition or documentation seemed sufficient to stop the stone that was our apprehension of politics from hurtling back downhill. The romance of New Hampshire would again be with us. The crucible event in the candidate's "character" would again be explored. Even that which seemed ineluctably clear would again vanish from collective memory, sink traceless into the stream of collapsing news and comment cycles that had become our national River Lethe. It was clear for example in 1988 that the political process had already become perilously remote from the electorate it was meant to represent. It was also clear in 1988 that the decision of the two major parties to obscure any possible perceived distinction between themselves, and by so doing to narrow the contested ground to a handful of selected "target" voters, had already imposed considerable strain on the basic principle of the democratic exercise, that of assuring the nation's citizens a voice in its affairs. It was also clear in 1988 that the rhetorical manipulation of resentment and anger designed to attract these target voters had reduced the nation's political dialogue to a level so dispiritingly low that its highest expression had come to be a pernicious nostalgia. Perhaps most strikingly of all, it was clear in 1988 that those inside the process had congealed into a permanent political class, the defining characteristic of which was its readiness to abandon those not inside the process. All of this was known. Yet by the time of the November 2000 presidential election and the onset of the thirty-six days that came to be known as "Florida," every aspect of what had been known in 1988 would again need to be rediscovered, the stone pushed up the hill one more time.

Perhaps the most persistent of the fables from which the political process proceeds has to do with the "choice" it affords the nation's citizens, who are seen to remain unappreciative. On the Saturday morning before the November 2000 presidential election, *The Washington Post* ran on its front page a piece by Richard Morin and Claudia Deane headlined "As Turnout Falls, Apathy Emerges As Driving Force." The thrust of this piece, which was based on polls of voter and nonvoter attitudes conducted both by the *Post* and by the Joan Shorenstein Center's "Vanishing Voter Project" at Harvard, was reinforced by a takeout about a Missouri citizen named Mike McClusky, a thirty-seven-year-old Army veteran who, despite "the 21-foot flagpole with the Stars and Stripes in the middle of the front yard," had never voted and did not now intend to vote. His wife, Danielle McClusky, did vote, and the *Post* noted the readiness with which she discussed "her take on Social Security, and health care, and health maintenance organizations, and what she heard on Larry King, and what she heard on Chris Matthews, and what George W. Bush would do, and what Al Gore would do." Meanwhile, the *Post* added, making it fairly clear which McClusky merited the approval of its Washington readers, "Mike McClusky pets the dogs and half-listens because he doesn't really have to sift through any of this." Accompanying the main story were graphs, purporting to show why Americans did not vote, and the *Post*'s analysis of its own graphs was this: "Apathy is the single biggest reason why an estimated 100 million Americans will not vote on Tuesday."

The graphs themselves, however, told a somewhat more complicated story: only thirty-five percent of nonvoters, or about seventeen percent of all adult Americans, fell into the "apathetic" category, which, according to a director of the Shorenstein study, included those who "have no sense of civic duty," "aren't interested in politics," and "have no commitment in keeping up with public affairs." Another fourteen percent of nonvoters were classified as "disconnected," a group including both those "who can't get to the polls because of advanced age or disability" and those "who recently changed addresses and are not yet registered"—in other words, people functionally unable to vote. The remaining fifty-one percent of these nonvoters, meaning roughly a quarter of all adult Americans, were classified as either "alienated" ("the angry men and women of U.S. politics . . . so disgusted with politicians and the political process that they've opted out") or "disenchanted" ("these nonvoters aren't so much repelled by politics as they are by the way politics is practiced"), in either case pretty much the polar opposite of "apathetic." According to the graphs, more than seventy percent of all nonvoters were in fact registered, a figure that cast some ambiguity on the degree of "apathy" even among the thirty-five percent categorized as "apathetic."

Study of the actual Shorenstein results clouded the *Post*'s "apathy" assessment still further. According to the Shorenstein Center's release dated the same Saturday as the *Post* story, its polling had shown that the attitudes toward politicians and the political process held by those who intended to vote differed—up to an interesting point—only narrowly from the attitudes held by those who did not intend to vote. Eighty-nine percent of nonvoters and seventy-six percent of voters agreed with the statement "most political candidates will say almost anything in order to get themselves elected." Seventy-eight percent of nonvoters and seventy percent of voters agreed with the statement "candidates are more concerned with fighting each other than with solving the nation's problems." Almost seventy percent of nonvoters and voters alike agreed with the statement "campaigns seem more like theater or entertainment than something to be taken seriously." The interesting point at which the attitudes of voters and nonvoters did diverge was that revealed by questioning about specific policies. Voters, for example, tended to believe that the federal budget surplus should go to a tax cut. Nonvoters, who on the whole had less education and lower income, more often said that the surplus should be spent on health, welfare, and education. "Nonvoters have different needs," is the way the *Post* summarized this. "But why should politicians listen?"

This notion of voting as a consumer transaction (the voter "pays" with his or her vote to obtain the ear of his or her professional politician, or his or her "leader," or by logical extension his or her "superior") might seem a spiritless social contract, although not—if it actually delivered on the deal—an intrinsically unworkable one. But of course the contract does not deliver: only sentimentally does "the vote" give "the voter" an empathetic listener in the political class, let alone any leverage on the workings of that class. When the chairman of Michael Dukakis's 1988 New York Finance Council stood barefoot on a table at the Atlanta Hyatt during that summer's Democratic convention (see page 33) and said "I've been around this process a while and one thing I've noticed, it's the people who write the checks who get treated as if they have a certain amount of power," she had a clear enough understanding of how the contract worked and did not work. When the only prominent Democrat on the west side of Los Angeles to raise money in 1988 for Jesse Jackson (see page 38) said "When I want something, I'll have a hard time getting people to pick up the phone, I recognize that, I made the choice," he had a clear enough understanding of how the contract worked and did not work.

When the same Democrat, Stanley Sheinbaum, said, in 1992 (see page 101), "I mean it's no longer a thousand dollars, to get into the act now you've got to give a hundred thousand," he had a clear enough understanding of how the contract worked and did not work. When Jerry Brown, who after eight years as governor of California had become the state party chairman who significantly raised the bar for Democratic fundraising in California, said at the 1992 Democratic convention in Madison Square Garden (see page 80) that the time had arrived to listen to "the people who fight our wars but never come to our receptions," he had a clear enough understanding of how the contract worked and did not work. When one of George W. Bush's lawyers told *The Los Angeles Times* in December 2000 that "if you were in this game, you had to be in Florida," he too had a clear enough understanding of how the contract worked and did not work. "Almost every lobbyist, political organizer, consulting group with ties to the Republicans was represented," a Republican official was quoted by Robert B. Reich, writing on the op-ed page of *The New York Times*, as having said to the same point. "If you ever were or wanted to be a Republican, you were down there."

Such clear understandings among the professionals of both major parties notwithstanding, the fact that the 2000 presidential election in Florida could come down to only a handful of votes would still be popularly presented as evidence that "every vote counts," conclusive proof of the absolute power of the American voter. "Whatever else one might conclude about the events of the past two weeks, they have awakened young people to election politics, to the daily news, and to the importance of the vote," a director of the Vanishing Voter project rather mysteriously concluded from data showing that although the attention level of younger respondents rose during the events in Florida, seventy percent of all Americans, young and old, reported themselves to be "discouraged" by those events and fifty percent to believe that the election had been "unfair to voters." Two weeks after the election, according to the Shorenstein Center's comparison of polling conducted just before the election and that conducted in its immediate aftermath, the number of Americans who answered "None" to the question "How much influence do you think people like you have on what the government does?" had increased from one in ten to one in four.

This "civics lesson" aspect of the thirty-six days that followed the election was much stressed, yet what those days actually demonstrated, from the morning on Day One when the candidate whose brother happened to be governor of Florida lined up the critical Tallahassee law firms until the evening on Day Thirty-five when the Supreme Court decided *Bush v. Gore* for the same candidate, was the immateriality of the voter against the raw power of being inside the process. "The Republicans didn't have to hire the big firms, or tie them up," a Gore strategist told *The Washington Post* about what happened on the morning of Day One. "Jeb Bush didn't need to send a note for them to know." About what happened on the evening of Day Thirty-five, Cokie Roberts, on *This Week*, made the case of the permanent political class for order, for continuity, for the perpetuation of the contract that delivered only to itself: "I think people do think it's political but they think that's okay. They expect the court to be political and—and they wanted this election to be over." In the absence of actual evidence to back up this arrestingly constructive reading of what "people" expected or wanted, she offered the rationale then common among those inside the process: "At least now, we are beginning to have that post-election coming together. Period."

The events that followed the November 2000 election were widely interpreted by those inside the process as aberrant, a source of outrage or education (the civics-lesson benefit again) but in any case an improbable random sequence thrown up by chance, in no way predictable and therefore dangerous: a "disaster," a "debacle," a disruption that could lead, in the absence of "closure," or of "that post-election coming together" longed for by Mrs. Roberts and by many others, only to "chaos." Yet the events in question were in many ways not only entirely predictable but entirely familiar: the reactive angers that drove this post-election period were not different in kind from the reactive angers that had driven American politics since the 1960s. Now as before, "the rule of law" was repeatedly invoked, although how a matter as demonstrably lawyered up as the Florida recount could be seen to threaten the rule of law was unclear. Now as before, the principal threat to "the rule of law" was construed to be the court system, which Robert H. Bork had described in *Slouching Towards Gomorrah* as the "enforcement arm" of what he called "the 'intellectual' class," the branch of government "responsible in no small measure for the spread of both radical individualism and radical egalitarianism." Now as before, the prevailing tone, on all sides, was self-righteous, victimized, grandiose; a quite florid instance of what Richard Hofstadter had identified in 1965 as the paranoid style in American politics.

This was all familiar, but the events that followed the 2000 presidential election represented something more than another airing of popular resentments to advance one or another element within the political process. The Democrats had lost that election, according to Al From of the Democratic Leadership Council, because their candidate's "populist" message had failed to resonate with the Democratic target voter, who was "affluent, educated, diverse, suburban, 'wired,' and moderate." That the same adjectives described the Republican target voter was, according to Mr. From, the point itself: the "true story" of the 2000 campaign was that the Republican and Democratic parties had at last achieved "parity," which meant that they were now positioned to split the remaining electorate, those "middle- and upper-middle-class Americans" who would be "the dominant voters of the Information Age." In other words we had reached the zero-sum point toward which the process had been moving, the moment in which the determination of the Republican Party to maximize its traditional low-turnout advantage was perfectly matched by the determination of the Democratic Party to shed any association with its traditional low-income base. "Who cares what every adult thinks," as one Republican strategist had presciently said to *The Washington Post* (see page 163) in 1998. "It's totally not germane to this election."

"Florida," in this light, could be seen as a perfectly legible ideogram of the process itself, and of where that process had taken us: the reduction of a national presidential election to a few hundred voters over which both parties could fight for thirty-six days was the logical imaginative representation of a process that had relentlessly worked, to the end of eliminating known risk factors, to restrict the contest to the smallest possible electorate. Fifty-three percent of voters in the 2000 election, Mr. From noted with what seemed genuine enthusiasm, had ("for the first time in our history") incomes above $50,000. Forty-three percent were suburban. Seventy-four percent had some higher education; forty-two percent had actual college degrees. Seventy percent said that they invested in the stock market. That this was not a demographic profile of the country at large, that half the nation's citizens had only a vassal relationship to the government under which they lived, that the democracy we spoke of spreading throughout the world was now in our own country only an ideality, had come to be seen, against the higher priority of keeping the process in the hands of those who already held it, as facts without application.

Insider Baseball

October 27, 1988

IT OCCURRED TO ME during the summer of 1988, in California and Atlanta and New Orleans, in the course of watching first the California primary and then the Democratic and Republican national conventions, that it had not been by accident that the people with whom I had preferred to spend time in high school had, on the whole, hung out in gas stations. They had not run for student body office. They had not gone to Yale or Swarthmore or DePauw, nor had they even applied. They had gotten drafted, gone through basic at Fort Ord. They had knocked up girls, and married them, had begun what they called the first night of the rest of their lives with a midnight drive to Carson City and a five-dollar ceremony performed by a justice of the peace still in his pajamas. They got jobs at the places that had laid off their uncles. They paid their bills or did not pay their bills, made down payments on tract houses, led lives on that social and economic edge referred to, in Washington and among those whose preferred locus is Washington, as "out there." They were never destined to be, in other words, communicants in what we have come to call, when we want to indicate the traditional ways in which power is exchanged and the status quo maintained in the United States, "the process."

"The process today gives everyone a chance to participate," Tom Hayden, by way of explaining "the difference" between 1968 and 1988, said to Bryant Gumbel on NBC at 7:50 A.M. on the day after Jesse Jackson spoke at the 1988 Democratic convention in Atlanta. This was, at a convention that had as its controlling principle the notably nonparticipatory goal of "unity," demonstrably not true, but people inside the process, constituting as they do a self-created and self-referring class, a new kind of managerial elite, tend to speak of the world not necessarily as it is but as they want people out there to believe it is. They tend to prefer the theoretical to the observable, and to dismiss that which might be learned empirically as "anecdotal."

They tend to speak a language common in Washington but not specifically shared by the rest of us. They talk about "programs," and "policy," and how to "implement" them or it, about "tradeoffs" and constituencies and positioning the candidate and distancing the candidate, about the "story," and how it will "play."

They speak of a candidate's "performance," by which they usually mean his skill at circumventing questions, not as citizens but as professional insiders, attuned to signals pitched beyond the range of normal hearing. "I hear he did all right this afternoon," they were saying to one another in the press section of the Louisiana Superdome in New Orleans on the evening in August 1988 when Dan Quayle was to be nominated for the vice presidency. "I hear he did all right with Brinkley." By the time the balloons fell that night the narrative had changed: "Quayle, zip," the professionals were saying as they brushed the confetti off their laptops. These were people who spoke of the process as an end in itself, connected only nominally, and vestigially, to the electorate and its possible concerns. "She used to be an issues person but now she's involved in the process," a prominent conservative said to me in New Orleans by way of suggesting why an acquaintance who believed Jack Kemp to be "speaking directly to what people out there want" had nonetheless backed George Bush. "Anything that brings the process closer to the people is all to the good," George Bush had declared in his 1987 autobiography, *Looking Forward*, accepting as given this relatively recent notion that the people and the process need not automatically be on convergent tracks.

When we talk about the process, then, we are talking, increasingly, not about "the democratic process," or the general mechanism affording the citizens of a state a voice in its affairs, but the reverse: a mechanism seen as so specialized that access to it is correctly limited to its own professionals, to those who manage policy and those who report on it, to those who run the polls and those who quote them, to those who ask and those who answer the questions on the Sunday shows, to the media consultants, to the columnists, to the issues advisers, to those who give the off-the-record breakfasts and those who attend them; to that handful of insiders who invent, year in and year out, the narrative of public life. "I didn't realize you were a political junkie," Martin Kaplan, the former *Washington Post* reporter and Mondale speechwriter who was married to Susan Estrich, the manager of the Dukakis campaign, said when I mentioned that I planned to write about the campaign; the assumption here, that the narrative should be not just written only by its own specialists but also legible only to its own specialists, is why, finally, an American presidential campaign raises questions that go so vertiginously to the heart of the structure.

2.

What strikes one most vividly about such a campaign is precisely its remoteness from the real life of the country. The figures are well known, and suggest a national indifference usually construed, by those inside the process, as ignorance, or "apathy," in any case a defect not in themselves but in the clay they have been given to mold. Only slightly more than half of those eligible to vote in the United States did vote in the 1984 presidential election. An average 18.5 percent of what Nielsen Media Research calls the "television households" in the United States tuned into network coverage of the 1988 Republican convention in New Orleans, meaning that 81.5 percent did not. An average 20.2 percent of those "television households" tuned into network coverage of the 1988 Democratic convention in Atlanta, meaning that 79.8 percent did not. The decision to tune in or out ran along predictable lines: "The demography is good even if the households are low," a programming executive at Bozell, Jacobs, Kenyon & Eckhardt told *The New York Times* in July 1988 about the agency's decision to buy "campaign event" time for Merrill Lynch on both CBS and CNN. "The ratings are about nine percent off 1984," an NBC marketing executive allowed, again to *The New York Times*, "but the upscale target audience is there."

When I read this piece I recalled standing, the day before the 1988 California primary, in a dusty central California schoolyard to which the leading Democratic candidate had come to speak one more time about what kind of president he wanted to be.

The crowd was listless, restless. There were gray thunderclouds overhead. A little rain fell. "We welcome you to Silicon Valley," an official had said by way of greeting the candidate, but this was not in fact Silicon Valley: this was San Jose, and a part of San Jose particularly untouched by technological prosperity, a neighborhood in which the lowering of two-toned Impalas remained a central activity. "I want to be a candidate who brings people together," the candidate was saying at the exact moment a man began shouldering his way past me and through a group of women with children in their arms. This was not a solid citizen, not a member of the upscale target audience. This was a man wearing a down vest and a camouflage hat, a man with a definite little glitter in his eyes, a member not of the 18.5 percent and not of the 20.2 percent but of the 81.5 percent, the 79.8. "I've got to see the next president," he muttered repeatedly. "I've got something to tell him."

". . . Because that's what this party is all about," the candidate said.

"Where is he?" the man said, confused. "Who is he?"

"Get lost," someone said.

". . . Because that's what this country is all about," the candidate said.

Here we had the last true conflict of cultures in America, that between the empirical and the theoretical. On the empirical evidence this country was about two-toned Impalas and people with camouflage hats and a little glitter in their eyes, but this had not been, among people inclined to the theoretical, the preferred assessment. Nor had it even been, despite the fact that we had all stood together on the same dusty asphalt, under the same plane trees, the general assessment: this was how Joe Klein, writing a few weeks later in *New York* magazine, had described those last days before the California primary:

> Breezing across California on his way to the nomination last week, Michael Dukakis crossed a curious American threshold. . . . The crowds were larger, more excited now; they seemed to be searching for reasons to love him. They cheered eagerly, almost without provocation. People reached out to touch him—not to shake hands, just to touch him. . . . Dukakis seemed to be making an almost subliminal passage in the public mind: he was becoming presidential.

Those June days in 1988 during which Michael Dukakis did or did not cross a curious American threshold had in fact been instructive. The day that ended in the schoolyard in San Jose had at first seemed, given that it was the day before the California primary, underscheduled, pointless, three essentially meaningless events separated by plane flights. At Taft High School in Woodland Hills that morning there had been little girls waving red and gold pom-poms in front of the cameras. "Hold that tiger," the band had played. "Dream . . . maker," the choir had crooned. "Governor Dukakis . . . this is . . . Taft High," the student body president had said. "I understand that this is the first time a presidential candidate has come to Taft High," Governor Dukakis had said. "Is there any doubt . . . under those circumstances . . . who you should support?"

"Jackson," a group of Chicano boys on the back sidewalk shouted in unison.

"That's what it's all about," Governor Dukakis had said, and "health care," and "good teachers and good teaching."

This event had been abandoned, and another materialized: a lunchtime "rally" in a downtown San Diego office plaza through which many people were passing on their way to lunch, a borrowed crowd but a less than attentive one. The cameras focused on the balloons. The sound techs picked up "La Bamba." "We're going to take child-support enforcement seriously in this country," Governor Dukakis had said, and "tough drug enforcement here and abroad." "Tough choices," he had said, and "we're going to make teaching a valued profession in this country."

Nothing said in any venue that day had seemed to have much connection with anybody listening ("I want to work with you and with working people all over this country," the candidate had said in the downtown San Diego office plaza, but people who work in offices in downtown San Diego do not think of themselves as "working people"), and late that afternoon, on the bus to the San Jose airport, I had asked a reporter who had traveled through the spring with the various campaigns (among those who moved from plane to plane it was agreed, by June, that the Bush plane had the worst access to the candidate and the best food, that the Dukakis plane had average access and average food, and that the Jackson plane had full access and no time to eat) if the candidate's appearances that day did not seem a little off the point.

"Not really," the reporter said. "He covered three major markets."

Among those who traveled regularly with the campaigns, in other words, it was taken for granted that these "events" they were covering, and on which they were in fact filing, were not merely meaningless but deliberately so: occasions in which film could be shot and no mistakes made ("They hope he won't make any mistakes," the NBC correspondent covering George Bush kept saying the evening of the September 25, 1988, debate at Wake Forest College, and, an hour and a half later, "He didn't make any big mistakes"), events designed only to provide settings for those unpaid television spots which in this case were appearing, even as we spoke, on the local news in California's three major media markets. "On the fishing trip, there was no way for the television crews to get videotapes out," *The Los Angeles Times* noted a few weeks later in a piece about how "poorly designed and executed events" had interfered with coverage of a Bush campaign "environmental" swing through the Pacific Northwest. "At the lumber mill, Bush's advance team arranged camera angles so poorly that in one setup only his legs could get on camera." A Bush adviser had been quoted: "There is no reason for camera angles not being provided for. We're going to sit down and talk about these things at length."

Any traveling campaign, then, was a set, moved at considerable expense from location to location. The employer of each reporter on the Dukakis plane the day before the California primary was billed, for a total flying time of under three hours, $1,129.51; the billing to each reporter who happened, on the morning during the Democratic convention in Atlanta when Michael Dukakis and Lloyd Bentsen met with Jesse Jackson, to ride along on the Dukakis bus from the Hyatt Regency to the World Congress Center, a distance of perhaps ten blocks, was $217.18. There was the hierarchy of the set: there were actors, there were directors, there were script supervisors, there were grips. There was the isolation of the set, and the arrogance, the contempt for outsiders. I recall pink-cheeked young aides on the Dukakis campaign referring to themselves, innocent of irony and so of history, as "the best and the brightest." On the morning after the Wake Forest debate, Michael Oreskes of *The New York Times* gave us this memorable account of Bush aides crossing the Wake Forest campus:

> The Bush campaign measured exactly how long it would take its spokesmen to walk briskly from the room in which they were watching the debate to the center where reporters were filing their articles. The answer was three and a half minutes—too long for Mr. Bush's strategists, Lee Atwater, Robert Teeter, and Mr. Darman. They ran the course instead as young aides cleared students and other onlookers from their path.

There was also the tedium of the set: the time spent waiting for the shots to be set up, the time spent waiting for the bus to join the motorcade, the time spent waiting for telephones on which to file, the time spent waiting for the Secret Service ("the agents," they were called on the traveling campaigns, never the Secret Service, just "the agents," or "this detail," or "this rotation") to sweep the plane. It was a routine that encouraged a certain passivity. There was the plane, or the bus, and one got on it. There was the schedule, and one followed it. There was time to file, or there was not. "We should have had a page-one story," a *Boston Globe* reporter complained to *The Los Angeles Times* after the Bush campaign had failed to provide the advance text of a Seattle "environment" speech scheduled to end only twenty minutes before the departure of the plane for California. "There are times when you sit up and moan, 'Where is Michael Deaver when you need him,'" an ABC producer said to the *Times* on this point.

A final victory, for the staff and the press on a traveling campaign, would mean not a new production but only a new location: the particular setups and shots of the campaign day (the walk on the beach, the meet-and-greet at the housing project) would dissolve imperceptibly, isolation and arrogance and tedium intact, into the South Lawns, the Oval Office signings, the arrivals and departures of the administration day. There would still be the "young aides." There would still be the "onlookers" to be cleared from the path. Another location, another stand-up: "We already shot a tarmac departure," they say on the campaign planes. "This schedule has two Rose Gardens," they say in the White House press room. Ronald Reagan, when asked by David Frost how his life in the Oval Office had differed from his expectation of it, said this: "I was surprised at how familiar the whole routine was—the fact that the night before I would get a schedule telling me what I'm going to do all day the next day and so forth."

3.

American reporters "like" covering a presidential campaign (it gets them out on the road, it has balloons, it has music, it is viewed as a big story, one that leads to the respect of one's peers, to the Sunday shows, to lecture fees and often to Washington), which is why there has developed among those who do it so arresting an enthusiasm for overlooking the contradictions inherent in reporting that which occurs only in order to be reported. They are willing, in exchange for "access," to transmit the images their sources wish transmitted. They are even willing, in exchange for certain colorful details around which a "reconstruction" can be built (the "kitchen table" at which the Dukakis campaign was said to have conferred on the night Lloyd Bentsen was added to the 1988 Democratic ticket, the "slips of paper" on which key members of the 1988 Bush campaign, aboard Air Force Two on their way to the Republican convention in New Orleans, were said to have written their choices for vice president), to present these images not as a story the campaign wants told but as fact. This was *Time*, reporting from New Orleans on George Bush's reaction to criticism of Dan Quayle, his chosen running mate:

> Bush never wavered in support of the man he had lifted so high. "How's Danny doing," he asked several times. But the Vice President never felt the compulsion to question Quayle face-to-face. The awkward interrogation was left to Baker. Around noon, Quayle grew restive about answering further questions. "Let's go," he urged, but Baker pressed to know more. By early afternoon, the mood began to brighten in the Bush bunker. There were no new revelations: the media hurricane had for the moment blown over.

"Appeal to the media by exposing the [Bush campaign's] heavy-handed spin-doctoring," William Safire advised the Dukakis campaign. "We hate to be seen being manipulated." This was Sandy Grady, reporting from Atlanta and the Dukakis campaign:

> Ten minutes before he was to face the biggest audience of his life, Michael Dukakis got a hug from his 84-year-old mother, Euterpe, who chided him, "You'd better be good, Michael." Dukakis grinned and said, "I'll do my best, Ma."

"Periodically," *The New York Times* reported in March 1988, "Martin Plissner, the political editor of CBS News, and Susan Morrison, a television producer and former political aide, organize gatherings of the politically connected at their house in Washington. At such parties, they organize secret ballots asking the assembled experts who will win. . . . By November 1, 1987, the results of Mr. Dole's organizing efforts were clear in a new Plissner-Morrison poll." The symbiosis here was complete, and the only outsider was the increasingly hypothetical voter, who was seen as responsive not to actual issues but to their adroit presentation: "At the moment the Republican message is simpler and more clear than ours," the Democratic chairman for California, Peter Kelly, said to *The Los Angeles Times* in August 1988, complaining, on the matter of what was called the Pledge of Allegiance issue, not that it was a false issue but that Bush had seized the initiative, or "the symbolism."

"Bush Gaining in Battle of TV Images," *The Washington Post* headlined a front-page story in September 1988, and quoted Jeff Greenfield, the ABC News political reporter: "George Bush is almost always outdoors, coatless, sometimes with his sleeves rolled up, and looks ebullient and Happy Warrior-ish. Mike Dukakis is almost always indoors, with his jacket on, and almost always behind a lectern." According to the same week's issue of *Newsweek*, the Bush campaign, which had the superior gift for getting film shot in "dramatic settings—like Boston Harbor," was winning "the all-important battle of the backdrops." A CBS producer covering the Dukakis campaign was quoted complaining about an occasion when Governor Dukakis, speaking to students on a California beach, had faced the students instead of the camera. "The only reason Dukakis was on the beach was to get his picture taken," the producer had said. "So you might as well see his face." Pictures, *Newsweek* had concluded, "often speak louder than words."

This "battle of the backdrops" story appeared on page 24 of the *Newsweek* dated September 12, 1988. On page 23 of the same issue there appeared, as illustrations for the lead National Affairs story ("Getting Down and Dirty: As the mudslinging campaign moves into full gear, Bush stays on the offensive—and Dukakis calls back his main street-fighting man"), two half-page color photographs, one of each candidate, which seemed designed to address the very concerns expressed on page 24 and in the *Post*. The photograph of George Bush showed him indoors, behind a lectern, with his jacket on. That of Michael Dukakis showed him outdoors, coatless, sleeves rolled up, looking ebullient, about to throw a baseball on an airport tarmac: something had been learned from Jeff Greenfield, or something had been told to Jeff Greenfield. "We talk to the press, and things take on a life of their own," Mark Siegel, a Democratic political consultant, said to Elizabeth Drew.

About this baseball on the tarmac. On the day that Michael Dukakis appeared at the high school in Woodland Hills and at the office plaza in San Diego and in the schoolyard in San Jose, there was, although it did not appear on the schedule, a fourth event, what was referred to among the television crews as a "tarmac arrival with ball tossing." This event had taken place in late morning, on the tarmac at the San Diego airport, just after the campaign's chartered 737 had rolled to a stop and the candidate had emerged. There had been a moment of hesitation, or decision. Then baseball mitts had been produced, and Jack Weeks, the traveling press secretary, had tossed a ball to the candidate. The candidate had tossed the ball back. The rest of us had stood in the sun and given this our full attention: some forty adults standing on a tarmac watching a diminutive figure in shirtsleeves and a red tie toss a ball, undeflected even by the arrival of an Alaska Airlines 767, to his press secretary.

"Just a regular guy," one of the cameramen had said, his inflection that of the "union official" who confided, in an early Dukakis commercial aimed at blue-collar voters, that he had known "Mike" a long time, and backed him despite his not being "your shot-and-beer kind of guy."

"I'd say he was a regular guy," another cameraman had said. "Definitely."

"I'd sit around with him," the first cameraman said.

Kara Dukakis, one of the candidate's daughters, had at that moment emerged from the 737.

"You'd have a beer with him?"

Jack Weeks had tossed the ball to Kara Dukakis.

"I'd have a beer with him."

Kara Dukakis had tossed the ball to her father. Her father had caught the ball and tossed it back to her.

"OK," one of the cameramen had said. "We got the daughter. Nice. That's enough. Nice."

The CNN producer then on the campaign told me, later in the day, that the first recorded ball tossing on the Dukakis campaign had been outside a bowling alley somewhere in Ohio. CNN had shot it. When the campaign realized that only one camera had it, they restaged it.

"We have a lot of things like the ball tossing," the producer said. "We have the Greek dancing, for example."

I asked if she still bothered to shoot it.

"I get it," she said, "but I don't call in anymore and say, 'Hey, hold it, I've got him dancing.'"

This sounded about right (the candidate might, after all, bean a citizen during the ball tossing, and CNN would need film), and not until I read Joe Klein's version of those days in California did it occur to me that this eerily contrived moment on the tarmac at San Diego could become, at least provisionally, history. "The Duke seemed downright jaunty," Joe Klein reported. "He tossed a baseball with aides. He was flagrantly multilingual. He danced Greek dances. . . ." In the July 25, 1988, issue of *U.S. News & World Report*, Michael Kramer opened his cover story ("Is Dukakis Tough Enough?") with a more developed version of the ball tossing:

> The thermometer read 101 degrees, but the locals guessed 115 on the broiling airport tarmac in Phoenix. After all, it was under a noonday sun in the desert that Michael Dukakis was indulging his truly favorite campaign ritual—a game of catch with his

> aide Jack Weeks. "These days," he has said, "throwing the ball around when we land somewhere is about the only exercise I get." For 16 minutes, Dukakis shagged flies and threw strikes. Halfway through, he rolled up his sleeves, but he never loosened his tie. Finally, mercifully, it was over and time to pitch the obvious tongue-in-cheek question: "Governor, what does throwing a ball around in this heat say about your mental stability?" Without missing a beat, and without a trace of a smile, Dukakis echoed a sentiment he has articulated repeatedly in recent months: "What it means is that I'm tough."

Nor was this the last word. On July 31, 1988, in *The Washington Post*, David S. Broder, who had also been with the Dukakis campaign in Phoenix, gave us a third, and, by virtue of his seniority in the process, perhaps the official version of the ball tossing:

> Dukakis called out to Jack Weeks, the handsome, curly-haired Welshman who goodnaturedly shepherds us wayward pressmen through the daily vagaries of the campaign schedule. Weeks dutifully produced two gloves and a baseball, and there on the tarmac, with its surface temperature just below the boiling point, the governor loosened up his arm and got the kinks out of his back by tossing a couple hundred 90-foot pegs to Weeks.

What we had in the tarmac arrival with ball tossing, then, was an understanding: a repeated moment witnessed by many people, all of whom believed it to be a setup and yet most of whom believed that only an outsider, only someone too "naive" to know the rules of the game, would so describe it.

4.

The narrative is made up of many such understandings, tacit agreements, small and large, to overlook the observable in the interests of obtaining a dramatic story line. It was understood, for example, that the first night of the 1988 Republican convention in New Orleans should be for Ronald Reagan "the last hurrah." "Reagan electrifies GOP" was the headline the next morning on the front page of *New York Newsday*; in fact the Reagan appearance, which was rhetorically pitched not to a live audience but to the more intimate demands of the camera, was, inside the Superdome, barely registered. It was understood, similarly, that Michael Dukakis's acceptance speech on the last night of the 1988 Democratic convention in Atlanta should be the occasion on which his "passion," or "leadership," emerged. "Could the no-nonsense nominee reach within himself to discover the language of leadership?" *Time* had asked. "Could he go beyond the pedestrian promise of 'good jobs at good wages' to give voice to a new Democratic vision?"

The correct answer, since the forward flow of the story here demanded the appearance of a genuine contender (a contender who could be seventeen points "up," so that George Bush could be seventeen points "down," a position from which he could rise to "claim" his own convention), was yes: "The best speech of his life," David S. Broder reported. Sandy Grady found it "superb," evoking "Kennedyesque echoes" and showing "unexpected craft and fire." *Newsweek* had witnessed Michael Dukakis "electrifying the convention with his intensely personal acceptance speech." In fact the convention that evening had been electrified, not by the speech, which was the same series of nonsequential clauses Governor Dukakis had employed during the primary campaign ("My friends . . . son of immigrants . . . good jobs at good wages . . . make teaching a valued and honored profession . . . it's what the Democratic Party is all about"), but because the floor had been darkened, swept with laser beams, and flooded with "Coming to America," played at concert volume with the bass turned up.

It is understood that this invented narrative will turn on certain familiar elements. There is the continuing story line of the "horse race," the reliable daily drama of one candidate falling behind as another pulls ahead. There is the surprise of the new poll, the glamour of the one-on-one colloquy on the midnight plane, a plot point (the nation sleeps while the candidate and his confidant hammer out its fate) pioneered by Theodore H. White. There is the abiding if unexamined faith in the campaign as personal odyssey, and in the spiritual benefits accruing to those who undertake it. There is, in the presented history of the candidate, the crucible event, the day that "changed the life." Robert Dole's life was understood to have changed when he was injured in Italy in 1945. George Bush's life is understood to have changed when he and his wife decided to "get out and make it on our own" (his words, or those of his speechwriter, Peggy Noonan, from the "lived the dream" acceptance speech at the 1988 convention, suggesting action, shirtsleeves, privilege cast aside) in west Texas. For Bruce Babbitt, "the dam just kind of broke" during a student summer in Bolivia. For Michael Dukakis, the dam was understood to have broken not during his own student summer in South America, in his case Peru, but after his 1978 defeat in Massachusetts: his tragic flaw, we read repeatedly during the 1988 campaign, was neither his evident sulkiness at losing that earlier election nor what many saw later as a rather dissociated self-satisfaction ("We're two people very proud of what we've done," he said on NBC in Atlanta, falling into a favorite speech pattern, "very proud of each other, actually . . . and very proud that a couple of guys named Dukakis and Jackson have come this far"), but the more attractive "hubris."

The narrative requires broad strokes. Michael Dukakis was physically small, and had associations with Harvard, which suggested that he could be cast as an "intellectual"; the "immigrant factor," on the other hand, could make him tough (as in "What it means is that I'm tough"), a "street-fighter." "He's cool, shrewd, and still trying to prove he's tough," the July 25, 1988, cover of *U.S. News & World Report* said about Dukakis. "Toughness is what it's all about," one of his advisers was quoted as having said. "People need to feel that a candidate is tough enough to be president. It is the threshold perception." George Bush had presented a more tortured narrative problem. The tellers of the story had not understood, or had not responded to, the essential Bush style, which was complex, ironic, the diffident edge of the Northeastern elite. This was what was at first identified as "the wimp factor," which was replaced not by a more complicated view of the personality but by its reverse: George Bush was by late August of 1988 no longer a "wimp" but someone who had "thrown it over," "struck out" to make his own way: no longer a product of the effete Northeast but someone who had thrived in Texas, and was therefore "tough enough to be president."

That George Bush might have thrived in Texas not in spite of being but precisely because he was a member of the Northeastern elite was a shading that had no part in the narrative: "He was considered back at that time one of the most charismatic people ever elected to public office in the history of Texas," Congressman Bill Archer of Houston said. "That charisma, people talked about it over and over again." People talked about it, probably, because Andover and Yale and the inheritable tax avoidance they suggested were, during the years George Bush lived in Texas, the exact ideals toward which the Houston and Dallas establishment aspired, but the narrative called for a less ambiguous version: "Lived in a little shotgun house, one room for the three of us," as Bush, or Peggy Noonan, had put it in the celebrated no-subject-pronoun cadences of the "lived the dream" acceptance speech. "Worked in the oil business, started my own. . . . Moved from the shotgun to a duplex apartment to a house. Lived the dream—high school football on Friday night, Little League, neighborhood barbecue . . . pushing into unknown territory with kids and a dog and a car. . . ."

All stories, of course, depend for their popular interest upon the invention of personality, or "character," but in the political narrative, designed as it is to maintain the illusion of consensus by obscuring rather than addressing actual issues, this invention served a further purpose. It was by 1988 generally if unspecifically agreed that the United States faced certain social and economic realities that, if not intractable, did not entirely lend themselves to the kinds of policy fixes that people who run for elected office, on whatever ticket, were likely to undertake. We had not yet accommodated the industrialization of parts of the third world. We had not yet adjusted to the economic realignment of a world in which the United States was no longer the principal catalyst for change. "We really are in an age of transition," Brent Scowcroft, Bush's leading foreign policy adviser, told Robert Scheer of *The Los Angeles Times* in the fall of 1988, "from a postwar world where the Soviets were the enemy, where the United States was a superpower and trying to build up both its allies and its former enemies and help the third world transition to independence. That whole world and all of those things are coming to an end or have ended, and we are now entering a new and different world that will be complex and much less unambiguous than the old one."

What continued to dominate the rhetoric of the 1988 campaign, however, was not this awareness of a new and different world but nostalgia for an old one, and coded assurance that any evidence of ambiguity or change, of what George Bush called the "deterioration of values," would be summarily dealt with by increased social control. It was not by accident that the word "enforcement," devoid of any apparent awareness that it had been tried before, played a large role in the language of both the Bush and Dukakis campaigns. Dukakis had promised, by way of achieving his goal of "no safe haven for dope dealers and drug profits anywhere on this earth," to "double the number" of Drug Enforcement Administration agents, not a promising approach. George Bush had repeatedly promised his support for the death penalty, and for both the Pledge of Allegiance and prayer, or "moments of silence," in public schools. "We've got to change this entire culture," he said in the Wake Forest debate; polling indicated that the electorate wanted "change," and this wish for change had been translated, by both campaigns, into the wish for a "change back," a regression to the "gentler America" of which George Bush repeatedly spoke.

To the extent that there was a "difference" between the candidates, the difference lay in just where on the time scale this "gentler America" could be found. The Dukakis campaign was oriented to "programs," and the programs it proposed were similar to those that had worked (the encouragement of private-sector involvement in low-cost housing, say) in the boom years after World War II. The Bush campaign was oriented to "values," and the values to which it referred were those not of a postwar but of a prewar America. In neither case did "ideas" play a part: "This election isn't about ideology, it's about competence," Michael Dukakis had said in Atlanta. "First and foremost, it's a choice between two persons," one of his senior advisers, Thomas Kiley, had told *The Wall Street Journal*. "What it comes down to, after all the shouting and the cheers, is the man at the desk," George Bush had said in New Orleans. In other words, what it "came down to," what it was "about," what was wrong or right with America, was not an historical shift largely unaffected by the actions of individual citizens but "character," and if "character" could be seen to count, then every citizen—since everyone was a judge of character, an expert in the field of personality—could be seen to count. This notion, that the citizen's choice among determinedly centrist candidates makes a "difference," is in fact the narrative's most central element, and its most fictive.

5.

The Democratic National Convention of 1968, during which the process was put to a popular vote on the streets of Chicago and after which it was decided that what had occurred could not be allowed to recur, is generally agreed to have prompted the increased emphasis on primaries, and the concomitant increased coverage of those primaries, that led to the end of the national party convention as a more than ceremonial occasion. Early in 1987, as the primary campaigns got underway for the 1988 election, David S. Broder, in *The Washington Post*, offered this compelling analysis of the power these "reforms" in the nominating procedure had vested not in the party leadership, which is where this power of choice ultimately resides, but in "the existing communications system," by which he meant the press, or the medium through which the party leadership sells its choice:

> Once the campaign explodes to 18 states, as it will the day after New Hampshire, when the focus shifts to a super-primary across the nation, the existing communications system simply will not accommodate more than two or three candidates in each party. Neither the television networks, nor the newspapers nor magazines, have the resources of people, space and time to describe and analyze the dynamics of two simultaneous half-national elections among Republicans and Democrats. That task is simply beyond us. Since we cannot reduce the number of states voting on Super Tuesday, we have to reduce the number of candidates treated as serious contenders. These news judgments will be arbitrary—but not subject to appeal. Those who finish first or second in Iowa and New Hampshire will get tickets from the mass media to play in the next big round. Those who don't, won't. A

minor exception may be made for the two reverends, Jesse L. Jackson and Marion G. (Pat) Robertson, who have their own church-based communications and support networks and are less dependent on mass-media attention. But no one else.

By the time the existing communications network set itself up in July and August 1988 in Atlanta and New Orleans, the priorities were clear. "NOTICE NOTICE NOTICE," read the typed note given to some print reporters when they picked up their credentials in Atlanta. "Because the Democratic National Convention Committee permitted the electronic media to exceed specifications for their broadcast booths, your assigned seat's sight line to the podium and the convention floor was obliterated." The network's skyboxes, in other words, had been built in front of the sections originally assigned to the periodical press. "This is a place that was chosen to be, for all intents and purposes, a large TV studio, to be able to project our message to the American people and a national audience," Paul Kirk, the chairman of the Democratic National Committee, said by way of explaining why the podium and the skyboxes had so reduced the size of the Omni Coliseum in Atlanta that some thousand delegates and alternates had been, on the evening Jesse Jackson spoke, locked out. Mayor Andrew Young of Atlanta apologized for the lockout, but said that it would be the same on nights to follow: "The one hundred and fifty million people in the country who are going to vote have got to be our major target." Still, convention delegates were seen to have a real role: "The folks in the hall are so important to how it looks," Lane Venardos, senior producer in charge of convention coverage for CBS News, said to *The New York Times* about the Republican convention. The delegates, in other words, were the dress extras who could make the set seem authentic.

During those eight summer evenings in 1988, four in Atlanta and four in New Orleans, when roughly eighty percent of the television sets "out there" were tuned somewhere else, the entire attention of those inside the process was directed toward the invention of this story in which they themselves were the principal players, and for which they themselves were the principal audience. The great arenas in which the conventions were held became self-contained worlds, constantly transmitting their own images back to themselves, connected by skywalks to interchangeable structures composed not of floors but of "levels," mysteriously separated by fountains and glass elevators and escalators that did not quite connect. In the Louisiana Superdome in New Orleans as in the Omni Coliseum in Atlanta, the grids of lights blazed and dimmed hypnotically. Men with rifles patrolled the high catwalks. The nets packed with balloons swung gently overhead, poised for that instant known as "the money shot," the moment, or "window," when everything was working and no network had cut to a commercial. Minicams trawled the floor, fishing in Atlanta for Rob Lowe, in New Orleans for Donald Trump. In the NBC skybox Tom Brokaw floated over the floor, adjusting his tie, putting on his jacket, leaning to speak to John Chancellor. In the CNN skybox Mary Alice Williams sat bathed in white light, the blond madonna of the skyboxes. On the television screens in the press section the images reappeared, but from another angle: Tom Brokaw and Mary Alice Williams again, broadcasting not just above us but also to us, the circle closed.

At the end of prime time, when the skyboxes went dark, the action moved across the skywalks and into the levels, into the lobbies, into one or another Hyatt or Marriott or Hilton or Westin. In the portage from lobby to lobby, level to level, the same people kept materializing, in slightly altered roles. On a level of the Hyatt in Atlanta I saw Ann Lewis in her role as a Jackson adviser. On a level of the Hyatt in New Orleans I saw Ann Lewis in her role as a correspondent for *Ms.* Some pictures were vivid: "I've been around this process a while, and one thing I've noticed, it's the people who write the checks who get treated as if they have a certain amount of power," I recall Nadine Hack, the chairman of New York fundraising for Dukakis, saying in a suite at the Hyatt in Atlanta: here was a willowy woman with long blond hair standing barefoot on a table and explaining to those present how they could buy into the action. "The great thing about those evenings was you could even see Michael Harrington there," I recall Richard Viguerie saying to me at a party in New Orleans: here was the man who managed the action for the American right sounding wishful about evenings he and I had spent together in the early 1960s at the Washington Square apartment of a mutual friend, a woman whose evenings had been at the time a kind of salon for the political edges.

There was in Atlanta in 1988, according to the Democratic National Committee, "twice the media presence" that there had been at the 1984 convention. There were in New Orleans "media workspaces" assigned not only to 117 newspapers and news services and to the American television and radio industry at full strength but to fifty-two foreign networks. On every corner one turned in the French Quarter someone was doing a standup. There were telephone numbers to be called for quotes: "Republican State and Local Officials," or "Pat Robertson Campaign," or "Richard Wirthlin, Reagan's Pollster." Newspapers came with teams of thirty, forty, fifty. In every lobby there were stacks of fresh newspapers, *The Atlanta Constitution*, *The New Orleans Times-Picayune*, *The Washington Post*, *The Miami Herald*, *The Los Angeles Times*. In Atlanta these papers were collected in bins and "recycled": made into thirty thousand posters, which were in turn distributed to the press in New Orleans.

This perfect recycling tended to present itself, in the narcosis of the event, as a model for the rest: like American political life itself, and like the printed and transmitted images on which that life depended, this was a world with no half-life. It was understood that what was said here would go on the wire and vanish. Garrison Keillor and his cute kids would vanish. Ann Richards and her peppery ripostes would vanish. Phyllis Schlafly and Olympia Snowe would vanish. All the opinions and all the rumors and all the housemaid Spanish spoken in both Atlanta and New Orleans would vanish, and all that would remain would be the huge arenas themselves, the arenas and the lobbies and the levels and the skywalks to which they connected, the agora, the symbolic marketplace in which the narrative was not only written but immediately, efficiently, entirely, consumed.

6.

A certain time lag exists between this world of the arenas and the world as we know it. One evening in New York between the Democratic and Republican conventions I happened to go down to Lafayette Street, to the Public Theater, to look at clips from documentaries on which the English-born filmmaker Richard Leacock had worked during his fifty years in America. We saw folk singers in Virginia in 1941 and oil riggers in Louisiana in 1946 (this was *Louisiana Story*, which Leacock had shot for Robert Flaherty) and tent performers in the Corn Belt in 1954; we saw Eddy Sachs preparing for the Indianapolis 500 in 1960 and Piri Thomas in Spanish Harlem in 1961. We saw parades, we saw baton twirlers. We saw quints in South Dakota in 1963. There on the screen in the Public Theater that night were images and attitudes from an America that had largely vanished, and what was striking was this: these were the very images and attitudes on which "the campaign" was predicated.

That "unknown territory" into which George Bush had pushed "with kids and a dog and a car" had existed in this vanished America, and had long since been subdivided, cut up for those tract houses on which the people who were not part of the process had made down payments. Michael Dukakis's "snowblower," and both the amusing frugality and the admirable husbandry of resources it was meant to suggest, derived from some half-remembered idea of what citizens of this vanished America had found amusing or admirable. "The Pledge" was an issue that referred back to that world. "A drug-free America" had perhaps seemed in that world an achievable ideal. I recall listening in Atlanta to Madeleine Albright, at that time Dukakis's foreign-policy adviser, as she conjured up, in the course of arguing against a "no first use" minority plank in the Democratic platform, a scenario in which "Soviet forces overrun Europe" and the United States has, by promising no first use of nuclear weapons, crippled its ability to act: she was talking about a world that had not turned since 1948. What was at work here seemed on the one hand a grave, although in many ways a comfortable, miscalculation of what people in America might have as their deepest concerns in 1988; it seemed on the other hand just another understanding, another of those agreements to overlook the observable.

It was into this sedative fantasy of a fixable imperial America that Jesse Jackson rode, on a Trailways bus. "You've never heard a sense of panic sweep the party as it has in the past few days," David Garth had told *The New York Times* during those perilous spring weeks in 1988 when there seemed a real possibility that a black candidate with no experience in elected office, a candidate believed to be so profoundly unelectable that he could take the entire Democratic Party down with him, might go to Atlanta with more delegates than any other Democratic candidate. "The party is up against an extraordinary endgame," the pollster Paul Maslin had said. "I don't know where this leaves us," Robert S. Strauss had said. One uncommitted super-delegate, *The New York Times* had reported, "said the Dukakis campaign changed its message since Mr. Dukakis lost the Illinois primary. Mr. Dukakis is no longer the candidate of 'inevitability' but the candidate of order, he said. 'They're not doing the train's leaving the station and you better be on it routine anymore,' this official said. 'They're now saying that the station's about to be blown up by terrorists and we're the only ones who can defuse the bomb.'"

The threat, or the possibility, presented by Jesse Jackson, the "historic" (as people liked to say after it became certain he would not have the numbers) part of his candidacy, derived from something other than the fact that he was black, a circumstance that had before been and could again be compartmentalized, segregated out. For example: "Next week, when we start doing our black media stuff, Jesse Jackson needs to be on the air in the black community on our behalf," Donna Brazile of the Dukakis campaign said to *The New York Times* in September 1988 by way of emphasizing how much the Dukakis campaign "sought to make peace" with Jackson. "Black," in other words, could be useful, and even a moral force, a way for white Americans to attain more perfect attitudes: "How moving it is, and how important, to see a black candidate meet and overcome the racism that lurks in virtually all of us white Americans," Anthony Lewis had noted in a March 1988 column explaining why the notion that Jesse Jackson could win was nonetheless "a romantic delusion" of the kind that had "repeatedly undermined" the Democratic Party. "You look at what Jesse Jackson has done, you have to wonder what a Tom Bradley of Los Angeles could have done, what an Andy Young of Atlanta could have done," I heard someone say on one of the Sunday shows after the Jackson campaign had entered its "historic," or in the candidate's word its "endless," phase.

"Black," by itself and in the right context—the right context being a reasonable constituency composed exclusively of blacks and supportive liberal whites—could be accommodated by the process. Something less traditional was at work in the 1988 Jackson candidacy. I recall having dinner, the weekend before the California primary, at the Pebble Beach house of the chairman of a large American corporation. There were sixteen people at the table, all white, all well off, all well dressed, all well educated, all socially conservative. During the course of the evening it came to my attention that six of the sixteen, or every one of the registered Democrats present, intended to vote on Tuesday for Jesse Jackson. Their reasons were unspecific, but definite. "I heard him, he didn't sound like a politician," one said. "He's talking about right now," another said. "You get outside the gate here, take a look around, you have to know we've got some problems, and he's talking about them."

What made the 1988 Jackson candidacy a bomb that had to be defused, then, was not that blacks were supporting a black candidate, but that significant numbers of whites were supporting—not only supporting but in many cases overcoming deep emotional and economic conflicts of their own in order to support—a candidate who was attractive to them not because of but in spite of the fact that he was black, a candidate whose most potent attraction was that he "didn't sound like a politician." "Character" seemed not to be, among these voters, the point-of-sale issue the narrative made it out to be: a number of white Jackson supporters to whom I talked would quite serenely describe their candidate as "a con man," or even, in George Bush's phrase, as "a hustler." "And yet . . . ," they would say. What "and yet" turned out to mean, almost without variation, was that they were willing to walk off the edge of the known political map for a candidate who was running against, as he repeatedly said, "politics as usual," against what he called "consensualist centrist politics"; against what had come to be the very premise of the process, the notion that the winning and maintaining of public office warranted the invention of a public narrative based at no point on observable reality.

In other words they were not idealists, these white Jackson voters, but empiricists. By the time Jesse Jackson got to California, where he would eventually win twenty-five percent of the entire white vote and forty-nine percent of the total vote from voters between the demographically key ages of thirty to forty-four, the idealists had rallied behind the sole surviving alternative, who was, accordingly, just then being declared "presidential." In Los Angeles, during May and early June 1988, those Democrats who had not fallen into line behind Michael Dukakis were described as "self-indulgent," or as "immature"; they were even described, in a dispiriting phrase that prefigured the tenor of the campaign to come, as "issues wimps." I recall talking to a rich and politically well-connected Californian who had been, during the primary season there, virtually the only Democrat on the famously liberal west side of Los Angeles who was backing Jackson. He said that he could afford "the luxury of being more interested in issues than in process," but that he would pay for it: "When I want something, I'll have a hard time getting people to pick up the phone. I recognize that. I made the choice."

7.

On the June night in 1988 when Michael Dukakis was declared the winner of the California Democratic primary, and the bomb officially defused, there took place in the Crystal Room of the Biltmore Hotel in downtown Los Angeles a "victory party" that was less a celebration than a ratification by the professionals, a ritual convergence of those California Democrats for whom the phones would continue to get picked up. Charles Manatt was there. John Emerson and Charles Palmer were there. John Van de Kamp was there. Leo McCarthy was there. Robert Shrum was there. All the custom-made suits and monogrammed shirts in Los Angeles that night were there, met in the wide corridors of the Biltmore to murmur assurances to one another. The ballroom had been cordoned as if to repel late invaders, roped off in such a way that once the Secret Service, the traveling press, the local press, the visiting national press, the staff, and the candidate himself had assembled, there would be room for only a controllable handful of celebrants, over whom the cameras would dutifully pan.

In fact the actual "celebrants" that evening were not at the Biltmore at all, but a few blocks away at the Los Angeles Hilton, dancing under the mirrored ceiling of the ballroom in which the Jackson campaign had gathered, its energy level in defeat notably higher than that of other campaigns in victory. Jackson parties tended to spill out of ballrooms onto several levels of whatever hotel they were in, and to last until three or four in the morning: anyone who wanted to be at a Jackson party was welcome at a Jackson party, which was unusual among the campaigns, and tended to reinforce the populist spirit that had given this one its extraordinary animation. Of that evening at the Los Angeles Hilton I recall a pretty woman in a gold lamé dress, dancing with a baby in her arms. I recall empty beer bottles, Corona and Budweiser and Excalibur, sitting among the loops of television cable. I recall the candidate, dancing on the stage, and, on this June evening when the long shot had not come in, this evening when his campaign was effectively over, giving the women in the traveling press the little parody wave they liked to give him, "the press chicks' wave," the stiff-armed palm movement they called "the Nancy Reagan wave"; then taking off his tie and throwing it into the crowd, like a rock star. This was of course a narrative of its own, but a relatively current one, and one that had, because it seemed at some point grounded in the recognizable, a powerful glamour for those estranged from the purposeful nostalgia of the traditional narrative.

In the end the predictable decision was made to go with the process, with predictable, if equivocal, results. On the last afternoon of the 1988 Republican convention in New Orleans I walked from the hotel in the Quarter where I was staying over to Camp Street. I wanted to see 544 Camp, a local point of interest not noted on the points-of-interest maps distributed at the convention but one that figures large in the literature of American conspiracy. "544 Camp Street" was the address stamped on the leaflets Lee Harvey Oswald was distributing around New Orleans between May and September of 1963, the "Fair Play for Cuba Committee" leaflets that, in the years after Lee Harvey Oswald assassinated John Fitzgerald Kennedy, suggested to some that he had been acting for Fidel Castro and suggested to others that he had been set up to appear to have been acting for Fidel Castro. Guy Bannister had his detective agency at 544 Camp. David Ferrie and Jack Martin frequented the coffee shop on the ground floor at 544 Camp. The Cuban Revolutionary Council, the members of which would have made up the provisional government of Cuba had the 1961 invasion of Cuba not ended at the Bay of Pigs, rented an office at 544 Camp. People had taken the American political narrative seriously at 544 Camp. They had argued about it, fallen out over it, hit each other over the head with pistol butts because of it.

In fact I never found 544 Camp, because there was no more such address: the small building had been bought and torn down and replaced by a new federal courthouse. Across the street in Lafayette Square that afternoon there had been a loudspeaker, and a young man on a makeshift platform talking about abortion, and unwanted babies being put down the Disposall and "clogging the main sewer drains of New Orleans," but no one except me had been there to listen. "*Satan, you're the liar*," the young woman with him on the platform had sung, lip-synching a tape originally made, she told me, by a woman who sang with an Alabama traveling ministry, the Ministry of the Happy Hunters. "*There's one thing you can't deny / You're the father of every lie. . .* ." The young woman had been wearing a black cape, and was made up to portray Satan, or Death, I was unclear which and it had not seemed a distinction worth pursuing.

Still, there were clouds off the Gulf that day and the air was wet and there was about the melancholy of Camp Street a certain sense of abandoned historic moment, heightened, quite soon, by something unusual: the New Orleans police began lining Camp Street, blocking every intersection from Canal Street west. I noticed a man in uniform on a roof. Before long there were Secret Service agents, with wires in their ears. The candidates, it seemed, would be traveling east on Camp Street on their way from the Republican National Committee Finance Committee Gala (Invitation Only) at the Convention Center to the Ohio Caucus Rally (Media Invited) at the Hilton. I stood for a while on Camp Street, on this corner that might be construed as one of those occasional accidental intersections where the remote narrative had collided with the actual life of the country, and waited until the motorcade itself, entirely and perfectly insulated, a mechanism dedicated like the process for which it stood only to the maintenance of itself, had passed, and then I walked to the Superdome. "I hear he did OK with Brinkley," they said that night in the Superdome, and, then, as the confetti fell, "Quayle, zip."

The West Wing of Oz

December 22, 1988

IN AUGUST 1986, George Bush, traveling in his role as vice president of the United States and accompanied by his staff, the Secret Service, the traveling press, and a personal camera crew wearing baseball caps reading "Shooters, Inc." and working on a $10,000 retainer paid by a Bush PAC called the Fund for America's Future, spent several days in Israel and Jordan. The schedule in Israel included, according to reports in *The Los Angeles Times* and *The New York Times*, shoots at the Western Wall, at the Holocaust memorial, at David Ben-Gurion's tomb, and at thirty-two other locations chosen to produce camera footage illustrating that George Bush was, as Marlin Fitzwater, at that time the vice-presidential press secretary, put it, "familiar with the issues." The Shooters, Inc. crew did not go on to Jordan (there was, an official explained to *The Los Angeles Times*, "nothing to be gained from showing him schmoozing with Arabs"), but the Bush advance team in Amman had nonetheless directed considerable attention to improving visuals for the traveling press.

Members of the advance team had requested, for example, that the Jordanian army marching band change its uniforms from white to red. They had requested that the Jordanians, who did not have enough equipment to transport Bush's traveling press corps, borrow the necessary helicopters to do so from the Israeli air force. In an effort to assure the color of live military action as a backdrop for the vice president, they had asked the Jordanians to stage maneuvers at a sensitive location overlooking Israel and the Golan Heights. They had asked the Jordanians to raise, over the Jordanian base there, the American flag. They had asked that Bush be photographed studying, through binoculars, "enemy territory," a shot ultimately vetoed by the State Department, since the "enemy territory" at hand was Israel. They had also asked, possibly the most arresting detail, that, at every stop on the itinerary, camels be present.

Some months later I happened to be in Amman, and mentioned reading about this Bush trip to several officials at the American embassy there. They could have, it was agreed, "cordially killed" the reporters in question, particularly Charles P. Wallace from *The Los Angeles Times*, but the reports themselves had been accurate. "You didn't hear this, but they didn't write the half of it," one said.

This is in fact the kind of story we expect to hear about our elected officials. We not only expect them to use other nations as changeable scrims in the theater of domestic politics but encourage them to do so. After the April 1961 failure of the Bay of Pigs, John Kennedy's job approval rating was four points higher than it had been in March. After the 1965 intervention in the Dominican Republic, Lyndon Johnson's job approval rating rose six points. After the 1983 invasion of Grenada, Ronald Reagan's job approval rating rose four points, and what was that winter referred to in Washington as "Lebanon"—the sending of American marines into Beirut, the killing of the 241, and the subsequent pullout—was, in the afterglow of this certified success in the Caribbean, largely forgotten. "Gemayal could fall tonight and it would be a two-day story," I recall David Gergen saying a few months later. In May 1984, Francis X. Klines of *The New York Times* described the view taken by James Baker, who was routinely described during his years in the Reagan White House as a manager of almost supernatural executive ability, the "ultimate pragmatist": "In attempting action in Lebanon, Baker argues, President Reagan avoided another 'impotent' episode, such as the taking of American hostages in Iran, and in withdrawing the Marines, the President avoided another 'Vietnam' . . . 'Pulling the Marines out put the lie to the argument that the President's trigger-happy,' he [Baker] said." The "issue," in other words, was one of preserving faith in President Reagan at home, a task that, after the ultimate pragmatist left the White House, fell into the hands of the less adroit.

History is context. At a moment when the nation had seen control of its economy pass to its creditors and when the administration-elect had for political reasons severely limited its ability to regain that control, this extreme reliance on the efficacy of faith over works meant something different from what it might have meant in 1984 or 1980. On the night in New Orleans in August 1988 when George Bush accepted the Republican nomination and spoke of his intention to "speak for freedom, stand for freedom, and be a patient friend to anyone, east or west, who will fight for freedom," the word "patient" was construed by some in the Louisiana Superdome as an abandonment of the Reagan Doctrine, a suggestion that a Bush administration would play a passive rather than an active role in any further dreams of rollback.

This overlooked the real nature of the Reagan Doctrine, the usefulness of which to the Reagan administration had been essentially political. Administrations with little room to maneuver at home have historically looked for sideshows abroad, for the creation of what pollsters call "a dramatic event," an external crisis, preferably one so remote that it remains an abstraction. On the evening of the November 1988 election and on several evenings that followed, I happened to sit at dinner next to men with considerable experience in the financial community. They were agreed that the foreign markets would allow the new Bush administration, which was seen to have limited its options by promising for political reasons not to raise taxes, only a limited time before calling in the markers; they disagreed only as to the length of that time and to the nature of the downturn. One thought perhaps two years, another six months. Some saw a blowout ("blowout" was a word used a good deal), others saw a gradual tightening, a slow transition to that era of limited expectations of which Jerry Brown had spoken when he was governor of California.

These men were, among themselves, uniformly pessimistic. They saw a situation in which the space available for domestic maneuvering had been reduced to zero. In this light it did not seem encouraging that George Bush, on the Thursday before he left for his post-election Florida vacation, found time to meet not with those investors around the world who were that week sending him a message (the dollar was again dropping against the yen, against the mark, and against the pound; the Dow was dropping 78.47 points), not with the Germans, not with the Japanese, not even with anyone from the American financial community, but with representatives of the Afghan resistance. "Once in a while I think about those things, but not much," the president-elect told the CBS News crew which asked him, a few days later in Florida, about the falling market.

2.

July 14, 1994

In December 1981 in El Salvador, twenty-one months after the murder of Archbishop Oscar Arnulfo Romero in San Salvador and twelve months after the murder of the four American Maryknoll women outside San Salvador and eleven months after the murder of the head of the Salvadoran land-reform agency and two of his American aides at the Sheraton Hotel in San Salvador, which is to say at a time when the Reagan administration had already demonstrated its ability to tolerate grave insults to its Central American policy, certain events occurred in certain remote villages north of the Torola River in Morazán province. In what has since become the most familiar of those villages, El Mozote, the events in question began late on a Thursday afternoon, December 10, at a time when the village was crowded with refugees from areas believed less safe, and were concluded at dawn on Saturday.

Later that day, in Los Toriles, two kilometers to the southeast, similar events occurred, as similar events had already occurred or would within a few hours occur in Arambala and La Joya and Jocote Amarillo and Cerro Pando and Joateca and La Rancheria. These events were later and variously described to the American writer Mark Danner by the two American embassy officials assigned to investigate them, Todd Greentree and Major John McKay, as "something bad," "something horrible," a case in which "there had probably been a massacre, that they had lined people up and shot them," a case in which "abuses against the civilian population probably took place"; a case that presented as its most urgent imperative the need to craft a report that would "have credibility among people who were far away and whose priorities were—you know, we're talking about people like Tom Enders—whose priorities were definitely not necessarily about getting at exactly what happened."

On December 10, 1992, eleven years to the day after the commencement of what has become known as the Mozote massacre (the largest number of those killed on that long December weekend were killed during the thirty-six hours spent in El Mozote by members of the Salvadoran army's Atlacatl Battalion), four American forensic experts submitted to the United Nations Truth Commission the results of their analysis of skeletal remains and artifacts recovered by a team of Argentinian forensic anthropologists originally assembled to reconstruct evidence of their own country's "dirty war." Working exclusively with material exhumed from what had been the sacristy of the Mozote church, the Americans were able to identify the bones of 143 human beings, 136 of whom were children and adolescents. Of the remaining seven adults, six were women, one in the third trimester of pregnancy. The average age of the children was six.

The report prepared for the United Nations noted that there may have been a greater number of deaths in the sacristy, which was one of several sites mentioned by survivors as places where bodies would be found, since "many young infants may have been entirely cremated" (much of the village had been burned before the Atlacatl left El Mozote) and "other children may not have been counted because of excessive fragmentation of body parts." Of the ten officers who commanded the units participating in the Morazán operation, according to the report prepared for the United Nations, three were by then dead, and four still serving in the Salvadoran army. None had been officially charged on any count related to the massacre. A year before, Tutela Legal, the human rights office of the Archbishopric of San Salvador, had compiled what may be the final and most comprehensive list of all those known or believed to have died in El Mozote and the surrounding villages. The Tutela Legal list numbered 767 men, women, and children, the youngest the two-day-old grandson of a day laborer named Miguel Marquez (the grandfather was also killed, as were his son, his daughter-in-law, two of his daughters, and seven of his other grandchildren), the oldest a man named Leoncio Diaz, who was said to be 105 years old and to have had a 100-year-old companion named Leoncia Marquez, who was also killed. Of the 767 victims cited on the Tutela Legal list, 358 were infants and children under the age of thirteen.

This was of course not a new story, and the fact that it was not a new story seems in many ways what moved Mark Danner to write his dispassionate, meticulously documented, and for these reasons conclusive *The Massacre at El Mozote: A Parable of the Cold War*. The essential facts of the Mozote massacre were published on January 27, 1982, on the front pages of both *The New York Times* and *The Washington Post*, accompanied by photographs taken by Susan Meiselas, who had walked into Morazán from Honduras with Raymond Bonner of the *Times*. Bonner reported seeing the charred skulls and bones of what appeared to him to be several dozen men, women, and children. Allowing that it was "not possible for an observer who was not present at the time of the massacre to determine independently how many people died or who killed them," he reported that the surviving relatives and friends of the victims believed the dead to number 733 and the killing to have been done "by uniformed soldiers" during an Atlacatl sweep of the region.

Alma Guillermoprieto, who was then a stringer for *The Washington Post* and who entered Mozote a few days after Bonner and Meiselas had left, also reported seeing bodies and body parts and quoted the same survivors, as well as the Salvadoran ambassador in Washington, Ernesto Rivas Gallont, who dismissed the reports from Morazán as the "type of story that leads us to believe there is a plan," the plan being either to derail the Salvadoran election scheduled for March 1982 or "to take credit away from the certification President Reagan must make to Congress." This "certification," during 1982 and 1983 a semiannual requirement for continued American aid to El Salvador, involved asserting that its government was "making a concerted and significant effort to comply with internationally recognized human rights" and was "achieving substantial control over all elements of its own armed forces, so as to bring to an end the indiscriminate torture and murder of Salvadoran citizens by those forces."

The Reagan administration made its certification to these points on January 28, 1982, one day after Bonner's and Alma Guillermoprieto's extensive reports from Morazán appeared in the *Times* and the *Post*. Mark Danner's true subject in *The Massacre at El Mozote*, then, was not the massacre itself but the way in which the story of the massacre, which was carried out by troops trained by the U.S. Special Forces and equipped with U.S.-manufactured M-16s and with ammunition manufactured for the U.S. government at Lake City, Missouri, came to be known and discounted in the United States, the way in which the story of El Mozote "was exposed to the light and then allowed to fall back into the dark."

Reports that something bad had happened in Morazán had begun to circulate almost immediately. The Reverend William L. Wipfler at the New York office of the National Council of Churches first heard the story from a contact at Socorro Juridico, which was then the legal aid office at the Archbishopric of San Salvador. Wipfler left a message for Raymond Bonner at the Mexico City bureau of the *Times*, and also sent a cable, dated December 15, 1981, asking Ambassador Deane Hinton in San Salvador for "confirmation or otherwise" of "reliable reports received here [indicating] that between December 10 and 13 a government joint military and security forces operation took place in Morazán Department which resulted in over 900 civilian deaths."

Hinton did not reply until January 8, by which time the guerrillas' Radio Venceremos was back in operation (to at least temporarily knock out the Venceremos transmitter had been one goal, perhaps the single successfully realized goal, of the Atlacatl's Morazán operation) and broadcasting a detailed account of the massacre from a survivor named Rufina Amaya. Rufina Amaya had witnessed the killing of her husband and four of her children, ages nine, five, three, and eight months, but in the confusion and terror of the event had herself been inadvertently overlooked as the soldiers corralled groups of struggling and screaming women, many of them torn from their infants and children, to be killed and then burned. "I do not know what your sources are but the only sources that I have seen alleging something like this are the clandestine

Radio Venceremos reports," Hinton's January 8 cable to the National Council of Churches read in part. "Frankly, I do not consider Radio Venceremos to be a reliable source." Since Radio Venceremos did not restore its ability to broadcast until well after the National Council of Churches query was sent, that Hinton would devote ten of this cable's twelve paragraphs to illustrations of Radio Venceremos's unreliability seems in retrospect to suggest a certain crisis of confidence, if not a panic, at the embassy.

In fact, definitely before January 8 and probably closer to mid-December, Todd Greentree, then a junior reporting officer at the embassy in San Salvador and later a desk officer for Nicaragua at the State Department, had relayed to Hinton not only a report from his own sources on the left about a massacre in Morazán but also an offer from the FMLN to guide him there. "I knew the guerrillas would never have masqueraded something like this, would never have fabricated it, if they were offering safe-conduct," Greentree told Danner. "I was convinced that something had gone on, and that it was bad. I mean, it was pretty clear, if they were going to do this, that something must have happened." Hinton's decision was that Greentree could not go in under guerrilla protection. "I should emphasize that I never got the feeling that they just wanted this to go away," Greentree told Danner about the meeting in which this decision was taken. "But there were political and military restraints that we were operating under."

What discussion there may have been of an independent investigation (at least ten of the fifty-five American military advisers Congress then allowed in El Salvador were assigned to the Atlacatl) is unknown, although Danner was told by one of the officers assigned to the Atlacatl that someone from the embassy Milgroup (Military Advisory Group) had called the Atlacatl base at La Libertad a few days after the massacre "and talked to the Special Forces people and told them they wanted Monterrosa [Lieutenant Colonel Domingo Monterrosa Barrios, the Atlacatl commander] to come in—they wanted to talk to him about something that had happened during the operation." Monterrosa had declined to come in, a suggestive illustration of the level of control the United States then had over the military forces it was funding. Whether or not the embassy decision to refuse the FMLN offer to guide Greentree to the site of the massacre was discussed with Washington also remains shrouded in the subjunctive. "However much we might have wanted more information, no one in State was going to make that call," Danner was told by Peter Romero, at the time of Mozote an El Salvador specialist at the State Department.

Most of the interested players, then, knew about Morazán, in outline if not in detail, well before January 6, when Raymond Bonner and Susan Meiselas, followed a few days later by Alma Guillermoprieto, first walked into El Mozote. Not until January 30, however, three days after the story had appeared on the front pages of the *Times* and the *Post*, did the embassy dispatch Todd Greentree and Major John McKay, who was then in the defense attaché's office at the embassy and was at the time Danner interviewed him a colonel attached to NATO in Brussels, to Morazán. Greentree and McKay did not exactly get to El Mozote, although they did fly over it. Greentree's impression from the air was that "El Mozote had been pretty much destroyed." Once on the ground in Morazán, although not in El Mozote, Greentree and McKay, accompanied by a squad of the Atlacatl, interviewed those residents of the northern villages who had reached the refugee camp outside San Francisco Gotera. Although the Americans later recalled being able to "observe and feel this tremendous fear," they did not elicit eyewitness accounts of a massacre, nor had they expected to.

"You had a bunch of very intimidated, scared people, and now the Army presence further intimidated them," McKay told Danner. "I mean, the Atlacatl had supposedly done something horrible, and now these gringos show up under this pretense of investigating it, but in the presence of these soldiers. It was probably the worst thing you could do. I mean, you didn't have to be a rocket scientist to know what the Army people were there for." Greentree and McKay then set out for El Mozote, and got to within an hour's walk of what had been the village when the Atlacatl soldiers accompanying them stopped, and refused to go further. "In the end, we went up there and we didn't want to find that anything horrible had happened," McKay told Danner. "And the fact that we didn't get to the site turned out to be very detrimental to our reporting—the Salvadorans, you know, were never very good about cleaning up their shell casings." That evening, back at the embassy in San Salvador, Greentree wrote a report, the overriding aim of which appears to have been "credibility," summarizing his and McKay's findings.

Here is the point at which El Mozote entered the thin air of Washington, where the official story was that El Salvador, with the inspiration of the Reagan administration, was at last "turning the corner" toward democracy. "The end of Bob White's tour, and the transition period before Hinton arrived [Robert White had preceded Hinton as ambassador], and the first six months of Hinton's tour—those were the absolute worst days, really out of control," Greentree told Danner by way of explaining why the conviction that what was known or suspected in country would not be "credible" in Washington had by then increased exponentially. "And the fact that Bob White and everybody in the embassy had been so thoroughly traumatized by the murders of the nuns, and the AFL-CIO guys [the two Americans who were killed with the head of the Salvadoran land-reform agency at the Sheraton in San Salvador], and just the general sort of out-of-control way the military was—it meant that everything we reported could be taken as suspect."

The following day, after review and revisions, Greentree's report went to the State Department over Hinton's name. This was the cable containing the careful and soon to be repeated assertions that it was "not possible to prove or disprove excesses of violence against the civilian population of El Mozote by government troops" and that "no evidence could be found to confirm that government forces systematically massacred civilians in the operation zone, nor that the number of civilians killed even remotely approached the number being cited in other reports circulating internationally." The Greentree cable also contained, deep in its text, a curious warning from one of the interviewees, the mayor of Jocoaitique, who according to the cable "intimated that he knew of violent fighting in El Mozote" but was "unwilling to discuss deportment of government troops" and who then made a comment so coded that it could stand as a veiled but exact expression of the embassy position on what did or did not take place in Morazán. What the cable quoted the mayor of Jocoaitique as having said to Todd Greentree and Major McKay was this: "This is something one should talk about in another time, in another country."

That part of the embassy cable did not appear in the statement made two days later to the House Subcommittee on Western Hemisphere Affairs by Assistant Secretary of State for Inter-American Affairs Thomas O. Enders. (Nor would it appear in the sanitized version of the cable released under the Freedom of Information Act to Raymond Bonner in 1983.) The Enders statement was arresting not only for what it said and did not say but for its tone, which suggested an extreme version of a kind of exaggerated hauteur commonly translated as entitlement in the northeastern United States. "Many of you have read," he said, addressing what he called "special pleading" in the matter of death and disappearance statistics, "about something called the Legal Aid Office of the Archbishopric—Socorro Judico [*sic*] is its Spanish name; it is often cited in the international media. It strangely lists no victims of guerrilla or terrorist violence. Apparently they do not commit violence."

This was a level of seigneurial dismissal often emulated but never quite mastered by Jeane Kirkpatrick and Elliott Abrams and other regular defenders of administration policy in Central America. "There is another organization, the Central American University, that collects statistics too," Enders continued, referring to UCA, the Jesuit-run José Simeón Cañas University of Central America. "Its bias may be apparent from the fact that it does include a category of persons killed by what I believe Congressman Bonker referred to as paramilitary organizations. And they are called in Spanish *ajusticiados*, referring to persons that have received justice at the hands of their executioners." Only then did Enders turn his attention to what he described as "allegations" of massacres, including Mozote. "We sent two embassy officers down to investigate the reports," Enders said, inadvertently illuminating the particular distance between Washington and Morazán, which in local usage is said to be not "down" but "up" from San Salvador. Enders continued:

> It is clear from the report they gave that there has been a confrontation between the guerrillas occupying Mozote and attack-

> ing Government forces last December. There is no evidence to confirm that Government forces systematically massacred civilians in the operations zone, or that the number of civilians remotely approached the 733 or 926 victims cited in the press. I note they asked how many people were in that canton and were told probably not more than 300 in December, and there are many survivors including refugees now.

Enders said this on February 2, 1982. On February 1, Deane Hinton, in response to what he apparently construed as careless use of his reply to the National Council of Churches, had sent a corrective cable to the State Department. This cable read in part:

> I would be grateful if department would use extreme care in describing my views on alleged massacre. Case in point is description in para 3 of *REFTEL* referring to my letter . . . as "denying the incident." My letter did not "deny" incident: it reported that at that time I had no confirmation and argued from available evidence from Radio Venceremos and from lack of other reports that I had no reason to believe Venceremos reports. I still don't believe Venceremos version but additional evidence strongly suggests that something happened that should not have happened and that it is quite possible Salvadoran military did commit excesses. Allegations that it was unit from Atlacatl battalion in El Mozote remain to be confirmed or discredited.

Several days later, this Hinton cable notwithstanding, Assistant Secretary of State for Human Rights and Humanitarian Affairs Elliott Abrams echoed Enders in his statement to the Senate Foreign Relations Committee. The Mozote case was, Abrams said, "a very interesting one in a sense." "Interesting" was at the time a word much in use, as were "strange" and "unusual." Enders, for example, had noted that Socorro Juridico "strangely lists no victims of guerrilla and terrorist violence." I recall watching Jeane Kirkpatrick during this period tease an audience to frenzy with little silken whips of innuendo as she described how "*interested*," even "*bemused*," she was by the "*unusual* standards," the "*extraordinarily*, even *uniquely* demanding standards" imposed by the certification requirement. The reason Elliott Abrams found El Mozote "interesting" was this: ". . . because we found, for example, that the numbers, first of all, were not credible, because as Secretary Enders notes, our information was that there were only three hundred people in the canton." Abrams went on to wonder why a massacre that had occurred in mid-December, if indeed it had occurred at all, had not been "publicized" until late January.

Ten years later, in an interview, Abrams was still asking the same question, to the same innuendo: "If it had really been a massacre and not a firefight, why didn't we hear about it right off from the FMLN? I mean, we didn't start hearing about it until a month later." Abrams, in other words, was still trying to negotiate what had become, with the exhumation of the sacristy, unnegotiable, still trying to return discussion to the familiar question of whether or not a massacre had occurred. Enders, when he talked to Danner, had transcended this now inoperative line of attack, ascending effortlessly to the big-picture argument against the existence of a massacre: "Coming on top of everything else, El Mozote, if true, might have destroyed the entire effort. Who knows? I certainly thought that when I first heard about it." In other words it had been necessary to deny the massacre because had there been a massacre the "effort" would have become, and this was the word Enders used, "unfundable."

The effort did not become unfundable. The effort instead became what was at that time the most expensive effort to support a foreign government threatened by an insurgency since Vietnam. Progressively cruder interpretations of what had been the surgically precise statements made by the embassy came to dominate, during the spring and summer of 1982, discussion of this country's role in Central America. By February 10 of that spring *The Wall Street Journal* was noting editorially that "extremists" in El Salvador had "learned long ago the trick of dressing in military uniforms to confuse their victims." (This appears to have been the source for Ronald Reagan's later assertion that "communist operatives" were dressing in "freedom fighter uniforms" to discredit the Nicaraguan contras.) Shrill excoriations of Raymond Bonner, who necessarily had to be cast as having what George Melloan of *The Wall Street Journal* called "a political orientation," became commonplace.

Bonner was a graduate of Stanford Law School, had been a

prosecutor in the San Francisco district attorney's office, and had served as a marine officer in Vietnam. John McKay, the marine major who went up to Morazán with Todd Greentree, had been with Bonner in Vietnam, where McKay lost an eye. "We could not have said, 'My God, there's been a massacre,'" McKay told Danner about the cable the embassy sent to Washington as a report of his and Greentree's trip to Morazán. "But, truth be known, the ambiguity of the cable that went out—in my own conscience I began to question it. And then when I saw the *New York Times* piece, and the picture, that really got me thinking. Bonner and I had gone to Quantico together, went to Vietnam together." In the late summer of 1980, at a time when Bonner had spent time in Bolivia and Guatemala but had made only a few short visits to El Salvador, he had been asked his opinion of U.S. policy in El Salvador. "Ask me about Bolivia, or Guatemala, or any country, I'll probably have an opinion," Bonner recalled having said. "But El Salvador, boy, I just don't know. I guess we're doing the right thing."

Bonner, then, might have seemed an unlikely target for the campaign then being mounted against him in Washington and New York. For those waging this campaign, however, the question of "political orientation" was answered once and for all in August 1982, when the *Times* abruptly withdrew Bonner from Central America. According to A. M. Rosenthal, then the executive editor of the *Times*, Bonner was withdrawn because he "didn't know the techniques of weaving a story together. . . . I brought him back because it seemed terribly unfair to leave him there without training." Actually Bonner had spent a good part of 1981 on the Metro desk at the *Times*, but Rosenthal suggested that those who believed Bonner to have been withdrawn for reasons other than "training" did so because they resented Rosenthal himself. "I was an agent of change in the *Times*," he said, "and a lot of people didn't like my politics."

This self-referential approach worked to blur the issue. Whatever reason or reasons Rosenthal may have had for withdrawing Bonner, it was the sheer fact of that withdrawal, the fact of that apparent failure to back up a reporter who had put the paper on the line with a story denied by the government, that spoke so eloquently to those who wanted to discredit the reporting on El Mozote. That the *Times* withdrew Bonner was seen, immediately and by larger numbers of people than were actually knowledgeable about El Salvador or administration policy, as "proof" that he had been wrong about El Mozote; as recently as a few years ago it was possible to hear it casually said about Bonner that the *Times* "had to pull him out," that he had "bought into a massacre."

"For more than a year now we've been following the campaign that we victimized former *New York Times* correspondent Raymond Bonner," *The Wall Street Journal* noted editorially in 1993. "The excavation of children's bones in El Mozote is supposed to vindicate Mr. Bonner and discredit what we said. . . . We did not fire Mr. Bonner in the first place. *The New York Times* did. Or, more precisely, after then Managing Editor A. M. Rosenthal undertook his own reporting visit to El Salvador, it pulled Mr. Bonner off the beat and back to New York, where he left the paper." In defense of its own reasonableness, the *Journal* noted that in its original 1982 attack on Bonner it had "offered not one word of criticism of Alma Guillermoprieto of *The Washington Post*."

Among the documents reproduced at the end of *The Massacre at El Mozote*, Danner included the full text of both Bonner's and Alma Guillermoprieto's stories. There was no substantive difference between the two in either the reporting or the qualifying of what had been observed, but there were certain marginal distinctions on which critics of Bonner could seize. Guillermoprieto referred to herself as "this correspondent" and said that she had been taken into Morazán by "the Farabundo Martí Liberation Front." Bonner referred to himself as "a visitor who traveled through the area with those who are fighting the junta that now rules El Salvador," i.e., the Farabundo Martí Liberation Front. Guillermoprieto began: "Several hundred civilians, including women and children, were taken from their homes in and around this village and killed by Salvadoran Army troops during a December offensive against leftist guerrillas, according to three survivors who say they witnessed the alleged massacres." She then proceeded to describe the bodies she herself had seen. Bonner began: "From interviews with people who live in this small mountain village and surrounding hamlets, it is clear that a massacre of major proportions occurred here last month." He then proceeded to describe the bodies he himself had seen. Bonner's statement is the less varnished of the two, but to call it different is to resort to a point of journalistic convention so narrowly defined as to be merely legalistic.

There seemed at the time at least two clear reasons that Bonner, not Guillermoprieto, became the target of choice. One reason was that Bonner, unlike Guillermoprieto, continued to report on a daily basis from El Salvador, and so, all through the spring and into the summer of 1982, remained a stubborn mote in Deane Hinton's ability to project the situation as the State Department wanted it projected. "I'm just afraid he's going to get himself killed," I recall an embassy official saying about Bonner during a lunch with Hinton in June of 1982; the tone here was the macho swagger never entirely absent from American embassies on hardship status. "That would be a tragedy." The other clear reason that Bonner was targeted, and Guillermoprieto was not, was this: Benjamin C. Bradlee and *The Washington Post* had backed up their reporter. A. M. Rosenthal and *The New York Times* had not.

The Mozote massacre occurred only six years after most of us watched the helicopters lift off the roof of the Saigon embassy and get pushed off the flight decks of the U.S. fleet into the South China Sea. There were by the time the bodies were exhumed from the sacristy of the Mozote church more than twice as many years between us and Mozote as there were between Mozote and those helicopters. This is not an insignificant time line, and suggests a third reason that Raymond Bonner's report from Morazán elicited an acrimony that Alma Guillermoprieto's did not. Bonner was an American. Alma Guillermoprieto had been born in and was then living in Mexico, a fact that was in some way understood to render her ineligible for casting as a member of what was sometimes called "the adversary culture," the culture that was construed as hostile to the interests of American business and the American government, the culture that had caused the United States to "lose" Vietnam, the culture that was even then drawing parallels between Vietnam and El Salvador.

Certain parallels were inescapable, since El Salvador was seen, by both the American military and the American policy community, as an opportunity to "apply the lesson" of Vietnam. The counterinsurgency doctrine that rationalized such operations as the 1981 sweep of Morazán was intended as a "revision" of the failed counterinsurgency effort in Vietnam (the "revision" for El Salvador emphasized a need to correct "root causes," or to win popular support by "democratizing" Salvadoran society), yet it had come to sound dispiritingly the same. The word "pacification" was in use, as was the phrase "third force," usually in reference to José Napoleón Duarte. "The only territory you want to hold is the six inches between the ears of the *campesino*," Colonel John C. Waghelstein, who took command of the Milgroup not long after Mozote, said when he spoke at the American Enterprise Institute in 1985 on "LIC [Low-Intensity Conflict] in the Post-Vietnam Period." As late as 1986, in *The Wall Street Journal*, an American military adviser was quoted describing a community event sponsored by a Salvadoran army unit as "winning hearts and minds." The event in question involved clowns, mariachis, and speeches from army officers calling on peasants to reject the guerrillas. "This is low-intensity-conflict doctrine in action," the adviser said.

Again as in Vietnam, the doctrine was met with resistance on the part of those charged with carrying it out. "Attempts to address root causes during [this] period enjoyed less success than did efforts to stabilize the military situation," four American military officers observed in their 1988 *American Military Policy in Small Wars: The Case of El Salvador*, the so-called "colonels' report" prepared for the Institute for Foreign Policy Analysis. "American officers recognized . . . [that] the government had to transform itself into an institution perceived as effective, impartial, and committed to bringing about genuine reform. Meaningful implementation of this concept has eluded the Salvadorans and their American advisers." In a 1991 Rand Institute report prepared for the Department of Defense, Benjamin C. Schwarz noted that "the greed and apparent tactical incompetence of Salvadoran officers has so exhausted American experts posted to El Salvador that all the individuals interviewed for this report who have served there in the past two years believe that the Salvadoran military does not wish to win the war because in so doing it would lose the American aid that has enriched it for the past decade."

In San Salvador as in Saigon, this had long been accepted as one of the many taxing givens that made the posting so difficult to share with those who were planning the effort in Washington. Deane Hinton, who would not talk to Danner, emerges in *The Massacre at El Mozote* as the ultimate example of the career foreign service officer trying to execute an extremely doubtful policy in an even more doubtful situation. In this role as the good soldier of American foreign policy, Hinton left El Salvador in 1983 for Pakistan, a more remote but equally doubtful situation, and then returned to Central America to mop up the debris left by the contra and then the Panama efforts. Alma Guillermoprieto, whose work after El Mozote was especially acute on the immediacy with which Washington dreams became Central and South American responsibilities, noted in *The Heart That Bleeds* that, as late as 1992 in Hinton's Panama embassy, the preferred way to refer to the 1989 invasion was as "*la liberación*."

"This is a suicide mission," an unidentified embassy official in San Salvador had said when Warren Hoge of *The New York Times* asked, not long after Mozote, if assignment to El Salvador could advance a foreign service career. "Someone's got to be nuts to be here. How many people do you think profited from having worked in Vietnam?" What made the San Salvador embassy a suicide mission was, of course, the certain knowledge that the facts of the situation would be less than welcome at the other end of the cable traffic. "There was no secret about who was doing the killing," Danner was told by Howard Lane, the public affairs officer at the embassy at the time of El Mozote. "I mean, you formed that view within forty-eight hours after arriving in the country, and there was no secret at all about it—except, maybe, in the White House."

What Mark Danner detailed in *The Massacre at El Mozote* was the process by which actual eyewitness accounts (Bonner, Guillermoprieto) and photographs (Meiselas) came to be discounted by large numbers of Americans for no other reason than that the government, presenting no evidence, referred to the accounts (the photographs seemed rather eerily not to exist in anyone's argument) as describing an event that was intrinsically unconfirmable, rendering the accounts by definition untrue. "Accurate information," Thomas Enders said as he began his February 2, 1982, statement on Capitol Hill. "I think we have all found out that is very hard to establish." He continued, first questioning the possibility of ever determining who had been responsible for the deaths—if indeed there had even been "deaths." Then he raised the ultimate question, the coup de grâce question, the question that had to do with the true interests or motives of those who reported such deaths: "The responsibility for the overwhelming number of deaths is never legally determined nor usually accounted for by clear or coherent evidence. Seventy percent of the political murders known to our embassy were committed by unknown assailants. And there is much special pleading going on also in this."

What is especially striking about Enders, as he presents himself in *The Massacre at El Mozote*, is his apparent inability to recognize any contradiction between what he said in 1982 to the House Subcommittee on Western Hemisphere Affairs and what he said a decade later to Danner. At one point Danner asked Enders about a rumor, believed by a number of prominent Salvadorans, that two American advisers had observed the Mozote operation from a base camp below the Torola River. This was the answer Enders gave: "Certainly, one of the issues I remember raising between us and the embassy was: Were there any American advisers on this sortie? The embassy made a great effort to talk to advisers who were with the Atlacatl to try to find out the truth." Any admission of knowledge, Enders conceded, "would have ruined those guys' careers—they would have been cashiered. So no one's going to volunteer, 'Hey, I was up there.'" The effect of such a disclosure on administration efforts to continue funding the war would have been "devastating," Enders said, and then: "American advisers with a unit that committed an atrocity? Can you imagine anything more corrosive of the entire military effort?"

Enders had recognized at the time, then, the existence of a "sortie." He had even recognized the possibility of an "atrocity." (The atrocity if not the sortie was in the subjunctive.) He had raised with the embassy the question of whether there had been "American advisers" present. Yet what Enders had said in 1982 was this: ". . . frankly, we do not have people who go out with the units as advisers, you know. These are military trainers. They stay behind." The idea that there was a difference between "advisers" and "trainers," another of the many legalistic distinctions at that time employed to rhetorical advantage, seems not to have been consistently held even by Enders.

Danner describes what happened to the story of El Mozote during the days and months after its disclosure as "a parable of the cold war." It was that, and as such a parable Mozote is irresistibly legible, but it was also something else. It was a parable of ideology, and of the apparently inconsolable anger it had become possible to feel toward those who were perceived as not sharing this ideology. "There have also been many fewer allegations of massacres during this reporting period than last," Thomas Enders was able to say in July 1982, when the question of certification once again came before the House Committee on Foreign Affairs. "This may be in part," he said, still the loyalist but still careful—*fewer* allegations, *may* be, *in part*—"because many earlier reports proved to be fabricated or exaggerated." At the same hearing, Nestor Sanchez, then deputy assistant secretary of defense for inter-American affairs, was able to single out "the first quick-reaction battalion trained by U.S. instructors in El Salvador" not only for "its tactical capability in fighting the guerrillas" but also for "its humane treatment of the people."

The "first quick-reaction battalion trained by U.S. instructors in El Salvador" was the Atlacatl. Just six years after Vietnam and in the face of what was beginning to seem a markedly similar American engagement, El Mozote, by which we have come to mean not exactly the massacre itself but the systematic obfuscation and prevarication that followed the disclosure of the massacre, was the first hard evidence that we had emerged a people again so yearning to accept the government version, or again so angry, as to buy into a revision of history in which those Americans who differed—those Americans who for reasons of their "political orientation" would "fabricate" reports of a massacre carried out by a unit noted for its "humane treatment of the people"—were again our true, and only truly sinister, enemy.

3.

December 18, 1997

The aides gave us the details, retold now like runes. Promptly at nine o'clock on most mornings of the eight years he spent as president of the United States, Ronald Reagan arrived in the Oval Office to find on his desk his personal schedule, printed on green stationery and embossed in gold with the presidential seal. Between nine and ten he was briefed, first by his chief of staff and the vice president and then by his national security adviser. At ten, in the absence of a pressing conflict, he was scheduled for downtime, an hour in which he answered selected letters from citizens and clipped items that caught his eye in *Human Events* and *National Review*. Other meetings followed, for example with the congressional leadership. "I soon learned that these meetings lasted just one hour, no more, no less," Tony Coelho, at the time majority whip in the House, told us in *Recollections of Reagan: A Portrait of Ronald Reagan*, a 1997 collection of reminiscences edited by Peter Hannaford. "If the agenda—which he had written out on cards—wasn't completed at the end of the hour, he would excuse himself and leave. If it was finished short of an hour, he would fill the rest of the time with jokes (and he tells a good one)." During some meetings, according to his press secretary, Larry Speakes, the president filled the time by reciting Robert Service's "The Cremation of Sam McGee."

When the entry on the schedule was not a meeting but an appearance or a photo opportunity, the president was rehearsed. "You'll go out the door and down the steps," Michael Deaver or someone else would say, we were told by Donald Regan, secretary of the treasury from 1981 until 1985 and White House chief of staff from 1985 until 1987. "The podium is ten steps to the right and the audience will be in a semi-circle with the cameras at the right end of the half-moon; when you finish speaking take two steps back, but don't leave the podium, because they're going to present you with a patchwork quilt." It was Larry Speakes, in his 1988 *Speaking Out: The Reagan Presidency from Inside the White House*, who told us how, at the conclusion of each meeting or appearance, the president would draw on his schedule a vertical line downward and an arrow pointing to the next event. "It gives me a feeling that I am accomplishing something," the president told Speakes. It was Donald Regan, in his 1988 *For the Record: From Wall Street to Washington*, who told us how the schedule reminded the president when it was time to give a birthday present ("a funny hat or a tee shirt bearing a jocular message") to one or another staff member. "These gifts were chosen by others, and sometimes Reagan barely knew the person to whom he was giving them, but his pleasure in these contacts was genuine. . . . On one occasion, when he was somehow given the wrong date for one man's birthday and called to offer congratulations, nobody had the heart to tell him about the mistake."

"I cannot remember a single case in which he changed a time or canceled an appointment or even complained about an item on his schedule," Regan noted, betraying a certain queasy wonder at his initial encounter with this apparently cheerful lack of interest: Regan, still at Treasury, found himself slotted into the schedule, along with James Baker and Michael Deaver, to introduce to the president the novel notion that he and Baker, then chief of staff, switch jobs. "Reagan listened without any sign of surprise," Regan recalled. "He seemed equable, relaxed—almost incurious. This seemed odd under the circumstances." Notwithstanding Regan's efforts to offer the possibility of further deliberation on so serious a move ("'I appreciate that, Don,' the President said with the bright courtesy that is typical of him. 'But I don't see why we shouldn't just go ahead with it'"), the meeting lasted, including an exchange of Christmas-vacation pleasantries, fewer than its allotted thirty minutes. "I did not know what to make of his passivity," Regan wrote. "He seemed to be absorbing a *fait accompli* rather than making a decision. One might have thought that the matter had already been settled by some absent party." On reflection, Regan understood:

> As President, Ronald Reagan acted on the work habits of a lifetime: he regarded his daily schedule as being something like a shooting script in which characters came and went, scenes were rehearsed and acted out, and the plot was advanced one day at a time, and not always in sequence. The Chief of Staff was a sort of producer, making certain that the star had what he needed to do his best; the staff was like the crew, invisible behind the lights, watching the performance their behind-the-scenes efforts

> had made possible. . . . Reagan's performance was almost always flawless. If he was scheduled to receive a visitor at ten o'clock, he would finish whatever else he was doing at 9:58, clear off his desk, clear his mind of whatever had gone before, and prepare himself for the next scene.

Dinesh D'Souza, when he arrived at the Reagan White House as a senior domestic policy analyst in 1987, was twenty-six years old, a resident of the United States only since 1978 but already a name within what had come on the right to be called "the movement." He was a native of India who seemed to have arrived in this country with preternatural pitch for the exact charged chords (affirmative action, multiculturalism, gender studies, the academy in general) that drove its politics of resentment, and he played them, first as a founding editor of *The Dartmouth Review*, then as editor of the equally strident Princeton *Prospect*, managing editor of the Heritage Foundation's *Policy Review*, and biographer of the Moral Majority's Jerry Falwell.

The 1980s were years in Washington when careers were made on undergraduate bliss. One of D'Souza's colleagues on *The Dartmouth Review* became a speechwriter for Reagan, another for George Bush. Another, Keeney Jones, the author of the notorious "Dis Sho' Ain't No Jive, Bro," a puerile but predictably inflammatory *Dartmouth Review* parody of black students ("Dese boys be sayin' that we be comin' here to Dartmut an' not takin' the classics. You know, Homa, Shakesphere; but I hea' dey all be co'd in da ground, six feet unda, and whatchu be askin' us to learn from dem?"), became a speechwriter for Secretary of Education William Bennett. Another, Laura Ingraham, who became famous at *The Dartmouth Review* for publishing the secretly taped transcript of a meeting of the Gay Students' Association and to whom D'Souza dedicated *Illiberal Education*, went on to clerk for Clarence Thomas and then to become one of the most visible blonde pundits on MSNBC. "What could be more exciting?" D'Souza, who had been editor of *The Dartmouth Review* at the time "Dis Sho' Ain't No Jive, Bro" was published, later wrote of those years in Washington when to be young and movement was very heaven. "We were a generation of young conservatives who came to Washington in the 1980s inspired by Reagan and the idea of America that he espoused and embodied. The world was changing, and we wanted to be instruments of that change. Reagan was a septuagenarian with a youthful heart. He hired people like me because he wanted fresh faces and new ideas in the White House. Full of vigor and determination, we rallied to his cause."

"He hired people like me" may seem to suggest excessive executive volition on the part of a president who by all accounts expressed no interest in who his secretary of the treasury or chief of staff was to be, but the choice of the active tense is key here. D'Souza's intention in his 1997 *Ronald Reagan: How an Ordinary Man Became an Extraordinary Leader* (which, like his 1991 *Illiberal Education: The Politics of Race and Sex on Campus* and his 1995 *The End of Racism: Principles for a Multiracial Society*, was written within the nurturing framework of the American Enterprise Institute) was to offer what he presented as a "revisionist" view of the Reagan years, a correction of the record for "a new generation of young people" who, because they have had "no alternative source of information," have been unable to detect the "transparent bias" of their teachers and the media.

It was D'Souza's thesis, honed by his useful and apparently inexhaustible ability to present himself as one of a besieged minority, that Reagan had been systematically misread. The misreading only began, in this view, with Reagan's "liberal critics," who were further identified as "the pundits, political scientists, and historians," "the wise men," "the intellectual elite," and "the cognoscenti." The more grave misreading, as D'Souza sees it, came from within Reagan's own party, not only from his more pragmatic aides (the "prags," or "ingrates and apostates," whose remarkably similar descriptions of the detachment at the center of the administration in which they served suggested to D'Souza "an almost defiant disloyalty") but even from his "hard-core" admirers, or "true believers," those movement conservatives who considered Reagan a "malleable figurehead" too often controlled by the pragmatists on his staff. "I was one of those conservatives," D'Souza allowed:

> Even when Reagan proved us wrong and showed how effective a president he was, many of us in his ideological camp nevertheless failed to understand the secret of his success. We could not fathom how he conceived and realized his grand objectives, effortlessly overcame his powerful adversaries, and won the respect of the American people. Many who worked with him are still bewildered. This study seeks to solve the mystery.

In his casuistical pursuit of the elusive frame in which Reagan can be seen as the "prime mover," the "decisive agent of change," and the "architect of his own success," D'Souza was not actually breaking new ground. Such attempts to "solve the mystery" date back at least to the 1980 transition, during which it became apparent to some that the president-elect, without benefit of constructive interpretation, could appear less than fully engaged. During a transition briefing on secret international agreements and commitments, according to Jimmy Carter, Reagan listened politely but asked no questions and took no notes. Two hours before his 1981 inauguration, according to Michael Deaver, he was still sleeping. Deaver did not actually find this extraordinary, nor would anyone else who had witnessed Reagan's performance as governor of California. "I remember sitting there in the governor's office with him, a couple of days after I had been elected to succeed him," Jerry Brown recalls in *Recollections of Reagan: A Portrait of Ronald Reagan*:

> We didn't have a nuts-and-bolts conversation about the transition that day. I didn't see Ronald Reagan as a nuts-and-bolts kind of guy. . . . He was definitely performing his ceremonial role as governor, and doing it quite well. I think a great deal of the job is ceremonial. The way I look at it now, most politicians holding office think they are doing things but it's all staffed out. . . . Most of the day-to-day stuff is very symbolic. That was one of the frustrations I found in being governor. At first, I took literally the nature of the material being presented at meetings, but I soon found that visiting delegations often were satisfied just being in the same room as the governor. There is something illusory about it, like a play. Then again, if that satisfies people, it has some value. Reagan seemed to understand all that.

This was in fact the very understanding that would come to power Reagan's performance as president, and many people knew it, but to have said so at the time would have been out of synch with the somewhat less Zen story line (West Wing lights burn late as dedicated workaholics hit the ground running) preferred in Washington. From the outset, then, the invention of a president who could be seen as active rather than passive, who could be understood to possess mysteriously invisible and therefore miraculously potent leadership skills, became a White House priority. "Reagan's aides have been telling reporters of decisions that the President himself has made, as if they found it necessary to explain that he has made some," Elizabeth Drew reported two months into the administration, when both NBC and *Time* had been enlisted to do "A Day with President Reagan" stories. "A White House aide told me, 'We thought it was important to do those, because of the perception out there that this is a marionette president. It's simply not true.'"

This president who was not a marionette would be shown making decisions, and not only that: the decisions he was shown making (or more often in this instance, where rhetoric was soon understood to be interchangeable with action, the speeches he was shown making) would have demonstrable, preferably Manichean, results. Victory, particularly in the realm of foreign affairs, which offered dramatic "standing tall" roles for the active president to play, would be narrowly defined: the barest suggestion of an election or a reform would serve to signal the enlistment of another fledgling democracy. So defined, all victories could assume equal import: the decision to invade Grenada, D'Souza tells us, reversed the Brezhnev Doctrine. "Reagan had listened intently but said little," D'Souza wrote about the moment of standing tall that preceded the Grenada invasion. "Finally he asked the Joint Chiefs of Staff whether they believed that a military operation was likely to succeed." The Joint Chiefs, according to D'Souza, who credits his account of this meeting to Edwin Meese and Caspar Weinberger, said they believed that the operation, which entailed landing six thousand marines and airborne rangers on an island significantly smaller than Barbados, "could be done."

"Very well," Reagan is said to have said. "In that case, let's go ahead."

The invasion of Grenada is instructive. The operation, which involved one of Reagan's few overt (and his only, on his own terms, "successful") uses of military power, was justified by the administration on the ground that a ten-thousand-foot landing strip was under construction on the island, but secondarily (or primarily, depending on who was talking) because American medical students were "captive" (in fact they could have left on either regularly scheduled or charter flights) at an island medical school. "I don't think it was an invasion," Jeane Kirkpatrick said on *Meet the Press* a few days after the operation. "I think it was a rescue, and I think that we ought to stop calling it an invasion." Norman Podhoretz, on the op-ed page of *The New York Times*, wrote that the invasion, or the rescue, suggested a return to "recovery and health" for "a United States still suffering from the shell-shocked condition that has muddled our minds and paralyzed our national will since Vietnam." D'Souza characterizes it as "Reagan's first opportunity to overthrow a communist regime," an occasion when "Reagan's leadership was exercised in the face of apprehension on the part of his staff and skepticism on the part of the congressional leadership."

Not long after the Grenada invasion, for which the number of medals awarded eventually exceeded the number of actual combatants, the president, in his commander-in-chief role, spoke at a ceremony honoring the nation's Medal of Honor recipients. "Our days of weakness are over," he declared, standing under a huge representation of the medal's pale-blue ribbon and five-pointed star. "Our military forces are back on their feet and standing tall." Grenada, then, virtually as it happened, had materialized into the symbolic centerpiece of the rollback scenario that was the Reagan Doctrine. In the first dozen pages of *Ronald Reagan: How an Ordinary Man Became an Extraordinary Leader*, D'Souza laid out, presumably for that "new generation of young people with no alternative source of information," a kind of Young Adults timeline in which the Reagan administration is seen to begin at modern history's lowest tide ("capitalism and democracy . . . on the retreat in much of the world," America itself facing "the greatest economic crisis since the Great Depression") and to conclude at its highest, the triumphal surge of reborn patriotism and purpose that was to raise all boats and end the cold war.

In this version of what happened between 1980 and 1988, Reagan's role as prime mover is seen to reside, before and after Grenada, less in actual actions than in his speeches, those moments when the president was primed to "go over the heads" of the Congress or the media or whoever was at the moment frustrating the aims of the administration. D'Souza, in *Ronald Reagan: How an Ordinary Man Became an Extraordinary Leader*, devoted four of his 264 pages to a close textual analysis of the 1983 "Evil Empire" speech (further comment appears on four more pages), which was, he assures us, "the single most important speech of the Reagan presidency, a classic illustration of what Václav Havel terms 'the power of words to change history.'"

This faith in the laser-like efficacy of Reagan's rhetoric seems undiminished by the fact that it remains largely a priori. "Going after a major policy change, crafting a practical policy initiative, and sticking with it is an accomplishment," Martin Anderson, who was Reagan's chief domestic policy adviser in the early administration, tells us in *Recollections of Reagan*. Yet the accomplishment he cites is the 1983 SDI, or "Star Wars," speech. "Another very important event in 1983 took place two weeks after the SDI speech," he adds, and, again, it develops that he is talking about not an actual "event" but another speech, in this instance the popular "Evil Empire."

William Kristol made recent reference to our need to credit Reagan's "magnificent" 1984 speech at Normandy, as if the speech, which was written by Peggy Noonan, were somehow at one on the "magnificence" scale with the invasion it was delivered to commemorate. ("The State/NSC draft that I'd been given weeks before wanted the president to go off on this little tangent about arms control," Miss Noonan later wrote about her Normandy speech, "and as I read it I thought, in the language of the day, Oh gag me with a spoon, this isn't a speech about arms negotiations, you jackasses, this is a speech about splendor.") As evidence that Reagan had the force of calculation behind his "predictions" and "prophecies," D'Souza offers the "tear down this wall" speech delivered at the Brandenburg Gate in 1987. "Not long after this," he writes, "the wall did come tumbling down, and Reagan's prophecies all came true. The most powerful empire in human history imploded. These were not just results Reagan predicted. He intended the outcome."

The consequences of reinventing Reagan as a leader whose leadership was seen to exist exclusively in his public utterances, the ultimate "charismatic" president, were interestingly studied by the political historian Jeffrey K. Tulis, who, in his 1987 *The Rhetorical Presidency*, outlined in some detail the dilemmas presented by a presidential style that tends to delegitimize both constitutional and bureaucratic authority, to depend for its effect on created crises (to "go over the heads" of the opposition requires the presence of some urgent message to be conveyed), and so to place unusual policy-making power in the hands of speechwriters:

> Many speeches are scheduled long before they are to be delivered. Thus the commitment to speak precedes the knowledge of any issue to speak about, often causing staff to find or create an issue for the speech. . . . The routinization of crisis, endemic to the rhetorical presidency, is accompanied by attempted repetitions of charisma. In Reagan's case this style was further reinforced by an ideology and a rhetoric opposed to the Washington establishment, to bureaucrats and bureaucracies. . . . He serves as a better illustration than any other president of the possibility and danger that presidents might come themselves to think in the terms initially designed to persuade those not capable of fully understanding the policy itself. Having reconfigured the political landscape, the rhetorical presidency comes to reconstitute the president's political understanding.

Since D'Souza's account of the Reagan presidency derived from and differed in no substantive factual detail from those of the "ingrates and apostates" who were already on their book tours when that presidency ended, the superimposition of the "leadership" narrative meant grappling with some fairly intractable material already on the record. The peculiarities noticed by others (the president was "detached," or "not entirely informed," or "vague on details," or "passive") would need to be translated into evidence of a grand design. Biographical details would need to be mined for "character" points, often to less than coherent effect. "Here was the son of the town drunk who grew up poor in the Midwest," D'Souza tells us on page

10. "Without any connections, he made his way to Hollywood and survived its cutthroat culture to become a major star."

This was not literally true: Reagan was never a "major star," but a reliable studio contract player who hit an era of diminished demand and was reduced, before finding a role as a spokesman for General Electric, to introducing a club act, The Continentals, at the Last Frontier in Las Vegas. "Survived its cutthroat culture to become a major star," however, fit the point D'Souza was trying to make on this page, which had to do with "the personal [and] political mystery" that had enabled Reagan to change "both his country and the rest of the world." By page 45, where the point to be made had to do with the president's flexibility and skill at "the art of negotiating and being part of a team," D'Souza had reworked the bio to yield what he needed: "Reagan was never a big enough star to permit himself such consuming narcissism. . . . When many actors were too fastidious to be seen on television, regarding it as inferior to film, Reagan obligingly switched to the new medium, thus guaranteeing himself more parts."

This constant trimming and tacking leads D'Souza into fairly choppy water, where logical connections tend to get jettisoned. If the famous Reagan "gaffes" were calculated, as D'Souza suggests ("When we recall Reagan's gaffes, we see that he sometimes used them as a kind of code to transmit important political messages that would be incomprehensible to a hostile media"), then could the president not be seen as a demagogue, deliberately manipulating the electorate with "facts" (the welfare queens, the student loans used to buy certificates of deposit, the young man who went into the grocery store and bought an orange with food stamps and a bottle of vodka with the change) he knew would never stand scrutiny? Not at all: the president dealt in "morality tales," in the "illustration of a broader theme," and "just because this or that particular detail might be erroneous did not mean that the moral of the story was invalid." If Reagan failed to recognize his black secretary of housing and urban development, Samuel Pierce, addressing him as "Mr. Mayor," did that not suggest a relationship both with his own administration and with urban America that remained casual at best? No, only an "oversight":

"He was wrong not to recognize Sam Pierce, but the reason for his oversight was that he had no interest in the Department of Housing and Urban Development, which he saw as a rat hole of public policy."

If Reagan set out to reduce the size and cost of the government and left it, in 1990 dollars, $1.5 trillion deeper in debt than when he started ("You and I, as individuals, can, by borrowing, live beyond our means, but only for a limited period of time," he had said in his 1981 inaugural address. "Why then should we think that collectively, as a nation, we are not bound by that same limitation?"), could not the president be said to have failed at his own mission? No, because Reagan's unique approach to that mission, which allowed him to cut taxes while increasing domestic entitlements and boosting defense spending to a rough total, for the eight years, of $2 trillion, turned out to have "a silver lining." D'Souza explains: "by a strange turn of fate, the deficit accomplished for Reagan what he was unable to achieve directly: for the first time in this century, Congress began to impose limits on the growth of government." If Reagan lacked, as D'Souza allows, not only "historical learning" and "encyclopedic knowledge" but also "the two characteristics of the liberally educated person: self-consciousness and open-mindedness," did dogmatism not tend to undermine the value of his opinions? Not exactly: Reagan "saw the world through the clear lens of right and wrong," and so possessed a knowledge that "came not from books but from within himself."

The knowledge that "came not from books but from within himself" is where we reenter the real woo-woo of the period, the insistence on the ineffable that began with the perceived need to front the administration with a "leader" and ended by transforming the White House into a kind of cargo cult. "There is no point in pining for 'another Ronald Reagan,'" D'Souza concludes, exactly if unwittingly capturing this aspect of the period. "He isn't returning, and there will never be another quite like him." Since it was the given of the Reagan administration that Reagan was at its helm, and since a good deal of the visible evidence suggested otherwise, the man must be a "mystery," with skills pitched, like a dog whistle, beyond our defective ability to hear them.

D'Souza tells us that Edmund Morris, Reagan's official biographer, in 1990 characterized his subject as the most incomprehensible figure he had ever encountered. He tells us that Lou Cannon, who covered Reagan in Sacramento and in Washington and wrote three books about him, regards Reagan as a puzzle, and is "still trying to understand the man." He tells us that Reagan and Edwin Meese, whose daily lives were inseparable in both Sacramento and Washington, never saw each other socially. Reagan had "countless acquaintances," D'Souza observes, but apparently only one close friend, the actor Robert Taylor. Nancy Reagan spoke regularly to friends on the telephone, but her husband did not: "He would say hello, exchange a few pleasantries, then hand the receiver to her." Frustrated by "the paradoxes of Reagan's personality," D'Souza writes, "some who worked with him for years have given up trying to understand him."

Yet these "paradoxes" existed only within what was essentially a category confusion. Defined as "president," or even as "governor," Reagan did indeed appear to have some flat sides, some missing pieces. Defined as "actor," however, he was from the beginning to the end of his public life entirely consistent, a knowable and in fact quite predictable quantity. D'Souza allows that Reagan's life as an actor was a significant part of his makeup, but sees "actor" as a stepping stone, a role the real Ronald Reagan, or "president," had mastered and shed, although not before absorbing certain lessons that "enabled him to govern more effectively": the importance of appealing to a mass audience, say, or the knowledge that "noble ideals" could be more effectively communicated "if they were not abstract but personalized and visualized." Grappling with the question of how Reagan could be "uniformly fair-minded and pleasant with aides" but "not get close to them personally," D'Souza, laboring from within the definition "president," extracts a "leadership" solution: "He saw them as instruments to achieve his goals."

"People would work for him for a decade, then they would leave, and he would not associate with them—not even a phone call," D'Souza notes, and again draws the "leadership" lesson: "Thus the conventional wisdom must be turned on its head: he wasn't their pawn; they were his." This fails to compute (if they were the pawns and he their leader, would he not instead be inclined to keep them on speed dial, available for further deployment?) and will continue to do so, since the category is wrong: what might be seen as mysterious behavior in one occupation can be standard operating procedure in another, and it is within the unique working rhythms of the entertainment industry that the "mysteries" of the man and the administration evaporate. Reagan could be "uniformly fair-minded and pleasant with aides" without getting close to them personally (or knowing where their offices were or even their names) not because he "saw them as instruments to achieve his goals" but because he saw them as members of the crew ("invisible behind the lights," in Donald Regan's words), as gaffers and best boys and script supervisors and even as day players, actors like himself but not featured performers whose names he need remember.

Similarly, the ability to work with people for a decade and never call them again precisely reflects the intense but temporary camaraderie of the set, the location, where the principals routinely exchange the ritual totems of bonding (unlisted home numbers, cell numbers, car numbers, triple-secret numbers, and hour-by-hour schedules for sojourns in Aspen and Sundance and Martha's Vineyard) in full and mutual confidence that the only calls received after the wrap will be for ADR, or for reshoots. Even that most minor of presidential idiosyncracies, the absolute adherence to the daily schedule remarked upon by virtually all Reagan's aides, the vertical line drawn through the completed task and the arrow pointing to the next task (D'Souza tells us again about the arrows, as evidence of "the brisk thoroughness with which he discharged his responsibilities"), derives from the habits of the set, where the revised shooting schedule is distributed daily. "SC. 183A—EXT. WASHINGTON STREET—MOTORCADE—DAY," such a schedule might read, and, once Scene 183A was completed, a vertical line would be drawn through it on the schedule, with an arrow pointing to "SC. 17—ANDREWS AFB—ESTABLISHING—DAY":

not in any sequence the principals need to understand, but the day's next task.

Asked whether he liked being president better than being an actor, Ronald Reagan, according to D'Souza, replied, "Yes, because here I get to write the script too." D'Souza presents this as the president's amusing deprecation of the way in which he achieved objectives "against the odds," and so it may have been intended, but the deeper peculiarities of Reagan's tenure could even at the time be seen to derive from his tendency to see the presidency as a script waiting to be solved. There is in the development of every motion picture a process known as "licking the script," that period during which the "story" is shaped and altered to fit the idealized character who must be at its center. A president who understands the "character clarity" that results from this process would sense immediately that a scene with, say, Prime Minister Yitzhak Shamir of Israel could be improved by a dramatization of how he, the president, or star, personally experienced the Holocaust.

It would be only logical, then, for Reagan to tell Shamir, as he did in 1983, that during World War II he had filmed Nazi death camps for the Signal Corps (in fact he had spent the entire war in Culver City, making training films at the Hal Roach studio), that he had (presciently) kept one reel in case the Holocaust was ever questioned, and that he had (just recently!) found occasion to convert a doubter by running this reel. A president who understands how a single scene can jump a script would naturally offer reporters in Charlotte, North Carolina, as Lou Cannon tells us that Reagan did during his 1975 primary campaign, this improved version of how segregation ended in the military:

> "When the Japanese dropped the bomb on Pearl Harbor there was a Negro sailor whose total duties involved kitchen-type duties. . . . He cradled a machine gun in his arms, which is not an easy thing to do, and stood on the end of a pier blazing away at Japanese airplanes that were coming down and strafing him and that [segregation] was all changed." When a reporter pointed out that segregation in the armed services actually had ended when President Truman signed an executive order in 1948 three

years after the war, Reagan stood his ground. "I remember the scene," Reagan told me on the campaign plane later. "It was very powerful."

The question most frequently asked in a script meeting is, in one variation or another, always this: *Why do we care, how can we up the stakes, what's going to make America root for this guy?* The "guy," of course is the main character, the star part, and infinite time and attention is devoted to finding his "hook," the secret to his character that gets hinted at in Act One, revealed at the end of Act Two, and turned in Act Three: "son of the town drunk," say, could even be the secret behind "stood on the burning pier and cradled in his arms the machine gun that would end segregation." Ronald Reagan, we later learned from his personal physician, Brigadier General John Hutton, first grasped the import of the AIDS epidemic in July 1985 (until then he had seemed to construe it as a punishment for bad behavior, and "would say words to the effect: 'Is there a message in this?'"), when he learned from a news report that it had happened to someone America could root for, Rock Hudson.

There is in *Ronald Reagan: How an Ordinary Man Became an Extraordinary Leader* one arresting account, which seems to be based not on D'Souza's access to the famous and less known movers of the period (his two-page list of acknowledgments recalls with considerable poignancy the fervor of the moment, including as it does such evocative names as "Elliott Abrams," "George Gilder," "Josh Gilder," "Michael Ledeen," "Joshua Muravchik," "Grover Norquist," "Robert Reilly," "Joseph Sobran," and "Faith Whittlesey") but on reporting done by Jane Mayer and Doyle McManus for their *Landslide: The Unmaking of the President, 1984–1988.* The place is the White House. The time is October 26, 1983, when the American students "rescued" by the invasion of Grenada were on their way to Charleston Air Force Base in South Carolina. "On the day of their arrival," D'Souza writes, "Oliver North, who had helped plan the Grenada operation, came rushing into the president's office."

> He said that the students had not been briefed on the reasons for the invasion, and no one knew what they would tell the press. "Come with me," Reagan said. He led North into a room with a television monitor. There the two of them watched as the first young man got off the plane, walked over to the runway, dropped to his knees, and kissed the soil of the United States. "You see, Ollie," Reagan said, "you should have more faith in the American people." Reagan knew that with the student's dramatic gesture, the national debate over the legitimacy of the Grenada invasion was effectively over.

Among the several levels on which this passage invites the reader to linger (Why would students in need of rescue need to be briefed on the reasons for the rescue? How exactly would "more faith in the American people" lead to the expectation that the first student off the plane would show the cameras what the administration wanted shown?), the most rewarding has to do with "Ollie," and his apparently easy access, as early as October 1983, to the president's office. It would, in due time, be repeatedly suggested that Lieutenant Colonel North was a rogue fantast who had inflated or even invented his proximity to the president. "He said he sometimes spent time alone with Ronnie in the Oval Office," Nancy Reagan wrote in *My Turn*, her own essay into correcting the record. "But that never happened." Larry Speakes called North's assertion that he had been in the Oval Office when the medical students arrived home from Grenada "an outright lie." "We researched the records," he wrote, "and there was never a time when Ollie was alone with the President in the Oval Office." Yet D'Souza's vignette casts North, whose several code names included "Mr. Goode" and "Mr. White," in what seems to have been his own preferred light: he was on the scene, he was in the picture, he was able in a moment of threatened crunch to regard the president as his confidant.

By October 1983, the sequence of events that became known as "Iran-contra," or, as D'Souza calls it, the "historical footnote that future generations will not even remember," was well underway, and the White House deep in that perilous territory where certain spectral missions were already coinciding, to deleterious effect, with the demands of the script. Iran-contra, D'Souza assures his Young Adult readers, "seems to have been transacted in the White House without Reagan's knowledge or approval," but even if we discount the assertions of Reagan's aides that he was briefed on every detail except possibly (this point remains unclear) the diversion of funds, and even if we discount the president's own statement that "it was my idea to begin with," Iran-contra was not a series of events that professionals of the Washington process would naturally think of transacting.

It was instead a scenario that suggested the addled inspiration of script meetings, the moment when the elusive line materializes: on the one hand we have the "lion in winter," as D'Souza calls Reagan, the aging freedom fighter (*NB, possible: we learn in Act Two he knows he has something terminal but hasn't told anybody???*) whose life has been dedicated to the eradication of tyranny and who is now, apparently alone (*NB, everyone opposes, scene where even trusted aide backs away*), facing his last and toughest battle with the forces of injustice. The inspiration, of course, the solution to the script, the always startlingly obvious idea that comes only when the table is littered with takeout and the producer is inventing pressing business elsewhere, is this: the lonely lion in winter turns out not to be alone after all, for we also have the young colonel, "Mr. Goode," a born performer, a larger-than-life character, a real character, actually, one who (according to Larry Speakes) "loved to operate big in the Situation Room . . . standing in the middle of the floor, a phone at each ear, barking cryptic orders to some faraway operative" and who (according to Peggy Noonan) could convincingly deliver such lines as "And don't forget this is in accord conversation Casey-North approximately 1500 this date" or "Don't talk to me about Pastora [the contra leader Eden Pastora, aka 'Comandante Zero'], I'm not speaking to Pastora."

For the "President," a man whose most practiced instincts had trained him to find the strongest possible narrative line in the scenes he was given, to clean out those extraneous elements that undermine character clarity, a man for whom historical truth had all his life run at twenty-four frames a second, Iran-contra would have been irresistible, a go project from concept, a script with two strong characters, the young marine officer with no aim but to serve his president, the aging president with no aim but to free the tyrannized (whether the tyrants were Nicaraguans or Iranians or some other nationality altogether was just a plot point, a detail to work out later), a story about male bonding, a story about a father who found the son he never (in this "cleaned out" draft of the script) had, a buddy movie, and better still than a buddy movie: a mentor buddy movie, with action.

"Reagan didn't violate the public trust in the pursuit of personal power," we are told by D'Souza, who, possibly because he noticed that he had "Ollie" running into the president's office on page 158, seems by page 247 of *Ronald Reagan: How an Ordinary Man Became an Extraordinary Leader* to have somewhat amended his earlier (page 16) assessment of Iran-contra as a series of events "transacted in the White House without Reagan's knowledge or approval." Here, on page 247, we see a change from passive to active voice: "He did it because he empathized with the suffering of the hostages and their families. . . . He refused to listen to Shultz and Weinberger's prudent recommendations that he avoid the foolish enterprise altogether." D'Souza seems not to entirely appreciate that for this actor, given this script, it would have been precisely the suggestion that he was undertaking a "foolish enterprise" that sealed his determination to go with it. "There are those who say that what we are attempting to do cannot be done," he had said in a hundred variations in as many speeches. This was a president who understood viscerally—as the young colonel also understood—that what makes a successful motion picture is exactly a foolish enterprise, a lonely quest, a lost cause, a fight against the odds: undertaken, against the best advice of those who say it cannot be done, by someone America can root for. *Cut, print.*

Eyes on the Prize

September 24, 1992

IN THE UNDERSTANDABLY general yearning for "change" in the governing of our country, we might pause to reflect on just what is being changed, and by whom, and for whom. At Madison Square Garden in New York from July 13, 1992, until the balloons fell on the evening of July 16, four days and nights devoted to heralding the perfected "centrism" of the Democratic Party, no hint of what had once been that party's nominal constituency was allowed to penetrate prime time, nor was any suggestion of what had once been that party's tacit role, that of assimilating immigration and franchising the economically disenfranchised, or what used to be called "co-opting" discontent. Jesse Jackson and Jimmy Carter got slotted in during the All-Star Game. Jerry Brown spoke of "the people who fight our wars but never come to our receptions" mainly on C-SPAN.

"This convention looks like our country, not like a country club," Representative Tom Foley declared, and a number of speakers echoed him. Yet the preferred images of the convention were those of a sun-belt country club, for example that of Tipper and Al Gore dancing sedately on the podium. The preferred sound was not "Happy Days Are Here Again" but Fleetwood Mac, Christine McVie's request before the New Hampshire primary that the Clinton campaign stop using her song "Don't Stop" notwithstanding. Those who wanted to dance with the Gores, join the club, made it clear that they were prepared to transcend, as their candidate had often put it, "the brain-dead policies in both parties," most noticeably their own. "Democrat" and "Republican," we heard repeatedly, as if a prayer for electoral rain, were old words, words without meaning, as were the words "liberal" and "conservative." "The choice we offer is not conservative or liberal, in many ways it is not even Republican or Democratic," the candidate told us. "It is different. It is new. . . . I call it a New Covenant."

What Governor Clinton had been calling "a New Covenant"

(for a while he had called it "a Third Way," which had sounded infelicitously Peruvian) was essentially the Democratic Leadership Council's "New Choice," or more recently its "New Social Contract," a series of policy adjustments meant to "reinvent government" (as in *Reinventing Government* by David Osborne, a Clinton adviser) not at all by diminishing but by repackaging its role. There was in the New Covenant or the Third Way or the New Choice or the New Social Contract much that was current in Republican as well as Democratic thinking, but there was also a shell game: part of the "New Covenant," for example, called for the federal government to "cut 100,000 bureaucrats" by attrition, but it was unclear who, if not a new hundred thousand bureaucrats, would administer the new federal programs ($133.7 billion to "Put America to Work," $22.5 billion to "Reward Work and Families," $63.3 billion to encourage "Lifetime Learning") promised in the ticket's *Putting People First: How We Can All Change America.* The "New Covenant" was nonetheless the candidate's "game plan," and it was also, covering another Republican base, his "new choice based on old values."

In certain ways this convention's true keynote address was delivered not by the keynote speakers of record but by the Democratic National Committee's finance chairman, Senator John D. (Jay) Rockefeller IV of West Virginia. Senator Rockefeller, describing himself as "one of those Democrats who doesn't threaten big donors," reported that this was a year in which it was possible to mount "the best financed Democratic presidential campaign ever," one in which the "donor base is bigger than ever," enabling the party to buy "focus groups, polling, research, whatever it takes to get the message out." The message was this: we're tough, kick ass, get a life. "We Democrats have some changing to do," the candidate said, accepting the nomination on behalf of those who "pay the taxes, raise the kids and play by the rules," by which he meant "the forgotten middle class" that had been the target of his campaign since New Hampshire. He had an ultimatum for "the fathers in this country who have chosen to abandon their children by neglecting their child support: take responsibility for your children or we will force you to do so." He had a promise to "end welfare as we know it," to put "100,000 more police on your streets," to set right a situation in which "the prime minister of Japan . . . actually said . . . he felt sympathy for America."

This world the candidate evoked, one in which the prime minister of Japan conspired with welfare queens and deadbeat dads (referred to in *Putting People First* as "deadbeat parents") to deride those who paid the taxes and raised the kids and played by the rules, began and ended with the woolly resentments of the focus group, and so remained securely distanced from what might be anyone's actual readiness to address actual concerns. The candidate spoke about "taking on the big insurance companies to lower costs and provide health care to all Americans," but *Putting People First* made it clear that this more comprehensive health care was to be paid for not only by decreasing Medicare benefits for those with incomes over $125,000, a proposal with which no one could argue, but also by "cutting medical costs," which, in practice, again means reducing benefits, this time at all income levels. (This is a thorny business. One reason medical costs keep rising is not necessarily because the insured consumer is being "gouged," as *Putting People First* suggests, but precisely because insured consumers now make up certain deficits incurred by the treatment of patients subject to the already restricted payment schedules specified by Medicare and Medicaid.)

The candidate spoke about "less entitlement" and more "empowerment," the preferred word among the Bush administration's own "New Paradigm" theorists for such doubtfully practicable ideas as selling housing projects to their tenants, but it remained unclear just what entitlement this particular candidate could have the political will to cut. The single "entitlement reform" detailed as an actual monetary saving in *Putting People First* was the Medicare cutback for those with incomes over $125,000, and it was hard not to remember that Governor Clinton, just four months before, had saturated Florida retirement condos with the news that Paul Tsongas, who had proposed to limit cost-of-living increases on Social Security benefits to recipients with incomes over $125,000, was against old people.

He spoke about reducing defense spending, but also about maintaining "the world's strongest defense"; the projected figure for "1993 defense cuts (beyond Bush)" offered by *Putting People First*, however, was only two billion dollars, and Governor Clinton, during the press of his losing primary campaign in Connecticut, had promised to save the Groton-based Seawolf submarine program, one multibillion-dollar defense expenditure marked for a cut by the Bush administration. He spoke about the need to "clean out the bureaucracy," as he had during all his primary campaigns except one, that in New York, where his key union endorsements included the Civil Service Employees Association (some 200,000 members in New York State) and District Council 37 (135,000 members in New York City) of the American Federation of State, County, and Municipal Employees. "There is a real opportunity in the citadel of the failures of the old bureaucratic approaches to talk about new ideas," Will Marshall, the president of the Democratic Leadership Council's Progressive Policy Institute and a Clinton adviser, had acknowledged to Ronald Brownstein of the *Los Angeles Times* on this point. "On the other hand, he's got a lot of support from public employee unions, he's fighting for his life and he needs support wherever he can get it."

These were Democrats, in other words, who accepted the responsibility with which Ron Brown had charged them: to "keep our eye on the prize, so to speak." These were Democrats who congratulated themselves for staying, as they put it, on message. Not much at their convention got left to improvisation. They spoke about "unity." They spoke about a "new generation," about "change," about "putting people first." As evidence of putting people first, they offered "real people" videos, soft-focus videos featuring such actual citizens as "Kyle Harrison," a student at the University of Arkansas in Fayetteville who cooperatively described himself as a member of "the forgotten middle class." Convention delegates were given what a Clinton aide called the "prayerbook," a set of six blue pocket cards covering questions they might be asked, for example about "The Real Bill Clinton." ("His father died before he was born and his mother had to leave home to study nursing. . . . Bill grew up in a home without indoor plumbing.") The volunteers who worked the DNC's "VVIP" skyboxes at the Garden were equipped with approved conversation, or "Quotable

Lines" ("Al Gore complements Bill Clinton, they are a strong team," or "The Republicans have run out of ideas, they're stuck in a rut . . . all Americans are losing out"), as well as with answers to more special, more VVIP-oriented questions, as in "Celebrity Talking Points" #3 and #4:

> 3. "Tipper Gore previously worked on a drive to put warning labels on albums classified violent or obscene. Isn't this a restriction of our 1st Amendment right to freedom of speech?"
>
> First, let's be clear—Al Gore is the Vice-Presidential candidate and this convention will determine the platform for this party and for this campaign. Second, Tipper Gore is entitled to her own opinions as is any other American. She is a good campaigner and will work hard on behalf of the platform of this party and the Clinton-Gore ticket.
>
> 4. "Why are some entertainment personalities who normally endorse Democratic candidates sitting this election year out or going to Ross Perot?"
>
> There are many other issues such as Human Rights, the Environment, Women Rights, AIDS and other such important issues which have become a priority for certain individuals. Also, those who have chosen other campaigns must have their reasons and I respect their right to do that.

"When in doubt," skybox volunteers were advised, "the best answer is, 'Thank you, I'll get a staff person to get you the campaign's position on that issue.'" It was frequently said to be the Year of the Woman, and the convention had clearly been shaped to make the ticket attractive to women, but its notion of what might attract women was clumsy, off, devised as it was by men who wanted simultaneously to signal the electorate that they were in firm control of any woman who might have her own agenda. There was the production number from *The Will Rogers Follies* with the poufs on the breasts. There was the transformation of two mature and reportedly capable women, Mrs. Clinton and Mrs. Gore, into double-the-fun blondes who jumped up and down, clapped on cue, and traveled, as Mrs. Reagan had, with a hairdresser on the manifest for comb-outs.

The party did introduce its five women candidates for the

Senate (Carol Moseley Braun, Jean Lloyd-Jones, Lynn Yeakel, Barbara Boxer, and Dianne Feinstein) as well as four of its most visible ingenues (Kathleen Brown, Barbara Roberts, Sharon Pratt Kelly, and Pat Schroeder), but had originally hedged the possibility that the presence of too many women might threaten any viewer by ghettoizing them, scheduling them, with Jimmy Carter and Jesse Jackson and the AIDS presentations, on Tuesday night, which on the Monday-through-Thursday convention schedule had traditionally been known as "losers' night." (After some complaints, the Senate candidates, although not the ingenues, got moved to the Monday schedule.) "What used to be losers' night we're making women's night," Ron Brown had said about this to one woman I know, a prominent Democrat in the entertainment industry.

The proceedings ran so relentlessly on schedule that it was sometimes necessary to pad out the pre-primetime events with unmotivated musical interludes, and on one occasion with an actual ten-minute recess. "The people running this convention are just impossible," an aide to Governor Ann Richards of Texas, who as convention chair might in past years have been thought to be one of the people running the convention, said on its second night. "Wouldn't give us a minute of time when the networks were on. Finally she [Governor Richards] said to us, girls, my ego doesn't need this, so don't let yourselves get dragged down." Jodie Evans, who managed Jerry Brown's campaign, was told that to enter his name in nomination would "clutter up the schedule."

Governor Brown, who did not get to be governor of California for eight years by misunderstanding either politics or the meaning of political gestures, remained a flaw in the convention's otherwise seamless projection of its talking points. It was not by accident that he had been the only one of the Democratic primary candidates who, on the evening of the primary campaign's first Washington debate, did not go to dinner at Pamela Harriman's. He maintained so apparently quixotic a guerrilla presence in New York that Maureen Dowd began referring to him in the *Times* as The Penguin. He worked out of the *Rolling Stone* office. He got messages at Dennis Rivera's Hospital Workers Union Local 1199. He camped one night at a homeless shelter and other nights at my husband's and my apartment. He passed up the balloon drop and the podium handshake to end the convention with his volunteers, finishing the night not at the DNC's four-million-dollar fundraising gala but at Elaine's.

He told Governor Clinton that the ticket would have his "full endorsement" in the unlikely eventuality that the platform was amended to include four provisions: "a $100 ceiling on all political contributions, a ban on political action committees (PACs), universal registration undertaken by government itself (together with same-day registration), and finally election day as a holiday." That these were not provisions the Clinton campaign was prepared to discuss ("I want to work with you on these critical issues throughout my campaign," the response went) freed Brown on what was for him, since he had shaped his campaign as a "fight for the soul of the Democratic Party," a quite sticky and isolating point, that of endorsing a ticket that could be seen as the very model of who his adversary might be in any "fight for the soul of the Democratic Party."

"I'd like to thank someone who's not here tonight," he said on the evening he declined to endorse but nonetheless did opt to clutter up the schedule. "Someone who's missing his first Democratic convention since the Depression. Someone I think of as the greatest Democrat of all. My father, Pat Brown." Referring as it did to a Democratic past, a continuum, a collective memory, this was jarring, off the beat of a party determined to present itself as devoid of all history save that one sunny day in the Rose Garden, preserved on film and repeatedly shown, when President John F. Kennedy shook the hand of the Boy's Nation delegate Bill Clinton, who could be seen on the film elbowing aside less motivated peers to receive the grail: the candidate's first useful photo opportunity.

2.

More recent opportunities had given us, early on, the outline of the campaign the Democrats planned to run. There was, first of all, the creation, or re-creation, of Governor Clinton. By all accounts, and particularly by certain contradictory threads within those accounts, this was a dramatically more interesting character than candidate, a personality so tightly organized around its own fractures that its most profound mode often appeared to be self-pity. "I was so young and inexperienced," Governor Clinton told *The Washington Post* about his 1980 Arkansas defeat, "I didn't understand how to break through my crisis and turn the situation around." In his famous and extremely curious letter to the director of the ROTC program at the University of Arkansas, Colonel Eugene Holmes, who could not reasonably have been thought to care, he had spoken of his "anguish," of his loss of "self-regard and self-confidence"; of a period during which, he said, he "hardly slept for weeks and kept going by eating compulsively and reading until exhaustion set in." He spoke of the continuing inclination of the press to dwell on this and other issues as "the trials which I endured."

"When people are criticizing me, they get to the old 'Slick Willie' business," he had explained before the New York primary to Jonathan Alter and Eleanor Clift of *Newsweek*. "Part of it is that I'm always smiling and try to make it look easy and all that. And part of it is the way I was raised. I had such difficulties in my childhood." Governor Clinton spoke often about these difficulties in his childhood, usually, and rather distressingly, in connection with questions raised about his adulthood. Such questions had caused him to wonder, he confided to *The Wall Street Journal*, "whether I'd ever be able to return to fighting for other people rather than for myself. I had to ask myself: what is it about the way I communicate or relate? Was it something in my childhood? I didn't wonder if I was a rotten person. I knew I was involved in a lifelong effort to be a better person."

He was sometimes demonstrably less than forthcoming when confronted with contradictions in this lifelong effort. By mid-May of the 1992 campaign he was still undertaking what he called an "enormous effort" to reconstruct his draft history, which had first come into question in Arkansas in October 1978, but was clear on one point: "Did I violate the laws of my state or nation? Absolutely not." Still, from the angle of "something in my childhood," this personal evasiveness could be translated into evidence of what came to be called his "reaching to please," his "need to bring people together": the heroic story required by the campaign coverage. "I'm always trying to work things out because that's the role I played for a long time," the candidate told David Maraniss of *The Washington Post* at one point, and, at another: "The personal pain of my childhood and my reluctance to be revealing in that sense may account for some of what may seem misleading."

He frequently referred to "my pain," and also to "my passion," or "my obsession," as in "it would be part of my obsession as president." He spoke of those who remained less than enthusiastic about allowing him to realize his passion or obsession as "folks who don't know me," and of his need to "get the people outside Arkansas to know me like people here do"; most of us do not believe that our best side is hidden. "I can feel other people's pain a lot more than some people can," he told Peter Applebome of *The New York Times*. What might have seemed self-delusion was transformed, in the necessary reinvention of the coverage, into "resilience," the frequently noted ability to "take the hits." "The comeback kid" was said at the convention to be Governor Mario Cuomo's tribute to the candidate, but of course it had initially been the candidate's own tribute, a way of positioning his second-place finish in New Hampshire as a triumph, and there was in Governor Cuomo's echo of it a grudging irony, a New York edge.

What else did we know about this candidate? We knew that he, or his campaign, was adept at what is generally called negative campaigning. There was the knockout punch in Florida, on the eve of Super Tuesday, when Clinton supporters distributed leaflets suggesting that his principal rival there, Senator Tsongas, besides being against old people, was against Israel. (Governor Clinton, who had himself campaigned in Delray Beach wearing a white yarmulke, allowed after the primary that the leaflets had been misleading.) There was, on the weekend before the New York primary, the Clinton radio commercial, run for a few hours before it was pulled off the air, accusing Jerry Brown, the only Clinton challenger then extant, of being against "choice," or the right to abortion. In fact Governor Brown's position on choice in California had been exactly that of Governor Cuomo in New York: each had said that he personally accepted the position of the Catholic Church on abortion but as governor supported both the right to choose and full public funding for abortion. This was a notably less equivocal position than that previously taken by Governor Clinton, who had signed into Arkansas law a measure requiring minors to notify both parents before abortion and had apparently taken no position on the state's 1988 constitutional amendment banning public financing for abortion.

There remained some cloudiness about this amendment. "I opposed the vote of the people to ban public funding on that," Governor Clinton had said, fairly unequivocally, when he was asked about it on WNBC the Sunday before the New York primary. That was April 1992. By July 1992, a letter dated 1986 (the year an earlier version of the Arkansas amendment was proposed) had turned up, and seemed equally unequivocal. This letter, which, according to *The New York Post*, was "made available" to news organizations by "Republican operatives," was from Governor Clinton to Arkansas Right to Life. "I do support the concept of the proposed Arkansas Constitutional Amendment 65 and agree with its stated purpose," the letter read. "I am opposed to abortion and to government funding of abortions. We should not spend state funds on abortions because so many people believe abortion is wrong."

Apparent accidents, and even some apparent mistakes in judgment, had emerged over time as less accidental than strategic. There was Hillary Clinton's "gaffe" in complaining to Gail Sheehy, interviewing her for *Vanity Fair*, that the press was following a "double standard" in dwelling on her husband's alleged friendship with Gennifer Flowers, since Anne Cox Chambers ("sittin' there in her sunroom") had told her about "Bush and his carrying on, all of which is apparently well known in Washington." This was an "embarrassment," a "mistake," and yet the appearance of the *Vanity Fair* piece coincided with Clinton strategists issuing the same preemptive warning to the Bush campaign; with Ron Brown suggesting that if questions about adultery were to persist, he thought similar questions should be put to Bush; and with Democratic consultant Robert Squier suggesting on the NBC *Today* show that Bush be asked what he called "the Jennifer question." Nor was just the single point scored: there was also considerable secondary gain in showing Mrs. Clinton as "feminine," a weaker vessel, gossiping with a friend over tea in the sunroom and then retailing the gossip to a new friend—who, in the "unfeminine" role of reporter, could be seen to have taken unfair advantage of the shared confidence, the wife's moment of indiscretion in her husband's defense. The erring but contrite wife could then be firmly but gently "reprimanded" by the presumptive CINC, her husband ("The main point is, she apologized . . . she made a mistake and she's acknowledged it"), an improved role for them both.

What else did we know? We knew that this was a candidate who arrived on the national scene with a quite identifiable set of regional mannerisms and attitudes, the residue of a culture that still placed considerable value on playing sports and taking charge and catting around with one kind of woman and idealizing the other kind. It was true that this "southernness" sometimes seemed in Governor Clinton's case less inherited than achieved; it was also true that the achievement seemed to have cost the candidate a certain reliability of pitch. "You're not worth being on the same platform as my wife," which is what he said to Governor Brown when the latter suggested a possible conflict of interest between Mrs. Clinton's law firm and the state of Arkansas, seemed so broad as to raise doubts that he really had the manner down. Yet the rudiments of the style were in place, and they worked to convey the image of a candidate uniquely free of entangling alliances with the exact "special interests" that many voters believed to be receiving undue attention.

Women were one such "special interest." Blacks were another. Appearing to take a firm line on women presented a delicate problem, since the party was increasingly dependent on the support of women who were declaring their intention to vote a single issue, that of choice; the candidate covered this by repeating that he wanted to see abortion made "safe, legal, and rare," an unarguable but safely paternalistic construction. When it came to blacks, the candidate claimed an ambiguous regional expertise. "Where I come from we know about race-baiting," Governor Clinton had said when he announced for the presidency at the Old State House in Little Rock, and in many variations, most of which made reference to "the politics of division," thereafter. "They've used it to divide us for years. I know this tactic well and I'm not going to let them get away with it." This was generally seen, for example in a *New York Newsday* editorial, as the candidate "at his most believable," evidence of his "fidelity to the cause of ending racial divisiveness in America." In *The Washington Post*, Richard Cohen even managed to cite, as "an early indication of why Bill Clinton enjoys such wide support in the black community," the draft letter, in which the twenty-three-year-old Clinton had told Colonel Holmes that his opposition to the Vietnam War had plumbed "a depth of feeling I had preserved solely for racism in America."

Yet there remained an odd undertone in what Governor Clinton actually said on this subject. The "race-baiting" about which he claimed the special southern knowledge, for example, worked more than one way: "race-baiting" was what Governor Clinton accused Senator Tsongas of doing, after Tsongas ran commercials in the South showing film on which Governor Clinton, unaware that a camera was running and enraged by a misunderstanding (he had just been told mistakenly that Jesse Jackson was endorsing Senator Harkin), spoke of Jackson's "backstabbing" and "dirty double-crossing." Similarly, letting "New York be split apart by race" was what Governor Clinton accused Governor Brown of doing, when the Clinton campaign wanted to remind New York primary voters that Brown had named Jesse Jackson as his choice for vice president. There was often this chance, when Governor Clinton spoke about race, to hear what he very clearly said and yet to understand it quite another way. The "them" who would not be allowed to "get away with it," for example, were clearly those who practiced "the politics of division," yet "the politics of division" remained, like "race-baiting," open to conflicting interpretation: it has been within memory the contention of large numbers of white Americans that civil rights legislation itself represented the politics of division.

This has not been a sphere in which very many American politicians have known how to talk straight. Susan Estrich, who managed Michael Dukakis's 1988 campaign, later pointed out to Peter Brown, the chief political writer for Scripps Howard and the author of *Minority Party: Why Democrats Face Defeat in 1992 and Beyond*, that she did not hear voters in the party's 1988 focus groups say they were "against" blacks. What she did hear, she said, was, "I want to get a decent job, send my kid to a good school." What was being said, as she saw it, was, "Are you the party that is going to bend over backwards for blacks when the rest of us just want to walk straight?" Although the Democratic Party's 1992 candidate told us in Madison Square Garden where he got what he called "my passionate commitment to bringing people together without regard to race" (from his grandfather, who ran a grocery in a black neighborhood and "just made a note of it" when customers couldn't pay), this was a campaign that took extraordinary care not to leave the impression that it was bending over backwards for blacks.

There was the picture, taken the day before the Georgia, Maryland, and Colorado primaries, showing Governor Clinton standing with Senator Sam Nunn of Georgia in front of a formation of mostly black prisoners at the Stone Mountain Correctional Facility, a less than conventional setting in which to make time for photos on the eve of three contested primaries. Senator Tom Harkin had promptly blanketed rural South Carolina with some eighty thousand copies of this Stone Mountain shot (juxtaposed with one of himself with Jesse Jackson), and its explication had for a while been a staple of Jerry Brown's stump speech: "Two white men and forty black prisoners, what's he saying? He's saying, We got 'em under control, folks, don't worry." There was, when Governor Clinton was campaigning in a white Detroit suburb before the Michigan primary, his rather unsettling take on the Bush campaign's 1988 use of Willie Horton: "This guy runs Willie Horton, scares the living daylights out of people, then cuts back on aid to local prosecutors, cuts back on aid to local law enforcement, cuts back Coast Guard, Customs, and Border Patrol funding to intercept drugs."

There was the apparently unmonitored decision, the day after the Illinois and Michigan primaries, to play nine holes of golf, accompanied by at least one television camera crew, at an unintegrated Little Rock country club, a recreational choice so outside the range of normal political behavior that it seemed aberrational, particularly since the issue was not unfamiliar in Little Rock; a group of twelve Arkansas legislators had a year or so before boycotted an event at another unintegrated local club, and both *The Boston Herald* and *The New York Post* had already run stories about Governor Clinton's honorary memberships in unintegrated Little Rock clubs. There was the equivocal response to the May 1992 Los Angeles riots (the desirability of "personal responsibility" and "an end to division" remained the unexceptionable but elusive Clinton position on discontent of all kinds), followed six weeks later by the campaign's cleanest surgical strike: the Sister Souljah moment.

Sister Souljah, born Lisa Williamson, was in 1992 a twenty-eight-year-old rap artist, writer, and community activist. She was a graduate of Rutgers. In high school she had won a prize in a constitutional oratory competition sponsored by the American Legion. Not long after the Los Angeles riots, in the course of an interview in *The Washington Post*, she had said this: "I mean, if black people kill black people every day, why not have a week and kill white people? You understand what I'm saying? In other words, white people, this government and that mayor were well aware of the fact that black people were dying every day in Los Angeles under gang violence. So if you're a gang member and you would normally be killing somebody, why not a white person?" What happened next was fortuitous, one of those random opportunities by which campaigns live or die: just a few weeks later, during a meeting of Jesse Jackson's Rainbow Coalition at which Governor Clinton was scheduled to speak, it came to the attention of the Clinton campaign that this same Sister Souljah had spoken the day before. A number of reporters had apparently been told in advance by Clinton aides that Governor Clinton would use his Rainbow Coalition speech to demonstrate his "independence" from Jesse Jackson, and the opportunity to signal white voters by denouncing Sister Souljah's "message of hate" was seamless, a gift from heaven, the most unassailable possible focus for such a signal. That this opportunity had been seized was precisely what constituted, for the campaign and for its observers, the incident's "success," and the candidate's "strength."

The extent to which many prominent Democrats perceived their party as hostage to Jesse Jackson was hard to overestimate. I recall being told by one of the party's 772 "superdelegates," a category devised to move control of the nominating process back from the primary electorate to the party leadership, that Jackson's speech at the 1988 Atlanta convention had been "a disaster" for the party, and had "lost the election for Dukakis." Duane Garrett, a San Francisco attorney and fundraiser, told the Scripps Howard political writer Peter Brown that "the key thing that would have helped Dukakis enormously would have been to go to war with Jesse at the convention. Not to be mean-spirited or petty, but to make it clear that Dukakis was the guy in charge." A good deal of Governor Clinton's 1992 campaign was about creating situations in which he could be seen to do what Dukakis had not done. Eleanor Clift, for example, on one of the Sunday-morning shows, interpreted "You're not worth being on the same platform with my wife" as a success on the not-Dukakis scale. The candidate, she said, had "needed to pass the Dukakis test, needed to show true strong emotion toward his wife." The Sister Souljah moment, in this view, represented a Clinton call for "an end to division" that had at once served to distance him from Jackson and to demonstrate that he was "the guy in charge," capable of dominating, or "standing up to," a kind of black anger that many white voters prefer to see as the basis for this country's racial division.

"It was a brilliant coup," Mary McGrory concluded in *The Washington Post*. "Clinton didn't take on Jackson directly. He didn't pick the fight on a central black concern." That Sister Souljah herself was a straw target was, then, beside the point, and what Clinton actually said at the Rainbow Coalition meeting (he said that Sister Souljah's comments in the *Post* had been "filled with the kind of hatred that you do not honor," that they were an example of "pointing the finger at one another across racial lines," and that "we have an obligation, all of us, to call attention to prejudice wherever we see it") was less important than the coverage of it, and the way in which the candidate capitalized on the coverage: the message had been sent and he reinforced it, just as he had reinforced his willingness to make "tough choices" by allowing the Arkansas execution of Rickey Ray Rector to proceed by lethal injection forty-eight hours before the Super Bowl Sunday on which Governor and Mrs. Clinton would address the Gennifer Flowers question on *60 Minutes*. The measures Governor Clinton had apparently taken to avoid the draft were adroitly reframed as another "tough choice," a decision to do what he saw as "right" ("I supported the Persian Gulf War because I thought it was right and in our national interest, just as I opposed the Vietnam War because I thought it was wrong and not in our national interest"); this was his commander-in-chief transformation, a mode in which he was moved to mention, as evidence of his ability to handle crises abroad, the several venues, including Honduras, to which he had deployed the Arkansas National Guard.

"If you want to be president you've got to stand up for what you think is right," Governor Clinton said about his Sister Souljah moment. "They have chosen to react against me, essentially taking the position, I guess, that because I'm white I shouldn't have said it, and I just disagree with that," he told *Larry King Live*. One of his principal advisers, Stuart Eizenstat, a former Carter adviser and then a lobbyist, for example representing the National Association of Manufacturers against a workers' right-to-know law on toxic chemicals, was more forthcoming: "Clinton's strategy is not without risk," he told *The New York Times* about the calculation that reaching out to unhappy white voters should be the campaign's first priority. "But we have no real choice. Our base is too small to win, even in a three-way race, so the old-time religion just won't work any more."

3.

This wisdom, that the failure of Democratic candidates in five of the six national elections preceding 1992 derived from an undesirable identification with the party's traditional base, was of course not new. It had its roots during the Vietnam War, with the 1968 and 1972 Nixon victories over the "liberals" Hubert Humphrey and George McGovern; was crystallized by Kevin Phillips's 1970 *The Emerging Republican Majority*; and became a fixed idea among the party's revisionist mainstream after the 1980 and 1984 defections of the so-called Reagan

Democrats. These "Reagan Democrats," statistically quite a small group of people, thereafter became the voters to whom all election appeals would be directed, a narrowing of focus with predictable results, not the least significant of which was that presidential elections would come to be conducted almost exclusively in code.

Governor Clinton, for example, did not speak of Reagan Democrats. He spoke instead of being stopped in an airport by a police officer who wanted to tell him that he was "dying to vote for a Democrat again." He spoke of "the forgotten middle class," or, in a 1991 speech to the Democratic Leadership Council, of "the very burdened middle class," also known as "the people who used to vote for us." The late Paul Tully, at that time the political director of the Democratic National Committee, described one of those hypothetical "people who used to vote for us" to *The New York Times* as "a suburbanite, in a household with about $35,000 income, younger than forty-five, with a child or two, and in a marriage in which both partners work." James Carville spoke of "a thirty-two-year-old with two kids in day care who works in some suburban office building."

The point on which everyone seemed to agree was that this suburban working parent of two was "middle class," which was, according to Ted Van Dyk, the Democratic strategist who advised Paul Tsongas, the phrase that signaled Reagan Democrats "that it is safe to come home to their party because poor, black, Hispanic, urban, homeless, hungry, and other people and problems out of favor in Middle America will no longer get the favored treatment they got from mushy 1960s and 1970s Democratic liberals." That "middle class" had been drained of any but this encoded meaning was clear when, at a Clinton rally in Atlanta, Governor Zell Miller of Georgia derided Senator Tsongas as "an anti-death-penalty, anti-middle-class politician." Middle class, Governor Clinton told the Rainbow Coalition, by way of answering a direct question, was not "a code word" for racism. In fact this was accurate, since the use of the code was never an appeal exclusively to racism; the appeal was broader, to an entire complex of attitudes held in common by those Americans who sensed themselves isolated and set adrift by the demographic and economic and cultural changes of the last half century. "Middle class," Governor Clinton explained, referred "to values nearly every American holds dear: support for family, reward for work, the willingness to change what isn't working."

This again was accurate, but since the phrase "nearly every American" raised the specter of unspecified other Americans who did not hold these values dear, it appealed to those who would prefer to see the changes of the last half century as reversible error, the detritus of too "liberal" a social policy. "I have spent most of my public life worrying about what it would take to give our children a safe place to live again," Governor Clinton also said, striking the same note of seductive nostalgia. Such reduction of political language to coded messages, to "middle class" and "reward for work," to safe children and Sister Souljah, has much to do with why large numbers of Americans report finding politics deeply silly, yet the necessity for this reduction is now accepted as a given: in his *Minority Party*, Peter Brown quoted suggestions made to Alabama party officials by the Democratic pollster Natalie Davis:

- Instead of talking about Democrats lifting someone out of poverty, describe the party's goal as helping average Americans live the good life.
- Instead of saying Democrats want to eliminate homelessness and educate the underclass, talk about finding a way for young couples to buy their first home and offer financial help to middle-class families to send their kids to college.
- Instead of saying the Democrats want to provide health care for the poor, focus on making sure all working Americans have coverage.

The way of talking here was familiar, that of salesmanship, or packaging. If this seemed a way of talking that the average "young couple" or "middle-class family" or "working American" could instinctively tune out, flick the channel, press the mute button, it was also a way of talking that the Democratic candidate nominated by the 1992 convention instinctively understood: Bill Clinton was the son of a traveling salesman, the stepson of a Buick dealer, he knew in his fingernails how the deal gets closed. "If we lead with class warfare, we lose," he had told Peter Brown after the 1988 campaign. With Governor James Blanchard of Michigan and Senators Nunn of Georgia and Charles Robb of Virginia, he had been a founder in 1985 of the Democratic Leadership Council, which was instrumental in reshaping the "image" of the Democratic Party to attract the money of major lobbyists. The chairman of this repackaged Democratic Party, Ron Brown, was himself a lobbyist, a partner at one of Washington's most influential law firms, Patton, Boggs, and Blow. Ron Brown was in 1988 lobbying for the Japanese electronics industry, including Hitachi, Mitsubishi, and Toshiba, but he was on the podium in Madison Square Garden on the evening when Governor Clinton got the delegates hissing and booing over how "the prime minister of Japan actually said he felt sympathy for America"; this was of course just more code, and accepted as such.

The role played by the Democratic Leadership Council was central to the eventual narrowing of American politics. It was the DLC that invented Super Tuesday, the strategy of concentrating primaries in southern states to "front-load" the process against visibly liberal candidates. After this backfired in 1988, enabling Jesse Jackson to gain enough momentum from newly registered voters on Super Tuesday to go on to Atlanta with a real hand to play, Jackson opened his remarks at a DLC-sponsored debate by thanking Senator Robb for Super Tuesday. This had, according to Peter Brown, so amused Governor Clinton, "sitting in the front row next to Robb," that he nearly fell off his chair, but it altered the thinking of the new Democratic leadership only to the extent that Ron Brown took care to deal Jackson out before play began for 1992.

The wisdom of the DLC analysis, which tacitly called for the party to jettison those voters who no longer turned out and target those who did, or "hunt where the ducks are," has not been universally shared. Jesse Jackson had tried to prove it was possible to just register more ducks, and appeared in Madison Square Garden to endorse the 1992 ticket as that classic tragic figure, a man who had tried and failed to incorporate his constituency into the system and who subsequently risked being overtaken by that constituency. Jerry Brown had tried to prove that what the political scientist Walter Dean Burnham had called "the largest political party in America," the party of those who see no reason to vote, could be given that reason within the Democratic Party, but had been led by his quite fundamental party allegiance into a campaign that remained for most Americans inexplicably internecine and finally recondite, a fight for the "soul" of a party about which they no longer or had never cared. "The last thing the Democratic Party has wanted to do is declare that there is a possibility for class struggle," Burnham noted in a discussion in *New Perspectives Quarterly*. "The Republicans, however, are perfectly happy to declare class struggle all the time. They are always waging a one-sided class war against the constituency the Democrats nominally represent. In this sense, the Republicans are the only real political party in the United States. They stand for ideology and interest, not compromise."

4.

The 1988 loss of Michael Dukakis was widely seen, both within the Democratic Party and outside it, as another example of the same malaise that had afflicted the party in 1968 and 1972 and in 1980 and 1984. Governor Dukakis, it was said after the fact, was not only "too liberal" but too northeastern, too closely identified with a section of the country that had once been a Democratic stronghold and no longer had the votes to elect a president. (Mario Cuomo, in this view, presented the same problem, one magnified by his very visibility and attractiveness as a candidate.) But in fact Governor Dukakis had not been nominated as a "liberal"; the party had closed ranks around him precisely because he had seemed at the time to offer the possibility of a "centrist" campaign, a campaign "not about ideology but about competence," which was what Governor Dukakis had promised in Atlanta in 1988 and which sounded not unlike what Governor Clinton promised (the choice that was "not conservative or liberal, Democratic or Republican" but "will work") in Madison Square Garden in 1992.

There were in fact a number of such dispiriting similarities between what was said at the Democratic convention in Atlanta in 1988 and what was said at the Democratic convention in New York in 1992. There was the same insistent stress on "unity," on "running on schedule." "This party's trains are running on time," I recall someone saying in Atlanta to dutiful applause. There was the same programmatic emphasis, tricked out in the same sentimental homilies. There were the same successful arguments to keep the platform free of any minority planks that could suggest less than total agreement with the platform, or lack of "unity." There was even the same emphasis on social control, on "enforcement," although nothing said in 1988 went quite so far in this direction, or suggested quite such a worrisome indifference to what such agencies of enforcement have meant in other countries, as the Clinton-Gore proposal to gather up "unemployed veterans and active military personnel" into what they called a "National Police Corps."

"Until now," Mary McGrory wrote in *The Washington Post* on the last day of the 1992 convention, the 1988 Democratic convention in Atlanta had been "considered the best." Clinton, she said, "hopes to top it, and of course, go on to a far different outcome in November." Not long after the 1988 defeat I was told by Stanley Sheinbaum, a major California Democratic fundraiser who had become distressed in the mid-1980s by the direction the party was taking, about having been excluded from a meeting at which leading Democrats had discussed the disaster and what to do next. "Don't ask Sheinbaum, I kept hearing from someone who was there, he'll only want to discuss issues," he said. It seemed that these Democrats had already convinced themselves that they had once again lost on "issues," specifically on what they saw as too close an association with Jesse Jackson, and they wanted now only to discuss mechanics, know-how, money: what Senator Rockefeller would describe, four years later at Madison Square Garden, as "focus groups, polling, research, whatever it takes to get the message out." The problem, as Sheinbaum saw it, was that there was no longer any message to get out:

> When you're caught up in this dance of how to run campaigns better, rather than what you can do for that constituency that used to be yours, you're not going to turn anybody on. The whole focus is on big money. The Democrats under Dukakis and this guy Bob Farmer mastered how to get around the campaign finance limitations, both with PACs and soft money. They were magnificent in what they raised and it didn't do them a fucking

> bit of good. I mean it's no longer a thousand dollars. To get into the act now you've got to give a hundred thousand. So who are the players? The players are the hundred-thousand people. Who are the hundred-thousand people? They're the people who don't go into Harlem, don't go into South Central. They don't even fly MGM [MGM Grand Air, at the time the transcontinental airline of choice for the entertainment industry] any more, they have their own planes. You get this whole DLC crowd, their rationale is that to talk about the issues will alienate too many people.

What was important, in 1992 as in 1988, was "winning this election," which was why each major DNC fundraiser, or "Managing Trustee," had been asked to raise for 1992 not $100,000 but $200,000. What was important, in 1992 as in 1988, was "not saddling the candidate with a position he'll have to defend." What was important, in 1992 as in 1988, was almost exclusively semantic, a way of presenting the party as free of unprofitable issues for which it might conceivably need to fight. "I don't only think George Bush is popular on many of these issues, I think he's absolutely right," the 1992 Democratic candidate had said in 1991 on one subject that might traditionally have been considered an issue, the incumbent Republican administration's foreign policy. By the time the candidate reached Madison Square Garden he had incorporated into his acceptance speech the very line with which the incumbent Republican president, in February 1992 at Concord, New Hampshire, had formally opened his campaign for reelection: "If we can change the world we can change America."

In this determined consensus on all but a few carefully chosen and often symbolic issues, American elections are necessarily debated on "character," or "values," a debate deliberately trivialized to obscure the disinclination of either party to mention the difficulties inherent in trying to resolve even those few problems that might lend themselves to a programmatic approach. A two-party system in which both parties are committed to calibrating the precise level of incremental tinkering required to get elected is not likely to be a meaningful system, nor is an election likely to be meaningful when it is specifically crafted as an exercise in *personalismo*, in "appearing presidential" to that diminishing percentage of the population that still pays attention. Governor Clinton, interestingly, began to "appear presidential" on the very morning he left New Hampshire, despite both his much-discussed "character problem" and the previous day's vote, which had shown him running eight points behind Senator Tsongas and incapable of raising more than twenty-five percent of the Democratic vote.

He appeared presidential largely because he was sufficiently well financed and sufficiently adroit to exit this disappointing performance via motorcade and private plane, in the authenticating presence of his own press entourage and ten-man Secret Service detail. By the day before the California primary he had begun to assume even the imperial untouchability of the presidency: plunging into a crowd on the UCLA campus, live on C-SPAN, the candidate and his Secret Service cordon became suddenly invisible in the sea of signs and faces. Only voices could be heard: "Bill, Bill, here, Bill," someone had kept saying. "You got a joint? Just one? I promise not to inhale?" And then, the same voice said, apparently to someone in the cordon of aides and agents: "I'm not touching him, hey, I said I'm not touching him, get your fucking hands off me."

Some weeks later, on the hot July morning when he stood outside the governor's mansion in Little Rock to introduce his choice for the vice-presidential nomination, Governor Clinton, in one simple but novel stroke, eliminated what some found the single remaining false note in this performance of presidentiality: he resolved the "character problem" by offering the electorate, as his running mate, an improvement on himself, a putatively more respectable Bill Clinton. In Senator Gore, he could present a version of himself already familiar to large numbers of Americans, a version of himself who had already produced the requisite book on a curve issue (Gore's *Earth in the Balance: Ecology and the Human Spirit*) and need not turn defensive about Arkansas whenever the subject of the environment was raised; a version of himself who, most importantly, had spent fifteen years in Congress free not only of identified character flaws but also of too many positions that might identify him as a Democrat.

Senator Gore, it was generally agreed, grounded the ticket, raised what had been its rather uneasy social comfort level: the Gore family had been with us for two generations now, and did not suggest, as the Clintons sometimes did, the sense of being about to spin free, back to the hollow. (This ungrounded quality reflects the oldest and deepest strain in actual American life, but we do not often see it in our candidates. We saw it in Gary Hart, where it was called "the weird factor," and engendered the distrust that ended his political career.) Senator Gore, moreover, lent Governor Clinton the gravitas of the Senate, and a presumed senatorial depth in foreign policy that the ticket might otherwise have been seen to lack. He supported the Bush administration on the use of force in the Persian Gulf. He had supported nonlethal aid to the Nicaraguan contras. He had supported the Reagan administration on the bombing of Libya. He had supported the Reagan administration on the invasion of Grenada.

Closer to home and to what his party had recently come to view as its terminal incubus, Senator Gore had been seen, during his aborted 1988 campaign for the presidency, as the only Democratic candidate willing to criticize, or "take on," Jesse Jackson. This was a Democratic candidate for vice president who could stand there in the hot midday sun in Little Rock and describe his birthplace—Carthage, Tennessee—as "a place where people know about it when you're born and care about it when you die." He could repeat this at Madison Square Garden, where he could also offer this capsule bio of his father, Senator Albert Gore Sr., who served seven terms in the House and three in the Senate before losing his seat in 1970 after opposing the war in Vietnam (a lesson learned for the son here): "a teacher in a one-room school who worked his way to the United States Senate." As presented by the younger Senator Gore, Carthage had its political coordinates somewhere in Reagan Country, as did the father's one-room school, as for that matter did the entire tableau on the lawn behind the governor's mansion in Little Rock, the candidate and the running mate and the wives and the children with the summer tans and the long straight sun-bleached hair that said *our kind, your kind, good parents, country club, chlorine in the swimming pool.* "This is what America looks like," Governor Clinton said on the eve of the nominating convention when he led the same successful cast off the plane at LaGuardia, "and we're going to give it to you."

5.

He said this in a summer during which one American city, Los Angeles, had already burned. He said this in another American city, New York, that had a week before in Washington Heights come close to the flashpoint at which cities burn. This was a year in which 944,000 American citizens and businesses filed for bankruptcy, a figure up twenty-one percent from the year before. This was a year in which 213,000 jobs vanished in the city of New York alone, or 113,000 more than the "100,000 bureaucrats" Governor Clinton proposed to lose by attrition from the federal government. This was a year in which the value of real property had sunk to a point at which Citicorp could agree to sell a vacant forty-four-story office tower at 45th Street and Broadway to Bertelsmann A.G. for $119 million, $134 million less than the $253 million mortgage Citicorp held on the property. Four years before, in the same 1988 interview in *New Perspectives Quarterly*, Walter Dean Burnham had argued that neither of the two existing parties would have sufficient political resources to impose the austerity required to resolve America's financial crisis, the Republicans because their base was narrow to begin with and the Democrats "because a substantial number of people who would be followers of the Democrats if they had credibility, have dropped out of the political system and don't vote":

> It is already clear that when the fiscal crunch gets serious enough, we are going to find ourselves further away from anything that can be called democracy . . . and the more turned off the public becomes, the more they drop out. There is probably no recourse for this situation. The system is becoming more conspicuously oligarchic all the time. Both the politics of deadlock and, increasingly the bipartisan politics of resolving the fiscal crisis, are accelerating this dynamic.

Half those eligible to vote did not do so in the 1988 presidential election. The percentage of those eligible to vote who actually did vote in the 1992 California primary was forty-four percent. Only twenty-six percent of those registered to vote, or seven percent of the actual voting-age population, voted in the 1992 New York primary. The question of what happens when fifty percent of the electorate (or fifty-six percent, or seventy-four percent, or, in the case of New York, ninety-three percent) believes itself insufficiently connected to either the common weal or the interests of the candidates to render a vote significant could mean, in hard times, something other than it might have meant in good times, and a working instinct for self-preservation might suggest that one's own well-being could well depend on increasing the numbers of those who feel they have a stake in the society.

Yet this was not a year in which the Democratic Party was inclined to address the question of bringing these nonvoting citizens into the process. The party leadership was focused instead on its phantom Reagan Democrats, on what Robert J. Shapiro, a Clinton adviser and vice president of the DLC's Progressive Policy Institute, described to Ronald Brownstein of *The Los Angeles Times* as "an attempt to take the traditional goals of the Democratic Party . . . and find means to achieve them that embody the values of the country." The "values of the country," which is to say the values of that fraction of the country that had come to matter, also known as "the swing vote," began to be defined in 1985, when the Michigan House Democratic Caucus commissioned Stanley Greenberg to do what became a seminal study of voters in Macomb County, Michigan. At a motel in Sterling Heights, Michigan, Greenberg assembled a focus group made up of three dozen registered Democrats who had voted for Ronald Reagan. According to Peter Brown,

> The voters were broken into four groups. Each participant was paid $35 for two hours and fed cold cuts. The tone was set when Greenberg read a quote from Robert Kennedy, a man held in reverence by these heavily Roman Catholic voters. The quote was RFK's eloquent call for Americans to honor their special obligation to black citizens whose forefathers had lived through the slave experience and who themselves were the victims of racial discrimination. . . .
>
> "That's bullshit," shouted one participant.

> "No wonder they killed him," said another.
>
> "I'm fed up with it," chimed a third. . . .
>
> The resulting report sent a shudder through state and national Democrats. It was the first of a continuing series of research projects during the latter half of the decade that explained the problem, quite literally, in black and white.
>
> The votes for Reagan among these traditional Democrats, Greenberg reported, stemmed from . . . a sense that "the Democratic Party no longer responded with genuine feeling to the vulnerabilities and burdens of the average middle-class person. Instead the party and government were preoccupied with the needs of minorities. . . . They advanced spending programs that offered no appreciable or visible benefit" for middle-class people.

"Traditional" has many meanings here. These were "traditional" Democrats, and yet black voters were those who tended to share what Shapiro had called "the traditional goals of the Democratic Party." A candidate bent on at once luring the former and holding the latter will predictably be less than entirely forthcoming on certain points, which is part of what lent the Clinton "program," as outlined in *Putting People First*, its peculiar evasiveness. In the first place its details were hard to extract, since *Putting People First* was essentially a paste job of speeches and position papers, with only the occasional and odd specific, for example a call to "end taxpayer subsidies for honey producers." Read one way, the program could seem largely based on transferring entitlements from what were called "special interests" to those who "work hard and play by the rules," in other words distributing what wealth there was among the voting percentage of the population. *Putting People First* spoke often and eloquently, and in many variations, of "rewarding work," of "providing tax fairness to working families," of "ending welfare as we know it," of "cracking down on deadbeat parents." Read another way, however, *Putting People First* could be seen to stress benefits to accrue to the formerly needy and about to be "empowered":

> *Empower people* with the education, training, and child care they need for up to two years, so they can break the cycle of dependency; expand programs to help people learn to read, get their high school diplomas or equivalency degrees, and acquire specific job skills; and ensure that their children are cared for while they learn.

> After two years, *require those who can work to go to work*, either in the private sector or in community service; provide placement assistance to help everyone find a job, and give the people who can't find one a dignified and meaningful community service job.
>
> *Expand the Earned Income Tax Credit* to guarantee a "working wage," so that no American with a family who works full-time is forced to raise children in poverty.

Clues as to how all this might be reconciled seemed absent in the text itself. Much of *Putting People First*, however, appeared to derive from the thinking of the Democratic Leadership Council, particularly as expressed in a document distributed as a "discussion guide" at a May 1992 meeting to which Governor Clinton, the former chairman made candidate, had returned in triumph. The thrust of this document was later refined as the DLC's "New Social Contract," outlined in the July 1992 issue of its bi-monthly publication, *The New Democrat*. It was this "New Social Contract" that provided an instructive subtext for the Clinton program. "Data suggest that the public is ready to shift the moral foundations of entitlements from a one-way street—if you need it, you are entitled to it—to a more balanced social contract," Daniel Yankelovich suggested in *The New Democrat*. "If the society gives you a benefit, you must, if you are able, pay it back in some appropriate form. This means no more 'freebies,' no more rip-offs, and no more unfairness to the middle class."

A few pages earlier, Will Marshall, president of the DLC's Progressive Policy Institute, quoted Yankelovich by way of explaining how to remedy the fact that an "explosion of new rights and entitlements," among which he counted the rights "to remedial and college education, to abortion, to equal pay for women, to child and health care, to free legal counsel, to public facilities for the disabled, and many, many more," had meant "higher taxes to pay for public transfers to 'special interests'": "What the public is saying is that government programs should require some form of reciprocity: people should no longer expect something for nothing."

"Freebies" and "rip-offs" and "something for nothing" are extremely loaded words to use in reference to entitlement programs already weighted, via Social Security and Medicare and tax exemptions for mortgage interest and for contributions to pension funds, to favor the voting class, but they are the words heard in focus groups. Similarly, the "new right" to abortion does not mean "higher taxes to pay for public transfers to 'special interests'"; women who need funded abortions would tend alternately to need funded births and Aid to Families with Dependent Children, clearly the more expensive choice, but the politics are different: abortion remains, among "swing voters," a deeply freighted issue.

The most discussed and ambitious parts of the Clinton program were his proposals to involve the federal government (in ways and at a cost not satisfactorily detailed in *Putting People First*) not only in medical care but in rebuilding infrastructure and retraining and educating the work force. Yet what was said in *The New Democrat* suggested that even these proposals may have been crafted to reflect "what the public is saying." Daniel Yankelovich, describing the results of a focus-group study conducted for the DLC to gauge the mood of the electorate, noted that since "the American people believe activist government is important in solving the great challenges facing our country,"

> they are rejecting calls to eliminate government and leave problems like helping their kids go to college to the whims of the marketplace. . . . While any proposal to help families send their children to college would appeal both to the growing emphasis on education and to the public's economic worries, national service is especially attractive because it emphasizes the value of reciprocity. [Clinton had proposed national service as a way to pay back universal college loans.] There is a strong belief among the public that "there is no free lunch." In nearly every focus group, people echoed the comments of the man in Detroit who said, "I believe in giving something in return, I don't think anyone should get a free ride." . . . .
>
> Welfare reform proposals that emphasize reciprocal obligation resonate well with the public, because they reinforce core American values. . . .
>
> There is virtual unanimity (76 percent) on the idea that the country's elected leaders are not paying attention to the long-range needs of the country. . . . They are convinced that education, training, and the dedication of the workforce are the keys to economic vitality. . . .

> All of this points to a possible solution involving a massive commitment to training, education, and outreach; a practical and realistic examination of what is meant by "most-qualified" so that minorities were not disqualified; and a serious good-faith effort to take black mistrust seriously and work at building a new structure of trust.
>
> This is not an easy or simple strategy to implement. But it offers a basis for compromise, rather than a sure formula for confrontation and defeat—moral as well as electoral.

What was striking about this "new social contract," then, was that its notion of what might resolve our social and economic woes, the "program," had been specifically shaped, like Governor Clinton's Madison Square Garden speech, to reflect what was said in focus groups. The "New Social Contract" talked not about what the Democratic Party should advocate but about what it "must be seen advocating," not about what might work but about what might have "resonance," about what "resonates most clearly with the focus-group participants." The "need for profound changes in the way progressives view economic policy" was confirmed, for Will Marshall and presumably for the new Democratic leadership, not by an economic reality but by an "evolution in the public's thinking."

The reliance on focus groups is not new, nor is it unique to the Democratic Party (the Willie Horton issue, most famously, was born in a 1988 focus group the Bush campaign ran in Paramus, New Jersey) or even to politics. Motion pictures are tested in focus groups at every stage of their production, sometimes even before production, in the "concept" stage. New products have been for at least the past several decades exhaustively exposed to focus research. The use of such groups in marketing, however, has as its general intention the sampling of public opinion at large, the extrapolation of the opinion of the majority from the opinion of a few. What seemed novel about the use of focus groups in the 1992 campaign was the increasingly narrow part of the population to which either party was interested in listening, and the extent to which this extreme selectivity had transformed the governing of the country, for most of its citizens, into a series of signals meant for someone else. "When people are asked to prioritize U.S. foreign policy," Daniel

Yankelovich noted, "they favor furthering our economic interests over support for democracy by a two to one margin."

This was what was meant by the DLC's "revolution in government," the revolution, according to *The New Democrat*, that the Democratic Party must lead if it "expects to win back the confidence of the American people." Out where confidence was harder to come by and the largest political party in America—those who did not vote—got larger as we watched, the questions raised in the focus groups of the two leading minority parties about "freebies" and "rip-offs" and "something for nothing," about Willie Horton and about Sister Souljah, remained less clear. At a time when the country's tolerance of participatory democracy had already shallowed, what remained less clear still, and a good deal more troubling, was what kind of revolution might be made after the focus session in Sterling Heights or Paramus or Costa Mesa when "the American people," which is the preferred way of describing the selected dozens of narrowly targeted registered voters who turn out for the cold cuts and the $35, decide to say something else.

Newt Gingrich, Superstar

August 10, 1995

AMONG THE PERSONALITIES and books and events that have "influenced" or "changed" or "left an indelible impression on" the thinking of the Honorable Newton Leroy Gingrich (R-Ga.), the Speaker of the House of Representatives and one of the leading beneficiaries of the nation's cultural and historical amnesia, are, by his own accounts, Abraham Lincoln, Thomas Jefferson, Franklin Roosevelt, Isaac Asimov, Alexis de Tocqueville, Tom Clancy, Allen Drury's *Advise and Consent*, Robert Walpole, William Gladstone, Gordon Wood, Peter Drucker, Arnold Toynbee's *A Study of History*, Napoleon Hill's *Think and Grow Rich*, the "Two Cultures" lectures of C. P. Snow (the lesson here for the Speaker was that "if you're capable of being glib and verbal, the odds are that you have no idea what you're talking about but it sounds good, whereas if you know a great deal of what you're saying the odds are you can't get on a talk show because nobody can understand you"), Adam Smith, *Zen and the Art of Archery*, "the great leader of Coca-Cola for many years, Woodruff," an Omaha entrepreneur named Herman Cain ("who's the head of Godfather Pizza, he's an African-American who was born in Atlanta and his father was Woodruff's chauffeur"), Ray Kroc's *Grinding It Out*, and Johan Huizinga's *The Waning of the Middle Ages*.

There were also: Daryl Conner's *Managing at the Speed of Change*, Sam Walton's *Made in America*, Stephen R. Covey's *The Seven Habits of Highly Effective People*, the 1913 *Girl Scout Handbook*, Alcoholics Anonymous's *One Day At A Time*, Gore Vidal's *Lincoln* ("even though I'm not a great fan of Vidal"), the Sydney Pollack/Robert Redford motion picture *Jeremiah Johnson* ("a great film and a useful introduction to a real authentic American"), commercial overbuilding in the sun belt ("I was first struck by this American passion for avoiding the lessons of history when I watched the Atlanta real-estate boom of the early 1970s"), the science fiction writer Jerry Pournelle, the business consultant W. Edwards Deming ("Quality as

Defined by Deming" is Pillar Five of Gingrich's Five Pillars of American Civilization), and, famously, the Tofflers, Alvin and Heidi, "important commentators on the human condition" and "dear friends" as well.

It was these and other influences that gave Mr. Gingrich what Dick Williams, an Atlanta newspaperman and the author of *Newt!*, called "an intellectual base that he has been developing since he was in high school, collecting quotes and ideas on scraps of paper stored in shoeboxes." It was in turn this collection of quotes and ideas on scraps of paper stored in shoeboxes (a classmate estimated that Mr. Gingrich had fifty such boxes, for use "in class and in politics") that led in 1984 to Mr. Gingrich's *Window of Opportunity* (described in its preface by Jerry Pournelle as "a detailed blueprint, a practical program that not only proves that we can all get rich, but shows how"); in 1993 to the televised "Renewing American Civilization" lectures that Mr. Gingrich delivered from Reinhardt College in Waleska, Georgia; and in 1995 to two books, the novel *1945* and the polemic *To Renew America*.

1945 is a fairly primitive example of the kind of speculative fiction known as "alternate history," the premise here being that Hitler "spent several weeks in a coma" after a plane crash on December 6, 1941, and so did not declare war on the United States. Now, in 1945, fully recovered, Hitler is poised to launch Operation Arminius, a manifold effort to seize England (which in 1943 had "agreed to a remarkably lenient armistice" after the collapse of the Churchill government) and cripple the ability of the United States to respond by sinking its fleet and knocking out Oak Ridge, where the development of the atomic bomb is still underway. "Kill every scientist at Oak Ridge and we kill their atomic program," the German officer charged with the facility's infiltration and destruction declares. "That is why the Führer is willing to go to war to stop the Americans before they beat us to this truly ultimate weapon." In *To Renew America*, for which HarperCollins originally offered $4.5 million, Mr. Gingrich recycles familiar themes from both *Window of Opportunity* and the "Renewing American Civilization" lectures as he endeavors to "restore our historic principles," most recently evidenced, as he sees it, in "the certainty and convictions of World War II and the Cold War."

To complain that Mr. Gingrich's thinking is "schematic," as some have, seems not exactly to describe the problem, which is that the "scheme," as revealed in his writing and lectures, remains so largely occult. The videotaped "Renewing American Civilization" lecture in which he discusses "The Historic Lessons of American Civilization" (Pillar One of the Five Pillars of American Civilization) offers, for example, clips from several television movies and documentaries about the Civil War, but not much clue about why the lessons of American civilization might be "historic," and no clue at all why the remaining four Pillars of American Civilization ("Personal Strength," "Entrepreneurial Free Enterprise," "The Spirit of Invention and Discovery," and "Quality as Defined by Deming") might not be more clearly seen as subsections of Pillar One, or lessons of civilization. Similarly, the attempt to track from one to five in Mr. Gingrich's "Five Reasons for Studying American History" ("One: History is a collective memory," "Two: American history is the history of our civilization," "Three: There is an American exceptionalism that can best be understood through history," "Four: History is a resource to be learned from and used," and "Five: There are techniques that can help you learn problem-solving from historic experience") leaves the tracker fretful, uneasy, uncertain just whose synapses are misfiring.

What has lent Mr. Gingrich's written and spoken work (or, as he calls it, his "teaching") the casual semblance of being based on some plainspoken substance, some rough-hewn horse sense, is that most of what he says reaches us in outline form, with topic points capitalized (the capitalization has been restrained in the more conventionally edited *To Renew America*) and systematically if inappositely numbered. There were "Seven key aspects" and "Nine vision-level principles" of "Personal Strength," Pillar Two of American Civilization. There were "Five core principles" of "Quality as Defined by Deming" (Pillar Five); there were "Three Big Concepts" of "Entrepreneurial Free Enterprise," Pillar Three. There were also, still under Pillar Three, "Five Enemies of Entrepreneurial Free Enterprise" ("Bureaucracy," "Credentialing," "Taxation," "Litigation," and "Regulation"), which might have seemed to replicate one another and would in any case have been pretty much identical to Pillar Four's "Seven welfare state cripplers of progress" had the latter not folded in "Centralization," "Anti-progress Cultural Attitude," and "Ignorance."

In *Window of Opportunity*, Mr. Gingrich advised us that "the great force changing our world is a synergism of essentially six parts," and offered "five simple steps to a bold future." On the health care issue, Mr. Gingrich posited "eight areas of necessary change." On the question of arms control, he saw "seven imperatives that will help the free world survive in the age of nuclear weapons." Down a few paragraphs the seven imperatives gave way to "two initiatives," then to "three broad strategic options for the next generation," and finally, within the scan of the eye, to "six realistic goals which would increase our children's chances of living in a world without nuclear war."

"Outlining" or "listing" remains a favored analytical technique among the management and motivational professionals whose approach Mr. Gingrich has so messianically adopted. (Balancing the budget and "finding a way to truly replace the current welfare state with an opportunity society" could both be done by the year 2002, he advised the Congress on the occasion of his swearing-in as Speaker, "if we apply the principles of Edwards Deming and Peter Drucker.") Yet, on examination, few of his own "areas" and "imperatives" and "initiatives," his "steps" and "options" and "goals," actually advance the discourse. The seventh of the seven steps necessary to solve the drug problem, as outlined in *To Renew America*, calls for the government to "intensify our intelligence efforts against drug lords across the planet and help foreign governments to trap them," in other words exactly what both the Drug Enforcement Administration and the United States Southern Command have been doing for some years now. No piety can long escape inclusion in one or another of Mr. Gingrich's five or four or eleven steps; another of the seven steps necessary to solve the drug problem is the reinvigoration of Mrs. Reagan's "Just Say No" campaign.

The first of the "eight areas of necessary change" in our health care system calls for "focusing on preventive medicine and good health," which meant, in *Window of Opportunity*, offering Medicare recipients $500 for not going to the doctor. *To Renew America* expands this notion to "employee insurance plans" that provide each employee with a $3,000 "Medisave" account to either spend on medical care or receive as a year-end bonus, i.e., a way of phasing out the concept of medical insurance by calling the phase-out "Medisave." Mr. Gingrich cites the "very large savings in medical expenses" achieved through Medisave accounts by the Golden Rule Insurance Company, the executives and employees of which happen to have put their savings to work, during the several years since Mr. Gingrich's ascendance into the national eye, by donating $42,510 to his campaign committee, $117,076 to his GOPAC, an undisclosed amount to the foundation that sponsors his lectures, and $523,775 to the Republican Party. The Golden Rule Insurance Company also sponsors *The Progress Report*, the call-in show Mr. Gingrich co-hosts on National Empowerment Television. "Linking their contributions to performance," Mr. Gingrich told us in *Window of Opportunity*, was "the first step for average Americans in learning to organize and systematize their new relationship with elected politicians."

Those arguments in *To Renew America* not immediately suggestive of ethical conflict tend to speed headlong into another kind of collision. We have, according to Mr. Gingrich, "an absolute obligation to minimize damage to the natural world," a "moral obligation to take care of the ecosystem." Since this collides with his wish to lift the "ridiculous burden" of "environmental regulations hatched in Washington," the fulfillment of our moral obligation to take care of the ecosystem is left to a constituent in Mr. Gingrich's district, Linda Bavaro, who turns two-liter Coca-Cola bottles into T-shirts, which she sells at Disney World. "Linda," Mr. Gingrich notes, "has a good chance of doing well financially by doing good environmentally. That is how a healthy free market in a free country ought to work."

Even Mr. Gingrich's most unexceptionable arguments can take these unpredictable detours. The "Third Wave Information Age" offers "potential for enormous improvement in the lifestyle choices of most Americans," opportunities for "continuous, lifelong learning" that can enable the outplaced or downsized to operate "*outside* corporate structures and hierarchies in the nooks and crannies that the Information Age creates" (so far, so good), but here is the particular cranny of the Information Revolution into which Mr. Gingrich skids:

> Say you want to learn batik because a new craft shop has opened at the mall and the owner has told you she will sell some of your work. First, you check in at the "batik station" on the Internet, which gives you a list of recommendations. . . . You may get a list of recommended video or audio tapes that can be delivered to your door the next day by Federal Express. You may prefer a more personal learning system and seek an apprenticeship with the nearest batik master. . . . In less than twenty-four hours, you have launched yourself on a new profession.

Similarly, what begins in *To Renew America* as a rational if predictable discussion of "New Frontiers in Science, Space, and the Oceans" takes this sudden turn: "Why not aspire to build a real Jurassic Park? . . . Wouldn't that be one of the most spectacular accomplishments of human history? What if we could bring back extinct species?" A few pages further into "New Frontiers in Science, Space, and the Oceans," we are careering into "honeymoons in space" ("Imagine weightlessness and its effects and you will understand some of the attractions"), a notion first floated in *Window of Opportunity*, in that instance as an illustration of how entrepreneurial enterprise could lead to job creation in one's own district: "One reason I am convinced space travel will be a growth industry is because I represent the Atlanta airport, which provides 35,000 aviation-related jobs in the Atlanta area."

The packaging of space honeymoons and recycled two-liter Coca-Cola bottles is the kind of specific that actually engages Mr. Gingrich: absent an idea that can be sold at Disney World, he has tended to lose interest. Asked, during a 1995 appearance at the 92nd Street YMHA in New York, what he would have done early on about Bosnia, he essayed "creating a Balkan-wide development zone." The somewhat anticlimactic ninth of his Nine Principles of Self-Government for an Opportunity Society was this: "Finally, try, try again. Self-government is an arduous, demanding task on which the survival of freedom depends." Many of the proposals in *Window of Opportunity* and *To Renew*

America fritter out this way, dwindle into the perfunctory, as if the proposer's attention had already hopped on. Mr. Gingrich, we are told by Dick Williams, manages his day in fifteen-minute increments, a lesson learned from Peter Drucker's *The Effective Executive.* Mr. Gingrich, he himself tells us, believes in dedicating as many as possible of those fifteen-minute increments to reading, particularly to the reading of biography, which is seen to offer direct personal benefit: "I don't care what you want to be. If you want to get rich, read the biographies of people who got rich. If you want to be a famous entertainer, read the biographies of people who got to be famous entertainers."

Reading can provide not only this kind of intravenous inspiration but also "quotes," what *Forbes* used to call "Thoughts on the Business of Life," rhetorical backup to be plucked from the shoebox and deployed, or "used." "I was very struck this morning by something Bill Emerson used," Mr. Gingrich said at his swearing-in as Speaker. "It's a fairly famous quote of Benjamin Franklin." Mr. Gingrich tends to weigh whatever he does on this scale of strategic applicability and immediate usefulness; the fourth and fifth, or clinching, of the "Five Reasons for Studying American History" are "History is a resource to be learned from and used" and "There are techniques that can help you learn problem-solving from historical experience."

A considerable amount of what Mr. Gingrich says has never borne extended study. There was the dispiriting view of the future as a kind of extended Delta hub, where "each news magazine would have a section devoted to the week's news from space," and from which we would "flow out to the Hiltons and Marriotts of the solar system, and mankind will have permanently broken free of the planet." There were the doubtful tales offered in evidence of the point at hand, the "personalization" (a key Gingrich concept) that did not quite add up. Mr. Gingrich learned that America was "in transition from one type of economy and lifestyle to another" from reading Peter Drucker's *The Age of Discontinuity* and John Naisbett's *Megatrends*, but the truth of this came home only when he was "shocked to discover" that he could telephone his oldest daughter on her junior year abroad "by first dialing the

001 code for the international telephone computer, then the code for France, then the area code for the region near Paris, and finally the code for my daughter's telephone."

That this discovery would seem to have taken place in 1982 or 1983 (his oldest daughter was born in 1963) was just one suggestion that this was not a mind that could be productively engaged on its own terms. There was also the casual relationship to accuracy, the spellings and names and ideas seized, in the irresistible momentum of outlining, in mid-flight. In *Window of Opportunity* and in the lectures, Peter Drucker's *The Age of Discontinuity* becomes *The Age of Discontinuities.* Garry Wills's *Inventing America* becomes "Garry Will's *Discovering America.*" Gordon Wood becomes Gordon Woods. *To Renew America* shows evidence of professional copy-editing, but it also defines what it calls "situational ethics" and "deconstructionism" as interchangeable terms for "the belief that there are no general rules of behavior." Alexis de Tocqueville is seen as a kind of visiting booster, whose privilege it was to "inform the world that 'Democracy in America' worked." De Tocqueville is also seen, even more peculiarly, as an exemplar of American culture: "From the Jamestown colony and the Pilgrims, through de Tocqueville's *Democracy in America*, up to the Norman Rockwell paintings of the 1940s and 1950s, there was a clear sense of what it meant to be an American."

There was the flirtation with the millennial, the almost astral insistence on the significance of specific but intrinsically meaningless dates and numbers. The "discontinuity" (Peter Drucker again) in American history lasted, according to Mr. Gingrich, from exactly 1965 until exactly 1994: "And what's been happening is that from 1965 to 1994, that America went off on the wrong track. Now that's an important distinction." "A year which ends in three zeroes is a rare thing indeed," he declared in *Window of Opportunity.* "We're starting the 104th Congress," he said at his swearing-in. "I don't know if you've ever thought about the concept: 208 years." This inclination toward the pointlessly specific (we have here a man who once estimated the odds on the survival of his second marriage at "53 to 47") is coupled with a tic to inflate what is actually specific into a general principle, a big concept. The cherry blossoms in Washington, he advised his constituents in 1984, remind us that "there's a rhythm and cycle to life. Winter goes and spring comes." *Forrest Gump* became for Mr. Gingrich "a reaffirmation that the counterculture destroys human beings and basic values." That *Star Wars* made more money than *The Right Stuff* instructs us that "we have allowed bureaucracies to dominate too many of our scientific adventures." In the absence of anything specific to either seize or inflate, he tends to spin perilously out of syntactical orbit:

> I think if you will consider for a moment—and this is part of why I wanted to pick up on the concept of "virtualness"—if you think about the notion that the great challenge of our lifetime is first to imagine a future that is worth spending our lives getting to, then because of the technologies and the capabilities we have today to get it up to sort of a virtual state, whether that's done in terms of actual levels of sophistication or whether it's just done in your mind, most studies of leadership argue that leaders actually are putting out past decisions, that part of the reason you get certainty in great leaders is that they have already thoroughly envisioned the achievement and now it's just a matter of implementation. And so it's very different. So in a sense, virtuality at the mental level is something I think you'd find in most leadership over historical periods.

2.

The real substance of Mr. Gingrich's political presence derives from his skill at massaging exhaustively researched voter preferences and prejudices into matters of lonely principle. The positions he takes are acutely tuned to the expressed fears and resentments of a significant number of Americans, yet he stands, in his rhetoric, alone, opposed by "the system," by "Washington," by "the liberal elite," by "the East Coast elite" (not by accident does a mention of Harvard in *1945* provoke the antipathy of the sympathetic president to "East Coast snobbery and intellectual hauteur"), or simply by an unspecified "they." "I kind of live on the edge," Mr. Gingrich told Dick Williams. "I push the system." When, in a famous GOPAC memo, Mr. Gingrich advised Republican candidates to characterize Democrats with the words "decay," "sick," "pathetic," "stagnation," "corrupt," "waste," and "traitors," and Republicans with the words "share," "change," "truth," "moral," "courage," "family," "peace," and "duty," each word had been tested and oiled in focus groups to function in what the memo called "Language, A Key Mechanism of Control."

The 1994 Contract with America was packaged as, and to a peculiar extent accepted even by its opponents as, a "bold agenda" (opponents said too bold, and were left arguing only to split the difference), a "vision for America's future" (opponents rushed to share the vision, and argued only the means), yet each of its ten items derived from and was later refined in focus groups run by Frank Luntz, who did the 1992 campaign polling first for Pat Buchanan and then for Ross Perot. "The Contract with America was specifically designed to appeal to the swing Perot voter who hates partisan politics," Mr. Gingrich said during his 1995 YMHA appearance. "The ten points basically selected themselves as deeply felt desires of the American people," is his somewhat cryptic version of this process in *To Renew America*. "It can literally be said that the Contract with America grew out of our conversations with the American people and out of our basic conservative values."

The preferences and attitudes discovered through opinion research tend to be, no matter who is paying for the research, fairly consistent. A majority of American voters who end up in political focus groups are displeased with the current welfare system, believe that affirmative action has been carried too far, are opposed to crime and in favor of "opportunity." They say this to researchers working for Republican candidates and they also say it to researchers working for Democratic candidates. Which was why, of course, anyone whose own researcher happened to be having identical conversations with the American people was left, up against the Contract with America, with nowhere to stand. "Now what you've got in this city is a simple principle," Mr. Gingrich told the Republican National Committee in January 1995. "I am a genuine revolutionary; they are the genuine reactionaries. We are going to change their world; they will do anything to stop us. They will use any tool—there is no grotesquerie, no distortion, no dishonesty too great for them to come after us." He described himself to Fred Barnes as "the leading revolutionary in the country. I'm trying to replace the welfare state and the counterculture and the old establishment with a system of opportunity and entrepreneurship and classic American civilization."

What seems grandiose melts down, on the floor, to business as usual. "Replacing the welfare state" turned out to mean, with the passage in the House of the Personal Responsibility and Senior Citizens Fairness Acts, phasing out a $16 billion welfare program for the poor (Aid to Families with Dependent Children) in order to expand, by lifting the level of its earnings test, what was already a $335 billion welfare program for the middle class, Social Security. The unfairness (Frank Luntz has isolated "fairness" and "unfairness" as hot words) of applying any earnings test at all to Social Security benefits was an issue seized early by Mr. Gingrich, who illustrated or "personalized" it in *Window of Opportunity* with another doubtful tale, this one featuring "Warren," a retiree who "wanted to do something to keep his mind and body busy and to contribute to the community and world he loves" but was forced to give up selling his contribution of choice, which happened to be scrimshaw, when the Social Security Administration threatened to reduce, or in Mr. Gingrich's telling "cut off," his benefits. When Dan Balz and Charles R. Babcock of *The Washington Post* suggested that this preference for what the Speaker calls "65 percent issues" could be construed as pandering to public opinion, Mr. Gingrich corrected them: "Politics," he said, "is about public opinion and gathering public support. It's like saying, isn't it pandering for Wal-Mart to stock everything people want to buy."

3.

"I teach a course which is an outline of my thoughts at 51 years of age, based on everything I've experienced, which is, frankly, rather more than most tenured faculty," Mr. Gingrich told *The New York Times* in January 1995. "I'm not credentialed as a bureaucratic academic. I haven't written 22 books that are meaningless." What details we have about the formative experience of the Speaker, who was born Newton Leroy McPherson and took the surname of his mother's second husband, describe a familiar postwar history, one not dissimilar from that of William Jefferson Clinton, who was born William Jefferson Blythe and took the surname of his mother's second husband. Each was the adored first-born son of a mother left largely, in the economic and social dislocations that transformed America during and immediately after World War II, to her own devices. Each was farmed out to relatives while the mother earned a living. Each appears to have reached adolescence firm in the conviction that these would be the make-or-break years, that the point of the exercise was to assert, win over, overcome.

The two relied on different means to this end, but the instinctive technique of each derived from the literature of personal improvement, effective self-presentation, salesmanship, five simple steps. Mr. Clinton, with his considerable personal magnetism, kept extensive lists of people he had met and on whom, when the time arrived, he could call. In the case of Mr. Gingrich, who after his mother remarried was repeatedly uprooted and moved from one army post to another, Kansas to France to Germany to Georgia, such social skills remained undeveloped, forcing him back on his reading, his self-education, his shoeboxes. He recalled being given an article when he was young. "It was about Lincoln's five defeats, I carried it in my wallet for years." At sixteen, en route from Stuttgart to Fort Benning, he concluded "that there was no moral choice except to immerse myself in the process of learning how to lead and how to be effective." His stepfather gave him a set of the *Encyclopedia Americana*, and he read it every night. At Baker High School near Fort Benning he yielded to the southern pressure to play sports, but was sidelined by headaches. His Democratic opponent in 1994 referred to him as a "wuss," and as "the guy who won the science project."

"I think I was very lonely and very driven," Mr. Gingrich told Dick Williams. "If you decide in your freshman year of high school that your job is to spend your lifetime trying to change the future of your people, you're probably fairly weird." The defense he adopted was the persona of "class brain" (his classmates voted him "Most Intellectual"), the one with the pens and slide rule in his shirt pocket, the one who could spark the debating society, tie for highest score in the county on the National Merit Scholarship test, make a strategic detour around his lack of aptitude for high school cool by tutoring the school beauty queen and not-quite-secretly dating the geometry teacher. As a freshman at Emory University he married the geometry teacher and co-founded the Emory Young Republican Club. As a graduate student at Tulane he organized a week-long protest against administration censorship of the college paper, discovered Alvin Toffler, and taught a noncredit class on the Year 2000.

He took for himself, in other words, the ritualized role of breaker of new ground, marcher to a different drummer, which happens to be the cast of mind in which speculative fiction finds its most tenacious hold. *What if* one or another event had not occurred, *what if* one or another historical figure had remained unborn, dropped into a coma, taken another turn: the contemplation of such questions has reliably occupied the different drummers of American secondary education. The impulse is anti-theological, which translates, for these readers, into thrilling iconoclasm. In Isaac Asimov's *Foundation* trilogy, according to Mr. Gingrich, "the Catholic Church's role in maintaining civilized knowledge through the Dark and Middle Ages is played by a secular group of intellectuals called 'The Foundation.'" The tendency is to see history as random but reversible, the sum of its own events and personalities. Isaac Asimov, Mr. Gingrich notes, "did not believe in a mechanistic world. Instead, to Asimov, human beings always hold their fate in their own hands."

It was this high school reading of Isaac Asimov, Mr. Gingrich tells us in *To Renew America*, that first "focused my attention on the fate of civilization. I came to realize that, while most people were immersed in day-to-day activities, daily behavior actually takes place within a much larger context of constantly changing global forces." Mr. Gingrich is frequently and often deprecatingly described as a "futurist," but even as he talks about those "constantly changing global forces," about a transformation "so large and historic that it can be compared with only two other great areas of human history—the Agricultural Revolution and the Industrial Revolution," his view of the future is a view of 1955, factory-loaded with Year 2000 extras. *To Renew America* asks us to "imagine a morning in just a decade or so":

> You wake up to a wall-size, high-definition television showing surf off Maui. (This is my favorite island—you can pick your own scene.) You walk or jog or do Stairmaster while catching up on the morning news and beginning to review your day's schedule. Your home office is filled with communications devices, so you can ignore rush-hour traffic. . . . When you are sick, you sit in your diagnostic chair and communicate with the local health clinic. Sensors take your blood pressure, analyze a blood sample, or do throat cultures. The results are quickly relayed to health aides, who make recommendations and prescribe medicine. . . . If you need a specialist, a databank at your fingertips gives you a wide range of choices based on cost, reputation, and outcome patterns. You can choose knowledgeably which risk you want to take and what price you want to pay.

The "diagnostic chair," or "personalized health chair," which could also be programmed to "monitor your diet over time and change recipes to minimize boredom while achieving the desired nutritional effect," appeared first in *Window of Opportunity*, which outlined a future in which we or our descendants would also use computer technology to correct golf swings, provide tax and IRA advice, and provide data on "literally thousands of vacation, recreation, and education opportunities," for example the Ocmulgee Indian Mounds Park in Macon, Georgia, with its "splendid natural walk area, a beautiful collection of ancient Indian ceremonial mounds, and fine museum on the history of the area from 900 A.D. to the present." For any among us whose view of the future might have been somewhat more forbidding or interesting (no Maui, no Macon, the IRAs all gone bust), Mr. Gingrich would recommend first the reading of science fiction, since "a generation that learns its magic from Tom Swift or Jules Verne has a much more optimistic outlook than one that is constantly being told that the planet is dying and that everything humanity is doing is wrong."

If wishes were horses, beggars would ride, as they said in the generation that learned its magic from Tom Swift and Jules Verne. To know that large numbers of Americans are concerned about getting adequate medical care is one thing; to give them the willies by talking about their "health chairs" is quite another, suggesting not the future but the past, the drone of the small-town autodidact, the garrulous bore in the courthouse square. There is about these dismal reductions something disarming and poignant, a solitary neediness, a dogged determination to shine in public that leads Mr. Gingrich to reveal to us, again and again, what his own interests dictate that we should not see. He concludes *To Renew America* with a "personalization" of his concern for voter concerns, an account of how he and his second wife, Marianne, spent the Christmas before he became Speaker in Leetonia, Ohio, "a wonderful small town that is like a scene from a Norman Rockwell *Saturday Evening Post* cover."

For much of this account Mr. Gingrich remains well within the secured territory of H.R. 0003–95 and H.R. 0006–95, the Taking Back Our Streets and American Dream Restoration Acts. He expresses concern for Marianne's eighty-year-old mother, who "worked and saved all her life" but now worries about "the reports that Medicare will go bankrupt by 2002." He worries that his eight-year-old nephew, Sean, "cannot walk around Youngstown the way I once wandered the streets of Harrisburg." He wonders how Marianne's sister and her husband will manage putting their boys, Jon and Mark, through college. Then, midway through this tuned and calculated Christmas reverie, Mr. Gingrich drops, abruptly and inexplicably, through the ice, off message: "At heart," he dismayingly confides, "I am still a happy four-year-old who gets up every morning hoping to find a cookie that friends or relatives may have left for me somewhere." This cookie is worrisome: Was it forgotten? Hidden? Why would they hide it? Where are they? Are they asleep, out, absentee friends, deadbeat relatives? The cookie was the treat and leaving is the trick? What we get from these problematic detours and revelations, from the cookies and the health chairs and the high-resolution views of Maui, from the Ten Steps and the Five Pillars and the thirty gigabytes to an improved golf swing, is a shadow of something unexplained, a scent of failure, which remains one reason why, in a country made even more uncomfortable by losers than Mr. Gingrich claims to be, personal popularity among large numbers of voters may continue to elude him.

Political Pornography

September 19, 1996

ON THE MORNING of Sunday, June 23, 1996, the day the pre-publication embargo on Bob Woodward's *The Choice* was lifted, *The Washington Post*, the paper for which Mr. Woodward has so famously been, since 1971, first a reporter and then an editor, published on the front page of its "A" section two stories detailing what its editors believed most newsworthy in *The Choice*. In columns one through four, directly under the banner and carrying the legend *The Choice—Inside the Clinton and Dole Campaigns*, there appeared passages from the book itself, edited into a narrative describing the meetings Hillary Clinton had from 1994 to 1996 with Jean Houston, who was characterized in the *Post* as "a believer in spirits, mythic and other connections to history and other worlds" and as "the most dramatic" of Mrs. Clinton's "10 to 11 confidants," a group that included her mother.

This account of Mrs. Clinton's not entirely remarkable and in any case private conversations with Jean Houston appeared under the apparently accurate if unsurprising headline "At a Difficult Time, First Lady Reaches Out, Looks Within," occupied one-hundred and fifty-four column inches, was followed by a six-column-inch box explaining the rules under which Mr. Woodward conducted his interviews, and included among similar revelations the news that, according to an unidentified source (Mr. Woodward tells us that some of his interviews were on the record, others "conducted under journalistic ground rules of 'background' or 'deep background,' meaning the information could be used but the sources of the information would not be identified"), Mrs. Clinton had at an unspecified point in 1995 disclosed to Jean Houston ("Dialogue and quotations come from at least one participant, from memos or from contemporaneous notes or diaries of a participant in the discussion") that "she was sure that good habits were the key to survival."

The remaining front-page columns above the fold in that

Sunday's *Post* were given over to a news story based on *The Choice*, written by Dan Balz, running seventy-nine column inches and headlined "Dole Seeks 'a 10' Among List of 15: Running Mate Must Not Anger Right, Book Says." Mr. Woodward, according to this story, "quotes Dole as saying he wants a running mate who will be 'a 10' in the eyes of the public, with the candidate telling the head of his search team, Robert F. Ellsworth, 'Don't give me someone who would send up [anger] the conservatives.'" Those *Post* readers sufficiently surprised by this disclosure to continue reading learned that "at the top of the list of 15 names, assembled in the late spring by Ellsworth and Dole's campaign manager, Scott Reed, was Colin L. Powell." When I read this in the *Post* I assumed that I would find some discussion of how or whether the vice-presidential search team had managed to construe their number-one choice of Colin L. Powell as consistent with the mandate "Don't give me someone who would send up the conservatives," but there was no such discussion to be found, neither in the *Post* nor in *The Choice* itself.

Mr. Woodward's aversion to engaging the ramifications of what people say to him has been generally understood as an admirable quality, at best a mandarin modesty, at worst a kind of executive big-picture focus, the entirely justifiable oversight of someone with a more important game to play. Yet what we see in *The Choice* is something more than a matter of an occasional inconsistency left unexplored in the rush of the breaking story, a stray ball or two left unfielded in the heat of the opportunity, as Mr. Woodward describes his role, "to sit with many of the candidates and key players and ask about the questions of the day as the campaign unfolded." What seems most remarkable in this Woodward book is exactly what seemed remarkable in the previous Woodward books, each of which was presented as the insiders' inside story and each of which went on to become a number-one bestseller: these are books in which measurable cerebral activity is virtually absent.

The author himself disclaims "the perspective of history." His preferred approach has been one in which "issues could be examined before the possible outcome or meaning was at all clear or the possible consequences were weighed." The refusal to consider outcome or meaning or consequence has, as a way of writing a book, a certain Zen purity, but tends toward a process in which no research method is so commonplace as to go unexplained ("The record will show how I was able to gain information from records or interviews. . . . I could then talk with other sources and return to most of them again and again as necessary"), no product of that research so predictable as to go unrecorded. The world rendered is an Erewhon in which not only inductive reasoning but ordinary reliance on context clues appear to have vanished. Any reader who wonders what Vice President Gore thought about Whitewater could turn to page 418 of *The Choice* and find that he believed the matter "small and unfair," but was sometimes concerned that "the Republicans and the scandal machinery in Washington" could keep it front and center. Any reader unwilling to hazard a guess about what Dick Morris's polling data told him about Medicare could turn to page 235 of *The Choice* and find that "voters liked Medicare, trusted it and felt it was the one federal program that worked."

This tabula rasa typing requires rather persistent attention on the part of the reader, since its very presence on the page works to suggest that significant and heretofore unrevealed information must have just been revealed by a reporter who left no stone unturned to obtain it. The weekly lunch shared by President Clinton and Vice President Gore, we learn in *The Choice*, "sometimes did not start until 3 P.M. because of other business." The president, "who had a notorious appetite, tried to eat lighter food." The reader attuned to the conventions of narrative might be led by the presentation of these quotidian details into thinking that a dramatic moment is about to occur, but the crux of the four-page prologue having to do with the weekly lunches turns out to be this: the president, according to Mr. Woodward, "thought a lot of the criticism he received was unfair." The vice president, he reveals, "had some advice. Clinton always had found excess reserve within himself. He would just have to find more, Gore said."

What Mr. Woodward chooses to leave unrecorded, or what he apparently does not think to elicit, is in many ways more instructive than what he commits to paper. "The accounts I have compiled may, at times, be more comprehensive than what a future historian, who has to rely on a single memo, letter, or recollection of what happened, might be able to piece together," he noted in the introduction to *The Agenda*, an account of certain events in the first years of the Clinton administration in which he endeavored, to cryogenic effect, "to give every key participant in these events an opportunity to offer his or her recollections and views." The "future historian" who might be interested in piecing together the details of how the Clinton administration arrived at its program for health care reform, however, will find, despite a promising page of index references, that none of the key participants interviewed for *The Agenda* apparently thought to discuss what might have seemed the central curiosity in that process, which was by what political miscalculation a plan initially meant to remove third-party profit from the health care equation (or to "take on the insurance industry," as *Putting People First*, the manifesto of the 1992 Clinton-Gore campaign, had phrased it) would become one distrusted by large numbers of Americans precisely because it seemed to enlarge and further entrench the role of the insurance industry.

This disinclination of Mr. Woodward's to exert cognitive energy on what he is told reaches critical mass in *The Choice*, where not much said to the author by a candidate or potential candidate appears to have been deemed too insignificant for inclusion, too casual for documentation. ("Most of them permitted me to tape-record the interviews; otherwise I took detailed notes.") President Clinton declined to be interviewed directly for this book, but Senator Dole "was interviewed for more than 12 hours and the typed transcripts run over 200 pages." Accounts of these interviews, typically including date, time, venue, weather, and apparel details (for one Saturday interview in his office the candidate was "dressed casually in a handsome green wool shirt") can be found, according to the index of *The Choice* ("Dole, Robert J. 'Bob,' interviews by author with"), on pages 87–89, 183, 214–215, 338, 345–348, 378, 414, and 423.

Study of these pages suggests the deferential spirit of the enterprise. In the course of the Saturday interview for which Senator Dole selected the "handsome green wool shirt," a ninety-minute session which took place on February 4, 1995, in Dole's office in the Hart Senate Office Building ("My tape recorder sat on the arm of his chair, and his press secretary, Clarkson Hine, took copious notes"), Mr. Woodward asked Dole if he had thought, in 1988, that he was the best candidate. He reports Dole's answer: "Thought I was." This gave Mr. Woodward the opportunity to ask what he had previously (and rather mystifyingly, since little else in *The Choice* tends to this point) defined for the reader as "an important question for my book": "You weren't elected," he reminded Senator Dole, "so you have to come out of that period feeling the system doesn't elect the best?"

Senator Dole, not unexpectedly, answered agreeably: "I think it's true. I think Elizabeth raises that a lot, whether it's president, or Senate or whatever, that a lot of the best—somebody people would describe [as] the best—doesn't make it. That's the way the system works. You also come out of that, even if you lose, if you still have enough confidence in yourself, that you didn't lose because you weren't the best candidate. You lost for other reasons. You can always rationalize these things."

On Saturday, July 1, 1995, again in Dole's Hart office (Senator Dole in "casual khaki pants, a blue dress shirt with cufflinks, and purple Nike tennis shoes"), Mr. Woodward elicited, in the course of a two-and-a-half-hour interview, these reflections from the candidate:

> *On his schedule*: "We're trying to pace ourselves. It's like today I'm not traveling, which is hard to believe. Tomorrow we go to Iowa, get back at 1 A.M. We're off all day Monday. Then we go to New Hampshire."
>
> *On his speechwriters*: "You can't just read something that somebody's written and say 'Oh, boy, this is dynamite.' You've got to have a feel for it and you've got to think, Jimminy, this might work. And this is the message. And I think we're still testing it, and I think you can't say that if I said this on day one, it's going to be written in stone forever."
>
> *On the message, in response to Mr. Woodward's suggestion that "there's something people are waiting for somebody to say that no one has said yet"*: "Right. I think you're right."

> *On his strategy*: "As long as we're on target, on message, and got money in the bank, and people are signing up, we're mostly doing the right thing. But I also have been around long enough to know that somebody can make a mistake and it'll be all over, too."
>
> *On the Senate*: "Somebody has to manage it. And it may not be manageable. It isn't, you know, it's a frustrating place sometimes but generally it works out."

"I was not out of questions," Mr. Woodward concludes, "but I too was growing tired, and it seemed time to stand up and thank him."

Mr. Woodward dutifully tries, in the note that prefaces *The Choice*, to provide the "why" paragraph, the "billboard," the sentence or sentences that explain to the reader why the book was written and what it is about. That these are questions with which he experiences considerable discomfort seems clear:

> Presidential elections are defining moments that go way beyond legislative programs or the role of the government. They are measuring points for the country that call forth a range of questions which every candidate must try to address. Who are we? What matters? Where are we going? In the private and public actions of the candidates are embedded their best answers. Action is character, I believe, and when all is said and sifted, character is what matters most.

This *quo vadis*, or valedictory, mode is one in which Mr. Woodward, faced with the question of what his books are about, has crashed repeatedly, as if his programming did not extend to this point. The "human story is the core" was his somewhat more perfunctory stab at explaining what he was up to in *The Commanders*. For *Wired*, his 1984 book about the life and death of the comic John Belushi, Mr. Woodward spoke to 217 people on the record and obtained access to "appointment calendars, diaries, telephone records, credit card receipts, medical records, handwritten notes, letters, photographs, newspaper and magazine articles, stacks of accountants' records covering the last several years of Belushi's life, daily movie production reports, contracts, hotel records, travel records, taxi receipts, limousine bills and Belushi's monthly cash disbursement records," only to arrive, not unlike HAL in *2001*, at these questions: "Why? What happened? Who was responsible, if anyone? Could it have been different or better? Those were the questions raised by his family, friends and associates. Could success have been something other than a failure? The questions persist. Nonetheless, his best and most definitive legacy is his work. He made us laugh, and now he can make us think."

In any real sense, these books are "about" nothing but the author's own method, which is not, on the face of it, markedly different from other people's. Mr. Woodward interviews people, he tapes or takes notes ("detailed" notes) on what they say. He takes "great care to compare and verify various sources' accounts of the same events." He obtains documents, he reads them, he files them: for *The Brethren*, the book he wrote with Scott Armstrong about the Supreme Court, the documents filled "eight file drawers." He consults *The Almanac of American Politics* ("the bible, and I relied on it"), he reads what others have written on the subject. "In preparation for my own reporting," he tells us about *The Choice*, "I and my assistant, Karen Alexander, read and often studied hundreds of newspaper and magazine articles."

Should the information he requires necessitate travel, he goes the extra mile: "I traveled from coast to coast many times, visiting everyone possible and everywhere possible," he tells us about the research for *Wired*. Since John Belushi worked in the motion-picture industry and died at the Chateau Marmont in Los Angeles, these coast-to-coast trips might have seemed to represent the minimum in dogged fact-gathering, but never mind: the author had even then, in 1984, transcended method and entered the heady ether of methodology, a discipline in which the reason for writing a book could be the sheer fact of being there. "I would like to know more and *Newsweek* magazine was saying that maybe that is the thing I should look at next," he allowed when a caller on *Larry King Live* asked if he might not want to write about Whitewater. "I don't know. I do not know about Whitewater and what it really means. I am waiting—if I can say this—for the call from somebody on the inside saying 'I want to talk.'"

Here is where we reach the single unique element in the method, and also the problem. As any prosecutor and surely Mr. Woodward knows, the person on the inside who calls and says "I want to talk" is an informant, or snitch, and is generally looking to bargain a deal, to improve his or her own situation, to place the blame on someone else in return for being allowed to plead down or out certain charges. Because the story told by a criminal or civil informant is understood to be colored by self-interest, the informant knows that his or her testimony will be unrespected, even reviled, subjected to rigorous examination and often rejection. The informant who talks to Mr. Woodward, on the other hand, knows that his or her testimony will be not only respected but burnished into the inside story, which is why so many people on the inside, notably those who consider themselves the professionals or managers of the process—assistant secretaries, deputy advisers, players of the game, aides who intend to survive past the tenure of the patron they are prepared to portray as hapless—do want to talk to him. Many Dole campaign aides did want to talk, for *The Choice*, about the herculean efforts and adroit strategy required to keep the candidate with whom they were saddled even marginally on message, on the program:

> Dole offered a number of additional references to the past, how it had been done before, and Reed [Dole campaign manager Scott Reed] countered with his own ideas about how he would handle similar situations. A sense of diffusion and randomness wouldn't work. Making seat-of-the-pants, airborne decisions was not the way he operated. . . . Dole needed a coherent and understandable message on which to run, Reed said. Deep down, he added, he knew Dole knew what he wanted to say, but he probably needed some help putting it together and delivering it. . . . Reed felt he had hit the right weaknesses.

Similarly, many Clinton foreign policy advisers did want to talk, again for *The Choice*, about the equally herculean efforts and strategy required to guide the president, on the question of Bosnia, from one of his "celebrated rages" ("I'm getting creamed!" Clinton, "unleashing his frustration" and "spewing forth profanity," is reported to have said on being told of the fall of Srebrenica) to a more nuanced appreciation of the policy options on which his aides—Deputy National Security Adviser Sandy Berger, say, and National Security Adviser Anthony Lake—had been laboring unappreciated. "Berger reminded him," Woodward tells us, "that Lake was trying to develop an Endgame Strategy." At a meeting a few days later in the Oval Office, when Vice President Gore mentioned a photograph in *The Washington Post* of a refugee from Srebrenica who had hanged herself from a tree, the adroit guidance continued:

> "My 21-year-old daughter asked about that picture," Gore said. "What am I supposed to tell her? Why is this happening and we're not doing anything?"
>
> It was a chilling moment. The vice president was directly confronting and criticizing the president. Gore believed he understood his role. He couldn't push the president too far, but they had built a good relationship and he felt he had to play his card when he felt strongly. He couldn't know precisely what going too far meant unless he occasionally did it.
>
> "My daughter is surprised the world is allowing this to happen," Gore said carefully. "I am too."
>
> Clinton said they were going to do something.

This is a cartoon, but not a cartoon in which anyone who spoke to the author will appear to have taken any but the highest ground. Asked, in the same appearance on *Larry King Live*, why he thought people talked to him, Mr. Woodward responded:

> Only because I get good information and I talk to people at the middle level, lower level, try to talk to the people at the top. They know that I am going to reflect their point of view. One of my earlier books, somebody called me who was in it and said "How am I going to come out?" and I said "Well, essentially, I write self-portraits." . . . They really are self-portraits, because I go to people and I double-check them but—but who are you? What are you doing? Where do you fit in? What did you say? What did you feel?

Those who talk to Mr. Woodward, in other words, can be confident that he will be civil ("I too was growing tired, and it seemed time to stand up and thank him"), that he will not feel impelled to make connections between what he is told and what is already known, that he will treat even the most patently self-serving account as if untainted by hindsight (that of Richard Darman, say, who in 1992 presented himself to Mr. Woodward, who in turn presented him to America, as the helpless Cassandra of the 1990 Bush budget deal); that he will be, above all, and herein can be found both Mr. Woodward's compass and the means by which he is set adrift, "fair."

I once heard a group of reporters agree that there were at most twenty people who run any story. What they meant by "running the story" was setting the terms, setting the pace, deciding the agenda, determining when and where the story exists, and shaping what the story will be. There were certain people who ran the story in Vietnam, there were certain people in Central America, there were certain people in Washington. An American presidential campaign is a Washington story, which means that the handful of people who run the story in Washington—the people who write the most influential columns, the people who conduct the Sunday shows on which Washington talks to itself—will also run the campaign. Bob Woodward, who is unusual in that he is not a regular participant in the television dialogue and appears in print, outside his books, only infrequently, is one of the people who run the story in Washington.

In this business of running the story, in fact in the business of news itself, certain conventions are seen as beyond debate. "Opinion" will be so labeled, and confined to the op-ed page or the television talk shows. "News analysis" will be so labeled, and will appear in a subordinate position to the "news" story it accompanies. In the rest of the paper as on the evening news, the story will be reported "impartially," the story will be "even-handed," the story will be "fair." "Fairness" is a quality Mr. Woodward seems particularly to prize ("I learned a long time ago," he told Larry King, "you take your opinions and your attitudes, your predispositions—get them in your back pocket, because they are only going to get in the way of doing your job"), and mentions repeatedly in his thanks to his assistants.

It was "Karen Alexander, a 1993 graduate of Yale University," who "brought unmatched intellect, grace and doggedness and an ingrained sense of fairness" to *The Choice*. On *The*

Agenda, it was "David Greenberg, a 1990 graduate of Yale University," who "repeatedly worked to bring greater balance, fairness, and clarity to our reporting and writing." It was "Marc E. Solomon, a 1989 Yale graduate," who "brought a sense of fairness and balance" to *The Commanders*. On *The Veil*, it was "Barbara Feinman, a 1982 graduate of the University of California at Berkeley," whose "friendship and sense of fairness guided the daily enterprise." For *The Brethren*, Mr. Woodward and his coauthor, Scott Armstrong, thank "Al Kamen, a former reporter for the *Rocky Mountain News*," for his "thoroughness, skepticism, and sense of fairness."

The genuflection toward "fairness" is a familiar newsroom piety, in practice the excuse for a good deal of autopilot reporting and lazy thinking but in theory a benign ideal. In Washington, however, a community in which the management of news has become the single overriding preoccupation of the core industry, what "fairness" has often come to mean is a scrupulous passivity, an agreement to cover the story not as it is occurring but as it is presented, which is to say as it is manufactured. Such institutionalized events as a congressional hearing or a presidential trip will be covered with due diligence, but the story will vanish the moment the gavel falls, the hour Air Force One returns to Andrews. "Iran-contra" referred exclusively, for many Washington reporters, to the hearings. The sequence of events that came to be known as "the S&L crisis," which was actually less a "crisis" than the structural malfunction that triggered an uncontrolled meltdown in middle-class confidence, existed as a "story" only on those occasions (hearings, indictments) when it showed promise of rising to its "crisis" slug. Similarly, "Whitewater" (as in "I do not know about Whitewater and what it really means") survived as a story only to the extent that it allowed those who covered it to calibrate the waxing or waning possibility of a "smoking gun," or "evidence."

"If there is evidence it should be pursued," Mr. Woodward told Larry King to this point. "In fairness to the Clintons. And it's—it—you know, we all in the news business, and in politics have to be very sensitive to the unfair smear. . . . It's not fair and again it goes back to what's the evidence?" Yet the actual interest of Whitewater lies in what has already been documented: it is "about" the S&L crisis, and thereby offers a detailed and specific look at the kinds of political and financial dealing that resulted in the meltdown in middle-class confidence. What Whitewater "really means" or offers, then, is an understanding of that meltdown, which has been reported as if it existed in a vacuum, an inexplicable phenomenon weirdly detached from the periodic growth figures produced in Washington. This could be a valuable story, but it is not one that will be put together by waiting for the call from somebody on the inside saying "I want to talk."

Every reporter, in the development of a story, depends on and coddles, or protects, his or her sources. Only when the protection of the source gets in the way of telling the story does the reporter face a professional, even a moral, choice: he can blow the source and move to another beat or he can roll over, shape the story to continue serving the source. The necessity for making this choice between the source and the story seems not to have come up in the course of writing Mr. Woodward's books, for good reason: since he proceeds from a position in which the very impulse to sort through the evidence and reach a conclusion is seen as suspect, something to be avoided in the higher interest of fairness, he has been able, consistently and conveniently, to define the story as that which the source tells him.

This fidelity to the source, whoever the source might be, leads Mr. Woodward down avenues that might at first seem dead-end. On page 16 of *The Choice* we have President Clinton, presumably on the word of a White House source, "thunderstruck" that Senator Dole, on the morning after Clinton's mother died in early 1994, should have described Whitewater on the network news shows as "unbelievable," "mind-boggling," "big, big news" that "cries out more than ever now for an independent counsel." On page 346 of *The Choice* we have Senator Dole, on December 27, 1995, telling Mr. Woodward "that he had never used Whitewater to attack the president personally," to which Mr. Woodward responds only: "What would be your criteria for picking a vice-president?" On page 423 of *The Choice* we have Mr. Woodward, on April 20, 1996, by which date he had apparently remembered what he said on page 16 that Senator Dole said, although not what he said on page 346 that Senator Dole said, advising Senator Dole that the president had resented his "aggressive call for a Whitewater independent counsel back in early 1994, the day Clinton's mother had died."

Only now do we arrive at what seems to be for Mr. Woodward the point, and it has to do with his own role as honest broker, or conscience to the candidates. He reports that Senator Dole was "troubled" by this disclosure, even "haunted by what he might have done," so much so that he was moved to write Clinton a letter of apology:

> Later that week, Dole was at the White House for an anti-terrorism bill signing ceremony. Clinton took him aside into a corridor so they could speak alone. The president thanked him for the letter. He said he had read it twice. He was touched and appreciated it very much.
>
> "Mothers are important," Dole said.
>
> Emotion rose up in both men. They looked at each other for an instant, then moved back to business. Soon they agreed on a budget for the rest of the year. It was not the comprehensive seven-year deal both had envisioned and worked on for months. But it was a start.

"This human story is the core," as Mr. Woodward said of *The Commanders.* To believe that this moment in the White House corridor occurred is not difficult: we know it occurred, precisely because whether or not it occurred makes no difference, has no significance, appears at first to tell us, like the famous moment described in *Veil*, the exchange between the author and William Casey in Room C6316 at Georgetown Hospital, nothing. "You knew, didn't you," Mr. Woodward thought to ask Casey on that occasion.

> The contra diversion had to be the first question: you knew all along.
>
> His head jerked up hard. He stared, and finally nodded yes.
>
> Why? I asked.
>
> "I believed."

What?
"I believed."
Then he was asleep, and I didn't get to ask another question.

This account provoked, in the immediate wake of *Veil*'s 1987 publication, considerable talk-show and dinner-table controversy (was Mr. Woodward actually in the room, did Mr. Casey actually nod, where were the nurses, what happened to the CIA security detail), including, rather astonishingly, spirited discussion of whether or not the hospital visit could be "corroborated." In fact there was so markedly little reason to think the account inauthentic that the very question seemed to obscure, as the account itself had seemed to obscure, the actual problem with the scene in Room C6316 at Georgetown Hospital, which had to do with timing, or with what did Mr. Woodward know and when did he know it.

The hospital visit took place, according to *Veil*, "several days" after Mr. Casey's resignation, which occurred on January 29, 1987. This was almost four months after the crash of the Hasenfus plane in Nicaragua, more than two months after the Justice Department disclosure that the United States had been selling arms to Iran in order to divert the profits to the contras, and a full month after both the House and Senate Permanent Subcommittees on Intelligence had completed reports on their investigations into the diversion. The inquiries of the two congressional investigating committees established in the first week of January 1987, the Senate Select Committee on Secret Military Assistance to Iran and the Nicaraguan Opposition and the House Select Committee to Investigate Covert Arms Transactions with Iran, were already underway. The report of the Tower Commission would be released in three weeks.

Against this background and this amount of accumulated information, the question of whether the director of Central Intelligence "knew" about the diversion was, at the time Mr. Woodward made his hospital visit and even more conclusively at the time he committed his account of the visit to paper, no longer at issue, no longer relevant, no longer a question. The hospital interview, then, exists on the page only as a prurient distraction from the real questions raised by the diversion, only as a dramatization of the preferred Washington view that

Iran-contra reflected not a structural problem but a "human story," a tale of how one man's hubris could have shaken the basically solid foundations of the established order, a disruption of the stable status quo that could be seen to end, satisfyingly, with that man's death.

Washington, as rendered by Mr. Woodward, is by definition basically solid, a diorama of decent intentions in which wise if misunderstood and occasionally misled stewards will reliably prevail. Its military chiefs will be pictured, as Colin Powell was in *The Commanders*, thinking on the eve of battle exclusively of their troops, the "kids," the "teenagers": a human story. The clerks of the Supreme Court will be pictured, as the clerks of the Burger court were in *The Brethren*, offering astute guidance as their justices negotiate the shoals of ideological error: a human story. The more available members of its foreign diplomatic corps will be pictured, as Saudi ambassador Prince Bandar bin Sultan was in *The Commanders* and *Veil*, gaining access to the councils of power not just because they have the oil but because of their "backslapping irreverence," their "directness," their exemplification of "the new breed of ambassador—activist, charming, profane": yet another human story. Its opposing leaders will be pictured, as President Clinton and Senator Dole are in *The Choice*, finding common ground on the importance of mothers: the ultimate human story.

That this crude personalization works to narrow the focus, to circumscribe the range of possible discussion or speculation, is, for the people who find it useful to talk to Mr. Woodward, its point. What they have in Mr. Woodward is a widely trusted reporter, even an American icon, who can be relied upon to present a Washington in which problematic or questionable matters will be definitively resolved by the discovery, or by the demonstration that there can be no discovery, of "the smoking gun," "the evidence." Should such narrowly defined "evidence" be found, he can then be relied upon to demonstrate, "fairly," that the only fingerprints on the smoking gun are those of the one bad apple in the barrel, the single rogue agent in the tapestry of good intentions.

"I kept coming back to the question of personal responsibility, Casey's responsibility," Mr. Woodward reports having mused (apparently for once prepared, at the moment when he is about to visit a source on his deathbed, to question the veracity of what he has been told) before his last visit to Room C6316 at Georgetown Hospital. "For a moment, I hoped he would take himself off the hook. The only way was an admission of some kind or an apology to his colleagues or an expression of new understanding. Under the last question on 'Key unanswered questions for Casey,' I wrote: 'Do you see now that it was wrong?'" To commit such Rosebud moments to paper is what it means to tell "the human story at the core," and it is also what it means to write political pornography.

Clinton Agonistes

October 22, 1998

NO ONE who ever passed through an American public high school could have watched William Jefferson Clinton running for office in 1992 and failed to recognize the familiar predatory sexuality of the provincial adolescent. The man was, Jesse Jackson said that year to another point, "nothing but an appetite." No one who followed his appearances on *The Road to the White House* on C-SPAN could have missed the reservoir of self-pity, the quickness to blame, the narrowing of the eyes, as in a wildlife documentary, when things did not go his way: a response so reliable that aides on Jerry Brown's 1992 campaign looked for situations in which it could be provoked. The famous tendency of the candidate to take a less than forthcoming approach to embarrassing questions had already been documented and discussed, most exhaustively in the matter of his 1969 draft status, and he remained the front-runner. The persistent but initially unpublished rumors about extramarital rovings had been, once Gennifer Flowers told her story to the *Star*, published and acknowledged, and he remained on his feet. "I have acknowledged wrongdoing," he had told America during his and his wife's rather premonitory *60 Minutes* appearances on Super Bowl Sunday of that year. "I have acknowledged causing pain in my marriage. I think most Americans who are watching this tonight, they'll know what we're saying, they'll get it, and they'll feel that we have been more than candid. And I think what the press has to decide is, are we going to engage in a game of gotcha?"

Nothing that is now known about the forty-second president of the United States, in other words, was not known before the New Hampshire primary in 1992. The implicit message in his August 1998 testimony to the Office of the Independent Counsel was not different in kind from that made explicit in January 1992: *I think most Americans who are watching this . . . they'll know what we're saying, they'll get it, and they'll feel that we have been more than candid*. By the time of the 1992 general election, the candidate was before us as he appears today: a more detailed and realized character than that presented in the Office of the Independent Counsel's oddly novelistic *Referral to the United States House of Representatives* but recognizably drawn to similar risk, voraciously needy, deeply fractured, and yet there, a force to contend with, a possessor of whatever manna accrues to those who have fought themselves and survived. The flaws already apparent in 1992 were by no means unreported, but neither, particularly in those parts of the country recently neutralized by their enshrinement as "the heartland," were they seized as occasions for rhetorical outrage. "With 16 million Americans unemployed, 40 million Americans without health care and 3 million Americans homeless, here's what we have to say about presidential aspirant Bill Clinton's alleged previous marital infidelity," the *Peoria Journal-Star* declared on its editorial page at the time of the *60 Minutes* appearance. "So what? And that's all."

There were those for whom the candidate's clear personal volatility suggested the possibility of a similar evanescence on matters of ideology or policy, but even the coastal opinion leaders seemed willing to grant him a *laissez-passer* on this question of sex: "To what degree, if any, is the private action relevant to the duties of the public office?" *The Los Angeles Times* asked on its editorial page in January 1992. "Shouldn't our right to know about a candidate's sex life be confined . . . to offenses such as rape, harassment, or sex discrimination?" *The New York Times* report on the *60 Minutes* interview, which appeared on page A14 and was headlined "Clinton Defends His Privacy and Says the Press Intruded," was followed the next day by an editorial ("Leers, Smears and Governor Clinton") not only commending the candidate for having drawn a line "between idle curiosity and responsible attention" but noting that "he won't provide details and he need not, unless it develops that his private conduct arguably touches his public performance or fitness for office." The same day, January 28, 1992, A. M. Rosenthal wrote in the *Times* that Governor and Mrs. Clinton had "presented to the American public a gift and a lasting opportunity":

> The gift is that they treated us as adults. The opportunity is for us to act that way. . . . We can at least treasure the hope that Americans would be fed up with the slavering inquisition on politicians' sexual history and say to hell with that and the torturers. That would be a thank-you card worthy of the gift from the Clinton couple—the presumption that Americans have achieved adulthood, at last.

Few in the mainstream press, in 1992, demanded a demonstration of "contrition" from the candidate. Few, in 1992, demanded "full remorse," a doubtful concept even in those venues, courtrooms in which criminal trials have reached the penalty phase, where "remorse" is most routinely invoked. Few, in 1992, spoke of the United States as so infantilized as to require a president above the possibility of personal reproach. That so few did this then, and so many have done this since, has been construed by some as evidence that the interests and priorities of the press have changed. In fact the interests and priorities of the press have remained reliably the same: then as now, the press could be relied upon to report a rumor or a hint down to the ground (tree it, bag it, defoliate the forest for it, destroy the village for it), but only insofar as that rumor or hint gave promise of advancing the story of the day, the shared narrative, the broad line of whatever story was at the given moment commanding the full resources of the reporters covering it and the columnists commenting on it and the on-tap experts analyzing it on the talk shows. (The 1998 *Yearbook of Experts, Authorities & Spokespersons* tellingly provides, for producers with underdeveloped Rolodexes of their own, 1,477 telephone numbers to call for those guests "who will drive the news issues in the next year.") In *Spin Cycle*, a book in which Howard Kurtz of *The Washington Post* endeavored to show the skill of the "Clinton propaganda machine" (similarly described by Joe Klein, despite what might seem impressive evidence to the contrary, as "the most sophisticated communications apparatus in the history of American politics") at setting the agenda for the press, there appears this apparently ingenuous description of how the press itself sets its agenda:

> A front-page exclusive would ripple through the rest of the press corps, dominate the briefing, and most likely end up on the network news. The newsmagazine reporters were not quite

> as influential as in years past, but they could still change the dialogue or cement the conventional wisdom with a cover story or a behind-the-scenes report. Two vital groups of reinforcements backed up the White House regulars. . . . One was the columnists and opinion-mongers—Jonathan Alter at *Newsweek*, Joe Klein at *The New Yorker*, William Safire and Maureen Dowd at *The New York Times*, E. J. Dionne and Richard Cohen at *The Washington Post*—who could quickly change the zeitgeist. . . . the other was the dogged band of investigative reporters—Jeff Gerth at the *Times*, Bob Woodward at the *Post*, Glenn Simpson at *The Wall Street Journal*, Alan Miller at *The Los Angeles Times*.

Once the "zeitgeist" has been agreed upon by this quite small group of people, any unrelated event, whatever its actual significance, becomes either non-news or, if sufficiently urgent, a news brief. An example of the relegation to non-news would be this: Robert Scheer, in his *Los Angeles Times* review of *Spin Cycle*, noted that its index included eighteen references to Paula Jones and sixteen to John Huang, but none to Saddam Hussein. An example of the relegation to news brief would be this: on August 16, 1998, after hearing flash updates on the Omagh bombing in Northern Ireland ("worst attack in almost thirty years of violence . . . latest figures as we have it are 28 people dead . . . 220 people injured . . . 103 still in hospital") and on the American embassy bombings in East Africa, Wolf Blitzer, on a two-hour *Late Edition with Wolf Blitzer* otherwise exclusively devoted to the "legal ramifications, political considerations, and historic consequences" of Monica Lewinsky, said this: "Catherine Bond, reporting live from Nairobi, thanks for joining us. Turning now to the story that has all of Washington holding its breath . . ."

In 1992, as in any election year, the story that had all of Washington holding its breath was the campaign, and since the guardians of the zeitgeist, taking their cue from the political professionals, had early on certified Governor Clinton as the most electable of the Democratic candidates, his personal failings could serve only as a step in his quest, a test of his ability to prevail. Before the New Hampshire primary campaign was even underway, Governor Clinton was reported to be the Democratic candidate with "centrist credentials," the

Democratic candidate who "offered an assessment of the state of the American economy that borrows as much from Republicans like Jack Kemp as it does from liberals," the Democratic candidate who could go to California and win support from "top Republican fundraisers," the candidate, in short, who "scored well with party officials and strategists." A survey of Democratic National Committee members had shown Clinton in the lead. The late Ronald H. Brown, at the time chairman of the Democratic Party, had been reported, still before a single vote was cast in New Hampshire, to have pressured Mario Cuomo to remove his name from the New York primary ballot, so that a divisive favorite-son candidacy would not impede the chosen front-runner.

By the morning of January 26, 1992, the Sunday of the *60 Minutes* appearance and shortly after the candidate sealed his centrist credentials by allowing the execution of the brain-damaged Rickey Ray Rector to proceed in Arkansas, William Schneider, in *The Los Angeles Times*, was awarding Governor Clinton the coveted "Big Mo," noting that "the Democratic Party establishment is falling in line behind Clinton." In a party that reserves a significant percentage of its convention votes (eighteen percent in 1996) for "superdelegates," the seven-hundred-some elected and party officials not bound by any popular vote, the message sent by this early understanding among the professionals was clear, as it had been when the professionals settled on Michael Dukakis in 1988: the train was now leaving the station, and, since the campaign, as "story," requires that the chosen candidates be seen as contenders who will go the distance, all inconvenient baggage, including "the character issue," would be left on the platform. What would go on the train was what Joe Klein, echoing the note of romantic credulity in his own 1992 coverage of the candidate Bill Clinton (that was before the zeitgeist moved on), recalled in 1998 in *The New Yorker* as the "precocious fizz" of the War Room, "the all-nighters . . . about policy or philosophy," the candidate who "loved to talk about serious things" and "seems to be up on every social program in America."

2.

It was January 16, 1998, when Kenneth W. Starr obtained authorization, by means of a court order opaquely titled "*In re* Madison Guaranty Savings & Loan Association," to extend his languishing Whitewater inquiry to the matter of Monica Lewinsky. It was also January 16 when Monica Lewinsky was detained for eleven hours and twenty-five minutes in Room 1016 of the Ritz-Carlton Hotel in Pentagon City, Virginia, where, according to the independent counsel's log of the "meeting," the FBI agent who undertook to read Miss Lewinsky "her rights as found on the form FD-395, Interrogation, Advice of Rights" was, for reasons the log does not explain, "unable to finish reading the FD-395." Miss Lewinsky herself testified:

> Then Jackie Bennett [of the Office of the Independent Counsel] came in and there was a whole bunch of other people and the room was crowded and he was saying to me, you know, you have to make a decision. I had wanted to call my mom, they weren't going to let me call my attorney, so I just—I just wanted to call my mom and they— Then Jackie Bennett said, "You're 24, you're smart, you're old enough, you don't need to call your mommy."

It was January 17 when President Clinton, in the course of giving his deposition in the civil suit brought against him by Paula Corbin Jones, either did or did not spring the perjury trap that Kenneth Starr either had or had not set. By the morning of January 21, when both Susan Schmidt in *The Washington Post* and ABC News correspondent Jackie Judd on *Good Morning America* jumped the stakes by quoting "sources" saying that Monica Lewinsky was on tape with statements that the president and Vernon Jordan had told her to lie, the "character issue" had gone from idle to full throttle, with Sam Donaldson and George Stephanopoulos and Jonathan Alter already on air talking about "impeachment proceedings."

In most discussions of how and why this matter came so incongruously to escalate, the press of course was criticized, and was in turn quick to criticize itself (or, in the phrasing preferred by many, since it suggested that any objection rested on hairsplitting, to "flagellate" itself), citing excessive and in some cases erroneous coverage. Perhaps because not all of the experts, authorities, and spokespersons driving this news had extensive experience with the kind of city-side beat on which it is taken for granted that the D.A.'s office will leak the cases they doubt they can make, selective prosecutorial hints had become embedded in the ongoing story as fact. "Loose attribution of sources abounded," Jules Witcover wrote in the March/April 1998 *Columbia Journalism Review*, although, since he tended to attribute the most egregious examples to "journalistic amateurs" and "journalistic pretenders" (Arianna Huffington and Matt Drudge), he could still express "hope," based on what he discerned two months into the story as "a tapering off of the mad frenzy of the first week or so," that, among "established, proven professional practitioners," any slip had been "a mere lapse of standards in the heat of a fast-breaking, incredibly competitive story of major significance."

For the same *CJR*, the cover line of which was "Where We Went Wrong . . . and What We Do Now," a number of other reporters, editors, and news executives were queried, and expressed similar hopes. The possibility of viewer confusion between entertainment and news shows was mentioned. The necessity for more careful differentiation among different kinds of leaks was mentioned. The "new technology" and "hyper-competition" and "the speed of news cycles these days" were mentioned, references to the way in which the Internet and the multiplication of cable channels had collapsed the traditional cyclical presentation of news into a twenty-four-hour stream of provisional raw takes. "We're in a new world in terms of the way information flows to the nation," James O'Shea, deputy managing editor for news of the *Chicago Tribune*, said. (The Lewinsky story had in fact first broken not in the traditional media but on the Internet, in a 1:11 A.M. January 18, 1998, posting on the *Drudge Report*.) "The days when you can decide not to print a story because it's not well enough sourced are long gone. When a story gets into the public realm, as it did with the *Drudge Report*, then you have to characterize it, you have to tell your readers, 'This is out there, you've probably been hearing about it on TV and the Internet. We have been unable to substantiate it independently.' And then give them enough information to judge the validity of it."

That the "story" itself might in this case be anything other than (in Witcover's words) "a fast-breaking, incredibly competitive story of major significance" was questioned by only one panelist, Anthony Lewis of *The New York Times*, who characterized "the obsession of the press with sex and public officials" as "crazy," but allowed that "after Linda Tripp went to the prosecutor, it became hard to say we shouldn't be covering this." The more general attitude seemed to be that there might have been an excess here or an error there, but the story itself was important by definition, significant because it was commanding the full resources of everyone on it—not unlike a campaign, which this story, in that it offered a particularly colorful version of the personalized "horse race" narrative that has become the model for most American political reporting, in fact resembled. "This is a very valid story of a strong-willed prosecutor and a president whose actions have been legitimately questioned," Walter Isaacson of *Time* said. "A case involving sex can be a very legitimate story, but we can't let our journalistic standards lapse simply because the sexual element makes everyone over-excited."

This, then, was a story "involving sex," a story in which there was a "sexual element," but, as we so frequently heard, it was not about sex, just as Whitewater, in the words of one of the several score editorials to this point published over the years by *The Wall Street Journal*, was "not merely about a land deal." What both stories were about, of course (although in the absence of both sex and evidence against the president one of them had proved a harder sell), was which of the contenders, the "strong-willed prosecutor" or his high-placed target, would go the distance, win the race. "The next forty-eight to seventy-two hours are critical," Tim Russert was saying on January 21, 1998, on MSNBC, where the daily recalibration of such sudden-death scenarios would by August raise the cable's Nielsen households from 49,000 a year before to 197,000. "I think his presidency is numbered in days," Sam Donaldson was saying by Sunday of the same week.

"On the high-status but low-interest White House beat, there is no story as exciting as that of the fall of a president," Jacob Weisberg observed in *Slate* in March. The president, everyone by then agreed, was "toast." The president "had to go," or "needed to go." The reasons the president needed to go had seemed, those last days in January and into February, crisp, easy to explain, grounded as they were in the galvanizing felony prospects set adrift without attribution by the Office of the Independent Counsel: obstruction of justice, subornation of perjury. Then, as questions threatened to slow the story (Would it not be unusual to prosecute someone for perjury in a civil suit? Did the chronology present a circumstantial case for, or actually against, obstruction? If someone lied in a deposition about a matter later ruled not essential to and so inadmissable in the case at hand, as Lewinsky had been ruled in *Jones v. Clinton*, was it in fact perjury?), the reasons the president "needed to go" became less crisp, more subjective, more a matter of "the mood here in the capital," and so, by definition, less open to argument from those not there in the capital.

This story was definitely moving, as they kept saying on MSNBC. By April 1, 1998, when U.S. District Court Judge Susan Webber Wright rendered the possibility of any felony technically remote by dismissing *Jones v. Clinton* altogether, the story had already rolled past its inconvenient legal (or "legalistic," a much-used word by then) limitations: ten weeks after America first heard the name Monica Lewinsky and still in the absence of any allegation bearing on the president's performance of his duties, the reasons the president needed to go were that he had been "weakened," that he would be "unable to function." The president's own former chief of staff, Leon Panetta, had expressed concern about "the slow drip-drip process and the price he's paying in terms of his ability to lead the country." When congressional staff members were asked in late March 1998 where they believed the situation was leading, twenty-one percent of Democratic staff members (forty-three percent of Republican) had foreseen, in the absence of resignation, impeachment proceedings.

The story was positioned, in short, for the satisfying long haul. By August 17, 1998, when the president confirmed the essential fact in the testimony Monica Lewinsky had given the grand jury eleven days before, virtually every "news analyst" on the eastern seaboard was on air (we saw the interiors of many attractive summer houses) talking about "the president's credibility," about "can he lead" or "still govern in any reasonably effective manner," questions most cogently raised that week by Garry Wills in *Time* and, to a different point, by Thomas L. Friedman in *The New York Times*. Proceeding from a belief both in President Clinton's underlying honor and in the redemptive power, if he was to be faced by crippling harassment, of the "principled resignation," Wills had tried to locate the homiletic possibilities in the dilemma, the opportunities for spiritual growth that could accrue to the country and to the president through resignation. The divergence between this argument and that made by Friedman was instructive. Friedman had seemed to be offering "can he lead" mainly as a strategy, an argument with which the professionals of the political process, who were increasingly bewildered by the public's apparent disinclination to join the rush to judgment by then general in the columns and talk shows, might most adroitly reeducate that "substantial majority" who "still feel that Mr. Clinton should remain in office."

In other words we had arrived at a dispiriting and familiar point, and would be fated to remain there even as telephone logs and Epass Access Control Reports and pages of grand-jury testimony floated down around us: "the disconnect," as it was now called, between what the professionals—those who held public office, those who worked for them, and those who wrote about them—believed to be self-evident and what a majority of Americans believed to be self-evident. John Kennedy and Warren Harding had both conducted affairs in the Oval Office (more recently known as "the workplace," or "under the same roof where his daughter lay sleeping"), and these affairs were by no means the largest part of what Americans thought about either of them. "If you step back a bit, it still doesn't look like a constitutional crisis," former federal prosecutor E. Lawrence Barcella told *The Los Angeles Times* to this point. "This is still a case about whether the President had sex with someone half his age. The American people have understood—certainly better than politicians, lawyers, and the press—that if this is ultimately about sex, it's really no one else's business. There are acceptable lies and unacceptable lies, and lying about someone's sex life is one of those tolerated lies."

Ten days after the president's August 17 admission to the nation, or ten days into the endless tape loop explicating the inadequacies of that admission, Mr. Clinton's own polls, according to *The Washington Post*, showed pretty much what everyone else's polls showed and would continue to show, notwithstanding the release first of Kenneth Starr's "narrative" and "grounds for impeachment" and then of Mr. Clinton's videotaped testimony and 3,183 pages of "supporting documents": that a majority of the public had believed all along that the president had some kind of involvement with Monica Lewinsky ("Cheat once, cheat twice, there's probably a whole line of them," a thirty-four-year-old woman told Democratic pollster Peter Hart in a focus session attended by *The Los Angeles Times*), continued to see it as a private rather than a political matter, believed Kenneth Starr to be the kind of sanctimonious hall monitor with sex on the brain they had avoided in their formative years (as in the jump-rope rhyme *Rooty-toot-toot! Rooty-toot-toot! / There go the boys from the Institute! / They don't smoke and they don't chew / And they don't go with the girls who do*), and, even as they acknowledged the gravity of lying under oath, did not wish to see the president removed from office.

The charge that he tried to conceal a personally embarrassing but not illegal liaison had not, it seemed, impressed most Americans as serious. Whether or not he had ever asked Vernon Jordan to call Ron Perelman and whether Vernon Jordan had in fact done so before or after the subpoena was issued to Monica Lewinsky had not, it seemed, much mattered to these citizens. Outside the capital, there had seemed to be a general recognition that the entire "crisis," although mildly entertaining, represented politics as usual, particularly since it had evolved from a case, the 1994 *Jones v. Clinton*, that would probably never have been brought and certainly never been funded had Mr. Clinton not been elected president. For Thomas L. Friedman, then, the way around this was to produce more desirable polling results by refocusing the question, steering the issue safely past the shoals of "should he be president," which was the essence of what the research was asking. "What might influence the public most," Friedman wrote, "is the question of 'can' Mr. Clinton still govern in any reasonably effective manner."

Since taking this argument to its logical conclusion raised, for a public demonstrably impatient with what it had come to see as a self-interested political class, certain other questions (If the president couldn't govern, who wouldn't let him? Was it likely that they would have let a lame duck govern anyway? What in fact was "governing," and did we want it?), most professionals fell back to a less vulnerable version of what the story was: a story so simple, so sentimental, as to brook no argument, no talking back from "the American people," who were increasingly seen as recalcitrant children, fecklessly resistant to responsible guidance. The story, William J. Bennett told us on *Meet the Press*, was about the "moral and intellectual disarmament" that befalls a nation when its president is not "being a decent example" and "teaching the kids the difference between right and wrong." The story, Cokie Roberts told us in the *New York Daily News*, was about reinforcing the lesson "that people who act immorally and lie get punished." The story, William Kristol told us on *This Week*, was about the president's "defiance," his "contempt," his "refusal to acknowledge some standards of public morality."

Certain pieties were repeated to the point where they could be referred to in shorthand. Although most Americans had an instinctive sense that Monica Lewinsky could well have been, as the *Referral* would later reveal her to have been, a less than entirely passive participant in whatever happened, we heard about the situational inviolability of interns (interns were "given into our care," interns were "lent to us by their parents") until Cokie Roberts's censorious cry to an insufficiently outraged congresswoman ("But with an *intern*?") could stand alone, a verdict that required no judge or jury. We heard repeatedly about "our children," or "our kids," who were, as presented, avid consumers of the *Nightly News* in whose presence sex had never before been mentioned and discussions of the presidency were routine. "I'd like to be able to tell my children, 'You should tell the truth,'" Stuart Taylor of the *National Journal* told us on *Meet the Press*. "I'd like to be able to tell them, 'You should respect the president.' And I'd like to be able to tell them both things at the same time." Jonathan Alter, in *Newsweek*, spoke of the president as someone "who has made it virtually impossible to talk to your kids about the American presidency or let them watch the news."

"I approach this as a mother," Cokie Roberts said on *This Week*. "We have a right to say to this president, 'What you have done is an example to our children that's a disgrace,'" William J. Bennett said on *Meet the Press*. The apparent inability of the public to grasp this *Kinder-Kirche* point (perhaps because not all Americans could afford the luxury of idealizing their own children) had itself become an occasion for outrage and scorn: the public was too "complacent," or too "prosperous," or too "fixed on the Dow Jones." The public in fact became the unindicted coconspirator: "This ought to be something that outrages us, makes us ashamed of him," Mona Charen complained on *Late Edition with Wolf Blitzer*. "This casts shame on the entire country because he behaved that way and all of the nation seems to be complicit now because they aren't rising up in righteous indignation."

This was the impasse (or, as it turned out, the box canyon) that led many into a scenario destined to prove wishful at best: "The American people," we heard repeatedly, would cast off their complicity when they were actually forced by the report of the independent counsel to turn their attention from the Dow and face what Thomas L. Friedman, in the *Times*, called "the sordid details that will come out from Ken Starr's investigation." "People are not as sophisticated as this appears to be," William Kristol had said hopefully the day before the president's televised address. "We all know, inside the Beltway, what's in that report," Republican strategist Mary Matalin said. "And I don't think . . . the country needs to hear any more about tissue, dresses, cigars, ties, anything else." George Will, on *This Week*, assured his co-panelists that support for the president would evaporate in the face of the *Referral*. "Because Ken Starr must—the president has forced his hand—must detail graphically the sexual activity that demonstrates his perjury. Once that report is written and published, Congress will be dragged along in the wake of the public. . . . Once the dress comes in, and some of the details come in from the Ken Starr report, people—there's going to be a critical mass, the yuck factor—where people say, 'I don't want him in my living room any more.'"

The person most people seemed not to want in their living rooms any more was "Ken" (as he was now called by those with an interest in protecting his story), but this itself was construed as evidence of satanic spin on the part of the White House. "The president's men," William J. Bennett cautioned in *The Death of Outrage: Bill Clinton and the Assault on American Ideals*, ". . . attempt relentlessly to portray their opposition as bigoted and intolerant fanatics who have no respect for privacy." He continued:

> At the same time they offer a temptation to their supporters: the temptation to see themselves as realists, worldly-wise, sophisticated: in a word, European. This temptation should be resisted by the rest of us. In America, morality is central to our politics and attitudes in a way that is not the case in Europe, and precisely this moral streak is what is best about us. . . . Europeans may have something to teach us about, say, wine or haute couture. But on the matter of morality in politics, America has much to teach Europe.

American innocence itself, then, was now seen to hang on the revealed word of the *Referral.* The report, Fox News promised, would detail "activities that most Americans would describe as unusual." These details, *Newsweek* promised, would make Americans "want to throw up." "Specifics about a half-dozen sex acts," *Newsday* promised, had been provided "during an unusual two-hour session August 26 in which Lewinsky gave sworn testimony in Starr's downtown office, not before the grand jury."

This is arresting, and not to be brushed over. On August 6, Monica Lewinsky had told the grand jury that sexual acts had occurred. On August 17, the president had tacitly confirmed this in both his testimony to the grand jury and his televised address to the nation. Given this sequence, the "unusual two-hour session August 26" might have seemed, to some, unnecessary, even excessive, not least because of the way in which, despite the full knowledge of the prosecutors that the details elicited in this session would be disseminated to the world in two weeks under the *Referral* headings "November 15 Sexual Encounter," "November 17 Sexual Encounter," "December 31 Sexual Encounter," "January 7 Sexual Encounter," "January 21 Sexual Encounter," "February 4 Sexual Encounter and Subsequent Phone Calls," "March 31 Sexual Encounter," "Easter Telephone Conversations and Sexual Encounter," "February 28 Sexual Encounter," and "March 29 Sexual Encounter," certain peculiar and warped proprieties had been so pruriently observed. "In deference to Lewinsky and the explicit nature of her testimony," *Newsday* reported, "all the prosecutors, defense lawyers and stenographers in the room during the session were women."

Since the "explicit nature of the testimony," the "unusual activity," the "throw-up details" everyone seemed to know about (presumably because they had been leaked by the Office of the Independent Counsel) turned out to involve masturbation, it was hard not to wonder if those in the know might not be experiencing some sort of rhetorical autointoxication, a kind of rapture of the feed. The average age of first sexual intercourse in this country has been for some years sixteen, and is younger in many venues. Since the average age of first marriage in this country is twenty-five for women and twenty-seven for men, sexual activity outside marriage occurs among Americans for an average of nine to eleven years. Six out of ten marriages in this country are likely to end in divorce, a significant percentage of those who divorce doing so after engaging in extramarital sexual activity. As of the date of the 1990 census, there were in this country 4.1 million households headed by unmarried couples. More than thirty-five percent of these households included children. Seventh-graders in some schools in this country were as early as the late 1970s reading the Boston Women's Health Book Collective's *Our Bodies, Ourselves*, which explained the role of masturbation in sexuality and the use of foreign objects in masturbation. The notion that Americans apparently willing to overlook a dalliance in the Oval Office would go pale at its rather commonplace details seemed puzzling in the extreme, as did the professed inability to understand why these Americans might favor the person who had engaged in a common sexual act over the person who had elicited the details of that act as evidence for a public stoning.

But of course these members of what Howard Fineman recently defined on MSNBC as "the national political class," the people "who read the *Hotline* or watch cable television political shows such as this one," were not talking about Americans at large. They did not know Americans at large. They occasionally heard from one, in a focus group or during the Q&A after a lecture date, but their attention, since it was focused on the political process, which had come to represent the concerns not of the country at large but of the organized pressure groups that increasingly controlled it, remained remote. When Howard Fineman, during the same MSNBC appearance, spoke of "the full-scale panic" that he detected "both here in Washington and out around the country," he was referring to calls he had made to "a lot of Democratic consultants, pollsters, media people and so forth," as well as to candidates: "For example one in Wisconsin, a woman running for the Democratic seat up there, she said she's beginning to get calls and questions from average folks wanting to know what her view of Bill Clinton is."

"Average folks," however, do not call their elected representatives, nor do they attend the events where the funds get raised and the questions asked. The citizens who do are the citizens with access, the citizens with an investment, the citizens who have a special interest. When Representative Tom Coburn (R-Okla.) reported to *The Washington Post* that during three days in September 1998 he received five hundred phone calls and 850 e-mails on the question of impeachment, he would appear to have been reporting, for the most part, less on "average folks" than on constituents who already knew, or had been provided, his telephone number or e-mail address; reporting, in other words, on an organized blitz campaign. When Gary Bauer of the Family Research Council seized the moment by test-running a drive for the presidency with a series of Iowa television spots demanding Mr. Clinton's resignation, he would appear to have been interested less in reaching out to "average folks" than in galvanizing certain caucus voters, the very caucus voters who might be expected to have already called or e-mailed Washington on the question of impeachment.

When these people on the political talk shows spoke about the inability of Americans to stomach "the details," then, they were speaking, in code, about a certain kind of American, a minority of the population but the minority to whom recent campaigns have been increasingly pitched. They were talking politics. They were talking about the "values" voter, the "pro-family" voter, and so complete by now was their isolation from the country in which they lived that they seemed willing to reserve its franchise for, in other words give it over to, that key core vote.

3.

The cost of producing a television show on which Wolf Blitzer or John Gibson referees an argument between an unpaid "former federal prosecutor" and an unpaid "legal scholar" is significantly lower than that of producing conventional programming. This is, as they say, the "end of the day," or the bottom-line fact. The explosion of "news comment" programming occasioned by this fact requires, if viewers are to be kept from tuning out, nonstop breaking stories on which the stakes can be raised hourly. The Gulf War made CNN, but it was the trial of O. J. Simpson that taught the entire broadcast industry how to perfect the pushing of the stakes. The crisis that led to the Clinton impeachment began as and remained a situation in which a handful of people, each of whom believed that he or she had something to gain (a book contract, a scoop, a sinecure as a network "analyst," contested ground in the culture wars, or, in the case of Starr, the justification of his failure to get either of the Clintons on Whitewater), managed to harness this phenomenon and ride it. This was not an unpredictable occurrence, nor was it unpredictable that the rather impoverished but generally unremarkable transgressions in question would come in this instance to be inflated by the rhetoric of moral rearmament.

"You cannot defile the temple of justice," Kenneth Starr told reporters during his many front-lawn and driveway appearances. "There's no room for white lies. There's no room for shading. There's only room for truth. . . . Our job is to determine whether crimes were committed." This was the authentic if lonely voice of the last American wilderness, the voice of the son of a Texas preacher in a fundamentalist denomination (the Churches of Christ) so focused on the punitive that it forbade even the use of instrumental music in church. This was the voice of a man who himself knew a good deal about risk-taking, an Ahab who had been mortified by his great Whitewater whale and so in his pursuit of what Melville called "the highest truth" would submit to the House, despite repeated warnings from his own supporters (most visibly on the editorial page of *The Wall Street Journal*) not to do so, a report in which his attempt to take down the government was based in its entirety on ten occasions of backseat intimacy as detailed by an eager but unstable participant who appeared to have memorialized the events on her hard drive.

This was a curious document. It was reported by *The New York Times*, on the day after its initial and partial release, to have been written in part by Stephen Bates, identified as a "part-time employee of the independent counsel's office and the part-time literary editor of *The Wilson Quarterly*," an apparent polymath who after his 1987 graduation from Harvard Law School "wrote for publications as diverse as *The Nation*, *The Weekly Standard*, *Playboy*, and *The New Republic*." According to the *Times*, Mr. Bates and Mr. Starr had together written a proposal for a book about a high school student in Omaha barred by her school from forming a Bible study group. The proposed book, which did not find a publisher, was to be titled *Bridget's Story*. This is interesting, since the "narrative" section of the *Referral*, including as it does a wealth of nonrelevant or "story" details (for example the threatening letter from Miss Lewinsky to the president which the president said he had not read, although "Ms. Lewinsky suspected that he had actually read the whole thing"), seems very much framed as "Monica's Story." We repeatedly share her "feelings," just as we might have shared Bridget's: "I left that day sort of emotionally stunned," Miss Lewinsky is said to have testified at one point, for "I just knew he was in love with me."

Consider this. The day in question, July 4, 1997, was six

weeks after the most recent of the president's attempts to break off their relationship. The previous day, after weeks of barraging members of the White House staff with messages and calls detailing her frustration at being unable to reach the president, her conviction that he owed her a job, and her dramatically good intentions ("I know that in your eyes I am just a hindrance—a woman who doesn't have a certain someone's best interests at heart, but please trust me when I say I do"), Miss Lewinsky had dispatched a letter that "obliquely," as the narrative has it, "threatened to disclose their relationship." On this day, July 4, the president has at last agreed to see her. He accuses her of threatening him. She accuses him of failing to secure for her an appropriate job, which in fact she would define in a later communiqué as including "anything at *George* magazine." "The most important things to me," she would then specify, "are that I am engaged and interested in my work, I am *not* someone's administrative/executive assistant, and my salary can provide me a comfortable living in NY."

At this point she cried. He "praised her intellect and beauty," according to the narrative. He said, according to Miss Lewinsky, "he wished he had more time for me." She left the Oval Office, "emotionally stunned," convinced "he was in love with me." The "narrative," in other words, offers what is known among students of fiction as an unreliable first-person narrator, a classic literary device whereby the reader is made to realize that the situation, and indeed the narrator, are other than what the narrator says they are. It cannot have been the intention of the authors to present their witness as the victimizer and the president her hapless victim, and yet there it was, for all the world to read. That the authors of the *Referral* should have fallen into this basic craft error suggests the extent to which, by the time the *Referral* was submitted, the righteous voice of the grand inquisitor had isolated itself from the more wary voices of his cannier allies.

That the voice of the inquisitor was not one to which large numbers of Americans would respond had always been, for these allies, beside the point: what it offered, and what less authentic voices obligingly amplified, was a platform for the reintroduction of fundamentalism, or "values issues," into the general discourse. "Most politicians miss the heart and soul of this concern," Ralph Reed wrote in 1996, having previously defined "the culture, the family, a loss of values, a decline in civility, and the destruction of our children" as the chief concerns of the Christian Coalition, which in 1996 claimed to have between a quarter and a third of its membership among registered Democrats. Despite two decades during which the promotion of the "values" agenda had been the common cause of both the "religious" (or Christian) and the neoconservative right, too many politicians, Reed believed, still "debate issues like accountants." John Podhoretz, calling on Republicans in 1996 to resist the efforts of Robert Dole and Newt Gingrich to "de-ideologize" the Republican Party, had echoed, somewhat less forthrightly, Reed's complaint about the stress on economic issues. "They do not answer questions about the spiritual health of the nation," he wrote. "They do not address the ominous sense we all have that Americans are, with every intake of breath, unconsciously inhaling a philosophy that stresses individual pleasure over individual responsibility; that our capacity to be our best selves is weakening."

That "all" of us did not actually share this "ominous sense" was, again, beside the point, since neither Reed nor Podhoretz was talking about all of us. Less than fifty percent of the voting-age population in this country actually voted (for anyone) for president in 1996. The figures in the previous five presidential-year elections ranged from fifty to fifty-five percent. Only between thirty-three and thirty-eight percent voted in any midterm election since 1974. The figures for those who vote in primary elections, where the terms on which the campaign will be waged are determined, drop even further, in some cases into the single digits. Ralph Reed and John Podhoretz had been talking in 1996, as William Kristol and Mary Matalin would be talking in 1998, about that small group of citizens for whom "the spiritual health of the nation" would serve as the stalking horse for a variety of "social," or control-and-respect, issues. They were talking, in other words, about that narrow subsection of the electorate known in American politics as most-likely-to-vote.

What the Christian Coalition and *The Weekly Standard* were asking the Republican Party and (by logical extension) its opponents to do in 1996 was to further narrow most-likely-to-vote, by removing from debate those issues that concerned the country at large. This might have seemed, at the time, a ticket only to marginalization. It might have seemed, as recently as 1996, a rather vain hope that the nation's opinion leaders would soon reach general agreement that the rearming of the citizenry's moral life required that three centuries of legal precedent and even constitutional protections be overridden in the higher interest of demonstrating the presence of moral error, or "determining whether a crime has been committed," as Kenneth Starr put it in the brief he submitted to the Supreme Court in the matter of whether Vincent Foster's lawyer could be compelled to turn over notes on conversations he had with Foster before his death. Yet by August 1998, here were two of those opinion leaders, George Will and Cokie Roberts, stiffening the spines of those members of Congress who might be tempted to share the inclination of their constituents to distinguish between mortal and venial sins:

> *G.W.*: Cokie, the metastasizing corruption spread by this man [the president] is apparent now. And the corruption of the very idea of what it means to be a representative. We hear people in Congress saying, "Our job is solely to read the public opinion polls and conform thereto. Well, if so, that's not intellectually complicated, it's not morally demanding. But it makes a farce of being a . . .
>
> *C.R.*: No, at that point, we should just go for direct democracy.
>
> *G.W.*: Exactly. Get them out of here and let's plug computers in. . . .
>
> *C.R.*: . . . I must say I think that letting the [impeachment] process work makes a lot of sense because it brings—then people can lead public opinion rather than just follow it through the process.
>
> *G.W.*: What a concept.
>
> *C.R.*: But we will see.

To talk about the failure of Congress to sufficiently isolate itself from the opinion of the electorate as a "corruption of the very idea of what it means to be a representative" is to talk (another kind of "end of the day," or bottom-line fact) about disenfranchising America. "The public was fine, the elites were not," an unnamed White House adviser had told *The Washington Post* about the difference of opinion, on the matter of the president's "apology" or "nonapology," between the political professionals and what had until recently been deferred to, if only pro forma, as the electorate. "You've got to let the elites win one."

No one should have doubted that the elites would in fact win this one, since, even before the somewhat dampening polling on the Starr report and on the president's videotaped testimony, the enterprise had achieved the perfect circularity toward which it had long been tending. "I want to find out who else in the political class thinks the way Mr. Clinton does about what is acceptable behavior," George Will had said in August, explaining why he favored impeachment proceedings over a resignation. "Let's smoke them out." That a majority of Americans seemed capable of separating Mr. Clinton's behavior in this matter from his performance as president had become, by that point, irrelevant, as had the ultimate outcome of the congressional deliberation. What was going to happen had already happened: since future elections could now be focused on the entirely spurious issue of correct sexual, or "moral," behavior, those elections would be increasingly decided by that committed and well-organized minority brought most reliably to the polls by "pro-family," or "values," issues. The fact that an election between two candidates arguing which has the more correct "values" left most voters with no reason to come to the polls had even come to be spoken about, by less wary professionals, as the beauty part, the bonus that would render the process finally and perpetually impenetrable. "Who cares what every adult thinks?" a Republican strategist asked *The Washington Post* to this point in early September 1998. "It's totally not germane to this election."

Vichy Washington

June 24, 1999

On an evening late in April 1999, some 350 survivors of what they saw as a fight for the soul of the republic gathered at the Mayflower Hotel in Washington to honor Representative Henry J. Hyde and the twelve House managers who, under his leadership, had carried the charges of impeachment to the floor of the Senate. C-SPAN caught the distinctive, familial fervor of the event, which was organized to benefit the Independent Women's Forum, an organization funded in part by Richard Mellon Scaife and the "women's group" in the name of which Kenneth Starr volunteered in 1994 to file an amicus curiae brief arguing that *Jones v. Clinton* should go forward. Live from the Mayflower, there on-screen were the familiar faces from the year-long entertainment that had preceded the impeachment, working the room amid the sedate din and the tinkling of glasses. There were the pretty women in country-club dinner dresses, laughing appreciatively at the bon mots of their table partners. There was the black-tie quartet, harmonizing on "Vive la, vive la, vive l'amour" and "Goodbye My Coney Island Baby" as Henry Hyde doggedly continued to spoon up his dessert, chocolate meeting mouth with metronomic regularity, his perseverance undeflected even by Bob Barr, leaning in to make a point.

The word "courage" was repeatedly invoked. Midge Decter, a director of the Independent Women's Forum, praised Henry Hyde's "manliness," and the way in which watching "him and his merry hand" on television during the impeachment trial had caused her to recall "whole chunks" of Rudyard Kipling's "If." Robert L. Bartley, the editor of *The Wall Street Journal*, had found similar inspiration in the way in which the managers had "exposed truths to the American people, and they did this in the face of all the polls and focus groups, and they were obviously doing an unpopular thing, and I think that is why they deserve our greatest credit." The words of Henry V before the Battle of Agincourt were recalled by Michael Novak, as they had been by Henry Hyde in his closing statement during the Senate impeachment trial, but for this occasion adapted to "our Prince Hal, our own King Henry": "He that outlives this day, and comes safe home, will stand at tiptoe when this day is named. . . . Then shall our names, familiar in his mouth as household words, Henry the King, Rogan and Hutchinson, Canady, Cannon, McCollum, Lindsey Graham, Gekas, Chabot, Bryant, Buyer, Barr, and Sensenbrenner."

This evening could have seemed, for those who still misunderstood the Reagan mandate to have been based on what are now called "social" issues, the last redoubt. Familiar themes were sounded, favorite notes struck. Even the most glancing reference to the depredations of "the Sixties" (". . . according to Sean Wilentz, a scholar who exemplifies all the intellectual virtues and glories of the Sixties . . .") proved a reliable crowd-pleaser. In deference to the man who had not only sponsored the Hyde Amendment (banning Medicaid payments for abortions) but who had a year before testified as a character witness for a defendant accused of illegally blockading abortion clinics ("He's a hero to me," Hyde had said. "He has the guts I wish more of us had"), the "unborn" were characterized as "the stranger, the other, the unwanted, the inconvenient."

Mentions of "Maxine Waters" were cues for derision. "Barney Frank" was a laugh line that required no explication. The loneliness of the shared position was assumed, and proudly stressed. Yet the mood of the evening was less elegiac than triumphal, less rueful than rededicated, as if there in a ballroom at the Mayflower was the means by which the American political dialogue could be finally reconfigured: on the sacrificial altar of the failed impeachment, in the memory of the martyred managers, the message of moral rearmament that has driven the conservative movement to what had seemed no avail might at last have met its moment. "As we were coming in," William J. Bennett told the guests that night, "I said to my friend Dan Oliver, I said 'Good group.' Dan said, 'Good group? This is it, pal. This is the army. This is all of it.'"

The notion that a failed attempt to impeach the president might nonetheless have accomplished exactly what it was meant to accomplish, that the desired phoenix might even then be rising from the ashes of acquittal, might have seemed to many, in the immediate wake of the November 1998 elections, when the disinclination of the American people to see the president impeached translated into the loss of five Republican congressional seats, wishful. "It's pretty clear that impeachment dropped off the public's radar screen," Henry Hyde said to a *Los Angeles Times* reporter as he realized on election night that he was losing not only his anticipated mandate but five of his votes. The next morning, in the O'Hare Hilton, he told three aides that his Judiciary Committee inquiry, which party leaders had inexplicably construed as so in tune with public sentiment as to promise a gain of twenty seats, would have to be telescoped, and impeachment delivered out of the House while his lame ducks could still vote.

Over the next several weeks, as they contemplated the unexpected hit they had taken by feeding the greed of their conservative base for impeachment, Republicans would float many fanciful scenarios by which the party could be extricated from its own device. Senator Arlen Specter of Pennsylvania argued on the op-ed page of *The New York Times* for "abandoning impeachment," in effect handing off this suddenly sticky wicket to the courts, where, since not many lawyers saw a makeable case for perjury, it could conveniently dematerialize. Robert Dole laid out a plan based on the distinctly improbable agreement of the president in his own censure. Even Henry Hyde saw a way for the president to save the day, by resigning: "I think he could be really heroic if he did that. He would be the savior of his party. . . . It would be a way of going out with honor." By mid-December 1998, former Senator Alan K. Simpson was expressing what had become by default the last-ditch position of most Republicans, which was that any hemorrhaging they were suffering outside their conservative base could be contained before 2000 by the putative inability of these less ideological voters to remember that long. "The attention span of Americans," Simpson said, "is 'which movie is coming out next month?' and whether the quarterly report on their stock will change."

This casual contempt for the electorate at large was by then sufficiently general to pass largely unremarked upon. A good deal of what seemed at the time opaque in the firestorm that consumed the attention of the United States from January 1998 until the spring of 1999 has since been illuminated, but what remains novel, and unexplained, was the increasingly histrionic insistence of the political establishment that it stood apart from, and indeed above, the country that had until recently been considered its validation. Under the lights at CNN and MSNBC and the Sunday shows, it became routine to declare oneself remote from "them," or "out there." The rhetorical expression of outrage, or "speaking out," became in itself a moral position, even when the reasons for having spoken out could not be recalled. ". . . Whether or not it happens," Robert H. Bork said to *The Washington Post* in December 1998 about impeachment, which he favored, "I will still think I was right. . . . I just spoke out. I think on a television show, maybe Larry King. I wish I could recall what I was concerned with, but I can't at the moment."

The electorate, as anyone who had turned on a television set since the spring of 1998 had heard repeatedly, was "complicit" in the "corruption" of the president, or of the administration, or of the country itself, which was therefore in need of the "purging" to be effected, as in myth, by the removal of the most visible figure on the landscape. "It would be an enormous emetic—culturally, politically, morally—for us to have an impeachment," the Reverend John Neuhaus, editor of the conservative monthly *First Things*, told Michael Powell of *The Washington Post*. "It would purge us." The reason the public was "complicit," and the country in need of "purging," was that the public was "materialistic," interested only in "the Dow," or, later, "their pension funds." The reason the public was "materialistic" was that the public had, well, no morals. "My wife likes to say they must be polling people coming out of Hooters on Saturday night," Senator Robert C. Smith of New Hampshire said at the time he was announcing his bid for the presidency. "I will not defend the public," William J. Bennett told *The New York Times* in February 1999, after Paul M. Weyrich had written to supporters of his Free Congress Foundation that since the nation was in the grip of an "alien ideology" they should abandon the idea that a moral majority existed and take steps to "quarantine" their families. "Absolutely not. If people want to pander to the public and say they're right they can. But they're not right on this one."

"What's popular isn't always what's right," Representative J. C. Watts of Oklahoma said, arguing in the House for impeachment. "Polls would have rejected the Ten Commandments. Polls would have embraced slavery and ridiculed women's rights." On the weekend in January 1999 when the "favorable" rating of the Republican Party dropped to thirty-six percent, the lowest point since Watergate, Senator Phil Gramm said on *Meet the Press* that the people of Texas "didn't elect me to read those polls." Not even when the bumper stickers of the John Birch Society were common road sightings had we been so insistently reminded that this was not a democracy but a republic, or a "representative form of government." For the more inductive strategists in the movement, the next logical step was obvious: since a republic depended by definition on an electorate, and since the electorate at hand had proved itself "complicit," the republic itself could be increasingly viewed as doubtful, open for rethinking. "The Clinton affair and its aftermath will, I think, turn out to be a defining moment that exposed the rot in the institutions of American republican government," Charles Murray wrote in *The Weekly Standard* in February 1999. "Whether the response will be to shore up the structure or abandon it remains an open question."

2.

On the morning of February 11, 1994, Michael Isikoff, at that time a reporter for *The Washington Post* and later the author of *Uncovering Clinton: A Reporter's Story*, received, from the conservative strategist Craig Shirley, a heads-up on what would be said that afternoon at the Conservative Political Action Conference at the Hotel Omni Shoreham, where a woman brought to Washington by Cliff Jackson, the Hot Springs lawyer who orchestrated Troopergate, was scheduled to give a press conference. Isikoff went over to the Shoreham, witnessed what would turn out to be the debut performance of Paula Jones, and the next morning conducted a three-hour interview with her, in a suite at the Shoreham where she was flanked by her husband and her then lawyer, Danny Traylor. Isikoff asked Paula Jones about her eighteen-month-old son, Madison, and told her about his own baby daughter. He asked her whether her parents had been Democrats or Republicans, a point about which she was uncertain. "I guess any man probably would be more [interested in politics] than a woman," she said. "That's just not my interest in life." Isikoff tells us that he questioned Traylor and Jackson independently about their initial involvement, and reports that the answers they gave "point toward an innocent explanation." If Isikoff did indeed choose to ask Paula Jones herself why, given her lack of interest in politics, her lawyer had hooked her up with Cliff Jackson and Craig Shirley and the Conservative Political Action Conference, he chose not to record her answer, although he renders certain details from that initial interview with some avidity:

> *Paula Jones*: "He had boxer shorts and everything and he exposed hisself [*sic*] with an erection . . . holding it . . . fiddling it or whatever. And he asked me to—I don't know his exact word—give him a blow job or—I know you gotta know his exact words."
>
> *Isikoff*: "Exact words."
>
> *Paula Jones*: "He asked me to do something. I know that. I'll tell you, I was so shocked. I think he wanted me to kiss it. . . . And he was saying it in a very disgusting way, just a horny-ass way . . ."
>
> *Isikoff*: "What do you mean in a very disgusting way?"
>
> *Paula Jones*: "Disgusting way, he just, it was *please, I want it so bad*—just that type of way, like he was wanting it bad, you know."

Over the next several years, first on the Paula Jones story for the *Post* and then on the Paula Jones and the Kathleen Willey and the Monica Lewinsky stories for *Newsweek*, Isikoff would encounter a number of such choices, moments in which a less single-minded reporter might well have let attention stray to the distinctly peculiar way the story was unfolding itself, the way in which corroborating witnesses and incriminating interviews would magically materialize, but Isikoff kept his eye on the ball, his story, which was, exactly, "uncovering" Clinton. There was for example the moment when Joe Cammarata, one of the lawyers chosen by those working behind the scenes on the Jones case to replace Danny Traylor, had accommodated Isikoff's need to find "evidence that Clinton did this to other women" by recalling a "mysterious phone call" he had received from a woman who would not give her name but said that "a similar thing" had happened to her when she was working in the White House. "This was weird, I thought," Isikoff recalls. "The caller had imparted a hell of a lot of detail. Cammarata, for his part, was more than happy to let me figure it out. If I could track this woman down, he reasoned, I'd probably pass it along to him. Then he could subpoena her. As he saw it, I would save him some legwork."

Examine this. Isikoff thought the call was "weird," but any suspicions this aroused seem not to have suggested to him that the Jones defense team, or someone working through the Jones defense team, might be planting a story. As might have been predicted, this tip led Isikoff to Kathleen Willey, at which point we enter another reportorial twilight zone. "A journalistic dance between aggressive reporter and reluctant source began," Isikoff writes, "a dance that was to continue for months." In the average reporting experience, reluctant sources hang up, or say no comment, then screen their calls, leave town. This "reluctant source," however, having extracted the promise that Isikoff would not publish her story "until she gave the green light," allowed herself to be interviewed for more than two hours, telling her story "in gripping and microscopic detail."

Asked by the "aggressive reporter" if anyone could corroborate her story, another point at which, if she did not want the story out, she could have recouped her losses by saying no, Kathleen Willey obligingly named two women. One of the women she named was Julie Hiatt Steele, to whom, on the spot, she placed a call, arranging a meeting later that day between Steele and Isikoff. The second woman was Linda Tripp, then at the Pentagon. Dutifully, a relentless op on the case,

Isikoff followed up his conveniently arranged meeting with Julie Hiatt Steele by tagging along with a *Newsweek* reporter who had access to the Pentagon. There, in a cubicle in the basement, Isikoff confronted Linda Tripp, who, within minutes, although "alarmed" by his visit, delivered the story's next reveal: "'There's something here, but the story's not what you think it is,' she said cryptically. 'You're barking up the wrong tree.'"

Note "cryptically." That was in March 1997. By April, Linda Tripp had delivered considerably more ("twenty-three-year-old former White House intern," got her job through "a wealthy campaign contributor," a "big insurance executive," "thrown out of the White House," "had gotten her a job at another federal agency," "hideaway off the Oval Office," "oral sex"), and had even let Isikoff listen in on a phone call from the former intern, "an excited and somewhat whiny young woman complaining about another woman named 'Marsha.'" Marsha, Linda Tripp explained, was Marsha Scott, the president's personnel aide. Marsha was supposed to have brought the young woman back to the White House after the 1996 election. Marsha had not. Marsha was giving the young woman the runaround.

No matter how many clues the remarkably patient Tripp provided, the story remained, Isikoff tells us, presenting himself as an impartial fact-gatherer to whom speculative connections were anathema, in the cryptic range. "I'm a reporter, not a voyeur," he tells us, appropriating the high-road benefit, and, also, "Tripp wouldn't give me the ex-intern's name or the agency she worked for." And there was something else: "Tripp was certain the relationship was entirely consensual. . . . That, it seemed to me, placed it outside the scope of the Paula Jones lawsuit—my main justification for proceeding down this path."

But wait, he surely said to himself at this point, or perhaps not. You got to Tripp via Willey. You got to Willey via the Jones defense team. Who gains here? Who wants what out? Why? Four months later, Isikoff was still refusing to acknowledge the possibility of connections. In August 1997, in a CNBC green room, he happened to be discussing legal strategy on the Jones case with Ann Coulter, one of the "movement," or conservative, lawyers who had become a fixture on the news-comment shows. According to Isikoff, he remarked to Coulter that she seemed to have inside knowledge of *Jones v. Clinton*, and she laughed. "Oh, yes," he reports her responding. "There are lots of us busy elves working away in Santa's workshop." "Busy elves?" Isikoff recalls having thought, and then: "I remembered something about George Conway in New York. Now Coulter. Who else? And what were they doing?"

Some might have seen this as a line of inquiry worth pursuing, but Isikoff, after a call to Conway's office at Wachtell, Lipton, Rosen & Katz in New York ("Conway and Coulter were fast friends" who "bonded over their common disdain for Clinton, and they loved nothing more than to gossip into the night about the latest developments in the Jones lawsuit"), seems to have satisfied himself that Conway and the other ardently conservative lawyers with whom Conway was in touch might be useful sources, but not themselves the story. Not until October 1997, when Linda Tripp summoned him to a meeting with Lucianne Goldberg and provided him with a beer, a bowl of pistachio nuts, and the name Monica Lewinsky, did his reporter's instincts briefly revive: "I stopped eating the nuts and started taking notes." There were, Linda Tripp said, tapes, and she was prepared to play them, but Isikoff, who "had been invited to appear on a CNBC talk show, *Hardball*," and so was "a bit pressed for time," refused, famously, to listen:

> It's an interesting journalistic issue. My hesitation was instinctive—but rooted in principles I had drummed into me when I first started as a young reporter at the *Post*. We don't tape without permission, the late Howard Simons, then the paper's managing editor, had decreed. . . . We reporters shouldn't deceive our sources, any more than we should deceive the public. Or so Simons—a wise and revered editor—had taught me.
>
> Of course, I wasn't being asked by Tripp to tape anybody secretly. But the distinction was a bit fuzzy. Tripp's taping of Lewinsky was ongoing. If I started to listen in on her conversations as she was taping them—as opposed to when she was finished—then I inevitably would have become part of the process. . . . And I was in a bit of a hurry to make it to *Hardball*.

"What do you do when you find yourself sucked into the story?" Isikoff asks rhetorically toward the end of *Uncovering Clinton*, the part in which he says mea culpa but not quite. "What happens when you become beholden to sources with an agenda? There are no easy answers here." Much that he learned later, he tells us, "cast a somewhat different light" on events. He was, for example, "chagrined to discover" that Linda Tripp and Lucianne Goldberg "had been talking about a book deal from the start." But what could there have been, in that, to "discover"? If Isikoff was, as he presents himself here, "an aggressive reporter" still unaware that there was more in this than met the eye, would not "a book deal" have been his first assumption? During his first meetings with Tripp, Isikoff had read part of her proposal for a book to be called *The President's Women*. He knew Lucianne Goldberg to be a literary agent. The idea of a book was nonetheless, Isikoff tells us, "well off my radar screen; indeed, it seemed a bit counterintuitive. Why were they wasting their time sharing information with me, if that was their purpose?"

If Isikoff asked himself this question, he seems to have adroitly avoided the answer, which might have led him to another aspect of the story that he was managing to keep well off his radar screen. What there was to "discover," of course, he already knew: by the time Linda Tripp and Lucianne Goldberg gave him Monica Lewinsky's name, any idea of "a book deal" would have been, as Lucianne Goldberg noted in her review of *Uncovering Clinton* in *Slate*, "a moot point that I can safely say faded to the vanishing point." The reason the point was moot was that, even by Isikoff's own account, Lucianne Goldberg was by then operating less as a lone agent than as a kind of useful front, a cutout for those unable to reveal themselves as running the same move: a cutout for Linda Tripp, a cutout for the ardent young movement lawyers (the "busy elves" Ann Coulter had mentioned) who made up the shadow legal team for *Jones v. Clinton*, and a cutout ultimately for the Office of the Independent Counsel.

"I had relied on the elves for information at critical junctures," Isikoff tells us on page 357 of *Uncovering Clinton*, still in his modified mea culpa mode, "even while they concealed from me their role in bringing the Lewinsky allegations to the Jones lawyers and later to Ken Starr." Among the "elves," whose contributions to *Jones v. Clinton* included writing briefs and arranging a moot court at which the nominal Jones lawyers were prepped for their argument before the Supreme Court by Robert H. Bork, the most frequently named were Jerome M. Marcus, an associate at Berger & Montague in Philadelphia, George T. Conway III at Wachtell Lipton in New York, and Richard W. Porter, a Chicago partner, as Kenneth Starr was a Washington partner, at Kirkland & Ellis. Jerome Marcus and Richard Porter had been classmates at the University of Chicago, as had Paul Rosenzweig, who was approached to work on *Jones v. Clinton* in 1994, decided against it, and in 1997 joined the Office of the Independent Counsel.

Review Isikoff's admission of imperfect prescience, the reporter's dilemma for which there were "no easy answers." The elves, he told us on page 357, had "concealed" from him their role in bringing the Lewinsky allegations to the Jones lawyers and later to Ken Starr. Go back to page 182 of *Uncovering Clinton*, the CNBC green room: when Ann Coulter said to Isikoff that there were "lots of us busy elves working away in Santa's workshop," was this not said to have been a response to his remark that she seemed to have "inside knowledge" of *Jones v. Clinton*? Or go back to page 135, where Isikoff gives a quite detailed account of what Linda Tripp told him during their early meetings, when she was not yet telling him the name of the intern. Linda Tripp told him, he reports, that "she herself had been asked by her White House–provided lawyer not to volunteer information about a memo she had seen about the White House travel office that implicated First Lady Hillary Rodham Clinton." Travel office? Travelgate? White House–provided lawyer? Did this not suggest a prior relationship with the Office of the Independent Counsel?

Given the players and the relationships already in place, would it not have been, as Isikoff said about the red herring that was the book deal, "counterintuitive" not to suspect that a certain amount of information was passing between the Jones team and the Office of the Independent Counsel and Linda Tripp? Did he not suspect it? If he suspected it, why did he not pursue it? Could it have been because he already knew it? This is an area that *Uncovering Clinton* was cannily designed, by virtue of the way its author chose to present himself, to leave safely uncharted. "As a reporter," the author tells us, "I don't think ideologically." And then, about his primary sources, Linda Tripp and Lucianne Goldberg: "I could not have cared less about their motives or their ultimate goal. My interest in them was quite simple and fairly well focused: Was the stuff they were telling me true? Could it be corroborated? Would it make a story for *Newsweek*?"

3.

When Paula Jones was brought to the 1994 Conservative Political Action Conference to air her charge against the president, Ralph Reed, under whose leadership the Christian Coalition had grown from fewer than five thousand members to a potent political force and whose presence might have lent the fateful press conference at the Shoreham a degree of legitimacy, was asked to participate. For what he seems to have seen as pragmatic reasons, he declined. As he explained in his 1996 *Active Faith: How Christians Are Changing the Soul of American Politics*, Reed considered it a mistake for conservatives to build their case against Clinton around Paula Jones: "When one of the nation's leading evangelical preachers suggests that the President may be a murderer, when a pro-life leader says that to vote for Clinton is to sin against God, and when conservative talk-show hosts lampoon the sexual behavior of the leader of the free world, the manner of their speech reflects poorly on the gospel and on our faith."

This was at a time when Jerry Falwell, on his *Old Time Gospel Hour*, was marketing *The Clinton Chronicles*, a forty-dollar video asserting that Clinton had ordered the murders of Arkansas opponents and governed the state "hooked on cocaine." A second video, *Circle of Power*, was suggesting that "countless people" who "had some connection to Bill Clinton" had "mysteriously died," and that "this is going on today." Even well in from the ideological frontiers of telemarketing, "impeachment" was already the word of the hour: a contributor to *The Weekly Standard*, Gary Schmitt, was calling for Clinton's impeachment on the grounds that the president had told Jim Lehrer during a PBS interview that he believed Kenneth Starr's

Whitewater investigation to be a partisan effort and so would not rule out the possibility of presidential pardons for those convicted in connection with that investigation. Reed, in his 1996 book, recalled attending a conservative dinner where the speaker had called for Clinton's impeachment and imprisonment on the grounds that he was "the most criminal president in our history."

Reed saw the feeding of this particular fire as a strategy only for self-immolation. "Like an army that overwhelms its enemies but leaves the land uninhabitable, some religious conservatives have come dangerously close to defining themselves in purely anti-Clinton terms," he wrote. "Those who are identified as followers of Christ should temper their disagreements with Clinton with civility and the grace of God, avoiding the temptation to personalize issues or demonize their opponents. This is critical to remember if our movement is to avoid the fate of its predecessors." Some of the harshest attacks on Clinton, Reed noted, had their origins in the "Christian nation" or "Reconstructionist" movement, the more unyielding proponents of which advocated "legislating the ancient Jewish law laid out in the Old Testament: stoning adulterers, executing homosexuals, even mandating dietary laws":

> There are historical precedents for Reconstructionist ideas stretching back to the millennialistic strains of Puritan thinking, American Revolutionary ideology, and even the anti-slavery movement. But those currents did not reflect the mainstream of Christian thinking then, and they certainly do not today. Reconstructionism is an authoritarian ideology that threatens the most basic civil liberties of a free and democratic society. If the pro-family movement hopes to realize its goals of relimiting government and reinstilling traditional values in our culture and in public policy, it must unequivocally dissociate itself from Reconstructionism and other efforts to use the government to impose biblical law through direct political action. It must firmly and openly exclude the triumphalist and authoritarian elements. . . .

That the fire had already jumped this break should have been, in retrospect, clear, since, even then, the word "authoritarian" no longer carried the exact freight it carried for Reed. The problem with rock music, Robert H. Bork told us in his

1996 *Slouching Towards Gomorrah*, was that it had encouraged the "subversion of authority," which in turn was the problem with the "baby boomers," who were already, principally because Clinton could be shoehorned into their number, a target of choice for the derision and excoriation engaged in even by many who were themselves members of the same generation. As this view took hold, the word "authority" was frequently preceded, as in William J. Bennett's *The Death of Outrage*, by the word "moral," "moral authority" being the manna allegedly possessed by all American presidents before William Clinton. Clinton, according to David S. Broder and Richard Morin of *The Washington Post*, confronted "his fellow citizens with choices between deeply held moral standards and an abhorrence of judging others' behavior, a conflict the baby boomers have stirred all their adult lives."

These "boomers," who had "no respect for authority," or who "flouted established moral standards," made increasingly frequent appearances. "The battle to dethrone Bill Clinton takes its place in the ongoing Boomer War, a three-decade struggle to define our culture and control our history and symbols," Michael Powell wrote in *The Washington Post*, citing Robert Bork, who had suggested in defense of Kenneth Starr that his was a useful effort to "kill off the lax moral spirit of the Sixties." The pollster Daniel Yankelovich, whose 1981 *New Rules* and later opinion surveys for the Democratic Leadership Council inspired the 1992 Clinton-Gore campaign's *Putting People First*, was quoted by Broder and Morin as having said that "we are beginning to measure a shift back toward absolute as opposed to relative values." The "shift back" was to a period before the mid-sixties, which had been marked, according to Yankelovich, by a "radical extension of individualism."

Reenter Robert Bork, who in *Slouching Towards Gomorrah* identified "radical individualism," or "the drastic reduction of limits to personal gratification," as one of the two "defining characteristics of modern liberalism" (the other being "radical egalitarianism") and, as such, a root cause of "Western decline." That Bork has tended to support his arguments with something other than a full deck of facts (as evidence of "Western decline," he asked us in 1996 to consider "the latest homicide figures for New York City, Los Angeles, or the District of Columbia," as well as "the rising rate of illegitimate births," both of which were dropping steadily during the 1990s) has never deflected his enthusiasm for taking positions, since facts seemed to exist for him in the same mutable state positions did, unfixed weapons to be deployed as needed in that day's sortie against the "leftist dream world."

Bork is worth some study, since it is to him that we owe the most forthright statements of what might be required to effect "a moral and spiritual regeneration," the necessity for which has since entered the talk-show and op-ed ether. Such a regeneration could be produced, Bork speculated in *Slouching Towards Gomorrah*, by one of four events: "a religious revival; the revival of public discourse about morality; a cataclysmic war; or a deep economic depression." As for the first of these options, Bork saw possibilities in "the rise of an energetic, optimistic, and politically sophisticated religious conservatism," but not in the "mainline churches," which no longer posited "a demanding God . . . who dictates how one should live and puts a great many bodily and psychological pleasures off limits." "The carrot alone has never been a wholly adequate incentive to desired behavior," Bork wrote. "It is not helpful that the ideas of salvation and damnation, of sin and virtue, which once played major roles in Christian belief, are now almost never heard of in the mainline churches."

It is of course not true that ideas of salvation and damnation or sin and virtue are "now almost never heard of in the mainline churches." Anyone who repeats the responses in the Episcopal litany asks for deliverance "from all evil and wickedness, from sin, from the crafts and assaults of the devil, from thy wrath and from everlasting damnation," and the Catholic baptismal sponsor swears in the name of the child to "reject Satan, father of sin and prince of darkness." Nor is it true, as Bork also wrote, that "the intellectual classes" view religion as "primitive superstition," or believe either that "science has left atheism as the only respectable intellectual stance" or that the question of faith was definitely answered by "Freud, Marx, and Darwin." These "atheists" and "mainline churches" that had abandoned sin and virtue had nonetheless become fixed stations in the conservative canon, recognizable cues, along with "Freud, Marx, and Darwin" and "the ACLU" and all the other calculated outrages; what John J. DiIulio Jr. described in *The Weekly Standard* as "the radical-feminist faithful, the non-judgmental clergy, the Hollywood crowd, and the abortion-on-demand minions."

The literal "truth" or "untruth" of what Bork wrote or said was, then, beside the point, since this was metaphor, and was so understood within the movement: polemic, political litany, a rhetorical incitement to the legislation of "desired behavior," which was to say the scourging of "immoral" behavior. That Bork himself understood this seems clear enough, since he seems to believe that Thomas Jefferson had some kind of similar intention—*this will raise the rabble*—when he wrote the Declaration of Independence. "It was indeed stirring rhetoric," Bork allows,

> entirely appropriate for the purpose of rallying the colonists and justifying their rebellion to the world. But some caution is in order. The ringing phrases are hardly useful, indeed may be pernicious, if taken, as they commonly are, as a guide to action, governmental or private. Then the words press inevitably towards extremes of liberty and the pursuit of happiness that court personal license and social disorder.

The extent to which "personal license" might be sought out for punishment was suggested by Bork in his earlier *The Tempting of America: The Political Seduction of the Law*: "Moral outrage is a sufficient ground for prohibitory legislation," he wrote. "Knowledge that an activity is taking place is a harm to those who find it profoundly immoral."

4.

"The Republican right wing in this country doesn't like it when we say coup d'etat, so I'll make it easier for them," Representative Jose E. Serrano (D-N.Y.) said on the floor of the House the day the impeachment vote was taken. "*Golpe de estado.* That's Spanish for overthrowing a government." The word "coup," which had begun to surface in the dialogue as the more ambiguous aspects of the Starr investigation became known, had predictably provoked impassioned objections, some of them reasoned (impeachment was a legitimate constitutional process, a conviction by the Senate on the impeachment charges brought by the House would result in the removal of the president but not of the political party holding the presidency) and others less reasoned (Hillary Rodham Clinton had said that there was a "vast right-wing conspiracy" to get her husband, ergo, there was not, or, alternately, it was not "vast," or it was not a "conspiracy"); and yet there were, in the sequence of events that culminated in impeachment, certain factors that seemed distinctly exotic to the politics of the United States.

There was, first of all, the sense of a "movement," an unchartered sodality that was dedicated to the "remoralization" (William Kristol's word) of the nation and that, for a variety of reasons (judicial activism, feminism, "nonjudgmentalism," what Bork called "the pernicious effects of our passion for equality"), believed itself inadequately represented in the nation's conventional electoral process. There was the reliance, as in the more authoritarian Latin American structures, on *orejas*, "ears," tale-tellers like Linda Tripp, citizens encouraged, whether directly or through the rhetoric of the movement, to obtain evidence against those perceived as enemies of the movement. There was the aid from the private sector, the dependence on such rich sympathizers as Richard Mellon Scaife and John Whitehead and the Chicago investment banker Peter W. Smith. There was the way in which it was seen as possible that the electoral process could be bypassed, that the desired change in the government could be effected by a handful of unseen individuals, like George Conway and Jerome Marcus and Richard Porter, working in concert.

There was the shared conviction of urgency, of mission, of an end so crucial to the fate of the republic as to sweep away possible reservations about means. If the Office of the Independent Counsel was violating Justice Department prosecutorial guidelines by prosecuting its case in the press, this had been justified, Kenneth Starr told Steven Brill, because it was "a situation where what we are doing is countering misinformation that is being spread about our investigation in order to discredit our office and our dedicated career prosecutors." If the treatment of Monica Lewinsky had seemed to some to violate her legal rights, this too had been justified by the imperative of the "prosecution," the "investigation." "When you're asked to cooperate in an investigation of this kind it's going to be hellish no matter how nice you are to her," Michael Emmick of the Office of the Independent Counsel told members of the American Bar Association in February 1999. "That's one of the ugly truths about law enforcement. It's very ugly at times. We tried to make it as undifficult as we could." Since the moral necessity and therefore the absolute priority of the "investigation" were assumed, any assertion of the right of the accused to defend himself could be construed only as prima facie evidence of guilt, which is what people meant when they condemned the president's defense as "legalistic."

In fact we had seen this willingness to sacrifice means to ends before, in the late 1980s, when it had seemed equally exotic. "Sometimes you have to go above the written law," Fawn Hall had testified on behalf of Lieutenant Colonel Oliver North, expressing a view shared, in that instance, by most conservatives. Representative Henry J. Hyde, for example, had argued that Fawn Hall was echoing Thomas Jefferson, who had written in an 1810 letter to John Colvin that to insist on "a strict observance of the written law" over "the laws of necessity, of self-preservation, of saving our country when in danger" would be "absurdly sacrificing the end to the means." "All of us," Hyde wrote in the "Supplemental Views" he attached to the 1987 *Report of the Congressional Committees Investigating the Iran-Contra Affair*, "at some time confront conflicts between rights and duties, between choices that are evil and less evil, and one hardly exhausts moral imagination by labeling every untruth and deception an outrage." Hyde continued:

> We have had a disconcerting and distasteful whiff of moralism and institutional self-righteousness in these hearings. . . . It has seemed to me that the Congress is usually more eager to assert authority than to accept responsibility, more ready to criticize than to constructively propose, more comfortable in the public relations limelight than in the murkier greyness of the real world, where choices must often be made, not between relative goods, but between bad and worse. . . .

The "less evil" choice at hand, of course, had been the covert support of the Nicaraguan contras, or "freedom fighters," who were for the conservative movement in the 1980s what the shifting cast of starring (Paula Jones, Monica Lewinsky) and day players (the Arkansas state troopers, Kathleen Willey, Dolly Kyle Browning, Juanita Broaddrick) who "proved" the moral perfidy of William Jefferson Clinton would become in the 1990s: flags around which the troops could be mobilized and an entire complex of "movement values" attached. For these symbolic purposes, the contras had proved the less fragile standard, since their support involved issues that could be sufficiently inflated to launch the entire matter into the ozone of "national security." Unlike "covert support for the freedom fighters," "Monica Lewinsky" remained resistant to inflation: no matter how many mentions of "perjury" and "rule of law" and "constitutional obligation" got pumped into the noise, the possibility of dallying and lying about it continued to be understood by, and regarded as irrelevant to the survival of the nation by, a majority of the nation's citizens.

This presented a problem. On a broad range of loosely cultural issues (the balanced budget, welfare reform, the death penalty), the positions shared by the president and the citizens in question could by no alchemy be presented as the products of "left-liberal ideology," which had been firmly established in the litany of the movement as the root cause of the nation's moral crisis. "For the model of cultural collapse to work," Andrew Sullivan observed in October 1998 in an analysis of the conservative dilemma in *The New York Times Magazine*, "Clinton must represent its nadir." It was the solution to this problem, the naming of the citizens themselves as co-conspirators in the nation's moral degradation, that remains the most strikingly exotic aspect of the events that came to dominate the late 1990s. "No analysis can absolve the people themselves of responsibility for the quandary we appear to be in," Don Eberly, director of the Civil Society Project in Harrisburg, Pennsylvania, told David S. Broder and Richard Morin of *The Washington Post*. "Non-judgmentalism, the trump card of moral debate, seems to have gained strength among the people, especially in the sexual realm, and this clearly does not bode well for America."

The citizens, it seemed, were running behind the zeitgeist, incapable of understanding momentous events. "The objection that the American people are opposed to impeachment ignores culture lags of historical frequency, including general opposition to the liberation of the slaves," William F. Buckley Jr. told *The New York Times*. The citizens were incapable of understanding momentous events because they had succumbed to the lures of hedonism, materialism, false modernity, "radical individualism" itself. "A certain portion of the American public is cowed by popular culture," Craig Shirley, the conservative strategist who gave Michael Isikoff the heads-up on the unveiling of Paula Jones at the 1994 Conservative Political Action Conference, told the *Times*. "They do not want to be thought of as not being modern or sophisticated." "Given their obstinate lack of interest in the subject, asking a group of average Americans about politics is like asking a group of stevedores to solve a problem in astrophysics," a senior editor of *The Weekly Standard*, Andrew Ferguson, had written in 1996. "Before long they're explaining, not merely that the moon is made of cheese, but what kind of cheese it is, and whether it is properly aged, and how it would taste on a Triscuit."

Within the movement, then, this censorious approach to the electorate was not entirely recent. What was recent was the extent to which the movement crusade to save America from its citizens would come to be acquiesced in by, which is to say aided and abetted by, that small but highly visible group of people who, day by day and through administration after administration, relay Washington to the world, tell its story, agree among themselves upon and then disseminate its narrative. They report the stories. They write the op-ed pieces. They appear on the talk shows. They consult, they advise, they swap jobs, they travel with unmarked passports between the public and the private, the West Wing and the green room. They make up the nation's permanent professional political class, and they are for the most part people who would say of themselves, as Michael Isikoff said of himself, that they "don't think ideologically."

And yet this was an instance in which the narrative they agreed upon, that the president's behavior had degraded and crippled the presidency and the government and the nation itself, worked at every point to obscure, in some cases by omission and in other cases through dismissal as "White House spin," what we now know to have been going on. It would have been possible to read the reports from Washington in four or five daily newspapers and still not know, until it was detailed by Renata Adler in *The Los Angeles Times Book Review* on March 14, 1999, that by the time Linda Tripp surfaced on the national screen as Monica Lewinsky's confidante she had already testified in four previous Office of the Independent Counsel investigations: Filegate, Travelgate, the Vincent Foster suicide, and Whitewater.

In the face of even this single piece of information, a good many of the attitudes struck during the past year might have seemed, if not deliberate obfuscation, at best perplexing digressions. "I couldn't buy the party line that this was more about Clinton's accusers than his own actions," George Stephanopoulous told us in his own mea culpa but not quite, *All Too Human.* On the first Sunday in February 1999, when it seemed clear that there were not enough votes for conviction in the Senate, Cokie Roberts was still on air calling for a censure vote, "a Democratic vote saying what he did was wrong." Otherwise, she said, "the way it will be written for history is that this was a partisan witch hunt, that it was an illegitimate process," and "the spinners could certainly win if you do it that way."

These people lived in a small world. Consider again the sentence that appears on page 357 of *Uncovering Clinton*, particularly its second clause: "*I had relied on the elves for information at critical junctures—even while they concealed from me their role in bringing the Lewinsky allegations to the Jones lawyers and later to Ken Starr.*" What we now know occurred was, in other words, a covert effort to advance a particular agenda by bringing down a president. We know that this covert effort culminated in the kind of sting operation that reliably creates a crime where a crime may or may not have otherwise existed. We knew all along that the "independence" of the independent prosecutor could have been, or should have been, open to some question, since, before his appointment as independent prosecutor, Kenneth Starr had consulted with the Jones legal team on the projected amicus curiae brief to be filed on behalf of the Independent Women's Forum arguing that

Jones v. Clinton should go forward. This had been reported, but was allowed to pass unremarked upon in what passed for the dialogue on the case. The Jones lawyer with whom Starr consulted, Isikoff tells us, was Gil Davis, whose billing records showed that the conversations with Starr covered four and a half hours, for which Davis billed Paula Jones $775.

The clues were always there, as they had been for Isikoff. There was always in the tale of the foolish intern and her disloyal friend a synchronicity that did not quite convince. There was from the outset the occasional odd reference in a news story, the name here or there that did not quite belong in the story, the chronology that did not quite tally, the curiously inexorable escalation of *Jones v. Clinton*. At least some of this, in other words, would appear to have been knowable, but it remained unacknowledged in the narrative that was the official story. "What drives Ken Starr onward?" Michael Winerip asked in *The New York Times Magazine* in September 1998. "Who is this minister's son in such relentless pursuit that he forced the president to admit his sins on national television?"

> Everyone has a theory on Starr. After the Lewinsky affair broke, Hillary Clinton called Starr "a politically motivated prosecutor who is allied with the right-wing opponents of my husband." Harold Ickes, the former Clinton aide, says he sees Starr as a dangerous moralist who views the Clintons "like Sodom and Gomorrah and is hell-bent on running them out of Washington."
>
> Even Starr's best friends don't know what to make of it all. They were caught off guard when he took the independent counsel's job in 1994 and are not sure why he wanted it. "I have no idea," says Theodore Olson, a prominent Washington lawyer. "He never asked me. I was shocked when I heard the news."

"*I was shocked when I heard the news.*" This was the same small world. Theodore Olson, whose wife, Barbara Olson, was a member of the National Advisory Board of the Independent Women's Forum, the group for which Kenneth Starr was to have written the amicus curiae brief urging that *Jones v. Clinton* go forward, was a Washington partner of the Los Angeles–based Gibson, Dunn & Crutcher. Gibson, Dunn had also been the firm of William French Smith, attorney general during the Reagan administration. Kenneth Starr had been William French Smith's chief of staff at the Justice Department, and it was William French Smith who in 1983 arranged Starr's appointment to the U.S. Circuit Court of Appeals for the District of Columbia, where he served with, and often voted with, Robert H. Bork. Olson was one of the lawyers, along with Robert Bork, enlisted by George Conway to prepare the Jones lawyers for the Supreme Court arguments that led to the Court's 9–0 decision denying a sitting president immunity from civil suits. The preparation took place at the Army-Navy Club in Washington. At a point after Christmas 1997, concerned about the ideological reliability of Linda Tripp's lawyer and under pressure to find a replacement before the cards started falling into place, Jerome Marcus and Richard Porter approached Theodore Olson about taking on Tripp's legal representation. Olson could not.

Ann Coulter, via George Conway, then suggested James Moody, who could, and did. James Moody was a Washington lawyer and a member, along with George Conway and Robert H. Bork and Kenneth Starr and Theodore and Barbara Olson, of the Federalist Society, an organization of conservative legal scholars and students that became influential during the Reagan administration and had been the recipient, according to *The Washington Post*, of at least $1.5 million from Richard Mellon Scaife's foundations and trusts. Moody was also an admirer of the Grateful Dead, and, with Ann Coulter, had flown to San Francisco for the memorial concert that followed the 1995 death of Jerry Garcia. James Moody and Ann Coulter called themselves, according to Isikoff, "the only two right-wing Deadheads in Washington."

"Even Starr's best friends don't know what to make of it all." Nor did we, since this was the tone in which the nation's permanent professional political class had chosen to tell us the story. To suggest that the investigation might be politically motivated, we were told repeatedly, was to misrepresent "Ken" Starr, whose own tendency to encourage this reading was understood in Washington as a badge of scholarly innocence, a "clumsiness," at worst an "amateurishness" (that was the editorial page of *The Washington Post*), the endearing "tin ear," not important. "What's important," the *Post* declared in a February 1999 editorial calling for a bipartisan censure, "is to have a clear record and a clear statement of the standard of conduct—the expectations—that this president has violated by the lying to escape being held to account that is a hallmark of his career." In the absence of censure, the *Post* warned: "The president and his people will end up portraying this sorry episode as mostly a partisan proceeding, an effort by his enemies to win through entrapment and impeachment what they could not at the polls. Mr. Clinton will be the victim in this telling, not a president who dishonored the office but one who was caught up in a politics of personal destruction."

This merits study. The word "partisan," as in "partisan proceeding," suggests, in the United States, a traditional process, "taking sides," "knows how to count," Democrats, Republicans, the ballot box. The word "partisan," then, worked to contain the suggestion that anything outside that tradition was at work here. Both the "president who dishonored the office" and the "one who was caught up in a politics of personal destruction" further trivialized what had taken place, reducing it to the "personal," to a parable about the "character" of either the president or his attackers. By reducing the matter to the personal as by labeling it "partisan" or "bipartisan," it was possible to divest what had taken place of its potentially disruptive gravity, possible to avoid all consideration of whether or not a move on the presidency had been covertly run, of whether or not the intent of such a move had been to legitimize a minority ideological agenda, and of whether or not—most disruptive of all—such a move was ongoing.

On November 2, 1998, the day before the midterm elections, *The Washington Post* published a much-discussed piece by Sally Quinn, a *Post* writer and the wife of former *Post* executive editor Benjamin Bradlee. Whether or not this piece should have been published became a matter of momentary controversy within the Washington establishment, precisely because it reported so accurately the collegial, even collaborative approach the establishment was taking toward the matter at hand, the unwillingness to consider the ramifications of the refusal to conjugate the verb *to conspire*, the way in which an institutional forgetfulness was serving to preserve the sanctity of the Washington status quo. “Privately,” Quinn wrote, “many in Establishment Washington would like to see Bill Clinton resign and spare the country, the presidency, and the city any more humiliation.”

In 1972, when word reached the *Post* that there had been a break-in at the Watergate office of the Democratic National Committee, those assigned to work the story were Metro reporters, Bob Woodward and Carl Bernstein. Woodward, Benjamin Bradlee wrote in his autobiography, *A Good Life*, was then “one of the new kids on the staff,” and Bernstein “the Peck’s Bad Boy of the Metro staff.” Woodward and Bernstein, in other words, were at that time Washington outsiders, and it was to their status as Washington outsiders that their ability to get “the real story” was commonly attributed. Those to whom Quinn spoke, on the other hand, seemed to believe that it was their own status as Washington insiders that gave them unique knowledge of the “real story” behind the drive for impeachment, which came down to what they saw as the president’s betrayal, by his failure to tell the truth, of the community and the country.

Those to whom Quinn spoke also seemed to believe that, despite their best efforts to disseminate it, this unique knowledge remained unshared by and unappreciated by the rest of the country. “Clinton’s behavior is unacceptable,” the pollster Geoff Garin told her. “If they did this at the local Elks Club hall in some other community it would be a big cause for concern.” “He came in here and he trashed the place, and it’s not his place,” David Broder of the *Post* said. “It’s a canard to say this is a private matter,” the *Wall Street Journal* columnist Albert R. Hunt said. “It’s had a profound effect on governance.” “There’s no way any president going through this process can be able to focus, whether on Kosovo or the economic crisis,” the NBC correspondent Andrea Mitchell said. “It’s just a tragedy for everyone.”

But not necessarily for everyone in Washington. The president would soon be, as David Broder would write in the *Post*, “disgraced and enfeebled.” The time would soon come for the president, as Broder would also write, to “step aside for the man he clearly believes is well qualified to be his successor, Vice-President Gore.” Since the matter had been so firmly established as "personal," there would be no need to pursue the possibility that the "process," or the "tragedy," or the "profound effect on governance," had been initiated by someone other than the president. In fact such a possibility need not even enter the picture, for this was a view from inside Washington, where those who did not "think ideologically" appreciated the drift, the climate, the wheeling of the ideological seasons, and also their access to whoever turns the wheel. As Quinn explained, "Starr is a Washington insider too."

God's Country

November 2, 2000

THE WORDS "compassionate conservatism" sound like and have often been dismissed as political rhetoric, a construction without intrinsic meaning, George W. Bush's adroit way of pitching the center, allowing middle-class voters to feel good about themselves while voting their interests. Former governor Lamar Alexander of Tennessee called them "weasel words." Joe Andrews, the national chairman of the Democratic National Committee, called them "a contrived copout." "You can't have these massive tax cuts and at the same time . . . be a compassionate conservative," Senator Paul Wellstone of Minnesota told *The New York Times*. To the extent that the words were construed to mean anything at all, then, they were misunderstood to suggest a warmer, more generous, more ameliorative kind of conservative. "I'm a conservative, and proud of it, but I'm a compassionate conservative," Senator Orrin Hatch told Judith Miller of *The New York Times* in March 1981. "I'm not some kind of ultra-right-wing maniac." Former governor Pete Wilson of California offered a still more centrist reading: compassionate conservatism, he was quoted as saying by *The Washington Post*, is "old-fashioned budget-balancing with spending for preventive health measures and protection of the environment, and a strong pro-choice position on abortion."

This suggests a pragmatic but still traditional economic conservatism into which many Americans could comfortably buy. Yet the phrase "compassionate conservatism" describes a specific and deeply radical experiment in social rearrangement, the aim of which was defined by Governor Bush, in his acceptance speech at the Republican convention in Philadelphia, with sufficient vagueness to signal the troops without alerting the less committed: what he meant by compassionate conservatism, he said, was "to put conservative values and conservative ideas into the thick of the fight for justice and opportunity." Marvin Olasky, the journalism professor at the University of Texas who became a Bush adviser in 1993 and is the author of the seminal work on the subject, *The Tragedy of American Compassion* (this was the 1992 book that Newt Gingrich received as a Christmas present from William J. Bennett in 1994 and promptly recommended to all Republican members of Congress), and of the more recent *Compassionate Conservatism*, has been more forthright. "Compassionate conservatism is neither an easy slogan nor one immune from vehement attack," he advises readers on page 1 of *Compassionate Conservatism*:

> It is a full-fledged program with a carefully considered philosophy. It will face in the twenty-first century not easy acceptance but dug-in opposition. It will have to cross a river of suspicion concerning the role of religion in American society. It will have to get past numerous ideological machine-gun nests. Only political courage will enable compassionate conservatism to carry the day and transform America.

The source of this "river of suspicion" and these "ideological machine-gun nests" becomes clear on reading the text, which is largely devoted to detailing a 1999 road trip during which Olasky, who before "God found me and changed me when I was twenty-six," had wrestled first with atheism ("I was bar mitzvahed at thirteen and an atheist by fourteen") and then with the Communist Party U.S.A. ("What if Lenin is wrong? What if there is a God?"), introduced his fourteen-year-old son, Daniel, to anti-poverty programs in Texas, the Midwest, and the Northeast. The drift soon emerges. "God's in charge," a couple who run a community center in South Dallas tell Olasky and Daniel. "I had to learn that God's in charge," they are told by a former user of heroin and cocaine who now runs the day-to-day operation of a recovery center in Minneapolis. A teacher at an evangelical summer school in Dallas explains how "curriculum is cleverly tied" to a pending mountain field trip, for example by assigning "Bible passages concerning mountains, eagles, and hawks."

Outside Houston, they visit "Youth-Reach Houston" and its founder, "Curt Williams, forty, who wears his long black hair pulled back in a pony tail" and who in 1984 "followed a pretty girl into a church and found welcome there. . . . Having hit bottom, he went to church and felt spiritually compelled to throw away his drugs and pornography." In Indianapolis, they meet with Mayor Stephen Goldsmith, chief domestic policy adviser to the Bush campaign and a civic leader who had studied "the negatives (high taxes, red tape, bad schools) that drive middle-class people away from the city" and found the answer in "using his bully pulpit to promote Catholic schools," since, as he tells Olasky and Daniel, "only hardened skeptics have trouble accepting that widespread belief in a Supreme Being improves the strength and health of our communities."

Again and again, Olasky and Daniel learn of successful recoveries effected in one or another "have-not" program, which is to say a program prevented from receiving the funding it deserves for the sole reason, Olasky suggests, that it is "faith-based." Again and again, they hear the same language ("hitting bottom," "putting God in charge," "changing one life at a time"), which is, not coincidentally, that of the faith-based twelve-step movement, from which a good deal of the "new thinking" on welfare derives. (Alcoholics Anonymous, according to James Q. Wilson, is "the single most important organized example of personal transformation we have.") Visiting a faith-based prison program outside Houston, they meet Donnie Gilmore, who was "pushing thirty with a resume of breaking into houses and stealing cars" when "his four-year-old daughter asked him about Jesus, and he realized he had never opened a Bible."

Gilmore then joined the "InnerChange" program ("Texas Governor George W. Bush gave the program a try, and state officials kept the American Civil Liberties Union at bay . . .") developed by Prison Fellowship Ministries, which is the organization founded by Charles ("Chuck") Colson after his release from the Maxwell Federal Prison Camp in Alabama and in which "the keys to success" are "God's grace and man's mentoring." "I have a couple of editions of the Bible with me," Colson reportedly said on the day he left for Maxwell to serve seven months of a one-to-three-year sentence for obstruction of justice in the prosecution of Daniel Ellsberg. "That's all."

"Repeatedly," Olasky notes with approval, "Daniel and I had found that the impetus for a compassionate conservative program came out of a Bible study or some other church or synagogue function." Both father and son are made "uneasy" by more secular programs, for example KIPP (Knowledge

Is Power Program) Academy, a charter school in Houston, where, despite the fact that it seemed "excellent," its public nature meant that "students miss out on that added dimension," i.e., prayer and Bible study. Similarly, in Minneapolis, they visit a Goodwill program that seemed to be successfully introducing women to the basic workplace manners (be on time, answer the phone politely) needed to make the transition from welfare to work. "All of this was impressive," Olasky allows, and yet, "as Daniel noted in comparing this helpful program to the faith-based equivalents we were seeing elsewhere, 'The absence of interest in God is glaring.'"

This use of "faith-based" is artful, and worth study. Goodwill was founded by a Methodist minister and run during its early years out of the Morgan Memorial Chapel in Boston, which would seem to qualify it as based in faith, although not, in the sense that Olasky apparently construes the phrase, as "faith-based." "Faith-based," then, is, as Olasky uses it, a phrase with a special meaning, a code phrase, employed to suggest that certain worthy organizations have been prevented from receiving government funding solely by virtue of their religious affiliation. This is misleading, since "religiously affiliated" organizations (for example Catholic Charities) can and do receive such funding. The organizations that have not are those deemed "pervasively sectarian," a judgment based on the extent to which they proselytize, or make religious worship or instruction a condition of receiving aid. This, the Supreme Court has to date maintained, would violate the establishment clause of the First Amendment, the original intent of which Olasky believes to have been warped. "Daniel and I spent some time talking about what happened 210 years ago," he wrote. "There's nothing about 'separation of church and state.' That was Thomas Jefferson's personal expression in a letter written over a decade after the amendment was adopted. . . . The founding fathers would be aghast at court rulings that make our part of the world safe for moral anarchy."

Olasky is insistent that the faith propagated by these "faith-based" organizations need by no means be exclusively Christian, and here we enter another area of artful presentation. "My tendency is to be inclusive," he told *The Los Angeles*

Times. "That can include Wiccans and Scientologists. If people are going to get mad at me, then so be it." The goal of compassionate conservatism, he has written repeatedly, is "faith-based diversity," a system in which the government would offer those in need of aid a choice of programs: "Protestant, Catholic, Jewish, Islamic, Buddhist, atheist." Perhaps because the theological imperative to convert nonbelievers runs with considerably more force among evangelical Christians than among Buddhists or atheists, most of the programs described in *Compassionate Conservatism* are nonetheless Christian, and, to one degree or another, evangelical. "All organizations, religious or atheistic, [had] the opportunity to propose values-based pre-release programs," Olasky notes by way of explaining how Texas state officials "kept the American Civil Liberties Union at bay" on behalf of Prison Fellowship, "but only Prison Fellowship went all the way."

In Philadelphia, Olasky and Daniel visit Deliverance Evangelistic, where John J. DiIulio Jr. "took his first steps toward faith in Christ" and where the pastor speaks of how "the ACLU is using and abusing" the First Amendment. They also visit the Bethel Community Bible Church, where they meet a paraplegic weight lifter who "sold drugs and saw no meaning to life until God grabbed him twelve years ago." Now he runs the Bethel weight room, which is "used by forty men each week, with no payment or conditions for use except one: the men need to attend church, Bible study, or church counseling at least once per week." Some of the programs Olasky describes refuse to compromise their evangelical mission by accepting government funding ("the reason we're here is that kids need to come to Christ"); others take the money, and devise ways of nominally separating it from the teaching mission.

Olasky and Daniel for example visit "the praying tailback," Herb Lusk, "the first National Football League player to use the end zone as the pulpit by crouching prayerfully following a touchdown." As pastor of the Greater Exodus Baptist Church in Philadelphia, Lusk does accept government funding for the church's welfare-to-work program, but works around it: "No, we don't talk about Christ during the training, but we promote our offer of a free lunch for participants, with Bible teaching during it." "Evangelism is central to everything we do," Olasky is told by a Dallas woman, Kathy Dudley, who left her suburban home for the inner city, where she defines her mission as "discipleship." "Early in the 1990s," Olasky reports, "one official offered her a $170,000 grant, but she asked, 'If I take this money and hire a housing director, I will hire a Christian and expect a certain standard of behavior. If the director has sex outside of marriage, I will fire him immediately. Do you have a problem with this?' Yes, the official told her. She spurned the grant."

2.

In addition to teaching at Austin, Marvin Olasky has written a number of books, none of which tapped into the national moment with the exact force that *The Tragedy of American Compassion* did but the range of which suggests the dexterity with which the excitable mind can divine the sermon in every stone. There was *Prodigal Press: The Anti-Christian Bias of the American News Media*. There was *Telling the Truth: How to Revitalize Christian Journalism*. There was *Corporate Public Relations: A New Historical Perspective*, drawn from five years Olasky spent writing speeches in the public affairs office at DuPont, an experience that led him to the Manichean conclusion that corporations were engaged in a liberal conspiracy to eliminate competition by supporting government regulation. "I wanted to work at DuPont because I was on the side of free enterprise," he told Michael King of *The Texas Observer*. "But I found out . . . you were largely lobbying government officials and others so that when they do the next set of regs—say environmental regs—that they write the regs in such a way that benefits you and hurts your smaller competitor."

There was *Fighting for Liberty and Virtue: Political and Cultural Wars in Eighteenth-Century America*. There was *The American Leadership Tradition: Moral Vision from Washington to Clinton*, which locates the "moral vision" of American presidents in their "religious beliefs and sexual morality" and offers a foreword by former Nixon aide Charles Colson, he of the career-making seven months at Maxwell, who speaks of "dedicated Olaskyites" and suggests that "a generation or two hence, historians will look back at this era and put Marvin

Olasky among the pantheon of seminal thinkers who have changed the way people and societies think."

From Austin, communicating largely by e-mail, Olasky also manages to both edit and write a column for every issue of a weekly magazine, *World*, which is published out of Asheville, North Carolina, and has as its national editor Bob Jones IV, the great-grandson of the founder and son of the current president of Bob Jones University. The "mission statement" of *World*, until it was edited into a slightly more elliptical version in February 1999, read this way:

> To help Christians apply the Bible to their understanding of and response to everyday current events. To achieve this by reporting the news on a weekly basis in an interesting, accurate, and arresting fashion. To accompany reporting with practical commentary on current events and issues from a perspective committed to the final authority of the Bible as the inerrant written Word of God. To assist in developing a Christian understanding of the world, rather than accepting existing secular ideologies.

Ninety-five percent of *World*'s 103,000 subscribers, according to its own 1999 survey, identify themselves as Caucasian. Ninety-eight percent attend church "usually every week." Twenty-two percent are Baptist, seventeen percent are Presbyterian or Reformed, twelve percent members of the Presbyterian Church in America (a fundamentalist breakaway from the mainline Presbyterian Church U.S.A. and the denomination to which Olasky himself belongs), and eleven percent pentecostal or charismatic. Forty-five percent of those with children "homeschool," or teach at least one child at home. Asked to rate twenty-six individuals and movements named by *World*, these readers think most highly of James Dobson (who as head of Focus on the Family threatened to leave the Republican Party if Bush chose a pro-choice running mate), of "crisis pregnancy centers," and of Charles Colson. They think least highly of President William Clinton, of the National Organization for Women, and of "the religious left."

Since *World* largely reflects or encourages these predispositions, its coverage tends to the predictable. "*Homosexuals take the offensive*," a 1999 cover line read. Onward *World* went, marching as to war through 1999 and into 2000: "*A teenage martyr: The funeral of Cassie Bernall.*" "*Battling the cultural menace.*" "*Abortion Speech Police.*" "*An inside look at the scary summer gathering of a fading feminist organization,*" i.e., the National Organization for Women. "*Armey: End Christian bashing.*" "*Texas students fight for pre-game prayers.*" "*Darwinists circle wagons against science teacher.*" Some stories are, for the general reader, more arresting, involving as they do people or issues or points of view somewhat outside the general discourse. This is a community of readers to whom a call to counter a "gay activist campaign" against "Dr. Laura" Schlessinger, the Orthodox Jewish talk-show host who referred to homosexuality as a "biological error," can serve as a summons to the barricades, in this case the main gate of Paramount Pictures. This is a community to which a "Pandora's box of controversies" can be opened by the question of whether Christians should continue to buy CDs featuring divorced Christian singers, or "fallen stars." "How credible can evangelicals be in condemning such sins as homosexuality and extramarital sex," *World* asked, "when many seem so tolerant of the sin of divorce?"

Olasky himself is divorced from his first wife. "I've been married since 1976, and in the early 1970s had a brief marriage followed by divorce," is the way he put it in a letter to *The New York Times Magazine* objecting to a piece that suggested he had "hidden his divorce from the press." He met his second wife, Susan, at the University of Michigan, where she was an undergraduate and he a graduate student in the throes of abandoning communism. "When I met him, he was definitely an anti-Communist, but I wouldn't say he was a Christian, at that point," Susan Olasky later told *The Texas Observer*. She said that Whittaker Chambers's *Witness*, which Olasky had recommended that she read, "described where he was then." After their arrival in Austin, Susan Olasky founded the Austin Crisis Pregnancy Center, the purpose for which Olasky believes "God brought about" the move. Charles Colson is also divorced from his first wife, which would not be worth mentioning had he not in summer 2000 called upon Charles Stanley, a fellow Christian broadcaster whose wife had recently divorced him, to resign as pastor of the thirteen-thousand-member First Baptist Church of Atlanta. "Given the already high divorce rate among Baptists," Colson declared (the highest 1998 divorce rates in the United States, according to the U.S. Census Bureau, were, outside Nevada, in the heavily Baptist states of Tennessee, Arkansas, Alabama, and Oklahoma), "the last thing we need to do is to give one of our own leaders a pass, no matter how much we may respect him." What Charles Stanley needed, Colson said, was "a time for personal repentance and healing."

Olasky, having had this time, now seems sufficiently cleansed of the sin of which too many evangelicals are tolerant to write frequently and enthusiastically about marriage, both his own and in general, as well as about the correct relative roles of men and women. "God does not forbid women to be leaders in society, generally speaking," he explained in a 1998 issue of the evangelical *Journal for Biblical Manhood and Womanhood*, "but when that occurs it's usually because of the abdication of men. . . . There's a certain shame attached. Why don't you have a man who's able to step forward?" An entire May 2000 issue of *World* was devoted to marriage and the family, with special emphasis on what remains a lively issue among evangelicals, this "headship and submission" question, which has to do with whether the language in Ephesians 5:22 and 5:23 commanding wives to "be subject" to their husbands "for the husband is the head of the wife as Christ is the head of the church" should be understood strictly or placed in the context of other biblical teachings. In the course of arguing for the latter position and against the extremity of the first ("The Bible advocates neither feminism nor sexual segregation"), Olasky inadvertently opened a window on a view of women not far from that of the Taliban:

> The Bible clearly shows the error both of feminists who claim no differences between men and women, and of sexual segregationists who argue that women are to be concerned "only" with marriage and motherhood. . . . Men go wrong, biblically, by either abdicating or waxing arrogant, either by running from God-given functions or refusing to hear what women have to say. In 1 Samuel 25, Abigail knows that her husband, Nabal, is a fool; when she acts to save her whole household, David tells her, "May you be blessed for your good judgment." I know that

my wife often has better judgment than I, and that if I am not to be Nabal Olasky I should listen. And so should we all. Today, some Christian men believe women should be co-leaders in everything. That leaves many men feeling emasculated and many women wishing that guys would step up and make a decision, already. Other Christian men go to the opposite extreme and assert that married women should not even be studying the Bible by themselves or in groups with other women; they should be taught only by their husbands.

3.

The intention that led Olasky to write *The Tragedy of American Compassion* ("I hoped to see welfare transformed, as much as possible, from government monopoly to faith-based diversity") might have well been dismissed as the evangelical impulse of someone operating at a considerable remove from the centrist American political tradition. Yet the book had a certain think-tank imprimatur that caused it to begin percolating through neoconservative circles. *The Tragedy of American Compassion* had been largely written during a year, 1990, that Olasky spent in Washington as a fellow at the Heritage Foundation. The book's central notions bore a reassuring resemblance to arguments already so much a part of the discourse that they had two years before inspired Peggy Noonan to incorporate the "thousand points of light" into the acceptance speech delivered by Governor Bush's father at the 1988 Republican convention. Alfred Regnery, who ultimately published the book, appeared in the acknowledgments, as did Patricia Bozell. Charles Murray, who was at the time writing *The Bell Curve* with Richard J. Herrnstein as a fellow at the American Enterprise Institute, wrote the preface.

The Tragedy of American Compassion was published in 1992, a year when certain key rhetorical assumptions, those having to do with the "moral depredations" of the 1960s and the "moral squalor" of American life since, were already in place. Robert H. Bork, having been sanctified as one of the two living martyrs of the judicial confirmation process, was already handing down the dicta that would shape his 1996 *Slouching Towards Gomorrah: Modern Liberalism and American Decline.*

William J. Bennett was about to publish his first book of moral teachings, *The Book of Virtues*, with *The Moral Compass* and *The Death of Outrage* still in the pipeline. This was a febrile moment, and the characteristically schematic ideas that emerged from it often seemed specifically crafted to support the mood of moral rearmament that was coming to dominate the dialogue. In January 1995, on C-SPAN, Marvin Olasky gave Brian Lamb an instructive precis of the process by which this moment had come to pass: "John Fund of *The Wall Street Journal* read it [*The Tragedy of American Compassion*] and wrote about it and liked it and talked about it with others. Bill Bennett read it and was talking about it. Some other people were, and then it got to the Speaker and he got excited about it and has been talking about it."

"Our models are Alexis de Tocqueville and Marvin Olasky," Newt Gingrich had just told the nation in his first 1995 address as Speaker of the House, apparently having already incorporated into his program the Christmas present William J. Bennett had given him a few weeks before. The "most important book on welfare and social policy in a decade," Bennett himself said about Olasky's book. Three years after the largely unnoticed initial publication of *The Tragedy of American Compassion*, then, its reductive and rather spookily utilitarian thesis, that the government should fund the faithful because faith "works," had become the idea whose time had come, the ultimate weapon in the "values" wars, a super stealth missile with first-strike capability, precisely aimed to simultaneously get welfare out of the system and get religion into it.

By his own account, Olasky wrote the book after comparing the evangelism of nineteenth-century philanthropy to secular welfare efforts, which he believed to be rendered useless by their lack of emphasis on personal responsibility. This belief was confirmed, he wrote, by taking "a first-hand look at contemporary compassion toward the poor" during two days he spent disguised as a beggar in order to visit Washington soup kitchens: "I put on three used T-shirts and two dirty sweaters, equipped myself with a stocking cap and a plastic bag, removed my wedding ring, got lots of dirt on my hands, and walked with the slow shuffle that characterizes the forty-year-old white homeless male of the streets." During his two days (no nights) as a street person, he was offered, he reported (and here we reach the germ of the experiment), "lots of food, lots of pills of various kinds, and lots of offers of clothing and shelter," but never a Bible.

There could never have been much doubt that the parable of the white homeless male in search of a Bible would resonate with George W. Bush. This was a man who not only grew up in Texas and did business in Texas but managed a Texas sports franchise, pretty much rendering him a market-maker in the secular God business. This was a man who, in the course of a primary-season debate, would famously name Jesus Christ as the "political philosopher" he most admires. This was a man who, when the Texas economy went belly-up in the mid-1980s, joined a group of Midland businessmen who met once a week under the guidance of a national group called Community Bible Study, the class format of which includes the twelve-step technique of personal testimony, in this case "seeing the truths of the Bible lived out in the lives of leaders and class members." The participants in Bush's class were "baby boomers, men with young families," a former member told Hanna Rosin of *The Washington Post*. "And we suddenly found ourselves in free fall. So we began to search for an explanation. Maybe we had been too involved with money. Maybe we needed to look inwardly and find new meaning in life."

It was 1993 when Marvin Olasky was first called to meet with Bush, who was at the time shopping for issues with which to defeat the incumbent governor of Texas, Ann Richards. Olasky and Bush, along with Bush adviser Karl Rove, talked for an hour, during which, according to Olasky, Bush "asked questions that went to the heart of issues involving children born out of wedlock and men slowly dying from drug abuse on the streets." Bush did not have occasion to call again on Olasky until 1995, when, as governor, he saw the political potential in taking up the side of a Christian drug program called Teen Challenge, which state regulators had tried to shut down because it refused to comply with certain state regulations, including one that required drug counselors to be trained in conventional anti-addiction techniques. (Conventional anti-addiction techniques in this country are largely based on the twelve-step regime, which carefully refers to an unspecified "Higher Power," or "God as we understand Him." The anti-addiction technique of choice at Teen Challenge was, in the words of its executive director, "Jesus Christ.") Over his next few years as governor, Bush not only made Texas the first state to sanction the redirection of state funds into faith-based programs but virtually dismantled state regulation of such programs, accruing, in the course of this pioneering endeavor, considerable political capital from the religious right. "An opportunity arose for a farsighted governor to take the lead" is how Olasky describes this. "George W. Bush was a natural, both because of his father's earlier interest in the 'thousand points of light' and his own personal, faith-based change in 1986 from heavy drinking at times to abstinence from alcohol."

Olasky was never a full-time Bush adviser, yet his involvement would seem to have been something more than "maybe they met once or twice," the version preferred by those Bush aides made nervous by the enthusiasm with which Olasky airs his less marketable positions, on the role of women, say, or on the necessity of conversion. T. Christian Miller of *The New York Times*, reporting in July 2000 on the campaign's "pattern of distancing Bush from the controversies that have dogged Olasky," quoted a Bush spokesman saying that the two had met only twice, once in 1996 and once in 1999, although the 1993 and 1995 meetings have been extensively documented. "Marvin is an evangelical Christian, and Bush is an evangelical Christian," John J. DiIulio Jr., a Bush adviser, told David Grann by way of suggesting the philosophical distance. "But Bush does not believe that every faith-based program is about religious conversion."

Olasky does believe this, and, on the basis of what Governor Bush himself has said, it would be hard to argue that Bush did not at some level, however unexamined, agree. "When asked why some faith-based groups succeed where secular organizations fail," Olasky wrote of Bush, "he praised programs that help to 'change the person's heart.'" "A person with a changed heart," Olasky quotes Bush as having told him, "is less likely to be addicted to drugs and alcohol. . . . I've had some personal experience with this. As has been reported, I quit drinking. The main reason I quit was because I accepted Jesus Christ into my life in 1986." To accept Jesus Christ as personal savior is pretty much the heart and soul of evangelical conversion (or of being "born again," which both Governor Bush and Vice President Gore claim to be), and incurs the obligation, for evangelical Christians who want to be saved, of converting others, which is to say, in Bush's words, changing the person's heart. The evangelical obligation to convert, the biblical basis for which is Matthew 28:19 ("Go therefore and make disciples of all nations, baptizing them in the name of the Father and of the Son and of the Holy Spirit"), rests on the belief that Bush notoriously expressed to a reporter for the *Austin American-Statesman* in 1993, that those who do not believe in Christ will go to hell. "Bush was giving the orthodox biblical answer," Marvin Olasky later explained to *Salon* on this point. "On the face of it, you have to believe in Christ to go to heaven; Jews don't believe in Christ; therefore, Jews don't go to heaven. So of course there was an uproar."

Olasky was made the head of Bush's policy sub-committee on religion in February 1999, after the two met for a four-hour session during which they and Bush aides hammered out policy with John J. DiIulio Jr., James Q. Wilson, and Robert L. Woodson Sr., the founder of the National Center for Neighborhood Enterprise and one of the people Olasky cites as a formative influence. In an October 1999 *World* column urging conservative Christians not to abandon the political process, Olasky himself described his role as "trying to walk the above talk by giving informal advice to one of the contenders for the G.O.P. nomination," a circumstance that had led him, he explained, to recuse himself from editing *World*'s campaign coverage. By the end of March 2000, however, in the wake of a small media storm over a column he had written for the *Austin American-Statesman* accusing three political commentators who happened to be Jews (David Brooks, William Kristol, and Frank Rich) of favoring John McCain because he lacked Bush's "Christian albatross" and so afforded them "a post-Clinton glow without pushing them to confront their own lives," Olasky downgraded his involvement to "my very minor Bush advising role last year" and declared that, since this involvement was no longer an issue and since Christian conservatives would "clearly favor the Bush position," he was now free to comment on the campaign.

However casually or occasionally delivered, Olasky's message demonstrably locked into certain of the candidate's established preferences, notably those for spinning off the government to the private sector and for taking a firm line with its less productive citizens. "Marvin offers not just a blueprint for government," Bush declared in the foreword he provided for *Compassionate Conservatism*, "but also an inspiring picture of the great resources of decency, caring, and commitment to one another that Americans share." Just how closely Olasky's "blueprint for government" would be followed was made clear on July 22, 1999, when Bush delivered, in Indianapolis, the speech that Olasky describes as the culmination of a process that began with the four-hour February meeting. "First, the ivy cabinet of policy conceptualizers came up with ideas and proposals," he wrote. "Second, Bush's kitchen cabinet of Austin advisers reviewed the proposals and tried to meld them. Third, Governor Bush decided which ones to run with and which to table."

"In every instance where my administration sees a responsibility to help people," Bush promised that day in Indianapolis, "we will look first to faith-based organizations, charities, and community groups that have shown their ability to save and change lives. . . . We will change the laws and regulations that hamper the cooperation of government and private institutions." The stories told that day as illustration of this "ability to save and change lives" now seem familiar, not only because they were so often repeated during the campaign but because they are identical in tone and venue to those told by Marvin Olasky. Bush for example cited the case in Texas of "a young man named James Peterson, who'd embezzled his way into a prison term" and who, as the time approached for his parole hearing, joined InnerChange, the faith-based program through which Olasky and Daniel met the similarly converted "Donnie Gilmore." Offered parole, "James" turned it down, electing to stay in prison "to finish the InnerChange course," a version of whatever happened that Bush seemed both to believe and to construe as a happy ending. "As James put it,

'There is nothing I want more than to be back in the outside world with my daughter Lucy, [but] I realized that this was an opportunity to become a living [witness] for my brothers [in prison] and to the world. I want to stay in prison to complete the transformation [God] has begun in me.'"

Among those present that day in Indianapolis were political reporters from America's three major newspapers, Adam Clymer for *The New York Times*, Terry M. Neal for *The Washington Post*, and Ronald Brownstein from *The Los Angeles Times.* "First major policy speech," their stories would read the next morning. "Most elaborate definition to date of his 'compassionate conservatism' credo." They would have heard the candidate say that federal money should be "devolved," not just to states but to "charities and neighborhood healers." They would have heard the candidate promise that his administration would expand the "role and reach" of such organizations "without changing them or corrupting them": a significant victory for Olasky, since the phrase would open the door to what he calls "theological conservatives," i.e., those whose aim is conversion. They would have heard the candidate, by way of forestalling any possible concern that an "unchanged" (or "uncorrupted") "neighborhood healer" might render "faith" the ultimate means test, offer the by now familiar but empirically ambiguous utilitarian argument. "It works," the candidate had said, and then: "Sometimes our greatest hope is not found in reform. It is found in redemption." That a mainstream American political candidate should make these remarkable statements might have seemed worth reporting, but did not: talk of "redemption" as a political platform had by July 1999 become sufficiently commonplace that neither the word "redemption" nor the words "without changing them or corrupting them" appeared the next day in any of the three major papers.

4.

Jeff Flock, CNN Correspondent: Well, Kyra, we've got our ear to the ground here in Wisconsin, this is Port Washington, north of Milwaukee, as you point out. We are inside the Allen-Edmonds shoe manufacturing plant . . . trying to get a sense [from] undecided voters if they made up their mind based on what they saw yesterday. . . . First of all is . . . the COO of Allen-Edmonds, I have got to ask you, you're on the fence. Have you made up your mind as a result of what you saw last night?

Unidentified Male: Well, I'm still undecided . . .

Flock: Now you tend to the Republican and vote Republican, but at this point, you are still undecided. Al Gore could get your vote.

Unidentified Male: Possibly, yes. . . . Certainly I'm going to listen to the next two debates, and I think not only are the issues important, but also the sincerity of the candidates. . . . Just a whole lot of honesty needs to be brought back into the candidacy.

—CNN *Early Edition*, OCTOBER 4, 2000

This question of the "undecided," or "swing," voter, about whom we have heard so much in recent elections, is interesting. "Scientific" political forecasting, that done not by professional pollsters but by a handful of political scientists around the country, for some months prior to the November 2000 election showed Vice President Gore the probable winner. In May 2000, when Robert G. Kaiser of *The Washington Post* reported on this academic forecasting, the only disagreement among the political scientists to whom he spoke had to do with the point spread by which Gore would win. Thomas M. Holbrook of the University of Wisconsin at Milwaukee gave Gore 59.6 percent, Christopher Wlezien of the University of Houston 56.1 percent, Alan I. Abramowitz of Emory University 53 or 54 percent, and Michael Lewis-Beck of the University of Iowa 56.2 percent. By the end of August 2000, when seven of these academic forecasters (including Robert S. Erickson of Columbia University, James E. Campbell of the University of Buffalo, and Helmut Norpoth of the State University of New York at Stony Brook) presented their forecasts at the annual meeting of the American Political Science Association in Washington, six of the seven had somewhat narrowed but not significantly changed the Gore lead, their August forecasts ranging from a 52.3 to a 55.4 Gore victory. The seventh, Holbrook, citing the record number of Americans who reported themselves satisfied with their personal financial situation, had slightly increased the Gore lead, to 60.3 percent.

This kind of forecasting, which was based on analyzing mathematical models of the thirteen presidential elections since 1948 and of the state of the economy (both actual and perceived) during each of these elections, had in the past proved remarkably accurate. Wlezien's early forecasts were accurate within six-tenths of one percent in 1988 and one-tenth of one percent in 1996. Lewis-Beck's early call on the 1996 election (in collaboration with Charles Tien of Hunter College) was, according to *The Washington Post*, not only closer to the ultimate result than polls conducted immediately before the election (Lewis-Beck and Tien gave Clinton 54.8 percent, the eventual recorded result was 54.7) but also closer, by almost three percentage points, than exit polls conducted while the election was actually in progress. "The outcome of a presidential election can be accurately predicted based on factors that are known well before the official campaign gets underway," Abramowitz told the *Post*. "Despite the time, effort and money devoted to campaigning, there is very little that the candidates can do during September and October to alter the eventual outcome of a presidential election."

Political reporters and operatives are nonetheless dismissive of this academic forecasting, since the models on which it is based, focusing as they do on economic indicators, relentlessly exclude the questions of personality or "positioning" that are seen as key to the "undecided" vote and so dominate discussion of presidential elections. The models largely discount the number of "undecided" answers that are elicited by polling, since, as James E. Campbell noted in *Before the Vote: Forecasting American National Elections*, "the 'socially desirable' answer . . . may be a late decision, both out of a sense of open-mindedness and because one may appear more deliberative in obtaining all possible information about the candidate before deciding how to vote." "Character," on which many polls seem to turn, plays no role in these projections. "Values," although much discussed in focus groups, go unmentioned.

Adam Clymer, covering the Washington meeting of the American Political Science Association for *The New York Times*, characterized the forecasters as "seven visitors [i.e., not Washington insiders] seeking to impose a precision and predictability on political life that even those working in its midst [i.e., the insiders the "visitors" will never be] cannot discern." At a time when conventional polling showed Bush running ahead of Gore by double digits, the Bush pollster Fred Steeper told *The Washington Post* that the academic models would necessarily prove wrong, since none factored in the opinion of voters on the question to which the professionals were at that time giving full focus, that of the country's presumed "decline in moral values."

Steeper said this in May 2000. The kind of polling or focus research that elicits opinions about "moral values" (where the "socially desirable" answer is even more clear than in preference polls) would have been, in May, not much more effective at projecting a November outcome than asking a ouija board. Until the final weeks of a presidential campaign, conventional opinion research has been notoriously unreliable. In May 1988, a not atypical *New York Times*/CBS News poll showed Dukakis leading Vice President Bush by ten points. In June 1992, the Field Institute showed Perot and by then President Bush dividing the bulk of the electoral vote, with Clinton "getting so few that he is currently not a factor." To the professionals of the political process, this indicates not an ambiguity in the research but an exciting volatility, the "horse race" construct, in which the election is seen to turn on the skill or lack of skill with which the candidates and their handlers "send signals," or deploy counters derived from the research.

Governor George W. Bush's acceptance speech at the 2000 Republican convention in Philadelphia was a string of such notational counters, each on the face of it deeply meaningless ("When I act, you will know my reasons. . . . When I speak, you will know my heart") but among which could be embedded such signals as "valuing the life of the unborn," or "We must renew our *values* to restore our *country*." Bush, it was immediately agreed, had sent the right signals, had at once positioned himself to seem, as they were saying on NBC while the confetti was still falling, "a very simple guy—loves his ranch, loves his family" and "also presidential." This instant positive judgment was entirely predictable, a phenomenon that occurs on the last night of every convention, but it was nonetheless seen, by those who made it and by those whose business it was to calibrate it, to significantly change the dynamic of the election. "My view of this process has totally changed," Robert Teeter, the longtime Republican pollster, told *The Washington Post* after the similarly predictable instant positive judgment on the naming of Richard Cheney (Cheney, it was said on CNN, was "one of the governing class") as Governor Bush's running mate. "You used to look for twenty-eight electoral votes or some demographic bloc. Now, the crucial question is how the press and public react in the first forty-eight hours."

That the press and the public might ultimately react in sharply divergent ways seemed not to enter Teeter's analysis, yet we had just lived through a period, that of the events leading up to and following impeachment, during which no political commentator in America failed to express bafflement at the mystery of what was called "the disconnect," which is to say the divergence between what the press thought and what the public thought about President Clinton. "It is impossible to overstate the extent to which the political community felt betrayed by the president and convinced that he would be forced from office," Thomas E. Mann of the Brookings Institution wrote in *Newsday* immediately after the November 1998 congressional elections, the occasion on which the prevailing view of the political community got put to a vote and lost. Mann continued:

> The public, on the other hand, while morally offended by the president's misbehavior and skeptical of the content of his character, has been steadfast in its belief that Clinton's personal failings did not compromise his ability to function successfully as chief executive. Each new public revelation of titillating details served mainly to reinforce their view that the effort to force the president from office was both unwise and, at least in part, politically motivated. This gap between Washington and public opinion had to close before the president's future could be resolved. Now that the election returns are in, we know how that gap will close. The message from the election is crystal-clear: The Washington community will have to accommodate itself to the views of the country.

In April 1999, two months after the Senate tried and acquitted President Clinton on the articles of impeachment brought by the House and three months before Governor George W. Bush would launch his redemption platform in Indianapolis, I happened to hear several prominent Democratic and Republican pollsters and strategists agree that the 2000 election would necessarily turn, in the absence of hard times, on "values." That these specialists in opinion research were hearing a certain number of Americans express concern about their own future and about the future of America seemed clear. What seemed less clear was the source of this concern, or what inchoate insecurity or nostalgia is actually being voiced when respondents address such questions as whether they fear that "this society will become too accepting of behaviors that are bad for people," say, or believe that "a president should set a moral tone for the country."

On the latter point, a 1998 poll conducted by *The Washington Post* in conjunction with Harvard University and the Kaiser Foundation found that fifty percent of those queried did believe the president should set a moral tone and forty-eight percent did not, a statistically insignificant difference but one cited in a later *Post* story bearing the headline "Polls Suggest Public Seeks Moral Leadership in Wake of White House Scandal." When Americans told researchers that they worried about the future of their family or the country, say, or that they did not believe their fellow citizens to be "as honest or moral as they used to be," what they were actually expressing, according to the *Post*, was their "yearning for a moral compass and virtuous leadership," a notion that tallied with what the nation's opinion leaders had been wishing they yearned for all year. Almost a year before the New Hampshire primary, then, the shape the campaign would take had already been settled upon, and it was not a shape that would require the Washington community to accommodate itself to the views of the country: what was concerning Americans, it had been decided, was the shame they had to date failed to recognize.

5.

More than two-thirds of Americans polled by *The Los Angeles Times* in February 1999, immediately after President Clinton was tried and acquitted by the Senate, said that his misconduct had not caused them to lose respect for the office of the presidency. Sixty-eight percent said that they did not want the issue raised in the 2000 presidential campaign. More than three in five said that Republicans pursued impeachment "primarily because they wanted to hurt President Clinton politically." Only one-third, or a number approximately the size of the Republican base, said that Republicans were motivated by concern about the effect of "Clinton's actions on the legal and moral fabric of the country."

The notional conviction that most Americans felt "revulsion" toward the Clinton administration, and the collateral conviction that this was damaging the Gore candidacy, nonetheless remained general, and, as became clear with the addition of Senator Joseph I. Lieberman to the Democratic ticket, would come to warp Gore's own conduct of his campaign. "The fundamentals are in Gore's favor," the political analyst Allan J. Lichtman acknowledged to *The New York Times* in September 2000. "Peace, prosperity, tranquility at home and a united incumbent party. Why has the race even been close? The Clinton scandals." A Republican pollster, Ed Goeas, suggested that Gore was suffering "the after-effect of impeachment. Voters didn't want Republicans to impeach Clinton because they thought it would rock the boat. Now that that is no longer an issue, they are indulging in a second emotion—they didn't want Clinton impeached, but they think what he did was wrong."

The choice of Senator Lieberman was widely construed as Gore's way of transcending this presumed public sentiment, of "sending a message" to the electorate. The actual message that got sent, however, was not to the electorate but to its political class—to that narrow group of those who wrote and spoke and remained fixed in the belief that "the Clinton scandals" constituted a weight that must be shed. Senator Lieberman, who had previously come to the nation's attention as the hedge player who had briefly seized center stage by managing both to denounce the president for "disgraceful" and "immoral" behavior and to vote against his conviction (similarly, he had in 1991 both voiced support for and voted against the confirmation of Clarence Thomas), was not, except to the press, an immediately engaging personality. There were, in those first wobbly steps as a vice-presidential candidate, the frequent references to "private moments of prayer" and to the "miracle" of his nomination. There were the insistent reminders of his own filial devotion, as displayed to the nation during his "only in America moment" at the Democratic convention: "Mom, thank you, I love you and you and I know how proud Pop would be tonight. Yes we do love you, Mom." There was the unsettling way in which he seemed to patronize his running mate, as if insensitive to the possibility that his unsolicited testimonials to Gore's character ("This is a man of courage! He showed it by picking me to be with him!") could suggest that it would otherwise be seen as doubtful.

His speech patterns, grounded as they were in the burden he bore for the rest of us and the personal rewards he had received from God for bearing it, tended to self-congratulation. In his *In Praise of Public Life*, a modest work in which he peculiarly defends his career as a professional politician, he noted that he must "endure the disdain" of those who distrust politicians, that he risks being "sullied by the fight for election," that winning the fight means only stepping "into yet another arena that has turned uglier than before." After his 1988 election to the Senate, he girded himself for the arena that had turned uglier than before by making "private visits to three religious leaders who meant a lot to me, to ask them for their prayers as I began this new chapter of my life." The religious leaders on whom he chose to call, already exhibiting his preference for hedge betting, were the Catholic archbishop of Hartford, an evangelical Protestant minister in Milford, and the Lubavitch rabbi Menachem Schneerson in Brooklyn.

There was, the reader of *In Praise of Public Life* learns, "no single reason" for the failure after sixteen years of his first marriage, and yet he does give reasons, each of which redounds to his credit. The president may have committed "disgraceful" and "immoral" acts, but Senator Lieberman had not, and the suggestion on a call-in radio show that he might have so upset his ex-wife that she had immediately called the show to say that "she knew I had never committed adultery." There had been instead "the fact that I had become much more religiously observant than I was when we met and married." There had been "the demands my political career put on our private life. That is surely one of the great costs and risks of public life."

There were, in the aftermath of Gore's decision to name Lieberman, many dispiriting reiterations of the benefit that would accrue. "Integrity on the Ticket" was the headline on the *Washington Post*'s lead editorial on the morning after the announcement. "A Gore-Lieberman ticket is not going to be associated with bad behavior," Al From of the Democratic Leadership Council told *The New York Times*, which obtained a similar encomium (to the "credibility" that "Mr. Lieberman brings to everything he touches") from the Reverend Jerry Falwell. Senator Lieberman, it was repeatedly said, gave the ticket "moral authority," the most frequently cited source for which was his having "fearlessly spoken out" or "fearlessly acted on his beliefs" to denounce both Clinton and popular culture. Hollywood, he had asserted, "doesn't understand piety." Although Hollywood, like Clinton at the time of his impeachment, might be considered something less than a moving target, there had been a further "fearless" aspect to Lieberman's crusade: just as he had teamed with Lynne Cheney to denounce "political correctness" (another fairly lethargic target), he had teamed with William J. Bennett to decry "the rising tide of sex and violence in our popular culture." This showed, it was said, Lieberman's "independence," his ability to "follow his conscience," which as presented came to seem a kind of golden retriever bounding ever to the right, determined to outrun his master and his ninety-five percent A.D.A. rating. "On issues that cut very close to the bone," Bennett explained to E. J. Dionne Jr., "he's there."

The rather histrionic humility with which Senator Lieberman accepted this nonpartisan admiration served only to further encourage those who wrote and spoke and offered opinions. "In the choice of a single man," Richard Cohen wrote on the *Washington Post*'s op-ed page, ". . . Gore shows he is comfortable with a running mate who was uncomfortable with Clinton's behavior." David Broder mentioned "the moral character he adds. . . . Lieberman embodies and defines the standards by which politicians should be judged." George Will spoke of the "unfeigned revulsion" with which Lieberman had denounced Clinton, and of the way in which that unfeigned revulsion could address "the national longing" to be rid of this president. To the same point, the editorial page of *The New York Times* saw the choice of Lieberman as "a signal that this ticket was moving beyond Mr. Clinton's behavioral—as opposed to his policy—legacy. Mr. Lieberman's authority in this regard derives from his moral bearing, embodied in his criticism of Mr. Clinton's conduct two years ago." Nor was this enthusiasm confined to the editorial and op-ed pages: on page 1 of a single issue, the *Times*, in its own reportorial voice, certified Mr. Lieberman's "moral rectitude," his "seriousness of purpose," his "integrity." He was "untainted." He was "regarded as one of the most upstanding public officials in the nation." He was a "moral compass in the wastelands of politics."

That the ticket would otherwise woefully lack this moral compass, and unless shriven by Senator Lieberman would reap the whirlwind of the assumed national yearning to punish Clinton, was accepted as given, since, for those who wrote and spoke and offered opinions, the furies and yearnings of the nation were necessarily indivisible from the furies and yearnings of its political class. The possibility that the yearnings of the nation might instead be expressed by the occasional actual citizen who managed to penetrate the cloud cover of the coverage seemed not to occur. On the morning of September 4, 2000, in a news-analysis piece headlined "Still Riding Wave, a Confident Gore Heads to Florida for Fall Push," Katharine G. Seelye of the *Times*, flying safely within the cloud cover, reminded readers of what was according to the story line the campaign's "central concern": that "while voters appreciate the good times, there is lingering resentment toward Mr. Clinton over his personal behavior, creating a complex web of emotions that still seems to ensnare Mr. Gore." This story appeared on page A14. Also on page A14, the same morning, in a report on a Gore-Lieberman event at a construction site in downtown Philadelphia, Richard Perez-Pena of the *Times* quoted a twenty-one-year-old electrician whom he had interviewed on the site. "Clinton did a real good job with the economy, and Gore was his V.P.," this actual citizen was reported to have said, "so he's the next best thing to Clinton if we can't have Clinton."

6.

Well, there's nothing wrong with candidates indicating what their faith [or] belief is. It's something else when they begin to put it into the public arena in terms of politics. And then what it starts becoming, as we've heard, Governor Bush this week talked about America being God's country. God created it. . . . Vice-Presidential candidate Cheney talked about [how] tolerance in this country should be the way Jesus Christ taught it. Now, that sounds like preaching from a pulpit. What's starting to happen is campaigning and candidates are beginning to outdo each other as [to] how godly they are and how much God has a part in their life. . . . All of a sudden, this new emphasis on faith and religion in—in—in a campaign that should deal with issues may move us off that experience of two hundred years.

—ABRAHAM H. FOXMAN, ON *This Week*,
SUNDAY, SEPTEMBER 3, 2000

Bill Clinton lowballed it to the White House with his yeomen telling themselves that "It's the economy, stupid," but the winning party has generally been the one that could claim the high moral ground. That's why Joe Lieberman's talk of God, which helps voters forget Bill Clinton's ungodly activity, has been so fruitful for Al Gore.

—MARVIN OLASKY, IN *World*,
SEPTEMBER 23, 2000

This was an election in which there were running for president and vice president on the Democratic ticket two professional politicians, one of whom was born to the game and the other of whom said that he was inspired to play it by the "figures of respect" already on the field, beginning with "the succession of dignified, personable mayors who ran Stamford." There was running for president on the Republican ticket someone whose most successful previous venture was based on his questionable readiness to accept, in the first year of his own father's presidency, a sweetheart ten percent "general partner interest" (aka "promote fee") in the 1989 purchase of the Texas

Rangers by a consortium of investors, an $86 million deal in which the candidate's personal investment was only $606,000. There was running for vice president on the Republican ticket someone who had parlayed his Gulf War credits in the Middle East into a $45.5 million stake in Halliburton, and who thought the thing to say when asked why he did not vote in the 2000 presidential primary in Texas (or for that matter in fourteen of the sixteen elections held while he was a resident of Dallas County) was that he had been focused on "global concerns," just as he had been focused on "other priorities" during the Vietnam years he spent failing to get a doctorate at the University of Wisconsin instead of getting drafted.

The grounds on which any one of the four could be construed as a candidate for the "high moral ground" remain obscure, yet their respective claims to this phantom venue, with Governor Bush and Senator Lieberman on point but Vice President Gore and Mr. Cheney not far behind, had come to dominate the campaign. Each had testified to the centrality of "faith" in his life and in that of the nation. Each had declared his intention to install "faith-based organizations" (by this point so obligatory a part of policy discussions that they were referred to by acronym, "FBOs") in the front lines of what had previously been the nation's social support system. "The Constitution guarantees freedom *of* religion, not freedom *from* religion," one or another of them could rather too frequently be heard saying, appropriating as new a line already familiar during the 1950s debate over adding the clause "under God" to the Pledge of Allegiance. ("It's not constitutional, so don't say it," I recall my grandfather instructing me to that point.) "I believe that faith in itself is sometimes essential to spark a personal transformation," Vice President Gore was already saying in May 1999 in Atlanta. By August 2000, Senator Lieberman was saying in Detroit that America was "moving to a new spiritual awakening," requiring only that we its people "reaffirm our faith and renew the dedication of our nation and ourselves to God and God's purpose."

There is a level at which many Americans simply discount what is said during a political campaign, dismiss it as loose talk. When Senator Lieberman tells us "never to indulge the supposition that morality can be maintained without religion," or when Governor Bush says "our nation is chosen by God," or when Vice President Gore talks about What Would Jesus Do or Mr. Cheney appears on a platform in Kansas City with a succession of athletes attesting to the personal role played in their lives by Jesus Christ and the Gospels, what gets said is often understood as no more than a tactical signal, a "message" sent to a certain constituency, a single fleeting moment in a moving campaign; a marker in a game with no causal connection to policy or legislation as it will actually evolve. Evangelical Christians, a spokesman for the National Association of Evangelicals told *The New York Times* in a discussion of Senator Lieberman's religiosity, "are very happy with everything the senator's been saying." They may well have been, and were meant to be, yet the senator had supported neither of two causes, authorization of student-led prayer or the mandatory posting of the Ten Commandments, recently of urgent interest to the evangelical community. Nor, despite what he has called in reference to abortion his "growing personal anxiety that something very wrong is happening in our country," had his votes on abortion legislation, a crucial evangelical concern, been other than generally pro-choice.

The expressed "personal anxiety that something very wrong is happening in our country," then, was exclusively rhetorical, or loose talk. As such, it could be set aside, understood as a nod to those "pro-family" or "values" voters who, although a minority, have been increasingly encouraged, by the way in which both parties have deliberately narrowed campaign dialogue to issues that concern those voters, to decide our elections. There is considerable evidence that this narrowing, which tends to alienate younger voters, has already had a deleterious effect on the electoral process. In the 1996 presidential election, the president of the ACLU Foundation of Southern California pointed out in *The Los Angeles Times*, the number of voters aged eighteen to twenty-one dropped from thirty-eight to thirty-one percent and the number of those aged twenty-one to twenty-four dropped from forty-five to thirty-three percent. In the 1998 congressional elections, the turnout in these age groups was less than seventeen percent, roughly half that of older voters. The competitive pieties of the 2000 campaign are not calibrated to reverse this estrangement of the young: in *What's God Got to Do with the American Experiment?*, a collection of studies and essays compiled under the auspices of the Brookings Institution, Richard N. Ostling noted that members of the generation now approaching voting age, to a greater extent than members of any previous generation, are "thoroughly detached from traditional Christian concepts . . . do not believe Jesus is the unique savior of mankind, do not read the Bible as God's word, and do not accept the idea of moral absolutes."

The September Sunday morning on which Abraham H. Foxman suggested to Cokie Roberts and the Reverend Pat Robertson that an excessive campaign emphasis on faith could "move us off that experience of two hundred years" ("So there's a tiny, tiny minority who consider themselves atheist," Pat Robertson said, "and you can't surrender the deeply held religious beliefs of the entire majority to please some tiny minority") followed several days of op-ed and talk-show debate prompted by the letter, making the same point, that Mr. Foxman had sent to Senator Lieberman after the latter's "new spiritual awakening" event in Detroit. In the course of this debate, the appropriate role of religion in American life had been discussed at some length. It had been widely agreed that the establishment clause of the First Amendment had been, to the extent that it had ensured the disestablishment of the Anglican or Episcopal Church, a good idea. It had also been widely agreed that the aim of the Founders had been not "atheism" (the straw man from the Scopes trial curiously back among us) but "diversity of faith." There had been areas of disagreement, hotly argued but narrow. Some held that one's faith was best practiced in private, others that faith practiced in private was no faith at all; a difference, as differences go, not entirely unlike the 1844 Philadelphia riot in which six people were killed over the issue of which version of the Ten Commandments should be posted in public schools.

Yet virtually all of the many positions and postures taken in this debate rested on a single and largely unchallenged assumption, that religion, whether public or private, was at the heart of the American experience, and that the "experience of two hundred years" to which Mr. Foxman referred had been in fact a record of serial awakenings, the eventual rightful end of which, once the obstructive element increasingly referred to as "the ACLU" had been shown the light, would be what both presidential candidates were now calling the "personal transformation" of the nation's citizens. "I need my civil liberties friends to tell me again the mortal danger of prayer—of religion generally—in public places," William Raspberry wrote in *The Washington Post.* "I keep forgetting it." "Separation between church and state never meant that religion had no place in American life," E. J. Dionne Jr. wrote in the *Post.* "Remember, this is a nation that still stamps 'In God We Trust' on its currency." The fact that the words "In God We Trust" were added to American currency during the same recent period and for the same political reason that the words "under God" were added to the Pledge of Allegiance, home-front ammunition in the Eisenhower administration's cold war arsenal, had vanished (like the fact that the number of Americans who belonged to churches during the American Revolution constituted only seventeen percent of the population) from the collective memory stream. "I confess," Dionne also wrote, "I love what Joe Lieberman is doing to our national debate about religion and public life":

> Lieberman is not the first politician to say how important faith is to our democracy. President Dwight Eisenhower offered the nation this notable sentiment: "Our government makes no sense unless it is founded on a deeply felt religious belief—and I don't care what it is." Today's discussion about religion and politics is much more serious than it was in the "I don't care what it is" past memorialized by Eisenhower. That's what makes so many people uncomfortable.

This was a meaningful shift in the national political dialogue. Politics, it had been until recently understood, is push and pull, give and take, the art of the possible, an essentially pragmatic process by which the differing needs and rights of the nation's citizens get balanced and to some degree met. The insertion into this process of a claim to faith, or to "the high moral ground," it also had been until recently understood, is perilous, permissible if at all only at moments of such urgent gravity as to warrant its inherent danger, which is that the needs and rights of some citizens might be overridden to accommodate the needs and rights of those holding the high ground. This was not such a moment in American life. The nation was not at war. A majority of its citizens seemed to understand that the demonstration of "full remorse" recently demanded of its president would prove less personally meaningful to their families than the skill or lack of skill with which he guided them through the rapids of the global economy.

The possible "legacy" of that president was popularly discussed in negative terms, as the redeeming grail he had hoped for and lost, but on any reasonable scale his legacy was already sizable: the country he would hand over to either Governor Bush or Vice President Gore was one in which median household income had reached an all-time high, the unemployment rate was at its lowest point in three decades, the rate of violent crime was down, and the digital national-debt clock in Manhattan was running, until its creator allowed that the device had outlived its effectiveness and stopped it, backward. It had been Clinton's "legacy," in short, to create the very conditions that had early on led the academic forecasters to call a presidential victory by the incumbent party the most probable outcome of the November 2000 election.

Yet so thin was the air on the high moral ground that none of this was seen as relevant, not even by the candidate who might have seemed poised to benefit from it. What had been for the past several decades the origin myth of the neoconservative right had become, in part because it so uniquely filled the need of the political class to explain its own estrangement from the electorate, the official story, shared by all participants in the process: America, in this apocalyptic telling, had been from its inception until the 1960s a deeply religious nation. During the 1960s, through the efforts of what Robert H. Bork called "the 'intellectual' class and that class's enforcement arm, the judiciary, headed by the Supreme Court of the United States," the nation and its citizens had been inexplicably and destructively "secularized," and were accordingly in need of "transformation," of "moral and intellectual rearmament," of "renewed respect for moral authority." In a country already so increasingly steeped in evangelical teaching that a significant number of its citizens had come to believe that "God created man pretty much in his present form at one time within the last ten thousand years" (forty-seven percent of Americans surveyed by Gallup in 1991 said they believed in such a fell swoop, or "recent special creation"), those who wrote and spoke were arguing about how the nation's political system could best revive those religious values allegedly destroyed (in an interestingly similar fell swoop) during the 1960s.

The delusionary notion that such a revival was now in progress, and would soon prove the correctness of the political class on the Clinton issue, is what lent the 2000 campaign its peculiar, and for the Democratic candidate its dangerous, distance from the electorate. President Clinton may have "escaped conviction," Marvin Olasky wrote in the preface to the most recent edition of *The American Leadership Tradition*, but was nonetheless "convicted in the court of public opinion." The electorate, he wrote, would no longer accept "an anything-goes moral vision." Accordingly, the 2000 election was one in which "the populace seemed to want the next president to be someone who would not disgrace the Oval Office, and that desire gave hope to those who want to revive a tradition of moral leadership."

The logic here, and it was the same logic that surfaced in response to the Lieberman nomination, was that of the origin myth, in which "the populace," once warned, could yet cast out its wicked allegiance to its disgraced leader and be saved before the final Rapture. This fable had been adjusted and trimmed with each retelling, yet one element, the disgraced leader, remained fixed, the rock on which the Bush campaign might have foundered early had the Gore campaign itself, in search of the chimerical "undecided" voter, not rushed to enter the fable's fatal eddy. The distinct possibility that an entire generation of younger voters might see no point in choosing between two candidates retelling the same remote story could benefit only one campaign, the Republican, and the failure of the Democratic campaign to recognize this could yet neutralize the advantage of the legacy it has worked so assiduously to disavow.

FIXED IDEAS

America Since 9.11

1

SEVEN DAYS AFTER September 11, 2001, I left New York to do two weeks of book promotion, under other circumstances a predictable kind of trip. You fly into one city or another, you do half an hour on local NPR, you do a few minutes on drive-time radio, you do an "event," a talk or a reading or an onstage discussion. You sign books, you take questions from the audience. You go back to the hotel, order a club sandwich from room service, and leave a 5 AM call with the desk, so that in the morning you can go back to the airport and fly to the next city. During the week between September 11 and the Wednesday morning when I went to Kennedy to get on the plane, none of these commonplace aspects of publishing a book seemed promising or even appropriate things to be doing. But—like most of us who were in New York that week—I was in a kind of protective coma, sleepwalking through a schedule made when planning had still seemed possible. In fact I was protecting myself so successfully that I had no idea how raw we all were until that first night, in San Francisco, when I was handed a book onstage and asked to read a few marked lines from an essay about New York I had written in 1967.

Later I remembered thinking: 1967, no problem, no land mines there.

I put on my glasses. I began to read.

"New York was no mere city," the marked lines began. "It was instead an infinitely romantic notion, the mysterious nexus of all love and money and power, the shining and perishable dream itself."

I hit the word "perishable" and I could not say it.

I found myself onstage at the Herbst Theater in San Francisco unable to finish reading the passage, unable to speak at all for what must have been thirty seconds. All I can say about the rest of that evening, and about the two weeks that followed, is that they turned out to be nothing I had expected, nothing I had ever before experienced, an extraordinarily open kind of traveling dialogue, an encounter with an America apparently immune to conventional wisdom. The book I was making the trip to talk about was *Political Fictions*, a series of pieces I had written for *The New York Review* about the American political process from the 1988 through the 2000 presidential elections. These people to whom I was listening—in San Francisco and Los Angeles and Portland and Seattle—were making connections I had not yet in my numbed condition thought to make: connections between that political process and what had happened on September 11, connections between our political life and the shape our reaction would take and was in fact already taking.

These people recognized that even then, within days after the planes hit, there was a good deal of opportunistic ground being seized under cover of the clearly urgent need for increased security. These people recognized even then, with flames still visible in lower Manhattan, that the words "bipartisanship" and "national unity" had come to mean acquiescence to the administration's preexisting agenda—for example the imperative for further tax cuts, the necessity for Arctic drilling, the systematic elimination of regulatory and union protections, even the funding for the missile shield—as if we had somehow missed noticing the recent demonstration of how limited, given a few box cutters and the willingness to die, superior technology can be.

These people understood that when Judy Woodruff, on the evening the President first addressed the nation, started talking on CNN about what "a couple of Democratic consultants" had told her about how the President would be needing to position himself, Washington was still doing business as usual. They understood that when the political analyst William Schneider spoke the same night about how the President had "found his vision thing," about how "this won't be the Bush economy any more, it'll be the Osama bin Laden economy," Washington was still talking about the protection and perpetuation of its own interests.

These people got it.

They didn't like it.

They stood up in public and they talked about it.

Only when I got back to New York did I find that people, if they got it, had stopped talking about it. I came in from Kennedy to find American flags flying all over the Upper East

Side, at least as far north as 96th Street, flags that had not been there in the first week after the fact. I say "at least as far north as 96th Street" because a few days later, driving down from Washington Heights past the big projects that would provide at least some of the manpower for the "war on terror" that the President had declared—as if terror were a state and not a technique—I saw very few flags: at most, between 168th Street and 96th Street, perhaps a half-dozen. There were that many flags on my building alone. Three at each of the two entrances. I did not interpret this as an absence of feeling for the country above 96th Street. I interpreted it as an absence of trust in the efficacy of rhetorical gestures.

There was much about this return to New York that I had not expected. I had expected to find the annihilating economy of the event—the way in which it had concentrated the complicated arrangements and misarrangements of the last century into a single irreducible image—being explored, made legible. On the contrary, I found that what had happened was being processed, obscured, systematically leached of history and so of meaning, finally rendered less readable than it had seemed on the morning it happened. As if overnight, the irreconcilable event had been made manageable, reduced to the sentimental, to protective talismans, totems, garlands of garlic, repeated pieties that would come to seem in some ways as destructive as the event itself. We now had "the loved ones," we had "the families," we had "the heroes."

In fact it was in the reflexive repetition of the word "hero" that we began to hear what would become in the year that followed an entrenched preference for ignoring the meaning of the event in favor of an impenetrably flattening celebration of its victims, and a troublingly belligerent idealization of historical ignorance. "Taste" and "sensitivity," it was repeatedly suggested, demanded that we not examine what happened. Images of the intact towers were already being removed from advertising, as if we might conveniently forget they had been there. The Roundabout Theatre had canceled a revival of Stephen Sondheim's *Assassins*, on the grounds that it was "not an appropriate time" to ask audiences "to think critically about various aspects of the American experience." The McCarter

Theatre at Princeton had canceled a production of Richard Nelson's *The Vienna Notes*, which involves a terrorist act, saying that "it would be insensitive of us to present the play at this moment in our history."

I found in New York that "the death of irony" had already been declared, repeatedly, and curiously, since irony had been declared dead at the precise moment—given that the gravity of September 11 derived specifically from its designed implosion of historical ironies—when we might have seemed most in need of it. "One good thing could come from this horror: it could spell the end of the age of irony," Roger Rosenblatt wrote within days of the event in *Time*, a thought, or not a thought, destined to be frequently echoed but never explicated. Similarly, I found that "the death of postmodernism" had also been declared. ("It seemed bizarre that events so serious would be linked causally with a rarified form of academic talk," Stanley Fish wrote after receiving a call from a reporter asking if September 11 meant the end of postmodernist relativism. "But in the days that followed, a growing number of commentators played serious variations on the same theme: that the ideas foisted upon us by postmodern intellectuals have weakened the country's resolve.") "Postmodernism" was henceforth to be replaced by "moral clarity," and those who persisted in the decadent insistence that the one did not necessarily cancel out the other would be subjected to what William J. Bennett would call—in *Why We Fight: Moral Clarity and the War on Terrorism*—"a vast relearning," "the reinstatement of a thorough and honest study of our history, undistorted by the lens of political correctness and pseudosophisticated relativism."

I found in New York, in other words, that the entire event had been seized—even as the less nimble among us were still trying to assimilate it—to stake new ground in old domestic wars. There was the frequent deployment of the phrase "the Blame America Firsters," or "the Blame America First crowd," the wearying enthusiasm for excoriating anyone who suggested that it could be useful to bring at least a minimal degree of historical reference to bear on the event. There was the adroit introduction of convenient straw men. There was Christopher Hitchens, engaging in a dialogue with Noam Chomsky, giving himself the opportunity to generalize whatever got said into "the liberal-left tendency to 'rationalize' the aggression of September 11." There was Donald Kagan at Yale, dismissing his colleague Paul Kennedy as "a classic case of blaming the victim," because the latter had asked his students to try to imagine what resentments they might harbor if America were small and the world dominated by a unified Arab-Muslim state. There was Andrew Sullivan, warning on his Web site that while the American heartland was ready for war, the "decadent left in its enclaves on the coasts" could well mount "what amounts to a fifth column."

There was the open season on Susan Sontag—on a single page of a single issue of *The Weekly Standard* that October she was accused of "unusual stupidity," of "moral vacuity," and of "sheer tastelessness"—all for three paragraphs in which she said, in closing, that "a few shreds of historical awareness might help us understand what has just happened, and what may continue to happen"; in other words that events have histories, political life has consequences, and the people who led this country and the people who wrote and spoke about the way this country was led were guilty of trying to infantilize its citizens if they continued to pretend otherwise.

Inquiry into the nature of the enemy we faced, in other words, was to be interpreted as sympathy for that enemy. The final allowable word on those who attacked us was to be that they were "evildoers," or "wrongdoers," peculiar constructions which served to suggest that those who used them were transmitting messages from some ultimate authority. This was a year in which it would come to seem as if we had been plunged at one fell stroke into a pre-modern world. The possibilities of the Enlightenment vanished. We had suddenly been asked to accept—and were in fact accepting—a kind of reasoning so extremely fragile that it might have been based on the promised return of the cargo gods.

I recall, early on, after John Ashcroft and Condoleezza Rice warned the networks not to air the bin Laden tapes because he could be "passing information," heated debate about the First Amendment implications of this warning—as if there were even any possible point to the warning, as if we had all forgotten that our enemies as well as we lived in a world where information gets passed in more efficient ways. A year later, we were still looking for omens, portents, the supernatural manifestations of good or evil. Pathetic fallacy was everywhere. The presence of rain at a memorial for fallen firefighters was gravely reported as evidence that "even the sky cried." The presence of wind during a memorial at the site was interpreted as another such sign, the spirit of the dead rising up from the dust.

This was a year when Rear Admiral John Stufflebeem, deputy director of operations for the Joint Chiefs of Staff, would say at a Pentagon briefing that he had been "a bit surprised" by the disinclination of the Taliban to accept the "inevitability" of their own defeat. It seemed that Admiral Stufflebeem, along with many other people in Washington, had expected the Taliban to just give up. "The more that I look into it," he said at this briefing, "and study it from the Taliban perspective, they don't see the world the same way we do." It was a year when the publisher of *The Sacramento Bee*, speaking at the midyear commencement of California State University, Sacramento, would be forced off the stage of the Arco Arena for suggesting that because of the "validity" and "need" for increased security we would be called upon to examine to what degree we might be "willing to compromise our civil liberties in the name of security." Here was the local verdict on this aborted speech, as expressed in one of many outraged letters to the editor of the *Bee*:

> It was totally and completely inappropriate for her to use this opportunity to speak about civil liberties, military tribunals, terrorist attacks, etc. She should have prepared a speech about the accomplishments that so many of us had just completed, and the future opportunities that await us.

In case you think that's a Sacramento story, it's not.

Because this was also a year when one of the student speakers at the 2002 Harvard commencement, Zayed Yasin, a twenty-two-year-old Muslim raised in a Boston suburb by his Bangladeshi father and Irish-American mother, would be caught in a swarm of protests provoked by the announced title of his talk, which was "My American Jihad." In fact the speech itself, which he had not yet delivered, fell safely within the commencement-address convention: its intention, Mr. Yasin told *The New York Times*, was to reclaim the original meaning of "jihad" as struggle on behalf of a principle, and to use it to rally his classmates in the fight against social injustice. Such use of "jihad" was not in this country previously uncharted territory: the Democratic pollster Daniel Yankelovich had only a few months before attempted to define the core values that animated what he called "the American jihad"—separation of church and state, the value placed on diversity, and equality of opportunity. In view of the protests, however, Mr. Yasin was encouraged by Harvard faculty members to change his title. He did change it. He called his talk "Of Faith and Citizenship." This mollified some, but not all. "I don't think it belonged here today," one Harvard parent told *The Washington Post*. "Why bring it up when today should be a day of joy?"

This would in fact be a year when it was to become increasingly harder to know who was infantilizing who.

2

California Monthly, the alumni magazine for the University of California at Berkeley, published in its November 2002 issue an interview with a member of the university's political science faculty, Steven Weber, who is the director of the MacArthur Program on Multilateral Governance at Berkeley's Institute of International Studies and a consultant on risk analysis to both the State Department and such private-sector firms as Shell Oil. It so happened that Mr. Weber was in New York on September 11, 2001, and for the week that followed. "I spent a lot of time talking to people, watching what they were doing, and listening to what they were saying to each other," he told the interviewer:

> The first thing you noticed was in the bookstores. On September 12, the shelves were emptied of books on Islam, on American foreign policy, on Iraq, on Afghanistan. There was a substantive discussion about what it is about the nature of the American presence in the world that created a situation in which movements like al-Qaeda can thrive and prosper. I thought that was a very promising sign.
>
> But that discussion got short-circuited. Sometime in late October, early November 2001, the tone of that discussion switched, and it became: What's wrong with the Islamic world that it failed to produce democracy, science, education, its own enlightenment, and created societies that breed terror?

The interviewer asked him what he thought had changed the discussion. "I don't know," he said, "but I will say that it's a long-term failure of the political leadership, the intelligentsia, and the media in this country that we didn't take the discussion that was forming in late September and try to move it forward in a constructive way."

I was struck by this, since it so coincided with my own impression. Most of us saw that discussion short-circuited, and most of us have some sense of how and why it became a discussion with nowhere to go. One reason, among others, runs back sixty years, through every administration since Franklin Roosevelt's. Roosevelt was the first American president who tried to grapple with the problems inherent in securing Palestine as a Jewish state. It was also Roosevelt who laid the groundwork for our relationship with the Saudis. There was an inherent contradiction here, and it was Roosevelt, perhaps the most adroit political animal ever made, who instinctively devised the approach adopted by the administrations that followed his: Stall. Keep the options open. Make certain promises in public, and conflicting ones in private. This was always a high-risk business, and for a while the rewards seemed commensurate: we got the oil for helping the Saudis, we got the moral credit for helping the Israelis, and, for helping both, we enjoyed the continuing business that accrued to an American defense industry significantly based on arming all sides.

Consider the range of possibilities for contradiction.

Sixty years of making promises we had no way of keeping without breaking the promises we'd already made.

Sixty years of long-term conflicting commitments, made in secret and in many cases for short-term political reasons.

Sixty years that tend to demystify the question of why we have become unable to discuss our relationship with the current government of Israel.

Whether the actions taken by that government constitute self-defense or a particularly inclusive form of self-immolation remains an open question. The question of course has a history, a background involving many complicit state and non-state actors and going back most recently to, but by no means beginning with, the breakup of the Ottoman Empire. This open question, and its history, are discussed rationally and with considerable intellectual subtlety in Jerusalem and Tel Aviv, as anyone who reads Amos Elon or Avishai Margalit in *The New York Review* or even occasionally sees *Ha'aretz* on-line is well aware. Where the question is not discussed rationally—where in fact the question is rarely discussed at all, since so few of us are willing to see our evenings turn toxic—is in New York and Washington and in those academic venues where the attitudes and apprehensions of New York and Washington have taken hold. The president of Harvard recently warned that criticisms of the current government of Israel could be construed as "anti-Semitic in their effect if not their intent."

The very question of the US relationship with Israel, in other words, has come to be seen—at Harvard as well as in New York and Washington—as unraisable, potentially lethal, the conversational equivalent of an unclaimed bag on a bus. We take cover. We wait for the entire subject to be defused, safely insulated behind baffles of invective and counterinvective. Many opinions are expressed. Few are allowed to develop. Even fewer change.

We have come in this country to tolerate many such fixed opinions, or national pieties, each with its own baffles of invective and counterinvective, of euphemism and downright misstatement, its own screen that slides into place whenever actual discussion threatens to surface. We have for example allowed American biological research to fall behind that in countries where stem cell programs are not confused with "cloning" and "abortion on demand," countries in other words where rationality is not held hostage to the posturing of the political process. We have allowed all rhetorical stops to be pulled out on non-issues, for example when the federal appeals court's Ninth Circuit ruled the words "under God" an unconstitutional addition to the Pledge of Allegiance. The Pledge was written in 1892 by a cousin of Edward Bellamy's, Francis Bellamy, a socialist Baptist minister who the year before had been pressured to give up his church because of the socialist thrust of his sermons. The clause "under God" was added in 1954 to distinguish the United States from the atheistic Soviet Union.

"Ridiculous" was the word from the White House about the ruling declaring the clause unconstitutional. "Junk justice," Governor Pataki said. "Just nuts," Senator Daschle said. "Doesn't make good sense to me," Representative Gephardt said. There was on this point a genuinely bipartisan rush to act out the extent of the judicial insult, the affront to all Americans, the outrage to the memory of the heroes of September 11. After the June 2002 ruling, members of the House met on the Capitol steps to recite the Pledge—needless to say the "under God" version—while the Senate interrupted debate on a defense bill to pass, unanimously, a resolution condemning the Ninth Circuit decision.

These were, some of them, the same elected representatives who had been quick to locate certain upside aspects to September 11. The events could offer, it was almost immediately perceived, an entirely new frame in which to present school prayer and the constitutional amendment to ban flag burning. To the latter point, an Iowa congressman running unsuccessfully for the Senate, Greg Ganske, marked Flag Day by posting a reminder on his Web site that his opponent, Senator Tom Harkin, who had spent five years during the Vietnam War as a Navy pilot, had in 1995 opposed the flag-burning amendment. "After the tragic events of September 11," the posting read, "America has a renewed sense of patriotism and a renewed appreciation for our American flag. Unfortunately, not everyone agrees." To the school prayer point, according to *The New York Times*, a number of politicians were maximizing the moment by challenging restrictions on school prayer established by courts over the past four decades. "Post–September 11," the *Times* was told by Richard D. Land, president of the Ethics and Religious Liberty Commission of the Southern Baptist Convention, "the secularists are going to have a harder time making their case."

One footnote on the Pledge issue, and the extent to which it intersects with the case the secularists are going to have a harder time making: a significant number of Americans now recite the Pledge with another new clause, which they hope to see made permanent by legislation. After the words "with liberty and justice for all," they add "born and unborn."

All of these issues or non-issues are, as they say, just politics, markers in a game. The flag-burning amendment is just politics, the school prayer issue is just politics—a bone to the Republican base on the Christian right and a way to beat up on the judiciary, red meat for the "Reagan Democrats" or "swing voters" who are increasingly seen as the base for both parties. The prohibition on the creation of new cell lines from discarded embryos that constituted the President's "compromise" on the stem cell question is politics. The fact that Israel has become the fulcrum of our foreign policy is politics. When it comes to any one of these phenomena that we dismiss as "politics," we tend to forgive, or at least overlook, the absence of logic or sense. We tell ourselves that this is the essential give and take of democracy, we tell ourselves that our elected representatives are doing the necessary work of creating consensus. We try to convince ourselves that somewhere, beneath the posturing, there is a hidden logic, there are minds at work, there is someone actually thinking out the future of the country beyond the 2004 election.

These would be comforting notions were they easier to maintain. In fact we have created a political process in which "consensus" is the last thing the professionals want or need, a process that works precisely by turning the angers and fears and energy of the few—that handful of voters who can be driven by the fixed aspect of their own opinions—against the rest of the country. During the past decade—through the several years of the impeachment process and through the denouement of the 2000 election—we had seen secular democracy itself put up for grabs in this country, and the response to September 11 could not have encouraged us to think that the matter was in any way settled.

We had seen the general acquiescence in whatever was presented as imperative by the administration. We had seen the persistent suggestions that anyone who expressed reservations about detentions, say, or military tribunals, was at some level "against" America. (As in the presidential formulation "you're either with us or you're with the terrorists.") We had seen, most importantly, the insistent use of September 11 to justify the reconception of America's correct role in the world as one of initiating and waging virtually perpetual war. And we had seen, buttressing this reconception, the demand that we interpret the war in Afghanistan as a decisive victory over al-Qaeda, the Taliban, and radical fundamentalism in general.

This was despite repeated al-Qaeda-linked explosions throughout Southeast Asia.

Despite continuing arson and rocket attacks on girls' schools in Afghanistan.

And despite the fact that the chairman of the Joint Chiefs said in November 2002 at the Brookings Institution that we had lost momentum in Afghanistan because the Taliban and al-Qaeda had been quicker to adapt to US tactics than the US had been to theirs.

3

In 1988, a few weeks after George W. Bush's father was elected president, I wrote a post-election note for *The New York Review* about a trip the senior Bush had made to Israel and Jordan in 1986, when he was still vice-president. He had his own camera crew with him in Israel, but not in Jordan, since, as an official explained to the *Los Angeles Times*, there was "nothing to be gained from showing him schmoozing with Arabs." Still, the Bush advance team in Amman had devoted considerable attention to crafting visuals for the traveling press. Members of the advance team had requested, for example, that the Jordanian army marching band change its uniforms from white to red. They had requested that the Jordanians, who did not have enough helicopters to transport Bush's traveling press corps, borrow the necessary helicopters to do so from the Israeli air force. In an effort to assure the color of live military action as a backdrop for the vice-president, they had asked the Jordanians to stage maneuvers at a sensitive location overlooking Israel and the Golan Heights. They had asked the Jordanians to raise, over the Jordanian base there, the American flag. They had asked that Bush be photographed studying, through binoculars, "enemy territory," a shot ultimately vetoed by the State Department, since the "enemy territory" at hand was Israel. They had also asked, possibly the most arresting detail, that, at every stop on the itinerary, camels be present.

"This is in fact the kind of story we expect to hear about our elected officials," I wrote in 1988:

> We not only expect them to use other nations as changeable scrims in the theater of domestic politics but encourage them to do so. After the April 1961 failure of the Bay of Pigs, John Kennedy's approval rating was four points higher than it had been in March. After the 1965 intervention in the Dominican Republic, Lyndon Johnson's approval rating rose six points. After the 1983 invasion of Grenada, Ronald Reagan's approval rating rose four points, and what was that winter referred to in Washington as "Lebanon"—the sending of American marines into Beirut, the

killing of 241, and the subsequent pullout—was, in the afterglow of this certified success in the Caribbean, largely forgotten.

That was 1988. Fourteen years later, we were again watching the scrims being changed, but in a theater we did not own. The Middle East was not Grenada. It was not the Dominican Republic. It was not, as they used to say in Washington about the Caribbean, "our lake." It was nitroglycerin, an unstable part of the world in which we had managed to make few friends and many enemies. And yet, all through the summer of 2002, the inevitability of going to war with Iraq was accepted as if predestined. The "when" had already been settled. "Time is getting short," *The New York Times* had warned us in July, "for decisions that have to be made if the goal is to take action early next year, before the presidential election cycle intrudes." That last clause bore study.

"Before the presidential election cycle intrudes." In case the priorities were still unclear.

The "why" had also been settled. The President had identified Saddam Hussein as one of the evildoers. Yes, there were questions about whether the evildoer in question had the weapons we feared he had, and yes, there were questions about whether he would use them if he did have them, and yes, there were questions about whether attacking Iraq might not in fact ensure that he would use them. But to ask those questions was sissy, not muscular, because the President had said we were going to do it and the President, if he were to back down, risked losing the points he got on the muscular "moral clarity" front.

"I made up my mind," he had said in April, "that Saddam needs to go." This was one of many curious, almost petulant statements offered in lieu of actually presenting a case. I've made up my mind, I've said in speech after speech, I've made myself clear. The repeated statements became their own reason: "Given all we have said as a leading world power about the necessity for regime change in Iraq," James R. Schlesinger, who is now a member of Richard Perle's Defense Policy Board, told *The Washington Post* in July, "our credibility would be badly damaged if that regime change did not take place."

There was of course, for better or for worse, a theory, or a fixed idea, behind these pronouncements from the President—actually not so much behind them as coinciding with them, dovetailing in a way that made it possible for many to suggest that the President was actually in on the thinking. The theory, or fixed idea, which not only predated September 11 but went back to the Reagan administration and its heady dreams of rollback, had already been employed to provide a rationale for the President's tendency to exhibit a certain truculence toward those who were not Americans. Within the theory, any such truculence could be inflated into "The Bush Doctrine," or "The New American Unilateralism." The theory was this: the collapse of the Soviet Union had opened the door to the inevitability of American preeminence, a mantle of beneficent power that all nations except rogue nations—whatever they might say on the subject—were yearning for us to assume. "We run a uniquely benign imperium," Charles Krauthammer had written in celebration of this point in a June 2001 issue of *The Weekly Standard*. "This is not mere self-congratulation; it is a fact manifest in the way others welcome our power."

Given this fixed idea, as if in a dream from which there is no waking, and given the correlative dream notion that an American president, Ronald Reagan, had himself caused the collapse of the Soviet Union with a specific magical incantation, the "Evil Empire" speech, the need to bring our force for good to bear on the Middle East could only become an imperative. By June 2002, Jim Hoagland was noting in *The Washington Post* that there was a growing acceptance at the White House of the need for an overwhelming US invasion force that will remain on the ground in Iraq for several years. The US presence will serve as the linchpin for democratic transformation of a major Arab country that can be a model for the region. A new Iraq would also help provide greater energy security for Americans.

A few weeks later in the *Post*, Michael Kelly was sketching an even rosier outcome, based on his eccentric reading of the generation now coming of age in the Middle East as a population poised by history to see the United States not as its enemy but as its "natural liberator." "It is right to think that we are living in a hinge moment in history," he wrote, and then argued against those who believe that the moment is not necessarily ours to control. "But it is wrong to think that the large forces of this moment act on the hinge to shut the door against American interests." The contrary may be true, he wrote, if only we take the next step, which is "to destroy the regime of Saddam Hussein and liberate the people of Iraq." This will be, he said, "when history really begins to turn on its hinge."

It so happened that I was traveling around the country again recently, talking and listening to people in St. Louis and Columbia and Philadelphia and San Diego and Los Angeles and San Francisco and Pittsburgh and Boston. I heard very few of the fixed ideas about America's correct role in the world that had come to dominate the dialogue in New York and Washington. I encountered many people who believed there was still what we had come to call a disconnect between the government and the citizens. I did not encounter conviction that going to war with Iraq would result in a democratic transformation of the Middle East. Most people seemed resigned to the prospect that we would nonetheless go to war with Iraq. Many mentioned a sense of "inevitability," or "dread." A few mentioned August 1914, and its similar sense of an irreversible drift toward something that would not work out well. Several mentioned Vietnam, and the similar bright hopefulness of those who had seen yet another part of the world as a blackboard on which to demonstrate their own superior plays. A few said that had they lost relatives on September 11, which they had not, they would be deeply angered at having those deaths cheapened by being put to use to justify this new war. They did not understand what this new war was about, but they knew it wasn't about that promising but never quite substantiated meeting in Prague between Iraqi intelligence and Mohamed Atta. They did not want to believe that it was about oil. Nor did they want to believe that it was about domestic politics. If I had to characterize a common attitude among them I would call it waiting to see. At a remove.

Like most of them, I no longer remembered all the arguments and inconsistencies and downright contradictions of the summer and early fall. I did remember one thing: a sequence of reports. It was June 1 when the President announced, in a commencement address at West Point, that the United

States military would henceforth act not defensively but preemptively against terrorists and hostile states in possession of chemical, biological, or nuclear weapons. It was June 6 when the secretary of state advised NATO in Brussels that NATO could no longer wait for "absolute proof" of such possession before taking action. It was June 10 when Thomas E. Ricks and Vernon Loeb reported in *The Washington Post* that under this new doctrine, according to Pentagon officials, the United States would consider using high-yield nuclear weapons on a first-strike basis. The use of such weapons would be reserved, according to these officials, for deployment "against biological weapons that can be best destroyed by sustained exposure to the high heat of a nuclear blast." Some bunkers in Iraq, the *Post* was told by Stephen M. Younger, the director of the Defense Department's Defense Threat Reduction Agency, are in fact "so incredibly hard" that "they do require high-yield nuclear weapons."

I never saw this mentioned again. I never heard anyone refer to it. Not even during the discussions of nuclear intentions that occurred six months later, after the administration released a reminder that the US reserved the right, if it or its allies were attacked with weapons of mass destruction, to respond with nuclear as well as conventional force. But let's look at where we are.

The idealists of the process are talking about the hinge of history.

And the Department of Defense was talking as early as last June about unloosing, for the first time since 1945, high-yield nuclear weapons.

In the early 1980s I happened to attend, at a Conservative Political Action conference in Washington, a session called "Rolling Back the Soviet Empire." One of the speakers that day was a kind of adventurer-slash-ideologue named Jack Wheeler, who was very much of the moment because he had always just come back from spending time with our freedom fighters in Afghanistan, also known as the Mujahideen. I recall that he received a standing ovation after urging that copies of the Koran be smuggled into the Soviet Union to "stimulate an Islamic revival" and the subsequent "death of a thousand cuts." We all saw that idea come home.

WHERE I WAS FROM

This book is for my brother
James Jerrett Didion,
and for our mother and father,
Eduene Jerrett Didion
and
Frank Reese Didion,
with love

PART ONE

1

MY GREAT-GREAT-GREAT-great-great-grandmother Elizabeth Scott was born in 1766, grew up on the Virginia and Carolina frontiers, at age sixteen married an eighteen-year-old veteran of the Revolution and the Cherokee expeditions named Benjamin Hardin IV, moved with him into Tennessee and Kentucky and died on still another frontier, the Oil Trough Bottom on the south bank of the White River in what is now Arkansas but was then Missouri Territory. Elizabeth Scott Hardin was remembered to have hidden in a cave with her children (there were said to have been eleven, only eight of which got recorded) during Indian fighting, and to have been so strong a swimmer that she could ford a river in flood with an infant in her arms. Either in her defense or for reasons of his own, her husband was said to have killed, not counting English soldiers or Cherokees, ten men. This may be true or it may be, in a local oral tradition inclined to stories that turn on decisive gestures, embroidery. I have it on the word of a cousin who researched the matter that the husband, our great-great-great-great-great-grandfather, "appears in the standard printed histories of Arkansas as 'Old Colonel Ben Hardin, the hero of so many Indian wars.'" Elizabeth Scott Hardin had bright blue eyes and sick headaches. The White River on which she lived was the same White River on which, a century and a half later, James McDougal would locate his failed Whitewater development. This is a country at some level not as big as we like to say it is.

I know nothing else about Elizabeth Scott Hardin, but I have her recipe for corn bread, and also for India relish: her granddaughter brought these recipes west in 1846, traveling with the Donner-Reed party as far as the Humboldt Sink before cutting north for Oregon, where her husband, the Reverend Josephus Adamson Cornwall, was determined to be the first Cumberland Presbyterian circuit rider in what was then called Oregon country. Because that granddaughter, Nancy Hardin Cornwall, was my great-great-great-grandmother, I have, besides her recipes, a piece of appliqué she made on the crossing. This appliqué, green and red calico on a muslin field, hangs now in my dining room in New York and hung before that in the living room of a house I had on the Pacific Ocean.

I also have a photograph of the stone marker placed on the site of the cabin in which Nancy Hardin Cornwall and her family spent the winter of 1846–47, still short of their destination in the Willamette Valley but unable to get their wagons through a steep defile on the Umpqua River without abandoning Josephus Cornwall's books. (This option seems to have presented itself only to his daughters.) "Dedicated to the memory of Rev. J. A. Cornwall and family," the engraving on the marker reads. "They built the first immigrant cabin in Douglas County near this site, hence the name Cabin Creek. The family wintered here in 1846–1847, were saved from extreme want by Israel Stoley, a nephew who was a good hunter. The Indians were friendly. The Cornwalls traveled part way westward with the ill-fated Donner Party."

My mother was sent the photograph of this marker by her mother's cousin Oliver Huston, a family historian so ardent that as recently as 1957 he was alerting descendants to "an occasion which no heir should miss," the presentation to the Pacific University Museum of, among other artifacts, "the old potato masher which the Cornwall family brought across the plains in 1846." Oliver Huston's letter continued: "By this procedure, such items can then be seen by all Geiger and Cornwall heirs at any time in the future by simply visiting the Museum." I have not myself found occasion to visit the potato masher, but I do have a typescript of certain memories, elicited from one of Nancy Hardin Cornwall's twelve children, Narcissa, of those months on what would later be called Cabin Creek:

> We were about ten miles from the Umpqua River and the Indians living there would come and spend the greater part of the day. There was one who spoke English, and he told Mother the Rogue River Indians were coming to kill us. Mother told them if they troubled us, in the spring the Bostons (the Indian name for the white people) would come out and kill them all off. Whether this had any effect or not I don't know, but anyway they did not kill us. But we always thought they would come one day for that purpose. One day Father was busy reading and did not notice

> the house was filling with strange Indians until Mother spoke about it. . . . As soon as Father noticed them he got up and got his pistols and asked the Indians to go out and see him shoot. They followed him out, but kept at a distance. The pistols were a great curiosity to them. I doubt if they had ever seen any before. As soon as they were all out of the cabin Mother barred the door and would not let them in any more. Father entertained them outside until evening, when they got on their ponies and rode away. They never returned to trouble us any more.

In another room of this house I had on the Pacific Ocean there hung a quilt from another crossing, a quilt made by my great-great-grandmother Elizabeth Anthony Reese on a wagon journey during which she buried one child, gave birth to another, twice contracted mountain fever, and took turns driving a yoke of oxen, a span of mules, and twenty-two head of loose stock. In this quilt of Elizabeth Reese's were more stitches than I had ever seen in a quilt, a blinding and pointless compaction of stitches, and it occurred to me as I hung it that she must have finished it one day in the middle of the crossing, somewhere in the wilderness of her own grief and illness, and just kept on stitching. From her daughter's account:

> Tom was sick with fever the first day of the crossing, no chance for a doctor. He was only sick a day or two when he died. He had to be buried right away, as the train of wagons was going right on. He was two years old, and we were glad to get a trunk to bury him in. A friend gave a trunk. My aunt, the following year, when her baby died, carried it for a long time in her arms without letting anyone know for fear they would bury the baby before coming to a station.

These women in my family would seem to have been pragmatic and in their deepest instincts clinically radical, given to breaking clean with everyone and everything they knew. They could shoot and they could handle stock and when their children outgrew their shoes they could learn from the Indians how to make moccasins. "An old lady in our wagon train taught my sister to make blood pudding," Narcissa Cornwall recalled. "After killing a deer or steer you cut its throat and catch the blood. You add suet to this and a little salt, and meal or flour if you have it, and bake it. If you haven't anything else to eat, it's pretty good." They tended to accommodate any means in pursuit of an uncertain end. They tended to avoid dwelling on just what that end might imply. When they could not think what else to do they moved another thousand miles, set out another garden: beans and squash and sweet peas from seeds carried from the last place. The past could be jettisoned, children buried and parents left behind, but seeds got carried. They were women, these women in my family, without much time for second thoughts, without much inclination toward equivocation, and later, when there was time or inclination, there developed a tendency, which I came to see as endemic, toward slight and major derangements, apparently eccentric pronouncements, opaque bewilderment and moves to places not quite on the schedule.

> Mother viewed character as being the mainspring of life, and, therefore, as regulating our lives here and indicating our destiny in the life to come. She had fixed and settled principles, aims and motives in life. Her general health was excellent and in middle life she appeared almost incapable of fatigue. Winter and summer, at all seasons and every day, except Sunday, her life was one ceaseless round of activity. The care of her family, to provide for hired help, to entertain visitors, and to entertain preachers and others during meetings which were frequent.

That was the view of Nancy Hardin Cornwall taken by her son Joseph, who was thirteen years old during the crossing. Nancy Hardin Cornwall's daughter Laura, two years old during the crossing, took a not dissimilar view: "Being a Daughter of the American Revolution, she was naturally a brave woman, never seeming afraid of Indians or shrinking from hardships."

A photograph:

A woman standing on a rock in the Sierra Nevada in perhaps 1905.

Actually it is not just a rock but a granite promontory: an igneous outcropping. I use words like "igneous" and "outcropping" because my grandfather, one of whose mining camps can be seen in the background of this photograph, taught me to use them. He also taught me to distinguish gold-bearing ores from the glittering but worthless serpentine I preferred as a child, an education to no point, since by that time gold was no more worth mining than serpentine and the distinction academic, or possibly wishful.

The photograph. The promontory. The camp in the background.

And the woman: Edna Magee Jerrett. She is Nancy Hardin Cornwall's great-granddaughter, she will in time be my grandmother. She is Black Irish, English, Welsh, possibly (this is uncertain) a fraction Jewish through her grandfather William Geiger, who liked to claim as an ancestor a German rabbi but was himself a Presbyterian missionary in the Sandwich Islands and along the Pacific coast; possibly (this is still more uncertain) a lesser fraction Indian, from some frontier somewhere, or maybe, because her skin darkens in the sun as she was told not to let it, she just likes to say that. She grew up in a house on the Oregon coast filled with the educational curiosities of the place and period: strings of shells and seeds from Tahiti, carved emu eggs, Satsuma vases, spears from the South Pacific, an alabaster miniature of the Taj Mahal and the baskets her mother was given by the local Indians. She is quite beautiful. She is also quite indulged, clearly given, although she knows enough about mountains to shake out her boots for snakes every morning, to more amenities than could have been offered in this mining camp in the Sierra Nevada at the time in question. In this photograph she is wearing, for example, a long suede skirt and jacket made for her by the most expensive tailor in San Francisco. "You couldn't pay for her *hats*," her father, a ship's captain, had told her suitors by way of discouragement, and perhaps they had all been discouraged but my grandfather, an innocent from the Georgetown Divide who read books.

It was an extravagance of spirit that would persist through her life. Herself a child, she knew what children wanted. When I was six and had the mumps she brought me, as solace, not a coloring book, not ice cream, not bubble bath, but an ounce of expensive perfume, Elizabeth Arden "On Dit," in a crystal bottle sealed with gold thread. When I was eleven and declined to go any longer to church she gave me, as inducement, not the fear of God but a hat, not any hat, not a child's well-mannered cloche or beret, but a *hat*, gossamer Italian straw and French silk cornflowers and a heavy satin label that read "Lilly Dache." She made champagne punch for the grandchildren left to sit with her on New Year's Eve. During World War II she volunteered to help salvage the Central Valley tomato crop by working the line at the Del Monte cannery in Sacramento, took one look at the moving conveyer belt, got one of those sick headaches her great-grandmother brought west with the seeds, and spent that first and only day on the line with tears running down her face. As atonement, she spent the rest of the war knitting socks for the Red Cross to send to the front. The yarn she bought to knit these socks was cashmere, in regulation colors. She had vicuña coats, hand-milled soap, and not much money. A child could make her cry, and I am ashamed to say that I sometimes did.

She was bewildered by many of the events in her adult life. One of her seafaring brothers became unstable when his ship hit a mine crossing the Atlantic; the son of another committed suicide. She witnessed the abrupt slide into madness of her only sister. Raised to believe that her life would be, as her great-grandmother's was said to have been, one ceaseless round of fixed and settled principles, aims, motives, and activity, she could sometimes think of nothing to do but walk downtown, check out the Bon Marché for clothes she could not afford, buy a cracked crab for dinner and take a taxi home. She died when I was twenty-three and I have of hers a petit-point evening bag, two watercolors she painted as a young girl in an Episcopal convent school (the watermelon still life, the mission she had never seen at San Juan Capistrano), twelve butter knives she had made at Shreve's in San Francisco, and fifty shares of Transamerica stock. I was instructed by her will to sell the stock for something I wanted and could not afford. "What will she have to look forward to," my mother scolded my grandmother on the occasions of the ounce of "On Dit," the Lilly Dache hat, the black scarf embroidered with jet to assuage the pain of dancing school. In the generational theater my mother, despite what I came to recognize as a recklessness quite outside my grandmother's range, had been assigned the role described in the stage directions as sensible. "She'll find something," my grandmother always said, a reassuring conclusion if not one entirely supported by her own experience.

Another photograph, another grandmother: Ethel Reese Didion, who I never knew. She caught fever during the waning days of the 1918 influenza epidemic and died, leaving a husband and two small boys, one of them my father, on the morning of the false armistice. Many times my father told me that she died thinking the war was over. He told me this each time as if it were a matter of considerable importance, and perhaps it was, since on reflection that is all he ever told me about what she thought on any subject. My great-aunt Nell, her younger sister, would say only that my grandmother had been "nervous," and "different." Different from what, I used to ask. Aunt Nell would light another cigarette, consign it immediately to a heavy quartz ashtray, and slide her big rings up and down her thin fingers. Ethel was nervous, she would finally repeat. You could never tease Ethel. Ethel was, well, different.

In this photograph, taken in about 1904, Ethel is at a Grange picnic in Florin, at that time a farm settlement south of Sacramento. She has not yet married the man, my grandfather, whose startling taciturnity would remain so inexplicable to her family, the man to whom I sometimes referred as "Grandfather Didion" but never addressed directly, from the time I was a small child until the day he died in 1953, by any form more familiar than "Mr. Didion." She is still Ethel Reese in this picture and she is wearing a white shirtwaist and a straw hat. Her brothers and cousins, ranchers' sons with a bent for good times and a gift for losing things without rancor, laugh at something outside the camera's range. Aunt Nell, the smallest, darts among their legs. My grandmother smiles tentatively. Her eyes are shut against the sun, or against the camera. I was said to have her eyes, "Reese eyes," eyes that reddened and watered at the first premonition of sun or primroses or raised voices, and I was also said to have some of her "difference," her way of being less than easy at that moment when the dancing starts, but there would be no way of knowing any of that from this picture of Ethel Reese at the Florin Grange picnic in about 1904. This is the memory of her aunt, Catherine Reese, a child during the Reese family's 1852 crossing, of the last stage and aftermath of the journey during which her mother made the quilt with the blinding compaction of stitches:

> Came by Carson City climbing mountains all the time, to Lake Tahoe and on down. Lived in the mountains as Father was sick with chills and fever. Had to give up our stock driver and Mother looked after the stock. Found two or three families of old country folk and lived with them until we got located in a sheep herder's house and lived the winter with him until Father got a house built on the hill ranch near Florin, $2 an acre government land. Father paid cash for 360 acres as he had sold the team and had some money. Went to raising grain and stock, had twelve cows and made and sold butter and eggs and chickens, once in a while a calf. Drove to Sacramento once a week to sell the stuff. Father and Dave did the churning, Mother and I did the milking. I walked six miles to school, to where the graveyard is now on Stockton Boulevard.

That first Reese ranch in Florin, enlarged after a few years from 360 to 640 acres, was into my adult life still owned by my family, or, more precisely, by a corporation called the Elizabeth Reese Estate Company, the shareholders in which were all members of my family. Occasionally, late at night, my father and brother and I would talk about buying out the interests of our cousins in what we still called "the hill ranch" (there was no actual "hill," but there was on the original acreage a rise of perhaps a foot), a move that would have pleased them, since most of them wanted to sell it. I was never able to ascertain whether my father's interest in holding this particular ranch was in any way sentimental; he spoke of it only as a cold property in the short term but a potentially hot one in the long. My mother had no interest in keeping the hill ranch, or in fact any California land: California, she said, was now too regulated, too taxed, too expensive. She spoke enthusiastically, on the other hand, about moving to the Australian outback.

"Eduene," my father would say, a remonstration.

"I would," she would insist, reckless.

"Just leave California? Give it all up?"

"In a *minute*," she would say, the pure strain talking, Elizabeth Scott's great-great-great-great-granddaughter. "Just *forget* it."

2

"ONE HUNDRED years ago, our great-great-grandparents were pushing America's frontier westward, to California." So began the speech I wrote to deliver at my eighth-grade graduation from the Arden School, outside Sacramento. The subject was "Our California Heritage." Developing a theme encouraged by my mother and grandfather, I continued, made rather more confident than I should have been by the fact that I was wearing a new dress, pale green organdy, and my mother's crystal necklace:

> They who came to California were not the self-satisfied, happy and content people, but the adventurous, the restless, and the daring. They were different even from those who settled in other western states. They didn't come west for homes and security, but for adventure and money. They pushed in over the mountains and founded the biggest cities in the west. Up in the Mother Lode they mined gold by day and danced by night. San Francisco's population multiplied almost twenty times, until 1906, when it burned to the ground, and was built up again nearly as quickly as it had burned. We had an irrigation problem, so we built the greatest dams the world has known. Now both desert and valley are producing food in enormous quantities. California has accomplished much in the past years. It would be easy for us to sit back and enjoy the results of the past. But we can't do this. We can't stop and become satisfied and content. We must live up to our heritage, go on to better and greater things for California.

That was June 1948.

The pale green of the organdy dress was a color that existed in the local landscape only for the few spring days when the rice first showed.

The crystal necklace was considered by my mother an effective way to counter the Valley heat.

Such was the blinkering effect of the local dreamtime that it would be some years before I recognized that certain aspects of "Our California Heritage" did not add up, starting with but by no means limited to the fact that I had delivered it to an audience of children and parents who had for the most part arrived in California during the 1930s, refugees from the Dust Bowl. It was after this realization that I began trying to find the "point" of California, to locate some message in its history. I picked up a book of revisionist studies on the subject, but abandoned it on discovering that I was myself quoted, twice. You will have perhaps realized by now (a good deal earlier than I myself realized) that this book represents an exploration into my own confusions about the place and the way in which I grew up, confusions as much about America as about California, misapprehensions and misunderstandings so much a part of who I became that I can still to this day confront them only obliquely.

3

A GOOD DEAL about California does not, on its own preferred terms, add up. The Sacramento River, the main source of surface water in a state where distrust of centralized governmental authority has historically passed for an ethic, has its headwaters in the far northern ranges of Siskiyou County. It picks up the waters of the McCloud and the Pit Rivers above Redding, of the Feather and the Yuba and the Bear below Knight's Landing, of the American at Sacramento, of the San Joaquin below Steamboat Slough; and empties through San Francisco Bay into the Pacific, draining the deep snowpacks of the southern Cascades and the northern Sierra Nevada. "The river here is about 400 yards wide," one of my great-great-grandfathers, William Kilgore, whose daughter Myra married into the Reese family, wrote in the journal of his arrival in Sacramento in August of 1850. "The tide raises the water about 2 ft. and steamboats and vessels are here daily. From this place to San Francisco is about 150 miles by water. All of this distance the river has low banks and is subject to inundation for several miles back." That the land to which he intended eventually to bring his wife and two children was "subject to inundation for several miles back" seems not to have presented itself as an argument against immediate settlement. "This is one of the trying mornings for me, as I now have to leave my family, or back out," he had written in his journal four months before. "Suffice it to say, we started." Yet this river that had been from the beginning his destination was one regularly and predictably given, during all but the driest of those years before its flow was controlled or rearranged, to turning its valley into a shallow freshwater sea a hundred miles long and as wide as the distance between the coast ranges and the foothills of the Sierra Nevada: a pattern of flooding, the Army Corps of Engineers declared in 1927, more intense and intractable than that on any other American river system including the Mississippi.

This annual reappearance of a marsh that did not drain to the sea until late spring or summer was referred to locally not as flooding but as "the high water," a seasonal fact of life, no more than an inconvenient but minor cost of the rich bottom land it created, and houses were routinely built with raised floors to accommodate it. Many Sacramento houses during my childhood had on their walls one or another lithograph showing the familiar downtown grid with streets of water, through which citizens could be seen going about their business by raft or rowboat. Some of these lithographs pictured the high water of 1850, after which a three-foot earthen levee between the river and the settlement was built. Others showed the high water of 1852, during which that first levee was washed out. Still others showed the high water of 1853 or 1860 or 1861 or 1862, nothing much changing except the increasing number of structures visible on the grid. "If you will take, on a map of California, Stockton, Sacramento, and San Francisco as guiding points, you will see that a large part of the land lying between these cities is marked 'swamp and overflowed,'" Charles Nordhoff, the grandfather of the co-author of *Mutiny on the Bounty*, wrote in his 1874 *Northern California, Oregon and the Sandwich Islands*:

> Until within five or six years these lands attracted but little attention. It was known that they were extremely fertile, but it was thought that the cost and uncertainty of reclaiming them were too great to warrant the enterprise. Of late, however, they have been rapidly bought up by capitalists, and their sagacity has been justified by the results on those tracts which have been reclaimed. These Tule lands . . . are simply deposits of muck, a mixture of the wash or sediment brought down by the Sacramento and San Joaquin rivers with the decayed vegetable matter resulting from an immense growth of various grasses, and of the reed called the "tule," which often grows ten feet high in a season, and decays every year. . . . The swamp and overflowed lands were given by Congress to the State, and the State has, in its turn, virtually given them to private persons. It has sold them for one dollar per acre, of which twenty percent was paid down, or twenty cents per acre; and this money, less some small charges for recording the transfer and for inspecting the reclamation, is returned by the State to the purchaser if he, within three years after the purchase, reclaims his land. That is to say, the State gives away the land on condition that it shall be reclaimed and brought into cultivation.

The creation of the entirely artificial environment that is now the Sacramento Valley was not achieved at one stroke, nor is it complete to this day. Bulletins on when and where the rivers would crest, on the conditions of levees and the addresses of evacuation centers, remained into my adult life the spring commonplaces of Sacramento life, as did rumors that one or another levee had been (or was being, or would be) covertly dynamited by one or another agency looking to save one or another downstream community. During years when repeated storms rolling in from the Pacific coincide with an early melting of the Sierra snowpack, levees still break, sections of interstate highways get destabilized by the rising water table, and the big dams go to crisis mode, trying to save themselves by releasing water as they get it, unchecked, no control, the runoff from the pack running free to the sea.

Reclamation of the tule lands has been a war, for those waging it, in which no armament could be too costly, no strategy too quixotic. By 1979, when the State of California published William L. Kahrl's *The California Water Atlas*, there were 980 miles of levee, 438 miles of canal. There were fifty miles of collecting canals and seepage ditches. There were three drainage pumping plants, five low-water check dams, thirty-one bridges, ninety-one gauging stations, and eight automatic shortwave water-stage transmitters. There were seven weirs opening onto seven bypasses covering 101,000 acres. There were not only the big headwater dams, Shasta on the Sacramento and Folsom on the American and Oroville on the Feather, but all their predecessors and collateral dams, their after-bays and forebays and diversions: Thermalito and Lake Almanor and Frenchman Lake and Little Grass Valley on the Feather, New Bullard's Bar and Englebright and Jackson Meadows and Lake Spaulding on the Yuba, Camp Far West and Rollins and Lower Bear on the Bear, Nimbus and Slab Creek and L. L. Anderson on the American, Box Canyon and Keswick on the Sacramento. The cost of controlling or rearranging the Sacramento, which is to say the "reclamation" of the Sacramento Valley, was largely borne, like the cost of controlling or rearranging many other inconvenient features of California life, by the federal government.

This extreme reliance of California on federal money, so

seemingly at odds with the emphasis on unfettered individualism that constitutes the local core belief, was a pattern set early on, and derived in part from the very individualism it would seem to belie. ("They didn't come west for homes and security, but for adventure and money," as "Our California Heritage" put it.) Charles Nordhoff complained of California in 1874 that "a speculative spirit invades even the farm-house," too often tempting its citizens "to go from one avocation to another, to do many things superficially, and to look for sudden fortunes by the chances of a shrewd venture, rather than be content to live by patient and continued labor." There had been from the beginning virtually no notion of "pushing America's frontier westward," my eighth-grade conception of it notwithstanding: the American traders and trappers who began settling in California as early as 1826 were leaving their own country for a remote Mexican province, Alta California. Many became naturalized Mexican citizens. Many married into Mexican and Spanish families. A fair number received grants of land from the Mexican authorities. As late as 1846, American emigrants were starting west with the idea of reaching territory at least provisionally Mexican, only to find on their arrival that the Bear Flag Revolt and the Mexican War had placed Alta California under American military authority. There it would remain—along with the other American spoil of that conquest, the territory that eventually became Nevada and Utah and New Mexico and Arizona and part of Colorado—until California was admitted to the union as a state in 1850.

Predicated as it was on this general notion of cutting loose and striking it rich, the California settlement had tended to attract drifters of loosely entrepreneurial inclination, the hunter-gatherers of the frontier rather than its cultivators, and to reward most fully those who perceived most quickly that the richest claim of all lay not in the minefields but in Washington. It was a quartet of Sacramento shopkeepers, Charles Crocker and Leland Stanford and Collis P. Huntington and Mark Hopkins, who built the railroad that linked California with the world markets and opened the state to extensive settlement, but it was the citizens of the rest of the country who paid for it, through a federal cash subsidy (sixteen thousand dollars a mile in the valley and forty-eight thousand dollars a mile in the "mountains," which were contractually defined as beginning six miles east of Sacramento) plus a federal land grant, ten or twenty checkerboarded square-mile sections, for each mile of track laid.

Nor did the role of the government stop with the construction of the railroad: the citizens of the rest of the country would also, in time, subsidize the crops the railroad carried, make possible the irrigation of millions of acres of essentially arid land, underwrite the rhythms of planting and not planting, and create, finally, a vast agricultural mechanism in a kind of market vacuum, quite remote from the normal necessity for measuring supply against demand and cost against return. As recently as 1993, eighty-two thousand acres in California were still planted in alfalfa, a low-value crop requiring more water than was then used in the households of all thirty million Californians. Almost a million and a half acres were planted in cotton, the state's second largest consumer of water, a crop subsidized directly by the federal government. Four hundred thousand acres were planted in rice, the cultivation of which involves submerging the fields under six inches of water from mid-April until the August harvest, months during which, in California, no rain falls. The 1.6 million acre feet of water this required (an acre foot is roughly 326,000 gallons) was made available, even in drought years, for what amounted to a nominal subsidized price by the California State Water Project and the Central Valley Project, an agency of the federal government, which, through the commodity-support program of the Department of Agriculture, also subsidized the crop itself. Ninety percent of this California rice was glutinous medium-grain Japonica, a type not popular in the United States but favored in both Japan and Korea, each of which banned the import of California rice. These are the kinds of contradictions on which Californians have tended to founder when they try to think about the place they come from.

4

JOSIAH ROYCE, who was from 1885 until his death in 1916 a central figure in what later became known as the "golden period" of the Harvard philosophy department, was born in Grass Valley, not far from Sacramento, grew up there and in San Francisco, and in some sense spent the rest of his life trying to make coherent the discontinuities implicit in this inheritance. "My native town was a mining town in the Sierra Nevada—a place five or six years older than myself," he said at a dinner given in his honor at the Walton Hotel in Philadelphia in 1915.

> My earliest recollections include a very frequent wonder as to what my elders meant when they said that this was a new community. I frequently looked at the vestiges left by the former diggings of miners, saw that many pine logs were rotten, and that a miner's grave was to be found in a lonely place not far from my own house. Plainly men had lived and died thereabouts. I dimly reflected that this sort of life had apparently been going on ever since men dwelt thereabouts. The logs and the grave looked old. The sunsets were beautiful. The wide prospects when one looked across the Sacramento Valley were impressive, and had long interested the people of whose love for my country I heard so much. What was there then in this place that ought to be called new, or for that matter crude? I wondered, and gradually came to feel that part of my life's business was to find out what all this wonder meant.

Here we come close to a peculiar California confusion: what Royce had actually made it his "life's business" to do, his work, did not resolve "what all this wonder meant." Instead, Royce invented an idealized California, an ethical system in which "loyalty" was the basic virtue, the moral law essential to the creation of "community," which was in turn man's only salvation and by extension the redeeming essence of the California settlement. Yet the California community most deeply recalled by the author of this system was what he acknowledged to have been "a community of irresponsible strangers" (or, in another reference, "a blind and stupid and homeless generation of selfish wanderers"), a community not of the "loyal" but of "men who have left homes and families, who have fled from before the word of the Lord, and have sought safety from their old vexatious duties in a golden paradise."

Such calls to dwell upon the place and its meaning (and, if the meaning proved intractable, to reinvent the place) had been general in California since the first American settlement, the very remoteness of which was sufficiently extreme to raise questions about why one was there, why one had come there, what the voyage would ultimately mean. The overland crossing itself had an aspect of quest: "One was going on a pilgrimage whose every suggestion was of the familiar sacred stories," Royce wrote. "One sought a romantic and far-off golden land of promise, and one was in the wilderness of this world, often guided only by signs from heaven. . . . The clear blue was almost perpetually overhead; the pure mountain winds were about one; and again, even in the hot and parched deserts, a mysterious power provided the few precious springs and streams of water."

Each arriving traveler had been, by definition, reborn in the wilderness, a new creature in no way the same as the man or woman or even child who had left Independence or St. Joseph however many months before: the very decision to set forth on the journey had been a kind of death, involving the total abandonment of all previous life, mothers and fathers and brothers and sisters who would never again be seen, all sentiment banished, the most elementary comforts necessarily relinquished. "I had for months anticipated this hour, yet, not till it came, did I realize the blank dreariness of seeing night come on without house or home to shelter us and our baby-girl," Josiah Royce's mother, Sarah, wrote of the day in 1849 on which she set off for Sacramento with her husband and first child.

The blank dreariness, Sarah Royce wrote.

Without house or home, Sarah Royce wrote.

Suffice it to say, we started, my great-great-grandfather William Kilgore wrote.

This moment of leaving, the death that must precede the rebirth, is a fixed element of the crossing story. Such stories are artlessly told. There survives in their repetition a problematic elision or inflation, a narrative flaw, a problem with point of view: the actual observer, or camera eye, is often hard to locate. This was Josephus Adamson Cornwall's goodbye to his mother, as related by a son who seems to have heard the story from his mother, Nancy Hardin Cornwall, she of the fixed and settled principles, aims, and motives in life, who had not herself been present: "Just ready to go, he entered his mother's parlor. She went out with him to his horse to say the last words and to see him depart. She told him that she would never again see him in this world, gave him her blessing, and commended him to God. He then mounted his horse and rode away, while she followed him with a last look, until he vanished from sight."

Who witnessed this moment of departure? Was the camera on Josephus Cornwall's mother, following her son with the last look? Or on the son himself, glancing back as he vanishes from sight? The gravity of the decisive break demands narrative. Conflicting details must be resolved, reworked into a plausible whole. Aging memories will be recorded as gospel. Children recount as the given of their personal and cultural history what neither they nor even their parents could possibly have known, for example the "providential interposition" that was said to have saved Josephus Cornwall's life when he was an infant in Georgia: "It was a peculiarity of that section of the state that mad dogs were very common. One day when his parents were busy he was left in the house alone in his cradle. A mad dog entered the room, walked around it and went away, but never molested him." What witness saw the mad dog enter the room? Did the witness take action, or merely observe and report, trusting the "providential interposition" to save the baby?

Yet it was through generations of just such apparently omniscient narrators that the crossing stories became elevated to a kind of single master odyssey, its stations of veneration fixed. There were the Platte, the Sandy, the Big and Little Sandys. There was the Green River. Fort Hall. Independence Rock. The Sweetwater. There were the Humboldt, the Humboldt Sink, the Hastings cut-off. The names were so deeply embedded in the stories I heard as a child that when I happened at age twenty to see the Green River, through the windows of a train crossing Wyoming, I was astonished by this apparent evidence that it actually existed, a fact on the ground, there to be seen—entirely unearned—by anyone passing by. Just as there were stations of veneration, so there were objects of veneration, relics of those who had made the redeeming journey. "The old potato masher which the Cornwall family brought across the plains in 1846" was not the only family totem given by my grandmother's cousins to the Pacific University Museum in 1957. "After consulting with certain of the heirs," Oliver Huston wrote, the cousins had also determined "that it will be advisable to turn over to the Museum at that time the small desk sent Grandfather in 1840 by William Johnson from Hawaii, and also certain mementoes of Grandmother Geiger," specifically "the blouse which formed part of her wedding costume" and "the old shawl or shoulder wrap she wore in her later years." So Saxon Brown, the heroine of Jack London's curious "California" novel *The Valley of the Moon*, could hold in her hands her mother's red satin corset ("the pioneer finery of a frontier woman who had crossed the plains") and see pass before her, "from East to West, across a continent, the great hegira of the land-hungry Anglo-Saxon. It was part and fiber of her. She had been nursed on its traditions and its facts from the lips of those who had taken part."

As repeated, this was an odyssey the most important aspect of which was that it offered moral or spiritual "tests," or challenges, with fatal consequences for failure. Josiah Royce's parents, traveling with only their two-year-old daughter, three other emigrants, and a manuscript list of landmarks that stopped at the Humboldt Sink, found themselves lost on the Carson desert, "confused, almost stupefied," "dazed," "half-senseless," suffering for a period "the same fatal horror of desolation and death that had assailed the Donner Party in the Truckee pass." Children who died of cholera got buried on the trail. Women who believed they could keep some token of their mother's house (the rosewood chest, the flat silver) learned to jettison memory and keep moving. Sentiment, like grief and dissent, cost time. A hesitation, a moment spent looking back, and the grail was forfeited. Independence Rock, west of Fort Laramie on the Sweetwater River, was so named because the traveler who had not reached that point by the Fourth of July, Independence Day, would not reach the Sierra Nevada before snow closed the passes.

The diaries of emigrants refer to the Sierra Nevada as "the most dreaded moment," "the Great Bugaboo," the source of "sleepless nights," "disturbed dreams." *Without house or home*: Sarah Royce and her husband and child abandoned their wagon and made it through the Sierra, with the help of a United States Army relief party, only ten days before the passes closed. Even while the passes remained open, there would be snow. There would be the repeated need to ford and again ford the Truckee or the Carson. There would be the repeated need to unload and reload the wagons. There would be recent graves, wrecked wagons, and, at Donner Lake, after the winter of 1846–47, human as well as animal bones, and the trees notched to show the depth of the fatal winter's snowpack. This is the entry in William Kilgore's diary for August 1, 1852:

> Ice and frost this morning. Four miles to Red Lake. This is . . . the head of Salmon Trout, or Carson River. It is a small lake and is within one mi. of the summit of the Sierra Nevada. From this lake to the summit the ascent is very great, some places being almost perpendicular. . . . Four mi. from the summit we cross a small creek, a tributary of the Sacramento. . . . At this creek we stop to noon. Here we help inter a young man who died last night of bilious fever. He was from Michigan. His name was Joseph Ricker. His parents reside in the state of Maine. Here we ascend another ridge of this mt. It is higher than the one we have just passed, being 9,339 ft. above the sea. From the foot to the summit it is five miles, and in ascending and descending we travel over four miles of snow, and it from two to 20 ft. deep. . . . 21 miles today.

To read these crossing accounts and diaries is to be struck by the regularity with which a certain apprehension of darkness enters the quest, a shadow of moral ambiguity that becomes steadily more pervasive until that moment when the traveler realizes that the worst of the Sierra is behind him. "The Summit is crossed!" one such diary reads. "We are in California! Far away in the haze the dim outlines of the Sacramento Valley are discernible! We are on the down grade now and our famished animals may pull us through. We are in the midst of huge pines, so large as to challenge belief. Hutton is dead. Others are worse. I am better." By this point, in every such journey, there would have been the accidents, the broken bones, the infected and even the amputated hands and feet. There would have been the fevers. Sarah Royce remembered staying awake all night after a man in her party died of cholera, and hearing the wind whip his winding sheet like "some vindictive creature struggling restlessly in bonds." There would have been the hurried burials, in graves often unmarked and sometimes deliberately obliterated. "Before leaving the Humboldt River there was one death, Miss Mary Campbell," Nancy Hardin Cornwall's son Joseph recalled. "She was buried right in our road and the whole train of wagons was driven over her grave to conceal it from the Indians. Miss Campbell died of mountain fever, and Mother by waiting on her caught the fever and for a long time she lingered, apparently between life and death, but at last recovered. Miss Campbell was an orphan, her mother having died at Green River."

There would have been, darkest of all, the betrayals, the suggestions that the crossing might not after all be a noble odyssey, might instead be a mean scrambling for survival, a blind flight on the part of Josiah Royce's "blind and stupid and homeless generation of selfish wanderers." Not all emigrants, to take just one example, cared for all orphans. It was on the Little Sandy that an emigrant named Bernard J. Reid, who had put down two hundred dollars to secure a place on an 1849 crossing, saw first "an emigrant wagon apparently abandoned by its owners" and then "a rude head-board indicating a new grave," which turned out to be that of the Reverend Robert Gilmore and his wife Mary, who had died the same day of cholera. This account comes to us from Reid's diary, which was found by his family in the 1950s, entrusted to Mary McDougall Gordon for editing, and published in 1983 by the Stanford University Press as *Overland to California with the Pioneer Line.* On turning from the grave to the apparently abandoned wagon, Reid tells us, he was "surprised to see a neatly dressed girl of about 17, sitting on the wagon tongue, her feet resting on the grass, and her eyes apparently directed at vacancy."

> She seemed like one dazed or in a dream and did not seem to notice me till I spoke to her. I then learned from her in reply to my questions that she was Miss Gilmore, whose parents had died

> two days before; that her brother, younger than herself, was sick in the wagon, probably with cholera; that their oxen were lost or stolen by the Indians; and that the train they had been traveling with, after waiting for three days on account of the sickness and death of her parents, had gone on that morning, fearful, if they delayed longer, of being caught by winter in the Sierra Nevada mountains. . . . The people of her train had told her that probably her oxen would yet be found, or at any rate some other train coming along with oxen to spare would take her and her brother and their wagon along.

"Who could tell the deep sense of bereavement, distress and desolation that weighed on that poor girl's heart, there in the wilderness with no telling what fate was in store for her and her sick brother?" Reid asks his readers and surely also himself. Such memories might have seemed difficult to reconcile with the conviction that one had successfully met the tests or challenges required to enter the new life. The redemptive power of the crossing was, nonetheless, the fixed idea of the California settlement, and one that raised a further question: for what exactly, and at what cost, had one been redeemed? When you jettison others so as not to be "caught by winter in the Sierra Nevada mountains," do you deserve not to be caught? When you survive at the cost of Miss Gilmore and her brother, do you survive at all?

5

I WAS BORN IN SACRAMENTO, and lived in California most of my life. I learned to swim in the Sacramento and the American, before the dams. I learned to drive on the levees up and downriver from Sacramento. Yet California has remained in some way impenetrable to me, a wearying enigma, as it has to many of us who are from there. We worry it, correct and revise it, try and fail to define our relationship to it and its relationship to the rest of the country. We make declamatory breaks with it, as Josiah Royce did when he left Berkeley for Harvard. "There is no philosophy in California—from Siskiyou to Ft. Yuma, and from the Golden Gate to the summit of the Sierras," he had written to William James, who eventually responded to this *cri de coeur* with the offer from Harvard. We make equally declamatory returns, as Frank Norris did, determined before his thirtieth birthday "to do some great work with the West and California as a background, and which will be at the same time thoroughly American." The intention, Norris wrote to William Dean Howells, who had reviewed *McTeague* favorably, was "to write three novels around the one subject of *Wheat*. First, a story of California (the producer), second, a story of Chicago (the distributor), third, a story of Europe (the consumer) and in each to keep the idea of this huge Niagara of wheat rolling from West to East. I think a big Epic trilogy could be made out of such a subject, that at the same time would be modern and thoroughly American. The idea is so big that it frightens me at times but I have about made up my mind to have a try at it."

Frank Norris's experience with his subject appears to have been exclusively literary. He was raised in Chicago and then San Francisco, where he met the young woman he would eventually marry at a debutante dance. He spent a year in Paris, studying art and writing a medieval romance, *Yvernelle, A Tale of Feudal France*, which his mother arranged to have published. He spent four years at Berkeley without taking the courses necessary for a degree, then a year as a non-degree student at Harvard. He covered the prelude to the Boer War for *Collier's* and *The San Francisco Chronicle*, the Santiago campaign in Cuba for *McClure's*. At the time he was seized by the trilogy-of-wheat notion, he was living in New York, at 61 Washington Square South.

The Octopus, published in 1901 and based on what was at the time quite recent history in the San Joaquin Valley, was, in the best sense, worked up: through well-situated friends, Ernest Peixotto and his wife (the Peixottos were a prominent San Francisco Jewish family, and Ernest Peixotto's older sister Jessica, an economist, was one of the first women on the faculty of the University of California), Norris managed an introduction to a couple who ran five thousand acres of wheat in San Benito County, and arranged to spend the summer of 1899 on their ranch near Hollister. San Benito County presented a gentler, more coastal landscape than the San Joaquin, which was where Norris intended to set his novel ("San Juan de Guadalajara," the mission in *The Octopus*, was a borrow from Mission San Juan Bautista near Hollister, there being no missions in the San Joaquin), but it was nonetheless a setting in which an attentive reporter could absorb the mechanics of a big wheat operation.

The Octopus opens on a day in "the last half of September, the very end of the dry season," a day when "all Tulare County, all the vast reaches of the San Joaquin Valley—in fact all South Central California, was bone dry, parched, and baked and crisped after four months of cloudless weather, when the day seemed always at noon, and the sun blazed white hot over the valley from the Coast Range in the west to the foothills of the Sierras in the east." The stuff of the novel, the incidents on which the narrative turns, came directly from actual events in what was then Tulare County. In 1893 in Tulare County there had been the killing by a sheriff's posse of John Sontag, an embittered Southern Pacific brakeman who had spent the previous three years dynamiting track and robbing trains, killing and wounding several lawmen. In *The Octopus* Sontag would become "Dyke," who commandeers an engineer to escape his pursuers, foils their attempt to derail him by reversing the engine, abandons it, and is taken by the posse.

Thirteen years before, in 1880, there had been, at a place then called Mussel Slough but after the incident renamed "Lucerne," the shootout between federal marshals acting for the

Southern Pacific, which had become through its federal land grants the largest landowner in California, and a group of local ranchers who were growing wheat on land leased from the railroad. The ranchers, under the rather willful misapprehension that their lease agreements gave them the right to buy the land at $2.50 an acre (the agreements were vaguely worded, but quite clearly stated that the land would be made available "at various figures from $2.50 upward per acre," "upward" being the word the ranchers preferred to miss), refused to pay the price, $17 to $40 an acre, ultimately set on the land. The railroad obtained eviction orders, the ranchers resisted, and both the ranchers and the federal marshals sent to evict them began firing. Six ranchers ultimately died in this confrontation, which not only provided the climactic incident for *The Octopus*—the showdown between eleven ranchers and the U.S. marshals sent in to enforce eviction orders—but also influenced the final scenes in Josiah Royce's only work of fiction, *The Feud of Oakfield Creek: A Novel of California Life*, based on the Sacramento squatters' riots of 1850.

For the San Francisco threads in his narrative, Norris drew on even more recent events: in 1899, there had been the celebrated publication in *The San Francisco Examiner* of Edwin Markham's "The Man with the Hoe," a rhetorical poem that decried the exploitation of labor. An epic poem in the style of "The Man with the Hoe" appears in *The Octopus* as "The Toilers," the newspaper poem that makes an instant celebrity of its author, Presley, the irresolute graduate of "an Eastern college" who is the novel's protagonist. The publication of "The Toilers" enables Presley to dine at the table of "the Railroad King" (Blue Point oysters, *purée a la Derby*, ortolan patties, *grenadins* of bass and stuffed salmon, Londonderry pheasants, *escalopes* of duck, *rissolettes á la pompadour*, asparagus rushed to the kitchen of the Railroad King by special train within hours of its cutting), even as, outside in the fog, the dispossessed widow of one of the evicted and killed San Joaquin wheat growers is literally starving to death, falling into her terminal coma on a vacant lot at the top of the Clay Street hill, her small daughter at her side, her older daughter already descended into prostitution.

Presley knows nothing of the fate of the widow, but had

by fortuitous narrative design run into the older daughter, her degradation apparent, that very afternoon, rendering this dinner an occasion for him of considerable clarity. He sits at the opulent table of the Railroad King as the Château Latour is poured and imagines the clink of the glasses "drowned in the explosion of revolvers" in the San Joaquin Valley. He sees, for an instant, "that splendid house sacked to its foundations, the tables overturned, the pictures torn, the hangings blazing, and Liberty, the red-handed Man in the Street, grimed with powder smoke, foul with the gutter, rush yelling, torch in hand, through every door." The intercutting from the dinner table inside to the dying widow and child outside is insistently allegorical, operatic, outsized, as is the subsequent death of the railroad's agent in the hold of a cargo ship taking on wheat destined for Asia, consigned there by the blind force of the market even as widows and orphans starve for want of a heel of bread on the streets of San Francisco:

> Deafened with the roar of the grain, blinded and made dumb with its chaff, he threw himself forward with clutching fingers, rolling upon his back, and lay there, moving feebly, the head rolling from side to side. The Wheat, leaping continuously from the chute, poured around him. It filled the pockets of the coat, it crept up the sleeves and trouser legs, it covered the great, protuberant stomach, it ran at last in rivulets into the distended, gasping mouth. It covered the face.
>
> Upon the surface of the Wheat, under the chute, nothing moved but the Wheat itself. There was no sign of life. Then, for an instant, the surface stirred. A hand, fat, with short fingers and swollen veins, reached up, clutching, then fell limp and prone. In another instant it was covered.

The Octopus has been, from the outset, a troubling work, in part because its apparent relentlessness could be so readily dismissed. As recently as 1991, in a discussion of the railroad's role in the development of California, the quarterly publication of the California Historical Society was trying to separate the significance of that role from Norris's "shrill, anti-corporate rhetoric," his "superficial and distorted tale," and pointing out that the cartoon image of the Southern Pacific as an octopus, with portraits of Leland Stanford and Charles Crocker for its eyes, long predated Norris's use of it. There would seem on the face of it to be nothing subtle in *The Octopus*: the novel is barely under way when Presley catches sight of a train, and immediately translates it into:

> the galloping monster, the terror of steel and steam, with its single eye, cyclopean, red, shooting from horizon to horizon . . . the symbol of a vast power, huge, terrible, flinging the echo of its thunder over all the reaches of the valley, leaving blood and destruction in its path; the leviathan, with tentacles of steel clutching into the soil, the soulless Force, the iron-hearted Power, the monster, the Colossus, the Octopus.

Yet *The Octopus* remains perhaps the most complex statement to date of the California condition, and a deeply ambiguous work. Nothing about the novel, on examination, is quite what it seems. Edwin Markham's "The Man with the Hoe" may have galvanized sentiment against the exploitation of labor, but it was said by its author to have been inspired, curiously, in one of the many apparent connections in California life that serve only as baffles to further inquiry, by study of a Millet painting owned by Charles Crocker, one of the Central and Southern Pacific's "Big Four," in other words a Railroad King. Frank Norris may have considered the Southern Pacific "the soulless Force, the iron-hearted Power, the monster, the Colossus, the Octopus," but two years before he conceived the novel he was an editor of, and writing regularly for, *The Wave*, a San Francisco weekly financed by the Southern Pacific to promote Charles Crocker's new Del Monte Hotel in Monterey. *The Octopus* is not, as it might logically seem to be, a story of an agrarian society overtaken by the brute momentum of industrialization: the octopus, if there is one, turns out to be neither the railroad nor corporate ownership but indifferent nature, which is characterized, to somewhat unsettling effect, in much the same language as the railroad was earlier: "a gigantic engine, a vast cyclopean power, huge, terrible, a leviathan with a heart of steel, knowing no compunction, no forgiveness, no tolerance; crushing out the human atom standing in its way, with nirvanic calm, the agony of destruction sending never a jar. . . ."

There are, as drawn by Norris, serious ambiguities about even the climactic shootout, not the least of which are that the ranchers had never owned the land in dispute, had chosen to misread the lease agreements on the gamble that other growers would band together in such force as to render the papers useless ("Oh, rot!" one of them cries when warned to take a closer look at the leases. "Of course the railroad will sell at two-fifty. We've got the contracts"), and had taken up raising wheat on railroad land in the first place only because the railroad was there to transport the wheat. These wheat ranchers in *The Octopus* are in no sense simple farmers. They are farmers with tickers in their offices, connecting the San Joaquin by wire with San Francisco and Chicago and New York and finally with Liverpool, at that time the nerve center of the wheat market. "Fluctuations in the price of the world's crop during and after the harvest," Norris wrote, "thrilled straight to the office of Los Muertos, to that of the Quien Sabe, to Osterman's, and to Broderson's [the ranches in the novel]. During a flurry in the Chicago wheat pits in the August of that year, which had affected even the San Francisco market, Harran and Magnus had sat up nearly half of one night watching the strip of white tape jerking unsteadily from the reel."

Nor are Magnus Derrick and his son Harran and Osterman and Broderson and Annixter even "farmers" at all, in the conventional sense of the word: they had come to the San Joaquin as an entrepreneurial move, after other ventures (in mining, in politics, in whatever had presented itself) had failed or gone dry, and after, most significantly and most ambiguously, the railroad had opened the San Joaquin to profitable cultivation by offering, for the first time, a way to move its crops to market. The proprietor of Los Muertos, Magnus Derrick, the nearest the novel gets to a tragic hero, is nonetheless characterized by Norris as a high-stakes gambler, a miner at heart, come to the San Joaquin in search of the quick killing that had eluded him in the Comstock Lode:

> It was the true California spirit that found expression through him, the spirit of the West, unwilling to occupy itself with details, refusing to wait, to be patient, to achieve by legitimate plodding; the miner's instinct of wealth acquired in a single night prevailed, in spite of all. It was in this frame of mind that Magnus and the multitude of other ranchers of whom he was a type, farmed their

> ranches. They had no love for their land. They were not attached to the soil. They worked their ranches as a quarter of a century before they had worked their mines. . . . To get all there was out of the land, to squeeze it dry, to exhaust it, seemed their policy. When, at last, the land worn out, would refuse to yield, they would invest their money in something else; by then, they would all have made fortunes. They did not care.

Norris's San Joaquin wheat growers, then, were of a type common enough in California: the speculators noted by Charles Nordhoff in 1874, entrepreneurs in search of the shrewd venture, men who might themselves have been running the railroad had they seen the opportunity, held the right cards, been quicker players. Confronted with the demands of the railroad (which was pressing not only to evict the ranchers but to raise freight rates) and its bought members of the Railroad Commission, the first response of the ranchers in *The Octopus* is to buy a commissioner of their own. Even in this venture not quick enough players, they buy the wrong man: Magnus Derrick's politically ambitious older son, who sells out to the railroad. That the only actual conflict in *The Octopus* turns out to be between successful and failed members of the same entrepreneurial class (members in some cases of the same families) creates a deep and troubled confusion in the novel, a dissonance its author grasped but failed to resolve. This dissonance, which had to do with the slippage between the way Californians perceived themselves and the way they were, between what they believed to be their unlimited possibilities and the limitations implicit in their own character and history, might have been Norris's great subject, but he died, at thirty-two, of peritonitis, before he could work it through. The confusions here have not been mine alone.

> In the 1860s . . . William Henry Brewer [the chief assistant to Josiah Dwight Whitney in his 1860–64 geological survey of California] . . . described the southwestern San Joaquin Valley as a "plain of absolute desolation." At the turn-of-the-century, the crusading novelist Frank Norris pictured the valley as "bone dry, parched, and baked and crisped" where the "day seemed always at noon." But, a century after Brewer's report, and less than half

> a century after Norris's observations, it became clear that by just adding water, this vale of sterility would bloom as the nation's garden.

Just by adding water. The above appears on the United States Bureau of Reclamation's web site, on the page prepared by the Bureau's History Program to deal with the Central Valley Project's San Luis Unit, West San Joaquin Division. *We had an irrigation problem, so we built the greatest dams the world has known*, was my equally can-do approach to the subject in "Our California Heritage." This, according to the same Bureau of Reclamation web page, is what it takes to "just add water" to the San Joaquin:

> Melting snow and runoff high in the mountains of Northern California are the first steps of a trek through the heart of the state. Once in the Sacramento–San Joaquin River Delta, water is released from storage and lifted 197 feet by the Tracy Pumping Plant. The flow is then conveyed about 70 miles south to the O'Neill Forebay via the California Aqueduct (a State Water Project, or SWP, feature) and the Federal Delta-Mendota Canal. Delta-Mendota carries water southeasterly from the Tracy Pumping Plant, eventually arriving at the O'Neill Pumping-Generating Plant. Running parallel to the Delta-Mendota Canal, the Edmund G. Brown California Aqueduct travels directly into the O'Neill Forebay. The O'Neill Dam, Pumping-Generating Plant and Forebay are all a half mile from the San Luis Dam and Reservoir. Units of the William R. Gianelli Pumping-Generating Plant (formerly known as the San Luis Pumping-Generating Plant) raises water from O'Neill Forebay into San Luis Reservoir. Releases from San Luis Reservoir are directed into the 101.3-mile-long San Luis Canal. Seventeen miles south of San Luis Reservoir, the Dos Amigos Pumping Station lifts the water again, so the flow can continue another 85 miles across central California. Journey's end for the San Luis Canal is the Federal terminus at Kettleman City. At Kettleman City, the SWP's California Aqueduct carries on to service farms, recreational users and municipalities as far south as Los Angeles. When drought strikes California, and Delta flows cannot supply State and Federal water projects, water is released back into the O'Neill Forebay, coursing southward through the California Aqueduct. During irrigation season, water is released from the

reservoir back through the pump-generator units of Gianelli to the O'Neill Forebay, generating electric power. Protecting the canal from streams crossing its path are the Los Banos and Little Panoche Detention Dams and Reservoirs. Other Unit features include the San Luis Drain, Pleasant Valley Pumping Plant, and the Coalinga Canal. The operation of the San Luis Unit is a fairly simple procedure for those brief periods when man and nature are in harmony, but both seldom have been in synchronization.

Just by adding water.

This vale of sterility would bloom as the nation's garden.

A fairly simple procedure for those brief periods when man and nature are in harmony.

The San Luis Dam, at the time it was completed in 1968, cost three billion dollars. What this taxpayer-financed investment meant to the San Joaquin's Westlands Water District was that several hundred growers, most of them corporate, would have the assurance of water, ditches, big automated Rain Birds moving all day with the sun. These growers would also have the assurance of "irrigation subsidies," which by 1987, according to Gerald Haslam's *The Great Central Valley*, amounted to twenty-seven million dollars, eleven million of which went to the Southern Pacific Land Company. "You can't buck the railroad" was a common phrase in my childhood, but I never ventured into its local application.

6

HOLLISTER, the San Benito County town near which Frank Norris spent the summer of 1899 researching *The Octopus*, was named for, and built on land at that time only recently owned by, an emigrant from Ohio named William Welles Hollister. In 1852, William Welles Hollister had driven some three hundred head of cattle from Ohio to California, sold them, and returned home. In 1853, he again made the crossing, this time driving not cattle but sheep, five thousand head. This time he stayed, and over the next twenty years he and two partners, Albert and Thomas Dibblee, accumulated some two hundred thousand acres of ranch land ranging from Monterey and San Benito Counties south to Santa Barbara. William Welles Hollister was the sole owner of thirty-nine thousand acres in Santa Barbara County alone, the several ranches collectively referred to as "the Hollister ranch," which at the time of its sale in the late 1960s incorporated the twenty miles of coastline running south from Point Conception and constituted one of the last intact coastal properties of its size between the Oregon and Mexican borders.

Such extensive holdings, typically acquired on very little equity, were not, at the time of their acquisition, entirely unusual, nor did William Welles Hollister and the Dibblee brothers even count among the largest private owners. In 1882, Richard O'Neill and James Flood together bought more than two hundred thousand acres straddling the line between Orange and San Diego Counties, a holding undivided until 1940, when the Flood heirs took the San Diego acreage and the O'Neill heirs took the Orange. Further north in Orange County, the heirs of James Irvine held the ninety-three thousand acres he had acquired in the 1870s by combining acreage originally granted to the Sepulveda and Yorba families, a property that stretched from the mountains to the sea and covered one-fifth of the county. By the time James Ben Ali Haggin and Lloyd Tevis consolidated their properties in 1890 as the Kern County Land Company, they had acquired, throughout the Southwest, almost a million and a half acres, roughly a third of them in the San Joaquin Valley. Henry Miller, another big holder, who once said that he could drive his cattle from Oregon to the Mexican border and sleep them every night on his own land, had arrived in San Francisco in 1850 with six dollars in his pocket and gone to work as a butcher. Within twenty years, he and his partner, Charles Lux, also a butcher in San Francisco, had gained control of ten to twelve million acres in California, a million and a half owned outright and grazing rights on the rest, vast tracts largely acquired through imaginative interpretation of the small print in federal legislation.

Miller, for example, made deals with cash-hungry veterans, buying up, at a discount, the land options to which they were entitled as a service benefit. He also made deft use of the federal Reclamation Act of 1850, which had granted California's "swamp and overflowed" land to the state, which in turn sold it (the "virtual gift" noted by Charles Nordhoff in 1874) for $1.15 to $1.25 an acre, an amount returned to any buyer who could demonstrate use of the land. Henry Miller was instrumental in getting large parts of California classified as swamp, in one favored telling by hooking up a team of horses to tow a rowboat over the land in question. Nor, at the time, was this even an obscure angle: *Power and Land in California*, the 1971 report prepared by the Ralph Nader Task Force and later published as *Politics of Land*, noted that two of the state surveyors responsible for classifying land as "swamp and overflowed" each left office with three hundred thousand acres.

Such landowners tended to have not much interest in presenting themselves as the proprietors of farms or estates on the eastern, which was to say the English, model. William Henry Brewer, when he came out from Pennsylvania in 1860 to assist Josiah Dwight Whitney in the first geological survey of California, complained that the owner of eighty thousand acres between Gaviota Pass and San Luis Obispo lived "about half as well as a man would at home who owned a hundred-acre farm paid for." Almost a century later, Carey McWilliams, in *California: The Great Exception*, remarked on the almost total absence of conventional "rural" life in California, which would have been, were it a country, the world's seventh-largest agricultural producer: "The large shipper-growers 'farm by phone' from headquarters in San Francisco or Los Angeles. Many of them travel, nowadays, exclusively by plane in visiting their various 'operations.' . . . Their relationship to the land is as casual as that of the migratory workers they employ." To live as farmers would have been, for the acquisitors of these operations, a bewilderingly alien concept, since their holdings were about something else altogether: they were temporary chips in the greater game of capital formation.

This is well known, yet remains an elusive point for many Californians, particularly those with a psychic investment in one or another heightened version of the founding period. The heroine of Jack London's *The Valley of the Moon*, Saxon Brown, when hard times and union troubles come to Oakland, finds herself "dreaming of the arcadian days of her people, when they had not lived in cities nor been vexed with labor unions and employers' associations. She would remember the old people's tales of self-sufficingness, when they shot or raised their own meat, grew their own vegetables, were their own blacksmiths and carpenters, made their own shoes—yes, and spun the cloth of the clothes they wore. . . . A farmer's life must be fine, she thought. Why was it that people had to live in cities? Why had times changed?" In fact almost no one in California speaks of "farmers," in the sense the word is used in the rest of the country, and yet this persistent suggestion of constructive husbandry continues to cloud the retrospect. What amounted to the subsidized monopolization of California tends to be reinvented either as "settlement" (the settlers came, the desert bloomed) or, even more ideally, as a kind of foresighted commitment on the part of the acquisitors, a dedication to living at one with both the elemental wilderness and an improved patrician past.

"We had all shared in the glamour of immense, privately owned land," one of William Welles Hollister's seven grandchildren, Jane Hollister Wheelwright, wrote in *The Ranch Papers: A California Memoir*, the book she published in 1988, some twenty years after the sale of the Hollister ranch. "We lived in a fantastic but real world of our own discovery: square miles of impassable terrain, wild cattle threatening on the trail, single coyotes caterwauling like a pack, pumas screaming, storms felling giant oaks, washouts that marooned us for days, wildfires that lasted weeks and scorched whole mountain ranges." Her father, she tells us, "rarely wore his *chapaderos*," and did not use his silver-inlaid saddle, "but our Mexican ranch hands knew him for what he was. They called him '*El Patrón*.'" In 1961, after the death of the father, the daughter returns alone to the ranch, the point at which there appears in her memoir the first shadow on the glamour: "No one was there to meet me—not even the ranch hands," she writes. "I had none of the honor and recognition given automatically to *El Patrón*. The ranch seemed deserted. I was being deliberately avoided. Wandering aimlessly, I found myself walking into the canyon that stretched in back of the old family home. . . . The disappointment at seeing no one quickly faded. At least the land was there to greet me."

Jane Hollister Wheelwright's sense of her entitlement seems, in *The Ranch Papers*, more layered than that of many inheritors, more complicated, even tortured. The Hollisters, she concludes, "had been given a chance to live a part of history, to experience an era virtually extinct elsewhere in California." She remains reluctant to confront the contradictions in that history. Her idea of what the land meant remains heightened, and in the familiar way. She mentions in passing that the ranch supported "a large herd of white-faced Hereford cattle," but offers no sense of a working cattle operation. She sees her father as "one of the last of the gentlemen cattlemen of the era of large family ranches in California." She tells us that she and her twin brother "had grown up in a trance, like sleepwalkers, muffled by the land's huge embrace," and accompanies a photograph of herself at twenty with an apparently meaningful quotation from Aldo Leopold's *A Sand County Almanac*: "There are two kinds of people: those who can live without wild things and those who cannot."

Yet she seems to have quite deliberately chosen, at age twenty-four, to live without wild things: she married a psychiatrist, Joseph Wheelwright, was herself analyzed by Carl Jung, became a lay analyst, gave birth to a daughter in China and a son in London, and returned to California with her husband to found, in 1943 in San Francisco, the world's first Jungian training center. The description she gives of her 1961 return to the ranch is suggestive. All such returns, she tells us, involved a learned process of "reaching into the mood of the place," of shedding "city demands." She had come to understand the necessity of cultivating "calming" through "the monotony of walking," of encouraging the accelerated onset of what others might call by other names but she called "the big letdown": "Our coast requires a descent always. For those new to the place the letdown is more often experienced as an unpleasant locked-in feeling, an immobilizing depression."

What we seem to have here, then, is a story of an acquisitive grandfather, a father who retreated into the huge holding that allowed him to play *El Patrón* (even the daughter who reveres him mentions, in the guise of a virtue, "his power of passivity"), and a daughter, Jane Hollister, who ran guiltily for daylight. It was nonetheless Jane Hollister Wheelwright, not her brothers or cousins, who inherited from the father in 1961 the power to vote more than half the shares in the ranches. "My father must have known that I was as stubborn as he and would try to tackle the problems; and as the only woman I would be outside male competition," she wrote in *The Ranch Papers.* "But the outrage it caused only compounded the existing situation, and so the struggle began amongst the seven of us." That the nature of this struggle is not described in *The Ranch Papers* is a telling lacuna. It would appear to have focused, since the need to sell was a given, on the terms of the sale: to whom, for how much, in return for what contingent agreements. One senses that the daughter may have favored, probably more than her brothers and cousins did, the ultimate buyer: a Los Angeles developer, described in *The Ranch Papers*, again ideally, as "an enterprising but environment-minded Los Angeles man," whose plan was to rezone the property into hundred-acre parcels and present the whole as an exclusive planned retreat.

In California as elsewhere, a buyer with a plan for this kind of low-density development signifies something quite specific: this is a buyer who means to pay less for the land than one with a plan for more intensive development. During the same years when the Hollisters were falling out over this issue, James Irvine's great-granddaughter, Joan Irvine Smith, someone else who had "shared in the glamour of immensely, privately owned land," was fighting the same kind of family fight, but from a different angle: it was Joan Irvine who successfully insisted, against the opposition of some in her own family, that the eighty-eight thousand acres that remained of the Irvine ranch in Orange County be intensively developed. Whether Jane Hollister's decision to divide her grandfather's ranch into hundred-acre parcels was in the end more intrinsically tuned to the spirit of the place than Joan Irvine's quite different decision remains an unresolved question. I recall in the early seventies seeing advertising for what came to be called "Hollister Ranch," emphasizing how very few select achievers could hope to live there. As it happens my father had been at Berkeley with one of the Hollisters, someone of an age to have been one of Jane Hollister's brothers or cousins; I do not remember his name and my father is dead. I remember this at all only because, every time we drove south and again at the time the ranch was sold, my father mentioned that the effort to keep their holding intact had left the Hollisters unable to afford, in the early 1930s, during the Depression, to let one of their children finish Berkeley. This was offered as a lesson, I am unsure to what point.

The lesson Jane Hollister Wheelwright took from the sale of her family's ranch, proceeding as she did from within what amounts to a fable of confusion, concerned what she called the "debatable" questions: "whether land can belong to anyone, or whether one belongs to the land." She concluded, unsurprisingly, that land belonged to no one. Yet it did: at the time the Hollister ranch was sold, in the late 1960s, according to a Ralph Nader Study Group report on land use in California, roughly two and a half million acres of California still belonged to the Southern Pacific. Almost half a million acres belonged to the Shasta Forest Company. A third of a million acres belonged to Tenneco, another third of a million each to the Tejon Ranch Company, Standard Oil, and Boise Cascade. Two hundred seventy-eight thousand acres belonged to Georgia Pacific. Two hundred and fifty thousand belonged to Pacific Gas & Electric. Two hundred thousand belonged to Occidental Petroleum, 192,000 to Sunkist, 171,062 to Pacific Lumber, 155,000 to Fibreboard Incorporated, and 152,000 to the Newhall Land and Farming Company. Another 1,350,045 acres belonged to, among them, American Forest Products, Times Mirror, the Penn Central, Hammond Lumber, Kaiser Industries, the Masonite Corporation, J. G. Boswell, International Paper, Diamond International Corporation, Vail, Miller & Lux, and the Irvine Ranch Company. Some of these were California companies; some were not. All played a role in determining which of California's possibilities would be realized and which limited. Most were diversified, no more interested in what grew or grazed on their land than Jane Hollister had been, to another point, in what grew or grazed on hers, but quicker players, all of them, than the Hollisters had proved to be.

Jane Hollister's mother, Lottie Steffens Hollister, was the sister of Lincoln Steffens, who wrote *The Shame of the Cities* and later said of the Soviet Union that he had seen the future and it worked. Lincoln Steffens was Jane Hollister's "Uncle Steffie," and she his "Lady Jane." The Steffens children had grown up in a house in Sacramento a few blocks from the house in which, in 1908, my father was born. The Steffens house later became the Governor's Mansion, in which both Jerry Brown and his sister Kathleen lived during the years their father, Edmund G. ("Pat") Brown, was the thirty-second governor of California. Jerry Brown was himself the thirty-fourth governor of California. Kathleen Brown, in 1994, tried and failed to become the thirty-seventh. I went to Berkeley with their sister Barbara. There are many connections in California life, and yet, like Charles Crocker's Millet as the source for Edwin Markham's "The Man with the Hoe," not much connects: my mother's father, who lived in Sacramento but grew up on the Georgetown Divide in El Dorado County, remained convinced to his death that Edwin Markham, who had been superintendent of schools in El Dorado County from 1882 until 1886, did not himself write "The Man with the Hoe," but was given the poem by, in my grandfather's words, "an emigrant wayfarer from whom Markham purchased it for a small amount of money, and thereby helped the traveler along his way." My grandfather seemed to have in his memory bank a fairly complete dossier on Edwin Markham (the names of his three wives, the dates of his and their arrivals in California, even the houses in which they had lived), and could be quite insistent about what he believed to be the true provenance of "The Man with the Hoe," but his attitude toward the alleged appropriation was sufficiently opaque to encourage me, as a child, to ask my mother if my grandfather had in fact been the emigrant wayfarer. "He wasn't an emigrant," my mother said, settling at least that question.

Jane Hollister Wheelwright, who was herself born in Sacramento, saw as a kind of death the intrusion onto the Hollister ranch of two Chevron pipelines ("I can only believe that their appearance on the ranch means just one thing: another expression of man's historical arrogance and hatred of nature") but, still operating within the fable of an ideal personal past, was untroubled, even comforted, by the presence of the Southern Pacific, which her grandfather had actively supported and to which he had given a sixty-foot right-of-way along the coast. On her farewell rides through the ranch she observed the daily appearance of *The Daylight*, the Southern Pacific's principal passenger train to Los Angeles, and noted that it "seemed to belong there, and did not jar the feeling of the coast in the slightest. The noises it made recalled my childhood when we had no other way of telling time, and the sound of a whistle in the distance meant we were hopelessly late for lunch."

The eighth governor of California, Leland Stanford, was at the time of his election the president of the Central Pacific and later the president of the Southern Pacific. Hiram Johnson, the twenty-third governor of California, was elected as a reform candidate pledged to break the power of the Southern Pacific. Hiram Johnson's father, Grove Johnson, had fled upstate New York under indictment for forgery in 1863, settled in Sacramento, become clerk of the county Swamp Land Board, been implicated in two vote-rigging scandals, and been elected, in 1877, to the California State Assembly. "The interests of the railroad and Sacramento are identical, and should always remain so," the elder Johnson declared during this campaign. "They should labor together like man and wife, only to be divorced by death."

When Hiram Johnson went to Berkeley in 1884 he lived in the Chi Phi house, as did, forty-five years later, my father and my uncle and the Hollister who had to drop out of school. When I went to Berkeley some years later I lived, as did Barbara Brown, at the Tri Delt house. Her father, not yet governor of California but its attorney general, spoke at our annual father-daughter dinners. When my brother went to Berkeley five years after I did he lived at the Phi Gamma Delta, or Fiji, house, as had, sixty-some years before, Frank Norris, who remained famous in the house for having initiated its annual celebratory "Pig Dinner." This was a California, into the nineteen-fifties, so hermetic, so isolated by geography and by history and also by inclination, that when I first read *The Octopus*, at age twelve or thirteen, in Sacramento, I did not construe it to have a personal relevance, since the events described took place not in the Sacramento Valley but somewhere else, the San Joaquin.

Not much about California, on its own preferred terms, has encouraged its children to see themselves as connected to one another. The separation, of north from south—and even more acutely of west from east, of the urban coast from the agricultural valleys and of both the coast and the valleys from the mountain and desert regions to their east—was profound, fueled by the rancor of water wars and by less tangible but even more rancorous differences in attitude and culture. My mother made the trip from Sacramento to Los Angeles in 1932, to see the Olympics, and did not find reason to make it again for thirty years. In the north we had San Francisco, with its Beaux Arts buildings and eucalyptus, its yearnings backward and westward, its resolutely anecdotal "color"; a place as remote and mannered as the melancholy colonial capitals of Latin America, and as isolated. When I was at Berkeley and had gone home to Sacramento for a weekend I would sometimes take the Southern Pacific's transcontinental *City of San Francisco* back down, not the most convenient train (for one thing it was always late) but one that suggested, carrying as it did the glamour of having come across the mountains from the rest of America, that our isolation might not be an indefinite sentence.

I see now that the life I was raised to admire was entirely the product of this isolation, infinitely romantic, but in a kind of vacuum, its only antecedent aesthetic, and the aesthetic only the determined "Bohemianism" of nineteenth-century San Francisco. The clothes chosen for me as a child had a strong element of the Pre-Raphaelite, muted greens and ivories, dusty rose, what seems in retrospect an eccentric amount of black. I still have the black mantilla I was given to wear over my shoulders when I started to go to dances, not the kind of handkerchief triangle Catholic women used to keep in their pockets and glove compartments but several yards of heavy black lace. It had been my great-grandmother's, I have no idea why, since this particular great-grandmother was from Oregon, with no reason to have bought into a romance-of-the-ranchos scenario. We lived in dark houses and favored, a preference so definite that it passed as a test of character, copper and brass that had darkened and greened. We also let our silver darken, which was said to "bring out the pattern." To this day I am put off by highly polished silver: it looks "new." This predilection for the "old" extended into all areas of domestic life: dried flowers were seen to have a more subtle charm than fresh, prints should be faded, rugs worn, wallpaper streaked by the sun. Our highest moment in this area was the acquisition, in 1951, of a house in Sacramento in which the curtains on the stairs had not been changed since 1907. These curtains, which were of unlined (and faded, naturally) gold silk organza, hung almost two stories, billowed iridescent with every breath of air, and, if touched, crumbled.

Stressing as it did an extreme if ungrounded individualism, this was not an ambiance that tended toward a view of life as defined or limited or controlled, or even in any way affected, by the social and economic structures of the larger world. To be a Californian was to see oneself, if one believed the lessons the place seemed most immediately to offer, as affected only by "nature," which in turn was seen to exist simultaneously as a source of inspiration or renewal ("Born again!" John Muir noted in the journal of his first trip into Yosemite) and as the ultimate brute reckoning, the force that by guaranteeing destruction gave the place its perilous beauty. Much of the California landscape has tended to present itself as metaphor, even as litany: the redwoods (*for a thousand years in thy sight are but as yesterday*), the Mojave (*in the midst of life we are in death*), the coast at Big Sur, Mono Lake, the great vistas of the Sierra, especially those of the Yosemite Valley, which, Kevin Starr has pointed out, "offered Californians an objective correlative for their ideal sense of themselves: a people animated by heroic imperatives." Thomas Starr King saw Yosemite in 1860 and went back to the First Unitarian Church of San Francisco determined to inspire "Yosemites in the soul." Albert Bierstadt saw Yosemite in 1863 and came back to do the grandiose landscapes that made him for a dozen years the most popularly acclaimed painter in America. "Some of Mr. Bierstadt's mountains swim in a lustrous, pearly mist," Mark Twain observed with some acerbity, "which is so enchantingly beautiful that I am sorry the Creator hadn't made it instead of him, so that it would always remain there."

Lessons could be found even in less obviously histrionic features: climbing Mt. Tamalpais in Marin County at sunrise was seen, in my grandmother's generation, as a convenient transformative experience, as was any contemplation of the opening to the Pacific that John C. Frémont, when he mapped the area in 1846, had named "Chrysopylae," or Golden Gate, "on the same principle that the harbor of Byzantium (Constantinople afterwards) was called Chrysoceras (golden horn)." Josiah Royce, in his 1879 essay "Meditation Before the Gate," reflected on the view of the Gate from Berkeley and pledged himself to pursue his philosophical inquiries "independently, because I am a Californian, as little bound to follow mere tradition as I am liable to find an audience by preaching in this wilderness; reverently, because I am thinking and writing face to face with a mighty and lovely Nature, by the side of whose greatness I am but as a worm."

This is interesting, a quite naked expression of what has been the California conundrum. Scaled against Yosemite, or against the view through the Gate of the Pacific trembling on its tectonic plates, the slightest shift of which could and with some regularity did destroy the works of man in a millisecond, all human beings were of course but as worms, their "heroic imperatives" finally futile, their philosophical inquiries vain. The population of California has increased in my lifetime from six million to close to thirty-five million people, yet the three phrases that come first to mind when I try to define California to myself refer exclusively to its topography, a landscape quite empty of people. The first of these phrases comes from the language of broadcast weather reports, the second from John

Muir. The third, and most persistent, comes from Robinson Jeffers. *Point Conception to the Mexican border. The Range of Light. Beautiful country burn again, / Point Pinos down to the Sur Rivers.*

This is the point in the California experience when discussion stops, and many voices fade. Broadcast weather reports could be seen as nominally neutral on the question of whether human beings have any rightful place in California, but John Muir and Robinson Jeffers could not. Muir traded the Calvinism of his Scottish childhood for an equally Calvinist wilderness, a landscape in which he could tolerate only Indians, because Indians "walk softly and hurt the landscape hardly more than the birds and squirrels, and their brush and bark huts last hardly longer than those of woodrats, while their more enduring monuments, excepting those wrought on the forests by the fires they made to improve their hunting grounds, vanish in a few centuries." Jeffers tolerated no one at all, taking this aversion to the point at which he came to favor war, which alone, as he saw it, could return the world to its "emptiness," to "the bone, the colorless white bone, the excellence." "Be in nothing so moderate as in love of man," he advised his twin sons, and referred to mankind as a "botched experiment that has run wild and ought to be stopped." He was accused of "proto-fascism." He called himself an "Inhumanist." (As in, from a posting on the Jeffers Studies web site, "I'm interested in the relationship between Inhumanism and Deep Ecology and would welcome any thoughts or comments.") He seemed to many an easy target: his poetry could be pretentious, his postures ugly. Read in situ, however, Jeffers makes fatally seductive sense: *Burn as before with bitter wonders, land and ocean and the Carmel water.* And: *When the cities lie at the monster's feet there are left the mountains.*

I am thinking and writing face to face with a mighty and lovely Nature, Josiah Royce wrote, *by the side of whose greatness I am but as a worm.* Royce in fact seems to have maintained an exhausting but finally vain alert against the undertow of this localized nihilism. His 1886 *California: A Study of American Character* bore on its title page these peculiar but premonitory lines, spoken by Mephistopheles in the Prologue to *Faust: On suns and worlds I can shed little light / I see but humans, and their piteous plight.* At sixty, in despair at the prospect of World War One and a few months short of what would be a fatal stroke, he encountered in Harvard Yard one of his students, Horace Kallen, who, according to Robert V. Hine's *Josiah Royce: From Grass Valley to Harvard*, reported of Royce that "When I greeted him, his round blue eyes looked staring, and without recognition. And then he said in a voice somehow thinner . . . 'You are on the side of humanity, aren't you?'" A few months before, describing himself as "socially ineffective as regards genuine 'team play,' ignorant of politics, an ineffective member of committees, and a poor helper of concrete social enterprises," as well as "a good deal of a non-conformist, and disposed to a certain rebellion," Royce had acknowledged that the idea of community to which he had devoted his career remained in some way alien to him: "When I review this whole process, I strongly feel that my deepest motives and problems have centered about the Idea of the Community, although this idea has only come gradually to my clear consciousness. This is what I was intensely feeling, in the days when my sisters and I looked across the Sacramento Valley, and wondered about the great world beyond our mountains. . . . So much of the spirit that opposes the community I have and have always had in me, simply, deeply, elementally."

So much of the spirit that opposes the community: of course he had it in him, considering what he was: ". . . *because I am a Californian*," he himself had written, "*as little bound to follow mere tradition*. . . ." In 1970 I spent a month in the South, in Louisiana and Alabama and Mississippi, under the misapprehension that an understanding of the differences between the West and the South, which had given California a good deal of its original settlement, would improve my understanding of California. Royce had fretted over the same question: "Very early . . . this relatively peaceful mingling of Americans from North and South had already deeply affected the tone of California life," he noted in *California: A Study of American Character*. "The type of the Northern man who has assumed Southern fashions, and not always the best Southern fashions at that, has often been observed in California life. . . . He often followed the Southerner, and was frequently, in time, partly assimilated by the Southern civilization." One difference between the West and the South, I came to realize in 1970, was this: in the South they remained convinced that they had bloodied their land with history. In California we did not believe that history could bloody the land, or even touch it.

7

THOMAS KINKADE was born in the late 1950s and raised in Placerville, El Dorado County, where his mother supported him and his siblings by working as a notary public, piecework, five dollars a document. The father had left. The family lived much of the time in a trailer. By the early 1990s "Thomas Kinkade" was a phenomenon, a brand on his own, a merchandiser who could touch a snow globe or a stoneware mug or a night-light or a La-Z-Boy chair with the magic of his name and turn it to money, a painter so successful that by the end of the decade there would be throughout the United States 248 Thomas Kinkade "signature galleries," seventy-eight of them in California alone, most of those in malls or tourist areas, four for example in Monterey and another four in Carmel, two exits down Highway 1. Since very few of Thomas Kinkade's original oil paintings were by that time available, and since those that were had risen in price from about $15,000 in the early 1990s to more than $300,000 by 1997, the pictures sold in these 248 "signature galleries" were canvas-backed reproductions, which themselves sold for $900 to $15,000 and were produced by the 450 employees who labored in the hundred-thousand-square-foot Morgan Hill headquarters of Media Arts Group Incorporated ("MDA" on the New York Stock Exchange), the business of which was Thomas Kinkade.

The passion with which buyers approached these Kinkade images was hard to define. The manager of one California gallery that handled them told me that it was not unusual to sell six or seven at a clip, to buyers who already owned ten or twenty, and that the buyers with whom he dealt brought to the viewing of the images "a sizeable emotional weight." A Kinkade painting was typically rendered in slightly surreal pastels. It typically featured a cottage or a house of such insistent coziness as to seem actually sinister, suggestive of a trap designed to attract Hansel and Gretel. Every window was lit, to lurid effect, as if the interior of the structure might be on fire. The cottages had thatched roofs, and resembled gingerbread houses. The houses were Victorian, and resembled idealized bed-and-breakfasts, at least two of which in Placerville, the Chichester-McKee House and the Combellack-Blair House, claimed to have been the models for Kinkade "Christmas" paintings. "There's a lot of beauty here that I present in a way that's whimsical and charming," Kinkade allowed to the Placerville *Mountain Democrat.* He branded himself the "Painter of Light," and the postcards Media Arts provided to his galleries each for a while bore this legend: "Thomas Kinkade is recognized as the foremost living painter of light. His masterful use of soft edges and luminous colors give his highly detailed oil paintings a glow all their own. This extraordinary 'Kinkade Glow' has created an overwhelming demand for Thomas Kinkade paintings and lithographs worldwide."

This "Kinkade Glow" could be seen as derived in spirit from the "lustrous, pearly mist" that Mark Twain had derided in the Bierstadt paintings, and, the level of execution to one side, there are certain unsettling similarities between the two painters. "After completing my recent plein air study of Yosemite Valley, the mountains' majesty refused to leave me," Kinkade wrote in June 2000 on his web site. "When my family wandered through the national park visitor center, I discovered a key to my fantasy—a recreation of a Miwok Indian Village. When I returned to my studio, I began work on *The Mountains Declare His Glory*, a poetic expression of what I felt at that transforming moment of inspiration. As a final touch, I even added a Miwok Indian Camp along the river as an affirmation that man has his place, even in a setting touched by God's glory."

Affirming that man has his place in the Sierra Nevada by reproducing the Yosemite National Park Visitor Center's re-creation of a Miwok Indian Village is identifiable as a doubtful enterprise on many levels (not the least of which being that the Yosemite Miwok were forcibly run onto a reservation near Fresno during the Gold Rush, and allowed to return to Yosemite only in 1855), but is Thomas Kinkade's Sierra in fact any more sentimentalized than that of Albert Bierstadt? Were not the divinely illuminated passes of Bierstadt's Sierra meant to confirm the successful completion of our manifest destiny? Was it by chance that Collis P. Huntington commissioned Bierstadt to undertake a painting celebrating the domination of Donner Pass by the Central Pacific Railroad? Was not Bierstadt's triumphalist *Donner Lake from the Summit* a willful revision to this point of the locale that most clearly embodied the moral ambiguity of the California settlement? This was the lesson drawn from the pass in question by one of the surviving children of the Donner Party, Virginia Reed, who wrote to her cousin: "Oh, Mary, I have not wrote you half of the trouble we've had, but I have wrote you enough to let you know what trouble is. But thank God, we are the only family that did not eat human flesh. We have left everything, but I don't care for that. We have got through with our lives. Don't let this letter dishearten anybody. Remember, never take no cutoffs and hurry along as fast as you can."

Remember, never take no cutoffs and hurry along as fast as you can.

Did the preferred version of our history reflect the artless horror and constricted moral horizon of Virginia Reed's first-hand account?

Or had it come more closely to resemble the inspirational improvement that was Bierstadt's *Donner Lake from the Summit*?

The confusions embedded in the crossing story can be seen in unintended relief in Jack London's *The Valley of the Moon*, the 1913 novel that has at its center the young woman Saxon Brown. At the time we meet Saxon she is orphaned, boarding with her hard-pressed socialist brother and his bad-tempered wife, and spending six hard days a week as a piecework ironer in an Oakland laundry. On their Saturday night off, Saxon and a friend from the laundry splurge on tickets to a Bricklayers' picnic, where Saxon meets a similarly orphaned teamster, Billy Roberts, to whom she confides that she was named for "the first English, and you know the Americans came from the English. We're Saxons, you an' me, an' Mary, an' Bert, and all the Americans that are real Americans, you know, and not Dagoes and Japs and such." If this seems a thin reed on which to hang one's identity, it would not have seemed so to London, who, Kevin Starr noted in *Americans and the California*

Dream, once protested an arrest for vagrancy by arguing to the court "that no old American whose ancestors had fought in the American Revolution should be treated this way." The moment in which the judge nonetheless sentenced him to thirty days is described by Starr as "one of the most traumatic" in London's life.

Assured by Billy Roberts that he too is a "real" American, that his mother's family "crossed to Maine hundreds of years ago," Saxon asks where his father was from. This extraordinary exchange ensues:

> "Don't know." Billy shrugged his shoulders. "He didn't know himself. Nobody ever knew, though he was American, all right, all right."
>
> "His name's regular old American," Saxon suggested. "There's a big English general right now whose name is Roberts. I've read it in the papers."
>
> "But Roberts wasn't my father's name. He never knew what his name was. Roberts was the name of a gold-miner who adopted him. You see, it was this way. When they was Indian-fightin' up there with the Modoc Indians, a lot of miners an' settlers took a hand. Roberts was captain of one outfit, and once, after a fight, they took a lot of prisoners—squaws, an' kids an' babies. An' one of the kids was my father. They figured he was about five years old. He didn't know nothin' but Indian."
>
> Saxon clapped her hands, and her eyes sparkled: "He'd been captured on an Indian raid!"
>
> "That's the way they figured it," Billy nodded. "They recollected a wagon-train of Oregon settlers that'd been killed by the Modocs four years before. Roberts adopted him, and that's why I don't know his real name. But you can bank on it, he crossed the plains just the same."
>
> "So did my father," Saxon said proudly.
>
> "An' my mother, too," Billy added, pride touching his own voice. "Anyway, she came pretty close to crossin' the plains, because she was born in a wagon on the River Platte on the way out."
>
> "My mother, too," said Saxon. "She was eight years old, an' she walked most of the way after the oxen began to give out."
>
> Billy thrust out his hand.
>
> "Put her there, kid," he said. "We're just like old friends, what with the same kind of folks behind us."

> With shining eyes, Saxon extended her hand to his, and gravely they shook.
>
> "Isn't it wonderful?" she murmured. "We're both old American stock."

To assume that London was employing irony here, that his intention was to underline the distance between Saxon and Billy's actual situation and their illusions of superior lineage, would be to misread *The Valley of the Moon.* "Times have changed," Saxon complains to Billy. "We crossed the plains and opened up this country, and now we're losing even the chance to work for a living in it." This strikes a chord in Billy, which resonates again when the two happen into a prosperous Portuguese settlement: "It looks like the free-born American ain't got no room left in his own land," Billy says to Saxon. A further thought from Billy: "It was our folks who made this country. Fought for it, opened it up, did everything—"

This truculence on the question of immigration was by no means an unfamiliar note in California, which by the time London wrote already had a tenacious history of vigilance committees and exclusionary legislation. "The fearful blindness of the early behavior of the Americans in California towards foreigners is something almost unintelligible," Josiah Royce wrote in 1886 of the violence and lynchings to which "foreigners"—mainly Sonorans but also Chinese and native Digger Indians—had been subjected in the gold fields. Sixty-some years after Royce, Carey McWilliams, in *California: The Great Exception*, characterized the pervasive local hostility toward Asians as "a social and psychic necessity of the situation," the "negative device" by which a state made up of newly arrived strangers had been able to achieve the illusion of a cohesive community joined against the menace of the foreign-born.

Such hostility was by no means unknown in more settled parts of the country, but rarely was it so intricately codified by law. The Foreign Miners' License Tax of 1850 had exacted a monthly fee of any non-citizen who wanted to work a claim. In 1854, an existing law prohibiting Negroes and Indians from testifying in court had been extended to also prohibit testimony by Chinese. The state legislature had barred "Mongolians,

Indians, and Negroes" from public schools in 1860; had barred Chinese from employment in corporations or on public works projects in 1879; and had amended an existing miscegenation law to include Chinese in 1906. The state Alien Land Acts of 1913 and 1920 would for more than thirty years effectively prohibit land ownership in California to both Asians and their American-born children.

It was in this spirit that the two "real" Americans, Saxon and Billy, set out in search of government land, the 160 free acres which were, as they saw it, their due. This conviction of entitlement was another familiar California note, and a particularly complicated one, since the idea of depending on the government of course ran counter to the preferred self-image of most Californians. Yet such dependence was, even then, almost total. It had been, as we have seen, federal money, spent on behalf of a broad spectrum of business interests, that built the railroad and opened the state to the rest of the world. It had been and would be, as we have seen, federal money, again spent on behalf of a large spectrum of business interests, that created what was no longer locally even called agribusiness, just "ag." The rationalization that resolves this contradiction is, in *The Valley of the Moon*, fairly primitive: the government owes Saxon and Billy free land, Billy reasons, "for what our fathers an' mothers done. I tell you, Saxon, when a woman walks across the plains like your mother done, an' a man an' wife gets massacred by the Indians like my grandfather an' mother done, the government does owe them something."

The land on which Saxon and Billy finally settle is the actual Valley of the Moon, in Sonoma County, and their discovery of it prefigures many of the doubtful sentiments that would later surface in the paintings of Thomas Kinkade. They arrive in the valley just as "sunset fires, refracted from the cloud-driftage of the autumn sky" turn the landscape "crimson." They see a stream, "singing" to them. They see "fairy circles" of redwoods. They see, at a distance, a man and a woman, "side by side, the delicate hand of the woman curled in the hand of the man, which looked as if made to confer benedictions." This magical bonding continues, again as if touched by the Kinkade Glow:

> Perhaps the picture made by Saxon and Billy was equally arresting and beautiful, as they drove down through the golden end of day. The two couples had eyes only for each other. The little woman beamed joyously. The man's face glowed into the benediction that had trembled there. To Saxon, like the field up the mountain, like the mountain itself, it seemed that she had always known this adorable pair. She knew that she loved them.

Only later does Saxon discover what the reader (by this point almost four hundred pages into *The Valley of the Moon*) may well have suspected early on: "this adorable pair" are in fact "old stock that had crossed the Plains," keepers perhaps of their own iconic potato masher, in any event kindred souls who "knew all about the fight at Little Meadow, and the tale of the massacre of the emigrant train of which Billy's father had been the sole survivor." Their rightful place in the California fable validated, Saxon and Billy settle in, determined to redeem the birthright of the "old stock" through the practice of scientific agronomy, which London himself imagined that he and his second wife, the woman he called his "Mate-Woman," Charmian Kittredge, were perfecting on their own Sonoma ranch. London's letters from this period speak of "making the dead soil live again," of leaving the land "better for my having been," of unremitting industry, transcendent husbandry. "No picayune methods for me," he wrote. "When I go in silence, I want to know that I left behind me a plot of land which, after the pitiful failures of others, I have made productive. . . . Can't you see? Oh, try to see!—In the solution of great economic problems of the present age, I see a return to the soil."

This was another confusion. His crops failed. His Wolf House, built to last a thousand years, burned to the ground before he and the Mate-Woman (or, as he alternately called Charmian, the Wolf-Mate) could move in. His health was gone. He battled depression. He battled alcoholism. At one point in 1913, the year Wolf House was completed and burned, he had only three dollars and forty-six cents left in the bank. In the end only the Mate-Woman kept the faith: "I am crazy for everyone to know about Jack's big experiment up here," Charmian Kittredge London wrote to a friend, Tom Wilkinson, on December 15, 1916. "So few persons think of it at all in connection with him—they slobber about his this and his that and his the other, and say nothing about his tremendous experiment—practical experiment—up here on Sonoma Mountain." Just three weeks before this letter was written, Jack London had died, at forty, of uremic poisoning and one final, fatal, dose of the morphine prescribed to calm his renal colic. In the last novel he was to write, *The Little Lady of the Big House*, he had allowed his protagonist and author-surrogate to ask these questions, a flash of the endemic empty in a work that is otherwise a fantasy of worldly and social success: "Why? What for? What's it worth? What's it all about?"

8

THE BOHEMIAN CLUB of San Francisco was founded, in 1872, by members of the city's working press, who saw it both as a declaration of unconventional or "artistic" interests and as a place to get a beer and a sandwich after the bulldog closed. Frank Norris was a member, as was Henry George, who had not yet published *Progress and Poverty*. There were poets: Joaquin Miller, George Sterling. There were writers: Samuel Clemens, Bret Harte, Ambrose Bierce, Jack London, who only a few months before his death managed to spend a week at Bohemian Grove, the club's encampment in the redwoods north of San Francisco. John Muir belonged to the Bohemian Club, and so did Joseph LeConte. For a few years the members appear to have remained resolute in their determination not to admit the merely rich (they had refused membership to William C. Ralston, the president of the Bank of California), but their over-ambitious spending, both on the club in town and on its periodic encampments, quite soon overwhelmed this intention. According to a memoir of the period written by Edward Bosqui, San Francisco's most prominent publisher during the late nineteenth century and a charter member of the Bohemian Club, it was at this point decided to "invite an element to join the club which the majority of the members held in contempt, namely men who had money as well as brains, but who were not, strictly speaking, Bohemians."

By 1927, a year after George Sterling committed suicide during a club dinner for H. L. Mencken by going upstairs to bed and swallowing cyanide (he had been depressed, he had been drinking, Frank Norris's brother had replaced him as toastmaster for the Mencken dinner), the Bohemian Club was banning from its annual art exhibit any entry deemed by the club "in radical and unreasonable departure from laws of art." By 1974, when G. William Domhoff, then a professor of sociology at the University of California at Santa Cruz, wrote *The Bohemian Grove and Other Retreats: A Study in Ruling-Class Cohesiveness*, one in five resident members and one in three nonresident members of the Bohemian Club was listed in

Standard & Poor's Register of Corporations, Executives, and Directors. Among those attending the summer encampment at Bohemian Grove in 1970, the year for which Domhoff obtained a list, "at least one officer or director from forty of the fifty largest industrial corporations in America was present. . . . Similarly, we found that officers and directors from twenty of the top twenty-five commercial banks (including all of the fifteen largest) were on our lists. Men from twelve of the first twenty-five life-insurance companies were in attendance (eight of these twelve were from the top ten)."

The summer encampment, then, had evolved into a special kind of enchanted circle, one in which these captains of American finance and industry could entertain, in what was to most of them an attractively remote setting, the temporary management of that political structure on which their own fortunes ultimately depended. When Dwight Eisenhower visited the Grove in 1950, eleven years before he made public his concern about the military-industrial complex, he traveled on a special train arranged by the president of the Santa Fe Railroad. Domhoff noted that both Henry Kissinger and Melvin Laird, then secretary of defense, were present at the 1970 encampment, as were David M. Kennedy, then secretary of the treasury, and Admiral Thomas H. Moorer, chairman of the Joint Chiefs of Staff. John Erlichman, as the guest of Leonard Firestone, represented the White House. Walter J. Hickel, at the time secretary of the interior, was the guest of Fred L. Hartley, the president of Union Oil.

The rituals of the summer encampment were fixed. There were, every day at twelve-thirty, "Lakeside Talks," informal speeches and briefings, off the record. Kissinger, Laird, and William P. Rogers, then secretary of state, gave Lakeside Talks in 1970; Colin Powell and the chairman of Dow Chemical were scheduled for 1999. Local color was measured: the fight songs sung remained those of the traditional California schools, Berkeley (or, in this venue, "Cal") and Stanford, yet it was a rule of the Bohemian Club that no Californian, unless he was a member, could be asked as a guest during the two-week midsummer encampment. (As opposed to the May "Spring Jinks" weekend, to which California non-members could be invited.) The list for the 1985 encampment, the most recent complete roster I have seen, shows the members and their "camps," the hundred-some self-selected groupings situated back through the hills and canyons and off the road to the Russian River. Each camp has a name, for example Stowaway, or Pink Onion, or Silverado Squatters, or Lost Angels.

For the 1985 encampment, Caspar Weinberger was due at Isle of Aves, James Baker III at Woof. "George H. W. Bush" appeared on the list for Hillbillies (his son, George W. Bush, seems not to have been present in 1985, but he was on the list, along with his father and Newt Gingrich, for 1999), as did, among others, Frank Borman, William F. Buckley, Jr., and his son Christopher, Walter Cronkite, A. W. Clausen of the Bank of America and the World Bank, and Frank A. Sprole of Bristol-Myers. George Shultz was on the list for Mandalay, along with William French Smith, Thomas Watson, Jr., Nicholas Brady, Leonard K. Firestone, Peter Flanigan, Gerald Ford, Najeeb Halaby, Philip M. Hawley, J. K. Horton, Edgar F. Kaiser, Jr., Henry Kissinger, John McCone, and two of the Bechtels. This virtual personification of Eisenhower's military-industrial complex notwithstanding, the Spirit of Bohemia, or California, could still be seen, in the traditional tableaux performed at every Grove encampment, to triumph over Mammon, God of Gold, and all his gnomes and promises and bags of treasure:

> SPIRIT: *Nay, Mammon. For one thing it cannot buy.*
> MAMMON: *What cannot it buy?*
> SPIRIT: *A happy heart!*

The transformation of the Bohemian Club from a lively if frivolous gathering of local free spirits to a nexus of the nation's corporate and political interests in many ways mirrored a larger transformation, that of California itself from what it had been, or from what its citizens preferred to believe that it had been, to what it is now, an entirely dependent colony of the invisible empire in which those corporate and political interests are joined. In 1868, four years before he helped to found the Bohemian Club, Henry George, twenty-nine years old and previously unpublished, wrote a piece in the *Overland Monthly* in which he tried to locate "the peculiar charm of California, which all who have lived here long enough feel." He concluded that California's charm resided in the character of its people: ". . . there has been a feeling of personal independence and equality, a general hopefulness and self-reliance, and a certain large-heartedness and open-handedness which were born of the comparative evenness with which property was distributed, the high standard of wages and of comfort, and the latent feeling of everyone that he might 'make a strike.'" This piece, "What the Railroad Will Bring Us," was intended, of course, as an antidote to the enthusiasm then general about the windfall to be realized by giving the state to the Southern Pacific:

> Let us see clearly whither we are tending. Increase in population and in wealth past a certain point means simply an approximation to the condition of older countries—the eastern states and Europe. . . . The truth is, that the completion of the railroad and the consequent great increase of business and population, will not be a benefit to all of us, but only to a portion. . . . This crowding of people into immense cities, this aggregation of wealth into large lumps, this marshalling of men into big gangs under the control of the great "captains of industry," does not tend to foster personal independence—the basis of all virtues—nor will it tend to preserve the characteristics which particularly have made Californians proud of their state.

Henry George asked what the railroad would bring, but not too many other people did. Many people would later ask whether it had served the common weal to transform the Sacramento and San Joaquin Valleys from a seasonal shallow sea to a protected hothouse requiring the annual application on each square mile of 3.87 tons of chemical pesticides, but not too many people asked this before the dams; those who did ask, for whatever reason, were categorized as "environmentalists," a word loosely used in this part of California to describe any perceived threat to the life of absolute personal freedom its citizens believe they lead. "California likes to be fooled," Cedarquist, the owner in *The Octopus* of a failed San Francisco ironworks, advises Presley when they happen to meet at (where else?) the Bohemian Club. "Do you suppose Shelgrim [the Collis P. Huntington figure] could convert the whole San Joaquin Valley into his back yard otherwise?"

"What the Railroad Will Bring Us" remained, into my generation at least, routine assigned reading for California children, one more piece of evidence that assigned reading makes nothing happen. I used to think that Henry George had overstated the role of the railroad, and in one sense he had: the railroad, of course, was merely the last stage of a process already underway, one that had its basis in the character of the settlement, in the very quality recommended by "What the Railroad Will Bring Us" as "a general hopefulness and self-reliance," or "a feeling of personal independence or equality," or "the latent feeling of everyone that he might 'make a strike.'" This process, one of trading the state to outside owners in exchange for their (it now seems) entirely temporary agreement to enrich us, in other words the pauperization of California, had in fact begun at the time Americans first entered the state, took what they could, and, abetted by the native weakness for boosterism, set about selling the rest.

Josiah Royce understood this negative side of the California character, but persisted in what was for him the essential conviction that the California community was so positive a force as to correct its own character. He allowed that "a general sense of social irresponsibility is, even today, the average Californian's easiest failing." Still, he seemed temperamentally unable to consider an "average Californian" who would not, in the end, see that his own best interests lay in cooperation, in the amelioration of differences, in a certain willingness to forego the immediate windfall for the larger or even his own long-term good. This was the same "average Californian" who, by the year Royce wrote, 1886, had already sold half the state to the Southern Pacific and was in the process of mortgaging the rest to the federal government. For most of the next hundred years, kept aloft first by oil and then by World War Two and finally by the Cold War and the largesse of the owners and managers who would arrive in Gulfstreams for the annual encampment at Bohemian Grove, that average Californian had seen his "easiest failing" yield only blue skies.

PART TWO

1

IN THE MAY 1935 issue of the *American Mercury*, William Faulkner published one of the few pieces of fiction he set in California, a short story he called "Golden Land." "Golden Land" deals with a day in the life of Ira Ewing, Jr., age forty-eight, a man for whom "twenty-five years of industry and desire, of shrewdness and luck and even fortitude," seem recently to have come to ashes. At fourteen, Ira Ewing had fled Nebraska on a westbound freight. By the time he was thirty, he had married the daughter of a Los Angeles carpenter, fathered a son and a daughter, and secured a foothold in the real estate business. By the time we meet him, eighteen years later, he is in a position to spend fifty thousand dollars a year, a sizable amount in 1935. He has been able to bring his widowed mother from Nebraska and install her in a house in Glendale. He has been able to provide for his children "luxuries and advantages which his own father not only could not have conceived in fact but would have condemned completely in theory."

Yet nothing is working out. Ira's daughter, Samantha, who wants to be in show business and has taken the name "April Lalear," is testifying in a lurid trial reported on page one ("April Lalear Bares Orgy Secrets") of the newspapers placed on the reading table next to Ira's bed. Ira, less bewildered than weary, tries not to look at the accompanying photographs of Samantha, the "hard, blonde, and inscrutable" daughter who "alternately stared back or flaunted long pale shins." Nor is Samantha the exclusive source of the leaden emptiness Ira now feels instead of hunger: there is also his son, Voyd, who continues to live at home but has not spoken unprompted to his father in two years, not since the morning when Voyd, drunk, was delivered home to his father wearing, "in place of underclothes, a woman's brassiere and step-ins."

Since Ira prides himself on being someone who will entertain no suggestion that his life is not the success that his business achievement would seem to him to promise, he discourages discussion of his domestic trials, and has tried to keep the newspapers featuring April Lalear and the orgy secrets away from his mother. Via the gardener, however, Ira's mother has learned about her granddaughter's testimony, and she is reminded of the warning she once gave her son, after she had seen Samantha and Voyd stealing cash from their mother's purse: "You make money too easy," she had told Ira. "This whole country is too easy for us Ewings. It may be all right for them that have been born here for generations, I don't know about that. But not for us."

"But these children were born here," Ira had said.

"Just one generation," his mother had said. "The generation before that they were born in a sod-roofed dugout on the Nebraska wheat frontier. And the one before that in a log house in Missouri. And the one before that in a Kentucky blockhouse with Indians around it. This world has never been easy for Ewings. Maybe the Lord never intended it to be."

"But it is from now on," the son had insisted. "For you and me too. But mostly for them."

"Golden Land" does not entirely hold up, nor, I would guess, will it ever be counted among the best Faulkner stories. Yet it retains, for certain Californians, a nagging resonance, and opens the familiar troubling questions. I grew up in a California family that derived, from the single circumstance of having been what Ira Ewing's mother called "born here for generations," considerable pride, much of it, it seemed to me later, strikingly unearned. "The trouble with these new people," I recall hearing again and again as a child in Sacramento, "is they think it's supposed to be easy." The phrase "these new people" generally signified people who had moved to California after World War Two, but was tacitly extended back to include the migration from the Dust Bowl during the 1930s, and often further. New people, we were given to understand, remained ignorant of our special history, insensible to the hardships endured to make it, blind not only to the dangers the place still presented but to the shared responsibilities its continued habitation demanded.

If my grandfather spotted a rattlesnake while driving, he would stop his car and go into the brush after it. To do less, he advised me more than once, was to endanger whoever later entered the brush, and so violate what he called "the code of the West." New people, I was told, did not understand their responsibility to kill rattlesnakes. Nor did new people understand that the water that came from the tap in, say, San Francisco, was there only because part of Yosemite had been flooded to put it there. New people did not understand the necessary dynamic of the fires, the seven-year cycles of flood and drought, the physical reality of the place. "Why didn't they go back to Truckee?" a young mining engineer from back East asked when my grandfather pointed out the site of the Donner Party's last encampment. I recall hearing this story repeatedly. I also recall the same grandfather, my mother's father, whose family had migrated from the hardscrabble Adirondack frontier in the eighteenth century to the hardscrabble Sierra Nevada foothills in the nineteenth, working himself up into writing an impassioned letter-to-the-editor over a fifth-grade textbook in which one of the illustrations summed up California history as a sunny progression from Spanish Señorita to Gold Miner to Golden Gate Bridge. What the illustration seemed to my grandfather to suggest was that those responsible for the textbook believed the settlement of California to have been "easy," history rewritten, as he saw it, for the new people. There were definite ambiguities in this: Ira Ewing and his children were, of course, new people, but so, less than a century before, had my grandfather's family been. New people could be seen, by people like my grandfather, as indifferent to everything that had made California work, but the ambiguity was this: new people were also who were making California rich.

Californians whose family ties to the state predate World War Two have an equivocal and often uneasy relationship to the postwar expansion. Joan Irvine Smith, whose family's eighty-eight-thousand-acre ranch in Orange County was developed during the 1960s, later created, on the twelfth floor of the McDonnell Douglas Building in Irvine, a city that did not exist before the Irvines developed their ranch, the Irvine Museum, dedicated to the California impressionist or plein air paintings she had begun collecting in 1991. "There is more nostalgia for me in these paintings than in actually going out to look at what used to be the ranch now that it has been developed, because I'm looking at what I looked at as a child," she told *Art in California* about this collection. Her attraction to the genre had begun, she said, when she was a child and would meet her stepfather for lunch at the California Club, where the few public rooms in which women were at that time allowed were decorated with California landscapes lent by the members. "I can look at those paintings and see what the ranch was as I remember it when I was a little girl."

The California Club, which is on Flower Street in downtown Los Angeles, was then and is still the heart of Southern California's old-line business establishment, the Los Angeles version of the Bohemian and Pacific Union Clubs in San Francisco. On any given day since World War Two, virtually everyone lunching at the California Club, most particularly not excluding Joan Irvine, has had a direct or indirect investment in the development of California, which is to say in the obliteration of the undeveloped California on display at the Irvine Museum. In the seventy-four paintings chosen for inclusion in *Selections from the Irvine Museum*, the catalogue published by the museum to accompany a 1992 traveling exhibition, there are hills and desert and mesas and arroyos. There are mountains, coastline, big sky. There are stands of eucalyptus, sycamore, oak, cottonwood. There are washes of California poppies. As for fauna, there are, in the seventy-four paintings, three sulphur-crested cockatoos, one white peacock, two horses, and nine people, four of whom are dwarfed by the landscape and two of whom are indistinct Indians paddling a canoe.

Some of this is romantic (the indistinct Indians), some washed with a slightly falsified golden light, in the tradition that runs from Bierstadt's "lustrous, pearly mist" to the "Kinkade Glow." Most of these paintings, however, reflect the way the place actually looks, or looked, not only to Joan Irvine but also to me and to anyone else who knew it as recently as 1960. It is this close representation of a familiar yet vanished landscape that gives the Irvine collection its curious effect, that of a short-term memory misfire: these paintings hang in a city, Irvine (population more than one hundred and fifty thousand, with a University of California campus enrolling some nineteen thousand students), that was forty years ago a mirror image of the paintings themselves, bean fields and grazing, the heart but by no means all of the cattle and sheep operation amassed by the great-grandfather of the founder of the Irvine Museum.

The disposition of such a holding can be, for its inheritors, a fraught enterprise. "On the afternoon of his funeral we gathered to honor this man who had held such a legacy intact for the main part of his ninety-one years," Jane Hollister Wheelwright wrote in *The Ranch Papers* about the aftermath of her father's death and the prospect of being forced to sell the Hollister ranch. "All of us were deeply affected. Some were stunned by the prospect of loss; others gloated, contemplating cash and escape. We were bitterly divided, but none could deny the power of that land. The special, spiritually meaningful (and often destructive) impact of the ranch was obvious. I proved it by my behavior, as did the others."

That was 1961. Joan Irvine Smith had replaced her mother on the board of the Irvine Company four years before, in 1957, the year she was twenty-four. She had seen, a good deal more clearly and realistically than Jane Hollister Wheelwright would see four years later, the solution she wanted for her family's ranch, and she had seen the rest of the Irvine board as part of the problem: by making small deals, selling off bits of the whole, the board was nibbling away at the family's principal asset, the size of its holding. It was she who pressed the architect William Pereira to present a master plan. It was she who saw the potential return in giving the land for a University of California campus. It was she, most importantly, who insisted on maintaining an interest in the ranch's development. And, in the end, which meant after years of internecine battles and a series of litigations extending to 1991, it was she who more or less prevailed. In 1960, before the Irvine ranch was developed, there were 719,500 people in all of Orange County. In 2000 there were close to 3 million, most of whom would not have been there had two families, the Irvines in the central part of the county and the inheritors of Richard O'Neill's Rancho Santa Margarita and Mission Viejo acreage in the southern, not developed their ranches.

This has not been a case in which the rising tide floated all boats. Not all of Orange County's new residents came to realize what would have seemed the middle-class promise of its growth. Not all of those residents even had somewhere to live: some settled into the run-down motels built in the mid-1950s, at the time Disneyland opened, and were referred to locally, because they had nowhere else to live and could not afford the deposits required for apartment rental, as "motel people." In his 1986 *The New California: Facing the 21st Century*, the political columnist Dan Walters quoted *The Orange County Register* on motel people: "Mostly Anglo, they're the county's newest migrant workers: instead of picking grapes, they inspect semiconductors." This kind of week-by-week or even day-by-day living arrangement has taken hold in other parts of the country, but remains particularly entrenched in Southern California, where apartment rents rose to meet the increased demand from people priced out of a housing market in which even the least promising bungalow can sell for several hundred thousand dollars. By the year 2000, according to *The Los Angeles Times*, some hundred Orange County motels were inhabited almost exclusively by the working poor, people who made, say, $280 a week sanding airplane parts, or $7 an hour at Disney's "California Adventure" park. "A land celebrating the richness and diversity of California, its natural resources, and pioneering spirit of its people," the web site for "California Adventure" read. "I can look at these paintings and look back," Joan Irvine Smith told *Art in California* about the collection she bought with the proceeds of looking exclusively, and to a famous degree, forward. "I can see California as it was and as we will never see it again." Hers is an extreme example of the conundrum that to one degree or another confronts any Californian who profited from the boom years: if we could still see California as it was, how many of us could now afford to see it?

2

> What is the railroad to do for us?—this railroad that we have looked for, hoped for, prayed for so long?
>
> —Henry George,
> "What the Railroad Will Bring Us"

LAKEWOOD, CALIFORNIA, the Los Angeles County community where in early 1993 an amorphous high school clique identifying itself as the Spur Posse achieved a short-lived national notoriety, lies between the Long Beach and San Gabriel Freeways, east of the San Diego, part of that vast grid familiar to the casual visitor mainly from the air, Southern California's industrial underbelly, the thousand square miles of aerospace and oil that powered the place's apparently endless expansion. Like much of the southern end of this grid, Lakewood was until after World War Two agricultural, several thousand acres of beans and sugar beets just inland from the Signal Hill oil field and across the road from the plant behind the Long Beach airport that the federal government completed in 1941 for Donald Douglas.

This Douglas plant, with the outsized American flag whipping in the wind and the huge forward-slanted letters *MCDONNELL DOUGLAS* wrapped around the building and the MD-11s parked like cars off Lakewood Boulevard, was at the time I first visited Lakewood in 1993 the single most noticeable feature on the local horizon, but for a while, not long after World War Two, there had been another: a hundred-foot pylon, its rotating beacon visible for several miles, erected to advertise the opening, in April 1950, of what was meant to be the world's biggest subdivision, a tract larger in conception than the original Long Island Levittown, 17,500 houses waiting to be built on the 3,400 dead-level acres that three California developers, Mark Taper and Ben Weingart and Louis Boyar, had purchased for $8.8 million from the Montana Land Company.

Lakewood, the sign read at the point on Lakewood Boulevard where Bellflower would become Lakewood, *Tomorrow's*

City Today. What was offered for sale in Tomorrow's City, as in most subdivisions of the postwar period, was a raw lot and the promise of a house. Each of the 17,500 houses was to be 950 to 1,100 square feet on a fifty-by-hundred-foot lot. Each was to be a one-story stucco (seven floor plans, twenty-one different exteriors, no identical models to be built next to or facing each other) painted in one of thirty-nine color schemes. Each was to have oak floors, a glass-enclosed shower, a stainless-steel double sink, a garbage disposal unit, and either two or three bedrooms. Each was to sell for between eight and ten thousand dollars. *Low FHA*, *Vets No Down*. There were to be thirty-seven playgrounds, twenty schools. There were to be seventeen churches. There were to be 133 miles of street, paved with an inch and a half of No. 2 macadam on an aggregate base.

There was to be, and this was key not only to the project but to the nature of the community which eventually evolved, a regional shopping center, "Lakewood Center," which in turn was conceived as America's largest retail complex: 256 acres, parking for ten thousand cars, anchored by a May Company. "Lou Boyar pointed out that they would build a shopping center and around that a city, that he would make a city for us and millions for himself," John Todd, a resident of Lakewood since its beginning and later its city attorney, wrote of the planning stage. "Everything about this entire project was perfect," Mark Taper said in 1969, when he sat down with city officials to work up a local history. "Things happened that may never happen again."

What he meant, of course, was the perfect synergy of time and place, the seamless confluence of World War Two and the Korean War and the G.I. Bill and the defense contracts that began to flood Southern California as the Cold War set in. Here on this raw acreage on the flood plain between the Los Angeles and San Gabriel Rivers was where two powerfully conceived national interests, that of keeping the economic engine running and that of creating an enlarged middle or consumer class, could be seen to converge.

The scene beneath the hundred-foot pylon during that spring of 1950 was Cimarron: thirty thousand people showed up for the first day of selling. Twenty thousand showed up on weekends throughout the spring. Near the sales office was a nursery where children could be left while parents toured the seven completed and furnished model houses. Thirty-six salesmen worked day and evening shifts, showing potential buyers how their G.I. benefits, no down payment, and thirty years of monthly payments ranging from $43 to $54 could elevate them to ownership of a piece of the future. Deals were closed on 611 houses the first week. One week saw construction started on 567. A new foundation was excavated every fifteen minutes. Cement trucks were lined up for a mile, waiting to move down the new blocks pouring foundations. Shingles were fed to roofers by conveyer belt. And, at the very point when sales had begun to slow, as Taper recalled at the 1969 meeting with city officials, "the Korean War was like a new stimulation."

"There was this new city growing—growing like leaves," one of the original residents, who with her husband had opened a delicatessen in Lakewood Center, said when she was interviewed for an oral history project undertaken by the city and Lakewood High School. "So we decided this is where we should start. . . . There were young people, young children, schools, a young government that was just starting out. We felt all the big stores were coming in. May Company and all the other places started opening. So we rented one of the stores and we were in business." These World War Two and Korean War veterans and their wives who started out in Lakewood were, typically, about thirty years old. They were, typically, not from California but from the Midwest and the border South. They were, typically, blue-collar and lower-level white collar. They had 1.7 children, they had steady jobs. Their experience tended to reinforce the conviction that social and economic mobility worked exclusively upward.

Donald J. Waldie, while he was working as the City of Lakewood's public information officer, wrote an extraordinary book, *Holy Land: A Suburban Memoir*, published in 1996, a series of interconnected essays about someone who, like their author, lived in Lakewood and worked at City Hall. "Naively, you could say that Lakewood was the American dream made affordable for a generation of industrial workers who in the preceding generation could never aspire to that kind of ownership," he said one morning when we were talking about the way the place was developed. "They were fairly but not entirely homogenous in their ethnic background. They were oriented to aerospace. They worked for Hughes, they worked for Douglas, they worked at the naval station and shipyard in Long Beach. They worked, in other words, at all the places that exemplified the bright future that California was supposed to be."

Donald Waldie grew up in Lakewood, and, after Cal State Long Beach and graduate work at the University of California at Irvine, had chosen to come back, as had a striking number of people who lived there. In a county increasingly populated by low-income Mexican and Central American and Asian immigrants and pressed by the continuing needs of its low-income blacks, almost sixty thousand of Lakewood's seventy-some thousand citizens were still, in the spring of 1993, white. More than half had been born in California, and most of the rest in the Midwest and the South. The largest number of those employed worked, just as their fathers and grandfathers had, for Douglas or Hughes or Rockwell or the Long Beach naval station and shipyard or for the many subcontractors and vendors that did business with Douglas and Hughes and Rockwell and the Long Beach naval station and shipyard.

People who lived in Lakewood did not necessarily think of themselves as living in Los Angeles, and could often list the occasions on which they had visited there, to see the Dodgers play, say, or to show a relative from out of state the Music Center. Their apprehension of urban woes remained remote: the number of homeless people in Lakewood either in shelters or "visible on street," according to the 1990 Census, was zero. When residents of Lakewood spoke about the rioting that had begun in Los Angeles after the 1992 Rodney King verdicts, they were talking about events that seemed to them, despite the significant incidence of arson and looting in such neighboring communities as Long Beach and Compton, to have occurred somewhere else. "We're far away from that element," one woman to whom I spoke said when the subject of the riots came up. "If you've driven around . . ."

"Little suburbia," a neighbor said.

"America U.S.A., right here."

The neighbor's husband worked at a nearby Rockwell plant,

not the Rockwell plant in Lakewood. The Rockwell plant in Lakewood had closed in 1992, a thousand jobs gone. The scheduled closing of the Long Beach naval station would mean almost nine thousand jobs gone. The Federal Base Closure and Realignment Commission had granted a provisional stay to the Long Beach naval shipyard, which adjoined the naval station and employed another four thousand people, but its prospects for survival remained dim. One thing that was not remote in Lakewood in 1993, one thing so close that not many people even wanted to talk about it, was the apprehension that what had already happened to the Rockwell plant and would happen to the Long Beach naval station and shipyard could also happen to the Douglas plant. I recall talking one day to Carl Cohn, then superintendent of the Long Beach Unified School District, which included Lakewood. "There's a tremendous fear that at some point this operation might go away entirely," he said. "I mean that's kind of one of the whispered things around town. Nobody wants it out there."

Douglas had already, in 1993, moved part of its MD-80 production to Salt Lake City. Douglas had already moved part of what remained of its C-17 production to St. Louis. Douglas had already moved the T-45 to St. Louis. In a 1992 study called *Impact of Defense Cuts on California*, the California Commission on State Finance had estimated nineteen thousand layoffs still to come from Hughes and McDonnell Douglas, but by 1992 there had already been, in Southern California, some twenty-one thousand McDonnell Douglas layoffs. According to a June 1993 report on aerospace unemployment prepared by researchers at the UCLA School of Architecture and Urban Planning, half the California aerospace workers laid off in 1989 were, two years later, either still unemployed or no longer living in California. Most of those who did find jobs had ended up in lower-income service jobs; only seventeen percent had gone back to work in the aerospace industry at figures approaching their original salaries. Of those laid off in 1991 and 1992, only sixteen percent, a year later, had found jobs of any kind.

It was the Douglas plant on the Lakewood city line, the one with the flag whipping in the wind and the logo wrapped around the building, that had by 1993 taken the hit for almost eighteen thousand of McDonnell Douglas's twenty-one thousand layoffs. "I've got two kids, a first and a third grader," Carl Cohn told me. "When you take your kid to a birthday party and your wife starts talking about so-and-so's father just being laid off—there are all kinds of implications, including what's going to be spent on a kid's birthday party. These concrete things really come home to you. And you realize, yeah, this bad economic situation is very real." The message on the marquee at Rochelle's Restaurant and Motel and Convention Center, between Douglas and the Long Beach airport, still read "Welcome Douglas Happy Hour 4–7," but the place was nailed shut, a door banging in the wind. "We've developed good citizens," Mark Taper said about Lakewood in 1969. "Enthusiastic owners of property. Owners of a piece of their country—a stake in the land." This was a sturdy but finally unsupportable ambition, sustained for forty years by good times and the good will of the federal government.

When people in Lakewood spoke about what they called "Spur," or "the situation at the high school," some meant the series of allegations that had led to the March 1993 arrests—with requests that charges be brought on ten counts of rape by intimidation, four counts of unlawful sexual intercourse, one count of forcible rape, one count of oral copulation, and one count of lewd conduct with a minor under the age of fourteen—of nine current or former Lakewood High School students who either happened to be or were believed to be members of an informal fraternity known locally as the Spur Posse. Others meant not the allegations, which they saw as either outright inventions or representations of events open to interpretation (the phrase "consensual sex" got heavy usage), but rather the national attention that followed those allegations, the invasion of Lakewood by what its residents called "you people," or "you folks," or "the media," and the appearance, on *Jenny Jones* and *Jane Whitney* and *Maury Povich* and *Nightline* and *Montel Williams* and *Dateline* and *Donahue* and *The Home Show*, of two hostile and briefly empowered arrangements of hormones, otherwise known as "the boys" and "the girls."

For a moment that spring they had seemed to be on view everywhere, those blank-faced Lakewood girls, those feral

Lakewood boys. There were the dead eyes, the thick necks, the jaws that closed only to chew gum. There was the refusal or inability to process the simplest statement without rephrasing it. There was the fuzzy relationship to language, the tendency to seize on a drifting fragment of something once heard and repeat it, not quite get it right, worry it like a bone. The news that some schools distributed condoms had been seized in mid-drift, for example, and pressed into service as an extenuating circumstance, the fact that Lakewood High School had never distributed condoms notwithstanding. "The schools, they're handing out condoms and stuff like that, and like, if they're handing out condoms, why don't they tell us you can be arrested for it?" one Spur asked Gary Collins and Sarah Purcell on *The Home Show*. "They pass out condoms, teach sex education and pregnancy this, pregnancy that, but they don't teach us any rules," another told Jane Gross of *The New York Times*. "Schools hand out condoms, teach safe sex," the mother of a Spur complained on *The Home Show*. "It's the society, they have these clinics, they have abortions, they don't have to tell their parents, the schools give out condoms, jeez, what does that tell you?" the father of one Lakewood boy, a sixteen-year-old who had just admitted to a juvenile-court petition charging him with lewd conduct with a ten-year-old girl, asked a television interviewer. "I think people are blowing this thing way out of proportion," David Ferrell of *The Los Angeles Times* was told by one Spur. "It's all been blown out of proportion as far as I'm concerned," he was told by another. "Of course there were several other sex scandals at the time, so this perfectly normal story got blown out of proportion," I was told by a Spur parent. "People, you know, kind of blow it all out of proportion," a Spur advised viewers of *Jane Whitney*. "They blow it out of proportion a lot," another said on the same show. A Spur girlfriend, "Jodi," called in to offer her opinion: "I think it's been blown way out of proportion, like way out of proportion."

Each of these speakers seemed to be referring to a cultural misery apprehended only recently, and then dimly. Those who mentioned "blowing it out of proportion" were complaining specifically about "the media," and its "power," but more generally about a sense of being besieged, set upon, at the mercy of forces beyond local control. "The whole society has changed," one Spur parent told me. "Morals have changed. Girls have changed. It used to be, girls would be more or less the ones in control. Girls would hold out, girls would want to be married at eighteen or nineteen and they'd keep their sights on having a home and love and a family." What seemed most perplexing to these Lakewood residents was that the disruption was occurring in what they uniformly referred to as "a middle-class community like this one," or sometimes "an upper-middle-class community like this one." "We're an upper-middle-class community," I was told one morning outside the Los Padrinos Juvenile Court in Downey, where a group of Lakewood women were protesting the decision of the Los Angeles County district attorney's office not to bring most of the so-called "sex charges" requested by the sheriff's department. "*It Wasn't The Bloods, Crips, Longos, It Was The Spurs*," the hand-lettered signs read that morning, "the Longos" being a Long Beach gang. "*What If One of the Victims Had Been Your Granddaughter, Huh, Mr. District Attorney?*" "It's a very hush-hush community," another protester said. "Very low profile, they don't want to make waves, don't want to step on anybody's toes." The following is an extract from the first page of Donald J. Waldie's *Holy Land: A Suburban Memoir*:

> He knew his suburb's first 17,500 houses had been built in less than three years. He knew what this must have cost, but he did not care.
>
> The houses still worked.
>
> He thought of them as middle class even though 1,100-square-foot tract houses on streets meeting at right angles are not middle class at all.
>
> Middle-class houses are the homes of people who would not live here.

This is in fact the tacit dissonance at the center of every moment in Lakewood, which is why the average day there raises, for the visitor, so many and such vertiginous questions:

What does it cost to create and maintain an artificial ownership class?

Who pays?

Who benefits?

What happens when that class stops being useful?

What does it mean to drop back below the line?

What does it cost to hang on above it, how do you behave, what do you say, what are the pitons you drive into the granite?

One of the ugliest and most revelatory of the many ugly and revelatory moments that characterized the 1993 television appearances of Lakewood's Spur Posse members occurred on *Jane Whitney*, when a nineteen-year-old Lakewood High School graduate named Chris Albert ("Boasts He Has 44 'Points' For Having Sex With Girls") turned mean with a member of the audience, a young black woman who had tried to suggest that the Spurs on view were not exhibiting what she considered native intelligence.

"I don't get—I don't understand what she's saying," Chris Albert had at first said, letting his jaw go slack as these boys tended to do when confronted with an unwelcome, or in fact any, idea.

Another Spur had interpreted: "We're dumb. She's saying we're dumb."

"What education does she have?" Chris Albert had then demanded, and crouched forward toward the young woman, as if trying to shake himself alert. "Where do you work at? McDonald's? Burger King?" A third Spur had tried to interrupt, but Chris Albert, once roused, could not be deflected. "Five twenty-five?" he said. "Five fifty?" And then, there it was, the piton, driven in this case not into granite but into shale, already disintegrating: "*I go to college.*" Two years later Chris Albert would be dead, shot in the chest and killed during a Fourth of July celebration on the Pacific Coast Highway in Huntington Beach.

3

LAKEWOOD EXISTS because at a given time in a different economy it had seemed an efficient idea to provide population density for the mall and a labor pool for the Douglas plant. There are a lot of towns like Lakewood in California. They were California's mill towns, breeder towns for the boom. When times were good and there was money to spread around, these were the towns that proved Marx wrong, that managed to increase the proletariat and simultaneously, by calling it middle class, to co-opt it. Such towns were organized around the sedative idealization of team sports, which were believed to develop "good citizens," and therefore tended to the idealization of adolescent males. During the good years, the years for which places like Lakewood or Canoga Park or El Segundo or Pico Rivera existed, the preferred resident was in fact an adolescent or post-adolescent male, ideally one already married and mortgaged, in harness to the plant, a good worker, a steady consumer, a team player, someone who played ball, a good citizen.

When towns like these came on hard times, it was the same adolescent males, only recently the community's most valued asset, who were most visibly left with nowhere to go. Among the Spur Posse members who appeared on the talk shows that spring, a striking number had been out of high school a year, or even two years, but did not seem actively engaged in a next step. "It was some of the older kids who were so obnoxious, so arrogant," one Spur father, Donald Belman, told me. "They're the ones who were setting up talk-show appearances just for the money. I had to kick them out of my house, they were answering my phone, monitoring my mail. They were just in it for the money, quick cash." Jane Gross of *The New York Times* asked one of these postgraduate Spurs what he had been doing since high school. "Partying," he said. "Playing ball."

Good citizens were encouraged, when partying failed, when playing ball failed, when they finally noticed that the jobs had gone to Salt Lake or St. Louis, to see their problem as one caused by "the media," or by "condoms in the schools," or by less-good citizens, or non-citizens. "Orange County is using illegal aliens now as a smoke-screen, as a scapegoat, because that's the way we get the white lower-income people to jump on board and say the immigrants are the problem," the wife of an aerospace engineer in Costa Mesa told Robert Scheer of *The Los Angeles Times.* "But we had our class differences before the immigrants. One of our sons was on the football team in the high school in Costa Mesa about twelve years ago. They had a great team and they were beating the pants off one of the schools in Newport Beach and the Newport stands started to cheer. '*Hey, hey, that's OK, you're gonna work for us one day.*'"

This is what it costs to create and maintain an artificial ownership class.

This is what happens when that class stops being useful.

Most adults to whom I spoke in Lakewood during that spring of 1993 shared a sense that something in town had gone wrong. Many connected this apprehension to the Spur Posse, or at least to certain Spur Posse members who had emerged, even before the arrests and for a variety of reasons, as the community's most visible males. Almost everyone agreed that this was a town in which what had been considered the definition of good parenting, the encouragement of assertive behavior among male children, had for some reason gotten badly out of hand. The point on which many people disagreed was whether sex was at the center of this problem, and some of these people felt troubled and misrepresented by the fact that public discussion of the situation in Lakewood had tended to focus exclusively on what they called "the sex charges," or "the sexual charges." "People have to understand," I was told by one plaintive mother. "This isn't about the sexual charges." Some believed the charges intrinsically unprovable. Others seemed simply to regard sex among teenagers as a combat zone with its own rules, a contained conflict from which they were prepared, as the district attorney was, to look away. Many seemed unaware of the extent to which questions of gender had come to occupy the nation's official attention, and so had failed to appreciate the ease with which the events in Lakewood could feed seamlessly into a discussion already in progress, offer a fresh context in which to recap Tailhook, Packwood, Anita Hill.

What happened that spring had begun, most people agreed, at least a year before, maybe more. Much of what got talked about had seemed, at first, suggestive mainly of underemployed teenagers playing at acting street. There had been threats, bully tactics, the systematic harassment of girls or younger children who made complaints or "stood up to" or in any way resisted the whim of a certain group of boys. Young children in Lakewood had come to know among themselves who to avoid in those thirty-seven playgrounds, what cars to watch for on those 133 miles of No. 2 macadam. "I'm talking about throughout the community," I was told by Karin Polacheck, who represented Lakewood on the board of education for the Long Beach Unified School District. "At the baseball fields, at the parks, at the markets, on the corners of schoolgrounds. They were organized enough that young children would say, 'Watch out for that car when it comes around,' 'Watch out for those boys.' I've heard stories of walking up and stealing baseball bats and telling kids, 'If you tell anyone I'll beat your head in.' I'm talking about young children, nine, ten years old. It's a small community. Younger kids knew that these older kids were out there."

"You're dead," the older boys would reportedly say, or "You're gonna get fucked up." "You're gonna get it." "You're gonna die." "I don't like who she's hanging with, why don't we just kill her now." There was a particular form of street terror mentioned by many people: invasive vehicular maneuvers construed by the targets as attempts to "run people down." "There were skid marks outside my house," one mother told me. "They were trying to scare my daughter. Her life was hell. She had chili-cheese nachos thrown at her at school." "They just like to intimidate people," I was repeatedly told. "They stare back at you. They don't go to school, they ditch. They ditch and then they beg the teacher to pass them, because they have to have a C average to play on the teams." "They came to our house in a truck to do something to my sister," one young woman told me. "She can't go anywhere. Can't even go to Taco Bell any more. Can't go to Jack-in-the-Box. They'll jump you. They followed me home not long ago, I just headed for the sheriff's office."

There had also been more substantive incidents, occurrences that could not be written off to schoolyard exaggeration or adolescent oversensitivity. There had been assaults in local parks, bicycles stolen and sold. There had been burglaries, credit cards and jewelry missing from the bedroom drawers of houses where local girls had been babysitting. There had even been, beginning in the summer of 1992, felony arrests: Donald Belman's son Dana, who was generally said to have "founded" the Spur Posse, was arrested on suspicion of stealing a certain number of guns from the bedroom of a house where he was said to have attended a party. Not long before that, in Las Vegas, Dana Belman and another Spur, Christopher Russo, had been detained for possession of stolen credit cards. Just before Christmas 1992, Dana Belman and Christopher Russo were detained yet again, and arrested for alleged check forgery.

There were odd quirks here, details not entirely consistent with the community's preferred view of itself. There were the high school trips to Vegas and to Laughlin, which is a Nevada casino town on the Colorado River below Las Vegas. There was the question of the certain number of guns Dana Belman was suspected of having stolen from the bedroom of the house where he was said to have attended the party: the number of guns mentioned was nineteen. Still, these details seemed to go unremarked upon, and the events unconnected. People who had been targeted by the older boys believed themselves, they said later, "all alone in this." They believed that each occasion of harassment was discrete, unique. They did not yet see a pattern in the various incidents and felonies. They had not yet made certain inductive leaps. That was before the pipe bomb.

The pipe bomb exploded on the front porch of a house not far from Lakewood High School between three and three-thirty on the morning of February 12, 1993. It destroyed one porch support. It tore holes in the stucco. It threw shrapnel into parked cars. One woman remembered that her husband was working the night shift at Rockwell and she had been sleeping light as usual when the explosion woke her. The next morning she asked a neighbor if she had heard the noise. "And she said,

'You're not going to believe it when I tell you what that was.' And she explained to me that a pipe bomb had blown up on someone's front porch. And that it had been a gang retaliatory thing. 'Gang thing?' I said. 'What are you *talking* about, a gang thing?' And she said, 'Well, you know, Spur Posse.' And I said, 'Spur Posse, what *is* Spur Posse?'"

This was the point at which the principal of Lakewood High School and the local sheriff's office, which had been trying to get a handle on the rash of felonies around town, decided to ask certain parents to attend a special meeting at the high school. Letters were sent to twenty-five families, each of which was believed to have at least one Spur Posse son. Only some fifteen people showed up at the March 2 meeting. Sheriff's deputies from both the local station and the arson-explosives detail spoke. The cause for concern, as the deputies then saw it, was that the trouble, whatever it was, seemed to be escalating: first the felonies, then a couple of car cherry bombs without much damage, now this eight-inch pipe bomb, which appeared to have been directed at one or more Spur Posse members and had been, according to a member of the arson-explosives detail, "intended to kill." It was during this meeting that someone, it was hard to sort out who, said the word "rape." Most people to whom I talked at first said that the issue had been raised by one of the parents, but those who said this had not actually been present at the meeting. Asking about this after the fact tended to be construed as potentially hostile, because the Los Angeles attorney Gloria Allred, a specialist in high-profile gender cases, had by then appeared on the scene, giving press conferences, doing talk shows, talking about possible civil litigation on behalf of the six girls who had become her clients, and generally making people in Lakewood a little sensitive about who knew what and when they had known it and what they had done about what they knew.

What happened next was also unclear. Lakewood High School students recalled investigators from the sheriff's Whittier-based sex-abuse unit coming to the school, calling people in, questioning anyone who had even been seen talking to boys who were said to be Spurs. "I think they came up with a lot of wannabe boys," one mother told me. "Boys who wanted to belong to something that had notoriety to it." The presence of the investigators at the school might well have suggested that arrests could be pending, but school authorities said that they knew nothing until the morning of March 18, when sheriff's deputies appeared in the principal's office and said that they were going into classrooms to take boys out in custody. "There was never any allegation that any of these incidents took place on school ground or at school events or going to and from school," Carl Cohn said on the morning we talked in his Long Beach Unified School District office. He had not been present the morning the boys were taken from their classrooms in cutoffs and handcuffs, but the television vans had been, as had *The Los Angeles Times* and *The Long Beach Press-Telegram*. "Arresting the youngsters at school might have been convenient, but it very much contributed to what is now this media circus," he said. "The sheriff's department had a press briefing. Downtown. Los Angeles. Where they notified the media that they were going in. All you have to do is mention that the perpetrators are students at a particular school and everybody gets on the freeway."

The boys arrested were detained for four nights. All but one sixteen-year-old, who was charged with lewd conduct against a ten-year-old girl, were released without charges. When those still enrolled at Lakewood High went back to school, they were greeted with cheers by some students. "Of *course* they were treated as heroes, they'd been wrongly accused," I was told by Donald Belman, whose youngest son, Kristopher, was one of those arrested and released. "These girls pre-planned these things. They wanted to be looked on favorably, they wanted to be part of the clique. They wanted to be, hopefully, the girlfriends of these studs on campus." The Belman family celebrated Kristopher's release by going out for hamburgers at McDonald's, which was, Donald Belman told *The Los Angeles Times*, "the American way."

Some weeks later the district attorney's office released a statement which read in part: "After completing an extensive investigation and analysis of the evidence, our conclusion is that there is no credible evidence of forcible rape involving any of these boys. . . . Although there is evidence of unlawful sexual intercourse, it is the policy of this office not to file criminal charges where there is consensual sex among teenagers. . . . The arrogance and contempt for young women which have been displayed, while appalling, cannot form the basis for criminal charges." "The district attorney on this did her homework," Donald Belman told me. "She questioned all these kids, she found out these girls weren't the victims they were made out to be. One of these girls had tattoos for chrissake." "If it's true about the ten-year-old, I feel bad for her and her family," one Spur told David Ferrell of *The Los Angeles Times.* "My regards go out to the family." As far as Lakewood High was concerned, it was time to begin, its principal said, "the healing process."

Donald and Dottie Belman, at the time they became the most public of the Spur Posse parents, had lived for twenty-two of their twenty-five years of marriage in a beige stucco house on Greentop Street in Lakewood. Donald Belman, who worked as a salesman for an aerospace vendor, selling to the large machine shops and to prime contractors like Douglas, had graduated in 1963 from Lakewood High School, spent four years in the Marine Corps, and come home to start a life with Dottie, herself a 1967 Lakewood High graduate. "I held out for that white dress," Dottie Belman told Janet Wiscombe of *The Long Beach Press-Telegram.* "The word 'sex' was never spoken in my home. People in movies went into the bedroom and closed the door and came out with a smile on their face. Now people are having brutal sex on TV. They aren't making love. There is nothing romantic about it."

This was a family that had been, by its own and other accounts, intensively focused on its three sons, Billy, then twenty-three, Dana, twenty, and Kristopher, eighteen, all of whom, at that time, still lived at home. "I'd hate to have my kids away from me for two or three days in Chicago or New York," Donald Belman told me by way of explaining why he had given his imprimatur to the appearance of his two younger sons on *The Home Show*, which was shot in Los Angeles, but not initially on *Jenny Jones*, which was shot in Chicago. "All these talk shows start calling, I said, 'Don't do it. They're just going to lie about you, they're going to set you up.' The more the boys said no, the more the shows enticed them. *The Home Show* was where I relented. They were offering a thousand dollars and a limo and it was in L.A. *Jenny Jones* offered I think fifteen hundred, but they'd have to fly."

During the years before this kind of guidance was needed, Donald Belman was always available to coach the boys' teams. There had been Park League, there had been Little League. There had been Pony League, Colt League, Pop Warner. Dottie Belman had regularly served as Team Mother, and remembered literally running from her job as a hairdresser so that she could have dinner on the table every afternoon at five-fifteen. "They would make a home run or a touchdown and I held my head high," she told the *Press-Telegram*. "We were reliving our past. We'd walk into Little League and we were hot stuff. I'd go to Von's and people would come up to me and say, 'Your kids are great.' I was so proud. Now I go to Von's at five A.M. in disguise. I've been Mother of the Year. I've sacrificed everything for my kids. Now I feel like I have to defend my honor."

The youngest Belman, Kristopher, who graduated from Lakewood High in June 1993, had been one of the boys arrested and released without charges that March. "I was crazy that weekend," his father told me. "My boy's in jail, Kris, he's never been in any trouble whatsoever, he's an average student, a star athlete. He doesn't even have to be in school, he has enough credits to graduate, you don't have to stay in school after you're eighteen. But he's there. Just to be with his friends." Around the time of graduation, Kristopher was arraigned on a charge of "forcible lewd conduct" based on an alleged 1989 incident involving a girl who was then thirteen; this charge was later dropped and Kristopher Belman agreed to do one hundred hours of community service. The oldest Belman son, Billy, according to his father, was working and going to school. The middle son, Dana, had graduated from Lakewood High in 1991 and had been named, as his father and virtually everyone else who mentioned him pointed out, "Performer of the Year 1991," for wrestling, in the Lakewood Youth Sports Hall of Fame. The Lakewood Youth Sports Hall of Fame is not at the high school, not at City Hall, but in a McDonald's, at the corner of Woodruff and Del Amo. "They're all standouts athletically," Donald Belman told me. "My psychology and philosophy is this: I'm a standup guy, I love my sons, I'm proud of their accomplishments." Dana, his father said, was at that time "looking for work," a quest complicated by the thirteen felony burglary and forgery charges on which he was then awaiting trial.

Dottie Belman, who had cancer surgery in April 1993, had filed for divorce in 1992 but for a year continued to live with her husband and sons on Greentop Street. "If Dottie wants to start a new life, I'm not going to hold her back," Donald Belman told the *Press-Telegram*. "I'm a solid guy. Just a solid citizen. I see no reason for any thought that our family isn't just all-American, basic and down-to-earth." Dottie Belman, when she spoke to the *Press-Telegram*, had been more reflective. "The wrecking ball shot right through the mantel and the house has crumbled," she said. "Dana said the other day, 'I want to be in the ninth grade again, and I want to do everything differently. I had it all. I was Mr. Lakewood. I was a star. I was popular. As soon as I graduated, I lost the recognition. I want to go back to the wonderful days. Now it's one disaster after another.'"

"You saw the papers," Ira Ewing says in "Golden Land" to the woman, a divorcée with a fourteen-year-old child of her own, who has become his sole consolation. "I can't understand it! After all the advantages that . . . after all I tried to do for them—"

The woman tries to calm him, offers him lunch.

"No. I don't want any lunch.—After all I have tried to give—"

Which was another way of saying: "The wrecking ball shot right through the mantel and the house has crumbled." It was 1996 when Dana Belman, convicted on three counts of burglary in the first degree, began serving a ten-year sentence at the California Men's Colony in San Luis Obispo. It was 1999 when he was discharged from prison, and a year later when he was released from parole.

4

ONCE WHEN I was twelve or thirteen and had checked the Lynds' *Middletown* and *Middletown in Transition* out of the Sacramento library, I asked my mother to what "class" we belonged.

"It's not a word we use," she said. "It's not the way we think."

On one level I believed this to be a willful misreading of what even a twelve-year-old could see to be the situation and on another level I understood it to be true: it was not the way we thought in California. We believed in fresh starts. We believed in good luck. We believed in the miner who scratched together one last stake and struck the Comstock Lode. We believed in the wildcatter who leased arid land at two and a half cents an acre and brought in Kettleman Hills, fourteen million barrels of crude in its first three years. We believed in all the ways that apparently played-out possibilities could while we slept turn green and golden. *Keep California Green and Golden*, was the state's Smokey the Bear fire motto around the time I was reading the Lynds. Put out your campfire, kill the rattlesnake and watch the money flow in.

And it did.

Even if it was somebody else's money.

The extent to which the postwar boom years confirmed this warp in the California imagination, and in the expectations of its citizens, would be hard to overestimate. Good times today and better times tomorrow were supposed to come with the territory, roll in with the regularity of the breakers on what was once the coast of the Irvine ranch and became Newport Beach, Balboa, Lido Isle. Good times were the core conviction of the place, and it was their only gradually apparent absence, in the early 1990s, that began to unsettle California in ways that no one exactly wanted to plumb. The recognition that the trend was no longer reliably up came late and hard to California. The 1987 market crash was widely if not consciously seen by its citizens as just one more of the problems that plagued the America they had left behind, evidence of a tiresome eastern negativity that would not travel. Even when the defense plants started closing down off the San Diego Freeway and the for-lease signs started going up in Orange County, very few people wanted to see a connection with the way life was going to be lived in the California that was not immediately identifiable as "aircraft."

This was in fact a state in which virtually every county was to one degree or another dependent on defense contracts, from the billions upon billions of federal dollars that flowed into Los Angeles County to the five-digit contracts in counties like Plumas and Tehama and Tuolomne, yet the sheer geographical isolation of different parts of the state tended to obscure the elementary fact of its interrelatedness. Even within Los Angeles County, there had seemed no meaningful understanding that if General Motors shut down its assembly plant in Van Nuys, say, as it did in fact do in 1992, twenty-six hundred jobs lost, the bell would eventually toll in Bel Air, where the people lived who held the paper on the people who held the mortgages in Van Nuys. I recall asking a real estate broker on the west side of Los Angeles, in June 1988, what effect a defense cutback would have on the residential real estate boom then in progress. She said that such a cutback would have no effect on the west side of Los Angeles, because people who worked for Hughes and Douglas did not live in Pacific Palisades or Santa Monica or Malibu or Beverly Hills or Bel Air or Brentwood or Holmby Hills. "They live in Torrance maybe, or Canoga Park or somewhere."

Torrance is off the San Diego Freeway, west of Lakewood and south of El Segundo and Hawthorne and Lawndale and Gardena. Canoga Park is in the San Fernando Valley. People who worked for Hughes did in 1988 live in Torrance and Canoga Park. Five years later, after passage by the Arizona state legislature of a piece of tax-incentive legislation known locally as "the Hughes bill," Hughes was moving a good part of its El Segundo and Canoga Park operations to Tucson, and a well-known residential real estate broker on the west side of Los Angeles was advising clients that the market in Beverly Hills was down 47.5 percent. I remember being told, by virtually everyone to whom I spoke in Los Angeles during the few months that followed the 1992 riot, how much the riot had "changed" the city. Most of those who said this had lived in Los Angeles, as I had, during the 1965 Watts riot, but 1992, they assured me, had been "different," 1992 had "changed everything." The words they used seemed overfreighted, ominous in an unspecific way, words like "sad" and "bad." Since these were largely not people who had needed a riot to tell them that a volatile difference of circumstance and understanding existed between the city's haves and its have-nots, what they said puzzled me, and I pressed for a closer description of how Los Angeles had changed. After the riot, I was told, it was impossible to sell a house in Los Angeles. The notion it might have been impossible to sell a house in Los Angeles that year for a simpler reason, the reason being that the money had gone away, was still in 1992 so against the grain of the place as to be largely rejected.

The sad, bad times had actually begun, most people later allowed, in 1989, when virtually every defense contractor in Southern California began laying off. TRW had already dropped a thousand jobs. Rockwell had dropped five thousand as its B-1 program ended. Northrop dropped three thousand. Hughes dropped six thousand. Lockheed's union membership had declined, between 1981 and 1989, from fifteen thousand to seven thousand. McDonnell Douglas asked five thousand managers to resign, then to compete against one another for 2,900 jobs. Yet there was still, in McDonnell Douglas towns like Long Beach and Lakewood, space to maneuver, space for a little reflexive optimism and maybe even a trip to Vegas or Laughlin, since the parent corporation's Douglas Aircraft Company, the entity responsible for commercial as opposed to defense aircraft, was hiring for what was then its new MD-11 line. "Douglas is going great guns right now because of the commercial sector," I had been told in 1989 by David Hensley, who then headed the UCLA Business Forecasting Project. "Airline traffic escalated tremendously after deregulation. They're all beefing up their fleets, buying planes, which means Boeing up in Washington and Douglas here. That's a buffer against the downturn in defense spending."

These early defense layoffs were described at the time as "correctives" to the buildup of the Reagan years. Later they became "reorganizations" or "consolidations," words that still suggested the normal trimming and tacking of individual companies; the acknowledgment that the entire aerospace industry might be in trouble did not enter the language until a few years later, when "the restructuring" became preferred usage. The language used, like the geography, had worked to encyst the problem in certain communities, enabling Los Angeles at large to see the layoffs as abstractions, the predictable if difficult detritus of geopolitical change, in no way logically connected to whether the mini-mall at the corner made it or went under. It had been August 1990 before anybody much noticed that the commercial and residential real estate markets had dried up in Los Angeles. It had been October 1990 before a *Los Angeles Times* business report tentatively suggested that a local slowdown "appears to have begun."

Before 1991 ended, California had lost sixty thousand aerospace jobs. Many of these jobs had moved to southern and southwestern states offering lower salary scales, fewer regulations, and state and local governments, as in Arizona, not averse to granting tax incentives. Rockwell was entertaining bids on its El Segundo plant. Lockheed had decided to move production on its Advanced Tactical Fighter from Burbank to Marietta, Georgia. By 1992, more than seven hundred manufacturing plants had relocated or chosen to expand outside California, taking with them 107,000 jobs. Dun & Bradstreet reported 9,985 California business failures during the first six months of 1992. Analysts spoke approvingly of the transition from large companies to small businesses. *The Los Angeles Daily News* noted the "trend toward a new, more independent work force that will become less reliant on the company to provide for them and more inclined toward entrepreneurship," in other words, no benefits and no fixed salary, a recipe for motel people. Early in 1991, the Arco oil refinery in Carson, near where the Harbor and San Diego Freeways intersect, had placed advertisements in *The Los Angeles Times* and *The Orange County Register* for twenty-eight jobs paying $11.42 to $17.45 an hour. By the end of a week some fourteen thousand applicants had appeared in person at the refinery, and an unspecified number more had mailed in resumes. "I couldn't get in the front gate," an Arco spokesman told the *Times.* "Security people were directing traffic. It was quite a sight to see."

According to the Commission on State Finance in Sacramento, which monitors federal spending and its impact on the state, some 800,000 jobs were lost in California between 1988 and 1993. More than half the jobs lost were in Los Angeles County. The commission's May 1993 report estimated the further loss, between 1993 and 1997, of another 90,000 aerospace jobs, as well as 35,000 civilian jobs at bases scheduled for closure, but warned that "the potential loss could be greater if the defense industry continues to consolidate operations outside California." The Bank of America estimated six to eight hundred thousand jobs lost between 1990 and 1993, but made an even more bleak projection: four to five hundred thousand more jobs lost, in the state's "downsizing industries," between 1993 and 1995. This was what people in Los Angeles were talking about when they talked about the 1992 riot.

5

People who worked on the line in the big California aerospace plants had constituted, in the good years, a kind of family. Many of them were second generation, and would mention the father who worked on the Snark missile, the brother who was foreman of a fabricating shop in Pico Rivera, the uncle who used to get what seemed like half the A-4 line out to watch Little League. These people might move among the half dozen or so major suppliers, but almost never outside them. The conventions of the marketplace remained alien to them. They worked to military specifications, or "milspec," a system that, *The Washington Post* noted, provided fifteen pages of specs for the making of chocolate cookies. They took considerable pride in working in an industry where decisions were not made in what Kent Kresa, then chairman of Northrop, dismissed as "a green eyeshade way." They believed their companies to be consecrated to what they construed as the national interest, and to deserve, in turn, the nation's unconditional support. They believed in McDonnell Douglas. They believed in Rockwell, Hughes, Northrop, Lockheed, General Dynamics, TRW, Litton Industries. They believed in the impossibility of adapting even the most elementary market principles to the manufacturing of aircraft. They believed the very notion of "fixed price," which was the shorthand contractors used to indicate that the government was threatening not to pay for cost overruns, to be antithetical to innovation, anathema to a process that was by its own definition undefined and uncertain.

Since this was an industry in which machine parts were drilled to within two-thousandths or even one-thousandth of an inch, tolerances that did not immediately lend themselves to automation, the people who worked in these plants had never, as they put it, gone robotic. They were the last of the medieval hand workers, and the spaces in which they worked, the huge structures with the immaculate white floors and the big rigs and the overhead cameras and the project banners and the flags of the foreign buyers, became the cathedrals of the Cold War, occasionally visited by but never entirely legible to the uninitiated. "Assembly lines are like living things," I was once told by the manager of assembly operations on the F/A-18 line at Northrop in El Segundo. "A line will gain momentum and build toward a delivery. I can touch it, I can feel it. Here on the line we're a little more blunt and to the point, because this is where the rubber meets the road. If we're going to ship an airplane every two days, we need people to respond to this." *Navy Pilots Are Depending On You*, a banner read in the high shadowy reaches above the F/A-18 line. *Build It As If You Were Going to Fly It*, another read. A toolbox carried this message: *With God & Guts & Guns Our Freedom Was Won!*

This was a world bounded by a diminishing set of coordinates. There were from the beginning a finite number of employers who needed what these people knew how to deliver, and what these people knew how to deliver was only one kind of product. "Our industry's record at defense conversion is unblemished by success," Norman Augustine, then the chairman and CEO of Martin Marietta, told *The Washington Post* in 1993. "Why is it rocket scientists can't sell toothpaste? Because we don't know the market, or how to research, or how to market the product. Other than that, we're in good shape."

Increasingly, the prime aerospace contractors had come to define themselves as "integrators," meaning that a larger and larger proportion of what they delivered, in some cases as much as seventy-five percent, had been supplied by subcontractors. The prime contractors were of course competitive with one another, but there was also an interdependence, a recognition that they had, vis-à-vis their shared principal customer, the federal government, a mutual interest. In this spirit, two or three competing contractors would typically "team" a project, submitting a joint bid, supporting one another during the lobbying phase, and finally dividing the spoils of production.

McDonnell Douglas had been the prime contractor on the F/A-18, an attack aircraft used by both the Navy and the Marine Corps and sold by the Air Force to such foreign users as the Republic of Korea, Malaysia, Australia, Canada, Spain, and Kuwait. McDonnell Douglas, however, teamed the F/A-18 with Northrop, which would every week send, from its El Segundo plant, two partial airplanes, called "shipsets," to the McDonnell Douglas facility in St. Louis. Each Northrop shipset for the F/A-18 included the fuselage and two tails, "stuffed," which is what aircraft people say to indicate that a piece of an airplane comes complete with its working components. McDonnell Douglas would then assemble the shipsets with the wings and other components, and roll the finished F/A-18s off its own line. Northrop and McDonnell Douglas again teamed on a prototype for the YF-23 Advanced Tactical Fighter, but lost the contract to Lockheed, which had teamed its own ATF prototype with Boeing and General Dynamics. Boeing, in turn, teamed its commercial 747 with Northrop, which supplied several 747 shipsets a month, each consisting of the center fuselage and associated sub-assemblies, or stuffing. General Dynamics had the prime contract with the Navy for the A-12 attack jet, but had teamed it with McDonnell Douglas.

The perfect circularity of the enterprise, one in which politicians controlled the letting of government contracts to companies which in turn utilized the contracts to employ potential voters, did not encourage natural selection. When any single element changed in this hermetic and interrelated world, for example a shift in the political climate enabling even one member of Congress to sense a gain in questioning the cost of even one DOD project, the interrelatedness tended to work against adaptation. One tree falls and the food chain fails: on the day in 1991 when Richard B. Cheney, then secretary of defense, finally canceled the Navy's contract with General Dynamics for the A-12, thousands of McDonnell Douglas jobs got wiped out in St. Louis, where McDonnell Douglas had been teaming the A-12 with General Dynamics.

To protect its headquarters plant in St. Louis, McDonnell Douglas moved some of the production on its own C-17 program from Long Beach to St. Louis. To protect the program itself, the company opened a C-17 plant in Macon, Georgia, what was called in the industry a "double-hitter," situated as it was in both the home state of Senator Sam Nunn, chairman of the Senate Armed Services Committee, and the home district of Rep. J. Roy Rowland, a member of the House Veterans' Affairs Committee. "It was smart business to put a plant in Macon," a former McDonnell Douglas executive told Ralph Vartabedian of *The Los Angeles Times.* "There wouldn't be a

C-17 without Nunn's support. There is nothing illegal or immoral about wanting to keep your program funded."

The C-17 was a cargo plane with a capacity for landing, as its supporters frequently mentioned, "on short runways like in Bosnia." It entered development in the mid-1980s. By the time the first plane was delivered in 1993 the number of planes on order from the Air Force had dropped from 210 to 120 and the projected cost of each had risen from $150 million to $380 million. The C-17, even more than most programs, had been plagued by cost overruns and technical problems. There were flaws in the landing gear, a problem with the flaps, trouble meeting range and payload specifications. One test aircraft leaked fuel. Another emerged from a ground strength-certification test with broken wings. Once off the ground, the plane showed a distressing readiness to pitch up its nose and go into a stall.

On June 14, 1993, the day the Air Force accepted delivery of its first C-17 Globemaster III, the plane was more than a year behind schedule, already $1.4 billion over budget, and not yet within sight of a final design determination. Considerable show attended this delivery. Many points were made. The ceremony took place at Charleston Air Force Base in South Carolina, the home state of Senator Strom Thurmond, then the ranking minority member of the Senate Armed Services Committee, as well as of Representatives Floyd Spence, John M. Spratt, Jr., and Arthur Ravenal, Jr., all members of the House Armed Services Committee. Some thirty-five hundred officials turned out. The actual aircraft, which was being delivered with 125 "waivers and deviations" from contract specifications and had been flown east with a load of ballast positioned to keep the nose from pitching up, was piloted on its delivery leg by General Merrill McPeak, the Air Force chief of staff. "We had it loaded with Army equipment . . . a couple of Humvees, twenty or thirty soldiers painted up for battle," General McPeak reported a few days later at a Pentagon briefing. "And I would just say that it's a fine airplane, wonderful capability when we get it fielded, it will make a big difference to us in terms of the global mobility requirement we have, and so I just think, you know, it's a home run."

At the time General McPeak pronounced the plane a home

run, 8,700 of the remaining employees at McDonnell Douglas's Long Beach plant were working on the C-17. What those 8,700 employees would be doing the month or the year after that remained, at that time, an open question, since even as the Air Force was demonstrating support of its own program, discussions had begun about how best to dispose of it. There were a number of options under consideration. One was to transfer program management from McDonnell Douglas to Boeing. Another was to further reduce the number of C-17s on order from 120 to as few as 25. The last-ditch option, the A-12 solution, was to just pull the plug. The Long Beach plant was the plant on the Lakewood city line, the plant with the American flag whipping in the wind and the forward-slanted logo and the boarded-up motel with the marquee that still read "Welcome Douglas Happy Hour 4–7." This was what people in Lakewood were talking about when they talked about the Spur Posse.

6

OF THE EIGHTY-NINE members of the Lakewood High School Class of 1989 who had responded, a year after graduation, to a school district questionnaire asking what they were doing, seventy-one said that they were attending college full or part time. Forty-two of those were enrolled at Long Beach Community College. Five were at community colleges in the neighboring communities of Cerritos and Cypress. Twelve were at various nearby California State University campuses: Fullerton, Long Beach, San Diego, Pomona. Two had been admitted to the University of California system, one to Irvine and one to Santa Barbara. One was at U.S.C. Nine were at unspecified other campuses. During the 1990–91 school year, 234 Lakewood High students were enrolled in the district's magnet program in aerospace technology, which channeled into Long Beach Community College and McDonnell Douglas. Lakewood High's SAT scores for that year averaged 362 verbal and 440 math, a total of ninety-five points below the state average.

This was not a community that pushed its children hard, or launched them into the far world. Males were encouraged to continue, after graduation and indeed into adulthood, playing ball (many kinds of ball, all kinds of ball) in the parks and on the schoolgrounds where they had grown up. Females were encouraged to participate in specific sports of their own, as well as to support the team activities of the ball players. Virtually everyone to whom I spoke in the spring of 1993 mentioned the city's superior sports program. "It's been a very clean community," I was told by John Todd, who had been instrumental in the city's 1954 incorporation and had served as city attorney ever since. "The people that made it up were sound American citizens. We were oriented to our schools and churches and other local activities. We have a tremendous park and recreation program here in Lakewood. And it tended to keep people here." Another longtime resident, whose oldest son worked for McDonnell Douglas and whose other grown children were all in school nearby, echoed this: "It's just a mass recreation program to keep them all busy."

People in Lakewood often mentioned to me how much there was going on in the area. There were the batting cages. There was bowling. There were many movies around. There was, nearby in Downey, the campaign to preserve the nation's last operating original McDonald's, a relic of 1953 at the corner of Lakewood Boulevard and Florence Avenue. "If they're going to tear this down, they might as well tell Clinton please take your business to Taco Bell," one observer told the *Press-Telegram*. And there was, always, the mall, Lakewood Center, the actual and figurative center of town. During the days I spent in Lakewood I had occasion to visit the mall now and then, and each time I found it moderately busy, the fact that its sales figures had decreased every quarter since 1990 notwithstanding. There was a reflecting pool, a carousel, a Burger King, a McDonald's, if not an original McDonald's. There was a booth offering free information on prescriptions. There was another displaying photographs of houses for sale. I said to a woman leafing through the listings that I had not before seen houses for sale in a mall. "H.U.D. and V.A. repos," she said.

One day at the mall I walked over to the freestanding Bullock's, which, because it was about to close its doors for good, was in the process of selling everything in the store at thirty-five percent off the ticket price. There were women systematically defoliating the racks in the men's-wear department, women dropping discards and hangers in tangles on the floor, women apparently undiscouraged by the scrawled sign warning that register lines were "currently in excess of 3+ hours long," women who had already staked out positions for the wait, women curled with their children on the floor, women who had bulwarked their positions with forts of quilts, comforters, bedspreads, mattress pads, Cuisinarts, coffee makers, sandwich grills, Juice Tigers, and Heart Wafflers. These were the women and the daughters and granddaughters of the women who had seen the hundred-foot pylon in 1950 and decided that this was the place to start. The clerks and security personnel monitoring the register lines were men. These were the men and the sons and grandsons of the men who used to get what seemed like half the A-4 line out to watch Little League.

7

"WE WANT GREAT CITIES, large factories, and mines worked cheaply, in this California of ours!" That was Henry George, in "What the Railroad Will Bring Us," rhetorically setting forth what was in 1868 popular local sentiment. Then he proceeded to count the cost:

> Would we esteem ourselves gainers if New York, ruled and robbed by thieves, loafers and brothel-keepers; nursing a race of savages fiercer and meaner than any who ever shrieked a war-whoop on the plains; could be set down on our bay tomorrow? Would we be gainers, if the cotton-mills of Massachusetts, with their thousands of little children who, official papers tell us, are being literally worked to death, could be transported to the banks of the American; or the file and pin factories of England, where young girls are treated worse than even slaves on southern plantations, be reared as if by magic at Antioch? Or if among our mountains we could by wishing have the miners, men, women and children, who work the iron and coal mines of Belgium and France, where the condition of production is that the laborer shall have meat but once a week—would we wish them here?
>
> Can we have one thing without the other?

In those towns off the San Diego Freeway that had seemed when times were good to answer Henry George's question in the affirmative, 1993 was a sullen spring. In April, about the time the Lakewood Center Bullock's was selling the last of its Heart Wafflers, the ten-year-old girl who said that she had been assaulted by a Spur Posse member gave her first press conference, in Gloria Allred's office. Her mother had been seen, on *Donahue*, *The Home Show*, and *20/20*, but the child, by that time eleven, had not. "I have been upset because I wanted to be on TV," she said at her press conference. "To show how I feel. I wanted to say it for myself." Also in April, Spur Posse members approached various talent agencies, trying to sell their story for a TV movie. An I.C.M. agent asked these Spurs if they were not concerned about how they might be presented. Their concern, they told him, was how much money they would make. I.C.M.

declined to represent the Spurs, as did, it was later reported, C.A.A., United Talent Agency, and William Morris.

It was April, too, at the Douglas plant on the Lakewood city line, when Teamsters Local 692 went on strike, over the issue of whether or not Douglas could contract out work previously done by union members. "They can't do that to people after twenty-seven years," the wife of one driver, for whom the new contract would mean a cut from $80,000 to $35,000 a year, told the *Press-Telegram*. "It's just not right." It was in April, again, that Finnair disclosed discussions about a switch from its mostly Douglas fleet to buying Boeing. It was in May that Continental, just out of bankruptcy reorganization, ordered ninety-two new planes, with options for ninety-eight more, all from Boeing.

In a town where it was possible to hear, unprompted, a spirited defense of the DC-10 ("Very quiet plane," John Todd told me, "nice flying plane, compared to those Boeings and those other airplanes it makes about half as much noise"), the involvement with Douglas went deeper than mere economic dependence. People in Lakewood had defined their lives as Douglas. I had lunch one day with a 1966 graduate of Lakewood High who had later spent time in the Peace Corps. It seemed that somewhere in the heart of Africa, he had hopped a ride on a DC-3. The DC-3 had a plate indicating that it had come off the Long Beach line, and he had thought, There it is, I've come as far as I can go and it's still Douglas. "It's a town on the plantation model," he said to me at lunch. "Douglas being the big house."

"They're history," an aircraft industry executive said that spring to *The Washington Post*. "I see a company going out of business, barring some miracle," Don E. Newquist, chairman of the International Trade Commission, said at a hearing on commercial aerospace competitiveness. Each was talking about Douglas, and by extension about the plant on the Lakewood city line, the plant with the flag and the forward-slanted logo and the MD-11s parked like cars and the motel with the marquee that still read "Welcome Douglas Happy Hour 4–7." "It's like a lifetime thing," one Lakewood High graduate said on *Jane Whitney*, trying to explain the Spur Posse and what held its members together. "We're all going to be friends for life, you know."

It was 1997 when Douglas was finally melted into Boeing, and the forward-slanted letters reading *MCDONNELL DOUGLAS* vanished from what was now the Boeing plant on the Lakewood city line.

It was 1999 when Boeing shut down Douglas's MD-90 program.

It was 2000 when Boeing shut down Douglas's MD-80 program, 2001 when Boeing shut down Douglas's MD-11 program.

It was 2000 when Boeing began talking about its plan to convert two hundred and thirty acres of what had been the Douglas plant into non-aircraft use, in fact a business park, "PacifiCenter," with its own condominium housing and the dream of attracting, with what inducements became increasingly unclear as the economy waned, such firms as Intel and Sun Microsystems.

It was 2002 when Boeing obtained an order from the Pentagon for sixty additional C-17s, another temporary stay of execution for what had been the Douglas program, which had been scheduled for closure in 2004. "It's a great day," the manager on the program told employees on the day he announced the order. "This is going to keep you employed through 2008, so rest tonight and start on sixty more tomorrow."

It was also 2002 when the first stage of a multi-billion-dollar public works project called the "Alameda Corridor" was completed, a $2.4 billion twenty-mile express railway meant to speed freight containers from the ports of Long Beach and Los Angeles to inland distribution points. This "Alameda Corridor" had been for some years a kind of model civic endeavor, one of those political mechanisms designed to reward old friends and make new ones. During the period when the Alameda Corridor was still only an idea, but an idea moving inexorably toward a start date, its supporters frequently framed it as the way to bring a "new economy" to the twenty-six "Gateway Cities" involved, all of which had been dependent on aerospace and one of which was Lakewood. This "new economy" was to be built on "international trade," an entirely theoretical replacement for the gold-standard money tree, the federal government, that had created these communities. Many seminars on "global logistics" were held. Many warehouses were built. The first stage of the Alameda Corridor was near completion before people started wondering what exactly these warehouses were to bring them; started wondering, for example, whether eight-dollars-an-hour forklift operators, hired in the interests of a "flexible" work force only on those days when the warehouse was receiving or dispatching freight, could ever become the "good citizens" of whom Mark Taper had spoken in 1969, the "enthusiastic owners of property," the "owners of a piece of their country—a stake in the land." *California likes to be fooled*, as Cedarquist, the owner in *The Octopus* of the failed San Francisco iron works, told Presley at the Bohemian Club.

In 1970 I was working for *Life*, and went up to eastern Oregon to do a piece on the government's storage of VX and GB nerve gas on twenty thousand acres near Hermiston, a farm town in Umatilla County, population then 5,300. It seemed that many citizens wanted the nerve gas, or, in the preferred term, "the defense material," the storage of which provided 717 civilian jobs and brought money into town. It seemed that other citizens, some of whom lived not in Hermiston but across the mountains in Portland and Salem, making them members of what was referred to in Hermiston as "the academic community and Other Mothers for Peace or whatever," saw the presence in Oregon of VX and GB as a hazard. The story was routine enough, and I had pretty much wrapped it up (seen the mayor, seen the city manager, seen the anti-gas district attorney in Pendleton, seen the colonel in charge of the depot and seen the rabbits they left in the bunkers to test for leaks) before I realized that the situation had for me an actual resonance: since well before Elizabeth Scott was born, members of my family had been moving through places in the same spirit of careless self-interest and optimism that now seemed to be powering this argument in Hermiston. Such was the power of the story on which I had grown up that this thought came to me as a kind of revelation: the settlement of the west, however inevitable, had not uniformly tended to the greater good, nor had it on every level benefitted even those who reaped its most obvious rewards.

One afternoon in September of 2002 I drove the length of the Alameda Corridor, north from the port through what had been the industrial heart of Southern California: Carson, Compton, Watts. Lynwood, South Gate. Huntington Park. Vernon. It was a few weeks before that fall's dockworkers' strike shut down Pacific trade, and I saw that afternoon no trains, no containers, only this new rail line meant to carry the freight and these new warehouses meant to house the freight, many of them bearing for-lease signs. On the first hill north of Signal Hill there was what appeared to be a new subdivision, with a sign, "Vista Industria." Past the sign that read Vista Industria there were only more warehouses, miles of warehouses, miles of empty intersections, one Gateway City after another, each indistinguishable from the last. Only when the Arco Towers began emerging from the distant haze over downtown Los Angeles did I notice a sign on a warehouse that seemed to suggest actual current usage. *165,000 Square Feet of T-Shirt Madness*, this sign read.

Save the Aero—See "Tadpole." This was the sign on the Aero Theatre on Montana Avenue in Santa Monica in September of 2002. The Aero Theatre was built in 1939 by Donald Douglas, as recreation for his workers when Douglas Aircraft was Santa Monica's biggest employer. During the ten years when I was living not far from the Aero, 1978 to 1988, I never saw anyone actually enter or leave the theatre. Douglas built Santa Monica and then left it, and the streets running south of what had been the first Douglas plant were now lined with body shops, mini-marts, Pentecostal churches and walk-in dentists. Still, Santa Monica had its ocean, its beaches, its climate, its sun and its fog and its climbing roses. The Gateway Cities will have only their warehouses.

PART THREE

1

"What had it all been about: all the manqué promises, the failures of love and faith and honor; Martha buried out there by the levee in a $250 dress from Magnin's with river silt in the seams; Sarah in Bryn Mawr, Pennsylvania; her father, who had not much cared, the easy loser (*He never could have been*, her mother had said and still loved him); her mother sitting alone this afternoon in the big house upriver writing out invitations for the Admission Day Fiesta and watching *Dick Clark's American Bandstand* because the Dodgers were rained out; Everett down there on the dock with his father's .38. She, her mother, Everett, Martha, the whole family gallery: they carried the same blood, come down through twelve generations of circuit riders, county sheriffs, Indian fighters, country lawyers, Bible readers, one obscure United States senator from a frontier state a long time ago; two hundred years of clearings in Virginia and Kentucky and Tennessee and then the break, the void into which they gave their rosewood chests, their silver brushes; the cutting clean which was to have redeemed them all. They had been a particular kind of people, their particular virtues called up by a particular situation, their particular flaws waiting there through all those years, unperceived, unsuspected, glimpsed only cloudily by one or two in each generation, by a wife whose bewildered eyes wanted to look not upon Eldorado but upon her mother's dogwood, by a blue-eyed boy who was at sixteen the best shot in the county and who when there was nothing left to shoot rode out one day and shot his brother, an accident. It had been above all a history of accidents: of moving on and of accidents. What is it you want, she had asked Everett tonight. It was a question she might have asked them all."

THAT passage is from the last few pages of a novel, *Run River*, published in 1963. The author of the novel was me. The protagonist, the "she" of the passage, is Lily McClellan, born Lily Knight, the wife of a hop grower on the Sacramento River. As the novel opens, Lily's husband, Everett McClellan, has just shot and killed the man with whom both Lily and his sister Martha have had affairs. This story, the "plot" of the novel, was imagined, but the impulse that initially led me to imagine this story and not another was real: I was a year or two out of Berkeley, working for *Vogue* in New York, and experiencing a yearning for California so raw that night after night, on copy paper filched from my office and the Olivetti Lettera 22 I had bought in high school with the money I made stringing for *The Sacramento Union* ("Big mistake buying Italian," my father had advised, "as you'll discover the first time you need a part replaced"), I sat on one of my apartment's two chairs and set the Olivetti on the other and wrote myself a California river.

The "stuff" of the novel, then, was the landscape and weather of the Sacramento Valley, the way the rivers crested and the way the tule fogs obscured the levees and the way the fallen camellias turned the sidewalks brown and slick during the Christmas rains. The stuff, too, was in the way those rains and those rivers had figured in the stories I had been told my entire life, stories predicated on the childhood memories of relatives (Kilgores and Reeses, Jerretts and Farnsworths, Magees and Cornwalls) who were by then long dead themselves, fragments of local oral history preserved by daughters and granddaughters on legal pads and the backs of envelopes:

> That winter was a very wet winter, raining night and day for weeks. It was always called the winter of the Flood as the levee broke on the east side of Sacramento and the city was a lake of water, boats running up and down the streets and small houses floating around like dry goods boxes. This was in 1861 and 1862.

> During the flood it was impossible to get any provisions out of Sacramento, only by boat, so three of our neighbors who were out of tobacco, Wm. Scholefield, Myron Smith and a man by the name of Sidell, built a boat out of rough boards and launched it in the creek on Scholefield's place and went to Sacramento by water, two rowing and one bailing the water out. They made the round trip and brought home their tobacco and some provisions.

> The downpour continued and the river swelled until the banks overflowed. The families were soon engulfed by the water. They gathered as much of their belongings as were salvageable and

> moved by rowboat to a two-story house on the Grape Vine Ranch, about one-half mile away.

The importance of recording these memories was unquestioned: the flood and the levees and the two-story house on the Grape Vine Ranch had become, like the potato masher that crossed the plains, like the books that did not get jettisoned on the Umpqua River, evidence of family endurance, proof of our worth, indistinguishable from the crossing story itself.

> During this time Elizabeth became critically ill. It was typhoid. Allen and one of the Kilgore cousins rowed through the storm to Sacramento for necessary supplies. The current of the rampant river flood raged about them and it took two days and nights to reach the settlement city. The morning following Allen's return, Elizabeth died. Allen built a coffin for Elizabeth and the women dressed her in a garment of coarse white cotton. The coffin was rowed to hilly ground where there were already other graves. The ground was so full of water that the grave was like a well. Here Elizabeth was buried as there was no other place available.

"Two hundred years of clearings in Virginia and Kentucky and Tennessee and then the break, the void into which they gave their rosewood chests, their silver brushes, the cutting clean which was to have redeemed them all." This was the crossing story as origin myth, the official history as I had learned it. Although certain other lines in that passage from *Run River* suggest that I was beginning to entertain some doubt ("what had it all been about," "a history of accidents: of moving on and of accidents"), the passage now raises questions that did not at the time occur to me. From what exactly was "the break" or "the void" or "the cutting clean" to have redeemed them? From their Scotch-Irish genes? From the idealization that had alchemized the luckless of Wales and Scotland and Ireland into classless western yeomen? From the confusions that led both Jack London and *The Valley of the Moon*'s Saxon Brown to claim the special rights they believed due them as "old American stock"? Or were they to have been redeemed from the break itself, the "cutting clean," "the void"? And the related question: for *what* were they to have been redeemed?

To make of their lives, as Nancy Hardin Cornwall was said to have made of hers, "one ceaseless round of activity"? To "live up to our heritage," as I put it in my eighth-grade graduation speech, and "go on to better and greater things for California"? What exactly was our heritage? *Remember*, as Virginia Reed wrote to her cousin, *never take no cutoffs and hurry along as fast as you can.*

Much in *Run River*, as I believed when I was writing it and as I read it now, some four decades later, has to do with the ways California was or is "changing," the detailing of which permeates the novel with a tenacious (and, as I see it now, pernicious) mood of nostalgia. The current action (much of the novel is past action) takes place in August 1959. Everett McClellan's sister Martha has been dead more than ten years, drowned when she took a boat onto the river in flood stage. On the March morning after Martha's death, as Everett and the ranch foreman dig the grave by the levee in which they will bury her, Lily concentrates on the river, on where and when the levee will go, on the "file of information, gathered and classified every year there was high water. . . . At what point had they opened the Colusa Weir. How many gates were open at the Sacramento Weir. When would the Bypass reach capacity. What was the flood stage at Wilkins Slough. At Rough and Ready Bend. Fremont Weir. Rio Vista."

As presented, Martha McClellan's burial on the ranch, with the river still rising and talk confined to speculation about whether the Army Engineers will dynamite an upstream levee, would seem to represent an idea of traditional, or "old," California. We are told that Martha herself, as a child, invented a game called "Donner Party," in which she herself starred as Tamsen Donner, and hung on the walls of her room "neither Degas ballet dancers nor scenes from *Alice in Wonderland* but a framed deed signed by John Sutter in 1847, a matted list of the provisions carried on an obscure crossing in 1852, a detailed relief map of the Humboldt Sink, and a large lithograph of Donner Pass on which Martha had printed, in two neat columns, the names of the casualties and survivors of the Donner-Reed crossing." To a similar point, Martha is buried in the sea chest in which her mother, long dead, had kept her linens, along with "ends of lace, a box of jet beading from a dress, and the ivory fan carried by Martha's great-great-grandmother Currier at Governor Leland Stanford's Inaugural Ball in 1862." To lay in the grave, Everett has torn down "whole branches" of camellias, which are presented in the novel as having, since they were planted locally in memory of the pioneers, a totemic significance. If the grave washes out, which it surely will if the river continues rising, Martha (and the totemic camellias) will be "free again in the water," at one with the river, a prospect that seems to deter, as "true" Californians, neither her brother nor her sister-in-law.

The year Martha dies is 1949. By 1959, as presented in *Run River*, this "true" California has been largely obliterated. The pear orchards on which Lily herself grew up are being relentlessly uprooted: her mother is selling off the acreage for development as fast as the bank will allow her to subordinate it. The ranches immediately upriver and downriver from the McClellan ranch are already subdivisions, Rancho Del Rio No. 1 and Rancho Del Rio No. 3. This is unsettling to Everett but not so to his and Lily's son, Knight. "They're just biding their time," Knight says. "Waiting it out for Rancho Del Rio No. 2." Knight is about to go east to college, to Princeton, a "new" kind of choice (the "traditional" choice would have been Berkeley or Stanford) and so, again, unsettling. Knight is full of himself, and lectures his mother, who has asked him, since he is driving to Berkeley, to pick up some new paperback books on Telegraph Avenue. From Knight's point of view:

> She did not seem to realize that there were now paperback bookstores in Sacramento. She and his father would never seem to get it through their heads that things were changing in Sacramento, that Aerojet General and Douglas Aircraft and even the State College were bringing in a whole new class of people, people who had lived back East, people who read things. She and his father were going to be pretty surprised if and when they ever woke up to the fact that nobody in Sacramento any more had even heard of the McClellans. Or the Knights. Not that he thought they ever would wake up. They'd just go right along dedicating their grubby goddamn camellia trees in Capitol Park to the memory of their grubby goddamn pioneers.

There are other signs of change, which, in the construct of the novel, is understood to mean decline. There is Everett's older sister, Sarah, who lives outside Philadelphia, another "new" kind of choice, with her third husband: again, a new kind of choice. Sarah has stopped by the ranch on her way to Maui (still another new choice, since the traditional Hawaiian destination would be Honolulu, on the *Lurline*), apologized to her husband for the Valley heat ("true" children of the Valley are made uneasy by summer temperatures that do not reach three digits), and made it clear to Everett that she tolerates his wish to keep as ranches rather than subdivide their joint inheritance, seven thousand acres on the Sacramento and Cosumnes Rivers, only as a provisional indulgence. "Surely we've had offers," Sarah suggests to Everett. Everett allows that interest has been expressed in the ranch on the Cosumnes. "I don't *care* so much about the Cosumnes," Sarah says. "The Cosumnes at least brings in a little cash."

There is also the man Everett will eventually shoot, Ryder Channing. Ryder Channing is the only character in the novel not "from" California, in other words one of the "new people." He first meets Martha in 1944, when he is stationed at Mather Field in Sacramento, and his appearances on the ranch to see her, which continue, inexplicably to Everett, after the war has ended and this person not from California should have gone home to wherever he came from, are presented as troubling elements. He has no intention of leaving, he tells Everett, because California is where the future is being made:

> Starting now. Channing had the hunch they were in on the ground floor of the biggest boom this country had ever seen. Talk about your gold rush. And he wasn't the only one who believed in Northern California. Just one example, the Keller Brothers believed in Northern California to the tune of five million berries.
>
> "The Keller Brothers," Everett said. "I don't believe I know them."
>
> The Keller Brothers, Channing explained patiently, were developers. Los Angeles developers who believed in Northern California, in the Valley specifically, to the tune of five million smackeroos. Which they were putting into the Natomas District.
>
> "I never heard of any Kellers in the Natomas," Everett said.

With what appeared to be infinite restraint, Channing inspected and crumpled three empty cigarette packages before answering. "They aren't in the Natomas right now. They want to develop the Natomas."

"Who's putting up the money? How can they raise five million dollars on land they haven't got?"

"Those sweethearts could raise five million dollars with a plot plan on the back of a goddamn napkin. Anyway," Channing added, apparently abandoning his effort to justify the Kellers' ways to Everett, "that's just one example. The point is we're sitting right here on the ground floor with the button pushed go."

Ryder, who because he has no California heritage is incapable of betraying it, not only sees the future but seizes it: he abandons Martha in 1948 to marry the daughter of a recently rich developer. ("Construction money, Everett believed. Wartime. It was all mixed up in his mind with Henry Kaiser.") Martha, about whom there have been previous suggestions of histrionic instability (at parties the year she was sixteen "it had been impossible not to notice her, as it might have been impossible not to notice someone running a high fever, or wearing a cellophane dress"), spends the winter between Ryder's marriage and her own death trying in vain to embrace this New California from which Ryder had come and to which she has now lost him: "She went everywhere, met everyone. She met builders, promoters, people looking for factory sites and talking about a deep-water channel and lobbying for federal dams; people neither Everett nor Lily would have known existed had she not told them. She went to large parties at new country clubs, went to small parties at new apartment houses, and went, almost every afternoon, to inspect subdivisions opened by one or another of the boys she knew who were going into the real estate business."

This is a not inaccurate characterization of the way Sacramento, or for that matter California itself, felt to a child growing up during the postwar boom years, the late 1940s and early 1950s; sometimes, say when I hear about what the Alameda Corridor will bring us, I still catch the echo of those years. It was true that it was suddenly possible, as if overnight, to buy paperback books at Levinson's bookstore downtown. It was true that it was suddenly possible, as if overnight, to see foreign movies—*Open City*, *The Bicycle Thief*, a lachrymose Swedish young-love picture called *One Summer of Happiness*—at the Guild Theater in Oak Park, although the only member of my family to regularly see them was a half-deaf great-aunt for whom subtitles offered the novel possibility of actually following the action onscreen. It was true that the habits and customs of "old Sacramento" (the school-vacation jobs on the ranches and at the canneries, the swimming in the rivers and wading in the ditches, the dutiful study of the agricultural exhibits at the California State Fair) were giving way to a more urban, or suburban, life, in which children swam in clear water in backyard pools lined with gunite and bought Italian typewriters and ate pears bought in supermarkets rather than dropped off in lugs by the relatives who grew them.

All this was true, and yet there was in *Run River* something that was not true, a warp, a persistent suggestion that these changes brought about by World War Two had in some way been resisted by "true" Californians. Had not any such resistance been confined to the retrospect? Were not "changes" and "boom years" what the California experience had been about since the first American settlement? Were we not still willing to traffic our own history to get what the railroad could bring us?

Take for example this business of laying the iconic camellias in Martha's grave: in point of fact the whole notion of planting camellias for the pioneers—there was in the park across from the state capitol building in Sacramento a "Camellia Grove" set aside for this purpose—had originated with my father's stepmother, Genevieve Didion, who was for many years the president of the Sacramento City Board of Education and was said by the rest of the family, not entirely approvingly, to be "political." All association of camellias with pioneers, in other words, derived from the same spirit of civic boosterism that would later turn Front Street, along the river, into the entirely ersatz "redevelopment" known as "Old Sacramento," twenty-eight riverfront acres of shops selling trinkets and souvenirs and popcorn. "The pioneers," in other words, had become a promotional tool, Sacramento's own unique selling proposition, a way of attracting tourists, conventions, a new kind of cash that did not depend on crops: one more version of the weakness for the speculative venture that Charles Nordhoff had noted in 1874.

"The pool kills me," Everett McClellan's sister Sarah says, in *Run River*, when she visits the ranch on which he and Lily live. "It looks like Pickfair."

The year Sarah says this is 1959. Although swimming pools were fairly general throughout California by 1959, this pool on the ranch represents, as presented, Everett's first concession to the postwar mood, and so cues the reader to yet another sign of decline. This did not exactly reflect any attitude toward pools with which I was familiar.

In 1948, when my mother and father and brother and I were living on some acreage outside Sacramento on which my father had built a house until the time seemed right to subdivide the property, my brother and I wanted a pool. We could have a pool, my father said, but only if we ourselves dug it. Every morning all that hot summer my brother, Jim, who was eight, took a shovel out to the middle of the field in front of the house and chipped in vain at the hardpan that underlay the inch or two of topsoil.

Five years older than Jim, doubtful that either he or I could dig a twenty-by-forty-foot hole eight feet deep, equally doubtful that our father—were such a hole to miraculously materialize—had any intention of following through (as I saw it, he might string a hose out there and turn on the tap, but no gunite, no filter, no tile coping), I declined to dig. Instead I spent the summer reading the plays of Eugene O'Neill and dreamed of escaping to Bennington, where I would prepare myself for a New York life in the theater by sitting in a tree in a leotard and listening to Francis Fergusson explain the difference between drama and melodrama. This was the year, 1948, when, already plotting my departure, I delivered the eighth-grade graduation speech on "Our California Heritage." This was also the year, 1948, when the Sacramento City Parks Department awarded, as prizes in its annual Easter egg hunt, what *The Sacramento Bee* described as "live bunnies named after pioneers," a teaching tool, it occurs to me now, that had "Genevieve Didion" written all over it. Ten years later I did have a New York life, although not in the theater, and I was writing the novel that would put such a protective distance between me and the place I came from.

2

THIS QUESTION OF "changes," involving as it does some reflexive suggestion of a birthright squandered, a paradise lost, is a vexed issue. I was many times told as a child that the grass in the Sacramento Valley had at the time the American settlers arrived in the 1840s grown so high that it could be tied over a saddle, the point being that it did no more. California, in this telling, had even then been "spoiled." The logical extension of this thought, that we were the people who had spoiled it, remained unexplored. Nor would it be explored in *Run River*, the inchoate intent of which was to return me to a California I wished had been there to keep me. "*Everything changes, everything changed*," one passage, obviously acutely felt at the time I wrote it, begins. "*Summer evenings driving downriver to auctions, past the green hops in leaf, blackbirds flying up from the brush in the dry twilight air, red Christmas-tree balls glittering in the firelight, a rush of autumn Sundays, all gone, when you drove through the rain to visit the great-aunts.*" The "change," the "all gone" part, is seen in *Run River* to have come only with the postwar boom years, the prosperous years when California "as it was" got bulldozed out of existence either for better (as Ben Weingart and Louis Boyar and Mark Taper saw it when they conceived Lakewood) or (as I then wished to see it) for worse.

Californians of more programmatic mind for many years presented these postwar changes as positive, the very genius of the place: it was conventional to mention the freeway system, the aerospace industry, the University of California Master Plan, Silicon Valley, the massive rearrangement of the water that got funded when Pat Brown was governor, the entire famous package, the celebrated promise that California was committed to creating and educating an apparently infinitely expandable middle class. The more recent programmatic attitude was to construe the same changes as negative, false promises: the freeways had encouraged sprawl, the aerospace industry had gone away, the University of California had lost faculty and classrooms to budget cuts, Silicon Valley had put housing beyond the means of non-tech California, and most of the state was still short water.

In a book of readings for students in freshman composition classes at California colleges, the editors and contributors speak of "the threats to the California dream," of the need to keep "the California dream in sight," of "the fashionable new mythology emerging nationwide in which California is being recast as a nightmare rather than a dream," and of which O. J. Simpson—O. J. Simpson as "the self-invented celebrity who climbed from poverty to the summit of fame and fortune" or O. J. Simpson in the white Bronco—"better reflects the truth about the California dream." In either case, genius of the place or its dystopian blight, the postwar changes that transformed California were understood to have been brought about by what was popularly seen as an unprecedented influx of population, what Pat Brown, in a 1962 issue of *Look*, called "the greatest mass migration in the history of the world" and George B. Leonard, in the same issue of *Look*, called "the migrating millions who vote with their wheels for California." During World War Two and the immediate postwar years, 1940 to 1950, the population of California did in fact increase 53 percent. During the next ten years, 1950 to 1960, the population of California did in fact increase 49 percent.

Yet such growth was in no way unprecedented. Nor, in a state that had seen its population increase in the first ten years of statehood by 245 percent, was it even remarkable. The decade between 1860 and 1870 brought a population increase to California of 47 percent, the decade that followed an increase of 54 percent. The years between 1900 and 1910 brought another 60 percent. Those were the years during which Faulkner's Ira Ewing, in "Golden Land," would have fled Nebraska on the night train to end up twenty-five years later sleepless in Beverly Hills. The years between 1910 and 1920 brought 44 percent. Those were the years when it came to the attention of Saxon Brown and Billy Roberts in *The Valley of the Moon* that "it looks like the free-born American ain't got no room left in his own land"—two babes convinced that they had been deprived of their Eden by industrialization, by immigration, by whatever it was that they could not name. The ten years that followed, between 1920 and 1930, when only shallowly settled arrivals were to find themselves further marginalized by the onset of the Depression, brought 66 percent. There had been, then, from the beginning, these obliterating increases, rates of growth that systematically erased freshly laid traces of custom and community, and it was from such erasures that many California confusions would derive.

There used to be on the main street through Gilroy, a farm town in Santa Clara County that billed itself as "The Garlic Capital of the World," a two- or three-story hotel, the Milias, where the dining room off the lobby had a black-and-white tiled floor and fans and potted palm trees and, in the opinion of my father, short ribs so succulent that they were worth a stop on any drive between Sacramento and the Monterey Peninsula. I remember sitting with him in the comparative cool of the Milias dining room (any claim of "cool" was at that time comparative, air conditioning not yet having taken widespread hold in Santa Clara County), eating short ribs and the cherries from his old-fashioned bourbon cocktail, the singular musky smell of garlic being grown and picked and processed permeating even the heavy linen napkins.

I am unsure at what point the Milias Hotel vanished (probably about the time Santa Clara County started being called Silicon Valley), but it did, and the "farm town" vanished too, Gilroy having reinvented itself as a sprawl of commuter subdivisions for San Jose and the tech industry. In the summer of 2001, a local resident named Michael Bonfante opened a ninety-million-dollar theme park in Gilroy, "Bonfante Gardens," the attractions of which were designed to suggest the agricultural: stage shows with singing tomatoes, rides offering the possibility of being spun in a giant garlic bulb or swung from a thirty-nine-foot-high mushroom. The intention behind Bonfante Gardens, according to its creator, was "to show how the county was in the 1950s and 1960s." The owner of a neighboring property was interviewed by *The New York Times* on the subject of Bonfante Gardens. "If it gets to be Disneyland, I am going to hate it," she said. "Right now it is pretty and beautiful. But who knows? Someone who has been here as long as I have has mixed feelings."

This interviewee, according to the *Times*, had been a resident of Gilroy, in other words "been here," for fifteen years. If fifteen years seems somewhat short of the longtime settlement suggested by "someone who has been here as long as I have," consider this: when my brother and I applied to change the zoning from agricultural to residential on a ranch we owned east of Sacramento, one of the most active opponents to the change, a man who spoke passionately to the folly of so altering the nature of the area, had moved to California only six months before, which suggested that he was living on a street that existed only because somebody else had developed a ranch. Discussion of how California has "changed," then, tends locally to define the more ideal California as that which existed at whatever past point the speaker first saw it: Gilroy as it was in the 1960s and Gilroy as it was fifteen years ago and Gilroy as it was when my father and I ate short ribs at the Milias Hotel are three pictures with virtually no overlap, a hologram that dematerializes as I drive through it.

Victor Davis Hanson is a professor of classics on the Fresno campus of California State University, a contributor of occasional opinion pieces to *The New York Times* and *The Wall Street Journal*, and the author of a number of books, including *The Land Was Everything: Letters from an American Farmer*, an impassioned polemic modeled on and informed by J. Hector St. John de Crèvecoeur's 1782 *Letters from an American Farmer*. Hanson has in fact for most of his life thought of himself as a farmer, either active or failed (he rejects the word "grower," more common in California, as "a term of self-approbation, used by those in California who often do not themselves grow anything"), with his brother and cousins a cultivator of grapevines and fruit trees on the same San Joaquin Valley land, fewer than two hundred acres, that their great-great-grandfather homesteaded in the 1870s. He sees himself as heir to the freeholding yeomen farmers who, in Crèvecoeur's and his own view, "created the American republican spirit." He tells us that his children are the sixth consecutive generation to live in the same house. The single photograph I have seen of him shows a man in his forties, wearing khakis and a T-shirt, his features and general stance so characteristic of the Central Valley (a good deal of sun exposure goes into this look, and a certain wary defiance) that the photograph could seem indistinguishable from snapshots of my father and cousins.

There is much in *The Land Was Everything* that catches exactly this Valley note. There is the smell of insecticides, fungicides, the toxic mists that constitute the smell of the place. ("What they're trying to do is generate a new fear of the word 'carcinogen,'" the corporate counsel for the J. G. Boswell Company, which operates fifty thousand acres in the Tulare Basin, famously said in response to certain restrictions placed during the mid-1980s on the use of toxic chemicals. "Chemicals are absolutely necessary for everyday life.") There is the sense of walking the ditches in an orchard, losing oneself among the propped limbs of the overburdened fruit trees. There is the visceral pleasure of cold Sierra water as it comes from the flume. There is the monosyllabic speech pattern, the directness to the point of rudeness, the abrupt way of launching and ending telephone calls with no niceties, no identification, no salutation, no goodbye, just a hangup. I never once heard my father's father, the grandfather who remained "Mr. Didion" to me, identify himself on the telephone. My mother frequently hung up without saying goodbye, sometimes in midsentence. "I do not think I shall leave the San Joaquin Valley of California," Hanson writes. "Courage, a friend tells me, requires me to grow up and leave, to get a better job elsewhere; cowardice, he says, is to stay put, possumlike, as the world goes on by. But at least my credentials as a San Joaquin Valley loyalist are unimpeachable, and thus my lament over its destruction is genuine."

Hanson lives on the family farm, but no longer actually farms it. "When we all went to the universities, when we abandoned what made us good and embraced what made us comfortable and secure, we lost something essential, knew we lost it and yet chose to lose," he writes. "Material bounty and freedom are so much stronger incentives than sacrifice and character." What was lost by the "we" of this passage, and in Hanson's view by America itself, was the pure hardship of the agrarian life, the yeoman ideal that constituted the country's "last link with the founding fathers of our political and spiritual past," its last line of defense against "market capitalism and entitlement democracy, the final stage of Western culture that is beyond good and evil."

This gets tricky. Notice the way in which the author implicitly frames his indictment of himself and his family for turning away from the pure agrarian life as an indictment of the rest of us, for failing to support that life. Notice, too, that the "destruction" of the San Joaquin Valley, as he sees it, began at the point when the small family farms on the east side of the Valley (the arid west side of the Valley, the part described by William Henry Brewer in the 1860s as a "plain of absolute desolation," belonged to the corporate growers) began giving way first to industrial parks and subdivisions and then to strip malls and meth labs. "Its Golden Age was therefore brief, no more than the beautiful century between 1870 and 1970, when gravity-fed irrigation in hand-dug ditches from the Sierra first turned a weed-infested desert into an oasis of small tree and vine farms and their quiet satellite communities."

This "Golden Age," in other words, began with the arrival of Hanson's own family, and ended with his own adolescence. "Times have changed," as the similarly focused Saxon Brown complained to Billy Roberts in *The Valley of the Moon*. "They've changed even since I was a little girl." There is a further possible mirage here: the San Joaquin Valley's "beautiful century" could have seemed, to those who were actually living it, perhaps not entirely golden: "Here, in this corner of a great nation, here, on the edge of the continent, here, in this valley of the West, far from the great centers, isolated, remote, lost, the great iron hand crushes life from us, crushes liberty and the pursuit of happiness from us. . . . Tell them, five years from now, the story of the fight between the League of the San Joaquin and the railroad and it will not be believed." That was Frank Norris, writing in *The Octopus*, on the slaughter that took place in 1880 at Mussel Slough, now Lucerne, now and then just fifteen miles from Selma, the site of the farmhouse in which six generations of Victor Davis Hanson's family have lived.

"There in my own small town," Hanson tells us in *The Land Was Everything*, "we have torn up vineyards and now have planted the following crops: Wal-Mart, Burger King, Food-4-Less, Baskin-Robbins, Cinema 6, Denny's, Wendy's, Payless, Andersen's Pea Soup, the Holiday Inn, McDonald's, Carl's

Jr., Taco Bell, four gas stations, three shopping centers, two videotape stores, and a car wash." In line with the thrust of his argument, Hanson offers this list as evidence of "change," specifically of the moral or spiritual impoverishment to which he believes the loss of the yeoman ethic in the San Joaquin Valley has led. Some readers—those, say, who remain unconvinced that there was ever a yeoman ethic in the San Joaquin Valley to lose—might take from the list evidence of a less elusive impoverishment: the enterprises named are in the main national chains, or franchises, not the kinds of entrepreneurial activity calculated to return either money or opportunity to the community.

According to a study conducted by the Public Policy Institute of California, the poverty rate in the San Joaquin Valley in the year 2000 was in fact twenty-two percent of the population, the highest in the state, which in turn had an overall poverty rate, when adjusted for cost of living, exceeded in the United States only by that of the District of Columbia. This overall California poverty rate began exceeding that of the rest of the nation only in the late 1980s, but being poor in the Central Valley was not a new condition. In 1980, of the ten American metropolitan areas most reliant on public assistance, six were in the Sacramento and San Joaquin Valleys, running south from Redding and Yuba City–Marysville and Stockton straight down through Modesto and Fresno and Visalia. Many assumed California's rising poverty rate to be a function of immigration, and to some degree, in the short term, it was: the foreign-born, particularly those from Southeast Asia and Hispanic America, who did have the highest rate of poverty in the state.

In the Central Valley, however, immigration did not tell the whole story. In 1998, Tulare County began paying its welfare clients the cost of relocating in other states, providing an average of $2,300 a client to rent a U-Haul van and buy gas and stay in motels en route and pay first-and-last-month rent on a place to live once they get there. This policy, which also includes e-mailing job applications and mining the Internet for apartment rentals, has since been adopted by four other San Joaquin counties, Kings, Madera, Fresno, and Kern. In June 2001 and June 2002, reporters from first *The New York Times* and then *The Washington Post* interviewed samplings of these relocated clients. There were David Langley and his wife and child, who moved from Visalia to Colorado, as did Jackie and Michael Foster, "with their year-old red-haired son." There was Lorrie Gedert, who moved with her two daughters from Ivanhoe, about ten miles outside Visalia, to Little Rock. There were Gloria and Nathan Dickerson, who moved with their two children, Emily and Drake, from Visalia to Ocala, Florida. There were Richard and Zena White, who moved from Fresno to Slidell, Louisiana, where, according to the *Post*, both are now working full-time, "Zena as an assistant manager at a Chevron gas station and Richard as a shift manager at McDonald's." What first strikes the reader of these reports is that the names of the former Californians interviewed do not uniformly suggest recent immigration from Southeast Asia or Hispanic America. What next strikes the reader is that even such marginal jobs as assistant manager at the Chevron station and shift manager at the McDonald's appear to have been unobtainable in the San Joaquin Valley, here where the vineyards got torn up so the Wal-Marts and the Burger Kings and the Taco Bells could grow, here, as Frank Norris saw it in 1901, *in this corner of a great nation, here, on the edge of the continent, here, in this valley of the West, far from the great centers, isolated, remote, lost.*

3

FOR MOST OF MY LIFE California felt rich to me: that was the point of it, that was the promise, the reward for having left the past on the Sweetwater, the very texture of the place. This was by no means to say that I believed all or even most Californians to be rich, only to suggest that the fact of having no money seemed to me to lack, in California, the immutable gravity that characterized the condition elsewhere. It was not designed to be a life sentence. You were meant, if you were a Californian, to know how to lash together a corral with bark, you were meant to know how to tent a raft and live on the river, you were meant to show spirit, kill the rattlesnake, keep moving. There were in California a lot of "dead brokes," Henry George had pointed out in 1868, in a passage from "What the Railroad Will Bring Us" that got read to me (rather selectively, in retrospect) by my grandfather, "but there never was a better country to be 'broken' in, and where almost every man, even the most successful, had been in the same position, it did not involve the humiliation and loss of hope which attaches to utter poverty in older and more settled communities."

That I should have continued, deep into adult life, to think of California as I was told as a child that it had been in 1868 suggests a confusion of some magnitude, but there it was. *It's not a word we use*, my mother had said about class. *It's not the way we think.* Only in the 1980s did certain facts—two of them, not unrelated—manage to penetrate what was clearly a fairly tenacious wish not to examine whatever it was I needed to believe. The first fact, which entered my attention as an almost personal affront, was that California no longer felt rich enough to adequately fund its education system. The second, or corollary, fact was that there seemed to be many towns in California—including towns I knew, towns I thought of as my own interior landscape, towns I had thought I understood, towns in the Sacramento and San Joaquin Valleys—so impoverished in spirit as well as in fact that the only way their citizens could think to reverse their fortunes was by getting themselves a state prison. Since the building and staffing of new prisons were major reasons why California no longer felt rich enough to adequately fund its education system, this second fact initially presented itself as an even deeper affront than the first, evidence that a "new" California had finally and fatally sold out the old.

Then I remembered, then I realized.

We were seeing nothing "new" here.

We were seeing one more version of making our deal with the Southern Pacific.

We were seeing one more version of making our bed with the federal government.

We were seeing one more enthusiastic fall into a familiar California error, that of selling the future of the place we lived to the highest bidder, which was in this instance the California Correctional Peace Officers Association.

The California Correctional Peace Officers Association is the prison guards' union, a 29,000-member force that has maintained for some years now the most effective lobbying operation in Sacramento. In the 1998 election cycle, for example, the union funneled over two million dollars to Grey Davis's gubernatorial campaign and another three million dollars to various other candidates and propositions. "All I've ever asked is that we get to play in the ballpark with all the big guys and gals out there," Don Novey told *The Los Angeles Times* in 2000. Don Novey is the former guard at Folsom State Prison who became in 1980 the president of the California Correctional Peace Officers Association. "They call us the 800-pound gorilla. But we're just taking care of our own like everybody else." Don Novey refers to those who consider the need for new prisons an arguable proposition as "the other element." He gave $75,000 to the opponent of a state senator who had once spoken against a prison bond issue. "If Don Novey ran the contractors' union," a Republican strategist told the *Times*, "there'd be a bridge over every puddle in the state." The prison guards were in California the political muscle behind the victims' rights movement. The prison guards were in California the political muscle behind the 1994 "three strikes" legislation and initiative, the act that mandated a sentence of twenty-five years to life for any third felony conviction, even for crimes as minor as growing a marijuana plant on a windowsill or shoplifting a bottle of Ripple. The prison guards were the political muscle that had by the year 2000 made the California corrections system, with thirty-three penitentiaries and 162,000 inmates, the largest in the western hemisphere.

Incarceration was not always a growth industry in California. In 1852 there was only San Quentin, by 1880 there was also Folsom. During the 104 years that followed, a century during which the population of California increased from 865,000 to 25,795,000 people, the state found need for only ten additional facilities, most of them low or medium security. It was only in 1984, four years after Don Novey took over the union, that the new max and supermax prisons began rolling online, Solano in 1984, "New Folsom" (a quarter mile removed from "Old Folsom") in 1986, Avenal and Ione and Stockton and San Diego in 1987, Corcoran and Blythe in 1988, Pelican Bay in 1989, Chowchilla in 1990, Wasco in 1991, Calipatria in 1992, Lancaster and Imperial and Centinela and Delano in 1993, Coalinga and a second prison at Blythe in 1994, second prisons at both Susanville and Chowchilla in 1995, Soledad in 1996, a second prison at Corcoran in 1997.

Delano, the town in the San Joaquin between Tulare and Bakersfield that became synonymous outside California with Cesar Chavez's farmworkers' union, still yearns for its own second prison, "New Delano," to be built just across the road from what is already called "Old Delano," the ten-year-old North Kern State Prison. Mendota, west of Fresno and south of Chowchilla, still waits for what was to have been its privately built and operated prison, on which construction was begun and then postponed by the Nashville-based Corrections Corporation of America, which had hit a snag trying to contract with the state for prisoners to fill the $100 million maximum-security prison it had already built in the Mojave desert. "They can build whatever prisons they want," Don Novey had said to this point. "But the hell if they're going to run them."

That these prisons should remain the objects of abject civic desire is curious, since they have not actually enriched the towns that got them. A new prison creates jobs, but few of those jobs go to local hires. The Department of Corrections allows that it imports half the "corrections workers" in any new prison, but "tries" to hire the rest from the community. Opponents to "New Delano" point out that only seven to nine percent of the jobs at these new prisons have typically been local hires, and that the local hires get the low-paid service jobs. Of the 1,600 projected jobs at "New Delano," only 72 would be local hires. There are, moreover, costs, both economic and social: when the families of inmates move into a prison town, they not only strain the limited resources of local schools and social service agencies but bring emotionally stressed children into the community and school system. "The students are all very high risk," a school official in Lassen County, where Susanville is located, told *The Los Angeles Times.* "They come from single-parent homes. They're latchkey kids, often on AFDC. It's very obvious they're from a whole different area. It creates societal conflicts. The child does not fit in."

It was 1993 when the California Department of Corrections activated its first "death fence," at Calipatria. It was 1994 when the second "death fence" was activated, at Lancaster, carrying a charge of 650 milliamperes, almost ten times the voltage required to cause instant death. "What the fence does is take out the human-error part," the warden at Lancaster was quoted as having said, explaining that the million-dollar fences would save money in the long run because armed officers could be removed from prison gun towers. "The fence never goes to sleep. It doesn't go to the bathroom. It doesn't do any of those things. It's always working." It was also 1994 when standardized testing of reading skills among California fourth-graders placed them last in the nation, below Mississippi, tied only with Louisiana. It was 1995 when, for the first time, California spent more on its prisons than on its two university systems, the ten campuses of the University of California and the twenty-four campuses of California State University.

Through most of my life I would have interpreted the growth of the prison system and the diminution of the commitment to public education as evidence of how California had "changed." Only recently did I come to see them as the opposite, evidence of how California had "not changed," and to understand "change" itself as one of the culture's most enduring misunderstandings about itself.

4

"The American community in early California fairly represented, as we shall see, the average national culture and character. But no other part of our land was ever so rapidly peopled as was California in the first golden days. Nowhere else were we Americans more affected than here, in our lives and conduct, by the feeling that we stood in the position of conquerors in a new land. Nowhere else, again, were we ever before so long forced by circumstance to live at the mercy of a very wayward chance, and to give to even our most legitimate business a dangerously speculative character. Nowhere else were we driven so hastily to improvise a government for a large body of strangers; and nowhere else did fortune so nearly deprive us for a little time of our natural devotion to the duties of citizenship. We Americans therefore showed, in early California, new failings and new strength. We exhibited a novel degree of carelessness and overhastiness, an extravagant trust in luck, a previously unknown blindness to our social duties, and an indifference to the rights of foreigners, whereof we cannot be proud. But we also showed our best national traits—traits that went far to atone for our faults. As a body, our pioneer community in California was persistently cheerful, energetic, courageous, and teachable. In a few years it had repented of its graver faults, it had endured with charming good humor their severest penalties, and it was ready to begin with fresh devotion the work whose true importance it had now at length learned—the work of building a well-organized, permanent, and progressive State on the Pacific Coast. In this work it has been engaged ever since."

—Josiah Royce,
California: A Study of American Character, 1886

JUST east of Sacramento, off Kilgore Road in what is now Rancho Cordova, a town with a population of almost fifty thousand that exists only because Aerojet General began manufacturing rockets there after World War Two, there is a three-acre family graveyard, the Matthew Kilgore Cemetery, its gates long gone, its two-hundred-some graves overgrown and many of its stone markers, a few of which are dated as recently as the

1970s, overturned. Two of my great-great-great-grandparents, Matthew Kilgore and his wife Massa McGuire Kilgore, were buried there, Massa Kilgore in 1876, Matthew Kilgore in 1882. When I was in high school and college and later I would sometimes drive out there, park the car and sit on the fender and read, but after the day I noticed, as I was turning off the ignition, a rattlesnake slide from a broken stone into the dry grass, I never again got out of the car.

In the 1980s, when the condition of the Kilgore Cemetery had become a matter of local concern (vandals had dug up a body and stolen its head), the president of the Rancho Cordova Chamber of Commerce appealed to "Cordovans" (residents of Rancho Cordova, in other words "new people") to join a volunteer effort to clean up the beer bottles and debris left by trespassers. "There are a lot of residents who would like to see this historic site preserved as it deserves to be," he was quoted as having said in the newspaper story my mother clipped and sent to me in Los Angeles.

I asked, when my mother and I next spoke, if the family—the seventy-some of my father's cousins who annually attended the Kilgore Family Reunion in McKinley Park in East Sacramento, say—was joining the effort to clean up the Kilgore Cemetery.

The family, my mother said, did not own the Kilgore Cemetery.

It occurred to me that neither did the president of the Rancho Cordova Chamber of Commerce own the Kilgore Cemetery, but I opted to go in a different direction. I asked how exactly it had come to pass that the family did not own the Kilgore Cemetery.

"I presume somebody sold it," my mother said.

I thought about this.

I also thought about having seen the rattlesnake slide from the broken stone into the grass.

I had seen the rattlesnake but I had failed to get out of the car and kill it, thereby violating, in full awareness that I was so doing, what my grandfather had told me was "the code of the West."

If "not killing the rattlesnake" violated "the code of the West," how about "selling the cemetery"? Would that qualify?

Not surprisingly, the Kilgore Cemetery makes an appearance of a kind in *Run River*. Lily's father, Walter Knight, after he misses a curve on the river road and drowns trapped in his car, is buried in what is described as a small family cemetery where the last previous burial had taken place in 1892. The burial is described from Lily's point of view: "There was a certain comfort in the unkempt graveyard. Dried grass obscured the markers, and the wings had been broken years before from the stone angels guarding the rusted wire gate; there was about the place none of the respect for death implicit in a well-tended plot."

Could this have been what I thought letting the Kilgore Cemetery go to ruin demonstrated? Some admirable wagons-west refusal to grant death its dominion? The idealization of the small family cemetery in *Run River* continues: "Once, a long time before, Walter Knight had brought Lily to see this graveyard. He had made her trace out with her finger the letters on the stones, the names and their dates, until she found the small, rough stone which marked the oldest grave." This "oldest grave" was that of a child not yet two, the first family member to die in California. "I think nobody owns land until their dead are in it," Walter Knight had said to Lily on this occasion. "Sometimes I think this whole valley belongs to me," Lily had said, and her father had responded sharply: "It does, you hear me? We made it."

Had I known when I was writing *Run River* that the Kilgore Cemetery had been or would be sold, was this the rationalization I would have worked out? Our dead were in it, so we owned it? Our deal, so we could sell it? Or would I have somehow managed to incorporate "selling the cemetery" into my bill of particulars against the "new people," against the "changes"? At what point exactly might I have asked: was it new people who sold the cemetery? Was it new people who ploughed under and grazed out the grass that could be tied over the saddle? How would Josiah Royce have construed "selling the cemetery"? "Novel degree of carelessness"? "Previously unknown blindness to social duties"? Or "building a well-organized, permanent, and progressive State on the Pacific Coast"? Or was that the same thing?

From the 1870s to the 1920s, according to Richard W. Fox's 1978 study *So Far Disordered in Mind: Insanity in California 1870–1930*, California had a higher rate of commitment for insanity than any other state in the nation, a disproportion most reasonably explained, Fox suggests, "by the zeal with which California state officials sought to locate, detain, and treat not only those considered 'mentally ill,' but also a wide variety of other deviants—including, as state hospital physicians put it, 'imbeciles, dotards, idiots, drunkards, simpletons, fools,' and 'the aged, the vagabond, the helpless.'" Not only did California have this notably higher rate of commitment but the institutions to which it committed its citizens differed fundamentally from those in the East, where the idea of how to deal with insanity had been from the beginning medicalized, based on regimes—however more honored in the breach—of treatment and therapy. The idea of how to deal with insanity in California began and ended with detention.

So broad were the standards for committal, and so general was the inclination to let the state take care of what might in another culture have been construed as a family burden, that even many of the doctors who ran the system were uneasy. As early as 1862, according to *So Far Disordered in Mind*, the resident physician at the Stockton State Asylum for the Insane complained of receiving patients "who, if affected in their minds at all, it is the weakness of old age, or intemperance, or perhaps most commonly both together." In 1870, the federal census classified one in every 489 Californians as insane. By 1880, the rate had risen to one in 345. After 1903, when the rate had reached one in 260 and the asylums had passed capacity, the notion of sterilizing inmates gained currency, the idea being that a certain number could then be released without danger of reproducing. Sterilization, or "asexualization," of inmates, which was legalized in some other states as early as 1907, was made legal in California in 1909. By 1917, the right of the state to sterilize had been extended twice, first to cases in which the patient did not agree to the procedure, then to cases in which the patient had not even been necessarily diagnosed with a hereditary or incurable disorder, but only with "perversion or marked departures from normal mentality." By the end of 1920, of the 3,233 sterilizations for insanity or feeblemindedness performed to that date throughout the United States, 2,558, or seventy-nine percent, had taken place in California.

What was arresting in this pattern of commitment was the extent to which it diverged from the California sense of itself as loose, less socially rigid than the rest of the country, more adaptable, more tolerant of difference. When Fox analyzed the San Francisco commitment records for the years 1906 to 1929, he found that the majority of those hospitalized, fifty-nine percent, had been committed not because they were violent, not because they presented a threat to others or to themselves, but simply because they had been reported, sometimes by a police officer but often by a neighbor or relative, to exhibit "odd or peculiar behavior." In 1914, for example, San Francisco medical examiners granted the wish of a woman to commit her thirty-seven-year-old unmarried sister, on the grounds that the sister, despite her "quiet and friendly" appearance during detention, had begun "to act silly, lost interest in all things which interest women, could no longer crochet correctly as formerly, takes no interest in anything at present." In 1915, a forty-year-old clerk was committed because "for three weeks he has been annoying the City Registrar, calling every day and insisting that he is a Deputy." In 1922, a twenty-three-year-old divorcée was committed after a neighbor reported that she was "lazy, slovenly, careless of personal appearance, stays away from home for days, neglecting self and consorting with men." The same year, a forty-eight-year-old pianist was committed on the grounds that "she has been irresponsible for years; has been a source of great annoyance to many institutions such as Y.W.C.A. Association, churches, etc."

The apparently pressing need to commit so many and in many cases such marginally troubled Californians to indefinite custodial detention seems not at the time to have struck their fellow citizens as an excessive lust for social control. Nor did these fellow citizens appear to see their readiness to slough off bothersome relatives and neighbors as a possible defect in their own socialization. Madness, it became convenient to believe quite early on, came with the territory, on the order of earthquakes. The first State Lunatic Asylum in California, that at Stockton, was established in 1853 specifically to treat those believed to have been driven mad by the goldfields. According to an 1873 State Board of Health report, this endemic madness had to do with "the speculative and gambling spirit" of the California settlement. It had to do with "heterogeneous elements," it had to do with "change of climate, habits, and modes of life," it had to do with being "isolated, without sympathy, and deprived of all home influences." California itself, then, according to its own Board of Health, was "well-calculated to break some link in reason's chain, and throw into confusion even the best balanced properties of mind."

I have on my desk a copy of the 1895 *California Blue Book, or State Roster*, family detritus, salvaged from a Goodwill box during a move of my mother's. I assumed at the time I retrieved it that the roster had been my grandfather's but I see now that the bookplate reads "Property of Chas. F. Johnson, Bakersfield, Calif., No. 230," in other words the detritus of someone else's family. The book is illustrated with etchings and photographs, a startling number of which feature what were in 1895 the state's five asylums for the insane, huge Victorian structures that appear to have risen from the deserts and fields of California's rural counties in a solitude more punitive than therapeutic. Among the illustrations are the facts, in neat columns: there were at the Napa State Asylum for the Insane thirty-five "Attendants," each of whom received an annual salary of $540. All were identified by name. There were, listed under the "Attendants" and also identified by name, sixty "Assistant Attendants," thirteen of whom received $480 a year and the rest $420. There were on the staff at the State Insane Asylum at Agnews, in Santa Clara County, more "Cooks" and "Assistant Cooks" and "Bakers" and "Assistant Bakers" than there appear to have been doctors (the only doctors listed are the "Medical Director," at $3,500, and two "Assistant Physicians," at $2,500 and $2,100 respectively), but the staff roster also includes—a note that chills by the dolorous entertainments it suggests—one "Musician, and Assistant Attendant," budgeted at $60 a year more than the other, presumably unmusical, Assistant Attendants.

These places survived through my childhood and adolescence into my adult life, sources of a fear more potent even than that of drowning in the rivers (drowning meant you had misread the river, drowning made sense, drowning you could negotiate), the fear of being sent away—no, worse—"put away." There was near Sacramento an asylum where I was periodically taken with my Girl Scout troop to exhibit for the inmates our determined cheerfulness while singing rounds, nine-year-olds with merit badges on our sleeves pressed into service as Musicians and Assistant Attendants. *White coral bells upon a slender stalk*, we sang in the sunroom, trying not to make eye contact, *lilies of the valley line your garden walk*. I could not have known at nine that my grandmother's sister, who arrived lost in melancholia to live with us after her husband died, would herself die in the asylum at Napa, but the possibility that such a fate could strike at random was the air we breathed.

Oh don't you wish that you could hear them ring, we sang, one by one faltering, only the strongest or most oblivious among us able to keep the round going in the presence of the put away, the now intractably lost, the abandoned, *that will happen only when the angels sing*. If it was going to be us or them, which of us in that sunroom would not have regressed in Royce's view to that "novel degree of carelessness," that "previously unknown blindness to social duties"? Which of us in that sunroom could not have abandoned the orphaned Miss Gilmore and her brother on the Little Sandy? Which of us in that sunroom did not at some level share in the shameful but entrenched conviction that to be weak or bothersome was to warrant abandonment? Which of us in that sunroom would not see the rattlesnake and fail to kill it? Which of us in that sunroom would not sell the cemetery? Were not such abandonments the very heart and soul of the crossing story? Jettison weight? Keep moving? Bury the dead in the trail and run the wagons over it? Never dwell on what got left behind, never look back at all? *Remember*, Virginia Reed had warned attentive California children, we who had been trained since virtual infancy in the horrors she had survived, *never take no cutoffs and hurry along as fast as you can*. Once on a drive to Lake Tahoe I found myself impelled to instruct my brother's small children in the dread lesson of the Donner Party, just in case he had thought to spare them. "Don't worry about it," another attentive California child, Patricia Hearst, recalled having told herself during the time she was locked in a closet by her kidnappers. "Don't examine your feelings. Never examine your feelings—they're no help at all."

PART FOUR

1

> To me as a child, the State was the world as I knew it, and I pictured other States and countries as pretty much "like this." I never felt the warm, colorful force of the beauty of California until I had gone away and come back over my father's route: dull plains; hot, dry desert; the night of icy mountains; the dawning foothills breaking into the full day of sunshine in the valley; and last, the sunset through the Golden Gate. And I came to it by railroad, comfortably, swiftly. My father, who plodded and fought or worried the whole long hard way at oxen pace, always paused when he recalled how they turned over the summit and waded down, joyously, into the amazing golden sea of sunshine—he would pause, see it again as he saw it then, and say, "I saw that this was the place to live."
>
> —Lincoln Steffens,
> *The Autobiography of Lincoln Steffens*

MY MOTHER died on May 15, 2001, in Monterey, two weeks short of her ninety-first birthday. The preceding afternoon I had talked to her on the telephone from New York and she had hung up midsentence, a way of saying goodbye so characteristic of her—especially by way of allowing her callers to economize on what she still called "long distance"—that it did not occur to me until morning, when my brother called, that in this one last instance she had been just too frail to keep the connection.

Maybe not just too frail.

Maybe too aware of what could be the import of this particular goodbye.

Flying to Monterey I had a sharp apprehension of the many times before when I had, like Lincoln Steffens, "come back," flown west, followed the sun, each time experiencing a lightening of spirit as the land below opened up, the checkerboards of the midwestern plains giving way to the vast empty reach between the Rockies and the Sierra Nevada; then *home, there, where I was from, me,* California. It would be a while before I realized that "me" is what we think when our parents die, even at my age, *who will look out for me now, who will remember me as I was, who will know what happens to me now, where will I be from.*

In the aftermath of my mother's death I found myself thinking a good deal about the confusions and contradictions in California life, many of which she had herself embodied. She despised, for example, the federal government and its "give-aways," but saw no contradiction between this view and her reliance on my father's military reserve status to make free use of Air Force doctors and pharmacies, or to shop at the commissaries and exchanges of whatever military installation she happened to be near. She thought of the true California spirit as one of unfettered individualism, but carried the idea of individual rights to dizzying and often punitive lengths. She definitely aimed for an appearance of being "stern," a word she seemed to think synonymous with what was not then called "parenting." As a child herself in the upper Sacramento Valley she had watched men hung in front of the courthouse. When John Kennedy was assassinated she insisted that Lee Harvey Oswald had "every right" to assassinate him, that Jack Ruby in turn had "every right" to kill Lee Harvey Oswald, and that any breakdown of natural order in the event had been on the part of the Dallas police, who had failed to exercise their own right, which was "to shoot Ruby on the spot." When I introduced her to my future husband, she advised him immediately that he would find her political beliefs so far to the right that he would think her "the original little old lady in tennis shoes." At Christmas that year he gave her the entire John Birch library, dozens of call-to-action pamphlets, boxed. She was delighted, amused, displaying the pamphlets to everyone who came by the house that season, but to the best of my knowledge she never opened one.

She was passionately opinionated on a number of points that reflected, on examination, no belief she actually held. She thought of herself as an Episcopalian, as her mother had been. She was married at Trinity Episcopal Pro-Cathedral in Sacramento. She had me christened there. She buried her mother there. My brother and I had her own funeral service at Saint John's Episcopal Chapel in Monterey, a church she had actually attended only two or three times but favored as an idea not only because it was a "California" church (it was built in the 1880s by Charles Crocker and C. P. Huntington on the grounds of the Southern Pacific's Del Monte Hotel) but also because the litany used was that from the 1928, as opposed to the revised, *Book of Common Prayer.* Yet she had herself at age twelve refused outright to be confirmed an Episcopalian: she had gone through the instruction and been presented to the bishop, but, when asked for the usual rote affirmation of a fairly key doctrinal point, had declared resoundingly, as if it were a debate, that she found herself "incapable of believing" that Christ was the son of God. By the time of my own confirmation, she had further hardened this position. "The only church I could possibly go to would be Unitarian," she announced when my grandmother asked why she never went to church with us.

"Eduene," my grandmother said, a soft keening. "How can you say that."

"I *have* to say it, if I want to be honest," my mother said, the voice of sweet reason. "Since I don't believe that Christ is the son of God."

My grandmother brightened, seeing space for resolution. "Then it's fine," she said. "Because nobody has to believe all *that.*"

Only in recent years did I come to realize that many of these dramatically pronounced opinions of my mother's were defensive, her own version of her great-grandmother's "fixed and settled principles, aims and motives in life," a barricade against some deep apprehension of meaninglessness. There had been glimpses of this apprehension all along, overlooked by me, my own barricade. She did not see a point in making beds, for example, since "they just get slept in again." Nor did she see a point in dusting, since dust just returned. "What difference does it make," she would often say, by way of ending a discussion of whether an acquaintance should leave her husband, say, or whether a cousin should drop out of school and become a manicurist. "What difference does it make," five words that had come to chill me at the bone, was what she said when I pressed her on the point about selling the cemetery. On the Good Friday after her own mother died she happened to be driving across the country with a friend from Sacramento. At the place where they stopped for dinner there had been no fish on the menu, only meat. "I took one bite and I thought of Mother and I wanted to throw up," my mother said when she arrived at my apartment in New York a few days later. Her mother, she said, would never eat meat on Good Friday. Her mother did not like to cook fish, but she would get a crab and crack it. I was about to suggest that cracked Dungeness crab was hard to come by on the average midwestern road trip, but before I could speak I noticed that she was crying. "What difference does it make," she said finally.

I had seen my mother cry only once before. The first time had been during World War Two, on a downtown street in some town where my father was stationed, Tacoma or Durham or Colorado Springs. My brother and I had been left in the car while our mother went into the military housing office that dealt with dependents. The office was crowded, women and children leaning against the plate glass windows and spilling outside. When our mother came back out onto the sidewalk she was crying: it seemed to be the end of some rope, one day too many on which there would be no place for us to stay.

The blank dreariness, Sarah Royce wrote.

Without house or home.

When she got into the car her eyes were dry and her expression was determinedly cheerful. "It's an adventure," she said. "It's wartime, it's history, you children will be thankful you got to see all this." In one of those towns we finally got a room in a hotel, with a shared bathtub, into which she poured a bottle of pine disinfectant every day before bathing us. In Durham we had one room, with kitchen privileges, in the house of a fundamentalist preacher and his family who sat on the porch after dinner and ate peach ice cream, each from his or her own quart carton. The preacher's daughter had a full set of *Gone With the Wind* paper dolls, off limits to me. It was in Durham where the neighborhood children crawled beneath the back stoop and ate the dirt, scooping it up with a cut raw potato and licking it off, craving some element their diet lacked.

Pica.

I knew the word even then, because my mother told me. "Poor children do it," she said, with the same determinedly cheerful expression. "In the South. You never would have learned that in Sacramento."

It was in Durham where my mother noticed my brother reaching for something through the bars of his playpen and froze, unable to move, because what he was reaching for was a copperhead. The copperhead moved on, possibly another instance of the "providential interposition" that had spared my mother's great-great-grandfather from the mad dog in Georgia.

Something occurs to me as I write this: my mother did not kill the copperhead.

Only once, in Colorado Springs, did we actually end up living in a house of our own—not much of a house, a four-room stucco bungalow, rented furnished, but a house. I had skipped part of first grade because we were moving around and I had skipped second grade because we were moving around but in Colorado Springs we had a house, in Colorado Springs I could go to school. I did. They were already doing multiplication and I had skipped learning how to subtract. Out at the base where my father was stationed pilots kept spiraling down through the high thin Colorado air. The way you knew was that you heard the crash wagons. A classmate told me that her mother did not allow her to play with military trash. My grandmother came by train to visit, bringing as usual material solace, thick blue towels and Helena Rubinstein soap in the shape of apple blossoms. I have snapshots of the two of us in front of the Broadmoor Hotel, my grandmother in a John Fredericks hat, me in a Brownie uniform. "You are just out of luck to be home because it's so nice and warm here," I wrote to her when she was gone. The letter, which I found with my mother's snapshots of the period, is decorated with gold and silver stars and cutout Christmas trees, suggesting that I had been trying hard for the upbeat. "But Mommy heard a girl say on the base that 'Remember last New Year's? It was eighteen below, and we had just this kind of weather.' We have a blue spruce Christmas tree. Jimmy and me are going to a party the 23rd at the base. They have a new name for the base. It's Peterson field."

I remember that my mother made me give the apple-blossom soap to the wife of a departing colonel, a goodbye present. I remember that she encouraged me to build many of those corrals that Californians were meant to know how to build, branches lashed together with their own stripped bark, ready for any loose livestock that might come our way, one of many frontier survival techniques I have never had actual occasion to use. I remember that once when we were snowbound she taught me how to accept and decline formal invitations, a survival technique from a different daydream: *Miss Joan Didion accepts with pleasure the kind invitation of*, *Miss Joan Didion regrets that she is unable to accept the kind invitation of*. Another time when we were snowbound she gave me several old copies of *Vogue*, and pointed out in one of them an announcement of the competition *Vogue* then had for college seniors, the Prix de Paris, first prize a job in *Vogue*'s Paris or New York office.

You could win that, she said. When the time comes. You could win that and live in Paris. Or New York. Wherever you wanted. But *definitely* you could win it.

A dozen-plus years later, my senior year at Berkeley, I did win it, and drove to Sacramento with the telegram from *Vogue* in my bag. I had found the yellow envelope with the glassine window slipped under my apartment door when I got back from a class that afternoon. *We are delighted to inform you*, the little strips of yellow tape read. *Miss Jessica Daves, Editor-in-Chief*, *Vogue*. When I showed the telegram to my mother I reminded her that it had been her idea in the first place.

"Really?" she said, doubtful.

This calls for a drink, my father said, his solution, as hanging up was my mother's solution, to any moment when emotion seemed likely to surface.

Colorado Springs, I said, prompting her. When we were snowbound.

"Imagine your remembering," she said.

I see now that World War Two was our own Big Sandy, Little Sandy, Humboldt Sink.

Imagine your remembering.

Something else I remembered: I remembered her telling me that when the war was over we would *all* go to live in Paris. *Toute la famille*. Paris had not yet been liberated but she already had a plan: my father was to reinvent himself as an architect, study architecture at the Sorbonne on the G.I. Bill.

To this end she tried to teach me the French she had learned at Lowell High School in San Francisco.

Pourquoi did we never go to live in Paris?

Je ne sais pas.

A few years after the war ended, when we were again living in Sacramento, I asked this question. My mother said that we had never gone to live in Paris because my father felt an obligation to his family to remain in Sacramento. I recall wondering how much of the plan she had actually discussed with him, since I had never been able to quite bring the picture of my father dropping everything and starting over in Paris into clear focus. The problem in the picture was not that he was risk-averse. Risk was in fact our bread and butter, risk was what put the lamb chops on the table. He had supported my mother and me during the Depression by playing poker with older and more settled acquaintances at the Sutter Club, a men's club in Sacramento to which he did not belong. Right now, after the war, he was supporting my mother and brother and me by buying houses and pieces of property with no money to speak of, then leveraging them, and buying some more. His idea of a relaxing way to make a payment was to drive to Nevada and shoot craps all night.

No.

"Risk" he definitely would have gone for.

The problem in the picture was "Paris."

One of the few perfectly clear points in his belief system (there was much that remained opaque) was the conviction that France, where he had never been, was a worthless country peopled exclusively by the devious, the corrupt, the frivolous, and the collaborating. The name "Didion," he insisted, was not French but German, the name of an ancestor who, although German, "happened to live in Alsace after the French took it over." The first time I went to Paris I sent him a page from a telephone book on which many apparently French Parisians named "Didion" were listed, but he never mentioned it.

One element in my mother's version of the chimerical Paris adventure did hold up: it was true that my father felt an obligation to his family to remain in Sacramento. The reason he felt this obligation had been distilled, within the family and over the years, into a plausible sequence of events, a story so reasonable that it seemed unconvincing, a kind of cartoon. Here was the story: when his mother was dying of influenza in 1918 she had told him to take care of his younger brother, and when his brother lost an eye in a fireworks accident my father thought he had failed. In fact whatever unfulfilled and unfulfillable obligation he felt was less identifiable than that. There was about him a sadness so pervasive that it colored even those many moments when he seemed to be having a good time. He had many friends. He played golf, he played tennis, he played poker, he seemed to enjoy parties. Yet he could be in the middle of a party at our own house, sitting at the piano—playing "Darktown Strutter's Ball," say, or "Alexander's Ragtime Band," a bourbon highball always within reach—and the tension he transmitted would seem so great that I would have to leave, run to my room and close the door.

It was during my first year at Berkeley when the physical manifestations of this tension became sufficiently troubling that he was referred to Letterman Hospital, at the Presidio in San Francisco, to undergo a series of tests. I am unsure how long he spent at Letterman, but it was a period covering some weeks or months. My mother would drive down from Sacramento on the weekends, either Saturday or Sunday, and pick me up at the Tri Delt house in Berkeley. We would cross the Bay Bridge and go out to the Presidio and pick up my father for lunch. I remember that all he would eat that year were oysters, raw. I remember that after the oysters we would spend the rest of the afternoon driving—not back into the city, because he did not like San Francisco, but through Golden Gate Park, down the beach, over into Marin County, anywhere he was likely to see a pickup baseball game he could stop and watch. I remember that at the end of the afternoon he would instruct my mother to drop him not at the Presidio but at the southwesternmost end of Golden Gate Park, so that he could walk back to the hospital along the beach. Sometimes during the week he would walk across the Golden Gate Bridge, visit a cousin at his Sausalito office, and walk back. Once I walked across the bridge with him. I remember that it swayed. In his letters to my mother he dismissed the Letterman psychiatrists as "the mind guys," or sometimes "the mind-over-matter guys," but a year or so before he died, in his eighties, he told me that there had been "this woman doctor" at Letterman who had been "actually very helpful" to him. "We talked about my mother," he said. It was several years after he died before I was able to fully articulate what could not have escaped either my or my mother's fixedly narrowed attention on those weekend afternoons in 1953: those were bad walks for someone under observation for depression.

It occurs to me how brave he must have been, to make those walks and come back.

It also occurs to me how brave my mother must have been, to drive back alone to Sacramento while he made those walks.

My father died in December of 1992. A few months later, in March, I happened to drive my mother from Monterey to Berkeley, where we were to spend a few nights at the Claremont Hotel and I was to speak at a University of California Charter Day ceremony.

"Are we on the right road," my mother had asked again and again as we drove up 101.

I had repeatedly assured her that we were, at last pointing out an overhead sign: *101 North.*

"Then where did it all go," she had asked.

She meant where did Gilroy go, where was the Milias Hotel, where could my father eat short ribs now. She meant where did San Juan Bautista go, why was it no longer so sweetly remote as it had been on the day of my wedding there in 1964. She meant where had San Benito and Santa Clara Counties gone as she remembered them, the coastal hills north of Salinas, the cattle grazing, the familiar open vista that had been relentlessly replaced (during the year, two years, three, the blink of the eye during which she had been caring for my father) by mile after mile of pastel subdivisions and labyrinthine exits and entrances to freeways that had not previously existed.

For some miles she was silent.

California had become, she said then, "all San Jose."

In the bar at the Claremont that evening someone was playing, as if to reinforce what had become a certain time-travel aspect in our excursion, "Only Make Believe," and "Where or When."

The smile you are smiling you were smiling then—
But I can't remember where or when—

I had last been in the bar at the Claremont in 1955, with the son of a rancher from Mendocino County. I recall that I had my roommate's driver's license and a crème de menthe frappé. Thirty-eight years later, from the platform at the Charter Day ceremony, I glanced at the row where my mother was seated and found her chair empty. When I located her outside she told me that it had been essential to leave. She said that "something terrible" had happened during the academic procession, something that had made her fear that she would "cry in front of everybody." It seemed that she had seen a banner reading "Class of 1931," and had realized that the handful of men straggling along behind it (if there were any women she did not mention them) were having trouble walking.

The Class of 1931 had been my father's class at Berkeley. "They were all old men," my mother said about those few of his former classmates who had made the procession. "They were just like your father." *Frank Reese "Jim" Didion*, the memorial note for my father had read in the alumni magazine. *December 19, in Carmel. A native of Sacramento, where he was active as a real estate investor, he majored in business at Cal and was a member of Chi Phi. He is survived by his wife, Eduene, two children, Joan Didion Dunne '56 and James '62, and four grandchildren, including Steven '88 and Lori '93.* There was no believable comfort I could offer my mother: she was right. They were all old men and it was all San Jose. Child of the crossing story that I was, I left my mother with Lori '93 and took the United redeye from San Francisco to Kennedy, the last plane to land before a storm CNN was calling "The Nor'easter of the Century" closed every airport and highway north of Atlanta. I remembered this abandonment the day she died.

2

I ALSO REMEMBERED THIS ONE.
Sacramento, July or August, 1971 or 1972.

I had brought Quintana—my daughter, then five or six—to spend a few days with my mother and father. Because it would be 105 at two and 110 before the sun went down, my mother and I decided to take Quintana out to lunch, somewhere with air conditioning.

My father did not believe in air conditioning.

My father in fact believed that Sacramento summers had been too cold since the dams.

We would go downtown, my mother said. We would have lunch in the Redevelopment. Old Sacramento. You haven't even *seen* Old Sacramento, she said.

I asked if she had seen Old Sacramento.

Not exactly, she said. But she definitely wanted to. We would see it together, it would be an adventure.

Quintana was wearing a pinafore, pale green, Liberty lawn.

My mother gave her a big straw hat to wear against the sun.

We drove downtown, we parked, we started walking on what had been Front Street, its view of the Tower Bridge pretty much constituting the "adventure" part.

The sidewalks in the Redevelopment were wooden, to give the effect of 1850.

Quintana was walking ahead of us.

The lawn pinafore, the big hat, the wooden sidewalk, the shimmer of the heat.

My father's great-grandfather had owned a saloon on Front Street.

I was about to explain this to Quintana—the saloon, the wooden sidewalk, the generations of cousins who had walked just as she was walking down just this street on days just this hot—when I stopped. Quintana was adopted. Any ghosts on this wooden sidewalk were not in fact Quintana's responsibility. This wooden sidewalk did not in fact represent anywhere Quintana was from. Quintana's only attachments on this wooden sidewalk were right now, here, me and my mother.

In fact I had no more attachment to this wooden sidewalk than Quintana did: it was no more than a theme, a decorative effect.

It was only Quintana who was real.

Later it seemed to me that this had been the moment when all of it—the crossing, the redemption, the abandoned rosewood chests, the lost flatware, the rivers I had written to replace the rivers I had left, the twelve generations of circuit riders and county sheriffs and Indian fighters and country lawyers and Bible readers, the two hundred years of clearings in Virginia and Kentucky and Tennessee and then the break, the dream of America, the entire enchantment under which I had lived my life—began to seem remote.

3

ON THE AFTERNOON after our mother's funeral my brother and I divided what few pieces of furniture she still had among her grandchildren, my brother's three children and Quintana. There was not much left; during the previous few years she had been systematically giving away what she had, giving back Christmas presents, jettisoning belongings. I do not remember what Quintana's cousins Kelley and Steven and Lori took. I do remember what Quintana took, because I have seen the pieces since in her apartment in New York. There was an oval Victorian table with a marble top that had come to my mother from some part of the family, I no longer remember which. There was a carved teak chest that had been in my mother and father's bedroom when I was a child. There was a small piecrust table that had been my grandmother's. There was, from among my mother's clothes, an Italian angora cape that she had been wearing ever since my father gave it to her, one Christmas in the late 1940s.

Actually I took the angora cape.

I remembered her wearing it the spring before, at the wedding in Pebble Beach, of my brother's youngest child. I remembered her wearing it in 1964 at my own wedding, wrapping herself in it for the drive from San Juan Bautista to the reception in Pebble Beach.

A representative from Allied came.

The pieces got tagged for shipment.

I put what I did not want to be thrown away—letters, photographs, clippings, folders and envelopes I could not that day summon up the time or the heart to open—in a large box.

Some weeks later the box arrived at my apartment in New York, where it sat in the dining room for perhaps a month, unopened. Finally I opened it. There were pictures of me on the beach at Carmel in 1936, pictures of me and my brother on the beach at Stinson Beach in 1946, pictures of me and my brother and my rabbit in the snow in Colorado Springs. There were pictures of great-aunts and cousins and great-great-grandparents who could be identified only because our mother, on the evening before she died, had thought to tell the names to my brother, who wrote them on the backing of the frames. There were pictures of my mother as a two-year-old visiting her grandmother in Oregon in 1912, there were pictures of my mother at a Peterson Field barbecue in 1943, a young woman in her early thirties wearing flowers in her hair as she makes hamburgers. There was an unframed watercolor of my grandmother's. There were letters my grandmother's brother Jim, like her father a merchant sea captain, had sent her in 1918 from England, where his ship, the S.S. *Armenia*, was in drydock at Southampton after having been torpedoed. There were letters my father had written to his own father in 1928, from a summer job on a construction crew outside Crescent City—my father asking, in letter after letter, if his father could please put in a word for him with an acquaintance who did the hiring for the State Fair jobs, a plea I happen to know was in vain.

I know this because I once wanted my father to make the same call for me.

My mother had told me to forget asking him, because *he's just like his own father, everybody in Sacramento picks up the phone to get their children jobs at the Fair but your father and his father never will, they won't ask for favors.*

There were also letters from me, letters I had written my mother from Berkeley, from the time I went down for summer school in 1952, making up credits between high school and college, until the time I graduated in 1956. These letters were in many ways unsettling, even dispiriting, in that I both recognized myself and did not. *Have never been so depressed as when I got back here Sunday night*, one of the first letters reads, from the summer of 1952. *I keep thinking about Sacramento and what people are doing. I got a letter from Nancy—she misses Sacramento too. They saw "The King and I," "Where's Charley," "Guys and Dolls," and "Pal Joey." A woman committed suicide by jumping out a window across from the Waldorf while they were there. Nancy said it was terrible, they had to clean up the street with fire hoses.*

Nancy was my best friend from Sacramento, traveling with her parents (this is only a guess, but an informed one, since another letter to my mother that summer mentions having "heard from Nancy who is at the Greenbrier and so bored") before beginning Stanford.

Nancy and I had known each other since we were five, when we had been in the same ballet class at Miss Marion Hall's dancing school in Sacramento.

In fact there was also, in the box that came from my mother's house, a program for a recital of that very ballet class: *Joan Didion and Nancy Kennedy*, the program read. "*Les Petites.*" There were also in the box many photographs of Nancy and me: modeling children's clothes in a charity fashion show, wearing matching corsages around our wrists at a high-school dance, standing on the lawn outside Nancy's house on the day of her wedding, Nancy in bouffant white, the bridesmaids in pale green organza, all of us smiling.

The last time I saw Nancy was at the Outrigger Canoe Club in Honolulu, during the Christmas season of the Iran hostage crisis. She was at the next table, having dinner with her husband and children. They were laughing and arguing and interrupting just as she and her brothers and her mother and father had laughed and argued and interrupted in the late 1940s and early 1950s, when I would have dinner at their house two or three times a week.

We kissed, we had a drink together, we promised to keep in touch.

A few months later Nancy was dead, of cancer, at Lenox Hill Hospital in New York.

I sent the recital program to Nancy's brother, to send on to her daughter.

I had my grandmother's watercolor framed and sent it to the next oldest of her three granddaughters, my cousin Brenda, in Sacramento.

I closed the box and put it in a closet.

There is no real way to deal with everything we lose.

When my father died I kept moving. When my mother died I could not. The last time I saw her was eight weeks before she died. She had been in the hospital, my brother and I had gotten her home, we had arranged for oxygen and shifts of nurses, we had filled the prescriptions for morphine and

Ativan. On the morning Quintana and I were to leave for New York, my mother insisted that we bring her a painted metal box that sat on a small table in her bedroom, a box in which she kept papers she thought might have importance, for example a copy of the deed to a gold mine in El Dorado County that she and her sister had inherited from their father and no longer owned. My brother said that she did not need the box, that he had already extracted any still operable papers and put them in safekeeping. She was insistent. She wanted the metal box. Quintana brought the box and set it on the bed. From it my mother took two pieces of silver flatware, a small ladle and a small serving spoon, each wrapped in smoothed scraps of used tissue paper. She gave the serving spoon to Quintana and the ladle to me. I protested: she had already given me all her silver, I had ladles, she had given me ladles. "Not this one," she said. She pointed out the curve of the handle. It seemed that she had what she called "a special feeling" for the way the handle curved on this particular ladle. It seemed that she found this ladle so satisfying to touch that she had set it aside, kept it. I said that since it gave her pleasure she should continue to keep it. "*Take* it," she said, her voice urgent. "I don't want it lost." I was still pretending that she would get through the Sierra before the snows fell. She was not.

THE YEAR OF MAGICAL THINKING

This book is for John and for Quintana

1

Life changes fast.
Life changes in the instant.
You sit down to dinner and life as you know it ends.
The question of self-pity.

THOSE WERE the first words I wrote after it happened. The computer dating on the Microsoft Word file ("Notes on change.doc") reads "May 20, 2004, 11:11 P.M.," but that would have been a case of my opening the file and reflexively pressing save when I closed it. I had made no changes to that file in May. I had made no changes to that file since I wrote the words, in January 2004, a day or two or three after the fact.

For a long time I wrote nothing else.

Life changes in the instant.

The ordinary instant.

At some point, in the interest of remembering what seemed most striking about what had happened, I considered adding those words, "the ordinary instant." I saw immediately that there would be no need to add the word "ordinary," because there would be no forgetting it: the word never left my mind. It was in fact the ordinary nature of everything preceding the event that prevented me from truly believing it had happened, absorbing it, incorporating it, getting past it. I recognize now that there was nothing unusual in this: confronted with sudden disaster we all focus on how unremarkable the circumstances were in which the unthinkable occurred, the clear blue sky from which the plane fell, the routine errand that ended on the shoulder with the car in flames, the swings where the children were playing as usual when the rattlesnake struck from the ivy. "He was on his way home from work—happy, successful, healthy—and then, gone," I read in the account of a psychiatric nurse whose husband was killed in a highway accident. In 1966 I happened to interview many people who had been living in Honolulu on the morning of December 7, 1941; without exception, these people began their accounts of Pearl Harbor by telling me what an "ordinary Sunday morning" it had been. "It was just an ordinary beautiful September day," people still say when asked to describe the morning in New York when American Airlines 11 and United Airlines 175 got flown into the World Trade towers. Even the report of the 9/11 Commission opened on this insistently premonitory and yet still dumbstruck narrative note: "Tuesday, September 11, 2001, dawned temperate and nearly cloudless in the eastern United States."

"And then—gone." *In the midst of life we are in death*, Episcopalians say at the graveside. Later I realized that I must have repeated the details of what happened to everyone who came to the house in those first weeks, all those friends and relatives who brought food and made drinks and laid out plates on the dining room table for however many people were around at lunch or dinner time, all those who picked up the plates and froze the leftovers and ran the dishwasher and filled our (I could not yet think *my*) otherwise empty house even after I had gone into the bedroom (our bedroom, the one in which there still lay on a sofa a faded terrycloth XL robe bought in the 1970s at Richard Carroll in Beverly Hills) and shut the door. Those moments when I was abruptly overtaken by exhaustion are what I remember most clearly about the first days and weeks. I have no memory of telling anyone the details, but I must have done so, because everyone seemed to know them. At one point I considered the possibility that they had picked up the details of the story from one another, but immediately rejected it: the story they had was in each instance too accurate to have been passed from hand to hand. It had come from me.

Another reason I knew that the story had come from me was that no version I heard included the details I could not yet face, for example the blood on the living room floor that stayed there until José came in the next morning and cleaned it up.

José. Who was part of our household. Who was supposed to be flying to Las Vegas later that day, December 31, but never went. José was crying that morning as he cleaned up the blood. When I first told him what had happened he had not understood. Clearly I was not the ideal teller of this story, something about my version had been at once too offhand and too elliptical, something in my tone had failed to convey the central fact in the situation (I would encounter the same failure later when I had to tell Quintana), but by the time José saw the blood he understood.

I had picked up the abandoned syringes and ECG electrodes before he came in that morning but I could not face the blood.

In outline.

It is now, as I begin to write this, the afternoon of October 4, 2004.

Nine months and five days ago, at approximately nine o'clock on the evening of December 30, 2003, my husband, John Gregory Dunne, appeared to (or did) experience, at the table where he and I had just sat down to dinner in the living room of our apartment in New York, a sudden massive coronary event that caused his death. Our only child, Quintana, had been for the previous five nights unconscious in an intensive care unit at Beth Israel Medical Center's Singer Division, at that time a hospital on East End Avenue (it closed in August 2004) more commonly known as "Beth Israel North" or "the old Doctors' Hospital," where what had seemed a case of December flu sufficiently severe to take her to an emergency room on Christmas morning had exploded into pneumonia and septic shock. This is my attempt to make sense of the period that followed, weeks and then months that cut loose any fixed idea I had ever had about death, about illness, about probability and luck, about good fortune and bad, about marriage and children and memory, about grief, about the ways in which people do and do not deal with the fact that life ends, about the shallowness of sanity, about life itself. I have been a writer my entire life. As a writer, even as a child, long before what I wrote began to be published, I developed a sense that meaning itself was resident in the rhythms of words and sentences and paragraphs, a technique for withholding whatever it was I thought or believed behind an increasingly impenetrable polish. The way I write is who I am, or have become, yet this is a case in which I wish I had instead of words and their rhythms a cutting room, equipped with an Avid, a digital editing system on which I could touch a key and collapse the sequence of time, show you simultaneously all the frames of memory that come to me now, let you pick the takes, the marginally different expressions, the variant readings of the same lines. This is a case in which I need more than words to find the meaning. This is a case in which I need whatever it is I think or believe to be penetrable, if only for myself.

2

DECEMBER 30, 2003, a Tuesday.

We had seen Quintana in the sixth-floor ICU at Beth Israel North.

We had come home.

We had discussed whether to go out for dinner or eat in.

I said I would build a fire, we could eat in.

I built the fire, I started dinner, I asked John if he wanted a drink.

I got him a Scotch and gave it to him in the living room, where he was reading in the chair by the fire where he habitually sat.

The book he was reading was by David Fromkin, a bound galley of *Europe's Last Summer: Who Started the Great War in 1914?*

I finished getting dinner, I set the table in the living room where, when we were home alone, we could eat within sight of the fire. I find myself stressing the fire because fires were important to us. I grew up in California, John and I lived there together for twenty-four years, in California we heated our houses by building fires. We built fires even on summer evenings, because the fog came in. Fires said we were home, we had drawn the circle, we were safe through the night. I lit the candles. John asked for a second drink before sitting down. I gave it to him. We sat down. My attention was on mixing the salad.

John was talking, then he wasn't.

At one point in the seconds or minute before he stopped talking he had asked me if I had used single-malt Scotch for his second drink. I had said no, I used the same Scotch I had used for his first drink. "Good," he had said. "I don't know why but I don't think you should mix them." At another point in those seconds or that minute he had been talking about why World War One was the critical event from which the entire rest of the twentieth century flowed.

I have no idea which subject we were on, the Scotch or World War One, at the instant he stopped talking.

I only remember looking up. His left hand was raised and he was slumped motionless. At first I thought he was making a failed joke, an attempt to make the difficulty of the day seem manageable.

I remember saying *Don't do that.*

When he did not respond my first thought was that he had started to eat and choked. I remember trying to lift him far enough from the back of the chair to give him the Heimlich. I remember the sense of his weight as he fell forward, first against the table, then to the floor. In the kitchen by the telephone I had taped a card with the New York–Presbyterian ambulance numbers. I had not taped the numbers by the telephone because I anticipated a moment like this. I had taped the numbers by the telephone in case someone in the building needed an ambulance.

Someone else.

I called one of the numbers. A dispatcher asked if he was breathing. I said *Just come.* When the paramedics came I tried to tell them what had happened but before I could finish they had transformed the part of the living room where John lay into an emergency department. One of them (there were three, maybe four, even an hour later I could not have said) was talking to the hospital about the electrocardiogram they seemed already to be transmitting. Another was opening the first or second of what would be many syringes for injection. (Epinephrine? Lidocaine? Procainamide? The names came to mind but I had no idea from where.) I remember saying that he might have choked. This was dismissed with a finger swipe: the airway was clear. They seemed now to be using defibrillating paddles, an attempt to restore a rhythm. They got something that could have been a normal heartbeat (or I thought they did, we had all been silent, there was a sharp jump), then lost it, and started again.

"He's still fibbing," I remember the one on the telephone saying.

"*V*-fibbing," John's cardiologist said the next morning when he called from Nantucket. "They would have said '*V*-fibbing.' V for ventricular."

Maybe they said "V-fibbing" and maybe they did not. Atrial

fibrillation did not immediately or necessarily cause cardiac arrest. Ventricular did. Maybe ventricular was the given.

I remember trying to straighten out in my mind what would happen next. Since there was an ambulance crew in the living room, the next logical step would be going to the hospital. It occurred to me that the crew could decide very suddenly to go to the hospital and I would not be ready. I would not have in hand what I needed to take. I would waste time, get left behind. I found my handbag and a set of keys and a summary John's doctor had made of his medical history. When I got back to the living room the paramedics were watching the computer monitor they had set up on the floor. I could not see the monitor so I watched their faces. I remember one glancing at the others. When the decision was made to move it happened very fast. I followed them to the elevator and asked if I could go with them. They said they were taking the gurney down first, I could go in the second ambulance. One of them waited with me for the elevator to come back up. By the time he and I got into the second ambulance the ambulance carrying the gurney was pulling away from the front of the building. The distance from our building to the part of New York–Presbyterian that used to be New York Hospital is six crosstown blocks. I have no memory of sirens. I have no memory of traffic. When we arrived at the emergency entrance to the hospital the gurney was already disappearing into the building. A man was waiting in the driveway. Everyone else in sight was wearing scrubs. He was not. "Is this the wife," he said to the driver, then turned to me. "I'm your social worker," he said, and I guess that is when I must have known.

"I opened the door and I seen the man in the dress greens and I knew. I immediately knew." This was what the mother of a nineteen-year-old killed by a bomb in Kirkuk said on an HBO documentary quoted by Bob Herbert in *The New York Times* on the morning of November 12, 2004. "But I thought that if, as long as I didn't let him in, he couldn't tell me. And then it—none of that would've happened. So he kept saying, 'Ma'am, I need to come in.' And I kept telling him, 'I'm sorry, but you can't come in.'"

When I read this at breakfast almost eleven months after the night with the ambulance and the social worker I recognized the thinking as my own.

Inside the emergency room I could see the gurney being pushed into a cubicle, propelled by more people in scrubs. Someone told me to wait in the reception area. I did. There was a line for admittance paperwork. Waiting in the line seemed the constructive thing to do. Waiting in the line said that there was still time to deal with this, I had copies of the insurance cards in my handbag, this was not a hospital I had ever negotiated—New York Hospital was the Cornell part of New York–Presbyterian, the part I knew was the Columbia part, Columbia-Presbyterian, at 168th and Broadway, twenty minutes away at best, too far in this kind of emergency—but I could make this unfamiliar hospital work, I could be useful, I could arrange the transfer to Columbia-Presbyterian once he was stabilized. I was fixed on the details of this imminent transfer to Columbia (he would need a bed with telemetry, eventually I could also get Quintana transferred to Columbia, the night she was admitted to Beth Israel North I had written on a card the beeper numbers of several Columbia doctors, one or another of them could make all this happen) when the social worker reappeared and guided me from the paperwork line into an empty room off the reception area. "You can wait here," he said. I waited. The room was cold, or I was. I wondered how much time had passed between the time I called the ambulance and the arrival of the paramedics. It had seemed no time at all (*a mote in the eye of God* was the phrase that came to me in the room off the reception area) but it must have been at the minimum several minutes.

I used to have on a bulletin board in my office, for reasons having to do with a plot point in a movie, a pink index card on which I had typed a sentence from *The Merck Manual* about how long the brain can be deprived of oxygen. The image of the pink index card was coming back to me in the room off the reception area: "Tissue anoxia for > 4 to 6 min. can result in irreversible brain damage or death." I was telling myself that I must be misremembering the sentence when the social worker reappeared. He had with him a man he introduced as "your husband's doctor." There was a silence. "He's dead, isn't he," I heard myself say to the doctor. The doctor looked at the social worker. "It's okay," the social worker said. "She's a pretty cool customer." They took me into the curtained cubicle where John lay, alone now. They asked if I wanted a priest. I said yes. A priest appeared and said the words. I thanked him. They gave me the silver clip in which John kept his driver's license and credit cards. They gave me the cash that had been in his pocket. They gave me his watch. They gave me his cell phone. They gave me a plastic bag in which they said I would find his clothes. I thanked them. The social worker asked if he could do anything more for me. I said he could put me in a taxi. He did. I thanked him. "Do you have money for the fare," he asked. I said I did, the cool customer. When I walked into the apartment and saw John's jacket and scarf still lying on the chair where he had dropped them when we came in from seeing Quintana at Beth Israel North (the red cashmere scarf, the Patagonia windbreaker that had been the crew jacket on *Up Close & Personal*) I wondered what an uncool customer would be allowed to do. Break down? Require sedation? Scream?

I remember thinking that I needed to discuss this with John.

There was nothing I did not discuss with John.

Because we were both writers and both worked at home our days were filled with the sound of each other's voices.

I did not always think he was right nor did he always think I was right but we were each the person the other trusted. There was no separation between our investments or interests in any given situation. Many people assumed that we must be, since sometimes one and sometimes the other would get the better review, the bigger advance, in some way "competitive," that our private life must be a minefield of professional envies and resentments. This was so far from the case that the general insistence on it came to suggest certain lacunae in the popular understanding of marriage.

That had been one more thing we discussed.

What I remember about the apartment the night I came home alone from New York Hospital was its silence.

In the plastic bag I had been given at the hospital there were a pair of corduroy pants, a wool shirt, a belt, and I think nothing else. The legs of the corduroy pants had been slit open, I supposed by the paramedics. There was blood on the shirt. The belt was braided. I remember putting his cell phone in the charger on his desk. I remember putting his silver clip in the box in the bedroom in which we kept passports and birth certificates and proof of jury service. I look now at the clip and see that these were the cards he was carrying: a New York State driver's license, due for renewal on May 25, 2004; a Chase ATM card; an American Express card; a Wells Fargo MasterCard; a Metropolitan Museum card; a Writers Guild of America West card (it was the season before Academy voting, when you could use a WGAW card to see movies free, he must have gone to a movie, I did not remember); a Medicare card; a Metro card; and a card issued by Medtronic with the legend "I have a Kappa 900 SR pacemaker implanted," the serial number of the device, a number to call for the doctor who implanted it, and the notation "Implant Date: 03 Jun 2003." I remember combining the cash that had been in his pocket with the cash in my own bag, smoothing the bills, taking special care to interleaf twenties with twenties, tens with tens, fives and ones with fives and ones. I remember thinking as I did this that he would see that I was handling things.

When I saw him in the curtained cubicle in the emergency room at New York Hospital there was a chip in one of his front teeth, I supposed from the fall, since there were also bruises on his face. When I identified his body the next day at Frank E. Campbell the bruises were not apparent. It occurred to me that masking the bruises must have been what the undertaker meant when I said no embalming and he said "in that case we'll just clean him up." The part with the undertaker remains remote. I had arrived at Frank E. Campbell so determined to avoid any inappropriate response (tears, anger, helpless laughter at the Oz-like hush) that I had shut down all response. After my mother died the undertaker who picked up her body left in its place on the bed an artificial rose. My brother had told me this, offended to the core. I would be armed against artificial roses. I remember making a brisk decision about a coffin. I remember that in the office where I signed the papers there was a grandfather's clock, not running. John's nephew Tony Dunne, who was with me, mentioned to the undertaker that the clock was not running. The undertaker, as if pleased to elucidate a decorative element, explained that the clock had not run in some years, but was retained as "a kind of memorial" to a previous incarnation of the firm. He seemed to be offering the clock as a lesson. I concentrated on Quintana. I could shut out what the undertaker was saying but I could not shut out the lines I was hearing as I concentrated on Quintana: *Full fathom five thy father lies / Those are pearls that were his eyes.*

Eight months later I asked the manager of our apartment building if he still had the log kept by the doormen for the night of December 30. I knew there was a log, I had been for three years president of the board of the building, the door log was intrinsic to building procedure. The next day the manager sent me the page for December 30. According to the log the doormen that night were Michael Flynn and Vasile Ionescu. I had not remembered that. Vasile Ionescu and John had a routine with which they amused themselves in the elevator, a small game, between an exile from Ceauşescu's Romania and an Irish Catholic from West Hartford, Connecticut, based on a shared appreciation of political posturing. "So where is bin Laden," Vasile would say when John got onto the elevator, the point being to come up with ever more improbable suggestions: "Could bin Laden be in the penthouse?" "In the maisonette?" "In the fitness room?" When I saw Vasile's name on the log it occurred to me that I could not remember if he had initiated this game when we came in from Beth Israel North in the early evening of December 30. The log for that evening showed only two entries, fewer than usual, even for a time of the year when most people in the building left for more clement venues:

> *NOTE: Paramedics arrived at 9:20 p.m. for Mr. Dunne. Mr. Dunne was taken to hospital at 10:05 p.m.*
> *NOTE: Lightbulb out on A-B passenger elevator.*

The A-B elevator was our elevator, the elevator on which the paramedics came up at 9:20 P.M., the elevator on which they took John (and me) downstairs to the ambulance at 10:05 P.M., the elevator on which I returned alone to our apartment at a time not noted. I had not noticed a lightbulb being out on the elevator. Nor had I noticed that the paramedics were in the apartment for forty-five minutes. I had always described it as "fifteen or twenty minutes." *If they were here that long does it mean that he was alive?* I put this question to a doctor I knew. "Sometimes they'll work that long," he said. It was a while before I realized that this in no way addressed the question.

The death certificate, when I got it, gave the time of death as 10:18 P.M., December 30, 2003.

I had been asked before I left the hospital if I would authorize an autopsy. I had said yes. I later read that asking a survivor to authorize an autopsy is seen in hospitals as delicate, sensitive, often the most difficult of the routine steps that follow a death. Doctors themselves, according to many studies (for example Katz, J. L., and Gardner, R., "The Intern's Dilemma: The Request for Autopsy Consent," *Psychiatry in Medicine* 3:197–203, 1972), experience considerable anxiety about making the request. They know that autopsy is essential to the learning and teaching of medicine, but they also know that the procedure touches a primitive dread. If whoever it was at New York Hospital who asked me to authorize an autopsy experienced such anxiety I could have spared him or her: I actively wanted an autopsy. I actively wanted an autopsy even though I had seen some, in the course of doing research. I knew exactly what occurs, the chest open like a chicken in a butcher's case, the face peeled down, the scale in which the organs are weighed. I had seen homicide detectives avert their eyes from an autopsy in progress. I still wanted one. I needed to know how and why and when it had happened. In fact I wanted to be in the room when they did it (I had watched those other autopsies with John, I owed him his own, it was fixed in my mind at that moment that he would be in the room if I were on the table) but I did not trust myself to rationally present the point so I did not ask.

If the ambulance left our building at 10:05 P.M., and death was declared at 10:18 P.M., the thirteen minutes in between were just bookkeeping, bureaucracy, making sure the hospital procedures were observed and the paperwork was done and the appropriate person was on hand to do the sign-off, inform the cool customer.

The sign-off, I later learned, was called the "pronouncement," as in "Pronounced: 10:18 P.M."

I had to believe he was dead all along.

If I did not believe he was dead all along I would have thought I should have been able to save him.

Until I saw the autopsy report I continued to think this anyway, an example of delusionary thinking, the omnipotent variety.

A week or two before he died, when we were having dinner in a restaurant, John asked me to write something in my notebook for him. He always carried cards on which to make notes, three-by-six-inch cards printed with his name that could be slipped into an inside pocket. At dinner he had thought of something he wanted to remember but when he looked in his pockets he found no cards. I need you to write something down, he said. It was, he said, for his new book, not for mine, a point he stressed because I was at the time researching a book that involved sports. This was the note he dictated: "Coaches used to go out after a game and say 'you played great.' Now they go out with state police, as if this were a war and they the military. The militarization of sports." When I gave him the note the next day he said "You can use it if you want to."

What did he mean?

Did he know he would not write the book?

Did he have some apprehension, a shadow? Why had he forgotten to bring note cards to dinner that night? Had he not warned me when I forgot my own notebook that the ability to make a note when something came to mind was the difference between being able to write and not being able to write? Was something telling him that night that the time for being able to write was running out?

One summer when we were living in Brentwood Park we fell into a pattern of stopping work at four in the afternoon and going out to the pool. He would stand in the water reading (he reread *Sophie's Choice* several times that summer, trying to see how it worked) while I worked in the garden. It was a small, even miniature, garden with gravel paths and a rose arbor and beds edged with thyme and santolina and feverfew. I had convinced John a few years before that we should tear out a lawn to plant this garden. To my surprise, since he had shown no previous interest in gardens, he regarded the finished product as an almost mystical gift. Just before five on those summer afternoons we would swim and then go into the library wrapped in towels to watch *Tenko*, a BBC series, then in syndication, about a number of satisfyingly predictable English women (one was immature and selfish, another seemed to have been written with *Mrs. Miniver* in mind) imprisoned by the Japanese in Malaya during World War Two. After each afternoon's *Tenko* segment we would go upstairs and work another hour or two, John in his office at the top of the stairs, me in the glassed-in porch across the hall that had become my office. At seven or seven-thirty we would go out to dinner, many nights at Morton's. Morton's felt right that summer. There was always shrimp quesadilla, chicken with black beans. There was always someone we knew. The room was cool and polished and dark inside but you could see the twilight outside.

John did not like driving at night by then. This was one reason, I later learned, that he wanted to spend more time in New York, a wish that at the time remained mysterious to me. One night that summer he asked me to drive home after dinner at Anthea Sylbert's house on Camino Palmero in Hollywood. I remember thinking how remarkable this was. Anthea lived less than a block from a house on Franklin Avenue in which we had lived from 1967 until 1971, so it was not a question of reconnoitering a new neighborhood. It had occurred to me as I started the ignition that I could count on my fingers the number of times I had driven when John was in the car; the single other time I could remember that night was once spelling him on a drive from Las Vegas to Los Angeles. He had been dozing in the passenger seat of the Corvette we then had. He had opened his eyes. After a moment he had said, very carefully, "I might take it a little slower." I had no sense of unusual speed and glanced at the speedometer: I was doing 120.

Yet.

A drive across the Mojave was one thing. There had been no previous time when he asked me to drive home from dinner in town: this evening on Camino Palmero was unprecedented. So was the fact that at the end of the forty-minute drive to Brentwood Park he pronounced it "well driven."

He mentioned those afternoons with the pool and the garden and *Tenko* several times during the year before he died.

Philippe Ariès, in *The Hour of Our Death*, points out that the essential characteristic of death as it appears in the *Chanson de Roland* is that the death, even if sudden or accidental, "gives advance warning of its arrival." Gawain is asked: "Ah, good my lord, think you then so soon to die?" Gawain answers: "I tell you that I shall not live two days." Ariès notes: "Neither his doctor nor his friends nor the priests (the latter are absent and forgotten) know as much about it as he. Only the dying man can tell how much time he has left."

You sit down to dinner.

"You can use it if you want to," John had said when I gave him the note he had dictated a week or two before.

And then—gone.

Grief, when it comes, is nothing we expect it to be. It was not what I felt when my parents died: my father died a few days short of his eighty-fifth birthday and my mother a month short of her ninety-first, both after some years of increasing debility. What I felt in each instance was sadness, loneliness (the loneliness of the abandoned child of whatever age), regret for time gone by, for things unsaid, for my inability to share or even in any real way to acknowledge, at the end, the pain and helplessness and physical humiliation they each endured. I understood the inevitability of each of their deaths. I had been expecting (fearing, dreading, anticipating) those deaths all my life. They remained, when they did occur, distanced, at a remove from the ongoing dailiness of my life. After my mother died I received a letter from a friend in Chicago, a former Maryknoll priest, who precisely intuited what I felt. The death of a parent, he wrote, "despite our preparation, indeed, despite our age, dislodges things deep in us, sets off reactions that surprise us and that may cut free memories and feelings that we had thought gone to ground long ago. We might, in that indeterminate period they call mourning, be in a submarine, silent on the ocean's bed, aware of the depth charges, now near and now far, buffeting us with recollections."

My father was dead, my mother was dead, I would need

for a while to watch for mines, but I would still get up in the morning and send out the laundry.

I would still plan a menu for Easter lunch.

I would still remember to renew my passport.

Grief is different. Grief has no distance. Grief comes in waves, paroxysms, sudden apprehensions that weaken the knees and blind the eyes and obliterate the dailiness of life. Virtually everyone who has ever experienced grief mentions this phenomenon of "waves." Eric Lindemann, who was chief of psychiatry at Massachusetts General Hospital in the 1940s and interviewed many family members of those killed in the 1942 Cocoanut Grove fire, defined the phenomenon with absolute specificity in a famous 1944 study: "sensations of somatic distress occurring in waves lasting from twenty minutes to an hour at a time, a feeling of tightness in the throat, choking with shortness of breath, need for sighing, and an empty feeling in the abdomen, lack of muscular power, and an intense subjective distress described as tension or mental pain."

Tightness in the throat.

Choking, need for sighing.

Such waves began for me on the morning of December 31, 2003, seven or eight hours after the fact, when I woke alone in the apartment. I do not remember crying the night before; I had entered at the moment it happened a kind of shock in which the only thought I allowed myself was that there must be certain things I needed to do. There had been certain things I had needed to do while the ambulance crew was in the living room. I had needed for example to get the copy of John's medical summary, so I could take it with me to the hospital. I had needed for example to bank the fire, because I would be leaving it. There had been certain things I had needed to do at the hospital. I had needed for example to stand in the line. I had needed for example to focus on the bed with telemetry he would need for the transfer to Columbia-Presbyterian.

Once I got back from the hospital there had again been certain things I needed to do. I could not identify all of these things but I did know one of them: I needed, before I did anything else, to tell John's brother Nick. It had seemed too late in the evening to call their older brother Dick on Cape Cod (he went to bed early, his health had not been good, I did not want to wake him with bad news) but I needed to tell Nick. I did not plan how to do this. I just sat on the bed and picked up the phone and dialed the number of his house in Connecticut. He answered. I told him. After I put down the phone, in what I can only describe as a new neural pattern of dialing numbers and saying the words, I picked it up again. I could not call Quintana (she was still where we had left her a few hours before, unconscious in the ICU at Beth Israel North) but I could call Gerry, her husband of five months, and I could call my brother, Jim, who would be at his house in Pebble Beach. Gerry said he would come over. I said there was no need to come over, I would be fine. Jim said he would get a flight. I said there was no need to think about a flight, we would talk in the morning. I was trying to think what to do next when the phone rang. It was John's and my agent, Lynn Nesbit, a friend since I suppose the late sixties. It was not clear to me at the time how she knew but she did (it had something to do with a mutual friend to whom both Nick and Lynn seemed in the last minute to have spoken) and she was calling from a taxi on her way to our apartment. At one level I was relieved (Lynn knew how to manage things, Lynn would know what it was that I was supposed to be doing) and at another I was bewildered: how could I deal at this moment with company? What would we do, would we sit in the living room with the syringes and the ECG electrodes and the blood still on the floor, should I rekindle what was left of the fire, would we have a drink, would she have eaten?

Had I eaten?

The instant in which I asked myself whether I had eaten was the first intimation of what was to come: if I thought of food, I learned that night, I would throw up.

Lynn arrived.

We sat in the part of the living room where the blood and electrodes and syringes were not.

I remember thinking as I was talking to Lynn (this was the part I could not say) that the blood must have come from the fall: he had fallen on his face, there was the chipped tooth I had noticed in the emergency room, the tooth could have cut the inside of his mouth.

Lynn picked up the phone and said that she was calling Christopher.

This was another bewilderment: the Christopher I knew best was Christopher Dickey, but he was in either Paris or Dubai and in any case Lynn would have said Chris, not Christopher. I found my mind veering to the autopsy. It could even be happening as I sat there. Then I realized that the Christopher to whom Lynn was talking was Christopher Lehmann-Haupt, who was the chief obituary writer for *The New York Times.* I remember a sense of shock. I wanted to say *not yet* but my mouth had gone dry. I could deal with "autopsy" but the notion of "obituary" had not occurred to me. "Obituary," unlike "autopsy," which was between me and John and the hospital, meant it had happened. I found myself wondering, with no sense of illogic, if it had also happened in Los Angeles. I was trying to work out what time it had been when he died and whether it was that time yet in Los Angeles. (Was there time to go back? Could we have a different ending on Pacific time?) I recall being seized by a pressing need not to let anyone at the *Los Angeles Times* learn what had happened by reading it in *The New York Times.* I called our closest friend at the *Los Angeles Times*, Tim Rutten. I have no memory of what Lynn and I did then. I remember her saying that she would stay the night, but I said no, I would be fine alone.

And I was.

Until the morning. When, only half awake, I tried to think why I was alone in the bed. There was a leaden feeling. It was the same leaden feeling with which I woke on mornings after John and I had fought. Had we had a fight? What about, how had it started, how could we fix it if I could not remember how it started?

Then I remembered.

For several weeks that would be the way I woke to the day.

I wake and feel the fell of dark, not day.

One of several lines from different poems by Gerard Manley Hopkins that John strung together during the months immediately after his younger brother committed suicide, a kind of improvised rosary.

O the mind, mind has mountains; cliffs of fall
Frightful, sheer, no-man-fathomed. Hold them cheap
May who ne'er hung there.
I wake and feel the fell of dark, not day.
And I have asked to be
Where no storms come.

I see now that my insistence on spending that first night alone was more complicated than it seemed, a primitive instinct. Of course I knew John was dead. Of course I had already delivered the definitive news to his brother and to my brother and to Quintana's husband. *The New York Times* knew. The *Los Angeles Times* knew. Yet I was myself in no way prepared to accept this news as final: there was a level on which I believed that what had happened remained reversible. That was why I needed to be alone.

After that first night I would not be alone for weeks (Jim and his wife Gloria would fly in from California the next day, Nick would come back to town, Tony and his wife Rosemary would come down from Connecticut, José would not go to Las Vegas, our assistant Sharon would come back from skiing, there would never not be people in the house), but I needed that first night to be alone.

I needed to be alone so that he could come back.

This was the beginning of my year of magical thinking.

3

THE POWER OF GRIEF to derange the mind has in fact been exhaustively noted. The act of grieving, Freud told us in his 1917 "Mourning and Melancholia," "involves grave departures from the normal attitude to life." Yet, he pointed out, grief remains peculiar among derangements: "It never occurs to us to regard it as a pathological condition and to refer it to medical treatment." We rely instead on "its being overcome after a certain lapse of time." We view "any interference with it as useless and even harmful." Melanie Klein, in her 1940 "Mourning and Its Relation to Manic-Depressive States," made a similar assessment: "The mourner is in fact ill, but because this state of mind is common and seems so natural to us, we do not call mourning an illness. . . . To put my conclusion more precisely: I should say that in mourning the subject goes through a modified and transitory manic-depressive state and overcomes it."

Notice the stress on "overcoming" it.

It was deep into the summer, some months after the night when I needed to be alone so that he could come back, before I recognized that through the winter and spring there had been occasions on which I was incapable of thinking rationally. I was thinking as small children think, as if my thoughts or wishes had the power to reverse the narrative, change the outcome. In my case this disordered thinking had been covert, noticed I think by no one else, hidden even from me, but it had also been, in retrospect, both urgent and constant. In retrospect there had been signs, warning flags I should have noticed. There had been for example the matter of the obituaries. I could not read them. This continued from December 31, when the first obituaries appeared, until February 29, the night of the 2004 Academy Awards, when I saw a photograph of John in the Academy's "In Memoriam" montage. When I saw the photograph I realized for the first time why the obituaries had so disturbed me.

I had allowed other people to think he was dead.

I had allowed him to be buried alive.

Another such flag: there had come a point (late February, early March, after Quintana had left the hospital but before the funeral that had waited on her recovery) when it had occurred to me that I was supposed to give John's clothes away. Many people had mentioned the necessity for giving the clothes away, usually in the well-intentioned but (as it turns out) misguided form of offering to help me do this. I had resisted. I had no idea why. I myself remembered, after my father died, helping my mother separate his clothes into stacks for Goodwill and "better" stacks for the charity thrift shop where my sister-in-law Gloria volunteered. After my mother died Gloria and I and Quintana and Gloria and Jim's daughters had done the same with her clothes. It was part of what people did after a death, part of the ritual, some kind of duty.

I began. I cleared a shelf on which John had stacked sweatshirts, T-shirts, the clothes he wore when we walked in Central Park in the early morning. We walked every morning. We did not always walk together because we liked different routes but we would keep the other's route in mind and intersect before we left the park. The clothes on this shelf were as familiar to me as my own. I closed my mind to this. I set aside certain things (a faded sweatshirt I particularly remembered him wearing, a Canyon Ranch T-shirt Quintana had brought him from Arizona), but I put most of what was on this shelf into bags and took the bags across the street to St. James' Episcopal Church. Emboldened, I opened a closet and filled more bags: New Balance sneakers, all-weather shoes, Brooks Brothers shorts, bag after bag of socks. I took the bags to St. James'. One day a few weeks later I gathered up more bags and took them to John's office, where he had kept his clothes. I was not yet prepared to address the suits and shirts and jackets but I thought I could handle what remained of the shoes, a start.

I stopped at the door to the room.

I could not give away the rest of his shoes.

I stood there for a moment, then realized why: he would need shoes if he was to return.

The recognition of this thought by no means eradicated the thought.

I have still not tried to determine (say, by giving away the shoes) if the thought has lost its power.

On reflection I see the autopsy itself as the first example of this kind of thinking. Whatever else had been in my mind when I so determinedly authorized an autopsy, there was also a level of derangement on which I reasoned that an autopsy could show that what had gone wrong was something simple. It could have been no more than a transitory blockage or arrhythmia. It could have required only a minor adjustment—a change in medication, say, or the resetting of a pacemaker. In this case, the reasoning went, they might still be able to fix it.

I recall being struck by an interview, during the 2004 campaign, in which Teresa Heinz Kerry talked about the sudden death of her first husband. After the plane crash that killed John Heinz, she said in the interview, she had felt very strongly that she "needed" to leave Washington and go back to Pittsburgh.

Of course she "needed" to go back to Pittsburgh.

Pittsburgh, not Washington, was the place to which he might come back.

The autopsy did not in fact take place the night John was declared dead.

The autopsy did not take place until eleven the next morning. I realize now that the autopsy could have taken place only after the man I did not know at New York Hospital made the phone call to me, on the morning of December 31. The man who made the call was not "my social worker," not "my husband's doctor," not, as John and I might have said to each other, our friend from the bridge. "Not our friend from the bridge" was family shorthand, having to do with how his Aunt Harriet Burns described subsequent sightings of recently encountered strangers, for example seeing outside the Friendly's in West Hartford the same Cadillac Seville that had earlier cut her off on the Bulkeley Bridge. "Our friend from the bridge," she would say. I was thinking about John saying "not our friend from the bridge" as I listened to the man on the telephone. I recall expressions of sympathy. I recall offers of assistance. He seemed to be avoiding some point.

He was calling, he said then, to ask if I would donate my husband's organs.

Many things went through my mind at this instant. The first word that went through my mind was "no." Simultaneously I remembered Quintana mentioning at dinner one night that she had identified herself as an organ donor when she renewed her driver's license. She had asked John if he had. He had said no. They had discussed it.

I had changed the subject.

I had been unable to think of either of them dead.

The man on the telephone was still talking. I was thinking: If she were to die today in the ICU at Beth Israel North, would this come up? What would I do? What would I do now?

I heard myself saying to the man on the telephone that my husband's and my daughter was unconscious. I heard myself saying that I did not feel capable of making such a decision before our daughter even knew he was dead. This seemed to me at the time a reasonable response.

Only after I hung up did it occur to me that nothing about it was reasonable. This thought was immediately (and usefully—notice the instant mobilization of cognitive white cells) supplanted by another: there had been in this call something that did not add up. There had been a contradiction in it. This man had been talking about donating organs, but there was no way at this point to do a productive organ harvest: John had not been on life support. He had not been on life support when I saw him in the curtained cubicle in the emergency room. He had not been on life support when the priest came. All organs would have shut down.

Then I remembered: the Miami-Dade Medical Examiner's office. John and I had been there together one morning in 1985 or 1986. There had been someone from the eye bank tagging bodies for cornea removal. Those bodies in the Miami-Dade Medical Examiner's office had not been on life support. This man from New York Hospital, then, was talking about taking only the corneas, the eyes. *Then why not say so? Why misrepresent this to me? Why make this call and not just say "his eyes"?* I took the silver clip the social worker had given me the night before from the box in the bedroom and looked at the driver's license. *Eyes: BL,* the license read. *Restrictions: Corrective Lenses.*

Why make this call and not just say what you wanted?

His eyes. His blue eyes. His blue imperfect eyes.

and what i want to know is
how do you like your blueeyed boy
Mister Death

I could not that morning remember who wrote those lines. I thought it was E. E. Cummings but I could not be sure. I did not have a volume of Cummings but found an anthology on a poetry shelf in the bedroom, an old textbook of John's, published in 1949, when he would have been at Portsmouth Priory, the Benedictine boarding school near Newport to which he was sent after his father died.

(His father's death: sudden, cardiac, in his early fifties, I should have taken that warning.)

If we happened to be anywhere around Newport John would take me to Portsmouth to hear the Gregorian chant at vespers. It was something that moved him. On the flyleaf of the anthology there was written the name *Dunne*, in small careful handwriting, and then, in the same handwriting, blue ink, fountain-pen blue ink, these guides to study: *1) What is the meaning of the poem and what is the experience? 2) What thought or reflection does the experience lead us to? 3) What* mood, feeling, emotion *is stirred or created by the poem as a whole?* I put the book back on the shelf. It would be some months before I remembered to confirm that the lines were in fact E. E. Cummings. It would also be some months before it occurred to me that my anger at this unknown caller from New York Hospital reflected another version of the primitive dread that had not for me been awakened by the autopsy question.

What was the meaning and what the experience?

To what thought or reflection did the experience lead us?

How could he come back if they took his organs, how could he come back if he had no shoes?

4

On most surface levels I seemed rational. To the average observer I would have appeared to fully understand that death was irreversible. I had authorized the autopsy. I had arranged for cremation. I had arranged for his ashes to be picked up and taken to the Cathedral of St. John the Divine, where, once Quintana was awake and well enough to be present, they would be placed in the chapel off the main altar where my brother and I had placed our mother's ashes. I had arranged for the marble plate on which her name was cut to be removed and recut to include John's name. Finally, on the 23rd of March, almost three months after his death, I had seen the ashes placed in the wall and the marble plate replaced and a service held.

We had Gregorian chant, for John.

Quintana asked that the chant be in Latin. John too would have asked that.

We had a single soaring trumpet.

We had a Catholic priest and an Episcopal priest.

Calvin Trillin spoke, David Halberstam spoke, Quintana's best friend Susan Traylor spoke. Susanna Moore read a fragment from "East Coker," the part about how "one has only learnt to get the better of words / For the thing one no longer has to say, or the way in which / One is no longer disposed to say it." Nick read Catullus, "On His Brother's Death." Quintana, still weak but her voice steady, standing in a black dress in the same cathedral where she had eight months before been married, read a poem she had written to her father.

I had done it. I had acknowledged that he was dead. I had done this in as public a way as I could conceive.

Yet my thinking on this point remained suspiciously fluid. At dinner in the late spring or early summer I happened to meet a prominent academic theologian. Someone at the table raised a question about faith. The theologian spoke of ritual itself being a form of faith. My reaction was unexpressed but negative, vehement, excessive even to me. Later I realized that my immediate thought had been: *But I did the ritual. I did it all.* I did St. John the Divine, I did the chant in Latin, I did the Catholic priest and the Episcopal priest, I did "For a thousand years in thy sight are but as yesterday when it is past" and I did "*In paradisum deducant angeli.*"

And it still didn't bring him back.

"Bringing him back" had been through those months my hidden focus, a magic trick. By late summer I was beginning to see this clearly. "Seeing it clearly" did not yet allow me to give away the clothes he would need.

In time of trouble, I had been trained since childhood, read, learn, work it up, go to the literature. Information was control. Given that grief remained the most general of afflictions its literature seemed remarkably spare. There was the journal C. S. Lewis kept after the death of his wife, *A Grief Observed*. There was the occasional passage in one or another novel, for example Thomas Mann's description in *The Magic Mountain* of the effect on Hermann Castorp of his wife's death: "His spirit was troubled; he shrank within himself; his benumbed brain made him blunder in his business, so that the firm of Castorp and Son suffered sensible financial losses; and the next spring, while inspecting warehouses on the windy landing-stage, he got inflammation of the lungs. The fever was too much for his shaken heart, and in five days, notwithstanding all Dr. Heidekind's care, he died." There were, in classical ballets, the moments when one or another abandoned lover tries to find and resurrect one or another loved one, the blued light, the white tutus, the *pas de deux* with the loved one that foreshadows the final return to the dead: *la danse des ombres*, the dance of the shades. There were certain poems, in fact many poems. There was a day or two when I relied on Matthew Arnold, "The Forsaken Merman":

Children's voices should be dear
(Call once more) to a mother's ear;
Children's voices, wild with pain—
Surely she will come again!

There were days when I relied on W. H. Auden, the "Funeral Blues" lines from *The Ascent of F6*:

Stop all the clocks, cut off the telephone,
Prevent the dog from barking with a juicy bone,
Silence the pianos and with muffled drum
Bring out the coffin, let the mourners come.

The poems and the dances of the shades seemed the most exact to me.

Beyond or below such abstracted representations of the pains and furies of grieving, there was a body of sub-literature, how-to guides for dealing with the condition, some "practical," some "inspirational," most of either useless. (Don't drink too much, don't spend the insurance money redecorating the living room, join a support group.) That left the professional literature, the studies done by the psychiatrists and psychologists and social workers who came after Freud and Melanie Klein, and quite soon it was to this literature that I found myself turning. I learned from it many things I already knew, which at a certain point seemed to promise comfort, validation, an outside opinion that I was not imagining what appeared to be happening. From *Bereavement: Reactions, Consequences, and Care*, compiled in 1984 by the National Academy of Sciences' Institute of Medicine, I learned for example that the most frequent immediate responses to death were shock, numbness, and a sense of disbelief: "Subjectively, survivors may feel like they are wrapped in a cocoon or blanket; to others, they may look as though they are holding up well. Because the reality of death has not yet penetrated awareness, survivors can appear to be quite accepting of the loss."

Here, then, we had the "pretty cool customer" effect.

I read on. Dolphins, I learned from J. William Worden of the Harvard Child Bereavement Study at Massachusetts General Hospital, had been observed refusing to eat after the death of a mate. Geese had been observed reacting to such a death by flying and calling, searching until they themselves became disoriented and lost. Human beings, I read but did not need to learn, showed similar patterns of response. They searched. They stopped eating. They forgot to breathe. They grew faint from lowered oxygen, they clogged their sinuses with unshed tears and ended up in otolaryngologists' offices with obscure ear infections. They lost concentration. "After a year I could read headlines," I was told by a friend whose husband had died three years before. They lost cognitive ability on all scales. Like Hermann Castorp they blundered in business and suffered sensible financial losses. They forgot their own telephone numbers and showed up at airports without picture ID. They fell sick, they failed, they even, again like Hermann Castorp, died.

This "dying" aspect had been documented, in study after study.

I began carrying identification when I walked in Central Park in the morning, in case it happened to me.

If the telephone rang when I was in the shower I no longer answered it, to avoid falling dead on the tile.

Certain studies, I learned, were famous. They were icons of the literature, benchmarks, referred to in everything I read. There was for example "Young, Benjamin, and Wallis, *The Lancet* 2:454–456, 1963." This study of 4,486 recent widowers in the United Kingdom, followed for five years, showed "significantly higher death rates for widowers in first six months following bereavement than for married." There was "Rees and Lutkins, *British Medical Journal* 4:13–16, 1967." This study of 903 bereaved relatives versus 878 non-bereaved matched controls, followed for six years, showed "significantly higher mortality for bereaved spouses in first year." The functional explanation for such raised mortality rates was laid out in the Institute of Medicine's 1984 compilation: "Research to date has shown that, like many other stressors, grief frequently leads to changes in the endocrine, immune, autonomic nervous, and cardiovascular systems; all of these are fundamentally influenced by brain function and neurotransmitters."

There were, I also learned from this literature, two kinds of grief. The preferred kind, the one associated with "growth" and "development," was "uncomplicated grief," or "normal bereavement." Such uncomplicated grief, according to *The Merck Manual*, 16th Edition, could still typically present with "anxiety symptoms such as initial insomnia, restlessness, and autonomic nervous system hyperactivity," but did "not generally cause clinical depression, except in those persons inclined to mood disorder." The second kind of grief was "complicated grief," which was also known in the literature as "pathological bereavement" and was said to occur in a variety of situations.

One situation in which pathological bereavement could occur, I read repeatedly, was that in which the survivor and the deceased had been unusually dependent on one another. "Was the bereaved actually very dependent upon the deceased person for pleasure, support, or esteem?" This was one of the diagnostic criteria suggested by David Peretz, M.D., of the Department of Psychiatry at Columbia University. "Did the bereaved feel helpless without the lost person when enforced separations occurred?"

I considered these questions.

Once in 1968 when I needed unexpectedly to spend the night in San Francisco (I was doing a piece, it was raining, the rain pushed a late-afternoon interview into the next morning), John flew up from Los Angeles so that we could have dinner together. We had dinner at Ernie's. After dinner John took the PSA "Midnight Flyer," a thirteen-dollar amenity of an era in California when it was possible to fly from Los Angeles to San Francisco or Sacramento or San Jose for twenty-six dollars round-trip, back to LAX.

I thought about PSA.

All PSA planes had smiles painted on their noses. The flight attendants were dressed in the style of Rudy Gernreich in hot-pink-and-orange miniskirts. PSA represented a time in our life when most things we did seemed without consequence, no-hands, a mood in which no one thought twice about flying seven hundred miles for dinner. This mood ended in 1978, when a PSA Boeing 727 collided with a Cessna 172 over San Diego, killing one hundred and forty-four.

It occurred to me when this happened that I had overlooked the odds when it came to PSA.

I see now that this error was not confined to PSA.

When Quintana at age two or three flew PSA to Sacramento to see my mother and father she referred to it as "going on the smile." John used to write down the things she said on scraps of paper and put them in a black painted box his mother had given him. This box, which remains with its scraps of paper on a desk in my living room, was painted with an American eagle and the words "E Pluribus Unum." Later he used some of the things she said in a novel, *Dutch Shea, Jr.* He gave them to Dutch Shea's daughter, Cat, who had been killed by an IRA bomb while having dinner with her mother in a restaurant on Charlotte Street in London. This is part of what he wrote:

> "Where you was?" she would say, and "Where did the morning went?" He wrote them all down and crammed them into the tiny secret drawer in the maple desk Barry Stukin had given him and Lee as a wedding present. . . . Cat in her school tartan. Cat who could call her bath a "bathment" and the butterflies for a kindergarten experiment "flybutters." Cat who had made up her first poem at the age of seven: "I'm going to marry / A boy named Harry / He rides horses / And handles divorces."
>
> The Broken Man was in that drawer. The Broken Man was what Cat called fear and death and the unknown. I had a bad dream about the Broken Man, she would say. Don't let the Broken Man catch me. If the Broken Man comes, I'll hang onto the fence and won't let him take me. . . . He wondered if the Broken Man had time to frighten Cat before she died.

I see now what I had failed to see in 1982, the year *Dutch Shea, Jr.* was published: this was a novel about grief. The literature would have said that Dutch Shea was undergoing pathological bereavement. The diagnostic signs would have been these: He is obsessed with the moment Cat died. He plays and replays the scene, as if rerunning it could reveal a different ending: the restaurant on Charlotte Street, the endive salad, Cat's lavender espadrilles, the bomb, Cat's head in the dessert trolley. He tortures his ex-wife, Cat's mother, with a single repeated question: why was she in the ladies' room when the bomb went off? Finally she tells him:

> You never gave me much credit for being Cat's mother, but I did raise her. I took care of her the day she got her period the first time and I remember when she was a little girl she called my bedroom her sweet second room and she called spaghetti buzzghetti and she called people who came to the house hellos. She said where you was and where did the morning went and you told Thayer, you son of a bitch, you wanted someone to remember her. So she told me she was pregnant, it was an accident, and she wanted to know what to do and I went into the ladies' room because I knew I was going to cry and I didn't want to cry in front of her and I wanted to get the tears out of the way so I could act sensibly and then I heard the bomb and when I

finally got out part of her was in the sherbet and part of her was in the street and you, you son of a bitch, you want someone to remember her.

I believe John would have said that *Dutch Shea, Jr.* was about faith.

When he began the novel he already knew what the last words would be, not only the last words of the novel but the last words thought by Dutch Shea before he shoots himself: "I believe in Cat. I believe in God." *Credo in Deum.* The first words of the Catholic catechism.

Was it about faith or was it about grief?

Were faith and grief the same thing?

Were we unusually dependent on one another the summer we swam and watched *Tenko* and went to dinner at Morton's?

Or were we unusually lucky?

If I were alone could he come back to me on the smile?

Would he say get a table at Ernie's?

PSA and the smile no longer exist, sold to US Airways and then painted off the planes.

Ernie's no longer exists, but was briefly re-created by Alfred Hitchcock, for *Vertigo.* James Stewart first sees Kim Novak at Ernie's. Later she falls from the bell tower (also re-created, an effect) at Mission San Juan Bautista.

We were married at San Juan Bautista.

On a January afternoon when the blossoms were showing in the orchards off 101.

When there were still orchards off 101.

No. The way you got sideswiped was by going back. The blossoms showing in the orchards off 101 was the incorrect track.

For several weeks after it happened I tried to keep myself on the correct track (the narrow track, the track on which there was no going back) by repeating to myself the last two lines of "Rose Aylmer," Walter Savage Landor's 1806 elegy to the memory of a daughter of Lord Aylmer's who had died at age twenty in Calcutta. I had not thought of "Rose Aylmer" since I was an undergraduate at Berkeley, but now I could remember not only the poem but much of what had been said about it in whichever class I had heard it analyzed. "Rose Aylmer" worked, whoever was teaching this class had said, because the overblown and therefore meaningless praise for the deceased in the first four lines ("Ah, what avails the sceptred race! / Ah, what the form divine! / What every virtue, every grace! / Rose Aylmer, all were thine") gets brought into sudden, even shocking relief by "the hard sweet wisdom" of the last two lines, which suggest that mourning has its place but also its limits: "A night of memories and sighs / I consecrate to thee."

"'A *night* of memories and sighs,'" I remembered the lecturer repeating. "A *night*. One night. It might be all night but he doesn't even say *all night*, he says *a night*, not a matter of a lifetime, a matter of some hours."

Hard sweet wisdom. Clearly, since "Rose Aylmer" had remained embedded in my memory, I believed it as an undergraduate to offer a lesson for survival.

December 30, 2003.

We had seen Quintana in the sixth-floor ICU at Beth Israel North.

Where she would remain for another twenty-four days.

Unusual dependency (is that a way of saying "marriage"? "husband and wife"? "mother and child"? "nuclear family"?) is not the only situation in which complicated or pathological grief can occur. Another, I read in the literature, is one in which the grieving process is interrupted by "circumstantial factors," say by "a delay in the funeral," or by "an illness or second death in the family." I read an explanation, by Vamik D. Volkan, M.D., a professor of psychiatry at the University of Virginia in Charlottesville, of what he called "re-grief therapy," a technique developed at the University of Virginia for the treatment of "established pathological mourners." In such therapy, according to Dr. Volkan, a point occurs at which:

> we help the patient to review the circumstances of the death—how it occurred, the patient's reaction to the news and to viewing the body, the events of the funeral, etc. Anger usually appears at this point if the therapy is going well; it is at first diffused, then directed toward others, and finally directed toward the dead. Abreactions—what Bibring [E. Bibring, 1954, "Psychoanalysis and the Dynamic Psycho-therapies," *Journal of the American Psycho-analytic Association* 2:745 ff.] calls "emotional reliving"—

> may then take place and demonstrate to the patient the actuality of his repressed impulses. Using our understanding of the psychodynamics involved in the patient's need to keep the lost one alive, we can then explain and interpret the relationship that had existed between the patient and the one who died.

But from where exactly did Dr. Volkan and his team in Charlottesville derive their unique understanding of "the psychodynamics involved in the patient's need to keep the lost one alive," their special ability to "explain and interpret the relationship that had existed between the patient and the one who died"? Were you watching *Tenko* with me and "the lost one" in Brentwood Park, did you go to dinner with us at Morton's? Were you with me and "the one who died" at Punchbowl in Honolulu four months before it happened? Did you gather up plumeria blossoms with us and drop them on the graves of the unknown dead from Pearl Harbor? Did you catch cold with us in the rain at the Jardin du Ranelagh in Paris a month before it happened? Did you skip the Monets with us and go to lunch at Conti? Were you with us when we left Conti and bought the thermometer, were you sitting on our bed at the Bristol when neither of us could figure how to convert the thermometer's centigrade reading into Fahrenheit?

Were you there?

No.

You might have been useful with the thermometer but you were not there.

I don't need to "review the circumstances of the death." I was there.

I didn't get "the news," I didn't "view" the body. I was there.

I catch myself, I stop.

I realize that I am directing irrational anger toward the entirely unknown Dr. Volkan in Charlottesville.

> Persons under the shock of genuine affliction are not only upset mentally but are all unbalanced physically. No matter how calm and controlled they seemingly may be, no one can under such circumstances be normal. Their disturbed circulation makes them cold, their distress makes them unstrung, sleepless. Persons they normally like, they often turn from. No one should ever be forced upon those in grief, and all over-emotional people, no

> matter how near or dear, should be barred absolutely. Although the knowledge that their friends love them and sorrow for them is a great solace, the nearest afflicted must be protected from any one or anything which is likely to overstrain nerves already at the threatening point, and none have the right to feel hurt if they are told they can neither be of use or be received. At such a time, to some people companionship is a comfort, others shrink from their dearest friends.

That passage is from Emily Post's 1922 book of etiquette, Chapter XXIV, "Funerals," which takes the reader from the moment of death ("As soon as death occurs, someone, the trained nurse usually, draws the blinds in the sick-room and tells a servant to draw all the blinds of the house") through seating instructions for those who attend the funeral: "Enter the church as quietly as possible, and as there are no ushers at a funeral, seat yourself where you approximately belong. Only a very intimate friend should take a position far up on the center aisle. If you are merely an acquaintance you should sit inconspicuously in the rear somewhere, unless the funeral is very small and the church big, in which case you may sit on the end seat of the center aisle toward the back."

This tone, one of unfailing specificity, never flags. The emphasis remains on the practical. The bereaved must be urged to "sit in a sunny room," preferably one with an open fire. Food, but "very little food," may be offered on a tray: tea, coffee, bouillon, a little thin toast, a poached egg. Milk, but only heated milk: "Cold milk is bad for someone who is already over-chilled." As for further nourishment, "The cook may suggest something that appeals usually to their taste—but very little should be offered at a time, for although the stomach may be empty, the palate rejects the thought of food, and digestion is never in best order." The mourner is prompted to practice economy as he or she accommodates the wearing of mourning: most existing garments, including leather shoes and straw hats, will "dye perfectly." Undertaking expenses should be checked in advance. A friend should be left in charge of the house during the funeral. The friend should see that the house is aired and displaced furniture put back where it belongs and a fire lit for the homecoming of the family. "It is also well to prepare a little hot tea or broth," Mrs. Post advised, "and it should be brought them upon their return without their being asked if they would care for it. Those who are in great distress want no food, but if it is handed to them, they will mechanically take it, and something warm to start digestion and stimulate impaired circulation is what they most need."

There was something arresting about the matter-of-fact wisdom here, the instinctive understanding of the physiological disruptions ("changes in the endocrine, immune, autonomic nervous, and cardiovascular systems") later catalogued by the Institute of Medicine. I am unsure what prompted me to look up Emily Post's 1922 book of etiquette (I would guess some memory of my mother, who had given me a copy to read when we were snowbound in a four-room rented house in Colorado Springs during World War Two), but when I found it on the Internet it spoke to me directly. As I read it I remembered how cold I had been at New York Hospital on the night John died. I had thought I was cold because it was December 30 and I had come to the hospital bare-legged, in slippers, wearing only the linen skirt and sweater into which I had changed to get dinner. This was part of it, but I was also cold because nothing in my body was working as it should.

Mrs. Post would have understood that. She wrote in a world in which mourning was still recognized, allowed, not hidden from view. Philippe Ariès, in a series of lectures he delivered at Johns Hopkins in 1973 and later published as *Western Attitudes toward Death: From the Middle Ages to the Present*, noted that beginning about 1930 there had been in most Western countries and particularly in the United States a revolution in accepted attitudes toward death. "Death," he wrote, "so omnipresent in the past that it was familiar, would be effaced, would disappear. It would become shameful and forbidden." The English social anthropologist Geoffrey Gorer, in his 1965 *Death, Grief, and Mourning*, had described this rejection of public mourning as a result of the increasing pressure of a new "ethical duty to enjoy oneself," a novel "imperative to do nothing which might diminish the enjoyment of others." In both England and the United States, he observed, the contemporary trend was "to treat mourning as morbid self-indulgence, and to give social admiration to the bereaved who hide their grief so fully that no one would guess anything had happened."

One way in which grief gets hidden is that death now occurs largely offstage. In the earlier tradition from which Mrs. Post wrote, the act of dying had not yet been professionalized. It did not typically involve hospitals. Women died in childbirth. Children died of fevers. Cancer was untreatable. At the time she undertook her book of etiquette, there would have been few American households untouched by the influenza pandemic of 1918. Death was up close, at home. The average adult was expected to deal competently, and also sensitively, with its aftermath. When someone dies, I was taught growing up in California, you bake a ham. You drop it by the house. You go to the funeral. If the family is Catholic you also go to the rosary but you do not wail or keen or in any other way demand the attention of the family. In the end Emily Post's 1922 etiquette book turned out to be as acute in its apprehension of this other way of death, and as prescriptive in its treatment of grief, as anything else I read. I will not forget the instinctive wisdom of the friend who, every day for those first few weeks, brought me a quart container of scallion-and-ginger congee from Chinatown. Congee I could eat. Congee was all I could eat.

5

THERE WAS SOMETHING ELSE I was taught growing up in California. When someone appears to have died you find out for sure by holding a hand mirror to the mouth and nose. If there is no exhaled moisture the person is dead. My mother taught me that. I forgot it the night John died. *Is he breathing*, the dispatcher had asked me. *Just come*, I had said.

December 30, 2003.

We had seen Quintana in the sixth-floor ICU at Beth Israel North.

We had noted the numbers on the respirator.

We had held her swollen hand.

We still don't know which way this is going, one of the ICU doctors had said.

We had come home. The ICU did not reopen after evening rounds until seven so it must have been past eight.

We had discussed whether to go out for dinner or eat in.

I said I would build a fire, we could eat in.

I have no memory of what we meant to eat. I do remember throwing out whatever was on the plates and in the kitchen when I came home from New York Hospital.

You sit down to dinner and life as you know it ends.

In a heartbeat.

Or the absence of one.

During the past months I have spent a great deal of time trying first to keep track of, and, when that failed, to reconstruct, the exact sequence of events that preceded and followed what happened that night. "At a point between Thursday, December 18, 2003, and Monday, December 22, 2003," one such reconstruction began, "Q complained of 'feeling terrible,' flu symptoms, thought she had strep throat." This reconstruction, which was preceded by the names and telephone numbers of doctors to whom I spoke not only at Beth Israel but at other hospitals in New York and other cities, continued. The heart of it was this: On Monday, December 22, she went with a fever of 103 to the emergency room at Beth Israel North, which had at the time a reputation for being the least-crowded emergency room on the Upper East Side of Manhattan, and was diagnosed with the flu. She was told to stay in bed and drink liquids. No chest X-ray was taken. On December 23 and 24 her fever fluctuated between 102 and 103. She was too ill to come to dinner on Christmas Eve. She and Gerry canceled plans to spend Christmas night and a few days after with his family in Massachusetts.

On Christmas Day, a Thursday, she called in the morning and said she was having trouble breathing. Her breathing sounded shallow, labored. Gerry took her back to the emergency room at Beth Israel North, where X-rays showed a dense infiltrate of pus and bacteria in the lower lobe of her right lung. Her pulse was elevated, 150-plus. She was extremely dehydrated. Her white count was almost zero. She was given Ativan, then Demerol. Her pneumonia, Gerry was told in the emergency room, was "a 5 on a scale of 10, what we used to call 'walking pneumonia.'" There was "nothing serious" (this may have been what I wanted to hear), but it was nonetheless decided to admit her to a sixth-floor ICU for monitoring.

By the time she reached the ICU that evening she was agitated. She was further sedated, then intubated. Her temperature was now 104-plus. One hundred percent of her oxygen was being supplied by the breathing tube; she was not at that point capable of breathing on her own. Late the next morning, Friday, December 26, it was learned that there was now pneumonia on both lungs, and that this pneumonia was, despite the massive IV administration of azithromycin, gentamicin, clindamycin, and vancomycin, growing. It was also learned—or assumed, since her blood pressure was dropping—that she was entering or had entered septic shock. Gerry was asked to allow two further invasive procedures, first the insertion of an arterial line and then the insertion of a second line that would go close to the heart to deal with the blood pressure problem. She was given neosynephrine to support her blood pressure at 90-plus over 60-plus.

On Saturday, December 27, we were told that she was being given what was then still a new Eli Lilly drug, Xigris, which would continue for ninety-six hours, four days. "This costs twenty thousand dollars," the nurse said as she changed the IV bag. I watched the fluid drip into one of the many tubes that were then keeping Quintana alive. I looked up Xigris on the Internet. One site said that the survival rate for sepsis patients treated with Xigris was 69 percent, as opposed to 56 percent for patients not treated with Xigris. Another site, a business newsletter, said that Eli Lilly's "sleeping giant," Xigris, was "struggling to overcome its problems in the sepsis market." This seemed in some ways a positive prism through which to view the situation: Quintana was not the child who had been a deliriously happy bride five months before and whose chance of surviving the next day or two could now be calibrated at a point between 56 and 69 percent, she was "the sepsis market," suggesting that there was still a consumer choice to be made. By Sunday, December 28, it had been possible to imagine that the sepsis market's "sleeping giant" was kicking in: the pneumonia had not decreased in size, but the neosynephrine supporting her blood pressure was stopped and the blood pressure was holding, at 95 over 40. On Monday, December 29, I was told by a physician's assistant that after his weekend absence he had come in that morning to find Quintana's condition "encouraging." I asked what exactly had encouraged him about her condition when he came in that morning. "She was still alive," the physician's assistant said.

On Tuesday, December 30, at 1:02 P.M. (according to the computer), I made these notes in anticipation of a conversation with one more specialist to whom I had placed a call:

> Any effect on brain—from oxygen deficit? From high fever? From possible meningitis?
>
> Several doctors have mentioned "not knowing if there is some underlying structure or blockage." Are they talking about a possible malignancy?
>
> The assumption here is that this infection is bacterial—yet no bacteria has shown up in the cultures—is there any way of knowing it's not viral?
>
> How does "flu" morph into whole-body infection?

The last question—*How does "flu" morph into whole-body infection?*—was added by John. By December 30 he had seemed fixed on this point. He had asked it many times in the preceding three or four days, of doctors and of physicians' assistants and of nurses and finally, most desperately, of me, and had never received an answer he found satisfactory. Something in this seemed to defy his understanding. Something in this defied my own understanding, but I was pretending that I could manage it. Here it was:

She had been admitted to the ICU on Christmas night.

She was in a hospital, we had kept telling each other on Christmas night. She was being taken care of. She would be safe where she was.

Everything else had seemed normal.

We had a fire. She would be safe.

Five days later everything outside the sixth-floor ICU at Beth Israel North still seemed normal: this was the part neither of us (although only John admitted it) could get past, one more case of maintaining a fixed focus on the clear blue sky from which the plane fell. There were still in the living room of the apartment the presents John and I had opened on Christmas night. There were still under and on a table in Quintana's old room the presents she had been unable to open on Christmas night because she was in the ICU. There were still on a table in the dining room the stacked plates and silver we had used on Christmas Eve. There were still on an American Express bill that came that day charges from the November trip we had made to Paris. When we left for Paris Quintana and Gerry had been planning their first Thanksgiving dinner. They had invited his mother and sister and brother-in-law. They were using their wedding china. Quintana had come by to get my mother's ruby crystal glasses. We had called them on Thanksgiving Day from Paris. They were roasting a turkey and pureeing turnips.

"And then—gone."

How does "flu" morph into whole-body infection?

I see the question now as the equivalent of a cry of helpless rage, another way of saying *How could this have happened when everything was normal.* In the cubicle where Quintana lay in the ICU, her fingers and face swollen with fluid, her lips cracked by fever around the breathing tube, her hair matted and soaked with sweat, the numbers on the respirator that night indicated that she was now receiving only 45 percent of her oxygen through the tube. John had kissed her swollen face.

"More than one more day," he had whispered, another part of our family shorthand. The reference was to a line from a movie, Richard Lester's *Robin and Marian*. "I love you more than even one more day," Audrey Hepburn as Maid Marian says to Sean Connery as Robin Hood after she has given them both the fatal potion. John had whispered this every time he left the ICU. On our way out we managed to maneuver a doctor into talking to us. We asked if the decrease in delivered oxygen meant that she was getting better.

There was a pause.

This was when the ICU doctor said it: "We're still not sure which way this is going."

The way this is going is up, I remember thinking.

The ICU doctor was still talking. "She's really very sick," he was saying.

I recognized this as a coded way of saying that she was expected to die but I persisted: *The way this is going is up. It's going up because it has to go up.*

I believe in Cat.

I believe in God.

"I love you more than one more day," Quintana said three months later standing in the black dress at St. John the Divine. "As you used to say to me."

We were married on the afternoon of January 30, 1964, a Thursday, at the Catholic Mission of San Juan Bautista in San Benito County, California. John wore a navy blue suit from Chipp. I wore a short white silk dress I had bought at Ransohoff's in San Francisco on the day John Kennedy was killed. Twelve-thirty P.M. in Dallas was still morning in California. My mother and I learned what happened only when we were leaving Ransohoff's for lunch and ran into someone from Sacramento. Since there were only thirty or forty people at San Juan Bautista on the afternoon of the wedding (John's mother, his younger brother Stephen, his brother Nick and Nick's wife Lenny and their four-year-old daughter, my mother and father and brother and sister-in-law and grandfather and aunt and a few cousins and family friends from Sacramento, John's roommate from Princeton, maybe one or two others), my intention for the ceremony had been to have no entrance, no "procession," to just stand up there and do it. "Principals emerge," I remember Nick saying helpfully: Nick got the plan, but the organist who had materialized did not, and suddenly I found myself on my father's arm, walking up the aisle and weeping behind my dark glasses. When the ceremony was over we drove to the lodge at Pebble Beach. There were little things to eat, champagne, a terrace that opened onto the Pacific, very simple. By way of a honeymoon we spent a few nights in a bungalow at the San Ysidro Ranch in Montecito and then, bored, fled to the Beverly Hills Hotel.

I had thought about that wedding on the day of Quintana's wedding.

Her wedding was simple too. She wore a long white dress and a veil and expensive shoes but her hair was in a thick braid down her back, as it had been when she was a child.

We sat in the choir at St. John the Divine. Her father walked her to the altar. There at the altar was Susan, her best friend in California since age three. There at the altar was her best friend in New York. There at the altar was her cousin Hannah. There was her cousin Kelley from California, reading a part of the service. There were the children of Gerry's stepdaughter, reading another part. There were the youngest children, small girls with leis, barefoot. There were watercress sandwiches, champagne, lemonade, peach-colored napkins to match the sorbet that came with the cake, peacocks on the lawn. She kicked off the expensive shoes and unpinned the veil. "Wasn't that just about perfect," she said when she called that evening. Her father and I allowed that it was. She and Gerry flew to St. Barth's. John and I flew to Honolulu.

July 26, 2003.

Four months and 29 days before she was admitted to the ICU at Beth Israel North.

Five months and four days before her father died.

During the first week or two after he died, at night, when the protective exhaustion would hit me and I would leave the relatives and friends talking in the living room and dining room and kitchen of the apartment and walk down the corridor to the bedroom and shut the door, I would avoid looking at the reminders of our early marriage that hung on the corridor walls. In fact I did not need to look, nor could I avoid them by not looking: I knew them by heart. There was a photograph of John and me taken on a location for *The Panic in Needle Park.* It was our first picture. We went with it to the Cannes festival. It was the first time I had ever been to Europe and we were traveling first-class on Twentieth Century–Fox and I boarded the plane barefoot, it was that period, 1971. There was a photograph of John and me and Quintana at Bethesda Fountain in Central Park in 1970, John and Quintana, age four, eating ice cream bars. We were in New York all that fall working on a picture with Otto Preminger. "She's in the office of Mr. Preminger who has no hair," Quintana advised a pediatrician who had asked where her mother was. There was a photograph of John and me and Quintana on the deck of the house we had in Malibu in the 1970s. The photograph appeared in *People.* When I saw it I realized that Quintana had taken advantage of a break in the day's shooting to apply, for the first time, eyeliner. There was a photograph Barry Farrell had taken of his wife, Marcia, sitting in a rattan chair in the house in Malibu and holding their then-baby daughter, Joan Didion Farrell.

Barry Farrell was now dead.

There was a photograph of Katharine Ross, taken by Conrad Hall during the Malibu period when she taught Quintana to swim by throwing a Tahitian shell in a neighbor's pool and telling Quintana the shell would be hers if she brought it up. This was a time, the early 1970s, when Katharine and Conrad and Jean and Brian Moore and John and I traded plants and dogs and favors and recipes and would have dinner at one or another of our houses a couple of times a week.

I remember that we all made soufflés. Conrad's sister Nancy in Papeete had shown Katharine how to make them work without effort and Katharine showed me and Jean. The trick was a less strict approach than generally advised. Katharine also brought back Tahitian vanilla beans for us, thick sheaves tied with raffia.

We did crème caramel with the vanilla for a while but nobody liked to caramelize the sugar.

We talked about renting Lee Grant's house above Zuma Beach and opening a restaurant, to be called "Lee Grant's House." Katharine and Jean and I would take turns cooking and John and Brian and Conrad would take turns running the front. This Malibu survivalist plan got abandoned because Katharine and Conrad separated and Brian was finishing a novel and John and I went to Honolulu to do a rewrite on a picture. We worked a lot in Honolulu. No one in New York could ever get the time difference straight so we could work all day without the phone ringing. There was a point in the 1970s when I wanted to buy a house there, and took John to look at many, but he seemed to interpret actually living in Honolulu as a less encouraging picture than staying at the Kahala.

Conrad Hall was now dead.

Brian Moore was now dead.

From an earlier house, a great wreck of a house on Franklin Avenue in Hollywood that we rented with its many bedrooms and its sun porches and its avocado trees and its overgrown clay tennis court for $450 a month, there was a framed verse that Earl McGrath had written on the occasion of our fifth anniversary:

This is the story of John Greg'ry Dunne
Who, with his wife Mrs. Didion Do,
Was legally married with family of one
And lived on Franklin Avenue.
Lived with their beautiful child Quintana
Also known as Didion D
Didion Dunne
And Didion Do.
And Quintana or Didion D.
A beautiful family of one Dunne Dunne Dunne
(I mean a family of three)
Living in a style best called erstwhile
On Franklin Avenue.

People who have recently lost someone have a certain look, recognizable maybe only to those who have seen that look on their own faces. I have noticed it on my face and I notice it now on others. The look is one of extreme vulnerability, nakedness, openness. It is the look of someone who walks from the ophthalmologist's office into the bright daylight with dilated eyes, or of someone who wears glasses and is suddenly made to take them off. These people who have lost someone look naked because they think themselves invisible. I myself felt invisible for a period of time, incorporeal. I seemed to have crossed one of those legendary rivers that divide the living from the dead, entered a place in which I could be seen only by those who were themselves recently bereaved. I understood for the first time the power in the image of the rivers, the Styx, the Lethe, the cloaked ferryman with his pole. I understood for the first time the meaning in the practice of suttee. Widows did not throw themselves on the burning raft out of grief. The burning raft was instead an accurate representation of the place to which their grief (not their families, not the community, not custom, *their grief*) had taken them. On the night John died we were thirty-one days short of our fortieth anniversary. You will have by now divined that the "hard sweet wisdom" in the last two lines of "Rose Aylmer" was lost on me.

I wanted more than a night of memories and sighs.

I wanted to scream.

I wanted him back.

6

SEVERAL YEARS AGO, walking east on Fifty-seventh Street between Sixth and Fifth Avenues on a bright fall day, I had what I believed at the time to be an apprehension of death. It was an effect of light: quick sunlight dappling, yellow leaves falling (but from what? were there even trees on West Fifty-seventh Street?), a shower of gold, spangled, very fast, a falling of the bright. Later I watched for this effect on similar bright days but never again experienced it. I wondered then if it had been a seizure, or stroke of some kind. A few years before that, in California, I had dreamed an image that, when I woke, I knew had been death: the image was that of an ice island, the jagged ridge seen from the air off one of the Channel Islands, except in this case all ice, translucent, a blued white, glittering in the sunlight. Unlike dreams in which the dreamer is anticipating death, inexorably sentenced to die but not yet there, there was in this dream no dread. Both the ice island and the fall of the bright on West Fifty-seventh Street seemed on the contrary transcendent, more beautiful than I could say, yet there was no doubt in my mind that what I had seen was death.

Why, if those were my images of death, did I remain so unable to accept the fact that he had died? Was it because I was failing to understand it as something that had happened to him? Was it because I was still understanding it as something that had happened to me?

Life changes fast.

Life changes in the instant.

You sit down to dinner and life as you know it ends.

The question of self-pity.

You see how early the question of self-pity entered the picture.

One morning during the spring after it happened I picked up *The New York Times* and skipped directly from the front page to the crossword puzzle, a way of starting the day that had become during those months a pattern, the way I had come to read, or more to the point not to read, the paper. I had never before had the patience to work crossword puzzles, but now imagined that the practice would encourage a return to constructive cognitive engagement. The clue that first got my attention that morning was 6 Down, "Sometimes you feel like . . ." I instantly saw the obvious answer, a good long one that would fill many spaces and prove my competency for the day: "a motherless child."

Motherless children have a real hard time—
Motherless children have such a real hard time—

No.

6 Down had only four letters.

I abandoned the puzzle (impatience died hard), and the next day looked up the answer. The correct answer for 6 Down was "anut." "Anut?" A nut? Sometimes you feel like *a nut*? How far had I absented myself from the world of normal response?

Notice: the answer most instantly accessed ("a motherless child") was a wail of self-pity.

This was not going to be an easy failure of understanding to correct.

Avid its rush, that reeling blaze!
Where is my father and Eleanor?
Not where are they now, dead seven years,
But what they were then?
No more? No more?

—DELMORE SCHWARTZ,
"Calmly We Walk Through This April's Day"

He believed he was dying. He told me so, repeatedly. I dismissed this. He was depressed. He had finished a novel, *Nothing Lost*, which was caught in the predictable limbo of a prolonged period between delivery and publication, and he was undergoing an equally predictable crisis of confidence about the book he was then beginning, a reflection on the meaning of patriotism that had not yet found its momentum. He had been dealing as well through most of the year with a series of enervating medical issues. His cardiac rhythm had been slipping with increasing frequency into atrial fibrillation. A normal sinus rhythm could be restored by cardioversion, an outpatient procedure in which he was given general anesthesia for a few minutes while his heart was electrically shocked, but a change in physical status as slight as catching a cold or taking a long plane flight could again disrupt the rhythm. His last such procedure, in April 2003, had required not one but two shocks. The steadily increasing frequency with which cardioversion had become necessary indicated that it was no longer a useful option. In June, after a series of consultations, he had undergone a more radical cardiac intervention, a radio-frequency ablation of the atrial-ventricular node and the subsequent implantation of the Medtronic Kappa 900 SR pacemaker.

During the course of the summer, buoyed by the pleasure of Quintana's wedding and by the apparent success of the pacemaker, his mood had seemed to lift. In the fall it dropped again. I recall a fight over the question of whether we should go to Paris in November. I did not want to go. I said we had too much to do and too little money. He said he had a sense that if he did not go to Paris in November he would never again go to Paris. I interpreted this as blackmail. That settles it then, I said, we're going. He left the table. We did not speak in any meaningful way for two days.

In the end we went to Paris in November.

I tell you that I shall not live two days, Gawain said.

A few weeks ago at the Council on Foreign Relations at Sixty-eighth and Park I noticed someone across from me reading the *International Herald Tribune*. One more example of slipping onto the incorrect track: I am no longer at the Council on Foreign Relations at Sixty-eighth and Park but sitting across from John at breakfast in the dining room of the Bristol in Paris in November 2003. We are each reading the *International Herald Tribune*, hotel copies, with little stapled cards showing the weather for the day. The cards for each of those November mornings in Paris showed an umbrella icon. We walked in the rain at the Jardin du Luxembourg. We escaped from the rain into St. Sulpice. There was a mass in progress. John took communion. We caught cold in the rain at the Jardin du Ranelagh. On the flight back to New York John's muffler and my jersey dress smelled of wet wool. On takeoff he held my hand until the plane began leveling.

He always did.

Where did that go?

In a magazine I see a Microsoft advertisement that shows the platform of the Porte des Lilas metro station in Paris.

I found yesterday in the pocket of an unworn jacket a used metro ticket from that November trip to Paris. "Only Episcopalians 'take' communion," he had corrected me one last time as we left St. Sulpice. He had been correcting me on this point for forty years. Episcopalians "took," Catholics "received." It was, he explained each time, a difference in attitude.

> *Not where are they now, dead seven years,*
> *But what they were then?*

That last cardioversion: April 2003. The one that had required two shocks. I remember a doctor explaining why it was done under anesthesia. "Because otherwise they jump off the table," he said. December 30, 2003: the sudden jump when the ambulance crew was using the defibrillating paddles on the living room floor. Was that ever a heartbeat or was it just electricity?

The night he died or the night before, in the taxi between Beth Israel North and our apartment, he said several things that for the first time made me unable to readily dismiss his mood as depression, a normal phase of any writer's life.

Everything he had done, he said, was worthless.

I still tried to dismiss it.

This might not be normal, I told myself, but neither was the condition in which we had just left Quintana.

He said that the novel was worthless.

This might not be normal, I told myself, but neither was it normal for a father to see a child beyond his help.

He said that his current piece in *The New York Review*, a review of Gavin Lambert's biography of Natalie Wood, was worthless.

This might not be normal, but what in the past several days had been?

He said he did not know what he was doing in New York. "Why did I waste time on a piece about Natalie Wood," he said.

It was not a question.

"You were right about Hawaii," he said then.

He may have meant that I had been right a day or so before when I said that when Quintana got better (this was our code for "if she lives") we could rent a house on the Kailua beach and she could recuperate there. Or he may have meant that I had been right in the 1970s when I wanted to buy a house in Honolulu. I preferred at the time to think the former but the past tense suggested the latter. He said these things in the taxi between Beth Israel North and our apartment either three hours before he died or twenty-seven hours before he died, I try to remember which and cannot.

7

WHY DID I KEEP STRESSING what was and was not normal, when nothing about it was?

Let me try a chronology here.

Quintana was admitted to the ICU at Beth Israel North on December 25, 2003.

John died on December 30, 2003.

I told Quintana that he was dead late on the morning of January 15, 2004, in the ICU at Beth Israel North, after the doctors had managed to remove the breathing tube and reduce sedation to a point at which she could gradually wake up. Telling her that day had not been the plan. The doctors had said that she would wake only intermittently, at first partially, and for a matter of days be able to absorb only limited information. If she woke and saw me she would wonder where her father was. Gerry and Tony and I had discussed this problem at length. We had decided that only Gerry should be with her when she first began to wake. She could focus on him, on their life together. The question of her father might not come up. I could see her later, maybe days later. I could tell her then. She would be stronger.

As planned, Gerry was with her when she first woke. As not planned, a nurse told her that her mother was outside in the corridor.

Then when is she coming in, she wanted to know.

I went in.

"Where's Dad," she whispered when she saw me.

Because three weeks of intubation had inflamed her vocal cords, even her whisper was barely audible. I told her what had happened. I stressed the history of cardiac problems, the long run of luck that had finally caught up with us, the apparent suddenness but actual inevitability of the event. She cried. Gerry and I each held her. She dropped back into sleep.

"How's Dad," she whispered when I saw her that evening.

I began again. The heart attack. The history. The apparent suddenness of the event.

"But how is he *now*," she whispered, straining to be audible.

She had absorbed the sudden event part but not the outcome.

I told her again. In the end I would have to tell her a third time, in another ICU, this one at UCLA.

The chronology.

On January 19, 2004, she was moved from the sixth-floor ICU at Beth Israel North to a room on the twelfth floor. On January 22, 2004, still too weak to stand or sit unsupported and running a fever from a hospital infection acquired in the ICU, she was discharged from Beth Israel North. Gerry and I put her to bed in her old room in my apartment. Gerry went out to fill the prescriptions she had been given. She got out of bed to get another quilt from the closet and collapsed on the floor. I could not lift her and needed to get someone from the building to put her back to bed.

On the morning of January 25, 2004, she woke, still in my apartment, with severe chest pain and increasing fever. She was admitted that day to the Milstein Hospital at Columbia-Presbyterian after a diagnosis of pulmonary emboli was reached in the Presbyterian emergency room. Given her prolonged immobility at Beth Israel, I know now but did not know then, this was an entirely predictable development that could have been diagnosed before discharge from Beth Israel by the same imaging that was done three days later in the Presbyterian emergency room. After she was admitted to Milstein her legs were imaged to see if further clots had formed. She was placed on anticoagulants to prevent such further formation while the existing clots were allowed to dissolve.

On February 3, 2004, she was discharged from Presbyterian, still on anticoagulants. She began physical therapy to regain strength and mobility. Together, with Tony and Nick, she and I planned the service for John. The service took place at four o'clock on a Tuesday afternoon, March 23, 2004, at the Cathedral of St. John the Divine, where, at three o'clock in the presence of the family, John's ashes had been placed as planned in the chapel off the main altar. After the service Nick had arranged a reception at the Union Club. Eventually thirty or forty members of the family made their way back to John's and my apartment. I lit a fire. We had drinks. We had dinner. Quintana, although still fragile, had stood up in her black dress at the Cathedral and laughed with her cousins at dinner. On the morning of March 25, a day and a half later, she and Gerry were going to restart their life by flying to California and walking on the beach at Malibu for a few days. I had encouraged this. I wanted to see Malibu color on her face and hair again.

The next day, March 24, alone in the apartment, the obligation to bury my husband and see our daughter through her crisis formally fulfilled, I put away the plates and allowed myself to think for the first time about what would be required to restart my own life. I called Quintana to wish her a good trip. She was flying early the next morning. She sounded anxious. She was always anxious before a trip. Decisions about what to pack had seemed since childhood to trigger some fear of lost organization. Do you think I'll be okay in California, she said. I said yes. Definitely she would be okay in California. Going to California would in fact be the first day of the rest of her life. It occurred to me as I hung up that cleaning my office could be a step toward the first day of the rest of my own life. I began doing this. During most of the following day, Thursday, March 25, I continued doing this. At points during the quiet day I found myself thinking that possibly I had come through into a new season. In January I had watched ice floes form on the East River from a window at Beth Israel North. In February I had watched ice floes break up on the Hudson from a window at Columbia-Presbyterian. Now in March the ice was gone and I had done what I had to do for John and Quintana would come back from California restored. As the afternoon progressed (her plane would have landed, she would have picked up a car and driven up the Pacific Coast Highway) I imagined her already walking on the beach with Gerry in the thin March Malibu sunlight. I typed the Malibu zip code, 90265, into AccuWeather. There was sun, a high and low I do not remember but do remember thinking satisfactory, a good day in Malibu.

There would be wild mustard on the hills.

She could take him to see the orchids at Zuma Canyon.

She could take him to eat fried fish at the Ventura County line.

She had arranged to take him to lunch one day at Jean Moore's, she would be in the places in which she had spent her childhood. She could show him where we had gathered mussels for Easter lunch. She could show him where the butterflies were, where she had learned to play tennis, where she had learned from the Zuma Beach lifeguards how to swim out of a riptide. On the desk in my office there was a photograph taken when she was seven or eight, her hair long and blonde from the Malibu sun. Stuck in the back of the frame there was a crayoned note, left one day on the kitchen counter in Malibu: *Dear Mom, when you opened the door it was me who ran away XXXXXX—Q.*

At ten minutes past seven that evening I was changing to go downstairs, for dinner with friends who live in the building. I say "at ten minutes past seven" because that was when the phone rang. It was Tony. He said he was coming right over. I noted the time because I was due downstairs at seven-thirty but Tony's urgency was such that I did not say so. His wife, Rosemary Breslin, had spent the past fifteen years dealing with an undiagnosable blood disorder. Since shortly after John died she had been on an experimental protocol that had left her increasingly weak and required intermittent hospitalization at Memorial Sloan-Kettering. I knew that the long day at the Cathedral and later with the family had been strenuous for her. I stopped Tony as he was about to hang up. I asked if Rosemary was back in the hospital. He said it was not Rosemary. It was Quintana, who, even as we spoke, at ten minutes past seven in New York and ten minutes past four in California, was undergoing emergency neurosurgery at UCLA Medical Center in Los Angeles.

8

THEY HAD GOTTEN off the plane.

They had picked up their shared bag.

Gerry was carrying the bag to the car rental shuttle, crossing the arrivals driveway ahead of Quintana. He looked back. Even today I have no idea what made him look back. I never thought to ask. I pictured it as one more case in which you heard someone talking and then you didn't, so you looked. *Life changes in the instant. The ordinary instant.* She was lying on her back on the asphalt. An ambulance was called. She was taken to UCLA. According to Gerry she was awake and lucid in the ambulance. It was only in the emergency room that she began convulsing and lost coherence. A surgical team was alerted. A CT scan was done. By the time they took her into surgery one of her pupils was fixed. The other became fixed as they wheeled her in. I would be told this more than once, in each case as evidence of the gravity of the condition and the critical nature of the intervention: "One pupil was fixed and the other went as we wheeled her in."

The first time I heard this I did not know the significance of what I was being told. By the second time I did. Sherwin B. Nuland, in *How We Die*, described having seen, as a third-year medical student, a cardiac patient whose "pupils were fixed in the position of wide black dilatation that signifies brain death, and obviously would never respond to light again." Again in *How We Die*, Dr. Nuland described the failing attempts of a CPR team to revive a patient who had suffered cardiac arrest in the hospital: "The tenacious young men and women see their patient's pupils become unresponsive to light and then widen until they are large fixed circles of impenetrable blackness. Reluctantly the team stops its efforts. . . . The room is strewn with the debris of the lost campaign." Was this what the New York–Presbyterian ambulance crew saw in John's eyes on our living room floor on December 30, 2003? Was this what the UCLA neurosurgeons saw in Quintana's eyes on March 25, 2004? "Impenetrable blackness?" "Brain death?" Was that what they thought? I look at a printout of that day's CT report from UCLA and still go faint:

> The scan shows right hemispheric subdural hematoma, with evidence of acute bleeding. Active bleeding cannot be excluded. The hematoma causes marked mass effect upon the right cerebrum, subfalcial and early uncal herniation, with 19 mm of midline shift from right to left at the level of the third ventricle. The right lateral ventricle is subtotally effaced and the left lateral ventricle shows early entrapment. There is moderate to marked midbrain compression and the perimesencephalic cistern is effaced. A thin posterior falcine and left tentorial subdural hematomas are noted. A small parenchymal bleed, likely contusional, is noted in the right inferolateral frontal lobe. The cerebellar tonsils are at the level of the foramen magnum. There is no skull fracture. There is a large right parietal scalp hematoma.

March 25, 2004. Ten minutes past seven in the evening in New York.

She had come back from the place where doctors said "We still don't know which way this is going" and now she was there again.

For all I knew it had already gone the wrong way.

They could have told Gerry and Gerry could be trying to absorb it before calling me.

She could already be on her way to the hospital morgue.

Alone. On a gurney. With a transporter.

I had already imagined this scene, with John.

Tony arrived.

He repeated what he had told me on the telephone. He had gotten the call from Gerry at UCLA. Quintana was in surgery. Gerry could be reached by cell phone in the hospital lobby, which happened to double (UCLA was building a new hospital, this one was overcrowded and outdated) as the surgical waiting area.

We called Gerry.

One of the surgeons had just come out to give him an update. The surgical team was now "fairly confident" that Quintana would "leave the table," although they could not predict in what condition.

I remember realizing that this was meant as an improved

assessment: the previous report from the operating room had been that the team was "not at all sure she would leave the table."

I remember trying and failing to understand the phrase "leave the table." Did they mean alive? Had they said "alive" and Gerry could not say it? *Whatever happens,* I remember thinking, *she will without question "leave the table."*

It was then maybe four-thirty in Los Angeles, seven-thirty in New York. I was not sure how long at that point the surgery had been in progress. I see now, since according to the CT report the scan had taken place at "15:06," six minutes past three in Los Angeles, that she had probably been in surgery only about half an hour. I got out an OAG guide to see who would still be flying that night to Los Angeles. Delta had a 9:40 P.M. out of Kennedy. I was about to call Delta when Tony said that he did not think that being in flight during the surgery was a good idea.

I remember a silence.

I remember setting aside the OAG.

I called Tim Rutten in Los Angeles, and asked him to go to the hospital to wait with Gerry. I called our accountant in Los Angeles, Gil Frank, whose own daughter had undergone emergency neurosurgery at UCLA a few months before, and he too said that he would go to the hospital.

That was as close as I could get to being there.

I set the table in the kitchen and Tony and I picked at coq au vin left from the dinner for the family after St. John the Divine. Rosemary arrived. We sat at the kitchen table and tried to develop what we referred to as a "plan." We used phrases like "the contingencies," delicately, as if one of the three of us might not know what "the contingencies" were. I remember calling Earl McGrath to see if I could use his house in Los Angeles. I remember using the words "if I need to," another delicate construction. I remember him cutting directly through this: he was flying to Los Angeles the next day on a friend's plane, I would go with them. Around midnight Gerry called and said that the surgery was finished. They would now do another CT scan to see if there was additional bleeding they had missed. If there was bleeding they would operate again. If there was not they would do a further procedure, the placement of a screen in the vena cava to prevent clots from entering the heart. About four A.M. New York time he called again, to say that the CT scan had shown no bleeding and they had placed the screen. He told me what the surgeons had told him about the operation itself. I made notes:

"Arterial bleed, artery gushing blood, like a geyser, blood all over the room, no clotting factor."

"Brain pushed to the left side."

When I got back to New York from Los Angeles late on the evening of April 30 I found these notes on a grocery list by the kitchen phone. I now know that the technical term for "brain pushed to the left side" is "midline shift," a significant predictive factor for poor outcome, but even then I knew that it was not good. What I had thought I needed on that March day five weeks before were Evian splits, molasses, chicken broth, and flaxseed meal.

Read, learn, work it up, go to the literature.

Information is control.

On the morning after the surgery, before I went to Teterboro to get on the plane, I looked on the Internet for "fixed and dilated pupils." I found that they were called "FDPs." I read the abstract of a study done by researchers in the Department of Neurosurgery at the University Clinic in Bonn. The study followed ninety-nine patients who had either presented with or developed one or two FDPs. The overall mortality rate was 75 percent. Of the 25 percent who were still alive twenty-four months later, 15 percent had what the Glasgow Outcome Scale defined as an "unfavorable outcome" and 10 percent a "favorable outcome." I translated the percentages: of the ninety-nine patients, seventy-four died. Of the surviving twenty-five, at the end of two years, five were vegetative, ten were severely disabled, eight were independent, and two had made a full recovery. I also learned that fixed and dilated pupils indicated injury or compression of the third cranial nerve and the upper brainstem. "Third nerve" and "brainstem" were words that I would hear more often than I wanted to during the weeks to come.

9

You're safe, I remember whispering to Quintana when I first saw her in the ICU at UCLA. *I'm here. You're going to be all right.* Half of her skull had been shaved for the surgery. I could see the long cut and the metal staples that held it closed. She was again breathing only through an endotracheal tube. *I'm here. Everything's fine.*

"When do you have to leave," she asked me on the day when she could finally speak. She said the words with difficulty, her face tensed.

I said I would not leave until we could leave together.

Her face relaxed. She went back to sleep.

It occurred to me during those weeks that this had been, since the day we brought her home from St. John's Hospital in Santa Monica, my basic promise to her. I would not leave. I would take care of her. She would be all right. It also occurred to me that this was a promise I could not keep. I could not always take care of her. I could not never leave her. She was no longer a child. She was an adult. Things happened in life that mothers could not prevent or fix. Unless one of those things killed her prematurely, as one had almost done at Beth Israel and another could still do at UCLA, I would die before she did. I remembered discussions in lawyers' offices during which I had become distressed by the word "predecease." The word could not possibly apply. After each of these discussions I would see the words "mutual disaster" in a new and favorable light. Yet once on a rough flight between Honolulu and Los Angeles I had imagined such a mutual disaster and rejected it. The plane would go down. Miraculously, she and I would survive the crash, adrift in the Pacific, clinging to the debris. The dilemma was this: I would need, because I was menstruating and the blood would attract sharks, to abandon her, swim away, leave her alone.

Could I do this?

Did all parents feel this?

When my mother was near death at age ninety she told me

that she was ready to die but could not. "You and Jim need me," she said. My brother and I were by then in our sixties.

You're safe.

I'm here.

One thing I noticed during the course of those weeks at UCLA was that many people I knew, whether in New York or in California or in other places, shared a habit of mind usually credited to the very successful. They believed absolutely in their own management skills. They believed absolutely in the power of the telephone numbers they had at their fingertips, the right doctor, the major donor, the person who could facilitate a favor at State or Justice. The management skills of these people were in fact prodigious. The power of their telephone numbers was in fact unmatched. I had myself for most of my life shared the same core belief in my ability to control events. If my mother was suddenly hospitalized in Tunis I could arrange for the American consul to bring her English-language newspapers and get her onto an Air France flight to meet my brother in Paris. If Quintana was suddenly stranded in the Nice airport I could arrange with someone at British Airways to get her onto a BA flight to meet her cousin in London. Yet I had always at some level apprehended, because I was born fearful, that some events in life would remain beyond my ability to control or manage them. Some events would just happen. This was one of those events. *You sit down to dinner and life as you know it ends.*

Many people to whom I spoke in those first days while Quintana lay unconscious at UCLA seemed free of this apprehension. Their initial instinct was that this event could be managed. In order to manage it they needed only information. They needed only to know how this had happened. They needed answers. They needed "the prognosis."

I had no answers.

I had no prognosis.

I did not know how this had happened.

There were two possibilities, both of them, I came to see, irrelevant. One possibility was that she had fallen and the trauma had caused a bleed into her brain, a danger of the anticoagulants she had been given to prevent emboli. The second possibility was that the bleed into her brain had occurred before the fall and in fact caused it. People on anticoagulants bleed. They bruise at a touch. The level of anticoagulant in the blood, which is measured by a number called the INR (International Normalized Ratio), is hard to control. The blood must be tested every few weeks and in some cases every few days. Minute and complicated changes must be made in dosage. The ideal INR for Quintana was, give or take a tenth of a point, 2.2. On the day she flew to Los Angeles it so happened that her INR was over 4, a level at which spontaneous bleeding can occur. When I got to Los Angeles and spoke to the chief surgeon, he said that he was "one hundred percent sure" the trauma had caused the bleed. Other doctors to whom I spoke were less certain. It was suggested by one that the flight alone could have caused sufficient changes in pressurization to precipitate a bleed.

I recall pressing the surgeon on this point, myself trying (one more time) to manage the situation, get answers. I was talking to him on a cell phone from the courtyard outside the UCLA Medical Center cafeteria. The cafeteria was named "Café Med." This was my first visit to Café Med and my introduction to its most noticeable regular, a small balding man (I assumed a Neuropsychiatric Institute patient with walkaround privileges) whose compulsion it was to trail one or another woman through the cafeteria, alternately spitting and mouthing enraged imprecations about how disgusting she was, how vile, what a piece of worthless trash. On this particular morning the small balding man had trailed me out to the courtyard and it was hard to make out what the surgeon was saying. "It was the trauma, there was a ruptured blood vessel, we saw it," I thought he said. This had not seemed to entirely address the question—a ruptured blood vessel did not categorically rule out the possibility that the ruptured blood vessel had preceded and caused the fall—but there in the Café Med courtyard with the small balding man spitting on my shoe I realized that the answer to the question made no difference. It had happened. It was the new fact on the ground.

During the course of this call from the surgeon, which took place on the first full day I spent in Los Angeles, I recall being told several other things.

I recall being told that her coma could continue for days or weeks.

I recall being told that it would be a minimum of three days before anyone could begin to know what shape her brain was in. The surgeon was "optimistic," but no prediction was possible. Many more urgent issues could come up in the next three or four or more days.

She could develop an infection.

She could develop pneumonia, she could develop an embolism.

She could develop further swelling, which would necessitate reoperating.

After I hung up I walked back into the cafeteria, where Gerry was having coffee with Susan Traylor and my brother's daughters, Kelley and Lori. I remember wondering whether to mention the more urgent issues the surgeon had mentioned. I saw when I looked at their faces that there was no reason not to: all four of them had been at the hospital before I got to Los Angeles. All four of them had already heard about the more urgent issues.

During the twenty-four December and January nights when Quintana was in the sixth-floor ICU at Beth Israel North I had kept on the table by my bed a paperback copy of *Intensive Care: A Doctor's Journal*, by John F. Murray, M.D., who had been from 1966 to 1989 chief of the Pulmonary and Critical Care Division at the University of California medical school in San Francisco. *Intensive Care* describes, day by day, a four-week period in a San Francisco General Hospital medical ICU for which Dr. Murray was at the time the attending physician responsible for all patients, residents, interns, and medical students. I had read this account over and over. I had learned much that proved useful in the calibration of my daily dealings with the ICU doctors at Beth Israel North. I had learned for example that it was often difficult to gauge when the time was right for extubation, the removal of an endotracheal tube. I had learned that a common barrier to extubation was the edema so predictably seen in intensive care. I had learned that this edema was less often the result of an underlying pathology than of an excess in the administration of intravenous fluid, a failure to observe the distinction between hydration and overhydration, an error of caution. I had learned that many young residents made a similar error of caution when it came to extubation itself: their tendency, because the outcome was uncertain, was to delay the procedure longer than necessary.

I had registered these lessons. I had made use of them: the tentative question here, the expressed wish there. I had "wondered" if she might not be "waterlogged." ("Of course I don't know, I just know how she looks.") I had deliberately used the word "waterlogged." I had noticed a stiffening when I used the word "edema." I had further "wondered" if she might not be better able to breathe if she was less waterlogged. ("Of course I'm not a doctor, but it just seems logical.") I had again "wondered" if the monitored administration of a diuretic might not allow extubation. ("Of course this is a home remedy, but if I felt the way she looks I'd take a Lasix.") With *Intensive Care* as my guide it had seemed straightforward, intuitive. There was a way to know if you had made headway. You knew you had made headway when a doctor to whom you had made one or another suggestion presented, a day later, the plan as his own.

This was different. A certain derisive phrase had occurred to me during the edema contest of wills at Beth Israel North: *It's not brain surgery.* This was. When these doctors at UCLA said "parietal" and "temporal" to me I had no idea where in the brain they were talking about, let alone what they meant. "Right frontal" I thought I could understand. "Occipital" I thought suggested "eye," but only on the misconceived reasoning that the word began with "oc," like "ocular." I went to the UCLA Medical Center bookstore. I bought a book described on its cover as a "concise overview of neuroanatomy and of its functional and clinical implications" as well as an "excellent review for the USMLE." This book was by Stephen G. Waxman, M.D., chief of neurology at Yale–New Haven, and was called *Clinical Neuroanatomy.* I skimmed successfully through some of the appendices, for example "Appendix A: The Neurologic Examination," but when I began to read the text itself I could think only of a trip to Indonesia during which I had become disoriented by my inability to locate the grammar in Bahasa Indonesia, the official language used on street signs and storefronts and billboards. I had asked someone at the American Embassy how to tell the verbs from the nouns. Bahasa was a language, he had said, in which the same word could be either a verb or a noun. *Clinical Neuroanatomy* seemed to be one more case in which I would be unable to locate the grammar. I put it on the table by my bed at the Beverly Wilshire Hotel, where it would remain for the next five weeks.

On further study of *Clinical Neuroanatomy*, say if I woke in the morning before *The New York Times* had arrived with its sedative crossword puzzle, even "Appendix A: The Neurologic Examination" seemed opaque. I had originally noticed the obvious familiar directives (ask the patient the name of the president, ask the patient to count backwards from one hundred by sevens), but as days passed I seemed focused on a mysterious narrative, identified in Appendix A as the "gilded-boy story," that could be used to test memory and comprehension. The patient could be told the story, Dr. Waxman suggested, then asked to retell it in his own words and explain its meaning. "At the coronation of one of the popes, about 300 years ago, a little boy was chosen to play the part of an angel."

So began the "gilded-boy story."

So far clear enough, although potentially troubling details (three hundred years ago? play the part of an angel?) for someone emerging from coma.

It continued: "So that his appearance might be as magnificent as possible, he was covered from head to foot with a coating of gold foil. The little boy fell ill, and although everything possible was done for his recovery except the removal of the fatal golden covering, he died within a few hours."

What was the "meaning" of the "gilded-boy story"? Did it have to do with the fallibility of "the popes"? With the fallibility of authority in general? With the specific fallibility (note that "everything possible was done for his recovery") of medicine? What possible point could there be in telling this story to a patient immobilized in a neuro ICU at a major teaching hospital? What lesson could be drawn? Did they think that because it was a "story" it could be told without consequence? There was a morning on which the "gilded-boy story" seemed to represent, in its utter impenetrability and apparent disregard for the sensitivity of the patient, the entire situation with which I was faced. I went back to the UCLA Medical Center bookstore with the thought of checking other sources for an elucidation, but there was no mention of the gilded-boy story in the first several textbooks I picked up. In lieu of checking further, I bought, since the afternoon highs in Los Angeles were by then in the eighties and I had flown west with only the late-winter clothes I had been wearing in New York, several sets of blue cotton scrubs. So profound was the isolation in which I was then operating that it did not immediately occur to me that for the mother of a patient to show up at the hospital wearing blue cotton scrubs could only be viewed as a suspicious violation of boundaries.

10

I HAD FIRST NOTICED what I came to know as "the vortex effect" in January, when I was watching the ice floes form on the East River from a window at Beth Israel North. At the join between the walls and the ceiling of the room from which I was watching the ice floes there happened to be a rose-patterned wallpaper border, a Dorothy Draper touch, left I supposed from the period when what was then Beth Israel North had been Doctors' Hospital. I myself had never been in Doctors' Hospital, but when I was in my twenties and working for *Vogue* it had figured in many conversations. It had been the hospital favored by *Vogue* editors for uncomplicated deliveries and for "resting," a kind of medical Maine Chance.

This had seemed a good line of thinking.

This had seemed better than thinking about why I was at Beth Israel North.

I had ventured further:

Doctors' Hospital was where X had the abortion that was bought and paid for by the district attorney's office. "X" was a woman with whom I had worked at *Vogue*. Seductive clouds of cigarette smoke and Chanel No. 5 and imminent disaster had trailed her through the Condé Nast offices, which were then in the Graybar Building. On a single morning, while I was attempting to put together a particularly trying *Vogue* feature called "People Are Talking About," she had found both that she needed an abortion and that her name had turned up in the files of a party girl operation under investigation by the district attorney's office. She had been cheerful about these two pieces of (what had seemed to me) devastating news. A deal had been struck. She had agreed to testify that she had been approached by the operation, and the district attorney's office had in turn arranged a D&C at Doctors' Hospital, no inconsiderable favor at a time when getting an abortion meant making a clandestine and potentially lethal appointment with someone whose first instinct in a crisis would be to vacate the premises.

The party girl operation and the arranged abortion and the

years in which I had spent mornings putting together "People Are Talking About" still seemed a good line of thinking.

I remembered having used such an incident in my second novel, *Play It As It Lays.* The protagonist, a former model named Maria, had recently had an abortion, which was troubling her.

> Once a long time before Maria had worked a week in Ocho Rios with a girl who had just had an abortion. She could remember the girl telling her about it while they sat huddled next to a waterfall waiting for the photographer to decide the sun was high enough to shoot. It seemed that it was a hard time for abortions in New York, there had been arrests, no one wanted to do it. Finally the girl, her name was Ceci Delano, had asked a friend in the district attorney's office if he knew of anyone. "Quid pro quo," he had said, and, late the same day that Ceci Delano testified to a blue-ribbon jury that she had been approached by a party girl operation, she was admitted to Doctors' Hospital for a legal D&C, arranged and paid for by the district attorney's office.
>
> It had seemed a funny story as she told it, both that morning at the waterfall and later at dinner, when she repeated it to the photographer and the agency man and the fashion coordinator for the client. Maria tried now to put what had happened in Encino into the same spirited perspective, but Ceci Delano's situation seemed not to apply. In the end it was just a New York story.

This seemed to be working.

I had avoided thinking for at least two minutes about why I was at Beth Israel North.

I had moved on, into the period during which I was writing *Play It As It Lays.* The rented wreck of a house on Franklin Avenue in Hollywood. The votive candles on the sills of the big windows in the living room. The *té de limón* grass and aloe that grew by the kitchen door. The rats that ate the avocados. The sun porch on which I worked. Watching from the windows of the sun porch as Quintana ran through a sprinkler on the lawn.

I recall recognizing that I had hit more dangerous water but there had seemed no turning back.

I had been writing that book when Quintana was three.

When Quintana was three.

There it was, the vortex.

Quintana at three. The night she had put a seed pod from the garden up her nose and I had driven her to Children's Hospital. The pediatrician who specialized in seed pods had arrived in his dinner jacket. The next night she had put another seed pod up her nose, wanting to repeat the interesting adventure. John and I walking with her around the lake in MacArthur Park. The old man lurching from a bench. "That child is the picture of Ginger Rogers," the old man cried. I finished the novel, I was under contract to begin a column for *Life*, we took Quintana to Honolulu. *Life*'s idea for the first column was that I should introduce myself, "let the readers know who you are." I planned to write it from Honolulu, the Royal Hawaiian Hotel, we used to get a lanai suite on the press rate for twenty-seven dollars a night. While we were there the news of My Lai broke. I thought about the first column. It seemed to me that given this news I should write it from Saigon. By then it was a Sunday. *Life* had given me a printed card with the home numbers of its editors and also of lawyers in cities around the world. I took out the card and called my editor, Loudon Wainwright, to say I was going to Saigon. His wife answered the phone. She said he would have to call me back.

"He's watching the NFL game," John said when I hung up. "He'll call you at halftime."

He did. He said that I should stay where I was and introduce myself, that as far as Saigon went "some of the guys are going out." The topic did not seem open to further discussion. "There's a world in revolution out there and we can put you in it," George Hunt had said when he was still the managing editor of *Life* and offering me the job. By the time I finished *Play It As It Lays* George Hunt had retired and some of the guys were going out.

"I warned you," John said. "I told you what working for *Life* would be like. Didn't I tell you? It would be like being nibbled to death by ducks?"

I was brushing Quintana's hair. The picture of Ginger Rogers.

I felt betrayed, humiliated. I should have listened to John.

I wrote the column letting the readers know who I was. It appeared. At the time it seemed an unexceptional enough eight hundred words in the assigned genre, but there was, at the end of the second paragraph, a line so out of synch with the entire *Life* mode of self-presentation that it might as well have suggested abduction by space aliens: "We are here on this island in the middle of the Pacific in lieu of filing for divorce." A week later we happened to be in New York. "Did you know she was writing it," many people asked John, sotto voce.

Did he know I was writing it?

He edited it.

He took Quintana to the Honolulu Zoo so I could rewrite it.

He drove me to the Western Union office in downtown Honolulu so I could file it.

At the Western Union office he wrote *REGARDS, DIDION* at the end of it. That was what you always put at the end of a cable, he said. Why, I said. Because you do, he said.

See where that particular vortex sucked me.

From the Dorothy Draper wallpaper border at Beth Israel North to Quintana at three and I should have listened to John.

I tell you that I shall not live two days, Gawain said.

The way you got sideswiped was by going back.

I saw immediately in Los Angeles that its potential for triggering this vortex effect could be controlled only by avoiding any venue I might associate with either Quintana or John. This would require ingenuity. John and I had lived in Los Angeles County from 1964 until 1988. Between 1988 and the time he died we had spent significant amounts of time there, usually at the very hotel in which I was now staying, the Beverly Wilshire. Quintana was born in Los Angeles County, at St. John's Hospital in Santa Monica. She went to school there, first in Malibu and later at what was then still the Westlake School for Girls (the year after she left it became coeducational, and was called Harvard-Westlake) in Holmby Hills.

For reasons that remain unclear to me the Beverly Wilshire itself only rarely triggered the vortex effect. In theory its every corridor was permeated with the associations I was trying to avoid. When we were living in Malibu and had meetings in town we would bring Quintana and stay at the Beverly Wilshire. After we moved to New York and needed to be in Los

Angeles for a picture we would stay there, sometimes for a few days, sometimes for weeks at a time. We set up computers and printers there. We had meetings there. *What if*, someone was always saying in these meetings. We could work until eight or nine in the evening there and transmit the pages to whichever director or producer we were working with and then go to dinner at a Chinese restaurant on Melrose where we did not need a reservation. We always specified the old building. I knew the housekeepers. I knew the manicurists. I knew the doorman who would give John the bottled water when he came back from walking in the morning. I knew by reflex how to work the key and open the safe and adjust the shower head: I had stayed over the years in some dozens of rooms identical to the one in which I was now staying. I had last stayed in such a room in October 2003, alone, doing promotion, two months before John died. Yet the Beverly Wilshire seemed when Quintana was at UCLA the only safe place for me to be, the place where everything would be the same, the place where no one would know about or refer to the events of my recent life; the place where I would still be the person I had been before any of this happened.

What if.

Outside the exempt zone that was the Beverly Wilshire, I plotted my routes, I remained on guard.

Never once in five weeks did I drive into the part of Brentwood in which we had lived from 1978 until 1988. When I saw a dermatologist in Santa Monica and street work forced me to pass within three blocks of our house in Brentwood, I did not look left or right. Never once in five weeks did I drive up the Pacific Coast Highway to Malibu. When Jean Moore offered me the use of her house on the Pacific Coast Highway, three-eighths of a mile past the house in which we had lived from 1971 until 1978, I invented reasons why it was essential for me to stay instead at the Beverly Wilshire. I could avoid driving to UCLA on Sunset. I could avoid passing the intersection at Sunset and Beverly Glen where for six years I had turned off to the Westlake School for Girls. I could avoid passing any intersection I could not anticipate, control. I could avoid keeping the car radio tuned to the stations I used to drive by, avoid locating KRLA, an AM station that had called itself "the heart and soul of rock and roll" and was still in the early 1990s programming the top hits of 1962. I could avoid punching in the Christian call-in station to which I had switched whenever the top hits of 1962 lost their resonance.

Instead I listened to NPR, a sedate morning show called *Morning Becomes Eclectic.* Every morning at the Beverly Wilshire I ordered the same breakfast, huevos rancheros with one scrambled egg. Every morning when I left the Beverly Wilshire I drove the same way to UCLA: out Wilshire, right on Glendon, slip left to Westwood, right on Le Conte and left at Tiverton. Every morning I noted the same banners fluttering from the light standards along Wilshire: *UCLA Medical Center—#1 in the West, #3 in the Nation.* Every morning I wondered whose ranking this was. I never asked. Each morning I inserted my ticket into the gate mechanism and each morning, if I inserted it right, the same woman's voice said "*Wel*-come to *U-C-L-A.*" Each morning, if I timed it right, I got a parking place outside, on the Plaza 4 level, against the hedge. Late each afternoon I would drive back to the Beverly Wilshire, pick up my messages, and return a few of them. After the first week Gerry was flying back and forth between Los Angeles and New York, trying to work at least a few days a week, and if he was in New York I would call to give him the day's information or lack of it. I would lie down. I would watch the local news. I would stand in the shower for twenty minutes and go out to dinner.

I went out to dinner every night I was in Los Angeles. I had dinner with my brother and his wife whenever they were in town. I went to Connie Wald's house in Beverly Hills. There were roses and nasturtiums and open fires in the big fireplaces, as there had been through all the years when John and I and Quintana would go there. Now Susan Traylor was there. I went to Susan's own house in the Hollywood hills. I had known Susan since she was three and I had known her husband Jesse since he and Susan and Quintana were in the fourth grade at the Point Dume School, and now they were looking after me. I ate in many restaurants with many friends. I had dinner quite often with Earl McGrath, whose intuitive kindness in this situation was to ask me every morning what I was doing that night and, if the answer was in any way vague, to arrange an untaxing dinner for two or three or four at Orso or at Morton's or at his house on Robertson Boulevard.

After dinner I would take a taxi back to the hotel and place my morning order for huevos rancheros. "One scrambled egg," the voice on the phone would prompt. "Exactly," I would say.

I plotted these evenings as carefully as I plotted the routes.

I left no time to dwell on promises I had no way of keeping.

You're safe. I'm here.

In the deep hush of *Morning Becomes Eclectic* the next day I would congratulate myself.

I could have been in Cleveland.

Yet.

I cannot count the days on which I found myself driving abruptly blinded by tears.

The Santa Ana was back.

The jacaranda was back.

One afternoon I needed to see Gil Frank, at his office on Wilshire, several blocks east of the Beverly Wilshire. In this previously untested territory (*terra cognita* for these purposes was west on Wilshire, not east) I caught sight, unprepared, of a movie theater in which John and I had in 1967 seen *The Graduate*. There had been no particular sense of moment about seeing *The Graduate* in 1967. I had been in Sacramento. John had picked me up at LAX. It had seemed too late to shop for dinner and too early to eat in a restaurant so we had gone to see *The Graduate* and then to dinner at Frascati's. Frascati's was gone but the theater was still there, if only to trap the unwary.

There were many such traps. One day I would notice a familiar stretch of coastal highway in a television commercial and realize it was outside the gate house, on the Palos Verdes Peninsula at Portuguese Bend, to which John and I had brought Quintana home from St. John's Hospital.

She was three days old.

We had placed her bassinet next to the wisteria in the box garden.

You're safe. I'm here.

Neither the house nor its gate could be seen in the commercial but I experienced a sudden rush of memories: getting out of the car on that highway to open the gate so that John could drive through; watching the tide come in and float a car that was sitting on our beach to be shot for a commercial; sterilizing bottles for Quintana's formula while the gamecock that lived on the property followed me companionably from window to window. This gamecock, named "Buck" by the owner of the house, had been abandoned on the highway, in the colorful opinion of the owner by "Mexicans on the run." Buck had a distinctive and surprisingly endearing personality, not unlike a Labrador. In addition to Buck this house also came equipped with peacocks, which were decorative but devoid of personality. Unlike Buck, the peacocks were fat and moved only as a last resort. At dusk they would scream and try to fly to their nests in the olive trees, a fraught moment because they would so often fall. Just before dawn they would scream again. One dawn I woke to the screaming and looked for John. I found him outside in the dark, tearing unripe peaches from a tree and hurling them at the peacocks, a characteristically straightforward if counterproductive approach to resolving an annoyance. When Quintana was a month old we were evicted. There was a clause in the lease that specified no children but the owner and his wife allowed that the baby was not the reason. The reason was that we had hired a pretty teenager named Jennifer to take care of her. The owner and his wife did not want strangers on the property, or as they said "behind the gate," particularly pretty teenagers named Jennifer, who would presumably have dates. We took a few months' lease on a house in town that belonged to Herman Mankiewicz's widow, Sara, who was going to be traveling. She left everything in the house as it was except one object, the Oscar awarded to Herman Mankiewicz for the screenplay of *Citizen Kane.* "You'll have parties, people will just get drunk and play with it," she said when she put it away. On the day we moved John was traveling with the San Francisco Giants, doing a piece on Willie Mays for *The Saturday Evening Post.* I borrowed my sister-in-law's station wagon, loaded it, put Quintana and Jennifer in the back seat, said goodbye to Buck, drove out, and let the totemic gate lock behind me for the last time.

All that and I had not even driven down there.

All I had done was catch sight of a commercial on television while I was dressing to go to the hospital.

Another day I would need to buy bottled water at the Rite

Aid on Canon and remember that Canon was where The Bistro had been. In 1964 and 1965, when we were living in the gate house with the beach and the peacocks but could not afford even to tip the parking boys at restaurants, let alone eat in them, John and I used to park on the street on Canon and charge dinner at The Bistro. We took Quintana there on the day of her adoption, when she was not quite seven months old. They had given us Sidney Korshak's corner banquette and placed her carrier on the table, a centerpiece. At the courthouse that morning she had been the only baby, even the only child; all the other adoptions that day had seemed to involve adults adopting one another for tax reasons. "*Qué bonita, qué hermosa*," the busboys at The Bistro crooned when we brought her in at lunch. When she was six or seven we took her there for a birthday dinner. She was wearing a lime-green ruana I had bought for her in Bogotá. As we were about to leave the waiter had brought the ruana and she had flung it theatrically over her small shoulders.

Qué bonita, qué hermosa, the picture of Ginger Rogers.

John and I had been in Bogotá together. We had escaped from a film festival in Cartagena and gotten on an Avianca flight to Bogotá. An actor who had been at the film festival, George Montgomery, had also been on the flight to Bogotá. He had gone up to the cockpit. From where I was sitting I could see him chatting with the crew, then sliding into the pilot's seat.

I had nudged John, who was sleeping. "They're letting George Montgomery fly this plane over the Andes," I had whispered.

"It beats Cartagena," John said, and went back to sleep.

I did not that day on Canon get as far as the Rite Aid.

11

SOMETIME IN JUNE, after she had left UCLA and was in the sixth of what would be fifteen weeks as an inpatient at the Rusk Institute of Rehabilitation Medicine at New York University Medical Center in New York, Quintana told me that her memory not only of UCLA but of her arrival at Rusk was "all mudgy." She could remember some things about UCLA, yes, as she could not yet remember anything else since before Christmas (she did not for example remember speaking about her father at St. John the Divine, nor, when she first woke at UCLA, did she remember that he had died), but it was still "mudgy." Later she corrected this to "smudgy," but she did not need to: I knew exactly what she meant. On the neuro floors at UCLA they had called it "spotty," as in "her orientation is improving but still spotty." When I try to reconstruct those weeks at UCLA I recognize the mudginess in my own memory. There are parts of days that seem very clear and parts of days that do not. I clearly remember arguing with a doctor the day they decided to do the tracheostomy. She had by then been intubated for almost a week, the doctor said. UCLA did not leave tubes in for more than a week. I said that she had been intubated for three weeks at Beth Israel in New York. The doctor had looked away. "The rule at Duke was also a week," he said, as if under the impression that mention of Duke would settle the question. Instead it enraged me: *What is Duke to me*, I wanted to say but did not. *What is Duke to UCLA. Duke is North Carolina. UCLA is California. If I wanted the opinion of somebody in North Carolina I would call somebody in North Carolina.*

Her husband is right now on a flight to New York, I said instead. Surely this can wait until he lands.

Not really, the doctor said. Since it's already on the schedule.

The day they decided to do the tracheostomy was also the day they turned off the EEG.

"Everything's looking good," they kept saying. "She's going to get better sooner once we do the trach. She's already off the EEG, maybe you didn't notice that."

Maybe I didn't notice that?

My only child?

My unconscious child?

Maybe I didn't notice when I walked into the ICU that morning that her brain waves were gone? That the monitor above her bed was dark, dead?

This was now being presented as progress but it had not seemed so when I first saw it. I remembered reading in *Intensive Care* that the ICU nurses at San Francisco General turned off the monitors when a patient was near death, because their experience was that family members would focus on the screens rather than on the dying patient. I wondered if such a determination had been made in this case. Even after I was assured that this was not the case, I found myself averting my eyes from the blank EEG screen. I had grown used to watching her brain waves. It was a way of hearing her talk.

I did not see why, since the equipment was sitting there unused, they could not keep the EEG on.

Just in case.

I had asked.

I do not remember getting an answer. It was a period when I asked many questions that did not get answered. What answers I did get tended to the unsatisfactory, as in, "It's already on the schedule."

Everyone in the neuro units got a trach, they had kept saying to me that day. Everyone in the neuro units had muscular weaknesses that rendered the removal of the breathing tube problematic. A trach involved less risk of windpipe damage. A trach involved less risk of pneumonia. Look to your right, look to your left, both sides have trachs. A trach could be done with fentanyl and a muscle relaxant, she would be under anesthesia no more than an hour. A trach would leave no cosmetic effect to speak of, "only a little dimple scar," "as time goes by maybe no scar at all."

They kept mentioning this last point, as if the basis for my resistance to the trach was the scar. They were doctors, however freshly minted. I was not. Ergo, any concerns I had must be cosmetic, frivolous.

In fact I had no idea why I so resisted the trach.

I think now that my resistance came from the same fund of superstition from which I had been drawing since John died. If she did not have a trach she could be fine in the morning, ready to eat, talk, go home. If she did not have a trach we could be on a plane by the weekend. Even if they did not want her to fly, I could take her with me to the Beverly Wilshire, we could have our nails done, sit by the pool. If they still did not want her to fly we could drive out to Malibu, spend a few restorative days with Jean Moore.

If she did not have a trach.

This was demented, but so was I.

Through the printed blue cotton curtains that separated the beds I could hear people talking to their functionally absent husbands, fathers, uncles, co-workers. In the bed to Quintana's right was a man injured in a construction accident. The men who had been on the site at the time of the accident had come to see him. They stood around his bed and tried to explain what had happened. The rig, the cab, the crane, I heard a noise, I called out to Vinny. Each man gave his version. Each version differed slightly from the others. This was understandable, since each witness proceeded from a different point of view, but I recall wanting to intercede, help them coordinate their stories; it had seemed too much conflicting data to lay on someone with a traumatic brain injury.

"Everything's going along as usual and then all shit breaks loose," one said.

The injured man made no response, nor could he, since he had a trach.

To Quintana's left lay a man from Massachusetts who had been in the hospital for several months. He and his wife had been in Los Angeles visiting their children, there had been a fall from a ladder, he had seemed all right. One more perfectly ordinary day. Then he had trouble speaking. *Everything's going along as usual and then all shit breaks loose.* Now he had pneumonia. The children came and went. The wife was always there, pleading with him in a low mournful voice. The husband made no response: he too had a trach.

They did the trach for Quintana on the first of April, a Thursday afternoon.

By Friday morning enough of the sedation for the breathing tube had been metabolized out that she could open her eyes and squeeze my hand.

On Saturday I was told that the next day or Monday she would be moved from the ICU into a step-down neuro-observational unit on the seventh floor. The sixth and seventh floors at UCLA were all neuro.

I have no memory of when she was moved but I think it was some days after that.

One afternoon after she had been moved to the step-down unit I ran into the woman from Massachusetts in the Café Med courtyard.

Her husband too had left the ICU, and was moving now to what she called a "subacute rehab facility." We each knew that "subacute rehab facilities" were what medical insurance carriers and hospital discharge coordinators called nursing homes but this went unmentioned. She had wanted him moved to the eleven-bed acute rehab unit at UCLA Neuropsychiatric but he had not been accepted. That was the phrase she used, "not been accepted." She was concerned about how she would get to the subacute facility—one of the two with an available bed was near LAX, the other in Chinatown—because she did not drive. The children had jobs, important jobs, they could not always be driving her.

We sat in the sun.

I listened. She asked about my daughter.

I did not want to tell her that my daughter would be moving to the eleven-bed acute rehab unit at Neuropsychiatric.

At some point I noticed that I was trying like a sheepdog to herd the doctors, pointing out edema to one intern, reminding another to obtain a urine culture to check out the blood in the Foley catheter line, insisting on a Doppler ultrasound to see if the reason for the leg pain could be emboli, doggedly repeating—when the ultrasound indicated that she was in fact again throwing clots—that I wanted a specialist on coagulation called in to consult. I wrote down the name of the specialist I wanted. I offered to call him myself. These efforts did not endear me to the young men and women who made up the house staff ("If you want to manage this case I'm signing off," one finally said) but they made me feel less helpless.

I remember learning at UCLA the names of many tests and scales. The Kimura Box Test. The Two-Point Discrimination Test. The Glasgow Coma Scale, the Glasgow Outcome Scale. My comprehension of the meaning of these tests and scales remained obscure. I also remember learning, both at UCLA and before, at Beth Israel and Columbia-Presbyterian, the names of many resistant hospital bacteria. At Beth Israel there had been *Acinetobacter baumannii*, which was resistant to vancomycin. "That's how you know it's a hospital infection," I recall being told by a doctor I asked at Columbia-Presbyterian. "If it's resistant to vanc it's hospital. Because vanc only gets used in hospital settings." At UCLA there had been MRSA, methicillin-resistant *Staphylococcus aureus*, as opposed to MRSE, methicillin-resistant *Staphylococcus epidermidis*, which was what they first thought they had cultured and which had seemed to more visibly alarm the staff. "I can't say why but since you're pregnant you may want to transfer off," one therapist advised another during the MRSE scare, glancing at me as if I might not understand. There were many other names of hospital bacteria, but those were the big hitters. Whatever bacteria was shown to be the source of the new fever or urinary tract infection, it would mandate gowns, gloves, masks. It would provoke heavy sighing among the aides who were required to suit up before entering the room to empty a wastebasket. The methicillin-resistant *Staphylococcus aureus* at UCLA was an infection in the bloodstream, a bacteremia. When I heard this I expressed concern to the doctor who was examining Quintana that an infection in her bloodstream might again lead to sepsis.

"Well, you know, sepsis, it's a clinical term," the doctor said, then continued examining her.

I had pressed him.

"She's already in some degree of sepsis." He had seemed cheerful. "But we're continuing vanc. And so far her blood pressure is holding."

So. We were back to waiting to see if she lost blood pressure.

We were back to watching for septic shock.

Next we would be watching for ice floes on the East River.

In point of fact what I watched from the windows at UCLA was a swimming pool. I never once saw anyone swim in this swimming pool, although it was filled, filtered (I could see the little swirl where the water entered the filter and the bubbling where it reemerged), sparkling in the sun, and surrounded by patio tables, with parasols. One day when I was watching it I had a sharp memory of having gotten the idea to float candles and gardenias in the pool behind the house in Brentwood Park. We were having a party. It was an hour before the party but I was already dressed when the gardenia idea presented itself. I knelt on the coping and lit the candles and used the pool skimmer to guide the gardenias and candles into a random pattern. I stood up, pleased with the result. I put the pool skimmer away. When I glanced back at the pool, the gardenias had vanished and the candles were out, tiny drenched hulks bobbing furiously around the filter intake. They could not be sucked in because the filter was already clogged with gardenias. I spent the remaining forty-five minutes before the party cleaning the sodden gardenias from the filter and scooping out the candles and drying my dress with a hair dryer.

So far so good.

A memory of the house in Brentwood Park that involved neither John nor Quintana.

Unfortunately I thought of another. I had been alone in the kitchen of that house, late twilight, early evening, feeding the Bouvier we then had. Quintana was at Barnard. John was spending a few days at the apartment we had in New York. This would have been late 1987, the period during which he had begun talking about wanting us to spend more time in New York. I had discouraged this idea. Suddenly a red flashing light had filled the kitchen. I had gone to the window. There was an ambulance in front of a house across Marlboro Street, visible beyond the coral tree and two cords of stacked wood in our side yard. This was a neighborhood in which many houses, including the one across Marlboro Street, had side yards in which there were two cords of stacked wood. I had watched the house until the last light was gone and the ambulance left. The next morning when I was walking the Bouvier a neighbor told me what had happened. Two cords of stacked wood had not kept the woman in the house across Marlboro Street from becoming a widow at dinner.

I had called John in New York.

The red flashing light had by then seemed an urgent warning.

I said maybe he was right, we should spend more time in New York.

Watching the empty swimming pool from the window at UCLA I could see the vortex coming but could not deflect it. The vortex in this instance would be the memory's insistent appointment-in-Samarra aspect. Had I not made that call would Quintana have moved back to Los Angeles when she graduated from Barnard? Had she been living in Los Angeles would Beth Israel North have happened, would Presbyterian have happened, would she be in UCLA today? Had I not misread the meaning of the red flashing light in late 1987 would I be able to get in my car today and drive west on San Vicente and find John at the house in Brentwood Park? Standing in the pool? Rereading *Sophie's Choice*?

Would I need to relive every mistake? If by accident I remembered the morning we drove down to St. Tropez from Tony Richardson's house in the hills and had coffee on the street and bought the fish for dinner would I also need to remember the night I refused to swim in the moonlight because the Mediterranean was polluted and I had a cut on my leg? If I remembered the gamecock at Portuguese Bend would I also need to remember the long drive home from dinner to that house, and how many nights as we passed the refineries on the San Diego Freeway one or the other of us had said the wrong thing? Or stopped speaking? Or imagined that the other had stopped speaking? "Each single one of the memories and expectations in which the libido is bound to the object is brought up and hypercathected, and detachment of the libido is accomplished in respect of it. . . . It is remarkable that this painful unpleasure is taken as a matter of course by us." So Freud explained what he saw as the "work" of grief, which as described sounded suspiciously like the vortex.

In point of fact the house in Brentwood Park from which I had seen the red flashing light and thought to evade it by moving to New York no longer existed. It was torn down to the ground and replaced (by a house marginally larger) a year after we sold it. The day we happened to be in Los Angeles and drove past the corner of Chadbourne and Marlboro and saw nothing left standing except the one chimney that allowed a tax advantage, I remembered the real estate agent telling me how meaningful it would be to the buyers were we to give them suitably inscribed copies of the books we had written in the house. We had done this. *Quintana and Friends*, *Dutch Shea, Jr.*, and *The Red White and Blue* for John, *Salvador*, *Democracy*, and *Miami* for me. When we saw the flattened lot from the car, Quintana, in the back seat, burst into tears. My first reaction was fury. I wanted the books back.

Did this corrective line of thinking stop the vortex?

Not hardly.

One morning when Quintana was still in the step-down unit because the persistence of her fever necessitated an echocardiogram to rule out endocarditis she lifted her right hand for the first time. This was significant because it was on the right side of her body that the effects of the trauma could be seen. Movement meant that the traumatized nerves remained alive. Later that day she kept wanting to get out of bed, and fell into a sulk like a child when I said I would not help her. My memory of that day is not at all mudgy.

It was decided in late April that sufficient time had passed since the surgery to allow her to fly to New York. The issue until then had been pressurization and the potential it presented for swelling. She would need trained personnel to accompany her. A commercial flight was ruled out. Arrangements were made to medevac her: an ambulance from UCLA to an airport, an air ambulance to Teterboro, and an ambulance from Teterboro to New York University Hospital, where she would do neuro-rehab at the Rusk Institute. Many conversations were held between UCLA and Rusk. Many records were faxed. A CD-ROM of CT scans was prepared. A date was set for what even I was now calling "the transfer": Thursday, April 29. Early that Thursday morning as I was about to check out of the Beverly Wilshire I got a call from somewhere in Colorado. The flight had been delayed. The plane was in Tucson, where it had landed with "mechanical difficulties." The mechanics in Tucson would look at it when they came in, at ten mountain time. By early afternoon Pacific time it was clear that the plane would not be flying. Another plane would be available the next morning, but the next morning was a Friday, and UCLA did not like to transfer on Fridays. At the hospital I pressed the discharge coordinator to agree to the Friday transfer.

To delay the transfer into the following week could only dispirit and confuse Quintana, I said, sure of my ground.

Rusk had no problem with a Friday night admission, I said, less sure.

There was nowhere I could stay over the weekend, I lied.

By the time the discharge coordinator had agreed to the Friday transfer Quintana was asleep. I sat for a while in the sun on the plaza outside the hospital and watched a helicopter circling to land on the roof. Helicopters were always landing on the roof at UCLA, suggesting trauma all over Southern California, remote scenes of highway carnage, distant falling cranes, bad days ahead for the husband or wife or mother or father who had not yet (even as the helicopter landed and the trauma team rushed the stretcher into triage) gotten the call. I remembered a summer day in 1970 when John and I stopped for a red light on St. Charles Avenue in New Orleans and noticed the driver of the next car suddenly slump over his steering wheel. His horn sounded. Several pedestrians ran up. A police officer materialized. The light changed, we drove on. John had been unable to get this image out of his mind. There he was, he had kept saying later. He was alive and then he was dead and we were watching. We saw him at the instant it happened. We knew he was dead before his family did.

Just an ordinary day.

"And then—gone."

The day of the flight, when it came, had seemed to unfold with the nonsequential inexorability of a dream. When I turned on the news in the early morning there was a guerrilla action on the freeways, truckers protesting the price of gasoline. Huge semi trucks had been deliberately jackknifed and abandoned on Interstate 5. Witnesses reported that the first semis to stop had carried the TV crews. SUVs had been waiting to take the truckers themselves from the blocked freeway. The video as I watched it had seemed dislocatingly French, 1968. "Avoid the 5 if you can," the newscaster advised, then warned that according to "sources" (presumably the same TV crews who were traveling with the truckers) the truckers would also block other freeways, specifically the 710, the 60, and the 10. In the normal course of this kind of disruption it would have seemed unlikely that we could get from UCLA to the plane, but by the time the ambulance arrived at the hospital the entire French event seemed to have dematerialized, that phase of the dream forgotten.

There were other phases to come. I had been told the plane would be at Santa Monica Airport. The ambulance crew had been told Burbank. Someone made a call and was told Van Nuys. When we reached Van Nuys there were no planes in sight, only helicopters. That must be because you're going by helicopter, one of the ambulance attendants said, clearly ready to hand us off and get on with his day. I don't think so, I said, it's three thousand miles. The ambulance attendant shrugged and disappeared. The plane was located, a jet Cessna with room for the two pilots, the two paramedics, the stretcher to which Quintana was strapped, and, if I sat on a bench over the oxygen canisters, me. We took off. We flew for a while. One of the paramedics had a digital camera and was taking pictures of what he kept referring to as the Grand Canyon. I said I believed it was Lake Mead, Hoover Dam. I pointed out Las Vegas.

The paramedic continued taking pictures.

He also continued referring to it as the Grand Canyon.

Why do you always have to be right, I remembered John saying.

It was a complaint, a charge, part of a fight.

He never understood that in my own mind I was never right. Once in 1971, when we were moving from Franklin Avenue to Malibu, I found a message stuck behind a picture I was taking down. The message was from someone to whom I had been close before I married John. He had spent a few weeks with us in the house on Franklin Avenue. This was the message: "You were wrong." I did not know what I had been wrong about but the possibilities seemed infinite. I burned the message. I never mentioned it to John.

All right it's the Grand Canyon, I thought, shifting position on the bench over the oxygen canisters so that I could no longer see out the window.

Later we landed in a cornfield in Kansas to refuel. The pilots struck a deal with the two teenagers who managed the airstrip: during the refueling they would take their pickup to a McDonald's and bring back hamburgers. While we waited the paramedics suggested that we take turns getting some exercise. When my turn came I stood frozen on the tarmac for a moment, ashamed to be free and outside when Quintana could not be, then walked to where the runway ended and the corn started. There was a little rain and unstable air and I imagined a tornado coming. Quintana and I were Dorothy. We were both free. In fact we were out of here. John had written a tornado into *Nothing Lost.* I remembered reading the last-pass galleys in Quintana's room at Presbyterian and crying when I hit the passage with the tornado. The protagonists, J.J. McClure and Teresa Kean, see the tornado "in the far distance, black and then milky when the sun caught it, moving like a huge reticulated vertical snake." J.J. tells Teresa not to worry, this stretch had been hit before, twisters never hit the same place twice.

> The tornado finally set down without incident just across the Wyoming line. That night in the Step Right Inn, at the junction between Higginson and Higgins, Teresa asked if it was true that tornadoes never hit the same place twice. "I don't know," J.J. said. "It seemed logical. Like lightning. You were worried. I didn't want you worried." It was as close a declaration of love as J.J. was capable of making.

Back in the plane, alone with Quintana, I took one of the hamburgers the teenagers had brought and tore it into pieces so that she and I could share. After a few bites she shook her head. She had been allowed solid food for only a week or so and could not eat more. There was still a feeding tube in place in case she could not eat at all.

"Am I going to make it," she asked then.

I chose to believe that she was asking if she would make it to New York.

"Definitely," I told her.

I'm here. You're safe.

Definitely she would be okay in California, I remembered telling her five weeks before.

That night when we arrived at the Rusk Institute Gerry and Tony were waiting outside to meet the ambulance. Gerry asked how the flight had been. I said that we had shared a Big Mac in a cornfield in Kansas. "It wasn't a Big Mac," Quintana said. "It was a Quarter Pounder."

It had seemed to me on the day in Quintana's room at Presbyterian when I read the final proof for *Nothing Lost* that there might be a grammatical error in the last sentence of the passage about J.J. McClure and Teresa Kean and the tornado. I never actually learned the rules of grammar, relying instead only on what sounded right, but there was something here that I was not sure sounded right. The sentence in the last-pass galleys read: "It was as close a declaration of love as J.J. was capable of making." I would have added a preposition: "It was as close *to* a declaration of love as J.J. was capable of making."

I sat by the window and watched the ice floes on the Hudson and thought about the sentence. *It was as close a declaration of love as J.J. was capable of making.* It was not the kind of sentence, if you had written it, you would want wrong, but neither was it the kind of sentence, if that was the way you had written it, you would want changed. How had he written it? What did he have in mind? How would he want it? The decision was left to me. Any choice I made could carry the potential for abandonment, even betrayal. That was one reason I was crying in Quintana's hospital room. When I got home that night I checked the previous galleys and manuscripts. The error, if it was an error, had been there from the beginning. I left it as it was.

Why do you always have to be right.

Why do you always have to have the last word.

For once in your life just let it go.

12

THE DAY ON WHICH Quintana and I flew east on the Cessna that refueled in the cornfield in Kansas was April 30, 2004. During May and June and the half of July that she spent at the Rusk Institute there was very little I could do for her. I could go down to East Thirty-fourth Street to see her in the late afternoons, and most afternoons I did, but she was in therapy from eight in the morning until four in the afternoon and exhausted by six-thirty or seven. She was medically stable. She could eat, the feeding tube was still in place but no longer necessary. She was beginning to regain movement in her right leg and arm. She was regaining the mobility in her right eye that she needed to read. On weekend days when she did not have therapy Gerry would take her to lunch and a movie in the neighborhood. He would eat dinner with her. Friends would join them for picnic lunches. For as long as she was at Rusk I could water the plants on her windowsill, I could find the marginally different sneakers her therapist had decreed, I could sit with her in the greenhouse off the Rusk lobby watching the koi in the pond, but once she left Rusk I would no longer be able to do even that. She was reaching a point at which she would need once again to be, if she was to recover, on her own.

I determined to spend the summer reaching the same point.

I did not yet have the concentration to work but I could straighten my house, I could get on top of things, I could deal with my unopened mail.

That I was only now beginning the process of mourning did not occur to me.

Until now I had been able only to grieve, not mourn. Grief was passive. Grief happened. Mourning, the act of dealing with grief, required attention. Until now there had been every urgent reason to obliterate any attention that might otherwise have been paid, banish the thought, bring fresh adrenaline to bear on the crisis of the day. I had passed an entire season during which the only words I allowed myself to truly hear were recorded: *Wel*-come to *U-C-L-A*.

I began.

Among the letters and books and magazines that had arrived while I was in Los Angeles was a thick volume called *Lives of '54*, prepared for what was by then the imminent fiftieth reunion of John's class at Princeton. I looked up John's entry. It read: "William Faulkner once said that a writer's obituary should read, 'He wrote books, then he died.' This is not an obit (at least as of 19 September 2002) and I am still writing books. So I'll stick with Faulkner."

I told myself: this was not an obit.

At least as of 19 September 2002.

I closed *Lives of '54*. A few weeks later I opened it again, and leafed through the other entries. One was from Donald H. ("Rummy") Rumsfeld, who noted: "After Princeton, the years seem like a blur, but the days seem more like rapid fire." I thought about this. Another, a three-page reflection by Lancelot L. ("Lon") Farrar, Jr., began: "Arguably our best-shared Princeton memory was Adlai Stevenson's address to the senior banquet."

I also thought about this.

I had been married to a member of the Class of '54 for forty years and he had never mentioned Adlai Stevenson's address to the senior banquet. I tried to think of anything at all he had mentioned about Princeton. He had many times mentioned the misguided entitlement he heard in the words "Princeton in the Nation's Service," the slogan Princeton had adopted from a speech by Woodrow Wilson. Other than that I could think of nothing except his saying a few days after our wedding (why did he say it? how had it come up?) that he had thought the Nassoons absurd. In fact, because he knew it amused me, he would sometimes impersonate the Nassoons in performance: the studied plunge of one hand into a pocket, the swirling of the ice cubes in the imaginary glass, the chin thrust into profile, the slight satisfied smile.

> *As I remember you—*
> *You stood there beside me on a high windy slope—*
> *Our faces to the wind and our hearts full of hope—*

For forty years this song had figured in a private joke between us and I could not remember its name, let alone the rest of its lyrics. Finding the lyrics became a matter of some urgency. I could find only a single reference on the Internet, in an obituary from the *Princeton Alumni Weekly*:

> John MacFadyen '46 *49: John MacFadyen died February 18, 2000, in Damariscotta, Maine, near the village of Head Tide, where he and his wife, Mary-Esther, made their home. The cause of death was pneumonia, but his health failed for some years, particularly after his wife's death in 1977. John came to Princeton from Duluth in the 'accelerated' summer of 1942. Gifted in music and arts, he contributed songs to Triangle, including, "As I Remember You," long a Nassoons favorite. John was the life of any party with a piano. Remembered was his rendition of "Shine, Little Glow Worm," played upside down from under the piano. After U.S. Army service in Japan, he returned to Princeton for a master's of fine arts in architecture. In the New York firm Harrison & Abramowitz, he designed a main United Nations building. John received the Rome Prize in architecture, and, newly wed to Mary-Esther Edge, spent 1952–53 at Rome's American Academy. His private architectural practice, noted especially for the design of the Wolf Trap Center for the Arts outside Washington, was interrupted by his service, during the 1960s, under Gov. Nelson Rockefeller, as executive director of the first state arts council. The class joins his children, Camilla, Luke, William, and John and three grandchildren in mourning the loss of one of our most unforgettable members.

"As I Remember You," long a Nassoons favorite.

But how about the death of Mary-Esther?

And how long ago was it when the life of any party last played "Shine, Little Glow Worm" upside down from under the piano?

What would I give to be able to discuss this with John?

What would I give to be able to discuss anything at all with John? What would I give to be able to say one small thing that made him happy? What would that one small thing be? If I had said it in time would it have worked?

A night or two before he died John asked me if I was aware how many characters died in the novel he had just sent to press, *Nothing Lost*. He had been sitting in his office making a list of them. I added one he had overlooked. Some months after he died I picked up a legal pad on his desk to make a note. On the legal pad, in very faint pencil, his handwriting, was the list. It read:

Teresa Kean
Parlance
Emmett McClure
Jack Broderick
Maurice Dodd
Four people in car
Charlie Buckles
Percy—electric chair (Percy Darrow)
Walden McClure

Why was the pencil so faint, I wondered.

Why would he use a pencil that barely left a mark.

When did he begin seeing himself as dead?

"It's not black and white," a young doctor at Cedars-Sinai Medical Center in Los Angeles had told me, in 1982, about the divide between life and death. We had been standing in an ICU at Cedars watching Nick and Lenny's daughter Dominique, who had the night before been strangled to the point of death. Dominique was lying there in the ICU as if she were asleep but she would not recover. She was breathing only on life support.

Dominique had been the four-year-old at John's and my wedding.

Dominique had been the cousin who supervised Quintana's parties and took her shopping for prom dresses and stayed with her if we were out of town. *Roses are red, violets are blue*, read the card on a glass of flowers Quintana and Dominique left on the kitchen table for our return from one such trip. *I wish you weren't home and Dominique does too. Love, Happy Mother's Day, D & Q.*

I remember thinking that the doctor was wrong. For as long as Dominique lay in this ICU she was alive. She could not keep herself alive unaided but she was alive. That was white. When they turned off the life support there would be a matter of some minutes before her systems shut down and then she would be dead. That was black.

There were no faint traces about dead, no pencil marks.

Any faint traces, any pencil marks, were left "a night or two before he died," or "a week or two before," in any case decisively *before he died.*

There was a divide.

The abrupt finality of this divide was something about which I thought a great deal during the late spring and summer after I came home from UCLA. A close friend, Carolyn Lelyveld, died in May, at Memorial Sloan-Kettering. Tony Dunne's wife, Rosemary Breslin, died in June, at Columbia-Presbyterian. In each of those cases the phrase "after long illness" would have seemed to apply, trailing its misleading suggestion of release, relief, resolution. In each of those long illnesses the possibility of death had been in the picture, in Carolyn's case for some months, in Rosemary's since 1989, when she was thirty-two. Yet having seen the picture in no way deflected, when it came, the swift empty loss of the actual event. It was still black and white. Each of them had been in the last instant alive, and then dead. I realized that I had never believed in the words I had learned as a child in order to be confirmed as an Episcopalian: *I believe in the Holy Ghost, the Holy Catholic Church, the Communion of Saints, the forgiveness of sins, the resurrection of the body, and the life everlasting, amen.*

I did not believe in the resurrection of the body.

Nor had Teresa Kean, Parlance, Emmett McClure, Jack Broderick, Maurice Dodd, the four people in the car, Charlie Buckles, Percy Darrow, or Walden McClure.

Nor had my Catholic husband.

I imagined this way of thinking to be clarifying, but in point of fact it was so muddled as to contradict even itself.

I did not believe in the resurrection of the body but I still believed that given the right circumstances he would come back.

He who left the faint traces before he died, the Number Three pencil.

One day it seemed important that I reread *Alcestis.* I had last read it at sixteen or seventeen, for a paper on Euripides, but recalled it as somehow relevant to this question of the "divide." I remembered the Greeks in general but *Alcestis* in particular as good on the passage between life and death. They visualized it, they dramatized it, they made the dark water and the ferry into the mise-en-scène itself. I did reread *Alcestis.* What happens in the play is this: Admetus, the young king of Thessaly, has been condemned by Death to die. Apollo has interceded, gaining a promise from the Fates that Admetus, if he can find another mortal to die in his place, need not die immediately. Admetus approaches his friends and his parents, in vain. "I tell myself that we are a long time underground and that life is short, but sweet," his father tells him after declining to take his place.

Only the wife of Admetus, the young queen, Alcestis, volunteers. There is much wailing about her approaching death, but no one steps in to save her. She dies, at length: "I see the two-oared boat, / I see the boat on the lake! / And Charon, / Ferryman of the Dead, / Calls to me, his hand on the oar . . ." Admetus is overcome by guilt and shame and self-pity: "Alas! How bitter to me is that ferrying of which you speak! O my unhappy one, how we suffer!" He behaves in every way badly. He blames his parents. He insists that Alcestis is suffering less than he. After some pages (and quite enough) of this, Alcestis, by means of a remarkably (even for 430 B.C.) clumsy deus ex machina, is allowed to come back. She does not speak, but this is explained, again clumsily, as temporary, self-correcting: "You may not hear her voice until she is purified from her consecration to the Lower Gods, and until the third dawn is risen." If we rely on the text alone, the play ends happily.

This was not my memory of *Alcestis*, which suggests that I was already given, at sixteen or seventeen, to editing the text as I read it. The principal divergences between the text and my memory appear toward the end, when Alcestis returns from the dead. In my memory, the reason Alcestis does not speak is that she declines to speak. Admetus, as I remembered it, presses her, at which point, to his distress, since what she turns out to have on her mind are his revealed failings, she does speak. Admetus, alarmed, shuts off the prospect of hearing more by calling for celebration. Alcestis acquiesces, but remains remote, other. Alcestis is on the face of it back with her husband and children, again the young queen of Thessaly, but the ending ("my" ending) could not be construed as happy.

In some ways this is a better (more "worked out") story, one that at least acknowledges that death "changes" the one who has died, but it opens up further questions about the divide. If the dead were truly to come back, what would they come back knowing? Could we face them? We who allowed them to die? The clear light of day tells me that I did not allow John to die, that I did not have that power, but do I believe that? Does he?

Survivors look back and see omens, messages they missed.

They remember the tree that died, the gull that splattered onto the hood of the car.

They live by symbols. They read meaning into the barrage of spam on the unused computer, the delete key that stops working, the imagined abandonment in the decision to replace it. The voice on my answering machine is still John's. The fact that it was his in the first place was arbitrary, having to do with who was around on the day the answering machine last needed programming, but if I needed to retape it now I would do so with a sense of betrayal. One day when I was talking on the telephone in his office I mindlessly turned the pages of the dictionary that he had always left open on the table by the desk. When I realized what I had done I was stricken: what word had he last looked up, what had he been thinking? By turning the pages had I lost the message? Or had the message been lost before I touched the dictionary? Had I refused to hear the message?

I tell you that I shall not live two days, Gawain said.

Later in the summer I received another book from Princeton. It was a first edition copy of *True Confessions*, in, as the booksellers say, "good condition, original dust jacket slightly frayed." In fact it was John's own copy: he had apparently sent it to a classmate who was organizing, for the fiftieth reunion of the Class of 1954, an exhibition of books written by class members. "It occupied the position of honor," the classmate wrote to me, "since John was unquestionably the most distinguished writer in our class."

I studied the original dust jacket, slightly frayed, on the copy of *True Confessions.*

I remembered the first time I saw this jacket, or a mock-up of this jacket. It had sat around our house for days, as proposed designs and type samples and jackets for new books always did, the idea being to gauge whether or not it would wear well, continue to please the eye.

I opened the book. I looked at the dedication. "For Dorothy Burns Dunne, Joan Didion, Quintana Roo Dunne," the dedication read. "Generations."

I had forgotten this dedication. I had *not sufficiently appreciated it*, a persistent theme by that stage of whatever I was going through.

I reread *True Confessions*. I found it darker than I had remembered it. I reread *Harp*. I found a different, less sunny, version of the summer we watched *Tenko* and went to dinner at Morton's.

Something else had happened toward the end of that summer.

In August there had been a memorial service for an acquaintance (this was not in itself the "something else" that happened), a French tennis player in his sixties who had been killed in an accident. The memorial service had been on someone's court in Beverly Hills. "I met my wife at the service," John had written in *Harp*, "coming directly from a doctor's appointment in Santa Monica, and as I sat there under the hot August sun, death was very much on my mind. I thought Anton had actually died under the best possible circumstances for him, a moment of terror as he realized the inevitable outcome of the accident, then an instant later the eternal dark."

> The service ended and the parking attendant brought my car. As we drove away, my wife said, "What did the doctor say?"
>
> There had not been an appropriate moment to mention my visit to the doctor in Santa Monica. "He scared the shit out of me, babe."
>
> "What did he say?"
>
> "He said I was a candidate for a catastrophic cardiac event."

A few pages further in *Harp*, the writer, John, examines the veracity of this (his own) account. He notes a name changed, a certain dramatic restructuring, a minor time collapse. He asks himself: "Anything else?" This was the answer he gave: "When I told my wife he scared the shit out of me, I started to cry."

Either I had not remembered this or I had determinedly chosen not to remember this.

I had *not sufficiently appreciated it.*

Was that what he experienced as he himself died? "A moment of terror as he realized the inevitable outcome of the accident, then an instant later the eternal dark"? In the sense that it happens one night and not another, the mechanism of a typical cardiac arrest could be construed as essentially accidental: a sudden spasm ruptures a deposit of plaque in a coronary artery, ischemia follows, and the heart, deprived of oxygen, enters ventricular fibrillation.

But how did he experience it?

The "moment of terror," the "eternal dark"? Did he accurately intuit this when he was writing *Harp*? Did he, as we would say to each other to the point of whether something was accurately reported or perceived, "get it right"? What about the "eternal dark" part? Didn't the survivors of near-death experiences always mention "the white light"? It occurs to me as I write that this "white light," usually presented dippily (evidence of afterlife, higher power), is in fact precisely consistent with the oxygen deficit that occurs as blood flow to the brain decreases. "Everything went white," those whose blood pressure has dropped say of the instant before they faint. "All the color drained out," those bleeding internally report of the moment when blood loss goes critical.

The "something else" that happened toward the end of that summer, which must have been 1987, was the series of events that followed the appointment with the doctor in Santa Monica and the memorial service on the tennis court in Beverly Hills. A week or so later an angiogram was done. The angiogram showed a 90 percent occlusion of the left anterior descending artery, or LAD. It also showed a long 90 percent narrowing in the circumflex marginal artery, which was considered significant mainly because the circumflex marginal artery fed the same area of the heart as the occluded LAD. "We call it the widow-maker, pal," John's cardiologist in New York later said of the LAD. A week or two after the angiogram (it was by then September of that year, still summer in Los Angeles) an angioplasty was done. The results after two weeks, as demonstrated by an exercise echocardiogram, were said to be "spectacular." Another exercise echo after six months confirmed this success. Thallium scans over the next few years and a subsequent angiogram in 1991 gave the same confirmation. I recall that John and I took different views of what had happened in 1987. As he saw it, he now had a death sentence, temporarily suspended. He often said, after the 1987 angioplasty, that he now knew how he was going to die. As I saw it, the timing had been providential, the intervention successful, the problem solved, the mechanism fixed. You no more know how you're going to die than I do or anyone else does, I remember saying. I realize now that his was the more realistic view.

13

I USED TO TELL JOHN my dreams, not to understand them but to get rid of them, clear my mind for the day. "Don't tell me your dream," he would say when I woke in the morning, but in the end he would listen.

When he died I stopped having dreams.

In the early summer I began to dream again, for the first time since it happened. Since I can no longer pass them off to John I find myself thinking about them. I remember a passage from a novel I wrote in the mid-1990s, *The Last Thing He Wanted*:

> Of course we would not need those last six notes to know what Elena's dreams were about.
>
> Elena's dreams were about dying.
>
> Elena's dreams were about getting old.
>
> Nobody here has not had (will not have) Elena's dreams.
>
> We all know that.
>
> The point is that Elena didn't.
>
> The point is that Elena remained remote most of all to herself, a clandestine agent who had so successfully compartmentalized her operation as to have lost access to her own cutouts.

I realize that Elena's situation is my own.

In one dream I am hanging a braided belt in a closet when it breaks. About a third of the belt just drops off in my hands. I show the two pieces to John. I say (or he says, who knows in dreams) that this was his favorite belt. I determine (again, I think I determine, I should have determined, my half-waking mind tells me to do the right thing) to find him an identical braided belt.

In other words to fix what I broke, *bring him back*.

The similarity of this broken braided belt to the one I found in the plastic bag I was given at New York Hospital does not escape my attention. Nor does the fact that I am still thinking *I broke it, I did it, I am responsible.*

In another dream John and I are flying to Honolulu. Many other people are going, we have assembled at Santa Monica

Airport. Paramount has arranged planes. Production assistants are distributing boarding passes. I board. There is confusion. Others are boarding but there is no sign of John. I worry that there is a problem with his boarding pass. I decide that I should leave the plane, wait for him in the car. While I am waiting in the car I realize that the planes are taking off, one by one. Finally there is no one but me on the tarmac. My first thought in the dream is anger: John has boarded a plane without me. My second thought transfers the anger: Paramount has not cared enough about us to put us on the same plane.

What "Paramount" was doing in this dream would require another discussion, not relevant.

As I think about the dream I remember *Tenko. Tenko*, as the series progresses, takes its imprisoned Englishwomen through their liberation from the Japanese camp and their reunions in Singapore with their husbands, which do not go uniformly well. There seemed for some a level at which the husband was held responsible for the ordeal of imprisonment. There seemed a sense, however irrational, of having been abandoned. Did I feel abandoned, left behind on the tarmac, did I feel anger at John for leaving me? Was it possible to feel anger and simultaneously to feel responsible?

I know the answer a psychiatrist would give to that question.

The answer would have to do with the well-known way in which anger creates guilt and vice versa.

I do not disbelieve this answer but it remains less suggestive to me than the unexamined image, the mystery of being left alone on the tarmac at Santa Monica Airport watching the planes take off one by one.

We all know that.

The point is that Elena didn't.

I wake at what seems to be three-thirty in the morning and find a television set on, MSNBC. Either Joe Scarborough or Keith Olbermann is talking to a husband and wife, passengers on a flight from Detroit to Los Angeles, "Northwest 327" (I actually write this down, to tell to John), on which "a terrorist tryout" is said to have occurred. The incident seems to have involved fourteen men said to be "Arabs" who, at some point after takeoff from Detroit, began gathering outside the coach lavatory, entering one by one.

The couple now being interviewed on-screen reports having exchanged signals with the crew.

The plane landed in Los Angeles. The "Arabs," all fourteen of whom had "expired visas" (this seemed to strike MSNBC as more unusual than it struck me), were detained, then released. Everyone, including the couple on-screen, had gone about their day. It was not, then, "a terrorist attack," which seemed to be what made it "a terrorist tryout."

I need in the dream to discuss this with John.

Or was it even a dream?

Who is the director of dreams, would he care?

Was it only by dreaming or writing that I could find out what I thought?

When the twilights got long in June I forced myself to eat dinner in the living room, where the light was. After John died I had begun eating by myself in the kitchen (the dining room was too big and the table in the living room was where he had died), but when the long twilights came I had a strong sense that he would want me to see the light. As the twilights began to shorten I retreated again to the kitchen. I began spending more evenings alone at home. I was working, I would say. By the time August came I was in fact working, or trying to work, but I also wanted not to be out, exposed. One night I found myself taking from the cupboard not one of the plates I normally used but a crackled and worn Spode plate, from a set mostly broken or chipped, in a pattern no longer made, "Wickerdale." This had been a set of dishes, cream with a garland of small rose and blue flowers and ecru leaves, that John's mother had given him for the apartment he rented on East Seventy-third Street before we were married. John's mother was dead. John was dead. And I still had, of the "Wickerdale" Spode, four dinner plates, five salad plates, three butter plates, a single coffee cup, and nine saucers. I came to prefer these dishes to all others. By the end of the summer I was running the dishwasher a quarter full just to make sure that at least one of the four "Wickerdale" dinner plates would be clean when I needed it.

At a point during the summer it occurred to me that I had no letters from John, not one. We had only rarely been far or long apart. There had been the week or two or three here and there when one of us was doing a piece. There had been a month in 1975 when I taught at Berkeley during the week and flew home to Los Angeles on PSA every weekend. There had been a few weeks in 1988 when John was in Ireland doing research for *Harp* and I was in California covering the presidential primary. On all such occasions we had spoken on the telephone several times a day. We counted high telephone bills as part of our deal with each other, the same way we counted high bills for the hotels that enabled us to take Quintana out of school and fly somewhere and both work at the same time in the same suite. What I had instead of letters was a souvenir of one such hotel suite: a small black wafer-thin alarm clock he gave me one Christmas in Honolulu when we were doing a crash rewrite on a picture that never got made. It was one of those many Christmases on which we exchanged not "presents" but small practical things to make a tree. This alarm clock had stopped working during the year before he died, could not be repaired, and, after he died, could not be thrown out. It could not even be removed from the table by my bed. I also had a set of colored Buffalo pens, given to me the same Christmas, in the same spirit. I did many sketches of palm trees that Christmas, palm trees moving in the wind, palm trees dropping fronds, palm trees bent by the December *kona* storms. The colored Buffalo pens had long since gone dry, but, again, could not be thrown out.

I remember having had on that particular New Year's Eve in Honolulu a sense of well-being so profound that I did not want to go to sleep. We had ordered mahimahi and Manoa lettuce vinaigrette for the three of us from room service. We had tried for a festive effect by arranging leis over the printers and computers we were using for the rewrite. We had found candles and lit them and played the tapes Quintana had wrapped up to put under the tree. John had been reading on the bed and had fallen asleep about eleven-thirty. Quintana had gone downstairs to see what was happening. I could see John sleeping. I knew Quintana was safe, she had been going downstairs to see what was happening in this hotel (sometimes alone, sometimes with Susan Traylor, who often came along with Quintana when we were working in Honolulu) since she was six or seven years old. I sat on a balcony overlooking the Waialae Country Club golf course and finished the bottle of wine we had drunk with dinner and watched the neighborhood fireworks all over Honolulu.

I remember one last present from John. It was my birthday, December 5, 2003. Snow had begun falling in New York around ten that morning and by evening seven inches had accumulated, with another six due. I remember snow avalanching off the slate roof at St. James' Church across the street. A plan to meet Quintana and Gerry at a restaurant was canceled. Before dinner John sat by the fire in the living room and read to me out loud. The book from which he read was a novel of my own, *A Book of Common Prayer*, which he happened to have in the living room because he was rereading it to see how something worked technically. The sequence he read out loud was one in which Charlotte Douglas's husband Leonard pays a visit to the narrator, Grace Strasser-Mendana, and lets her know that what is happening in the country her family runs will not end well. The sequence is complicated (this was in fact the sequence John had meant to reread to see how it worked technically), broken by other action and requiring the reader to pick up the undertext in what Leonard Douglas and Grace Strasser-Mendana say to each other. "Goddamn," John said to me when he closed the book. "Don't ever tell me again you can't write. That's my birthday present to you."

I remember tears coming to my eyes.

I feel them now.

In retrospect this had been my omen, my message, the early snowfall, the birthday present no one else could give me.

He had twenty-five nights left to live.

14

THERE CAME A TIME in the summer when I began feeling fragile, unstable. A sandal would catch on a sidewalk and I would need to run a few steps to avoid the fall. What if I didn't? What if I fell? What would break, who would see the blood streaming down my leg, who would get the taxi, who would be with me in the emergency room? Who would be with me once I came home?

I stopped wearing sandals. I bought two pairs of Puma sneakers and wore them exclusively.

I started leaving lights on through the night. If the house was dark I could not get up to make a note or look for a book or check to make sure I had turned off the stove. If the house was dark I would lie there immobilized, entertaining visions of household peril, the books that could slide from the shelf and knock me down, the rug that could slip in the hallway, the washing machine hose that could have flooded the kitchen unseen in the dark, the better to electrocute whoever turned on a light to check the stove. That this was something more than prudent caution first came to my attention one afternoon when an acquaintance, a young writer, came by to ask if he could write a profile about me. I heard myself say, too urgent, that I could not possibly be written about. I was in no shape to be written about. I heard myself overstressing this, fighting to regain balance, avert the fall.

I thought about this later.

I realized that for the time being I could not trust myself to present a coherent face to the world.

Some days later I was stacking some copies of *Daedalus* that were lying around the house. Stacking magazines seemed at that point the limit of what I could do by way of organizing my life. Careful not to push this limit too far, I opened one of the copies of *Daedalus*. There was a story by Roxana Robinson, called "Blind Man." In this story, a man is driving in the rain at night to deliver a lecture. The reader picks up danger signals: the man cannot immediately recall the subject of his lecture, he takes his small rented car into the fast lane oblivious to an approaching SUV; there are references to someone, "Juliet," to whom something troubling has happened. Gradually we learn that Juliet was the man's daughter, who, on her first night alone after a college suspension and rehab and a restorative few weeks in the country with her mother and father and sister, had done enough cocaine to burst an artery in her brain and die.

One of the several levels on which the story disturbed me (the most obvious being the burst artery in the child's brain) was this: the father has been rendered fragile, unstable. The father is me.

In fact I know Roxana Robinson slightly. I think of calling her. She knows something I am just beginning to learn. But it would be unusual, intrusive, to call her: I have met her only once, at a cocktail party on a roof. Instead I think about people I know who have lost a husband or wife or child. I think particularly about how these people looked when I saw them unexpectedly—on the street, say, or entering a room—during the year or so after the death. What struck me in each instance was how exposed they seemed, how raw.

How fragile, I understand now.

How unstable.

I open another issue of *Daedalus*, this one devoted to the concept of "happiness." One piece on happiness, the joint work of Robert Biswas-Diener of the University of Oregon and Ed Diener and Maya Tamir of the University of Illinois, Champaign-Urbana, noted that although "research has shown that people can adapt to a wide range of good and bad life events in less than two months," there remained "some events to which people are slow or unable to adapt completely." Unemployment was one such event. "We also find," the authors added, "that it takes the average widow many years after her spouse's death to regain her former level of life satisfaction."

Was I "the average widow"? What in fact would have been my "former level of life satisfaction"?

I see a doctor, a routine follow-up. He asks how I am. This should not be, in a doctor's office, an unforeseeable question. Yet I find myself in sudden tears. This doctor is a friend. John and I went to his wedding. He married the daughter of friends who lived across the street from us in Brentwood Park. The ceremony took place under their jacaranda tree. In the first days after John died this doctor had come by the house. When Quintana was at Beth Israel North he had gone up with me on a Sunday afternoon and talked to the doctors on the unit. When Quintana was at Columbia-Presbyterian, his own hospital although she was not his patient, he had stopped in to see her every evening. When Quintana was at UCLA and he happened to be in California he had taken an afternoon to come by the neuroscience unit and talk to the doctors there. He had talked to them and then he had talked to the neuro people at Columbia and then he had explained it all to me. He had been kind, helpful, encouraging, a true friend. In return I was crying in his office because he asked how I was.

"I just can't see the upside in this," I heard myself say by way of explanation.

Later he said that if John had been sitting in the office he would have found this funny, as he himself had found it. "Of course I knew what you meant to say, and John would have known too, you meant to say you couldn't see the light at the end of the tunnel."

I agreed, but this was not in fact the case.

I had meant pretty much exactly what I said: I couldn't see the upside in this.

As I thought about the difference between the two sentences I realized that my impression of myself had been of someone who could look for, and find, the upside in any situation. I had believed in the logic of popular songs. I had looked for the silver lining. I had walked on through the storm. It occurs to me now that these were not even the songs of my generation. They were the songs, and the logic, of the generation or two that preceded my own. The score for my generation was Les Paul and Mary Ford, "How High the Moon," a different logic altogether. It also occurs to me, not an original thought but novel to me, that the logic of those earlier songs was based on self-pity. The singer of the song about looking for the silver lining believes that clouds have come her way. The singer of the song about walking on through the storm assumes that the storm could otherwise take her down.

I kept saying to myself that I had been lucky all my life. The point, as I saw it, was that this gave me no right to think of myself as unlucky now.

This was what passed for staying on top of the self-pity question.

I even believed it.

Only at a later point did I begin to wonder: what exactly did "luck" have to do with it? I could not on examination locate any actual instances of "luck" in my history. ("That was lucky," I once said to a doctor after a test revealed a soluble problem that would have been, untreated, less soluble. "I wouldn't call it lucky," she said, "I'd call it the game plan.") Nor did I believe that "bad luck" had killed John and struck Quintana. Once when she was still at the Westlake School for Girls, Quintana mentioned what she seemed to consider the inequable distribution of bad news. In the ninth grade she had come home from a retreat at Yosemite to learn that her uncle Stephen had committed suicide. In the eleventh grade she had been woken at Susan's at six-thirty in the morning to learn that Dominique had been murdered. "Most people I know at Westlake don't even know anyone who died," she said, "and just since I've been there I've had a murder and a suicide in my family."

"It all evens out in the end," John said, an answer that bewildered me (what did it mean, couldn't he do better than that?) but one that seemed to satisfy her.

Several years later, after Susan's mother and father died within a year or two of each other, Susan asked if I remembered John telling Quintana that it all evened out in the end. I said I remembered.

"He was right," Susan said. "It did."

I recall being shocked. It had never occurred to me that John meant that bad news will come to each of us. Either Susan or Quintana had surely misunderstood. I explained to Susan that John had meant something entirely different: he had meant that people who get bad news will eventually get their share of good news.

"That's not what I meant at all," John said.

"I knew what he meant," Susan said.

Had I understood nothing?

Consider this matter of "luck."

Not only did I not believe that "bad luck" had killed John and struck Quintana but in fact I believed precisely the opposite: I believed that I should have been able to prevent whatever happened. Only after the dream about being left on the tarmac at the Santa Monica Airport did it occur to me that there was a level on which I was not actually holding myself responsible. I was holding John and Quintana responsible, a significant difference but not one that took me anywhere I needed to be. *For once in your life just let it go.*

15

A FEW MONTHS AFTER JOHN died, in the late winter of 2004, after Beth Israel and Presbyterian but before UCLA, I was asked by Robert Silvers at *The New York Review of Books* if I wanted him to submit my name for credentials to cover the Democratic and Republican summer conventions. I had looked at the dates: late July in Boston for the Democratic convention, the week before Labor Day in New York for the Republican convention. I had said yes. At the time it had seemed a way of committing to a normal life without needing actually to live it for another season or two, until spring had come and summer had come and fall was near.

Spring had come and gone, largely at UCLA.

In the middle of July Quintana was discharged from the Rusk Institute.

Ten days later I went to Boston for the Democratic convention. I had not anticipated that my new fragility would travel to Boston, a city devoid, I thought, of potentially tricky associations. I had been with Quintana in Boston only once, on a book tour. We had stayed at the Ritz. Her favorite stop on this tour had been Dallas. She had found Boston "all white." "You mean you didn't see many black people in Boston," Susan Traylor's mother had said when Quintana got back to Malibu and reported on her trip. "No," Quintana had said. "I mean it's not in color." The last several times I had needed to be in Boston I had gone alone, and in each case arranged the day so as to get the last shuttle back; the single time I could remember being there with John was for a preview of *True Confessions*, and all I remembered of that was having lunch at the Ritz and walking with John to Brooks Brothers to pick up a shirt and hearing, after the picture was shown and the response evaluated, this disheartening assessment of its commercial prospects: *True Confessions* could do very well, the market researcher said, among adults with sixteen-plus years of education.

I would not be staying at the Ritz.

There would be no need to go to Brooks Brothers.

There would be market researchers, but what bad news they delivered would not be mine.

I did not realize that there was still room for error until I was walking to the Fleet Center for the opening of the convention and found myself in tears. The first day of the Democratic convention was July 26, 2004. The day of Quintana's wedding had been July 26, 2003. Even as I waited in the security line, even as I picked up releases in the press center, even as I located my seat and stood for the national anthem, even as I bought a hamburger at the McDonald's in the Fleet Center and sat on the lowest step of a barricaded stairway to eat it, the details sprang back. "In another world" was the phrase that would not leave my mind. Quintana sitting in the sunlight in the living room having her hair braided. John asking me which of two ties I preferred. Opening the boxes of flowers on the grass outside the cathedral and shaking the water off the leis. John giving a toast before Quintana cut the cake. The pleasure he took in the day and the party and her transparent happiness. "More than one more day," he had whispered to her before he walked her to the altar.

"More than one more day," he had whispered to her on the five days and nights he saw her in the Beth Israel North ICU.

"More than one more day," I had whispered to her in his absence on the days and nights that followed.

As you used to say to me, she had said when she stood in her black dress at St. John the Divine on the day we committed his ashes.

I recall being seized by the overwhelming conviction that I needed to get out of the Fleet Center, now. I have only rarely experienced panic but what set in next was recognizably panic. I remember trying to calm myself by seeing it as a Hitchcock movie, every shot planned to terrify but ultimately artifice, a game. There was the proximity of my assigned section to the netting that held the balloons for the balloon drop. There were the shadowy silhouettes moving on the high catwalks. There was the steam or smoke leaking from a vent over the sky boxes. There were, once I fled my seat, the corridors that seemed to go nowhere, mysteriously emptied, the walls slanted and distorted (the Hitchcock movie I was seeing would have to be *Spellbound*) ahead of me. There were the immobilized escalators. There were the elevators that did not respond to the push of the button. There were, once I managed to get downstairs, the empty commuter trains frozen in place beyond the locked glass wall (again, slanted and distorted as I approached it) that opened to the North Station tracks.

I got out of the Fleet Center.

I watched the end of that night's session on television in my room at the Parker House. There had seemed about this room at the Parker House when I first walked into it the day before something déjà vu, which I had put from my mind. Only now, as I was watching C-SPAN and listening to the air conditioner cycle on and off on its own schedule, did I remember: I had stayed in just such a room at the Parker House for a few nights between my junior and senior years at Berkeley. I had been in New York for a college promotion *Mademoiselle* then ran (the "Guest Editor" program, memorialized by Sylvia Plath in *The Bell Jar*) and was returning to California via Boston and Quebec, an "educational" itinerary arranged, in retrospect dreamily, by my mother. The air conditioner had been cycling on and off on its own schedule even in 1955. I could remember sleeping until afternoon, miserable, then taking a subway to Cambridge, where I must have walked around aimlessly and taken the subway back.

These shards from 1955 were coming to me in such shredded (or "spotty," or even "mudgy") form (what did I do in Cambridge, what possibly could I have done in Cambridge?) that I had trouble holding them, but I tried, because for so long as I was thinking about the summer of 1955 I would not be thinking about John or Quintana.

In the summer of 1955 I had taken a train from New York to Boston.

In the summer of 1955 I had taken another train from Boston to Quebec. I stayed in a room at the Château Frontenac that did not have its own bathtub.

Did mothers always try to press on their daughters the itineraries of which they themselves had dreamed?

Did I?

This was not working.

I tried going further back, earlier than 1955, to Sacramento, high school dances at Christmastime. This felt safe. I thought about the way we danced, close. I thought about the places on the river we went after the dances. I thought about the fog on the levee driving home.

I fell asleep maintaining focus on the fog on the levee.

I woke at four A.M. The point about the fog on the levee was that you couldn't see the white line, someone had to walk ahead to guide the driver. Unfortunately there had been another place in my life where the fog got so thick that I had to walk ahead of the car.

The house on the Palos Verdes Peninsula.

The one to which we brought Quintana when she was three days old.

When you came off the Harbor Freeway and through San Pedro and onto the drive above the sea you hit the fog.

You (I) got out of the car to walk the white line.

The driver of the car was John.

I did not risk waiting for the panic to follow. I got a taxi to Logan. I avoided looking, as I bought a coffee at the Starbucks franchise outside the Delta shuttle, at its decorative garland of red-white-and-blue foil strips, presumably conceived as a festive "convention" touch but instead glittering forlornly, Christmas in the tropics. *Mele Kalikimaka*. Merry Christmas in Hawaiian. The little black alarm clock I could not throw away. The dried-out Buffalo pens I could not throw away. On the flight to LaGuardia I remember thinking that the most beautiful things I had ever seen had all been seen from airplanes. The way the American west opens up. The way in which, on a polar flight across the Arctic, the islands in the sea give way imperceptibly to lakes on the land. The sea between Greece and Cyprus in the morning. The Alps on the way to Milan. I saw all those things with John.

How could I go back to Paris without him, how could I go back to Milan, Honolulu, Bogotá?

I couldn't even go to Boston.

A week or so before the Democratic convention, Dennis Overbye of *The New York Times* had reported a story involving Stephen W. Hawking. At a conference in Dublin, according to the *Times*, Dr. Hawking said that he had been wrong thirty years before when he asserted that information swallowed by a black hole could never be retrieved from it. This change of mind was "of great consequence to science," according to the *Times*, "because if Dr. Hawking had been right, it would have violated a basic tenet of modern physics: that it is always possible to reverse time, run the proverbial film backward and reconstruct what happened in, say, the collision of two cars or the collapse of a dead star into a black hole."

I had clipped this story, and carried it with me to Boston.

Something in the story seemed urgent to me, but I did not know what it was until a month later, the first afternoon of the Republican convention in Madison Square Garden. I was on the Tower C escalator. The last time I had been on such an escalator in the Garden was with John, in November, the night before we flew to Paris. We had gone with David and Jean Halberstam to see the Lakers play the Knicks. David had gotten seats through the commissioner of the NBA, David Stern. The Lakers won. Rain had been sluicing down the glass beyond the escalator. "It's good luck, an omen, a great way to start this trip," I remembered John saying. He did not mean the good seats and he did not mean the Laker win and he did not mean the rain, he meant we were doing something we did not ordinarily do, which had become an issue with him. We were not having any fun, he had recently begun pointing out. I would take exception (didn't we do this, didn't we do that) but I had also known what he meant. He meant doing things not because we were expected to do them or had always done them or should do them but because we wanted to do them. He meant wanting. He meant living.

This trip to Paris was the one over which we had fought.

This trip to Paris was the one he said he needed to take because otherwise he would never see Paris again.

I was still on the Tower C escalator.

Another vortex revealed itself.

The last time I covered a convention at Madison Square Garden had been 1992, the Democratic convention.

John would wait until I came uptown at eleven or so to have dinner with me. We would walk to Coco Pazzo on those hot July nights and split an order of pasta and a salad at one of the little unreserved tables in the bar. I do not think we ever discussed the convention during these late dinners. On the Sunday afternoon before it began I had talked him into going uptown with me to a Louis Farrakhan event that never materialized, and between the improvisational nature of the scheduling and the walk back downtown from 125th Street his tolerance for the 1992 Democratic convention was pretty much exhausted.

Still.

He waited every night to eat with me.

I thought about all this on the Tower C escalator and suddenly it occurred to me: I had spent a minute or two on this escalator thinking about the November night in 2003 before we flew to Paris and about those July nights in 1992 when we would eat late at Coco Pazzo and about the afternoon we had stood around 125th Street waiting for the Louis Farrakhan event that never happened. I had stood on this escalator thinking about those days and nights without once thinking I could change their outcome. I realized that since the last morning of 2003, the morning after he died, I had been trying to reverse time, run the film backward.

It was now eight months later, August 30, 2004, and I still was.

The difference was that all through those eight months I had been trying to substitute an alternate reel. Now I was trying only to reconstruct the collision, the collapse of the dead star.

16

I SAID I KNEW what John meant when he said we were not having any fun.

What he meant was something that had to do with Joe and Gertrude Black, a couple we had met in Indonesia in December 1980. We were there on a USIA trip, giving lectures and meeting Indonesian writers and academics. The Blacks had shown up in a classroom one morning at Gadjah Mada University in Jogjakarta, an American couple apparently at home in the remote and in many ways alien tropic of central Java, their faces open and strikingly luminous. "The critical theories of Mr. I. A. Richards," I remember a student asking me that morning. "What think?" Joe Black was then in his fifties, Gertrude a year or two younger but again, I suppose in her fifties. He had retired from the Rockefeller Foundation and come to Jogjakarta to teach political science at Gadjah Mada. He had grown up in Utah. As a young man he had been an extra in John Ford's *Fort Apache*. He and Gertrude had four children, one of whom had been, he said, hit hard by the 1960s. We talked to the Blacks only twice, once at Gadjah Mada and a day later at the airport, when they came to see us off, but each of these conversations was curiously open, as if we had found ourselves stranded together on an island. Over the years John mentioned Joe and Gertrude Black frequently, in each case as exemplary, what he thought of as the best kind of American. They represented something personal to him. They were models for the life he wanted us eventually to live. Because he had mentioned them again a few days before he died I searched his computer for their names. I found the names in a file called "AAA Random Thoughts," one of the files in which he kept notes for the book he was trying to get off the ground. The note after their names was cryptic: "Joe and Gertrude Black: The concept of service."

I knew what he meant by that too.

He had wanted to be Joe and Gertrude Black. So had I. We hadn't made it. "Fritter away" was a definition in the crossword that morning. The word it defined was five letters, "waste."

Was that what we had done? Was that what he thought we had done?

Why didn't I listen when he said we weren't having any fun?

Why didn't I move to change our life?

According to the computer dating the file called "AAA Random Thoughts" was last amended at 1:08 P.M. on December 30, 2003, the day of his death, six minutes after I saved the file that ended *how does "flu" morph into whole-body infection.* He would have been in his office and I would have been in mine. I cannot stop where this leads me. We should have been together. Not necessarily in a classroom in central Java (I do not have a sufficiently deluded view of either of us to see that scenario intact, nor was a classroom in central Java what he meant) but together. The file called "AAA Random Thoughts" was eighty pages long. What it was he added or amended and saved at 1:08 P.M. that afternoon I have no way of knowing.

17

GRIEF TURNS OUT to be a place none of us know until we reach it. We anticipate (we know) that someone close to us could die, but we do not look beyond the few days or weeks that immediately follow such an imagined death. We misconstrue the nature of even those few days or weeks. We might expect if the death is sudden to feel shock. We do not expect this shock to be obliterative, dislocating to both body and mind. We might expect that we will be prostrate, inconsolable, crazy with loss. We do not expect to be literally crazy, cool customers who believe that their husband is about to return and need his shoes. In the version of grief we imagine, the model will be "healing." A certain forward movement will prevail. The worst days will be the earliest days. We imagine that the moment to most severely test us will be the funeral, after which this hypothetical healing will take place. When we anticipate the funeral we wonder about failing to "get through it," rise to the occasion, exhibit the "strength" that invariably gets mentioned as the correct response to death. We anticipate needing to steel ourselves for the moment: will I be able to greet people, will I be able to leave the scene, will I be able even to get dressed that day? We have no way of knowing that this will not be the issue. We have no way of knowing that the funeral itself will be anodyne, a kind of narcotic regression in which we are wrapped in the care of others and the gravity and meaning of the occasion. Nor can we know ahead of the fact (and here lies the heart of the difference between grief as we imagine it and grief as it is) the unending absence that follows, the void, the very opposite of meaning, the relentless succession of moments during which we will confront the experience of meaninglessness itself.

As a child I thought a great deal about meaninglessness, which seemed at the time the most prominent negative feature on the horizon. After a few years of failing to find meaning in the more commonly recommended venues I learned that I could find it in geology, so I did. This in turn enabled me to find meaning in the Episcopal litany, most acutely in the words *as it was in the beginning, is now and ever shall be, world without end*, which I interpreted as a literal description of the constant changing of the earth, the unending erosion of the shores and mountains, the inexorable shifting of the geological structures that could throw up mountains and islands and could just as reliably take them away. I found earthquakes, even when I was in them, deeply satisfying, abruptly revealed evidence of the scheme in action. That the scheme could destroy the works of man might be a personal regret but remained, in the larger picture I had come to recognize, a matter of abiding indifference. No eye was on the sparrow. No one was watching me. *As it was in the beginning, is now and ever shall be, world without end.* On the day it was announced that the atomic bomb had been dropped on Hiroshima those were the words that came immediately to my ten-year-old mind. When I heard a few years later about mushroom clouds over the Nevada test site those were again the words that came to mind. I began waking before dawn, imagining that the fireballs from the Nevada test shots would light up the sky in Sacramento.

Later, after I married and had a child, I learned to find equal meaning in the repeated rituals of domestic life. Setting the table. Lighting the candles. Building the fire. Cooking. All those soufflés, all that crème caramel, all those daubes and albóndigas and gumbos. Clean sheets, stacks of clean towels, hurricane lamps for storms, enough water and food to see us through whatever geological event came our way. *These fragments I have shored against my ruins*, were the words that came to mind then. These fragments mattered to me. I believed in them. That I could find meaning in the intensely personal nature of my life as a wife and mother did not seem inconsistent with finding meaning in the vast indifference of geology and the test shots; the two systems existed for me on parallel tracks that occasionally converged, notably during earthquakes. In my unexamined mind there was always a point, John's and my death, at which the tracks would converge for a final time. On the Internet I recently found aerial photographs of the house on the Palos Verdes Peninsula in which we had lived when we were first married, the house to which we had brought Quintana home from St. John's Hospital in Santa Monica and put her in her bassinet by the wisteria in the box garden. The photographs, part of the California Coastal Records Project, the point of which was to document the entire California coastline, were hard to read conclusively, but the house as it had been when we lived in it appeared to be gone. The tower where the gate had been seemed intact but the rest of the structure looked unfamiliar. There seemed to be a swimming pool where the wisteria and box garden had been. The area itself was identified as "Portuguese Bend landslide." You could see the slumping of the hill where the slide had occurred. You could also see, at the base of the cliff on the point, the cave into which we used to swim when the tide was at exactly the right flow.

The swell of clear water.

That was one way my two systems could have converged.

We could have been swimming into the cave with the swell of clear water and the entire point could have slumped, slipped into the sea around us. The entire point slipping into the sea around us was the kind of conclusion I anticipated. I did not anticipate cardiac arrest at the dinner table.

You sit down to dinner and life as you know it ends.

The question of self-pity.

People in grief think a great deal about self-pity. We worry it, dread it, scourge our thinking for signs of it. We fear that our actions will reveal the condition tellingly described as "dwelling on it." We understand the aversion most of us have to "dwelling on it." Visible mourning reminds us of death, which is construed as unnatural, a failure to manage the situation. "A single person is missing for you, and the whole world is empty," Philippe Ariès wrote to the point of this aversion in *Western Attitudes toward Death*. "But one no longer has the right to say so aloud." We remind ourselves repeatedly that our own loss is nothing compared to the loss experienced (or, the even worse thought, not experienced) by he or she who died; this attempt at corrective thinking serves only to plunge us deeper into the self-regarding deep. *(Why didn't I see that, why am I so selfish.)* The very language we use when we think about self-pity betrays the deep abhorrence in which we hold it: self-pity is *feeling sorry for yourself*, self-pity is *thumb-sucking*, self-pity is *boo hoo poor me*, self-pity is the condition in which those feeling sorry for themselves *indulge*, or even *wallow*. Self-pity remains both the most common and the most universally reviled of our character defects, its pestilential destructiveness accepted as given. "Our worst enemy," Helen Keller called it. *I never saw a wild thing / sorry for itself*, D. H. Lawrence wrote, in a much-quoted four-line homily that turns out on examination to be free of any but tendentious meaning. *A small bird will drop frozen dead from a bough / without ever having felt sorry for itself.*

This may be what Lawrence (or we) would prefer to believe about wild things, but consider those dolphins who refuse to eat after the death of a mate. Consider those geese who search for the lost mate until they themselves become disoriented and die. In fact the grieving have urgent reasons, even an urgent need, to feel sorry for themselves. Husbands walk out, wives walk out, divorces happen, but these husbands and wives leave behind them webs of intact associations, however acrimonious. Only the survivors of a death are truly left alone. The connections that made up their life—both the deep connections and the apparently (until they are broken) insignificant connections—have all vanished. John and I were married for forty years. During all but the first five months of our marriage, when John was still working at *Time*, we both worked at home. We were together twenty-four hours a day, a fact that remained a source of both merriment and foreboding to my mother and aunts. "For richer for poorer but never for lunch," one or another of them frequently said in the early years of our marriage. I could not count the times during the average day when something would come up that I needed to tell him. This impulse did not end with his death. What ended was the possibility of response. I read something in the paper that I would normally have read to him. I notice some change in the neighborhood that would interest him: Ralph Lauren has expanded into more space between Seventy-first and Seventy-second Streets, say, or the empty space where the Madison Avenue Bookshop used to be has finally been leased. I recall coming in from Central Park one morning in mid-August with urgent news to report: the deep summer green has faded overnight from the trees, the season is already changing. *We need to make a plan for the fall*,

I remember thinking. *We need to decide where we want to be at Thanksgiving, Christmas, the end of the year.*

I am dropping my keys on the table inside the door before I fully remember. There is no one to hear this news, nowhere to go with the unmade plan, the uncompleted thought. There is no one to agree, disagree, talk back. "I think I am beginning to understand why grief feels like suspense," C. S. Lewis wrote after the death of his wife. "It comes from the frustration of so many impulses that had become habitual. Thought after thought, feeling after feeling, action after action, had H. for their object. Now their target is gone. I keep on through habit fitting an arrow to the string, then I remember and have to lay the bow down. So many roads lead thought to H. I set out on one of them. But now there's an impassable frontierpost across it. So many roads once; now so many cul de sacs."

We are repeatedly left, in other words, with no further focus than ourselves, a source from which self-pity naturally flows. Each time this happens (it happens still) I am struck again by the permanent impassibility of the divide. Some people who have lost a husband or wife report feeling that person's presence, receiving that person's advice. Some report actual sightings, what Freud described in "Mourning and Melancholia" as "a clinging to the object through the medium of a hallucinatory wishful psychosis." Others describe not a visible apparition but just a "very strongly felt presence." I experienced neither. There have been a few occasions (the day they wanted to do the trach at UCLA, for example) on which I asked John point blank what to do. I said I needed his help. I said I could not do this alone. I said these things out loud, actually vocalized the words.

I am a writer. Imagining what someone would say or do comes to me as naturally as breathing.

Yet on each occasion these pleas for his presence served only to reinforce my awareness of the final silence that separated us. Any answer he gave could exist only in my imagination, my edit. For me to imagine what he could say only in my edit would seem obscene, a violation. I could no more know what he would say about UCLA and the trach than I could know whether he meant to leave the "to" out of the sentence about

J.J. McClure and Teresa Kean and the tornado. We imagined we knew everything the other thought, even when we did not necessarily want to know it, but in fact, I have come to see, we knew not the smallest fraction of what there was to know.

When something happens to me, he would frequently say.

Nothing will happen to you, I would say.

But if it does.

If it does, he would continue. If it did, for example, I was not to move to a smaller apartment. If it did I would be surrounded by people. If it did I would need to make plans to feed these people. If it did I would marry again within the year.

You don't understand, I would say.

And in fact he did not. Nor did I: we were equally incapable of imagining the reality of life without the other. This will not be a story in which the death of the husband or wife becomes what amounts to the credit sequence for a new life, a catalyst for the discovery that (a point typically introduced in such accounts by the precocious child of the bereaved) "you can love more than one person." Of course you can, but marriage is something different. Marriage is memory, marriage is time. "She didn't know the songs," I recall being told that a friend of a friend had said after an attempt to repeat the experience. Marriage is not only time: it is also, parodoxically, the denial of time. For forty years I saw myself through John's eyes. I did not age. This year for the first time since I was twenty-nine I saw myself through the eyes of others. This year for the first time since I was twenty-nine I realized that my image of myself was of someone significantly younger. This year I realized that one reason I was so often sideswiped by memories of Quintana at three was this: when Quintana was three I was thirty-four. I remember Gerard Manley Hopkins: *Margaret, are you grieving / Over Goldengrove unleaving?* and *It is the blight man was born for, / It is Margaret you mourn for.*

It is the blight *man* was born for.

We are not idealized wild things.

We are imperfect mortal beings, aware of that mortality even as we push it away, failed by our very complication, so wired that when we mourn our losses we also mourn, for better or for worse, ourselves. As we were. As we are no longer. As we will one day not be at all.

Elena's dreams were about dying.

Elena's dreams were about getting old.

Nobody here has not had (will not have) Elena's dreams.

Time is the school in which we learn, / Time is the fire in which we burn: Delmore Schwartz again.

I remember despising the book Dylan Thomas's widow Caitlin wrote after her husband's death, *Leftover Life to Kill.* I remember being dismissive of, even censorious about, her "self-pity," her "whining," her "dwelling on it." *Leftover Life to Kill* was published in 1957. I was twenty-two years old. Time is the school in which we learn.

18

AT THE TIME I began writing these pages, in October 2004, I still did not understand how or why or when John died. I had been there. I had watched while the EMS team tried to bring him back. I still did not know how or why or when. In early December 2004, almost a year after he died, I finally received the autopsy report and emergency room records I had first requested from New York Hospital on the fourteenth of January, two weeks after it happened and one day before I told Quintana that it had happened. One reason it took eleven months to receive these records, I realized when I looked at them, was that I myself had written the wrong address on the hospital's request form. I had at that time lived at the same address on the same street on the Upper East Side of Manhattan for sixteen years. Yet the address I had given the hospital was on another street altogether, where John and I had lived for the five months immediately following our wedding in 1964.

A doctor to whom I mentioned this shrugged, as if I had told him a familiar story.

Either he said that such "cognitive deficits" could be associated with stress or he said that such cognitive deficits could be associated with grief.

It was a mark of those cognitive deficits that within seconds after he said it I had no idea which he had said.

According to the hospital's Emergency Department Nursing Documentation Sheet, the Emergency Medical Services call was received at 9:15 P.M. on the evening of December 30, 2003.

According to the log kept by the doormen the ambulance arrived five minutes later, at 9:20 P.M. During the next forty-five minutes, according to the Nursing Documentation Sheet, the following medications were given, by either direct injection or IV infusion: atropine (times three), epinephrine (times three), vasopressin (40 units), amiodarone (300 mg), high-dose epinephrine (3 mg), and high-dose epinephrine again (5 mg). According to the same documentation the patient was intubated at the scene. I have no memory of an intubation. This may be an error on the part of whoever did the documentation, or it may be another cognitive deficit.

According to the log kept by the doormen the ambulance left for the hospital at 10:05 P.M.

According to the Emergency Department Nursing Documentation Sheet the patient was received for triage at 10:10 P.M. He was described as asystolic and apneic. There was no palpable pulse. There was no pulse via sonography. The mental status was unresponsive. The skin color was pale. The Glasgow Coma Scale rating was 3, the lowest rating possible, indicating that eye, verbal, and motor responses were all absent. Lacerations were seen on the right forehead and the bridge of the nose. Both pupils were fixed and dilated. "Lividity" was noted.

According to the Emergency Department Physician's Record the patient was seen at 10:15 P.M. The physician's notation ended: "Cardiac arrest. DOA—likely massive M.I. Pronounced 10:18 P.M."

According to the Nursing Flow Chart the IV was removed and the patient extubated at 10:20 P.M. At 10:30 P.M. the notation was "wife at bedside—George, soc. worker, at bedside with wife."

According to the autopsy report, examination showed a greater than 95 percent stenosis of both the left main and the left anterior descending arteries. Examination also showed "slight myocardial pallor on TCC staining, indicative of acute infarct in distribution of left anterior descending artery."

I read this paperwork several times. The elapsed time indicated that the time spent at New York Hospital had been, as I had thought, just bookkeeping, hospital procedure, the regularization of a death. Yet each time I read the official sheets I noticed a new detail. On my first reading of the Emergency Department Physician's Record I had not for example registered the letters "DOA." On my first reading of the Emergency Department Physician's Record I was presumably still assimilating the Emergency Department Nursing Documentation Sheet.

"Fixed and dilated" pupils. FDPs.

Sherwin Nuland: "The tenacious young men and women see their patient's pupils become unresponsive to light and then widen until they are large fixed circles of impenetrable blackness. Reluctantly the team stops its efforts. . . . The room is strewn with the debris of the lost campaign . . ."

Fixed circles of impenetrable blackness.

Yes. That was what the ambulance crew saw in John's eyes on our living room floor.

"Lividity." Post-mortem lividity.

I knew what "lividity" meant because it is an issue in morgues. Detectives point it out. It can be a way of determining time of death. After circulation stops, blood follows the course of gravity, pooling wherever the body is resting. There is a certain amount of time before this pooled blood becomes visible to the eye. What I could not remember was what that amount of time was. I looked up "lividity" in the handbook on forensic pathology that John kept on the shelf above his desk. "Although lividity is variable, it normally begins to form immediately after death and is usually clearly perceptible within an hour or two." If lividity was clearly perceptible to the triage nurses by 10:10 P.M., then, it would have started forming an hour before.

An hour before was when I was calling the ambulance.

Which meant he was dead then.

After that instant at the dinner table he was never not dead.

I now know how I'm going to die, he had said in 1987 after the left anterior descending artery had been opened by angioplasty.

You no more know how you're going to die than I do or anyone else does, I had said in 1987.

We call it the widowmaker, pal, his cardiologist in New York had said about the left anterior descending artery.

Through the summer and fall I had been increasingly fixed on locating the anomaly that could have allowed this to happen.

In my rational mind I knew how it happened. In my rational mind I had spoken to many doctors who told me how it happened. In my rational mind I had read David J. Callans in *The New England Journal of Medicine*: "Although the majority of cases of sudden death from cardiac causes involve patients with preexisting coronary artery disease, cardiac arrest is the first manifestation of this underlying problem in 50 percent of patients. . . . Sudden cardiac arrest is primarily a problem in patients outside of the hospital; in fact, approximately 80 percent of cases of sudden death from cardiac causes occur at home. The rate of success of resuscitation in patients with out-of-hospital cardiac arrest has been poor, averaging 2 to 5 percent in major urban centers. . . . Resuscitation efforts initiated after eight minutes are almost always doomed to fail." In my rational mind I had read Sherwin Nuland in *How We Die*: "When an arrest occurs elsewhere than the hospital, only 20 to 30 percent survive, and these are almost always those who respond quickly to the CPR. If there has been no response by the time of arrival in the emergency room, the likelihood of survival is virtually zero."

In my rational mind I knew that.

I was not however operating from my rational mind.

Had I been operating from my rational mind I would not have been entertaining fantasies that would not have been out of place at an Irish wake. I would not for example have experienced, when I heard that Julia Child had died, so distinct a relief, so marked a sense that *this was finally working out*: John and Julia Child could have dinner together (this had been my immediate thought), she could cook, he could ask her about the OSS, they would amuse each other, like each other. They had once done a breakfast together, in a season when each was promoting a book. She had inscribed a copy of *The Way to Cook* and given it to him.

I found the copy of *The Way to Cook* in the kitchen and looked at the inscription.

"*Bon appetit* to John Gregory Dunne," it read.

Bon appetit to John Gregory Dunne and Julia Child and the OSS.

Nor, had I been operating from my rational mind, would I have given such close attention to "health" stories on the Internet and pharmaceutical advertising on television. I fretted for example over a Bayer commercial for a low-dose aspirin that was said to "significantly reduce" the risk of a heart attack. I knew perfectly well how aspirin reduces the risk of heart attack: it keeps the blood from clotting. I also knew that John was taking Coumadin, a far more powerful anticoagulant. Yet I was seized nonetheless by the possible folly of having overlooked low-dose aspirin. I fretted similarly over a study done by UC–San Diego and Tufts showing a 4.65 percent increase in cardiac death over the fourteen-day period of Christmas and New Year's. I fretted over a study from Vanderbilt demonstrating that erythromycin quintupled the risk of cardiac arrest if taken in conjunction with common heart medications. I fretted over a study on statins, and the 30 to 40 percent jump in the risk of heart attack for patients who stopped taking them.

As I recall this I realize how open we are to the persistent message that we can avert death.

And to its punitive correlative, the message that if death catches us we have only ourselves to blame.

Only after I read the autopsy report did I begin to believe what I had been repeatedly told: nothing he or I had done or not done had either caused or could have prevented his death. He had inherited a bad heart. It would eventually kill him. The date on which it would kill him had already been, by many medical interventions, postponed. When that date did come, no action I could have taken in our living room—no home defibrillator, no CPR, nothing short of a fully equipped crash cart and the technical facility to follow cardioversion within seconds with IV medication—could have given him even one more day.

The one more day *I love you more than.*

As you used to say to me.

Only after I read the autopsy report did I stop trying to reconstruct the collision, the collapse of the dead star. The collapse had been there all along, invisible, unsuspected.

Greater than 95 percent stenosis of both the left main and the left anterior descending arteries.

Acute infarct in distribution of left anterior descending artery, the LAD.

That was the scenario. The LAD got fixed in 1987 and it stayed fixed until everybody forgot about it and then it got unfixed. *We call it the widowmaker, pal*, the cardiologist had said in 1987.

I tell you that I shall not live two days, Gawain said.

When something happens to me, John had said.

19

I HAVE TROUBLE THINKING of myself as a widow. I remember hesitating the first time I had to check that box on the "marital status" part of a form. I also had trouble thinking of myself as a wife. Given the value I placed on the rituals of domestic life, the concept of "wife" should not have seemed difficult, but it did. For a long time after we were married I had trouble with the ring. It was loose enough to slip off my left ring finger, so for a year or two I wore it on my right. After I burned the right finger taking a pan from the oven, I put the ring on a gold chain around my neck. When Quintana was born and someone gave her a baby ring I added her ring to the chain.

This seemed to work.

I still wear the rings that way.

"You want a different kind of wife," I frequently said to John in the first years of our marriage. I usually said this on the way back to Portuguese Bend after dinner in town. It was typically the initial volley in those fights that started as we passed the refineries off the San Diego Freeway. "You should have married someone more like Lenny." Lenny was my sister-in-law, Nick's wife. Lenny entertained and had lunch with friends and ran her house effortlessly and wore beautiful French dresses and suits and was always available to look at a house or give a baby shower or take visitors from out of town to Disneyland. "If I wanted to marry someone more like Lenny I would have married someone more like Lenny," John would say, at first patiently, then less so.

In fact I had no idea how to be a wife.

In those first years I would pin daisies in my hair, trying for a "bride" effect.

Later I had matching gingham skirts made for me and Quintana, trying for "young mother."

My memory of those years is that both John and I were improvising, flying blind. When I was clearing out a file drawer recently I came across a thick file labeled "Planning." The very fact that we made files labeled "Planning" suggests how little of it we did. We also had "planning meetings," which consisted of sitting down with legal pads, stating the day's problem out loud, and then, with no further attempt to solve it, going out to lunch. Such lunches were festive, as if to celebrate a job well done. Michael's, in Santa Monica, was a typical venue. In this particular "Planning" file I found several Christmas lists from the 1970s, a few notes on telephone calls, and, the bulk of the file, many notes, again dating from the 1970s, having to do with projected expenses and income. A mood of desperation permeates these notes. There was a note made for a meeting with Gil Frank on April 19, 1978, when we were trying to sell the house in Malibu to pay for the house in Brentwood Park on which we had already put down a $50,000 deposit. We could not sell the house in Malibu because it rained all that spring. Slopes fell. The Pacific Coast Highway was closed. No one could even look at the house unless they already lived on the Malibu side of the washout. Over a period of some weeks we had only one viewer, a psychiatrist who lived in the Malibu Colony. He left his shoes outside in the driving rain to "get the feel of the house," walked around barefoot on the tile floor, and reported to his son, who reported to Quintana, that the house was "cold." This was the note made on April 19 of that year: *We must assume we will not sell Malibu until end of year. We have to assume the worst so that any improvement will seem better.*

A note made a week later, I can only think for a "planning meeting": *Discuss: Abandon Brentwood Park? Eat the $50,000?*

Two weeks later we flew to Honolulu, thinking to escape the rain and sort out our dwindling options. The next morning when we came in from swimming there was a message: the sun had come out in Malibu and we had an offer within range of the asking.

What had encouraged us to think that a resort hotel in Honolulu was the place to solve a cash shortfall?

What lesson did we take from the fact that it worked?

Twenty-five years later, confronted with a similar shortfall and similarly deciding to sort it out in Paris, how could we have seen it as economizing because we got one ticket free on the Concorde?

In the same file drawer I found a few paragraphs John had

written in 1990, on our twenty-sixth anniversary. "She wore sunglasses throughout the service the day we got married, at the little mission church in San Juan Bautista, California; she also wept through the entire ceremony. As we walked down the aisle, we promised each other that we could get out of this next week and not wait until death did us part."

That worked too. Somehow it had all worked.

Why did I think that this improvisation could never end?

If I had seen that it could, what would I have done differently?

What would he?

20

I AM WRITING NOW as the end of the first year approaches. The sky in New York is dark when I wake at seven and darkening again by four in the afternoon. There are colored Christmas lights on the quince branches in the living room. There were also colored Christmas lights on quince branches in the living room a year ago, on the night it happened, but in the spring, not long after I brought Quintana home from UCLA, those strings burned out, went dead. This served as a symbol. I bought new strings of colored lights. This served as a profession of faith in the future. I take the opportunity for such professions where and when I can invent them, since I do not yet actually feel this faith in the future.

I notice that I have lost the skills for ordinary social encounters, however undeveloped those skills may have been, that I had a year ago. During the Republican convention I was invited to a small party at a friend's apartment. I was happy to see the friend and I was happy to see her father, who was the reason for the party, but I found conversation with others difficult. I noticed as I was leaving that the Secret Service was there but lacked even the patience to stay long enough to learn what important person was coming. On another evening during the Republican convention I went to a party given by *The New York Times* in the Time Warner building. There were candles and gardenias floating in glass cubes. I could not focus on whoever I was talking to. I was focused only on the gardenias getting sucked into the filter at the house in Brentwood Park.

On such occasions I hear myself trying to make an effort and failing.

I notice that I get up from dinner too abruptly.

I also notice that I do not have the resilience I had a year ago. A certain number of crises occur and the mechanism that floods the situation with adrenaline burns out. Mobilization becomes unreliable, slow or absent. In August and September, after the Democratic and Republican conventions but before the election, I wrote, for the first time since John died, a piece. It was about the campaign. It was the first piece I had written since 1963 that he did not read in draft form and tell me what was wrong, what was needed, how to bring it up here, take it down there. I have never written pieces fluently but this one seemed to be taking even longer than usual: I realized at some point that I was unwilling to finish it, because there was no one to read it. I kept telling myself that I had a deadline, that John and I never missed deadlines. Whatever I finally did to finish this piece was as close as I have ever come to imagining a message from him. The message was simple: *You're a professional. Finish the piece.*

It occurs to me that we allow ourselves to imagine only such messages as we need to survive.

The trach at UCLA, I recognize now, was going to happen with or without me.

Quintana resuming her life, I recognize now, was going to happen with or without me.

Finishing this piece, which was to say resuming my own life, was not.

When I checked the piece for publication I was startled and unsettled by how many mistakes I had made: simple errors of transcription, names and dates wrong. I told myself that this was temporary, part of the mobilization problem, further evidence of those cognitive deficits that came with either stress or grief, but I remained unsettled. Would I ever be right again? Could I ever again trust myself not to be wrong?

Do you always have to be right? He had said that.

Is it impossible for you to consider the possibility that you might be wrong?

Increasingly I find myself focusing on the similarities between these December days and the same December days a year ago. In certain ways those similar days a year ago have more clarity for me, a sharper focus. I do many of the same things. I make the same lists of things undone. I wrap Christmas presents in the same colored tissue, write the same messages on the same postcards from the Whitney gift shop, affix the postcards to the colored tissue with the same gold notary seals. I write the same checks for the building staff, except the checks are now imprinted with only my name. I would not have changed the checks (any more than I would change the voice on the answering machine) but it was said to be essential that John's name now appear only on trust accounts. I order the same kind of ham from Citarella. I fret the same way over the number of plates I will need on Christmas Eve, count and recount. I keep an annual December dentist's appointment and realize as I am putting the sample toothbrushes into my bag that no one will be waiting for me in the reception room, reading the papers until we can go to breakfast at 3 Guys on Madison Avenue. The morning goes empty. When I pass 3 Guys I look the other way. A friend asks me to go with her to hear the Christmas music at St. Ignatius Loyola, and we walk home in the dark in the rain. That night the first snow falls, although only a dusting, no avalanching off the roof of St. James', nothing like my birthday a year ago.

My birthday a year ago when he gave me the last present he would ever give me.

My birthday a year ago when he had twenty-five nights left to live.

On the table in front of the fireplace I notice something out of place in the stack of books nearest the chair in which John sat to read when he woke in the middle of the night. I have deliberately left this stack untouched, not from any shrine-building impulse but because I did not believe that I could afford to think about what he read in the middle of the night. Now someone has placed on top of the stack, balanced precariously, a large illustrated coffee-table book, *The Agnelli Gardens at Villar Perosa*. I move *The Agnelli Gardens at Villar Perosa*. Beneath it is a heavily marked copy of John Lukacs's *Five Days in London: May 1940*, in which there is a laminated bookmark that reads, in a child's handwriting, *John—happy reading to you—from John, age 7*. I am at first puzzled by the bookmark, which under the lamination is dusted with festive pink glitter, then remember: the Creative Artists Agency, as a Christmas project every year, "adopts" a group of Los Angeles schoolchildren, each of whom in turn makes a keepsake for a designated CAA client.

He would have opened the box from CAA on Christmas night.

He would have stuck the bookmark in whatever book was on top of that stack.

He would have had one hundred and twenty hours left to live.

How would he have chosen to live those one hundred and twenty hours?

Beneath the copy of *Five Days in London* is a copy of *The New Yorker* dated January 5, 2004. A copy of *The New Yorker* with that issue date would have been delivered to our apartment on Sunday, December 28, 2003. On Sunday, December 28, 2003, according to John's calendar, we had dinner at home with Sharon DeLano, who had been his editor at Random House and was at that time his editor at *The New Yorker*. We would have had dinner at the table in the living room. According to my kitchen notebook we ate linguine Bolognese and a salad and cheese and a baguette. At that point he would have had forty-eight hours left to live.

Some premonition of this timetable was why I had not touched the stack of books in the first place.

I don't think I'm up for this, he had said in the taxi on our way down from Beth Israel North that night or the next night. He was talking about the condition in which we had once again left Quintana.

You don't get a choice, I had said in the taxi.

I have wondered since if he did.

21

"SHE'S STILL BEAUTIFUL," Gerry had said as he and John and I left Quintana in the ICU at Beth Israel North.

"He said she's still beautiful," John said in the taxi. "Did you hear him say that? She's still beautiful? She's lying there swollen up with tubes coming out of her and he said—"

He could not continue.

That happened on one of those late December nights a few days before he died. Whether it happened on the 26th or the 27th or the 28th or the 29th I have no idea. It did not happen on the 30th because Gerry had already left the hospital by the time we got there on the 30th. I realize that much of my energy during the past months has been given to counting back the days, the hours. At the moment he was saying in the taxi on the way down from Beth Israel North that everything he had done was worthless did he have three hours left to live or did he have twenty-seven? Did he know how few hours there were, did he feel himself going, was he saying that he did not want to leave? *Don't let the Broken Man catch me*, Quintana would say when she woke from bad dreams, one of the "sayings" John put in the box and borrowed for Cat in *Dutch Shea, Jr.* I had promised her that we would not let the Broken Man catch her.

You're safe.

I'm here.

I had believed that we had that power.

Now the Broken Man was in the ICU at Beth Israel North waiting for her and now the Broken Man was in this taxi waiting for her father. Even at three or four she had recognized that when it came to the Broken Man she could rely only on her own efforts: *If the Broken Man comes I'll hang onto the fence and won't let him take me.*

She hung onto the fence. Her father did not.

I tell you I shall not live two days.

What gives those December days a year ago their sharper focus is their ending.

22

> As the grandchild of a geologist I learned early to anticipate the absolute mutability of hills and waterfalls and even islands. When a hill slumps into the ocean I see the order in it. When a 5.2 on the Richter Scale wrenches the writing table in my own room in my own house in my own particular Welbeck Street I keep on typing. A hill is a transitional accommodation to stress, and ego may be a similar accommodation. A waterfall is a self-correcting maladjustment of stream to structure, and so, for all I know, is technique. The very island to which Inez Victor returned in the spring of 1975—Oahu, an emergent post-erosional land mass along the Hawaiian Ridge—is a temporary feature, and every rainfall or tremor along the Pacific plates alters its shape and shortens its tenure as Crossroads of the Pacific. In this light it is difficult to maintain definite convictions about what happened down there in the spring of 1975, or before.

THIS PASSAGE is from the beginning of a novel I wrote during the early 1980s, *Democracy.* John named it. I had begun it as a comedy of family manners with the title *Angel Visits*, a phrase defined by *Brewer's Dictionary of Phrase and Fable* as "delightful intercourse of short duration and rare occurrence," but when it became clear that it was going in a different direction I had kept writing without a title. When I finished John read it and said I should call it *Democracy.* I looked up the passage after the 9.0 Richter earthquake along a six-hundred-mile section of the Sumatran subduction zone had triggered the tsunami that wiped out large parts of coastline bordering the Indian Ocean.

I am unable to stop trying to imagine this event.

There is no video of what I try to imagine. There are no beaches, no flooded swimming pools, no hotel lobbies breaking up like rotted pilings in a storm. What I want to see happened under the surface. The India Plate buckling as it thrust under the Burma Plate. The current sweeping unseen through the deep water. I do not have a depth chart for the Indian Ocean but can pick up the broad outline even from my Rand McNally cardboard globe. Seven hundred and eighty meters off Banda Aceh. Twenty-three hundred between Sumatra and Sri Lanka. Twenty-one hundred between the Andamans and Thailand and then a long shallowing toward Phuket. The instant when the leading edge of the unseen current got slowed by the continental shelf. The buildup of water as the bottom of the shelf began to shallow out.

As it was in the beginning, is now and ever shall be, world without end.

It is now December 31, 2004, a year and a day.

On December 24, Christmas Eve, I had people for dinner, just as John and I had done on Christmas Eve a year before. I told myself that I was doing this for Quintana but I was also doing it for myself, a pledge that I would not lead the rest of my life as a special case, a guest, someone who could not function on her own. I built a fire, I lit candles, I laid out plates and silver on a buffet table in the dining room. I put out some CDs, Mabel Mercer singing Cole Porter and Israel Kamakawiwo'ole singing "Over the Rainbow" and an Israeli jazz pianist named Liz Magnes playing "Someone to Watch Over Me." John had been seated next to Liz Magnes once at a dinner at the Israeli mission and she had sent him the CD, a Gershwin concert she had given in Marrakech. In its ability to suggest drinks at the King David Hotel in Jerusalem during the British period this CD had seemed to John spectrally interesting, recovered evidence of a vanished world, one more reverberation from World War One. He referred to it as "the Mandate music." He had put it on while he was reading before dinner the night he died.

About five in the afternoon on the 24th I thought I could not do the evening but when the time came the evening did itself.

Susanna Moore sent leis from Honolulu for her daughter Lulu and Quintana and me. We wore the leis. Another friend brought a gingerbread house. There were many children. I played the Mandate music, although the noise level was such that no one heard it.

On Christmas morning I put away the plates and silver and in the afternoon I went up to St. John the Divine, where there were mainly Japanese tourists. There were always Japanese tourists at St. John the Divine. On the afternoon Quintana got married at St. John the Divine there had been Japanese tourists snapping pictures as she and Gerry left the altar. On the afternoon we placed John's ashes in the chapel off the main altar at St. John the Divine an empty Japanese tour bus had caught fire and burned outside, a pillar of flame on Amsterdam Avenue. On Christmas Day the chapel off the main altar was blocked off, part of the cathedral reconstruction. A security guard took me in. The chapel was emptied, filled only with scaffolding. I ducked under the scaffolding and found the marble plate with John's name and my mother's name. I hung the lei from one of the brass rods that held the marble plate to the vault and then I walked from the chapel back into the nave and out the main aisle, straight toward the big rose window.

As I walked I kept my eyes on the window, half blinded by its brilliance but determined to keep my gaze fixed until I caught the moment in which the window as approached seems to explode with light, fill the entire field of vision with blue. The Christmas of the Buffalo pens and the black wafer alarm clock and the neighborhood fireworks all over Honolulu, the Christmas of 1990, the Christmas during which John and I had been doing the crash rewrite on the picture that never got made, had involved that window. We had staged the denouement of the picture at St. John the Divine, placed a plutonium device in the bell tower (only the protagonist realizes that the device is at St. John the Divine and not the World Trade towers), blown the unwitting carrier of the device straight out through the big rose window. We had filled the screen with blue that Christmas.

I realize as I write this that I do not want to finish this account.

Nor did I want to finish the year.

The craziness is receding but no clarity is taking its place.

I look for resolution and find none.

I did not want to finish the year because I know that as the days pass, as January becomes February and February becomes summer, certain things will happen. My image of John at the instant of his death will become less immediate, less raw. It will become something that happened in another year. My sense of John himself, John alive, will become more remote, even "mudgy," softened, transmuted into whatever best serves my life without him. In fact this is already beginning to happen.

All year I have been keeping time by last year's calendar: what were we doing on this day last year, where did we have dinner, is it the day a year ago we flew to Honolulu after Quintana's wedding, is it the day a year ago we flew back from Paris, *is it the day*. I realized today for the first time that my memory of this day a year ago is a memory that does not involve John. This day a year ago was December 31, 2003. John did not see this day a year ago. John was dead.

I was crossing Lexington Avenue when this occurred to me.

I know why we try to keep the dead alive: we try to keep them alive in order to keep them with us.

I also know that if we are to live ourselves there comes a point at which we must relinquish the dead, let them go, keep them dead.

Let them become the photograph on the table.

Let them become the name on the trust accounts.

Let go of them in the water.

Knowing this does not make it any easier to let go of him in the water.

In fact the apprehension that our life together will decreasingly be the center of my every day seemed today on Lexington Avenue so distinct a betrayal that I lost all sense of oncoming traffic.

I think about leaving the lei at St. John the Divine.

A souvenir of the Christmas in Honolulu when we filled the screen with blue.

During the years when people still left Honolulu on the Matson Lines the custom at the moment of departure was to throw leis on the water, a promise that the traveler would return. The leis would get caught in the wake and go bruised and brown, the way the gardenias in the pool filter at the house in Brentwood Park had gone bruised and brown.

The other morning when I woke I tried to remember the arrangement of the rooms in the house in Brentwood Park. I imagined myself walking through the rooms, first on the ground floor and then on the second. Later in the day I realized that I had forgotten one.

The lei I left at St. John the Divine would have gone brown by now.

Leis go brown, tectonic plates shift, deep currents move, islands vanish, rooms get forgotten.

I flew into Indonesia and Malaysia and Singapore with John, in 1979 and 1980.

Some of the islands that were there then would now be gone, just shallows.

I think about swimming with him into the cave at Portuguese Bend, about the swell of clear water, the way it changed, the swiftness and power it gained as it narrowed through the rocks at the base of the point. The tide had to be just right. We had to be in the water at the very moment the tide was right. We could only have done this a half dozen times at most during the two years we lived there but it is what I remember. Each time we did it I was afraid of missing the swell, hanging back, timing it wrong. John never was. You had to feel the swell change. You had to go with the change. He told me that. No eye is on the sparrow but he did tell me that.

THE YEAR OF MAGICAL THINKING

The Play

THE YEAR OF MAGICAL THINKING

Production Details

OPENING PERFORMANCE:

March 29, 2007

Booth Theatre

222 West 45th Street

New York, NY

Starring Vanessa Redgrave

Directed by David Hare

Produced by Scott Rudin, Roger Berlind, Debra Black, Daryl Roth, and The Shubert Organization.

Stuart Thompson and John Barlow, Executive Producers.

Set design by Bob Crowley

Costume design by Ann Roth

Lighting design by Jean Kalman

Sound design by Paul Arditti

1

THIS HAPPENED ON DECEMBER 30, 2003. That may seem a while ago but it won't when it happens to you.

And it will happen to you. The details will be different, but it will happen to you.

That's what I'm here to tell you.

We had come home. "Home" meaning an apartment on the Upper East Side of Manhattan. Early evening, maybe eight o'clock. We discussed whether to go out or eat in. I said we could stay in, I would build a fire.

The fire was the point.

In California we heated our houses by building fires. In Malibu we built fires even on summer evenings, because the fog came in. Fires said we were home, we had drawn the circle, we were safe through the night.

I built the fire. I drew the circle.

I have no memory of what I meant to have for dinner.

Memory stops. The frame freezes. You'll find that's something that happens.

I warned you. I'm telling you what you need to know.

You see me on this stage, you sit next to me on a plane, you run into me at dinner, you know what happened to me.

You don't want to think it could happen to you.

That's why I'm here.

John was in his office. I got him a drink. He sat down by the fire to read. He was reading a bound galley of David Fromkin's *Europe's Last Summer: Who Started the Great War in 1914?* I set the table in the living room, where we could see the fire.

I must have noticed that later. The name of the book. I eventually read it myself, but found no clues.

Wait. I was telling you what happened.

He wanted a second drink. I got it. He asked if I had used single-malt scotch for the second drink. I said I had used whatever I used for the first drink. "Good," he said. "I don't know why but I don't think you should mix them."

I was at the table, making a salad. He was sitting across from me, talking. Either he was talking about why World War One was the event from which the entire rest of the twentieth century flowed or he was talking about the scotch, I have no idea which.

Then he wasn't. Wasn't talking.

I looked up. I said, "Don't do that." I thought he was making a joke.

Slumping over. Pretending to be dead. You've seen people make that kind of tiresome joke. Maybe you've done it yourself. Meaning "this was a hard day, we got through it, we're having dinner, we've got a fire."

In fact neither of us had yet said out loud how hard that day had been.

My next thought was that he had started to eat and choked. I tried to move him so I could do the Heimlich.

He fell onto the table, then to the floor. There was a dark liquid pooling beneath his face.

Within what *I now know* to have been exactly five minutes, two ambulances came. The crews worked on the living room floor for what *I now know* to have been exactly forty-five minutes.

I now know these facts because I obtained the documents. I obtained the Emergency Department Nursing Documentation Sheet. I obtained the Nursing Flow Chart. I obtained the Physician's Record. I obtained the log kept by the doormen in our building. "*Paramedics arrived at 9:20 p.m. for Mr. Dunne,*" the log read. "*Mr. Dunne was taken to the hospital at 10:05 p.m.*"

The distance from our apartment to the ambulance entrance of New York Cornell is six crosstown blocks. I do not remember traffic. I do not remember sirens. When I got out of the ambulance the gurney was already being pushed inside. Everyone was in scrubs. I noticed one man who was not in scrubs. "Is this the wife," he said to the driver. Then he looked at me. "I'm your social worker."

And I guess that was when I knew.

That's something else to remember. If they give you a social worker, you're in trouble.

Life changes fast.
Life changes in the instant.
You sit down to dinner and life as you know it ends.
The question of self-pity.

Those were the first words I wrote after it happened.
And after that—
I'm a writer—
But after that I didn't write anything for a long while.

For several weeks after it happened I tried different strategies for keeping on the correct track. One that worked for a while was repeating to myself the last two lines of "Rose Aylmer," Walter Savage Landor's 1806 elegy to the memory of a daughter of Lord Aylmer's who had died at age twenty in Calcutta. I had not thought of "Rose Aylmer" since I was at Berkeley, but now I could remember not only the poem but much of what was said about it in whichever class I heard it analyzed. "*Ah what avails the sceptred race!*" it begins. "*Ah what the form divine! When every virtue, every grace, Rose Aylmer, all were thine!*" "Rose Aylmer" worked, the lecturer said, because the overblown and therefore meaningless praise in those first lines gets thrown into sudden, even shocking relief by what he called "the hard sweet wisdom" of the last, which suggest that grief has its place but also its limits: "*A night of memories and sighs / I consecrate to thee.*"

“A night of memories and sighs,” he repeated. “*A* night. One night. It might be all night but he doesn’t say *all night*, he says *a night*, not a matter of a lifetime, a matter of some hours.”

Hard sweet wisdom. Clearly, since “Rose Aylmer” remained embedded in my memory, I believed it to offer a lesson for survival.

2

I TOLD YOU I KNEW WHEN I SAW the social worker but I didn't really.

Or more correctly—"correctly" is important to me—I knew but I refused to know.

There's a certain kind of personality—my own, maybe yours—that sets great store on seeing it straight. For certain of us this is a big ego point.

You might think you'll see it straight but you won't.

You'll be standing in some ER and at one level you'll have a pretty clear idea of whatever it was that just happened but you'll see it as a kind of first draft.

Notice the evasion there. "Whatever it was that just happened." The actual words will have vanished from your accessible vocabulary. The only words at hand will have to do with how this can be corrected.

Reversible error.

If you're a lawyer you're probably thinking she doesn't know what "reversible error" means, but I do.

There was a verdict here. Find the right error and the verdict gets thrown out.

And errors are easy to find.

If you're me.

For example this is the wrong hospital.

This is a perfectly good hospital but it's not "our" hospital. It's New York Presbyterian Cornell. "Our" hospital is New York Presbyterian Columbia, a hundred blocks uptown. So while I stand in line to show the insurance cards—nobody told me to stand in this line but I see it as a constructive step, proof that I'm handling the situation—I tell myself that as soon as he is stabilized I can move him to Columbia.

He will need a bed with telemetry. When I arrange the move I need to specify this.

Notice that only "I" can do this. I do not distrust those in charge here, but I do feel compelled to manage them.

I go further. I see a plan falling into place. Once Quintana is stabilized I can also move her to Columbia.

Maybe I didn't mention this before.

New York Cornell is not our first hospital of the evening.

The first hospital of the evening was Beth Israel North. You know, the one that used to be Doctors' Hospital. Across from Gracie Mansion. Where our daughter has been in an induced coma in the sixth-floor ICU since Christmas night with what began as the flu and is now septic shock.

Another case of the wrong hospital.

From my point of view.

But just try telling a grown child that the easiest emergency room on the Upper East Side doesn't necessarily add up to the right hospital.

Try telling her anything, once they sedate her for the endotracheal tube.

Must you always have the last word, John said when we fought. Which was often. *Must you always be right. For once in your life just let it go.*

When we saw her tonight in the ICU her hair was damp and matted from the fever. No one seems to have brushed it. I have been trying to brush it since the day after Christmas but cannot. I could always brush her hair. I could brush her hair even in Malibu, when it was long and bleached from the sun and green from the chlorine in swimming pools and she had been in the water all day. She would come up from the beach and John would wrap her in towels on the deck outside his office and I would brush her hair.

"I love you more than even one more day," he said to her tonight in the ICU.

He said that on each of the five nights he saw her there.

On the chance she could hear.

He said it tonight just before we came home and discussed whether to go out for dinner or eat in. Just before I built the fire—

No.

The lights are too bright in this hospital. It's too cold.

If I hold focus I can arrange for both of them to recuperate at Columbia. Adjoining rooms. The McKeen Pavilion. I can go up in the afternoons and have tea with them in the atrium while the volunteer pianist in scrubs plays "Isn't It Romantic." I can stay until eight and the car will be waiting and I'll come downtown and build a fire and make myself a hamburger. I'll think about John and Quintana in their adjoining rooms but I'll still have a fire and I'll still eat the hamburger and I'll still watch Chris Matthews on rerun.

Because I will have arranged for them to be safe. I will have brought in the appropriate specialists. I will have made sure that each of these specialists appreciates the entire picture. I will have managed the situation.

My social worker reappears. He leads me out of the insurance line and into an empty room away from the triage area. He tells me to wait. Part of my mind is thinking that this does not look good and part is trying to remember the words on a pink index card I have in my office.

When he comes back he has a subteen in a white coat with him. He introduces the subteen as "your husband's doctor."

There is a silence.

I hear my own voice. What I hear it saying is this: "He's dead, isn't he."

The doctor looks at the social worker. "It's okay," the social worker says. "She's a pretty cool customer."

They take me to the cubicle where he is. They ask if I want a priest. I say yes. A priest comes. He says the words. I thank him. They give me the silver clip in which John kept his driver's license and credit cards. They give me the cash from his pocket.

They give me his watch. They give me his cell phone. They give me a plastic bag in which they say I will find his clothes. I thank them. The social worker asks if he can do anything more for me. I say he can put me in a taxi. He does. I thank him. He asks if I have money for the fare. I say I do, the cool customer.

He uses that word, the "fare."

Wouldn't it have been more colloquial to say the "taxi"? Do you have money for the *taxi*? Wouldn't that have been less troubling? Less as if I were taking some kind of mystery tour?

When I walk back into the apartment I see John's jacket still lying on the chair where he dropped it. I pick it up. A Patagonia windbreaker, the crew jacket from *Up Close & Personal.* All pictures have crew jackets, there used to be a joke about a picture so bad the crew won't wear the jacket.

The dark liquid is still pooled on the living room floor. I see now that it is blood.

The EKG electrodes are still on the floor.

The empty syringes are still on the floor.

The pink index card.

I had typed the words on the card because they had to do with a plot point in another picture, one we started and abandoned because we could not figure out how the accidental killer who is also the DA gets the body out of the house. Here are the words, which I had copied from the Merck Manual: "Tissue anoxia for >4–6 minutes can result in irreversible brain damage or death."

I consider irreversible brain damage. I stop.

That isn't exactly what happened.

Something else happened but I can't afford to access the word.

There are people I need to call. I can't call Quintana, Quintana is where we left her, unconscious in the ICU, the IV lines still dripping the medications that are what they mean when they say "We're giving it everything we've got."

"Everything we've got" doesn't do it for me.

I want the names. I wrote them down. I looked them up. There were the antibiotics. Vancomycin. They call it "vanc." By now so do I. Azithromycin. Gentamicin. Clindamycin.

Then there was Xigris.

Xigris is Eli Lilly's drug for septic shock.

Said to improve the survival rate from 56 to 69 percent.

You might want to file that.

For when you're standing by your child's ICU bed and the vanc isn't working and somebody mentions Xigris.

Spelled X-I-G-R-I-S, pronounced *ZY-griss.*

"This costs twenty thousand dollars," the nurse said tonight when she changed the IV bag.

"We still don't know which way this is going," one of the ICU doctors said.

Did he say that tonight?

Or did he say it last night?

You want to know how this happened.

John asked that question.

A perfectly healthy young woman.

Married five months.

She and Gerry had just had their first Thanksgiving dinner. They pureed turnips, they unpacked their wedding china.

The weekend before Christmas she "felt terrible." She went with a fever of 103 to the Beth Israel emergency room and was diagnosed with the flu. Stay in bed, drink liquids, it's going around. No chest X-ray was taken. Three days later she went back to the emergency room. Her pulse was elevated, 150-plus. Her white count was almost zero. There was pneumonia on one lung. She would go to an ICU overnight for monitoring but it was "nothing, what we used to call walking pneumonia." By morning her fever had passed 104, she was intubated, there was pneumonia on both lungs, her blood pressure was dropping, she had entered septic shock, and they did not know which way this was going.

Reconstructing this sequence did not answer John's question.

He said "how did this happen" but what he meant was "why."

If I could answer that question would he still be—

I decide to make the calls from the bedroom.

In the hall outside the bedroom there is a photograph of John and me taken on a location for *The Panic in Needle Park.* It was our first picture. We went with it to the Cannes Festival. It was the first time I had ever been to Europe and we flew first-class on Twentieth Century–Fox and I boarded the plane barefoot, it was that period, 1971. One or the other of us sent Quintana a postcard every day. She was five, at home in Malibu. "*Mon cher pamplemousse*," these postcards began.

There is also a photograph of Katharine Ross, taken by Conrad Hall during the Malibu period when she taught Quintana to swim by throwing a Tahitian shell in a neighbor's pool and telling Quintana that the shell was hers if she brought it up. This was a time when Katharine and Conrad and Jean and Brian Moore and John and I traded plants and dogs and favors and recipes and would have dinner at one or another of our houses a couple of times a week.

We all made soufflés.

Once on Quintana's birthday I made two dozen chocolate soufflés and watched two dozen six-year-olds mash them into chocolate pudding.

We talked about renting Lee Grant's house above Zuma Beach and opening a restaurant, to be called Lee Grant's House. Katharine and Jean and I would take turns cooking and Conrad and Brian and John would take turns running the front.

Conrad Hall is now dead.

Brian Moore is now dead.

I do not further pursue this update on who is now dead.

The telephone rings. It is Lynn Nesbit. I am unclear how she knows but she does and she is on her way over.

This is all happening too fast.

I need to discuss this with John. There is nothing I do not discuss with John. I do not always think he is right nor does he always think I am right but we are each the person the other trusts. There is no separation between our interests and investments in any given situation. Many people assume that we must be competitive, that our private life must be a minefield of professional envies and resentments. This is so far from the case that the general insistence on it has come to suggest certain lacunae in the popular understanding of marriage.

When Lynn arrives we do not sit in the part of the living room where the blood and the syringes and the EKG electrodes are still on the floor.

She has a telephone in her hand. I realize that she is talking to Christopher Lehmann-Haupt.

If she is talking to Christopher Lehmann-Haupt she is talking about an obituary in *The New York Times.*

An obituary means he is dead.

I am seized by the need not to let anyone at the *Los Angeles Times* read this in *The New York Times.* I call a friend at the *Los Angeles Times.* As he picks up I realize that I have made a mistake. It's still early in Los Angeles, is John even dead there? What time was it here when they said he was dead? Is it that time yet in Los Angeles? If there's time left on the West Coast, does it even need to happen there? Should I be taking him there right now? If I hang up and fly out can we have a different ending on Pacific time?

Lynn says she will spend the night.

I say no, I'm fine.

And I am.

Until the morning. When I wake and he still isn't here.

Let me make myself clear. Of course I knew he was dead. Of course I had already delivered the definitive news to *The New York Times* and the *Los Angeles Times.* Yet I was myself in no way prepared to accept this news as final: there was a level on which I believed that whatever had happened remained open to revision.

That was why I needed to be alone.

I needed to be alone so that he could come back.

That was the beginning of my year of magical thinking.

When I wake and he still isn't here I try not to move.

I lie very still.

I analyze the situation.

Maybe it takes time for people to come back.

Maybe you have to wait.

Maybe you need to play along, maybe you need to make what everyone is calling "the arrangements." John's nephew Tony comes down from Connecticut to help me, he used to be a construction coordinator on pictures shooting in New York, he learned how to deal with the mob and the city, he knows how to make arrangements.

I do not mention to Tony that I am just playing along while I wait.

We go to Frank E. Campbell, I sign the papers, we bring the clothes, we identify the body.

On most surface levels I seem rational. To the average observer I would appear to fully understand that death is irreversible. I have authorized an autopsy. I have arranged for cremation.

Still.

He does not look as if he needs to be dead.

He looks pale and a tooth is chipped from the fall but he is wearing faded jeans and a checked shirt and a navy-blue blazer from Sills and he does not necessarily look dead.

If he does not even look dead he is doing *his* part.

There must be more *I* need to do.

There must be more to this bargain than I know.

Further arrangements.

It occurs to me that one of these arrangements could be planning a funeral.

This funeral part will not be easy.

We can't plan a funeral while Q is in a coma.

She was christened Quintana but we called her "Q." Or "Q Roo."

When she was sixteen years old at the Westlake School for Girls in Holmby Hills he gave her a red car with the plate "Q ROO."

You're safe, I say. I'm here.

I say it every time I walk into the ICU.

I have been saying it to her all her life. The first time I said it was in the nursery at St. John's Hospital in Santa Monica, the day she was born.

We took her home and put her in the bassinette overlooking the point.

The point with the cave where the sea ran in.

If the tide was right and you caught a swell of clear water you could swim into the cave.

After we brought Quintana home we never did it.

The obituaries were already on the wires. We told the resident on duty in the ICU that the television in her room had to be turned off.

The resident said that television news could be helpful in maintaining mentation in unconscious patients.

We said her father had died. It was a news story. She could not be allowed to learn from CNN that her father was dead.

The television set was turned off.

When we came back that evening the set was back on.

We said it again.

The next day when I walked into the ICU there was a sign taped up. "DEAD FATHER. NO TV."

3

FOR ALL I KNOW NOW I IMAGINED THAT.

For all I know now it was a metaphor for how hard I had to work at that hospital to get my point across.

To keep her alive.

To do for her what I failed to do for her father.

One morning in Malibu when John and I were having a fight he took it out on Quintana. She cried. I told her she and I were leaving, she and I were going to LAX, she and I were flying away from him.

She told me we couldn't do that to him.

Even at six did she think herself safer with him than with me?

Were they safe only with each other?

Would I fail her as I failed him?

I continue to wait.

I continue to play along.

I mention this to no one.

For one thing no one wants to hear it.

They want to believe that I am "being strong."

To myself I am invisible, incorporeal. I have crossed one of those rivers that divide the living from the dead. I feel for the first time the power in the image of the rivers, the Styx, the Lethe, the cloaked ferryman with his pole.

I saw the ferryman.

I heard the ferryman speak.

It was the ferryman who asked if I had the *fare*.

He believed he was dying. He told me so, repeatedly. I dismissed this. I assured him that he was merely depressed. I said he was being Irish.

But what did he mean when he said in the taxi that everything he had done was worthless?

Why was he assessing his life?

Why was he taking so final a view?

What view did I take, what did I say, did I say the equivalent of don't be ridiculous, don't pull focus, what shall we do for dinner?

Is that what the living always say to the dying?

What shall we do for dinner?

I am reading the literature, I am searching for clues.

Philippe Ariès, in *The Hour of Our Death*, points out that death as it appears in the literature of the Middle Ages "gives advance warning of its arrival" even if sudden or accidental.

What did Gawain say when he is asked, "Ah good my lord, think you then so soon to die?"

"I tell you that I shall not live two days."

And didn't he call that one right?

Do they get a message? Or do they will it?

Do you know what else he said that night?

When we were leaving Beth Israel?

He said "I don't think I'm up for this."

I said "You don't get a choice."

I have wondered since if he did.

For some months he had been saying that we weren't having any fun.

He meant doing things not because we were expected to do them or had always done them or should do them but because we wanted to do them. He meant wanting. He meant living.

He wanted for example to go to Paris.

I said we had too much to do.

He said he had a sense that if he did not go to Paris right now, November, he would never again go to Paris.

"That settles it then, we're going," I said. Meaning this isn't a discussion anymore, it's blackmail, you just escalated it.

"All right, you did it, you got the last word," he said as he left the table.

We did not speak in any meaningful way for thirty-six hours.

When we resumed speaking we went to Paris.

We walked in the rain in the Luxembourg Gardens.

When it got dark at three in the afternoon we swam in the pool on the Bristol roof and watched the lights on the Eiffel Tower.

How could I have so missed the signals?

Had he not told me?

Once in 1987 his cardiologist was talking about the artery he had just fixed, the left anterior descending, the LAD.

The word I took from this discussion was "fixed."

Restored. Cured.

A timely and successful intervention.

But the cardiologist said something else about the LAD: "We call it the widowmaker, pal."

I tell you that I shall not live two days.

From the last afternoon we swam in the pool on the Bristol roof he lived thirty-two days.

There came a day when it occurred to me that I was supposed to give his clothes away. Many people had mentioned the necessity for doing this, usually in the guise of offering to help, but I had resisted.

I did not need help. I could manage this.

I began. I filled many bags with T-shirts, sweatpants, socks, Brooks Brothers shorts.

A few weeks later I assembled more empty bags. I was not yet prepared to address suits or shirts or jackets but thought I could handle the shoes.

I stopped at the door to the room.

I could not give away his shoes.

I stood there a moment, then realized why: he would need shoes if he was to return.

The recognition of this thought by no means eradicated the thought.

"Magical thinking" is a phrase I learned when I was reading anthropology.

Primitive cultures operate on magical thinking. "*If*" thinking.

If we sacrifice the virgin—the rain will come back.

If I keep his shoes—

I now see the autopsy as an early example of this line of thinking.

I wanted the autopsy.

In the course of doing research I had watched autopsies. I knew exactly what happens, the face peeled down, the chest open like a chicken in a butcher's case.

I still wanted the autopsy.

In fact I wanted to be in the room when they did it, but I didn't think I could present this point rationally so I didn't ask.

Here was my reasoning, which for some months remained hidden even from me: an autopsy could show that what had gone wrong was no more than a transitory blockage or arrhythmia.

If so, the reasoning went, they might be able to fix it.

Quintana is out of the hospital.

We can do the funeral.

St. John the Divine.

A Catholic priest and an Episcopal priest. Gregorian chant. Gerry walked Quintana to the pulpit. Still weak but standing very straight in a black dress in the same cathedral where she had eight months before been married, she read a poem she had written to her father. "I love you more than even one more day," she said.

Everyone except Quintana referred to John in the past tense.

I had succeeded.

I had convinced them.

They had said good-bye.

I had done it.

I had made this happen.

I had played along, I had followed the ritual, I had made the arrangements.

I had acknowledged that he was dead.

I had done this in as public a way as I could conceive.

And it still didn't bring him back.

After Quintana said "I love you more than even one more day," she said something else.

This is what she said: "As you used to say to me."

Yes. Many people have pointed out that John and Quintana and I were "unusually dependent" on one another.

Is "unusual dependency" another way of saying "marriage"? Husband and wife? Parent and child?

On the occasion when John gave Q the red car with the "Q ROO" plate I gave her a gold Tiffany bangle.

(Shows her bracelet)

Like this one.

The day I finally told Quintana her father was dead was January 15, 2004, the day the sedation had been sufficiently metabolized to remove the endotracheal tube.

I did not intend to tell her that day.

I did not intend even to see her. If she saw me she would ask where her father was and I would have to tell her.

Our plan was that she would wake and see Gerry and for as many hours or days as she was in and out she would not think to ask where her mother and father were. We conveyed this plan to the ICU team. We got the ICU team on board.

Nevertheless.

She was barely awake when an aide volunteered that her mother was just down the hall.

She asked the logical question.

"If she's just down the hall," she whispered, "then why doesn't she come in."

"Where's Dad," she whispered when she saw me.

I told her.

I stressed the long history of cardiac problems, the apparent suddenness but actual inevitability of the event.

I did not in fact believe this but it was the story I was telling.

She cried. Gerry and I each held her. She tried to talk. She believed that she had spent the past month in Taipei. The space shuttle to Tokyo had developed mechanical difficulties and been diverted to Taipei.

She dropped back into sleep.

"How's Dad," she whispered when I saw her that evening.

I told her again.

"But how is he *now*." She had absorbed the event but not the outcome.

That was the flaw in the story I was telling.

I could never make the outcome convincing.

In the end I would have to tell her again, in another intensive care unit, this one at UCLA.

4

LET ME DO SOME CHRONOLOGY HERE.

Just to assure you I can still do dates.

Neurologists are very big on dates.

I would learn later.

When they kept asking Q what "the date" was and I never knew myself.

When it was all I could do to get up in the morning and do the crossword with breakfast.

One more thing to remember: mornings are when you need to mount a frontal assault on the self-pity question. Get out of bed. Eat breakfast, work the crossword, memorize the date. Walk briskly into the unit and go hand to hand with whichever resident is hapless enough to get caught in your eye line. "If you want to manage this case I'm signing off," one of them finally said to me.

I counted that a victory.

Must you always be right?

John said that in Malibu. The morning I told Q we would go to LAX and fly away from him.

We can't do that to him, she said.

And we didn't. We stayed. It was he who walked out of the house in Malibu that particular morning. Slammed the kitchen door and shot zero to sixty onto the PCH.

In my Corvette.

Must you always have the last word? Can you once in your life just let it go?

Why was I the one who had to let it go?

Since I was the one in charge of assembling the facts?

Since I was the one who cross-checked the EMT records against the Emergency Department Nursing Documentation Sheet against the Nursing Flow Chart against the log kept by the doormen, which is how I happen to know that the ambulances arrived exactly five minutes after I called them? Which is also how I happen to know that the crews worked on the living room floor for exactly forty-five minutes? Which is also how I happen to know that at the time of triage he was asystolic, apneic, had no pulse via sonography, and had a Glasgow Coma Scale rating of 3, indicating that eye, verbal, and motor responses were all absent?

Clearly I am not on top of the self-pity question.

Am I failing to understand this as something that happened to him?

Am I still understanding it as something that happened to me?

The crossword clue that first gets my attention this morning is 6-Down, "Sometimes you feel like . . ."

I instantly see the answer, a good long one that will fill many spaces and prove my competence for the day: ". . . a motherless child."

Motherless children have a real hard time—

Motherless children have such a real hard time—

No.

6-Down has only four letters.

I abandon the puzzle and look up the answer. The correct answer for 6-Down is "A-N-U-T." A nut? Sometimes you feel like a nut? How far have I absented myself from the world of normal response?

Notice: the answer most instantly accessed—"a motherless child"—is a wail of self-pity.

The chronology. The dates.

On Saturday, March 25, two days after we put John's ashes in the vault at St. John the Divine, Quintana and Gerry flew to California to spend a few days in Malibu.

I encouraged this.

I even pressed it.

When she wondered if she was well enough I spoke of how restorative it would be to walk on the beach.

I wanted to see Malibu color on her face and hair again.

I had another reason.

I wanted her to be a child again.

(After a beat)

I will tell you one thing about slamming the kitchen door

and walking out of a house in Malibu and hitting the PCH at sixty in your wife's Corvette.

Unless you've got all day to make your statement, there's nowhere to go, so you tend to come back.

And finish the picture you wanted to quit.

Which as I recall was the issue in that particular walkout.

Quintana.

Malibu.

March 25.

I talked to her before she left. She sounded anxious. She always sounded anxious before a trip. Do you think I'll be okay in California, she asked.

I said yes. Definitely she would be okay in California.

In January I had watched ice floes on the East River from a window at Beth Israel North.

In February I had watched ice floes on the Hudson from a window at Columbia Presbyterian.

Now in March the ice was gone and Quintana would come back from Malibu restored.

That afternoon I imagined her already walking on the beach.

Her plane would have landed, they would have picked up a car and driven up the Pacific Coast Highway.

There would be wild mustard on the hills.

She could take Gerry to see the orchids at Zuma Canyon.

She could take him to eat fried fish at the Ventura County line.

She could take him to lunch at Jean Moone's, she could show him where she had played tennis, where she had learned from the Zuma lifeguards how to swim out of a riptide. On the desk in my office there is a photograph taken when she was seven or eight, her hair white from the sun. Stuck in the frame is a crayoned note, left one day on the kitchen counter in Malibu: "Dear Mom," the note reads. "When you opened the door it was me who ran away. XXXXX—Q."

At ten minutes past seven that evening Tony called. He said he was on his way over. I noted the time because I was due for dinner at seven-thirty but his urgency was such that I did not say so. His wife had been ill. As he was about to hang up I asked if Rosemary was back in the hospital.

He said it was not Rosemary.

It was Quintana.

They had gotten off the plane.

They had picked up their shared bag.

Gerry was carrying the bag to the car rental shuttle, crossing the arrivals driveway ahead of her.

He looked back. She was lying on her back on the asphalt.

Life changes in the instant. The ordinary instant.

I checked to see who was still flying to Los Angeles.

Delta had a 9:40 out of Kennedy.

I was picking up the phone to call Delta when Tony said he did not think being in flight during the surgery was a good idea.

I put down the phone.

"Midline shift."

"Brain pushed to left side."

"Massive arterial bleed."

"Blood everywhere, like a geyser, no clotting factor."

"One pupil was fixed and the other went as we wheeled her in."

Those are some of the things the neurosurgeon said when I got to Los Angeles.

I walked into the ICU. She was in a coma. The neurosurgeon said the coma could continue for days or weeks. The bleed into her brain could have been caused by the fall or the fall could have been caused by the bleed. New problems could present themselves in the immediate days ahead. Those problems included but were not limited to seizures, fever, infection, emboli, pneumonias, and further swelling in the brain, which would require further surgery. Half her skull was stapled, the staples still oozing blood.

"You're safe. I'm here."

Have you noticed?

The way people always describe the ordinary nature of the circumstances in which the disaster occurred?

The clear blue sky from which the plane fell?

The way the children were playing on the swings as usual when the rattlesnake struck from the ivy?

5

JOHN AND I WERE MARRIED on the afternoon of January 30, 1964, a Thursday, at the Catholic Mission of San Juan Bautista in San Benito County, California. John wore a navy blue suit from Chipp. I wore a short white silk dress I bought at Ransohoff's in San Francisco the day John Kennedy was killed. My plan for San Juan Bautista was to have no entrance, no "procession," just stand up there and do it. It never occurred to me to take off my dark glasses.

I thought about that wedding on the day of Quintana's wedding.

She wore a long dress and a veil and expensive shoes but her hair was in a thick braid down her back, as it had been when she was a child in Malibu. We sat in the choir at St. John the Divine. There were small girls with leis, barefoot. There were watercress sandwiches, champagne, lemonade, peacocks on the lawn. She kicked off the expensive shoes and unpinned the veil. "Wasn't that just about perfect," she said when she called that evening.

July 26, 2003.

All gone.

Over.

In another world.

I cannot think of what is gone.

If I think of what is gone the difference between then and now will take me.

I won't be there when she needs me.

"When do you have to leave," she asked me at UCLA the day she could finally speak.

I promised I would not leave until we could leave together.

It occurred to me that this had been, since the day she was born, my basic promise to her. I would not leave.

The neurologists who ask her what day it is also ask her what city it is.

One day she gets it, although not the next.

I report this limited advance to a friend who calls.

There is a silence.
He asks for "the prognosis."
I notice his uneasiness when I have none to offer.
That doesn't matter to me.
If I can keep her alive John will come back.
He and I will go to Paris again.
She and Gerry will have Thanksgiving again.
I am keeping her alive.

To keep her alive I need to focus.
I need to avoid noticing anything that might lead me back into the past.
Going back has trick currents, unrevealed eddies, you can be skimming along on what looks like clear water and suddenly go under.
Get sucked down.
Get caught in the vortex and let go of her hand.
Lose control.
Lose her.
Feel the water take her.

I first identified this vortex effect when I was watching the ice floes from Beth Israel North. There happened to be a rose-patterned wallpaper border left from the period when Beth Israel North was Doctors' Hospital. Doctors' Hospital led directly to someone I knew when I was working for *Vogue*, a woman who moved through the Condé Nast offices trailing clouds of cigarette smoke and Chanel No. 5 and imminent disaster.

This seems a safe line of thinking.
Clear water.
I sail on.
I should see it coming but I don't.
I used a version of this character in *Play It As It Lays.*
Because there was a snake on the jacket of *Play It As It Lays* Quintana called it "Mommy's snake book."
I recognize, too late, that I have entered marked water with "Mommy's snake book."
I was writing that book when Quintana was three.

I am in the vortex.

The night she put a seedpod up her nose and we drove her to Children's Hospital. The pediatrician who specialized in seedpods arrived in his dinner jacket. The next night she put another seedpod up her nose, wanting to repeat the interesting adventure. John and I walking her around the lake in MacArthur Park. The old man lurching from the bench. "That child is the picture of Ginger Rogers," the old man cried. I finish the novel, I am under contract to begin a column for *Life*, we take her to Honolulu. *Life*'s idea for the first column is that I should tell the readers who I am. I plan to write it from Honolulu, but once we are there the My Lai massacre breaks. It seems clear that I should forget telling the readers who I am. I should go instead to Saigon and do My Lai. I call my editor. He instructs me to stay in Honolulu and tell the readers who I am, that as far as Saigon goes, "some of the guys are going out."

"I warned you," John says. "I told you what working for *Life* would be like. Didn't I tell you? It would be like being nibbled to death by ducks?"

I am brushing Quintana's hair. The picture of Ginger Rogers.

I feel betrayed, humiliated. I should have listened to John.

See where that particular vortex sucked me.

From the wallpaper border at Beth Israel North to Quintana at three and I should have listened to John.

I tell you that I shall not live two days, Gawain said.

You will have divined that the "hard sweet wisdom" of "Rose Aylmer" is now lost on me.

I need more than a night of memories and sighs.

I need him back.

I need him to hold on to her in the water.

I see immediately in Los Angeles that its potential for triggering this vortex effect can be controlled only by avoiding any venue I might associate with either John or Quintana. This will require ingenuity. She was born here. John and I lived here most of the time we were married. Even after we moved to New York we spent weeks at a time here, usually at the very hotel in which I am now staying, the Beverly Wilshire.

For reasons that remain unclear, the Beverly Wilshire itself only rarely triggers the vortex effect.

Outside the Beverly Wilshire I plot my routes, I remain on guard.

Never once in five weeks do I drive up the Pacific Coast Highway. When Jean Moore offers me her house in Malibu I invent reasons why it is necessary to stay instead at the Beverly Wilshire. Not driving to Malibu means John can still be wrapping Quintana in towels on the deck outside his office. Not driving to Malibu means her hair can still be bleached from the sun and green from the chlorine in swimming pools.

I even avoid driving to UCLA on Sunset.

Sunset was how we drove to Malibu.

I avoid tuning the car radio to the stations I used to drive by. I avoid locating KRLA, an AM station that when I was driving to Malibu called itself "the heart and soul of rock and roll."

Instead I listen to NPR, a sedate morning show called *Morning Becomes Eclectic.*

Every morning at the Beverly Wilshire I order the same breakfast, huevos rancheros with only one scrambled egg.

Every morning when I drive to UCLA on Wilshire I notice the same banners on the light standards: *UCLA Medical Center—#1 in the West, #3 in the Nation.* Every morning I wonder whose ranking this is. I never ask.

In the deep hush of *Morning Becomes Eclectic* I congratulate myself.

I am outmaneuvering the vortex.

The trick is to remain flexible.

Take the morning I need to buy bottled water at the Rite-Aid and turn up Canon.

I see trouble ahead, but I have already turned up Canon.

Canon is where The Bistro used to be. When Quintana was six or seven John and I took her to The Bistro for a birthday lunch. She was wearing a lime green ruana I brought her from Bogotá. *Qué bonita, qué hermosa*, the busboys crooned.

I realize that if I continue up Canon I will be walking through the Rite-Aid in tears.

There is also the blood running down my leg.

I just noticed the blood.

The blood must have something to do with trying to use the self-serve island at the Union 76 on Wilshire this morning.

That did not go well.

Was it the car door?

If I walk into the Rite-Aid in this condition someone will alert security. Tears, blood, Aisle 3.

Scratch bottled water. Order bottled water from room service.

Did she ever read *Play It As It Lays*?

Did she ever read anything we wrote?

I don't mean dutifully turning the pages and saying "very good, really interesting," I mean actually read it?

John asked her that once. I never would have.

This was her answer: "When you read something you make a judgment on it and you don't want to make a judgment on your mother and father."

Very good. Really interesting.

Were we always so afraid of each other?

What were we afraid of?

Does she know I still see her as a child?

I am driving west on Santa Monica, to see a dermatologist about my leg—

Exactly, still bleeding—

Precisely, I should have gotten a stitch but I had to get to UCLA—

In any case.

I am on my way to this dermatologist for what they are now calling "wound care" when I see that roadwork will force me to take San Vicente. If I take San Vicente I will pass within three blocks of the house in Brentwood Park to which we moved when Quintana started Westlake.

I try to catch this one early.

I take out my cell phone on Santa Monica Boulevard and reschedule the appointment.

What I do next makes no sense at all.

What I do next is everything I have been working not to do.

I take the detour I cannot take.

I lose all control.

I stop the car on San Vicente.

I let the vortex take me.

There are girls in school uniforms outside the Brentwood Mart so it must be after school—

Hours must have passed—

How long have I been gone, did she wake?

Does she think I left her?

She could be alone thinking I broke the promise—

Pleated uniform skirts chopped off into minis—

Angel tenth-graders pushing the dress code—

Black wing, brown wing, hover over—

Twenty years and the spring is over—

I would read her that poem to go to sleep—

In the back of a closet I still have one of her chopped-off Westlake skirts—

Along with her St. John's Hospital volunteer pinafore and a black challis dress I bought her when she was three—

Today grieves, tomorrow grieves—

Cover me over, light-in-leaves—

She always woke in Malibu when the tide turned and the sea went silent—

This was never supposed to happen to her.

When I got to the hospital this morning I could not find a parking place on the Plaza 4 level.

Plaza 4 means you park outside, not in the structure.

Plaza 4 is important to me. Plaza 4 represents a routine.

On Plaza 4 you park against the hedge and you leave your pass on the dashboard and you lock the car and you walk up the terraces to the lobby and by the time you get there you are ready.

Prepared. You have willed this day to go as you need it to go.

This morning when I could not find the parking place I lost that sequence. I sat in the car waiting for a space. And I realized that I cannot will her to be safe.

I saw the extent to which I have been operating on magic.

If I follow the rules—

If I learn the language—

I followed the rules.

I learned the language.

I learned how to assess kidney function by the lab values. I learned how the placement of a screen in the vena cava prevents emboli from stopping the heart. I learned the significance of midline shift. Fixed and dilated pupils. The difference between a methicillin-resistant staph A hospital infection and a methicillin-resistant staph E hospital infection and what it will mean when each becomes resistant to vanc.

And I still can't keep her safe.

What was in my mind when I bought the blue cotton scrubs at the UCLA Medical Center bookstore?

Did it never occur to me that for the mother of a patient to show up at the hospital wearing blue cotton scrubs could only be construed as a suspicious violation of boundaries?

Has my isolation become this profound?

Must you always be right? Must you always have the last word?

I certainly don't have it now, do I?

If I can get her pronounced stable and discharged I can remove her from here.

We have had enough of IVs and PIC lines and CAT scans and swallow tests.

See where they are getting us. Nowhere.

She needs to be in the water.

She needs to let what hair she has go green from the chlorine.

They cut off half her hair in the OR and the rest got cut in the ICU but it is already growing back, baby hair, feathers, like a duck.

We can get her hair properly washed at the Beverly Wilshire.

We can sit by the pool and have our nails done together.

You think I'm crazy.

You think I'm crazy because otherwise I'm dangerous.

Radioactive.

If I'm sane, what happened to me could happen to you.

You don't want to hear what I have to tell you.

You want me to give you a good prognosis.

I can't. So it's safer to think I'm crazy.

Fine. It doesn't matter to me.

I was crazy for a while but I'm not now.

6

AFTER FIVE WEEKS they have pronounced her stable enough to be transferred for neurorehabilitation.

I have made arrangements with the Rusk Institute at NYU.

This transfer will require trained medical personnel.

Arrangements are made to medevac her: an ambulance from UCLA to an airport, an air ambulance to Teterboro, and an ambulance from Teterboro to NYU Hospital.

Records are faxed.

A CD-ROM of CAT scans is prepared.

A date is set: Friday, April 30.

The arrangement complete, I sit in the sun outside the hospital and watch a helicopter circling to land on the roof. Helicopters are always landing on this roof, suggesting trauma all over Southern California, remote scenes of highway carnage, distant falling cranes, bad days ahead for the husband or wife or mother or father who has not yet gotten the call.

My call is behind me.

I am taking her home.

The day of the flight unfolds with the nonsequential inexorability of a dream.

There is the question of whether the plane is at Santa Monica or Burbank or Van Nuys.

There is the insistence of the ambulance attendant that since no plane is in sight we must be going by helicopter.

I don't think so, I say, it's three thousand miles.

The plane is finally located, a jet Cessna with room for two pilots, two paramedics, the stretcher to which Quintana is strapped, and, if I sit on the bench over the oxygen canisters, me.

We take off.

I have with me a red suede Prada bag she was carrying the day she flew to California.

When I opened the safe at the Beverly Wilshire this morning I took out the plastic pouch reading *UCLA Medical Center Specimen for Laboratory* and put it in the Prada bag. By smoothing the plastic I can see what they sealed inside while they were taking her into surgery: her watch and her wedding rings and the little diamond earrings Susan Traylor's mother gave her.

When Quintana was part of Susan's family and Susan part of ours.

When Susan would go to Honolulu with us.

One morning in Honolulu John insisted that Susan and Quintana come in from the water and go with us to the Honolulu courthouse, where we were following a prostitution trial.

It was his way of keeping them safe from drowning.

Improvised, like everything else in our life. Flying blind.

Why did I think this improvisation could never end?

I put something else in Quintana's bag this morning. The copy of *Clinical Neuroanatomy* I bought at the UCLA Medical Center bookstore when I could not understand what the doctors were saying. This book has been by my bed at the Beverly Wilshire for five weeks and I still do not understand what the doctors are saying. I do not even understand "the gilded boy story," a mysterious test for memory and comprehension that appears in "Appendix A: The Neurologic Examination."

The patient should be told the gilded boy story, according to Appendix A, and then asked to retell it and explain its meaning. Quote: "At the coronation of one of the popes, about 300 years ago, a little boy was chosen to play the part of an angel."

So far clear enough, although potentially troubling details for someone emerging from coma.

I mean "300 years ago"?

"Play the part of an angel"?

The narrative continues: "So that his appearance might be as magnificent as possible, he was covered from head to foot with gold foil. The little boy fell ill, and although everything possible was done for his recovery, he died within a few hours."

What is the meaning of the gilded boy story?

Does it have to do with the fallibility of "the popes"?

With the fallibility of authority in general?

Given that "everything possible was done for his recovery," does it have to do with the specific fallibility of medicine?

What possible point could there be in telling this story to a patient immobilized in a neuro ICU at a major teaching hospital?

What lesson could be drawn?

Do they think that because it's a "story" it can be told without consequence?

It occurs to me that the gilded boy story represents, in its utter impenetrability and apparent disregard for the sensitivity of the patient, the entire situation that Quintana and I are right now leaving behind.

We fly for a while.

I keep checking the bag to make sure I have not lost her rings.

I have her rings, I have her.

It might take six weeks, even the whole summer and fall, but she will play tennis again.

She will take pictures again.

She will swim out of a riptide.

I turn my attention to the paramedics.

One of them has a digital camera and is taking pictures of what he keeps calling the Grand Canyon. I correct him. I say it is not the Grand Canyon but Lake Mead, Hoover Dam.

I point out Las Vegas.

He continues taking pictures.

He also continues calling it the Grand Canyon.

All right, I think. It's the Grand Canyon. I shift position on the bench over the oxygen canisters so I can no longer see out the window.

We land in a cornfield in Kansas to refuel. The pilots strike a deal with the two teenagers who manage the strip: during the refueling they will take their pickup to a McDonald's and bring back hamburgers. While we wait I walk to where the tarmac ends and the corn begins. There is a little rain and unstable air and I imagine a tornado coming.

John wrote a tornado into his last novel.

Six weeks after he died I read the galleys in Quintana's room at Columbia Presbyterian.

In the passage about the tornado there was what could have been a typo, a dropped word. I considered adding the word but did not.

If I added a word he did not want he might not come back.

Today at the end of the tarmac I realize something:

I am no longer waiting for him to come back.

That's gone. I lost it. He's dead. He can't come back. He can't hold on to her in the water.

Any more than she and I can go back to Malibu.

The Malibu house was a teardown.

As was the house in Brentwood Park.

Black wing, brown wing, hover over—

Twenty years and the spring is over—

What exactly was wrong with thinking he could come back?

Wasn't it getting us through this?

What can get us through this now?

Back in the plane I take one of the hamburgers from the McDonald's bag and tear it into pieces so that Quintana and I can share. After a few bites she shakes her head. She has been allowed solid food for only a week and cannot eat more. There is still a feeding tube in place in case she cannot eat at all.

"Am I going to make it," she asks then.

I choose to believe that she is asking if she will make it to New York.

"Definitely," I say.

Definitely you will be okay in California, I said five weeks ago.

That night when we arrive at NYU Gerry and Tony are standing outside to meet the ambulance. Gerry asks how the flight was. I say we shared a Big Mac in a cornfield in Kansas. "It wasn't a Big Mac," Quintana says. "It was a Quarter-Pounder."

Do you remember I said I gave her a bracelet like this one?

(Shows her bracelet)

I gave her this one.

I have the Prada bag too.

And the black dress she bought for John's funeral.

I sent the dress to Susan Traylor.

And the little diamond earrings Susan's mother gave Quintana.

7

HOW DID THIS HAPPEN.

On the fifteenth of July 2004 she was discharged from the Rusk Institute to continue neurorehabilitation on an outpatient basis.

A week later I went back to work. Because I was committed to write a piece on the campaign, I flew to Boston for the Democratic convention. When it was time to stand for the national anthem I could see myself pitching forward, in free fall. I became convinced that the Fleet Center escalators were locked to prevent my exit. I watched the rest of the convention on C-SPAN.

I realized that I *was* in fact in free fall.

Rendered incapable. Gone.

That I was only then beginning the process of mourning did not occur to me.

I began making notes.

They became a book. Because the book was about events that touched the heart of Quintana's life and of which she had no firsthand memory, I asked her to read the manuscript.

She said it was "very good."

"Really interesting."

Had we all along been distant from each other?

Or had we each been too acutely aware of how it would be to lose the other?

In June 2005 she was admitted to another ICU through another ER, this one at Cornell.

The same ER where her father had been pronounced dead on arrival.

She had been at home with Gerry, Sunday lunch, sudden nausea, probably a stomach bug, it's going around.

The less casual diagnosis was acute pancreatitis.

Followed by septic shock.

We were back to vanc. We were back to Xigris.

At Beth Israel she had gone to the edge of death. At UCLA she had again gone to the edge.

Does going that close leave its mark?

Are you ever again as you were?

Or does the damage hide, pick its time, line up its target, kick back in just when you think you're safe?

Say at Sunday lunch with your husband? A lazy afternoon? The *Times* half read?

Don't let the Broken Man catch me, she would say when she was three or four and woke from bad dreams. *If the Broken Man comes I'll hang on to the fence and not let him take me.*

She let go of the fence on August 26, 2005.

There were days in July when everyone said "we're really very hopeful." There was the promise of a step-down unit. Physical therapists came by. Psychiatric residents came by. The last day she was awake she was perfectly lucid but anxious, the way she was before a trip. They were taking her down for a procedure. You're going to be fine, I said. It's nothing, it's diagnostic, they'll find out what's wrong and they'll fix it.

Definitely you will be okay in California.

You're safe.

I'm here.

If you have never seen this happen you won't believe it's going to happen.

They will have been telling you for days that it could happen—"could" meaning "will"—but you won't have believed it.

Somewhere in there someone will have said something like "we're not giving up on this" and that's what you will have heard.

You'll come into the ICU as usual one morning and there'll be fifteen or twenty people in scrubs and masks and gowns and gloves and one of them will tell you you can't come in.

Then the attending will notice you and come out.

And he'll mention the sixteen units of blood they have used since the numbers started dropping and the four more on their way.

And he'll explain that they are doing hand compression because the vent can't get enough oxygen into the lungs.

And then he'll take you in.

And he won't seem to care about the mask and the gown and the gloves.

And that's when you'll know.

Except you won't really.

Am I going to make it, she asked me in the cornfield in Kansas.

Definitely, I promised.

I watched the river as it happened.

Have you ever wondered why the ICUs in New York hospitals have such high-rent river views? Why you can watch the tide turn in the East River from the ICUs at Cornell? Why you can watch the sea surge press back the Hudson from the ICUs at Columbia?

I have a few more questions I need to ask her.

Did I lie to you?

Did I lie to you all your life?

When I said you're safe, I'm here, was that a lie or did you believe it?

Is a lie only a story that the hearer disbelieves?

Is that the only definition of a lie?

Or did you believe it?

8

THERE WAS ONE CHRISTMAS.

We were in Honolulu, doing a crash rewrite on a picture that never got made.

On that particular Christmas we ordered mahi-mahi and Manoa lettuce vinaigrette from room service. We tried for a holiday effect by arranging leis over the printers and computers we were using for the rewrite. We found candles and lit them. John fell asleep about eleven thirty. Quintana and Susan went downstairs to see what was happening.

I could see John sleeping.

I knew Quintana and Susan were safe, they had been going downstairs to see what was happening in this hotel since they were seven.

I had a sense of well-being so profound that I did not want to go to sleep. Everyone was so safe that I could sit on a balcony overlooking the Waialae Country Club golf course and finish the wine we drank with dinner and watch neighborhood fireworks all over Honolulu.

9

I TOLD YOU I WROTE A BOOK.

(Reads from page 188)

"Grief turns out to be a place none of us know until we reach it. We know that someone close to us could die. We might expect to feel shock. We do not expect this shock to be obliterative, dislocating to both body and mind. We might expect to be prostrate, inconsolable, crazy with loss. We do not expect to be literally crazy, cool customers who believe that their husband is about to return and need his shoes. Nor can we know ahead of the fact—and here lies the heart of the difference between grief as we imagine it and grief as it is—the unending absence that follows, the void, the relentless succession of moments during which we will confront the experience of meaninglessness itself."

(Not reading)

I went on to explain that as a child I thought a great deal about meaninglessness, which seemed at the time the most prominent negative feature on the horizon.

(Reading)

"After a few years of failing to find meaning in the more commonly recommended venues I learned that I could find it in geology, so I did. This in turn enabled me to find meaning in the Episcopal litany, most acutely in the words *as it was in the beginning, is now and ever shall be, world without end*, which I interpreted as a literal description of the constant changing of the earth, the unending erosion of the shores and mountains, the inexorable shifting of the geological structures that could throw up mountains and islands and could just as reliably take them away. No eye was on the sparrow. No one was watching me."

(Closes the book)

After the book was published many people asked me if this view had not changed.

Been modified.

If "what I had been through"—this was always the phrase

—had not offered me a more "comforting" version of the meaning of life and death. "Comforting" was always the word.

When I am asked this question I consider the solace I found in geology.

In its promise that the world will change but also continue.

Do I still find that solace?

How about those river views from the ICUs?

Those eddies, those tidal bores, those currents, those floes?

If those aren't about geology, what are they about?

As it was in the beginning, is now and ever shall be, world without end?

Do we get more "comfort" than that?

We all know that if we are to live ourselves there comes a time when we must relinquish the dead, let them go, keep them dead.

Let them become the photograph on the table.

Let them become the name on the trust accounts.

Let go of them in the water.

Knowing this does not make it any easier to let go of them in the water.

I did not want the year after either of them died to end. I knew that as the second year began and the days passed, certain things would happen. My image of them at the instant of death would become something that happened in another year. My sense of John and Quintana themselves, John and Quintana alive, would become more remote, softened, transmuted into whatever best served my life without them.

In fact this is already happening.

For once in your life just let it go.

During the years when people still left Honolulu on the Matson Lines the custom at the moment of departure was to throw leis on the water, a promise that the traveler would return. The leis would get caught in the wake and go bruised and brown.

Leis go brown, tectonic plates shift, deep currents change.

I think about bringing her home from St. John's Hospital in

Santa Monica and placing her in the bassinette that overlooked the point where the sea ran into the cave.

The cave into which we never again swam after the day we brought her home.

One more improvised way of keeping her from drowning.

You're safe. I'm here.

He checked every few minutes to see if she was breathing.

When she was five days old he christened her himself, in a sink.

Just in case she didn't live until we could do the ceremony.

She did live that long.

She lived long enough to stand up in her black dress at his funeral and say "I love you more than even one more day. As you used to say to me."

Maybe she did.

Maybe he did.

I think about swimming with him into that cave, about the swell of clear water, the way it changed, the swiftness and power it gained as it narrowed through the rocks at the base of the point.

The tide had to be just right.

We had to be in the water at the very moment the tide was right.

We could only have done this a half dozen times at most during the two years we lived there but it is what I remember. Each time we did it I was afraid of missing the swell, hanging back, timing it wrong. He never was. You had to feel the swell change. You had to go with the change. He told me that. No eye is on the sparrow but he did tell me that.

BLUE NIGHTS

This book is for Quintana

1

In certain latitudes there comes a span of time approaching and following the summer solstice, some weeks in all, when the twilights turn long and blue. This period of the blue nights does not occur in subtropical California, where I lived for much of the time I will be talking about here and where the end of daylight is fast and lost in the blaze of the dropping sun, but it does occur in New York, where I now live. You notice it first as April ends and May begins, a change in the season, not exactly a warming—in fact not at all a warming—yet suddenly summer seems near, a possibility, even a promise. You pass a window, you walk to Central Park, you find yourself swimming in the color blue: the actual light is blue, and over the course of an hour or so this blue deepens, becomes more intense even as it darkens and fades, approximates finally the blue of the glass on a clear day at Chartres, or that of the Cerenkov radiation thrown off by the fuel rods in the pools of nuclear reactors. The French called this time of day "l'heure bleue." To the English it was "the gloaming." The very word "gloaming" reverberates, echoes—the gloaming, the glimmer, the glitter, the glisten, the glamour—carrying in its consonants the images of houses shuttering, gardens darkening, grass-lined rivers slipping through the shadows. During the blue nights you think the end of day will never come. As the blue nights draw to a close (and they will, and they do) you experience an actual chill, an apprehension of illness, at the moment you first notice: the blue light is going, the days are already shortening, the summer is gone. This book is called "Blue Nights" because at the time I began it I found my mind turning increasingly to illness, to the end of promise, the dwindling of the days, the inevitability of the fading, the dying of the brightness. Blue nights are the opposite of the dying of the brightness, but they are also its warning.

2

JULY 26, 2010.

Today would be her wedding anniversary.

Seven years ago today we took the leis from the florist's boxes and shook the water in which they were packed onto the grass outside the Cathedral of St. John the Divine on Amsterdam Avenue. The white peacock spread his fan. The organ sounded. She wove white stephanotis into the thick braid that hung down her back. She dropped a tulle veil over her head and the stephanotis loosened and fell. The plumeria blossom tattooed just below her shoulder showed through the tulle. "Let's do it," she whispered. The little girls in leis and pale dresses skipped down the aisle and walked behind her up to the high altar. After all the words had been said the little girls followed her out the front doors of the cathedral and around past the peacocks (the two iridescent blue-and-green peacocks, the one white peacock) to the Cathedral house. There were cucumber and watercress sandwiches, a peach-colored cake from Payard, pink champagne.

Her choices, all.

Sentimental choices, things she remembered.

I remembered them too.

When she said she wanted cucumber and watercress sandwiches at her wedding I remembered her laying out plates of cucumber and watercress sandwiches on the tables we had set up around the pool for her sixteenth-birthday lunch. When she said she wanted leis in place of bouquets at her wedding I remembered her at three or four or five getting off a plane at Bradley Field in Hartford wearing the leis she had been given when she left Honolulu the night before. The temperature in Connecticut that morning was six degrees below zero and she had no coat (she had been wearing no coat when we left Los Angeles for Honolulu, we had not expected to go on to Hartford) but she had seen no problem. Children with leis don't wear coats, she advised me.

Sentimental choices.

On the day of that wedding she got all her sentimental

choices except one: she had wanted the little girls to go barefoot in the cathedral (memory of Malibu, she was always barefoot in Malibu, she always had splinters from the redwood deck, splinters from the deck and tar from the beach and iodine for the scratches from the nails in the stairs in between) but the little girls had new shoes for the occasion and wanted to wear them.

MR. AND MRS. JOHN GREGORY DUNNE

REQUEST THE HONOR OF YOUR PRESENCE

AT THE MARRIAGE OF THEIR DAUGHTER,

QUINTANA ROO

TO

MR. GERALD BRIAN MICHAEL

ON SATURDAY THE TWENTY-SIXTH OF JULY

AT TWO O'CLOCK

The stephanotis.

Was that another sentimental choice?

Did she remember the stephanotis?

Is that why she wanted it, is that why she wove it into her braid?

At the house in Brentwood Park in which we lived from 1978 until 1988, a house so determinedly conventional (two stories, center-hall plan, shuttered windows, and a sitting room off every bedroom) as to seem in situ idiosyncratic ("their suburbia house in Brentwood" was how she referred to the house when we bought it, a twelve-year-old establishing that it was not her decision, not her taste, a child claiming the distance all children imagine themselves to need), there was stephanotis growing outside the terrace doors. I would brush the waxy flowers when I went out to the garden. Outside the same doors there were beds of lavender and also mint, a tangle of mint, made lush by a dripping faucet. We moved into that house the summer she was about to start the seventh grade at what was then still the Westlake School for Girls in Holmby Hills. This was like yesterday. We moved out of that house the year she was about to graduate from Barnard. This too was like yesterday. The stephanotis and mint were dead by then, killed when the man who was buying the house insisted that we rid it of termites by tenting it and pumping in Vikane and chloropicrin. At the time this buyer bid on the house he sent us word via the brokers, apparently by way of closing the deal, that he wanted the house because he could picture his daughter marrying in the garden. This was a few weeks before he required us to pump in the Vikane that killed the stephanotis, killed the mint, and also killed the pink magnolia into which the twelve-year-old who took so assiduously removed a view of our suburbia house in Brentwood had until then been able to look from her second-floor sitting-room windows. The termites, I was quite sure, would come back. The pink magnolia, I was also quite sure, would not.

We closed the deal and moved to New York.

Where in fact I had lived before, from the time I was twenty-one and just out of the English Department at Berkeley and starting work at *Vogue* (a segue so profoundly unnatural that when I was asked by the Condé Nast personnel department to name the languages in which I was fluent I could think only of Middle English) until I was twenty-nine and just married.

Where I have lived again since 1988.

Why then do I say I lived much of this time in California?

Why then did I feel so sharp a sense of betrayal when I exchanged my California driver's license for one issued by New York? Wasn't that actually a straightforward enough transaction? Your birthday comes around, your license needs renewing, what difference does it make where you renew it? What difference does it make that you have had this single number on your license since it was assigned to you at age fifteen-and-a-half by the state of California? Wasn't there always an error on that driver's license anyway? An error you knew about? Didn't that license say you were five-foot-two? When you knew perfectly well you were at best—(max height, top height ever, height before you lost a half inch to age)—when you knew perfectly well you were at best five-foot-one-and-three-quarters?

Why did I make so much of the driver's license?

What was that about?

Did giving up the California license say that I would never again be fifteen-and-a-half?

Would I want to be?

Or was the business with the license just one more case of "the apparent inadequacy of the precipitating event"?

I put "the apparent inadequacy of the precipitating event" in quotes because it is not my phrase.

Karl Menninger used it, in *Man Against Himself*, by way of describing the tendency to overreact to what might seem ordinary, even predictable, circumstances: a propensity, Dr. Menninger tells us, common among suicides. He cites the young woman who becomes depressed and kills herself after cutting her hair. He mentions the man who kills himself because he has been advised to stop playing golf, the child who commits suicide because his canary died, the woman who kills herself after missing two trains.

Notice: not one train, *two* trains.

Think that over.

Consider what special circumstances are required before this woman throws it all in.

"In these instances," Dr. Menninger tells us, "the hair, the golf, and the canary had an exaggerated value, so that when they were lost or when there was even a threat that they might be lost, the recoil of severed emotional bonds was fatal."

Yes, clearly, no argument.

"The hair, the golf, and the canary" had each been assigned an exaggerated value (as presumably had the second of those two missed trains), but why? Dr. Menninger himself asks this question, although only rhetorically: "But why should such extravagantly exaggerated over-estimations and incorrect evaluations exist?" Did he imagine that he had answered the question simply by raising it? Did he think that all he had to do was formulate the question and then retreat into a cloud of theoretical psychoanalytic references? Could I seriously have construed changing my driver's license from California to New York as an experience involving "severed emotional bonds"?

Did I seriously see it as loss?

Did I truly see it as separation?

And before we leave this subject of "severed emotional bonds":

The last time I saw the house in Brentwood Park before its title changed hands we stood outside watching the three-level Allied van pull away and turn onto Marlboro Street, everything we then owned, including a Volvo station wagon, already inside and on its way to New York. After the van moved out of sight we walked through the empty house and out across the terrace, a good-bye moment rendered less tender by the lingering reek of Vikane in the house and the stiff dead leaves where the pink magnolia and stephanotis had been. I smelled Vikane even in New York, every time I unpacked a carton. The next time I was in Los Angeles and drove past the house it was gone, a teardown, to be replaced a year or two later by a house marginally bigger (a new room over the garage, an additional foot or two in a kitchen already large enough to accommodate a square Chickering grand piano that remained mostly unnoticed) but lacking (for me) the resolute conventionality of the original. Some years later in a Washington bookstore I met the daughter, the one the buyer had said he could picture marrying in the garden. She was at school somewhere in Washington (Georgetown? George Washington?), I was there to give a reading at Politics and Prose. She introduced herself. I grew up in your house, she said. Not exactly, I refrained from saying.

John always said we moved "back" to New York.

I never did.

Brentwood Park was then, New York was now.

Brentwood Park before the Vikane had been a time, a period, a decade, during which everything had seemed to connect.

Our suburbia house in Brentwood.

It was exactly that. She called it.

There had been cars, a swimming pool, a garden.

There had been agapanthus, lilies of the Nile, intensely blue starbursts that floated on long stalks. There had been gaura, clouds of tiny white blossoms that became visible at eye level only as the daylight faded.

There had been English chintzes, chinoiserie toile.

There had been a Bouvier des Flandres motionless on the stair landing, one eye open, on guard.

Time passes.

Memory fades, memory adjusts, memory conforms to what we think we remember.

Even memory of the stephanotis in her braid, even memory of the plumeria tattoo showing through the tulle.

It is horrible to see oneself die without children. Napoléon Bonaparte said that.

What greater grief can there be for mortals than to see their children dead. Euripedes said that.

When we talk about mortality we are talking about our children.

I said that.

I think now of that July day at St. John the Divine in 2003 and am struck by how young John and I appeared to be, how well. In actual fact neither of us was in the least well: John had that spring and summer undergone a series of cardiac procedures, most recently the implantation of a pacemaker, the efficacy of which remained in question; I had three weeks before the wedding collapsed on the street and spent the several nights following in a Columbia Presbyterian ICU being transfused for an unexplained gastrointestinal bleed. "You're just going to swallow a little camera," they said in the ICU when they were trying to demonstrate to themselves what was causing the bleed. I recall resisting: since I had never in my life been able to swallow an aspirin it seemed unlikely that I could swallow a camera.

"Of course you can, it's only a *little* camera."

A pause. The attempt at briskness declined into wheedling:

"It's really a *very* little camera."

In the end I did swallow the very little camera, and the very little camera transmitted the desired images, which did not demonstrate what was causing the bleed but did demonstrate that with sufficient sedation anyone could swallow a very little camera. Similarly, in another less than entirely efficient use of high-tech medicine, John could hold a telephone to his heart, dial a number, and get a reading on the pacemaker, which proved, I was told, that at the given instant he dialed the number (although not necessarily before or after) the device was operating.

Medicine, I have had reason since to notice more than once, remains an imperfect art.

Yet all had seemed well when we were shaking the water off the leis onto the grass outside St. John the Divine on July 26, 2003. Could you have seen, had you been walking on Amsterdam Avenue and caught sight of the bridal party that day, how utterly unprepared the mother of the bride was to accept what would happen before the year 2003 had even ended? The father of the bride dead at his own dinner table? The bride herself in an induced coma, breathing only on a respirator, not expected by the doctors in the intensive care unit to live the night? The first in a cascade of medical crises that would end twenty months later with her death?

Twenty months during which she would be strong enough to walk unsupported for possibly a month in all?

Twenty months during which she would spend weeks at a time in the intensive care units of four different hospitals?

In all of those intensive care units there were the same blue-and-white printed curtains. In all of those intensive care units there were the same sounds, the same gurgling through plastic tubing, the same dripping from the IV line, the same rales, the same alarms. In all of those intensive care units there were the same requirements to guard against further infections, the donning of the double gowns, the paper slippers, the surgical cap, the mask, the gloves that pulled on only with difficulty and left a rash that reddened and bled. In all of those intensive care units there was the same racing through the unit when a code was called, the feet hitting the floor, the rattle of the crash cart.

This was never supposed to happen to her, I remember thinking—outraged, as if she and I had been promised a special exemption—in the third of those intensive care units.

By the time she reached the fourth I was no longer invoking this special exemption.

When we talk about mortality we are talking about our children.

I just said that, but what does it mean?

All right, of course I can track it, of course you can track it, another way of acknowledging that our children are hostages to fortune, but when we talk about our children what are we saying? Are we saying what it meant to us to have them? What it meant to us not to have them? What it meant to let them go? Are we talking about the enigma of pledging ourselves to protect the unprotectable? About the whole puzzle of being a parent?

Time passes.

Yes, agreed, a banality, of course time passes.

Then why do I say it, why have I already said it more than once?

Have I been saying it the same way I say I have lived most of my life in California?

Have I been saying it without hearing what I say?

Could it be that I heard it more this way: *Time passes, but not so aggressively that anyone notices?* Or even: *Time passes, but not for me?* Could it be that I did not figure in either the general nature or the permanence of the slowing, the irreversible changes in mind and body, the way in which you wake one summer morning less resilient than you were and by Christmas find your ability to mobilize gone, atrophied, no longer extant? The way in which you live most of your life in California, and then you don't? The way in which your awareness of this passing time—this permanent slowing, this vanishing resilience—multiplies, metastasizes, becomes your very life?

Time passes.

Could it be that I never believed it?

Did I believe the blue nights could last forever?

3

LAST SPRING, 2009, I had some warnings, flags on the track, definite notices of darkening even before the blue nights came.

L'heure bleue. The gloaming.

Not even yet evident when that year's darkening gave its first notices.

The initial such notice was sudden, the ringing telephone you wish you had never answered, the news no one wants to get: someone to whom I had been close since her childhood, Natasha Richardson, had fallen on a ski slope outside Quebec (spring break, a family vacation, a bunny slope, *this was never supposed to happen to her*) and by the time she noticed that she did not feel entirely well she was dying, the victim of an epidural hematoma, a traumatic brain injury. She was the daughter of Vanessa Redgrave and Tony Richardson, who was one of our closest friends in Los Angeles. The first time I ever saw her she had been maybe thirteen or fourteen, not yet entirely comfortable in her own skin, an uncertain but determined adolescent with a little too much makeup and startlingly white stockings. She had come from London to visit her father at his house on Kings Road in Hollywood, an eccentrically leveled structure that had belonged to Linda Lovelace, the star of *Deep Throat*. Tony had bought the house and proceeded to fill it with light and parrots and whippets. When Tasha arrived from London he had brought her to dinner with us at La Scala. The dinner had not been planned as a party for her arrival but there had happened to be many people her father and we knew at La Scala that night and her father had made it feel like one. She had been pleased. A few years later Quintana had been at the same uncertain age and Tasha, by then seventeen, was spending the summer at Le Nid du Duc, the village her father had invented, an entertainment of his own, a director's conceit, in the hills of the Var above Saint-Tropez.

To say that Tasha was spending the summer at Le Nid du Duc fails to adequately suggest the situation. In fact, by the time John and I arrived in France that summer, Tasha was running Le Nid du Duc, the seventeen-year-old chatelaine of what amounted to a summer-long house party for a floating thirty people. Tasha was managing the provisioning of the several houses that made up the compound. Tasha was cooking and serving, entirely unaided, three meals a day for the basic thirty as well as for anyone else who happened up the hill and had a drink and waited for the long tables under the lime trees to be set—not only cooking and serving but, as Tony noted in his memoir *The Long-Distance Runner*, "completely unfazed when told that there'd be an extra twenty for lunch."

Most astonishingly, at seventeen, Tasha was undertaking the induction into adult life not only of her sisters Joely and Katharine but of two Los Angeles eighth-graders, one of them Quintana, the other Kenneth and Kathleen Tynan's daughter Roxana, both avid to grow up, each determined to misbehave. Tasha made certain that Quintana and Roxana got to the correct spot on the beach at Saint-Tropez every afternoon, that summer's correct spot of choice being the Aqua Club. Tasha made certain that Quintana and Roxana got a proper introduction to the Italian boys who trailed them on the beach, a "proper introduction" for Tasha entailing a meal at the long tables under the lime trees at Le Nid du Duc. Tasha came up from the Aqua Club and Tasha did a perfect beurre blanc for the fish Tony had bought that morning and Tasha watched Quintana and Roxana mesmerize the Italian boys into believing that they were dealing not with fourteen-year-olds last seen in the pastel cotton uniforms of the Westlake and Marlborough Schools for Girls in Los Angeles but with preternaturally sophisticated undergraduates from UCLA.

And never ever, not once, not ever, did I hear Tasha blow the whistle on that or on any other of the summer's romantic fables.

Au contraire.

Tasha devised the fables, Tasha wrote the romance.

The last time I ever saw her was a few nights after she fell on the bunny slope outside Quebec, in a room at Lenox Hill Hospital in New York, lying as if about to wake.

She was not about to wake.

She had been flown down from Montreal while her family met in New York.

When I left the hospital after seeing her there were photographers outside, waiting for clear camera lines on the family.

I circled around them onto Park Avenue and walked on home.

Her first marriage, to the producer Robert Fox, had taken place in my apartment. She had filled the rooms with quince blossoms for the ceremony. The blossoms had eventually fallen but the branches had remained, brittle and dusty, twigs breaking off, nonetheless still passing as decorative elements in the living room. When I walked in from Lenox Hill that night the apartment seemed full of photographs of Tasha and of her father and mother. Her father on location for *The Border*, riding a Panavision camera. Her father on location in Spain, wearing a red windbreaker, directing Melanie Griffith and James Woods on an HBO project he and John and I did together. Her mother backstage at the Booth Theater on West Forty-fifth Street, the year she and I did a play together. Tasha herself, talking to John at one of the long tables she had arranged outside for the wedding dinner on her farm in Millbrook when she was married a second time, this time to Liam Neeson.

She had managed that wedding on the farm as before and after she managed summers at Le Nid du Duc.

She had managed even a priest, a wedding mass. She had kept referring to the priest as "Father Dan." It was only when he stood to actually do the ceremony that I realized that "Father Dan" was Daniel Berrigan, one of the activist Berrigan brothers. It seemed that Daniel Berrigan had been an advisor on Roland Joffé's *The Mission*. It seemed that Liam had played a role in *The Mission*. Tasha had designed the entire event, in other words, as a piece of theater, the very kind of moment Tony liked best in the world. He particularly would have liked Tasha forgetting the wafers for the mass, tearing up long baguettes to pass in their place, but Tony was dead by the day of that wedding.

Tasha died in March 2009.

This was never supposed to happen to her.

On her twenty-first birthday her father had made a film of the lunch he gave in her honor at Linda Lovelace's former house on Kings Road. John had wished her happy birthday, on film. Quintana and Fiona Lewis and Tamara Asseyev had sung "Girls Just Want to Have Fun," on film. After lunch we had untied rafts of white balloons and watched them drift over the Hollywood hills, on film. These are the lines from W. H. Auden that Tony quoted that afternoon as "the best twenty-first birthday wish you can make for anyone":

> *So I wish you first a*
> *Sense of theatre; only*
> *Those who love illusion*
> *And know it will go far—*

Tasha and her father and John and Quintana and the whippets and the parrots and the white balloons, all still there, on film.

I have a copy of the film.

So I wish you first a sense of theatre—

So her father would have said at the wedding in Millbrook.

The second such warning, this one not at all sudden, came in April 2009.

Because I had been showing symptoms of neuritis, or neuropathy, or neurological inflammation (there seemed no general agreement on what to call it), an MRI was done, then an MRA. Neither suggested a definitive reason for the symptoms at hand but images of the Circle of Willis showed evidence of a 4.2 mm by 3.4 mm aneurysm deep in that circle of arteries—the anterior cerebral, the anterior communicating, the internal carotid, the posterior cerebral, and the posterior communicating—at the base of my brain. This finding, the several neurologists who examined the images stressed, was "entirely incidental," had "nothing to do with what we're looking for," and was not even necessarily significant. One of the neurologists ventured that this particular aneurysm "doesn't look ready to blow"; another suggested that "if it does blow, you won't live through it."

This seemed to be offered as encouraging news, and I accepted it as such. At that instant in April 2009 I realized that I was no longer, if I had ever been, afraid to die: I was now afraid not to die, afraid that I might damage my brain (or my heart or my kidneys or my nervous system) and survive, continue living.

Had there been an instant when Tasha was afraid not to die?

Had there been an instant when Quintana was afraid not to die?

Toward the very end, say, for example on the August morning when I walked into the ICU overlooking the river at New York–Cornell and one of what must have been twenty doctors in the unit happened to mention (a point of interest, a teachable moment, Grand Rounds for two students, the husband and the mother of the patient) that they were doing hand compression because the patient could no longer get enough oxygen through the ventilator? Only he did not say "the ventilator," he said "the vent"? And I asked dutifully (the attentive student, up on the vernacular) how long it had been since the patient could get enough oxygen through the vent? And the doctor said it had been at least an hour?

Did I get this all wrong?

Did I misunderstand a key point?

Could they have actually let an hour go by without mentioning to me that her brain had already been damaged by insufficient oxygen?

Put the question another way: what if the attentive student had never asked?

Would they have mentioned it at all?

One further turn of the screw: if I had never asked would she still be alive?

Warehoused somewhere?

No longer sentient but alive, not dead?

What greater grief can there be for mortals than to see their children dead?

Was there an instant when she knew what was in store for her that August morning in the ICU overlooking the river at New York–Cornell?

Did the instant occur that August morning when she was in fact dying?

Or had it occurred years before, when she thought she was?

4

"WHEN QUINTANA was a little girl, we moved to Malibu, to a house overlooking the Pacific." So began the toast John delivered in the Cathedral house at St. John the Divine on the afternoon she wove the stephanotis into her braid and cut the peach-colored cake from Payard. There were aspects of living in that house overlooking the Pacific that he failed to mention—he failed to mention for example the way the wind would blow down through the canyons and whine under the eaves and lift the roof and coat the white walls with ash from the fireplace, he failed to mention for example the king snakes that dropped from the rafters of the garage into the open Corvette I parked below, he failed to mention for example that king snakes were locally considered a valuable asset because the presence of a king snake in your Corvette was understood to mean (I was never convinced that it did) that you didn't have a rattlesnake in your Corvette—but the following is what he did mention. I can quote what he mentioned exactly because after he mentioned it he wrote it down. He wanted her to have it in his words, his exact memory, in his exact words, of her childhood:

> The house didn't have any heat—it had old baseboard heaters, but we were always afraid they'd burn the place up—and so we heated it from this huge walk-in fireplace in the living room. In the morning I'd get up and bring in wood for the day—we used about a cord of wood a week—and then I'd get Q up and make her breakfast and get her ready for school. Joan was trying to finish a book that year, and she would work until two or three in the morning, then have a drink and read some poetry before she came to bed. She always made Q's lunch the night before, and put it in this little blue lunchbox. You should have seen those lunches: they weren't your basic peanut butter and jelly school-box lunch. Thin little sandwiches with their crusts cut off, cut into four triangular pieces, kept fresh in Saran Wrap. Or else there would be homemade fried chicken, with little salt and pepper shakers. And for dessert, stemmed strawberries, with sour cream and brown sugar.

> So I'd take Q to school, and she'd walk down this steep hill. All the kids wore uniforms—Quintana wore a plaid jumper and a white sweater, and her hair—she was a towhead in that Malibu sun—her hair was in a ponytail. I would watch her disappear down that hill, the Pacific a great big blue background, and I thought it was as beautiful as anything I'd ever seen. So I said to Joan, "You got to see this, babe." The next morning Joan came with us, and when she saw Q disappear down that hill she began to cry.
>
> Today Quintana is walking back up that hill. She's not the towhead with the plaid jumper and the blue lunchbox and the ponytail. She's the Princess Bride—and at the top of that hill stands her Prince. Will you join me please in toasting Gerry and Quintana.

We did.

We joined him in toasting Gerry and Quintana.

We toasted Gerry and Quintana at St. John the Divine and a few hours later, in their absence, at a Chinese restaurant on West Sixty-fifth Street with my brother and his family, we toasted Gerry and Quintana again. We wished them happiness, we wished them health, we wished them love and luck and beautiful children. On that wedding day, July 26, 2003, we could see no reason to think that such ordinary blessings would not come their way.

Do notice:

We still counted happiness and health and love and luck and beautiful children as "ordinary blessings."

5

SEVEN YEARS LATER.
July 26, 2010.

Laid out on a table in front of me today is a group of photographs sent to me only recently but all taken in 1971, summer or fall, in or around the unheated house in Malibu mentioned in the wedding toast. We had moved into that house in January 1971, on a perfectly clear day which turned so foggy that by the time I drove back to the house from a late-day run to the Trancas Market, three-and-a-half miles down the Pacific Coast Highway, I could no longer find the driveway. Since sundown fogs in January and February and March turned out to be as much a given of that stretch of coast as wildfires would be in September and October and November, this disappearance of the driveway was by no means an unusual turn of events: the preferred method for finding it was to hold your breath, avert your mind from the unseeable cliff below, rising two-hundred-some feet from open ocean, and turn left.

Neither the fogs nor the wildfires figure in the photographs.

There are eighteen images.

Each is of the same child at the same age, Quintana at five, her hair, as noted in the wedding toast, bleached by the beach sun. In some she is wearing her plaid uniform jumper, also noted in the toast. In a few she is wearing a cashmere turtleneck sweater I brought her from London when we went that May to do promotion for the European release of *The Panic in Needle Park*. In a few she is wearing a checked gingham dress trimmed in eyelet, a little faded and a little too big for her, the look of a hand-me-down. In others she has on cutoff jeans and a denim Levi jacket with metal studs, a bamboo fishing pole against her shoulder, artfully arranged there (by her) in a spirit less of fishing than of styling, a prop to accessorize the outfit.

The photographs were taken by one of her West Hartford cousins, Tony Dunne, who had arrived on leave from Williams to spend a few months in Malibu. He had been in Malibu only a day or two when she began to lose her first baby tooth. She had noticed the tooth loosening, she had wiggled the tooth, the tooth loosened further. I tried to remember how this situation had been handled in my own childhood. My most coherent memory involved my mother tying a piece of thread around the loose tooth, attaching the thread to a doorknob, and slamming the door. I tried this. The tooth stayed fixed in place. She cried. I grabbed the car keys and screamed for Tony: tying the thread to the doorknob had so exhausted my aptitude for improvisational caretaking that my sole remaining thought was to get her to the emergency room at UCLA Medical Center, thirty-some miles into town. Tony, who grew up with three siblings and many cousins, tried without success to convince me that UCLA Medical Center might be overkill. "Just let me try just this one thing first," he said finally, and pulled the tooth.

The next time a tooth got loose she pulled it herself. I had lost my authority.

Was I the problem? Was I always the problem?

In the note Tony included when he sent the photographs a few months ago he said that each image represented something he had seen in her. In some she is melancholy, large eyes staring directly into the lens. In others she is bold, daring the camera. She covers her mouth with her hand. She obscures her eyes with a polka-dotted cotton sun hat. She marches through the wash at the edge of the sea. She bites her lip as she swings from an oleander branch.

A few of these photographs are familiar to me.

A copy of one of them, one in which she is wearing the cashmere turtleneck sweater I bought her in London, is framed on my desk in New York.

There is also on my desk in New York a framed photograph she herself took one Christmas on Barbados: the rocks outside the rented house, the shallow sea, the wash of surf. I remember the Christmas she took that picture. We had arrived on Barbados at night. She had gone immediately to bed and I had sat outside listening to a radio and trying to locate a line I believed to be from Claude Lévi-Strauss's *Tristes Tropiques* but was never able to find: "The tropics are not exotic, they are merely out of date." At some point after she went to sleep news had come on the radio: since our arrival on Barbados the United

States had invaded Panama. When the first light came I had woken her with this necessary, or so it seemed to me, information. She had covered her face with the sheet, clearly indicating no interest in pursuing the topic. I had nonetheless pressed it. I knew "exactly yesterday" we were going to invade Panama last night, she had said. I asked how she had known "exactly yesterday" we were going to invade Panama last night. Because all the SIPA photographers were stopping by the office yesterday, she said, picking up credentials for the Panama invasion. SIPA was the photo agency for which she then worked. She had again burrowed beneath the sheet. I did not ask why she had not thought the invasion of Panama worth a mention on the five-hour flight down. "*For Mom and Dad*," the inscription on the photograph reads. "*Try to imagine the seductive sea if you can, love XX, Q.*"

She had known exactly yesterday we were going to invade Panama last night.

The tropics were not exotic, they were merely out of date.

Try to imagine the seductive sea if you can.

Even in those Malibu photographs which are unfamiliar, I recognize certain elements: the improvised end table by a chair in the living room, one of my mother's "Craftsman" dinner knives on the table we identified as "Aunt Kate's," the straightbacked wooden Hitchcock chairs my mother-in-law had painted black-and-gold to send to us from Connecticut.

The oleander branch on which she swings is familiar, the curve of the beach on which she kicks through the wash is familiar.

The clothes of course are familiar.

I had for a while seen them every day, washed them, hung them to blow in the wind on the clotheslines outside my office window.

I wrote two books watching her clothes blow on those lines.

Brush your teeth, brush your hair, shush I'm working.

So read the list of "Mom's Sayings" that she posted one day in the garage, an artifact of the "club" she had started with a child who lived down the beach.

What remained until now unfamiliar, what I recognize in the photographs but failed to see at the time they were taken, are the startling depths and shallows of her expressions, the quicksilver changes of mood.

How could I have missed what was so clearly there to be seen?

Did I not read the poem she brought home that year from the school on the steep hill? The school to which she wore the plaid uniform jumper and carried the blue lunchbox? The school to which John watched her walk every morning and thought it was as beautiful as anything he had ever seen?

"The World," this poem is called, and I recognize her careful printing, quixotically executed on a narrow strip of construction paper fourteen inches long but only two inches wide. I see that careful printing every day: the strip of construction paper is now framed on a wall behind my kitchen in New York, along with a few other mementos of the period: a copy of Karl Shapiro's "California Winter," torn from *The New Yorker*; a copy of Pablo Neruda's "A Certain Weariness," typed by me on one of the several dozen Royal manuals my father had bought (along with a few mess halls, a fire tower, and the regulation khaki Ford jeep on which I learned to drive) at a government auction; a postcard from Bogotá, sent by John and me to Quintana in Malibu; a photograph showing the coffee table in the beach house living room after dinner, the candles burning down and the silver baby cups filled with santolina; a mimeographed notice from the Topanga–Las Virgenes Fire District instructing residents of the district what to do "when the fire comes."

Do note: not "*if* the fire comes."

When the fire comes.

No one at the Topanga–Las Virgenes Fire District was talking about what most people see when they hear the words "brush fire," a few traces of smoke and an occasional lick of flame: at the Topanga–Las Virgenes Fire District they were talking about fires that burned on twenty-mile fronts and spotted ahead twelve-foot flames as they moved.

This was not forgiving territory: consider finding the driveway.

Also consider "The World" itself, its eccentric strip of construction paper and careful printing obscuring one side of the mimeographed notice from the Topanga–Las Virgenes Fire District. Since the choices made by the careful printer may or may not have meaning, I give you the text of "The World" with her spacing, her single misspelling:

THE
WORLD

The world
Has nothing
But morning
And night
It has no
Day or lunch
So this world
Is poor and desertid.
This is some
Kind of an
Island with
Only three
Houses on it
In these
Families are
2,1,2, people
In each house
So 2,1,2 make
Only 5 people
On this
Island.

In point of fact the beach on which we lived, our personal "some Kind of an Island," did have "Only three Houses on it," or, more correctly, it had only three houses that were occupied year-round. One of these three houses was owned by Dick Moore, a cinematographer who, when he was not on a location, lived there with his two daughters, Marina and Tita. It was Tita Moore who started the club with Quintana that entailed posting "Mom's Sayings" in our garage. Tita and Quintana also had an entrepreneurial enterprise, "the soap factory," the business mission of which was to melt down and reshape all remaining bars of the gardenia-scented I. Magnin soap I used to order by the box and sell the result to passers-by on the beach. Since both ends of this beach were submerged by the tide, no more than two or three passers-by would actually materialize during the soap factory's operating hours, enabling me to buy back my own I. Magnin soap, reconfigured from pristine ivory ovals into gray blobs. I have no memory of the other "Families" in these houses, but in our own I would have said that there were not "2, 1, 2, people" but "3 people."

Possibly Quintana saw our personal "some Kind of an Island" differently.

Possibly she had reason to.

Brush your teeth, brush your hair, shush I'm working.

Once when we were living in the beach house we came home to find that she had placed a call to what was known familiarly on our stretch of the coast as "Camarillo." Camarillo was at that time a state psychiatric facility twenty-some miles north of us in Ventura County, the hospital in which Charlie Parker once detoxed and then memorialized in "Relaxin' at Camarillo," the institution sometimes said to have provided inspiration to the Eagles for "Hotel California."

She had called Camarillo, she advised us, to find out what she needed to do if she was going crazy.

She was five years old.

On another occasion we came home to the beach house and found that she had placed a call to Twentieth Century–Fox.

She had called Twentieth Century–Fox, she explained, to find out what she needed to do to be a star.

Again, she was five years old, maybe six.

Tita Moore is dead now, she died before Quintana did.

Dick Moore is dead now too, he died last year.

Marina called me recently.

I do not remember what Marina and I talked about but I know we did not talk about the club with "Mom's Sayings" in the garage and I know we did not talk about the soap factory and I know we did not talk about how the ends of the beach got submerged by the tide.

I say this because I do not believe that either Marina or I could have managed such a conversation.

Relax, said the night man—
We are programmed to receive—
You can check out any time you like—
But you can never leave—

So goes the lyric to "Hotel California."
Depths and shallows, quicksilver changes.
She was already a person. I could never afford to see that.

6

WHAT ABOUT THE "Craftsman" dinner knife of my mother's?

The "Craftsman" dinner knife on Aunt Kate's table, the one I recognize in the photographs? Was it the same "Craftsman" dinner knife that dropped through the redwood slats of the deck into the iceplant on the slope? The same "Craftsman" dinner knife that stayed lost in the iceplant until the blade was pitted and the handle scratched? The knife we found only when we were correcting the drainage on the slope in order to pass the geological inspection required to sell the house and move to Brentwood Park? The knife I saved to pass on to her, a memento of the beach, of her grandmother, of her childhood?

I still have the knife.

Still pitted, still scratched.

I also still have the baby tooth her cousin Tony pulled, saved in a satin-lined jeweler's box, along with the baby teeth she herself eventually pulled and three loose pearls.

The baby teeth were to have been hers as well.

7

In fact I no longer value this kind of memento.

I no longer want reminders of what was, what got broken, what got lost, what got wasted.

There was a period, a long period, dating from my childhood until quite recently, when I thought I did.

A period during which I believed that I could keep people fully present, keep them with me, by preserving their mementos, their "things," their totems.

The detritus of this misplaced belief now fills the drawers and closets of my apartment in New York. There is no drawer I can open without seeing something I do not want, on reflection, to see. There is no closet I can open with room left for the clothes I might actually want to wear. In one closet that might otherwise be put to such use I see, instead, three old Burberry raincoats of John's, a suede jacket given to Quintana by the mother of her first boyfriend, and an angora cape, long since moth-eaten, given to my mother by my father not long after World War Two. In another closet I find a chest of drawers and perilously stacked assortment of boxes. I open one of the boxes. I find photographs taken by my grandfather when he was a mining engineer in the Sierra Nevada in the early years of the twentieth century. In another of the boxes I find the scraps of lace and embroidery that my mother had salvaged from her own mother's boxes of mementos.

The jet beads.

The ivory rosaries.

The objects for which there is no satisfactory resolution.

In the third of the boxes I find skein after skein of needlepoint yarn, saved in the eventuality that remedial stitches might ever be required on a canvas completed and given away in 2001. In the chest of drawers I find papers written by Quintana when she was still at the Westlake School for Girls: the research study on stress, the analysis of Angel Clare's role in *Tess of the d'Urbervilles*. I find her Westlake summer uniforms, I find her navy-blue gym shorts. I find the blue-and-white pinafore she wore for volunteering at St. John's Hospital in Santa

Monica. I find the black wool challis dress I bought her when she was four at Bendel's on West Fifty-seventh Street. When I bought that black wool challis dress Bendel's was still on West Fifty-seventh Street. It was that long ago. Bendel's became after Geraldine Stutz stopped running it just another store but when it was still on West Fifty-seventh Street and I bought that dress it was special, it was everything I wanted either one of us to wear, it was all Holly's Harp chiffon and lettuce edges and sizes zero and two.

Other objects for which there is no satisfactory resolution.

I continue opening boxes.

I find more faded and cracked photographs than I want ever again to see.

I find many engraved invitations to the weddings of people who are no longer married.

I find many mass cards from the funerals of people whose faces I no longer remember.

In theory these mementos serve to bring back the moment.

In fact they serve only to make clear how inadequately I appreciated the moment when it was here.

How inadequately I appreciated the moment when it was here is something else I could never afford to see.

8

HER DEPTHS AND SHALLOWS, her quicksilver changes. Of course they were not allowed to remain just that, depths, shallows, quicksilver changes.

Of course they were eventually assigned names, a "diagnosis." The names kept changing. Manic depression for example became OCD and OCD was short for obsessive-compulsive disorder and obsessive-compulsive disorder became something else, I could never remember just what but in any case it made no difference because by the time I did remember there would be a new name, a new "diagnosis." I put the word "diagnosis" in quotes because I have not yet seen that case in which a "diagnosis" led to a "cure," or in fact to any outcome other than a confirmed, and therefore an enforced, debility.

Yet another demonstration of medicine as an imperfect art.

She was depressed. She was anxious. Because she was depressed and because she was anxious she drank too much. This was called medicating herself. Alcohol has its own well-known defects as a medication for depression but no one has ever suggested—ask any doctor—that it is not the most effective anti-anxiety agent yet known. This would seem a fairly straightforward dynamic, yet, once medicalized—once the depths and shallows and quicksilver changes had been assigned names—it appeared not to be. We went through many diagnoses, many conditions that got called by many names, before the least programmatic among her doctors settled on one that seemed to apply. The name of the condition that seemed to apply was this: "borderline personality disorder." "Patients with this diagnosis are a complex mixture of strengths and weaknesses that confuse the diagnostician and frustrate the psychotherapist." So notes a 2001 *New England Journal of Medicine* review of John G. Gunderson's *Borderline Personality Disorder: A Clinical Guide*. "Such patients may seem charming, composed, and psychologically intact one day and collapse into suicidal despair the next." The review continues: "Impulsivity, affective lability, frantic efforts to avoid abandonment, and identity diffusion are all hallmarks."

I had seen most of these hallmarks.

I had seen the charm, I had seen the composure, I had seen the suicidal despair.

I had seen her wishing for death as she lay on the floor of her sitting room in Brentwood Park, the sitting room from which she had been able to look into the pink magnolia. *Let me just be in the ground*, she had kept sobbing. *Let me just be in the ground and go to sleep.*

I had seen the impulsivity.

I had seen the "affective lability," the "identity diffusion."

What I had not seen, or what I had in fact seen but had failed to recognize, were the "frantic efforts to avoid abandonment."

How could she have ever imagined that we could abandon her?

Had she no idea how much we needed her?

I recently read for the first time several fragments of what she had referred to at the time she wrote them as "the novel I'm writing just to show you." She must have been thirteen or fourteen when this project occurred to her. "Some of the events are based on the truth and the others are fictitious," she advises the reader at the outset. "The names have not yet been definitively changed." The protagonist in these fragments, also fourteen and also named Quintana (although sometimes referred to by other names, presumably trials for the definitive changes to come), believes she may be pregnant. She consults, in a plot point that seems specifically crafted to "confuse the diagnostician and frustrate the psychotherapist," her pediatrician. The pediatrician advises her that she must tell her parents. She does so. Her idea of how her parents would respond seems, like the entire rest of the plot point involving the pregnancy, confused, a fantasy, a manifestation of what might be extreme emotional distress or might be no more than narrative inventiveness: "They said that they would provide the abortion but after that they did not even care about her any more. She could live in their suburbia house in Brentwood, but they didn't even care what she did any more. That was fine in her book. Her father had a bad temper, but it showed that they cared very much about their only child. Now, they didn't even care any more. Quintana would lead her life any way she wanted."

At this point the fragment skids to an abrupt close: "On the next pages you will find out why and how Quintana died and her friends became complete burnouts at the age of eighteen."

So ended the novel she was writing just to show us.

Show us what?

Show us that she could write a novel?

Show us why and how she would die?

Show us what she believed our reaction would be?

Now, they didn't even care any more.

No.

She had no idea how much we needed her.

How could we have so misunderstood one another?

Had she chosen to write a novel because we wrote novels? Had it been one more obligation pressed on her? Had she felt it as a fear? Had we?

What follows are notes I made about a figure who at an earlier point had populated her nightmares, a fantast she called The Broken Man and described so often and with such troubling specificity that I was frequently moved to check for him on the terrace outside her second-floor windows. "He has on a blue work shirt, like a repair man," she repeatedly told me. "Short sleeves. He has his name always on his shirt. On the right-hand side. His name is David, Bill, Steve, one of those common names. I would guess this man is maybe age fifty to fifty-nine. Cap like a Dodger cap, navy blue, *GULF* on it. Brown belt, navy-blue pants, black really shiny shoes. And he talks to me in a really deep voice: *Hello, Quintana. I'm going to lock you here in the garage.* After I became five I never ever dreamed about him."

David, Bill, Steve, one of those common names?

Name always on his shirt? On the right-hand side?

Cap like a Dodger cap, navy blue, *GULF* on it?

After she became five she never ever dreamed about him?

It was when she said "I would guess this man is maybe age fifty to fifty-nine" that I realized my fear of The Broken Man to be as unquestioning as her own.

9

ON THIS QUESTION of fear.

When I began writing these pages I believed their subject to be children, the ones we have and the ones we wish we had, the ways in which we depend on our children to depend on us, the ways in which we encourage them to remain children, the ways in which they remain more unknown to us than they do to their most casual acquaintances; the ways in which we remain equally opaque to them.

The ways in which for example we write novels "just to show" each other.

The ways in which our investments in each other remain too freighted ever to see the other clear.

The ways in which neither we nor they can bear to contemplate the death or the illness or even the aging of the other.

As the pages progressed it occurred to me that their actual subject was not children after all, at least not children *per se*, at least not children *qua* children: their actual subject was this refusal even to engage in such contemplation, this failure to confront the certainties of aging, illness, death.

This fear.

Only as the pages progressed further did I understand that the two subjects were the same.

When we talk about mortality we are talking about our children.

Hello, Quintana. I'm going to lock you here in the garage.

After I became five I never ever dreamed about him.

Once she was born I was never not afraid.

I was afraid of swimming pools, high-tension wires, lye under the sink, aspirin in the medicine cabinet, The Broken Man himself. I was afraid of rattlesnakes, riptides, landslides, strangers who appeared at the door, unexplained fevers, elevators without operators and empty hotel corridors. The source of the fear was obvious: it was the harm that could come to her. A question: if we and our children could in fact see the other clear would the fear go away? Would the fear go away for both of us, or would the fear go away only for me?

10

SHE WAS BORN in the first hour of the third day of March, 1966, at St. John's Hospital in Santa Monica. We were told that we could adopt her late the afternoon of the same day, March third, when Blake Watson, the obstetrician who delivered her, called the house at Portuguese Bend in which we then lived, forty-some miles down the coast from Santa Monica. I was taking a shower and burst into tears when John came into the bathroom to report what Blake Watson had said. "I have a beautiful baby girl at St. John's," is what he had said. "I need to know if you want her." The baby's mother, he had said, was from Tucson. She had been staying with relatives in California for the birth of the baby. An hour later we stood outside the window of the nursery at St. John's looking at an infant with fierce dark hair and rosebud features. The beads on her wrist spelled out not her name but "N.I.," for "No Information," which was the hospital's response to any questions that might be asked about a baby being placed for adoption. One of the nurses had tied a pink ribbon in the fierce dark hair. "Not *that* baby," John would repeat to her again and again in the years that followed, reenacting the nursery scene, the recommended "choice" narrative, the moment when, of all the babies in the nursery, we picked her. "Not *that* baby . . . *that* baby. The baby with the ribbon."

"Do *that baby*," she would repeat in return, a gift to us, an endorsement of our wisdom in opting to follow the recommended choice narrative. The choice narrative is no longer universally favored by professionals of child care, but it was in 1966. "Do it again. Do the baby with the ribbon."

And later: "Do the part about Dr. Watson calling." Blake Watson was already a folk figure in this recital.

And then: "Tell the part about the shower."

Even the shower had become part of the recommended choice narrative.

March 3, 1966.

After we left St. John's that night we stopped in Beverly Hills to tell John's brother Nick and his wife, Lenny. Lenny offered to meet me at Saks in the morning to buy a layette. She was taking ice from a crystal bucket, making celebratory drinks. Making celebratory drinks was what we did in our family to mark any unusual, or for that matter any usual, occasion. In retrospect we all drank more than we needed to drink but this did not occur to any of us in 1966. Only when I read my early fiction, in which someone was always downstairs making a drink and singing "Big Noise blew in from Winnetka," did I realize how much we all drank and how little thought we gave to it. Lenny added more ice to my glass and took the crystal bucket to the kitchen for a refill. "Saks because if you spend eighty dollars they throw in the bassinette," she added as she went.

I took the glass and put it down.

I had not considered the need for a bassinette.

I had not considered the need for a layette.

The baby with the fierce dark hair stayed that night and the next two in the nursery at St. John's and at some point during each of those nights I woke in the house at Portuguese Bend to the same chill, hearing the surf break on the rocks below, dreaming that I had forgotten her, left her asleep in a drawer, gone into town for dinner or a movie and made no provision for the infant who could even then be waking alone and hungry in the drawer in Portuguese Bend.

Dreaming in other words that I had failed.

Been given a baby and failed to keep her safe.

When we think about adopting a child, or for that matter about having a child at all, we stress the "blessing" aspect.

We omit the instant of the sudden chill, the "what-if," the free fall into certain failure.

What if I fail to take care of this baby?

What if this baby fails to thrive, what if this baby fails to love me?

And worse yet, worse by far, so much worse as to be unthinkable, except I did think it, everyone who has ever waited to bring a baby home thinks it: *what if I fail to love this baby?*

March 3, 1966.

Until that instant when Lenny mentioned the bassinette it had all happened very fast. Until the bassinette it had all seemed casual, even blithe, not different in spirit from the Jax jerseys and printed cotton Lilly Pulitzer shifts we were all wearing that year: on New Year's weekend 1966 John and I had gone to Cat Harbor, on the far side of Catalina Island, on Morty Hall's boat. Morty Hall was married to Diana Lynn. Diana was a close friend of Lenny's. At some point on the boat that weekend (presumably at a point, given the drift of the excursion, when we were having or thinking about having or making or thinking about making a drink) I had mentioned to Diana that I was trying to have a baby. Diana had said I should talk to Blake Watson. Blake Watson had delivered her and Morty's four children. Blake Watson had also delivered the adopted daughter of Howard and Lou Erskine, old friends of Nick and Lenny's (Howard had gone to Williams with Nick) who happened to be on the boat that weekend. Maybe because the Erskines were there or maybe because I had mentioned wanting a baby or maybe because we had all had the drink we were thinking about having, the topic of adoption had entered the ether. Diana herself, it seemed, had been adopted, but this information had been withheld from her until she was twenty-one and it had become necessary for some financial reason that she know. Her adoptive parents had handled the situation by revealing the secret to (this had not seemed unusual at the time) Diana's agent. Diana's agent had handled the situation by taking Diana to lunch at (nor at the time had this) the Beverly Hills Hotel. Diana got the news in the Polo Lounge. She could remember fleeing into the bougainvillea around the bungalows, screaming.

That was all.

Yet the next week I was meeting Blake Watson.

When he called us from the hospital and asked if we wanted the beautiful baby girl there had been no hesitation: we wanted her. When they asked us at the hospital what we would call the beautiful baby girl there had been no hesitation: we would call her Quintana Roo. We had seen the name on a map when we were in Mexico a few months before and promised each other that if ever we had a daughter (dreamy speculation, no daughter had been in the offing) Quintana Roo would be her name. The place on the map called Quintana Roo was still not yet a state but a territory.

The place on the map called Quintana Roo was still frequented mainly by archaeologists, herpetologists, and bandits. The institution that became spring break in Cancún did not yet exist. There were no bargain flights. There was no Club Med.

The place on the map called Quintana Roo was still terra incognita.

As was the infant in the nursery at St. John's.

L'adoptada, she came to be called in the household. The adopted one.

M'ija she was also called. My daughter.

Adoption, I was to learn although not immediately, is hard to get right.

As a concept, even what was then its most widely approved narrative carried bad news: if someone "chose" you, what does that tell you?

Doesn't it tell you that you were available to be "chosen"?

Doesn't it tell you, in the end, that there are only two people in the world?

The one who "chose" you?

And the other who didn't?

Are we beginning to see how the word "abandonment" might enter the picture? Might we not make efforts to avoid such abandonment? Might not such efforts be characterized as "frantic"? Do we want to ask ourselves what follows? Do we need to ask ourselves what words come next to mind? Isn't one of those words "fear"? Isn't another of those words "anxiety"?

Terra incognita, as I had seen it until then, meant free of complications.

That terra incognita could present its own complications had never occurred to me.

11

ON THE DAY her adoption became legal, a hot September afternoon in 1966, we took her from the courthouse in downtown Los Angeles to lunch at The Bistro in Beverly Hills. At the courthouse she had been the only baby up for adoption; the other prospective adoptees that day were all adults, petitioning to adopt one another for one or another tax advantage. At The Bistro, too, more predictably, she was the only baby. *Qué hermosa*, the waiters crooned. *Qué chula*. They gave us the corner banquette usually saved for Sidney Korshak, a gesture the import of which would be clear only to someone who had lived in that particular community at that particular time. "Let's just say a nod from Korshak, and the Teamsters change management," the producer Robert Evans would later write by way of explaining who Sidney Korshak was. "A nod from Korshak, and Vegas shuts down. A nod from Korshak, and the Dodgers suddenly can play night baseball." The waiters placed her carrier on the table between us. She was wearing a blue-and-white dotted organdy dress. She was not quite seven months old. As far as I was concerned this lunch at Sidney Korshak's banquette at The Bistro was the happy ending to the choice narrative. We had chosen, the beautiful baby girl had accepted our choice, no natural parent had stood up at the courthouse and exercised his or her absolute legal right under the California law covering private adoptions to simply say no, she's mine, I want her back.

The issue, as I preferred to see it, was now closed.

The fear was now gone.

She was ours.

What I would not realize for another few years was that I had never been the only person in the house to feel the fear.

What if you hadn't answered the phone when Dr. Watson called, she would suddenly say. *What if you hadn't been home, what if you couldn't meet him at the hospital, what if there'd been an accident on the freeway, what would happen to me then?*

Since I had no adequate answer to these questions, I refused to consider them.

She considered them.

She lived with them.

And then she didn't.

"You have your wonderful memories," people said later, as if memories were solace. Memories are not. Memories are by definition of times past, things gone. Memories are the Westlake uniforms in the closet, the faded and cracked photographs, the invitations to the weddings of the people who are no longer married, the mass cards from the funerals of the people whose faces you no longer remember. Memories are what you no longer want to remember.

12

SIDNEY KORSHAK, *88, Dies; Fabled Fixer for the Chicago Mob:* So read the headline on Sidney Korshak's obituary, when he died in 1996, in *The New York Times.* "It was a tribute to Sidney Korshak's success that he was never indicted, despite repeated Federal and state investigations," the obituary continued. "And the widespread belief that he had in fact committed the very crimes the authorities could never prove made him an indispensable ally of leading Hollywood producers, corporate executives and politicians."

Thirty years before Morty Hall had declared on principle that he and Diana would refuse to go to any party given by Sidney Korshak.

I remember Morty and Diana arguing heatedly at dinner one night over this entirely hypothetical point.

Morty and Diana and the heated argument at dinner about whether or not to refuse to go to a party given by Sidney Korshak are, I have to conclude, what people mean when they mention my wonderful memories.

I recently saw Diana in an old commercial, one of those curiosities that turn up on YouTube. She is wearing a pale mink stole, draping herself over the hood of an Olds 88. In her smoky voice, she introduces the Olds 88 as "the hottest number I know." The Olds 88 at this point begins to talk to Diana, mentioning its own "rocket engine" and "hydra-matic drive." Diana wraps herself in the pale mink stole. "This is *great*," she replies to the Olds 88, again in the smoky voice.

It occurs to me that Diana does not sound in this Olds 88 commercial as if she would necessarily refuse to go to a party given by Sidney Korshak.

It also occurs to me that no one who now comes across this Olds 88 commercial on YouTube would know who Sidney Korshak was, or for that matter who Diana was, or even what an Olds 88 was.

Time passes.

Diana is dead now. She died in 1971, at age forty-five, of a cerebral bleed.

She had collapsed after a wardrobe fitting for a picture she was due to start in a few days, the third lead, after Tuesday Weld and Anthony Perkins, in *Play It As It Lays*, for which John and I had written the screenplay and in which she was replaced by Tammy Grimes. The last time I saw her was in an ICU at Cedars-Sinai in Los Angeles. Lenny and I had gone together to Cedars to see her. The next time Lenny and I were in an ICU at Cedars together it was to see her and Nick's daughter Dominique, who had been strangled outside her house in Hollywood. "She looks even worse than Diana did," Lenny whispered when she saw Dominique, her intake of breath so sudden that I could barely hear her. I knew what Lenny was saying. Lenny was saying that Diana had not lived. Lenny was saying that Dominique was not going to live. I knew this—I suppose I had known it from the time the police officer who called identified himself as "Homicide"—but did not want to hear anyone say it. I ran into one of Diana's daughters a few months ago, in New York. We had lunch in the neighborhood. Diana's daughter remembered that we had last seen each other when Diana was still alive and living in New York and I had brought Quintana to play with her daughters. We promised to keep in touch. It occurred to me as I walked home that I had seen too many people for the last time in one or another ICU.

13

FOR EVERYTHING *there is a season.*

Ecclesiastes, yes, but I think first of The Byrds, "Turn Turn Turn."

I think first of Quintana Roo sitting on the bare hardwood floors of the house on Franklin Avenue and the waxed terra-cotta tiles of the house in Malibu listening to The Byrds on eight-track.

The Byrds and The Mamas and the Papas, "Do You Wanna Dance?"

"I wanna dance," she would croon back to the eight-track.

For everything there is a season. *I'd miss having the seasons*, people from New York like to say by way of indicating the extraordinary pride they take in not living in Southern California. In fact Southern California does have seasons (it has for example "fire season" or "the season when the fire comes," and it also has "the season when the rain comes," but such Southern California seasons, arriving as they do so theatrically as to seem strokes of random fate, do not inexorably suggest the passage of time.) Those other seasons, the ones so prized on the East Coast, do. Seasons in Southern California suggest violence, but not necessarily death. Seasons in New York—the relentless dropping of the leaves, the steady darkening of the days, the blue nights themselves—suggest only death. For my having a child there was a season. That season passed. I have not yet located the season in which I do not hear her crooning back to the eight-track.

I still hear her crooning back to the eight-track.

I wanna dance.

The same way I still see the stephanotis in her braid, the plumeria tattoo through her veil.

Something else I still see from that wedding day at St. John the Divine: the bright red soles on her shoes.

She was wearing Christian Louboutin shoes, pale satin with bright red soles.

You saw the red soles when she kneeled at the altar.

14

BEFORE SHE WAS BORN we had been planning a trip to Saigon.

We had assignments from magazines, we had credentials, we had everything we needed.

Including, suddenly, a baby.

That year, 1966, during which the American military presence in Vietnam would reach four hundred thousand and American B-52s had begun bombing the North, was not widely considered an ideal year to take an infant to Southeast Asia, yet it never occurred to me to abandon or even adjust the plan. I even went so far as to shop for what I imagined we would need: Donald Brooks pastel linen dresses for myself, a flowered Porthault parasol to shade the baby, as if she and I were about to board a Pan Am flight and disembark at *Le Cercle Sportif.*

In the end this trip to Saigon did not take place, although its cancellation was by no means based on what might have seemed the obvious reason—we canceled, it turned out, because John had to finish the book he had contracted to write about César Chávez and his National Farm Workers Association and the DiGiorgio grape strike in Delano—and I mention Saigon at all only by way of suggesting the extent of my misconceptions about what having a child, let alone adopting one, might actually entail.

How could I not have had misconceptions?

I had been handed this perfect baby, out of the blue, at St. John's Hospital in Santa Monica. She could not have been more exactly the baby I wanted. In the first place she was beautiful. *Hermosa, chula.* Strangers stopped me on the street to tell me so. "I have a beautiful baby girl at St. John's," Blake Watson had said, and he did. Everyone sent dresses, an homage to the beautiful baby girl. There the dresses were in her closet, sixty of them (I counted them, again and again), immaculate little wisps of batiste and Liberty lawn on miniature wooden hangers. The miniature wooden hangers, too, were a gift to the beautiful baby girl, another homage from her instantly acquired relatives, besotted aunts and uncles and cousins in

West Hartford (John's family) and Sacramento (mine). I recall changing her dress four times on the afternoon the State of California social worker made her mandated visit to observe the candidate for adoption in the home environment.

We sat on the lawn.

The candidate for adoption played at our feet.

I did not mention to the social worker that Saigon had until recently figured in the candidate's future.

Nor did I mention that current itineraries called for her to sojourn instead at the Starlight Motel in Delano.

Arcelia, who cleaned the house and laundered the wisps of batiste, busied herself watering, as anticipated.

"As anticipated" because I had prepped Arcelia for the visit.

The thought of an unstructured encounter between Arcelia and a State of California social worker had presented spectral concerns from the outset, imagined scenarios that kept me awake at four in the morning and only multiplied as the date of the visit approached: what if the social worker were to notice that Arcelia spoke only Spanish? What if the social worker were to happen into the question of Arcelia's papers? What would the social worker put in her report if she divined that I was entrusting the perfect baby to an undocumented alien?

The social worker remarked, in English, on the fine weather.

I tensed, fearing a trap.

Arcelia smiled, beatific, and continued watering.

I relaxed.

At which point Arcelia, no longer beatific but dramatic, flung the hose across the lawn and snatched up Quintana, screaming "*Víbora!*"

The social worker lived in Los Angeles, she had to know what *víbora* meant, *víbora* in Los Angeles meant snake and snake in Los Angeles meant rattlesnake. I was relatively certain that the rattlesnake was a fantasy but I nonetheless guided Arcelia and Quintana inside, then turned to the social worker. It's a game, I lied. Arcelia pretends she sees a snake. We all laugh. Because you can see. There is no snake.

There could be no snake in Quintana Roo's garden.

Only later did I see that I had been raising her as a doll.

She would never have faulted me for that.

She would have seen it as a logical response to my having

been handed, out of the blue at St. John's Hospital in Santa Monica, the beautiful baby girl, herself. At the house after her christening at St. Martin of Tours Catholic Church in Brentwood we had watercress sandwiches and champagne and later, for anyone still around at dinner time, fried chicken. The house we were renting that spring belonged to Sara Mankiewicz, Herman Mankiewicz's widow, who was traveling for six months, and although she had packed away the china she did not want used along with Herman Mankiewicz's Academy Award for *Citizen Kane* (you'll have friends over, she had said, they'll get drunk, they'll want to play with it) she had left out her Minton dinner plates, the same pattern as the Minton tiles that line the arcade south of Bethesda Fountain in Central Park, for me to use. I had not used the Minton dinner plates before the christening but I put them on a buffet table that night for the fried chicken. I remember Diana eating a chicken wing off one of them, a fleck of rosemary from the chicken the only blemish on her otherwise immaculate manicure. The perfect baby slept in one of her two long white christening dresses (she had two long white christening dresses because she had been given two long white christening dresses, one batiste, the other linen, another homage) in the Saks bassinette. John's brother Nick took photographs. I look at those photographs now and am struck by how many of the women present were wearing Chanel suits and David Webb bracelets, and smoking cigarettes. It was a time of my life during which I actually believed that somewhere between frying the chicken to serve on Sara Mankiewicz's Minton dinner plates and buying the Porthault parasol to shade the beautiful baby girl in Saigon I had covered the main "motherhood" points.

15

THERE WAS A REASON why I told you about Arcelia and the sixty dresses.

I was not unaware as I did so that a certain number of readers (more than some of you might think, fewer than the less charitable among you will think) would interpret this apparently casual information (she dressed her baby in clothes that needed washing and ironing, she had help in the house to do this washing and ironing) as evidence that Quintana did not have an "ordinary" childhood, that she was "privileged."

I wanted to lay this on the table.

"Ordinary" childhoods in Los Angeles very often involve someone speaking Spanish, but I will not make that argument.

Nor will I even argue that she had an "ordinary" childhood, although I remain unsure about exactly who does.

"Privilege" is something else.

"Privilege" is a judgment.

"Privilege" is an opinion.

"Privilege" is an accusation.

"Privilege" remains an area to which—when I think of what she endured, when I consider what came later—I will not easily cop.

I look again at the photographs Nick took at the christening.

In fact the afternoon these photographs were taken, the afternoon at St. Martin of Tours and Sara Mankiewicz's house, the afternoon when Quintana wore the two christening dresses and I wore one of the pastel linen Donald Brooks dresses I had bought under the misunderstanding that they would be needed in Saigon, was never what I considered her "real" christening. (One question: would you have called buying pastel linen dresses for Saigon a mark of "privilege"? Or would you have called it more a mark of bone stupidity?) Her "real" christening had taken place in a tiled sink at the house in Portuguese Bend, a few days after we brought her home from the nursery at St. John's Hospital in Santa Monica. John had christened her himself, and told me only after the fact.

I recall a certain defensiveness on this issue.

What he said when he told me was not exactly along the lines of "I thought we might christen the baby, what do you think."

What he said when he told me was more along the lines of "I just christened the baby, take it or leave it."

It seemed that he had worried because the date I had arranged at St. Martin of Tours was two months away.

It seemed that he had not wanted to risk consigning our not yet christened baby to limbo.

I knew why he had not told me this before the fact.

He had not told me this before the fact because I was not a Catholic, and he had imagined objection.

Of the two of us, however, it was I who thought of that day in the tiled sink as the "real" christening.

The other christening, the christening at which the photographs were taken, was the "dress-up" christening.

Certain faces spring out at me from the photographs.

Connie Wald, wearing one of the several Chanel suits in evidence that afternoon, in her case one of blue-and-cream tweed lined in cyclamen-pink silk. It was Connie who gave Quintana one of the two long white dresses she wore at the church and after. Until Connie was in her nineties, when she developed a neuropathy, she still swam every day of her life. She cut back on the regimen of daily laps and stopped driving herself around Beverly Hills in an aged Rolls-Royce but otherwise continued exactly as before. She still wore the Claire McCardell dresses she had been given when she was a McCardell model in the 1940s. She still gave two or three dinner parties a week, cooked herself, mixed young and old in a way that flattered everyone present, lit huge fires in her library and filled the tables with salted almonds and fat pitchers of nasturtiums and the roses she still grew herself. Connie had been married to the producer Jerry Wald, who was said to have been Budd Schulberg's model for Sammy Glick in *What Makes Sammy Run* and who had died a few years before I met her. She once told me about the six weeks she spent in Nevada establishing the residency she needed to divorce her previous husband and marry Jerry Wald. She did not spend the six weeks in Las Vegas, because Las Vegas as we later knew it did not yet exactly exist. She spent the six weeks twenty miles from Las Vegas, in Boulder City, which had been built by the Bureau of Reclamation as the construction camp for Hoover Dam and in which both gambling and union membership were prohibited by law. I asked her what she had found to do for six weeks in Boulder City. She said that Jerry had given her a dog, which she walked, every day, through the identical streets lined with matching government bungalows that constituted Boulder City and on across the dam. I recall this striking me as the most intrepid story I ever heard about how someone did or did not stay in Las Vegas, a topic not entirely deficient in intrepid stories.

Diana.

Diana Lynn, Diana Hall.

Hers is another face that springs out from the photographs taken that day.

In this photograph she is holding a champagne flute and smoking a cigarette. It occurs to me as I look at her photograph that it was Diana who had made that day possible. It was Diana who had drawn me into the conversation about adoption over the New Year's weekend on Morty's boat. It was Diana who had talked to Blake Watson, it was Diana who had intuited how deeply I needed Quintana. It was Diana who had changed my life.

16

SOME OF US FEEL this overpowering need for a child and some of us don't. It had come over me quite suddenly, in my mid-twenties, when I was working for *Vogue*, a tidal surge. Once this surge hit I saw babies wherever I went. I followed their carriages on the street. I cut their pictures from magazines and tacked them on the wall next to my bed. I put myself to sleep by imagining them: imagining holding them, imagining the down on their heads, imagining the soft spots at their temples, imagining the way their eyes dilated when you looked at them.

Until then pregnancy had been only a fear, an accident to be avoided at any cost.

Until then I had felt nothing but relief at the moment each month when I started to bleed. If that moment was delayed by even a day I would leave my office at *Vogue* and, looking for instant reassurance that I was not pregnant, go see my doctor, a Columbia Presbyterian internist who had come to be known, because his mother-in-law had been editor in chief of *Vogue* and his office was always open to fretful staff members, as "the *Vogue* doctor." I recall sitting in his examining room on East Sixty-seventh Street one morning waiting for the results of the most recent rabbit test I had implored him to do. He came into the room whistling, and began misting the plants on the window sill.

The test, I prompted.

He continued misting the plants.

I needed to know the results, I said, because I was leaving to spend Christmas in California. I had the ticket in my bag. I opened the bag. I showed him.

"You might not need a ticket to California," he said. "You might need a ticket to Havana."

I correctly understood this to be intended as reassuring, his baroque way of saying that I might need an abortion and that he could help me get one, yet my immediate response was to vehemently reject the proposed solution: it was delusional, it was out of the question, it was beyond discussion.

I couldn't possibly go to Havana.

There was a revolution in Havana.

In fact there was: it was December 1958, Fidel Castro would enter Havana within days.

I mentioned this.

"There's always a revolution in Havana," the *Vogue* doctor said.

A day later I started to bleed, and cried all night.

I thought I was regretting having missed this interesting moment in Havana but it turned out the surge had hit and what I was regretting was not having the baby, the still unmet baby, the baby I would eventually bring home from St. John's Hospital in Santa Monica. *What if you hadn't been home, what if you couldn't meet Dr. Watson at the hospital, what if there'd been an accident on the freeway, what would happen to me then.* Not long ago, when I read the fragment of the novel written just to show us, the scrap in which the protagonist thinks she might be pregnant and elects to address the situation by consulting her pediatrician, I remembered that morning on East Sixty-seventh Street. *Now, they didn't even care any more.*

17

There are certain moments in those first years with her that I remember very clearly.

These very clear moments stand out, recur, speak directly to me, on some levels flood me with pleasure and on others still break my heart.

I remember very clearly for example that her earliest transactions involved what she called "sundries." She invested this word, which she used as a synonym for "possessions" but seemed to derive from the "sundries shops" in the many hotels to which she had already been taken, with considerable importance, dizzying alternations of infancy and sophistication. One day after she had asked me for a Magic Marker I found her marking off an empty box into "drawers," or areas meant for specific of these "sundries." The "drawers" she designated were these: "Cash," "Passport," "My IRA," "Jewelry," and, finally—I find myself hardly able to tell you this—"Little Toys."

Again, the careful printing.

The printing alone I cannot forget.

The printing alone breaks my heart.

Another moment, not, on examination, dissimilar: I remember very clearly the Christmas night at her grandmother's house in West Hartford when John and I came in from a movie to find her huddled alone on the stairs to the second floor. The Christmas lights were off, her grandmother was asleep, everyone in the house was asleep, and she was patiently waiting for us to come home and address what she called "the new problem." We asked what the new problem was. "I just noticed I have cancer," she said, and pulled back her hair to show us what she had construed to be a growth on her scalp. In fact it was chicken pox, obviously contracted before she left nursery school in Malibu and just now surfacing, but had it been cancer, she had prepared her mind to be ready for cancer.

A question occurs to me:

Did she emphasize "new" when she mentioned "the new problem"?

Was she suggesting that there were also "old" problems,

undetailed, problems with which she was for the moment opting not to burden us?

A third example: I remember very clearly the doll's house she constructed on the bookshelves of her bedroom at the beach. She had worked on it for several days, after studying a similar improvisation in an old copy of *House & Garden* ("Muffet Hemingway's doll's house" was how she identified the prototype, taking her cue from the *House & Garden* headline), but this was its first unveiling. Here was the living room, she explained, and here was the dining room, and here was the kitchen, and here was the bedroom.

I asked about an undecorated and apparently unallocated shelf.

That, she said, would be the projection room.

The projection room.

I tried to assimilate this.

Some people we knew in Los Angeles did in fact live in houses with projection rooms but to the best of my knowledge she had never seen one. These people who lived in houses with projection rooms belonged to our "working" life. She, I had imagined, belonged to our "private" life. Our "private" life, I had also imagined, was separate, sweet, inviolate.

I set this distinction to one side and asked how she planned to furnish the projection room.

There would need to be a table for the telephone to the projectionist, she said, then stopped to consider the empty shelf.

"And whatever I'll need for Dolby Sound," she added then.

As I describe these very clear memories I am struck by what they have in common: each involves her trying to handle adult life, trying to be a convincing grown-up person at an age when she was still entitled to be a small child. She could talk about "My IRA" and she could talk about "Dolby Sound" and she could talk about "just noticing" she had cancer, she could call Camarillo to find out what she needed to do if she was going crazy and she could call Twentieth Century–Fox to find out what she needed to do to be a star, but she was not actually prepared to act on whatever answers she got. "Little Toys" could still assume equal importance. She could still consult her pediatrician.

Was this confusion about where she stood in the chronological scheme of things our doing?

Did we demand that she be an adult?

Did we ask her to assume responsibility before she had any way of doing so?

Did our expectations prevent her from responding as a child?

I recall taking her, when she was four or five, up the coast to Oxnard to see *Nicholas and Alexandra.* On the drive home from Oxnard she referred to the czar and czarina as "Nicky and Sunny," and said, when asked how she had liked the picture, "I think it's going to be a big hit."

In other words, despite having just been told what had seemed to me as I watched it a truly harrowing story, a story that placed both parents and children in unthinkable peril—a peril to children more unthinkable still because its very source lay in the bad luck of having been born to these particular parents—she had resorted without hesitation to the local default response, which was an instant assessment of audience potential. Similarly, a few years later, taken to Oxnard to see *Jaws*, she had watched in horror, then, while I was still unloading the car in Malibu, skipped down to the beach and dove into the surf. About certain threats I considered real she remained in fact fearless. When she was eight or nine and enrolled in Junior Lifeguard, a program run by the Los Angeles County lifeguards that entailed being repeatedly taken out beyond the Zuma Beach breakers on a lifeguard boat and swimming back in, John and I arrived to pick her up and found the beach empty. Finally we saw her, alone, huddled in a towel behind a dune. The lifeguards, it seemed, were insisting, "for absolutely no reason," on taking everyone home. I said there must be a reason. "Only the sharks," she said. I looked at her. She was clearly disappointed, even a little disgusted, impatient with the turn the morning had taken. She shrugged. "They were just blues," she said then.

When I remember the "sundries" I am forced to remember the hotels in which she had stayed before she was five or six or seven. I say "forced to remember" because my images of her in these hotels are tricky. On the one hand those images survive as my truest memories of the paradox she was—of the child trying not to appear as a child, of the strenuousness with which she tried to present the face of a convincing adult. On the other hand it is just such images—the same images—that encourage a view of her as "privileged," somehow deprived of a "normal" childhood.

On the face of it she had no business in these hotels.

The Lancaster and the Ritz and the Plaza Athénée in Paris.

The Dorchester in London.

The St. Regis and the Regency in New York, and also the Chelsea. The Chelsea was for those trips to New York when we were not on expenses. At the Chelsea they would find her a crib downstairs and John would bring her breakfast from the White Tower across the street.

The Fairmont and the Mark Hopkins in San Francisco.

The Kahala and the Royal Hawaiian in Honolulu. "Where did the morning went," she would ask at the Royal Hawaiian when she woke, still on mainland time, and found the horizon dark. "Imagine a five-year-old walking to the reef," she would say at the Royal Hawaiian, near a swoon, when we held her hands and swung her through the shallow sea.

The Ambassador and the Drake in Chicago.

It was at the Ambassador, in the Pump Room at midnight, that she ate caviar for the first time, a mixed success since she wanted it again at every meal thereafter and did not yet entirely understand the difference between "on expenses" and "not on expenses." She had happened to be in the Pump Room at midnight because we had taken her that night to Chicago Stadium to see a band we were following, Chicago, research for *A Star Is Born*. She had sat through the concert onstage, on one of the amps. The band had played "Does Anybody Really Know What Time It Is," and "25 or 6 to 4." She had referred to the band as "the boys."

When we left Chicago Stadium with the boys that night the crowd had rocked the car, delighting her.

She did not want to go to her grandmother's in West Hartford the next day, she had advised me when we got back to the Ambassador, she wanted to go to Detroit with the boys.

So much for keeping our "private" life separate from our "working" life.

In fact she was inseparable from our working life. Our

working life was the very reason she happened to be in these hotels. When she was five or six, for example, we took her with us to Tucson, where *The Life and Times of Judge Roy Bean* was shooting. The Hilton Inn, where the production was based during its Tucson location, sent a babysitter to stay with her while we watched the dailies. The babysitter asked her to get Paul Newman's autograph. A crippled son was mentioned. Quintana got the autograph, delivered it to the babysitter, then burst into tears. It was never clear to me whether she was crying about the crippled son or about feeling played by the babysitter. Dick Moore was the cinematographer on *The Life and Times of Judge Roy Bean* but she seemed to make no connection between this Dick Moore she encountered at the Hilton Inn in Tucson and the Dick Moore she encountered on our beach. On our beach everyone was home, and so was she. At the Hilton Inn in Tucson everyone was working, and so was she. "Working" was a way of being she understood at her core. When she was nine I took her with me on an eight-city book tour: New York, Boston, Washington, Dallas, Houston, Los Angeles, San Francisco, Chicago. "How do you like our monuments," Katharine Graham had asked her in Washington. She had seemed mystified but game. "What monuments," she had asked with interest, entirely unaware that most children who visited Washington were shown the Lincoln Memorial instead of National Public Radio and *The Washington Post.* Her favorite city on this tour had been Dallas. Her least favorite had been Boston. Boston, she had complained, was "all white."

"You mean you didn't see many black people in Boston," Susan Traylor's mother had suggested when Quintana got back to Malibu and reported on her trip.

"No," Quintana said, definite on this point. "I mean it's not in color."

She had learned to order triple lamb chops from room service on this trip.

She had learned to sign her room number for Shirley Temples on this trip.

If a car or an interviewer failed to show up at the appointed time on this trip she had known what to do: check the schedule and "call Wendy," Wendy being the publicity director at Simon & Schuster. She knew which bookstores reported to which best-seller lists and she knew the names of their major buyers and she knew what a green room was and she knew what agents did. She knew what agents did because before she was four, on a day when my schedule for household help had fallen apart, I had taken her with me to a meeting at the William Morris office in Beverly Hills. I had prepared her, explained that the meeting was about earning the money that paid for the triple lamb chops from room service, impressed on her the need for not interrupting or asking when we could leave. This preparation, it turned out, was entirely unnecessary. She was far too interested to interrupt. She accepted a glass of water when one was offered to her, managed the heavy Baccarat glass without dropping it, listened attentively but did not speak. Only at the end of the meeting did she ask the William Morris agent the question apparently absorbing her: "But when do you give her the money?"

When we noticed her confusions did we consider our own?

I still have the "Sundries" box in my closet, marked as she marked it.

18

I DO NOT KNOW many people who think they have succeeded as parents. Those who do tend to cite the markers that indicate (their own) status in the world: the Stanford degree, the Harvard MBA, the summer with the white-shoe law firm. Those of us less inclined to compliment ourselves on our parenting skills, in other words most of us, recite rosaries of our failures, our neglects, our derelictions and delinquencies. The very definition of success as a parent has undergone a telling transformation: we used to define success as the ability to encourage the child to grow into independent (which is to say into adult) life, to "raise" the child, to let the child go. If a child wanted to try out his or her new bicycle on the steepest hill in the neighborhood, there may have been a pro forma reminder that the steepest hill in the neighborhood descended into a four-way intersection, but such a reminder, because independence was still seen as the desired end of the day, stopped short of nagging. If a child elected to indulge in activity that could end badly, such negative possibilities may have gotten mentioned once, but not twice.

It so happened that I was a child during World War Two, which meant that I grew up in circumstances in which even more stress than usual was placed on independence. My father was a finance officer in the Army Air Corps, and during the early years of the war my mother and brother and I followed him from Fort Lewis in Tacoma to Duke University in Durham to Peterson Field in Colorado Springs. This was not hardship but neither was it, given the overcrowding and dislocation that characterized life near American military facilities in 1942 and 1943, a sheltered childhood. In Tacoma we were lucky enough to rent what was called a guest house but was actually one large room with its own entrance. In Durham we again lived in one room, this one not large and not with its own entrance, in a house that belonged to a Baptist preacher and his family. This room in Durham came with "kitchen privileges," which amounted in practice to occasional use of the family's apple butter. In Colorado Springs we lived, for the first time, in an actual house, a four-room bungalow near a psychiatric hospital, but did not unpack: there was no point in unpacking, my mother pointed out, since "orders"—a mysterious concept that I took on faith—could arrive any day.

My brother and I were expected in each of these venues to adapt, make do, both invent a life and simultaneously accept that any life we invented would be summarily upended by the arrival of "orders." Who gave the orders was never clear to me. In Colorado Springs, where my father was stationed for longer than he had been in either Tacoma or Durham, my brother scouted the neighborhood, and made friends. I trolled the grounds of the psychiatric hospital, recorded the dialogue I overheard, and wrote "stories." I did not at the time think this an unreasonable alternative to staying in Sacramento and going to school (later it occurred to me that if I had stayed in Sacramento and gone to school I might have learned to subtract, a skill that remains unmastered), but it would have made no difference if I had. There was a war in progress. That war did not revolve around or in any way hinge upon the wishes of children. In return for tolerating these home truths, children were allowed to invent their own lives. The notion that they could be left to their own devices—were in fact best left so—went unquestioned.

Once the war was over, and we were again home in Sacramento, this laissez-faire approach continued. I remember getting my learner's driving permit at age fifteen-and-a-half and interpreting it as a logical mandate to drive from Sacramento to Lake Tahoe after dinner, two or three hours up one of the switchbacked highways into the mountains and, if you just turned around and kept driving, which was all we did, since we already had whatever we wanted to drink in the car with us, two or three hours back. This disappearance into the heart of the Sierra Nevada on what amounted to an overnight DUI went without comment from my mother and father. I remember, above Sacramento at about the same age, getting sluiced into a diversion dam while rafting on the American River, then dragging the raft upstream and doing it again. This too went without comment.

All gone.

Virtually unimaginable now.

No time left on the schedule of "parenting" for tolerating such doubtful pastimes.

Instead, ourselves the beneficiaries of this kind of benign neglect, we now measure success as the extent to which we manage to keep our children monitored, tethered, tied to us. Judith Shapiro, when she was president of Barnard, was prompted to write an op-ed piece in *The New York Times* advising parents to show a little more trust in their children, stop trying to manage every aspect of their college life. She mentioned the father who had taken a year off from his job to supervise the preparation of his daughter's college applications. She mentioned the mother who had accompanied her daughter to a meeting with her dean to discuss a research project. She mentioned the mother who had demanded, on the grounds that it was she who paid the tuition bills, that her daughter's academic transcript be sent to her directly.

"You pay $35,000 a year, you want services," Tamar Lewin of *The New York Times* was told by the director of "the parents' office" at Northeastern in Boston, an office devoted to the tending of parents having become a virtually ubiquitous feature of campus administration. For a *Times* piece a few years ago on the narrowing of the generation gap on campus, Ms. Lewin spoke not only to the tenders of the parents but also to the students themselves, one of whom, at George Washington University, allowed that she used well over three thousand cellphone minutes a month talking to her family. She seemed to view this family as an employable academic resource. "I might call my dad and say, 'What's going on with the Kurds?' It's a lot easier than looking it up. He knows a lot. I would trust almost anything my dad says." Asked if she ever thought she might be too close to her parents, another George Washington student had seemed only puzzled: "They're our parents," she had said. "They're supposed to help us. That's almost their job."

We increasingly justify such heightened involvement with our children as essential to their survival. We keep them on speed dial. We watch them on Skype. We track their movements. We expect every call to be answered, every changed plan reported. We fantasize unprecedented new dangers in their every unsupervised encounter. We mention terrorism, we share anxious admonitions: "It's different now." "It's not the way it was." "You can't let them do what we did."

Yet there were always dangers to children.

Ask anyone who was a child during the supposedly idyllic decade advertised to us at the time as the reward for World War Two. New cars. New appliances. Women in high-heeled pumps and ruffled aprons removing cookie sheets from ovens enameled in postwar "harvest" colors: avocado, gold, mustard, brown, burnt orange. This was as safe as it got, except it wasn't: ask any child who was exposed during this postwar harvest fantasy to the photographs from Hiroshima and Nagasaki, ask any child who saw the photographs from the death camps.

"I *have to know* about this."

So Quintana said when I found her hiding under the covers of her bed in Malibu, stunned, disbelieving, flashlight in hand, studying a book of old *Life* photographs that she had come across somewhere.

There were blue-and-white checked gingham curtains in the windows of her room in Malibu.

I remember them blowing as she showed me the book.

She was showing me the photographs Margaret Bourke-White did for *Life* of the ovens at Buchenwald.

That was what she *had to know*.

Or ask the child who would not allow herself to fall asleep during most of 1946 because she feared the fate of six-year-old Suzanne Degnan, who on January seventh of that year had been kidnapped from her bed in Chicago, dissected in a sink, and disposed of in pieces in the sewers of the far north side. Six months after Suzanne Degnan's disappearance a seventeen-year-old University of Chicago sophomore named William Heirens was arrested and sentenced to life imprisonment.

Or ask the child who nine years later followed the California search for fourteen-year-old Stephanie Bryan, who vanished while walking home from her Berkeley junior high school through the parking lot of the Claremont Hotel, her customary shortcut, and was next seen several hundred miles from Berkeley, buried in a shallow grave in California's most northern mountains. Five months after Stephanie Bryan's disappearance a twenty-seven-year-old University of California accounting student was arrested, charged with her death, and within two years convicted and executed in the gas chamber at San Quentin.

Since the events surrounding the disappearances and deaths of both Suzanne Degnan and Stephanie Bryan occurred in circulation areas served by aggressive Hearst papers, both cases were extensively and luridly covered. The lesson taught by the coverage was clear: childhood is by definition perilous. To be a child is to be small, weak, inexperienced, the dead bottom of the food chain. Every child knows this, or did.

Knowing this is why children call Camarillo.

Knowing this is why children call Twentieth Century–Fox.

"This case has been a haunting one all my life as I was a grown-up eight-year-old when it happened and followed it every day in the *Oakland Tribune* from day one till the end." So wrote an internet correspondent in response to a recent look back at the Stephanie Bryan case. "I had to read it when my parents weren't around as they didn't think it was fitting to be reading about a homicide at my age."

As adults we lose memory of the gravity and terrors of childhood.

Hello, Quintana. I'm going to lock you here in the garage.

After I became five I never ever dreamed about him.

I have to know about this.

One of her abiding fears, I learned much later, was that John would die and there would be no one but her to take care of me.

How could she have even imagined that I would not take care of her?

I used to ask that.

Now I ask the reverse:

How could she have even imagined that I *could* take care of her?

She saw me as needing care myself.

She saw me as frail.

Was that her anxiety or mine?

I learned about this fear when she was temporarily off the ventilator in one or another ICU, I have no memory which.

I told you, they were all the same.

The blue-and-white printed curtains. The gurgling through plastic tubing. The dripping from the IV line, the rales, the alarms.

The codes. The crash cart.

This was never supposed to happen to her.

It must have been the ICU at UCLA.

Only at UCLA was she off the ventilator long enough to have had this conversation.

You have your wonderful memories.

I do, but they blur.

They fade into one another.

They become, as Quintana a month or two later described the only memory she could summon of the five weeks she spent in the ICU at UCLA, "all mudgy."

I tried to tell her: I too have trouble remembering.

Languages mingle: do I need an *abogado* or do I need an *avocat*?

Names vanish. The names for example of California counties, once so familiar that I recited them in alphabetized order (Alameda and Alpine and Amador, Calaveras and Colusa and Contra Costa, Madera and Marin and Mariposa) now elude me.

The name of one county I do remember.

The name of this single county I always remember.

I had my own Broken Man.

I had my own stories about which I had to know.

Trinity.

The name of the county in which Stephanie Bryan had been found buried in the shallow grave was Trinity.

The name of the test site at Alamogordo that had led to the photographs from Hiroshima and Nagasaki was also Trinity.

19

"WHAT WE NEED here is a montage, music over. *How she*: talked to her father and xxxx and xxxxx—

"xx," he said.

"xxx," she said.

"*How she*:

"*How* she did this and *why* she did that and *what the music was* when they did x and x and xxx—

"How he, and also she—"

The above are notes I made in 1995 for a novel I published in 1996, *The Last Thing He Wanted*. I offer them as a representation of how comfortable I used to be when I wrote, how easily I did it, how little thought I gave to what I was saying until I had already said it. In fact, in any real sense, what I was doing then was never writing at all: I was doing no more than sketching in a rhythm and letting that rhythm tell me what it was I was saying. Many of the marks I set down on the page were no more than "xxx," or "xxxx," symbols that meant "copy tk," or "copy to come," but do notice: such symbols were arranged in specific groupings. A single "x" differed from a double "xx," "xxx" from "xxxx." The number of such symbols had a meaning. The arrangement was the meaning.

The same passage, rewritten, which is to say "written" in any real sense at all, became more detailed: "What we want here is a montage, music over. *Angle on Elena*. Alone on the dock where her father berthed the *Kitty Rex*. Working loose a splinter on the planking with the toe of her sandal. Taking off her scarf and shaking out her hair, damp from the sweet heavy air of South Florida. *Cut to Barry Sedlow*. Standing in the door of the frame shack, under the sign that read RENTALS GAS BAIT BEER AMMO. Leaning against the counter. Watching Elena through the screen door as he waited for change. *Angle on the manager*. Sliding a thousand-dollar bill beneath the tray in the cash register, replacing the tray, counting out the hundreds. No place you could not pass a hundred. There in the sweet heavy air of South Florida. Havana so close you could see the two-tone Impalas on the Malecón. Goddamn but we had some fun there."

More detailed, yes.

"She" now has a name: Elena.

"He" now has a name: Barry Sedlow.

But again, do notice: it had all been there in the original notes. It had all been there in the symbols, the marks on the page. It had all been there in the "xxx" and the "xxxx."

I supposed this process to be like writing music.

I have no idea whether or not this was an accurate assessment, since I neither wrote nor read music. All I know now is that I no longer write this way. All I know now is that writing, or whatever it was I was doing when I could proceed on no more than "xxx" and "xxxx," whatever it was I was doing when I imagined myself hearing the music, no longer comes easily to me. For a while I laid this to a certain weariness with my own style, an impatience, a wish to be more direct. I encouraged the very difficulty I was having laying words on the page. I saw it as evidence of a new directness. I see it differently now. I see it now as frailty. I see it now as the very frailty Quintana feared.

We are moving into another summer.

I find myself increasingly focused on this issue of frailty.

I fear falling on the street, I imagine bicycle messengers knocking me to the ground. The approach of a child on a motorized scooter causes me to freeze mid-intersection, play dead. I no longer go for breakfast to Three Guys on Madison Avenue: what if I were to fall on the way?

I feel unsteady, unbalanced, as if my nerves are misfiring, which may or may not be an exact description of what my nerves are in fact doing.

I hear a new tone when acquaintances ask how I am, a tone I have not before noticed and find increasingly distressing, even humiliating: these acquaintances seem as they ask impatient, half concerned, half querulous, as if no longer interested in the answer.

As if all too aware that the answer will be a complaint.

I determine to speak, if asked how I am, only positively.

I frame the cheerful response.

What I believe to be the cheerful response as I frame it emerges, as I hear it, more in the nature of a whine.

Do not whine, I write on an index card. *Do not complain. Work harder. Spend more time alone.*

I push-pin the index card to the corkboard on which I collect notes.

"*Struck by a train nine days before our wedding*," one note on the corkboard reads. "*Left the house that morning and was killed that afternoon in the crash of a small plane*," another reads. "*It was the second of January, 1931*," a third reads. "*I ran a little coup. My brother became president. He was more mature. I went to Europe.*"

These notes I push-pin to the corkboard are intended at the time I make them to restore my ability to function, but have so far not done so. I study the notes again. *Who* was struck by the train nine days before her wedding? Or was it nine days before *his* wedding? *Who* left the house that morning and was killed that afternoon in the crash of the small plane? *Who*, above all, ran the little coup on the second of January, 1931? And in what country?

I abandon the attempt to answer these questions.

The telephone rings.

Grateful for the interruption, I pick it up. I hear the voice of my nephew Griffin. He feels the need to report that he has been getting calls from "concerned friends." The focus of their concern is my health, specifically my weight. I am no longer grateful. I point out that I have weighed the same amount since the early 1970s, when I picked up paratyphoid during a film festival on the Caribbean coast of Colombia and by the time I got home had dropped so much weight that my mother had to fly to Malibu to feed me. Griffin says that he recognizes this. He is aware that my weight has not fluctuated since he was old enough to notice it. He is reporting only what these "concerned friends" have mentioned to him.

Griffin and I understand each other, which means in this case that we are able to change the subject. I consider asking him if he knows who it was who ran the little coup on the second of January, 1931, and in what country, but do not. In the absence of another subject I tell him about a taxi driver I recently encountered on my way from the Four Seasons Hotel in San Francisco to SFO. This taxi driver told me that he had been analyzing drill sites around Houston until the oil boom went belly up. His father had been a construction supervisor, he said, which meant that he had grown up on the construction sites of the big postwar high dams and power reactors. He mentioned Glen Canyon on the Colorado. He mentioned Rancho Seco outside Sacramento. He mentioned, when he learned that I was a writer, wanting himself to write a book about "intercourse between the United States and Japan." He had proposed such a book to Simon & Schuster but Simon & Schuster, he now believed, had passed the proposal on to another writer.

"Fellow by the name of Michael Crichton," he said. "I'm not saying he stole it, I'm just saying they used my ideas. But hey. Ideas are free."

Around San Bruno he began mentioning Scientology.

I tell you this true story just to prove that I can.

That my frailty has not yet reached a point at which I can no longer tell a true story.

Weeks pass, then months.

I go to a rehearsal room on West Forty-second Street to watch a run-through of a play, a new production of a Broadway musical for which two close friends wrote the lyrics in the 1970s.

I sit on a folding metal chair. Behind me I hear voices I recognize (the two close friends and their collaborator, who wrote the book) but I feel too uncertain to turn around. The songs, some familiar and some new, continue. The reprises roll around. As I sit on the folding metal chair I begin to fear getting up. As the finale approaches, I experience outright panic. What if my feet no longer move? What if my muscles lock? What if this neuritis or neuropathy or neurological inflammation has evolved into a condition more malign? I once in my late twenties had an exclusionary diagnosis of multiple sclerosis, believed later by the neurologist who made the diagnosis to be in remission, but what if it is no longer in remission? What if it never was? What if it has returned? What if I stand up from this folding chair in this rehearsal room on West Forty-second Street and collapse, fall to the floor, the folding metal chair collapsing with me?

Or what if—

(Another series of dire possibilities occurs to me, this series even more alarming than the last—)

What if the damage extends beyond the physical?

What if the problem is now cognitive?

What if the absence of style that I welcomed at one point—the directness that I encouraged, even cultivated—what if this absence of style has now taken on a pernicious life of its own?

What if my new inability to summon the right word, the apt thought, the connection that enables the words to make sense, the rhythm, the music itself—

What if this new inability is systemic?

What if I can never again locate the words that work?

20

I SEE A NEW neurologist, at Columbia Presbyterian.

The new neurologist has answers: all new neurologists have answers, usually wishful. New neurologists remain the last true believers in the power of wishful thinking. The answers offered by this particular new neurologist are for me to gain weight and devote a minimum of three hours a week to physical therapy.

I have been through this catechism before.

I happen to have been a remarkably small child. I say remarkably for a reason: something about my size was such that perfect strangers could always be relied upon to remark on it. "You're not very thick," I recall a French doctor saying when I went to see him in Paris for an antibiotic prescription. This was true enough, but I grew tired of hearing it. I grew particularly tired of hearing it when it was presented as something I might otherwise have missed. I was short, I was thin, I could circle my wrists with my thumb and index finger. My earliest memories involve being urged by my mother to gain weight, as if my failure to do so were willful, an act of rebellion. I was not allowed to get up from the table until I had eaten everything on my plate, a rule that led mainly to new and inventive ways of eating nothing on my plate. The "clean-plate club" was frequently mentioned. "Good eaters" were commended. "She's not a human garbage can," I recall my father exploding in my defense. As an adult I came to see this approach to food as more or less guaranteeing an eating disorder, but I never mentioned this theory to my mother.

Nor do I mention it to the new neurologist.

Actually the new neurologist offers, in addition to gaining weight and doing physical therapy, a third, although equally wishful, answer: the exclusionary diagnosis I received in my late twenties notwithstanding, I do not have multiple sclerosis. He is vehement on this point. There is no reason to believe that I have multiple sclerosis. Magnetic Resonance Imaging, a technique not yet available when I was in my late twenties, conclusively demonstrates that I do not have multiple sclerosis.

In that case, I ask, trying to summon an appearance of faith in whatever he chooses to answer, what is it that I do have?

I have neuritis, a neuropathy, a neurological inflammation.

I overlook the shrug.

I ask what caused this neuritis, this neuropathy, this neurological inflammation.

Not weighing enough, he answers.

It does not escape me that the consensus on what is wrong with me has once again insinuated the ball into my court.

I am referred to a dietitian on this matter of gaining weight.

The dietitian makes (the inevitable) protein shakes, brings me freshly laid eggs (better) from a farm in New Jersey and perfect vanilla ice cream (better still) from Maison du Chocolat on Madison Avenue.

I drink the protein shakes.

I eat the freshly laid eggs from the farm in New Jersey and the perfect vanilla ice cream from Maison du Chocolat on Madison Avenue.

Nonetheless.

I do not gain weight.

I have an uneasy sense that the consensus solution has already failed.

I find, on the other hand, somewhat to my surprise, that I actively like physical therapy. I keep regular appointments at a Columbia Presbyterian sports medicine facility at Sixtieth and Madison. I am impressed by the strength and general tone of the other patients who turn up during the same hour. I study their balance, their proficiency with the various devices recommended by the therapist. The more I watch, the more encouraged I am: *this stuff really works*, I tell myself. The thought makes me cheerful, optimistic. I wonder how many appointments it will take to reach the apparently effortless control already achieved by my fellow patients. Only during my third week of physical therapy do I learn that these particular fellow patients are in fact the New York Yankees, loosening up between game days.

21

TODAY AS I WALK home from the Columbia Presbyterian sports medicine facility at Sixtieth and Madison I find the optimism engendered by proximity to the New York Yankees fading. In fact my physical confidence seems to be reaching a new ebb. My cognitive confidence seems to have vanished altogether. Even the correct stance for telling you this, the ways to describe what is happening to me, the attitude, the tone, the very words, now elude my grasp.

The tone needs to be direct.

I need to talk to you directly, I need to *address the subject as it were*, but something stops me.

Is this another kind of neuropathy, a new frailty, am I no longer able to talk directly?

Was I ever?

Did I lose it?

Or is the subject in this case a matter I wish not to address?

When I tell you that I am afraid to get up from a folding chair in a rehearsal room on West Forty-second Street, of what am I really afraid?

22

W*HAT IF YOU hadn't been home when Dr. Watson called—*
What if you couldn't meet him at the hospital—
What if there'd been an accident on the freeway—
What would happen to me then?

All adopted children, I am told, fear that they will be abandoned by their adoptive parents as they believe themselves to have been abandoned by their natural. They are programmed, by the unique circumstances of their introduction into the family structure, to see abandonment as their role, their fate, the destiny that will overtake them unless they outrun it.

Quintana.

All adoptive parents, I do not need to be told, fear that they do not deserve the child they were given, that the child will be taken from them.

Quintana.

Quintana is one of the areas about which I have difficulty being direct.

I said early on that adoption is hard to get right but I did not tell you why.

"Of course you won't tell her she's adopted," many people said at the time she was born, most of these people the age of my parents, a generation, like that of Diana's parents, for which adoption remained obscurely shameful, a secret to be kept at any cost. "You couldn't possibly tell her."

Of course we could possibly tell her.

In fact we had already told her. *L'adoptada, m'ija.* There was never any question of not telling her. What were the alternatives? Lie to her? Leave it to her agent to take her to lunch at the Beverly Hills Hotel? Before too many years passed I would write about her adoption, John would write about her adoption, Quintana herself would agree to be one of the children interviewed for a book by the photographer Jill Krementz called *How It Feels to Be Adopted.* Over those years we had received periodic communications from women who had seen these mentions of her adoption and believed her to be their own lost daughter, women who had themselves given up infants for adoption and were now haunted by the possibility that this child about whom they had read could be that missing child.

This beautiful child, this perfect child.

Qué hermosa, qué chula.

We responded to each of these communications, we followed up, we explained how the facts did not coincide, the dates did not tally, why the perfect child could not be theirs.

We considered our role fulfilled, the case closed.

Still.

The recommended choice narrative did not end, as I had imagined it would (hoped it would, dreamed it would), with the perfect child placed on the table between us for lunch at The Bistro (Sidney Korshak's corner banquette, the blue-and-white dotted organdy dress) on the hot day in September 1966 when the adoption became final.

Thirty-two years later, in 1998, on a Saturday morning when she was alone in her apartment and vulnerable to whatever bad or good news arrived at her door, the perfect child received a Federal Express letter from a young woman who convincingly identified herself as her sister, her full sister, one of two younger children later born, although we had not before known this, to Quintana's natural mother and father. At the time of Quintana's birth the natural mother and father had not yet been married. At a point after her birth they married, had the two further children, Quintana's full sister and brother, and then divorced. According to the letter from the young woman who identified herself as Quintana's sister, the mother and sister lived now in Dallas. The brother, from whom the mother was estranged, lived in another city in Texas. The father, who had remarried and fathered another child, lived in Florida. The sister, who had learned from her mother only a few weeks before that Quintana existed, had determined immediately, against the initial instincts of her mother, to locate her.

She had resorted to the internet.

On the internet she had found a private detective who said that he could locate Quintana for two hundred dollars.

Quintana had an unlisted telephone number.

The two hundred dollars was for accessing her Con Ed account.

The sister had agreed to the deal.

It had taken the detective only ten further minutes to call the sister back with a street address and apartment number in New York.

14 Sutton Place South. Apartment 11D.

The sister had written the letter.

She had sent it to Apartment 11D at 14 Sutton Place South via Federal Express.

"Saturday delivery," Quintana said when she showed us the letter, still in its Federal Express envelope. "The FedEx came *Saturday delivery*." I remember her repeating these words, emphasizing them, *Saturday delivery, the FedEx came Saturday delivery*, as if maintaining focus on this one point could put her world back together.

23

I CANNOT EASILY EXPRESS what I thought about this.

On the one hand, I told myself, it could hardly be a surprise. We had spent thirty-two years considering just such a possibility. We had for many of those years seen such a possibility even as a probability. Quintana's mother, through a bureaucratic error on the part of the social worker, had been told not only our names and Quintana's name but the name under which I wrote. We did not lead an entirely private life. We gave lectures, we attended events, we got photographed. We could be easily found. We had discussed how it would happen. There would be a letter. There would be a phone call. The caller would say such and such. Whichever one of us took the call would say such and such and such. We would meet.

It would be logical.

It would all, when it happened, make sense.

In an alternate scenario, Quintana herself would choose to undertake the search, initiate the contact. Should she wish to do so, the process would be simple. Through another bureaucratic error, a bill from St. John's Hospital in Santa Monica had reached us without the mother's name redacted. I had seen the name only once but it had remained imprinted on my memory. I had thought it a beautiful name.

We had discussed this with our lawyer. We had authorized him, should Quintana ask, to give her whatever help she wanted or needed.

This too would be logical.

This too would all, when it happened, make sense.

On the other hand, I told myself, it now seemed too late, not the right time.

There comes a point, I told myself, at which a family is, for better or for worse, finished.

Yes. I just told you. *Of course* I had considered this possibility.

Accepting it would be something else.

A while back, to another point, I mentioned that we had taken her with us to Tucson while *The Life and Times of Judge Roy Bean* was shooting there.

I mentioned the Hilton Inn and I mentioned the babysitter and I mentioned Dick Moore and I mentioned Paul Newman but there was a part of that trip that I did not mention.

It happened on our first night in Tucson.

We had left her with the babysitter. We had watched the dailies. We had met in the Hilton Inn dining room for dinner. Halfway through dinner—a few too many people at the table, a little too much noise, just another working dinner on a motion picture on just another location—it had struck me: this was not, for me, just another location.

This was Tucson.

We had not been told much about her natural family but we had been told one thing: her mother was from Tucson. Her mother was from Tucson and I knew her mother's name.

I never considered not doing what I did next.

I got up from dinner and found a pay phone with a Tucson telephone book.

I looked up the name.

I showed the name to John.

Without discussion we went back to the crowded table in the dining room and told the producer of *The Life and Times of Judge Roy Bean* that we needed to speak to him. He followed us into the lobby. There in a corner of the lobby of the Hilton Inn we talked to him for three or four minutes. It was imperative, we said, that no one should know we were in Tucson. It was especially imperative, we said, that no one should know Quintana was in Tucson. I did not want to pick up the Tucson paper, I said, and see any cute items about children on the *Judge Roy Bean* location. I asked him to alert the unit publicity people. I stressed that under no condition should Quintana's name appear in connection with the picture.

There was no reason to think that it would but I had to be sure.

I had to cover that base.

I had to make that effort.

I believed as I did so that I was protecting both Quintana and her mother.

I tell you this now by way of suggesting the muddled impulses that can go hand in hand with adoption.

A few months after the arrival of the FedEx Saturday delivery, Quintana and her sister met, first in New York and then in Dallas. In New York Quintana showed her visiting sister Chinatown. She took her shopping at Pearl River. She brought her to dinner with John and me at Da Silvano. She invited her friends and cousins to her apartment for drinks so that they and her sister could all meet. The two sisters looked like twins. When Griffin walked into Quintana's apartment and saw the sister he inadvertently greeted her as "Q." Margaritas were mixed. Guacamole was made. There was about this initial weekend meeting a spirit of willed excitement, determined camaraderie, resolute discovery.

It would be a month or so later, in Dallas, before the will and the determination and the resolution all failed her.

When she called after twenty-four hours in Dallas she had seemed distraught, on the edge of tears.

In Dallas she had been introduced for the first time not only to her mother but to many other members of what she was now calling her "biological family," strangers who welcomed her as their long-missing child.

In Dallas these strangers had shown her snapshots, remarked on her resemblance to one or another cousin or aunt or grandparent, seemingly taken for granted that she had chosen by her presence to be one of them.

On her return to New York she had begun getting regular calls from her mother, whose initial resistance to the idea of a reunion (in the first place it wasn't a reunion, her mother had punctiliously pointed out, since they had never met in the first place) seemed to have given way to a need to discuss the events that had led to the adoption. These calls came in the morning, typically at a time when Quintana was just about to leave for work. She did not want to cut her mother short but neither did she want to be late for work, particularly because *Elle Décor*, the magazine for which she was at that time the photography editor, was undergoing a staff realignment and she felt her job to be in jeopardy. She discussed this conflict with a psychiatrist. After the discussion with the psychiatrist she wrote to her mother and sister saying that "being found" ("I was found" had evolved into her arrestingly equivocal way of referring to what had happened) was proving "too much to handle," "too much and too soon," that she needed to "step back," "catch up for a while" with what she still considered her real life.

In reply she received a letter from her mother saying that she did not want to be a burden and so had disconnected her telephone.

This was the point at which it seemed clear that not one of us would escape those muddled impulses.

Not Quintana's mother, not Quintana's sister, certainly not me.

Not even Quintana.

Quintana who referred to the shattering of her known world as "being found."

Quintana who had called Nicholas and Alexandra "Nicky and Sunny" and seen their story as "a big hit."

Quintana who had imagined The Broken Man in such convincing detail.

Quintana who told me that after she became five she never ever dreamed about The Broken Man.

A few weeks after her mother disconnected her telephone another message arrived, although not from her mother and not from her sister.

She received a letter from her natural father in Florida.

Over the time that passed between the time she knew herself to have been adopted and the time she was "found," a period of some thirty years, she had many times mentioned her other mother. "My other mommy," and later "my other mother," had been from the time she first spoke the way she referred to her. She had wondered who and where this other mother was. She had wondered what she looked like. She had considered and ultimately rejected the possibility of finding out. John had once asked her, when she was small, what she would do if she met her "other mommy." "I'd put one arm around Mom," she had said, "and one arm around my other mommy, and I'd say 'Hello, Mommies.'"

She had never, not once, mentioned her other father.

I have no idea why but the picture in her mind seemed not to include a father.

"What a long strange journey this has been," the letter from Florida read.

She burst into tears as she read it to me.

"On top of everything else," she said through the tears, "my father has to be a Deadhead."

Three years later the final message arrived, this one from her sister.

Her sister wanted her to know that their brother had died. The cause of death was unclear. His heart was mentioned.

Quintana had never met him.

I am not sure of the dates but I think he would have been born the year she was five.

After I became five I never ever dreamed about him.

This call to say that he had died may have been the last time the sisters spoke.

When Quintana herself died, her sister sent flowers.

24

I FIND MYSELF leafing today for the first time through a journal she kept in the spring of 1984, a daily assignment for an English class during her senior year at the Westlake School for Girls. "I had an exciting revelation while studying a poem by John Keats," this volume of the journal begins, on a page dated March 7, 1984, the one-hundred-and-seventeenth entry since she had begun keeping the journal in September of 1983. "In the poem, 'Endymion,' there is a line that seems to tell my present fear of life: *Pass into nothingness.*"

This March 7, 1984, entry continues, moves into a discussion of Jean-Paul Sartre and Martin Heidegger and their respective understandings of the abyss, but I am no longer following the argument: automatically, without thinking, appallingly, as if she were still at the Westlake School and had asked me to take a look at her paper, I am editing it.

For example:

Delete commas setting off title "Endymion."

"Tell," as in "a line that seems to tell my present fear of life," is of course wrong.

"Describe" would be better.

"Suggest" would be better still.

On the other hand: "tell" might work: try "tell" as she uses it.

I try it: *She "tells" her present fear of life in relation to Sartre.*

I try it again: *She "tells" her present fear of life in relation to Heidegger. She "tells" her understanding of the abyss. She qualifies her understanding of the abyss: "This is merely how I interpret the abyss; I could be wrong."*

Considerable time passes before I realize that my preoccupation with the words she used has screened off any possible apprehension of what she was actually saying when she wrote her journal entry on that March day in 1984.

Was that deliberate?

Was I screening off what she said about her fear of life the same way I had screened off what she said about her fear of The Broken Man?

Hello, Quintana? I'm going to lock you here in the garage?

After I became five I never ever dreamed about him?

Did I all her life keep a baffle between us?

Did I prefer not to hear what she was actually saying?

Did it frighten me?

I try the passage again, this time reading for meaning.

What she said: *My present fear of life.*

What she said: *Pass into nothingness.*

What she was actually saying: *The World has nothing but Morning and Night. It has no Day or Lunch. Let me just be in the ground. Let me just be in the ground and go to sleep.* When I tell you that I am afraid to get up from a folding chair in a rehearsal room on West Forty-second Street, is this what I am actually saying?

Does it frighten me?

25

LET ME AGAIN try to talk to you directly.

On my last birthday, December 5, 2009, I became seventy-five years old.

Notice the odd construction there—*I became seventy-five years old*—do you hear the echo?

I *became* seventy-five? I *became* five?

After I became five I never ever dreamed about him?

Also notice—in notes that talk about aging in their first few pages, notes called *Blue Nights* for a reason, notes called *Blue Nights* because at the time I began them I could think of little other than the inevitable approach of darker days—how long it took me to tell you that one salient fact, how long it took me to *address the subject as it were*. Aging and its evidence remain life's most predictable events, yet they also remain matters we prefer to leave unmentioned, unexplored: I have watched tears flood the eyes of grown women, loved women, women of talent and accomplishment, for no reason other than that a small child in the room, more often than not an adored niece or nephew, has just described them as "wrinkly," or asked how old they are. When we are asked this question we are always undone by its innocence, somehow shamed by the clear bell-like tones in which it is asked. What shames us is this: the answer we give is never innocent. The answer we give is unclear, evasive, even guilty. Right now when I answer this question I find myself doubting my own accuracy, rechecking the increasingly undoable arithmetic (born December 5, 1934, subtract 1934 from 2009, do this in your head and watch yourself get muddled by the interruption of the entirely irrelevant millennium), insisting to myself (no one else particularly cares) that there must be a mistake: only yesterday I was in my fifties, my forties, only yesterday I was thirty-one.

Quintana was born when I was thirty-one.

Only yesterday Quintana was born.

Only yesterday I was taking Quintana home from the nursery at St. John's Hospital in Santa Monica.

Enveloped in a silk-lined cashmere wrapper.

Daddy's gone to get a rabbit skin to wrap his baby bunny in.

What if you hadn't been home when Dr. Watson called?

What would happen to me then?

Only yesterday I was holding her in my arms on the 405.

Only yesterday I was promising her that she would be safe with us.

We then called the 405 the San Diego Freeway.

It was only yesterday when we still called the 405 the San Diego, it was only yesterday when we still called the 10 the Santa Monica, it was only the day before yesterday when the Santa Monica did not yet exist.

Only yesterday I could still do arithmetic, remember telephone numbers, rent a car at the airport and drive it out of the lot without freezing, stopping at the key moment, feet already on the pedals but immobilized by the question of which is the accelerator and which the brake.

Only yesterday Quintana was alive.

I disengage my feet from the pedals, first one, then the other.

I invent a reason for the Hertz attendant to start the rental car.

I am seventy-five years old: this is not the reason I give.

26

A DOCTOR to whom I occasionally talk suggests that I have made an inadequate adjustment to aging.

Wrong, I want to say.

In fact I have made no adjustment whatsoever to aging.

In fact I had lived my entire life to date without seriously believing that I would age.

I had no doubt that I would continue to wear the red suede sandals with four-inch heels that I had always preferred.

I had no doubt that I would continue to wear the gold hoop earrings on which I had always relied, the black cashmere leggings, the enameled beads.

My skin would develop flaws, fine lines, even brown spots (this, at seventy-five, was what passed for a realistic cosmetic assessment), but it would continue to look as it had always looked, basically healthy. My hair would lose its original color but color could continue to be replaced by leaving the gray around the face and twice a year letting Johanna at Bumble and Bumble highlight the rest. I would recognize that the models I encountered on these semiannual visits to the color room at Bumble and Bumble were significantly younger than I was, but since these models I encountered on my semiannual visits to the color room at Bumble and Bumble were at most sixteen or seventeen there could be no reason to interpret the difference as a personal failure. My memory would slip but whose memory does not slip. My eyesight would be more problematic than it might have been before I began seeing the world through sudden clouds of what looked like black lace and was actually blood, the residue of a series of retinal tears and detachments, but there would still be no question that I could see, read, write, navigate intersections without fear.

No question that it could not be fixed.

Whatever "it" was.

I believed absolutely in my own power to surmount the situation.

Whatever "the situation" was.

When my grandmother was seventy-five she experienced a

cerebral hemorrhage, fell unconscious to the sidewalk not far from her house in Sacramento, was taken to Sutter Hospital, and died there that night. This was "the situation" for my grandmother. When my mother was seventy-five she was diagnosed with breast cancer, did two cycles of chemotherapy, could not tolerate the third or fourth, nonetheless lived until she was two weeks short of her ninety-first birthday (when she did die it was of congestive heart failure, not cancer) but was never again exactly as she had been. Things went wrong. She lost confidence. She became apprehensive in crowds. She was no longer entirely comfortable at the weddings of her grandchildren or even, in truth, at family dinners. She made mystifying, even hostile, judgments. When she came to visit me in New York for example she pronounced St. James' Episcopal Church, the steeple and slate roof of which constitute the entire view from my living room windows, "the single ugliest church I have ever seen." When, on her own coast and at her own suggestion, I took her to see the jellyfish at the Monterey Bay Aquarium, she fled to the car, pleading vertigo from the movement of the water.

I recognize now that she was feeling frail.

I recognize now that she was feeling then as I feel now.

Invisible on the street.

The target of any wheeled vehicle on the scene.

Unbalanced at the instant of stepping off a curb, sitting down or standing up, opening or closing a taxi door.

Cognitively challenged not only by simple arithmetic but by straightforward news stories, announced changes in traffic flow, the memorization of a telephone number, the seating of a dinner party.

"Estrogen actually made me feel better," she said to me not long before she died, after several decades without it.

Well, yes. Estrogen had made her feel better.

This turns out to have been "the situation" for most of us.

And yet:

And still:

Despite all evidence:

Despite recognizing that my skin and my hair and even my cognition are all reliant on the estrogen I no longer have:

Despite recognizing that I will not again wear the red suede sandals with the four-inch heels and despite recognizing that the gold hoop earrings and the black cashmere leggings and the enameled beads no longer exactly apply:

Despite recognizing that for a woman my age even to note such details of appearance will be construed by many as a manifestation of misplaced vanity:

Despite all that:

Nonetheless:

That being seventy-five could present as a significantly altered situation, an altogether different "it," did not until recently occur to me.

27

SOMETHING HAPPENED TO ME early in the summer. Something that altered my view of my own possibilities, shortened, as it were, the horizon.

I still have no idea what time it was when it happened, or why it was that it happened, or even in any exact way what it was that happened. All I know is that midway through June, after walking home with a friend after an early dinner on Third Avenue in the eighties, I found myself waking on the floor of my bedroom, left arm and forehead and both legs bleeding, unable to get up. It seemed clear that I had fallen, but I had no memory of falling, no memory whatsoever of losing balance, trying to regain it, the usual preludes to a fall. Certainly I had no memory of losing consciousness. The diagnostic term for what had happened (I was to learn before the night ended) was "syncope," fainting, but discussions of syncope, centering as they did on "pre-syncope symptoms" (palpitations, light-headedness, dizziness, blurred or tunnel vision), none of which I could identify, seemed not to apply.

I had been alone in the apartment.

There were thirteen telephones in the apartment, not one of which was at that moment within reach.

I remember lying on the floor and trying to visualize the unreachable telephones, count them off room by room.

I remember forgetting one room and counting off the telephones a second and then a third time.

This was dangerously soothing.

I remember deciding in the absence of any prospect of help to go back to sleep for a while, on the floor, the blood pooling around me.

I remember pulling a quilt down from a wicker chest, the only object I could reach, and folding it under my head.

I remember nothing else until I woke a second time and managed on this attempt to summon enough traction to pull myself up.

At which point I called a friend.

At which point he came over.

At which point, since I was still bleeding, we took a taxi to the emergency room at Lenox Hill Hospital.

It was I who said Lenox Hill.

Let me repeat: it was I who said Lenox Hill.

Weeks later, this one fact was still troubling me as much as anything else about the entire sequence of events that night: *it was I who said Lenox Hill.* I got into a taxi in front of my apartment, which happens to be equidistant from two hospitals, Lenox Hill and New York Cornell, *and I said Lenox Hill.* Saying Lenox Hill instead of New York Cornell did not demonstrate a developed instinct for self-preservation. Saying Lenox Hill instead of New York Cornell demonstrated only that I was at that moment incapable of taking care of myself. Saying Lenox Hill instead of New York Cornell proved the point humiliatingly made by every nurse and aide and doctor to whom I spoke in the two nights I would eventually spend at Lenox Hill, the first night in the emergency room and the second in a cardiac unit, where a bed happened to be available and where it was erroneously assumed that because I had been given a bed in the cardiac unit I must have a cardiac problem: I was old. I was too old to live alone. I was too old to be allowed out of bed. I was too old even to recognize that if I had been given a bed in the cardiac unit I must have a cardiac problem.

"Your cardiac problem isn't showing up on the monitors," one nurse kept reporting, accusingly.

I tried to process what she was saying.

Processing what people were saying was not at that moment my long suit, but this nurse seemed to be suggesting that my "cardiac problem" was not showing up on the monitors because I had deliberately detached the electrodes.

I countered.

I said that to the best of my knowledge I did not have a cardiac problem.

She countered.

"Of course you have a cardiac problem," she said. And then, closing the issue: "Because otherwise you wouldn't be in the cardiac unit."

I had no answer for that.

I tried to pretend I was home.

I tried to figure out whether it was day or night: if it was day

I had a shot at going home, but in the hospital there was no day or night.

Only shifts.

Only waiting.

Waiting for the IV nurse, waiting for the nurse with the narcotics key, waiting for the transporter.

Will someone please take the catheter out.

That transfusion was ordered at eleven this evening.

"How do you normally get around your apartment," someone in scrubs kept asking, marveling at what he seemed to consider my entirely unearned mobility, finally providing his own answer: "Walker?"

Demoralization occurs in the instant: I have trouble expressing the extent to which two nights of relatively undemanding hospitalization negatively affected me. There had been no surgery. There had been no uncomfortable procedures. There had been no real discomfort at all, other than emotional. Yet I felt myself to be the victim of a gross misunderstanding: I wanted only to go home, get the blood washed out of my hair, stop being treated as an invalid. Instead the very opposite was happening. My own doctor, who was based at Columbia Presbyterian, happened to be in St. Petersburg with his family: he called me at Lenox Hill during an intermission at the Kirov Ballet. He wanted to know what I was doing at Lenox Hill. So, at that point, did I. The doctors on the scene, determined to track down my phantom "cardiac problem," seemed willing to permanently infantilize me. Even my own friends, dropping by after work, very much in charge, no blood in their hair, sentient adults placing and receiving calls, making arrangements for dinner, bringing me perfect chilled soups that I could not eat because the hospital bed was so angled as to prevent sitting upright, were now talking about the need to get me "someone in the house": it was increasingly as if I had taken a taxi to Lenox Hill and woken up in *Driving Miss Daisy*.

With effort, I managed to convey this point.

I got released from Lenox Hill.

My own doctor got back from St. Petersburg.

After further days of unproductive cardiac monitoring the cardiac hypothesis was abandoned.

An appointment was made with yet another new neurologist, this one at New York Cornell.

Many tests were scheduled and done.

A new MRI, to establish whether or not there had been significant changes.

There had not been.

A new MRA, to see whether or not there had been any enlargement of the aneurysm visualized on the previous MRAs.

There had not been.

A new ultrasound, to establish whether or not there had been increased calcification of the carotid artery.

There had not been.

And, finally, a full-body PET scan, meant to show any abnormalities in the heart, the lungs, the liver, the kidneys, the bones, the brain: in fact anywhere in the body.

I repeatedly slid in and out of the PET scanner.

Forty minutes passed, then a change of position and another fifteen.

I lay motionless on the scanner.

It seemed impossible to imagine this coming up clean.

It would be one more version of the bed in the cardiac unit: a full-body PET scan had been ordered, *ergo*, as night follows day, there would need to be abnormalities for the full-body PET scan to show.

A day later I was given the results.

There were, surprisingly, no abnormalities seen in the scan.

Everyone agreed on this point. Everyone used the word "surprisingly."

Surprisingly, there were no abnormalities to explain why I felt as frail as I did.

Surprisingly, there were no abnormalities to tell me why I was afraid to get up from a folding chair in a rehearsal room on West Forty-second Street.

Only then did I realize that during the three weeks that had passed between taking the taxi to Lenox Hill, on the fourteenth of June, and receiving the results of the full-body PET scan, on the eighth of July, I had allowed this year's most deeply blue nights to come and go without my notice.

What does it cost to lose those weeks, that light, the very nights in the year preferred over all others?

Can you evade the dying of the brightness?

Or do you evade only its warning?

Where are you left if you miss the message the blue nights bring?

"Have you ever had a moment where everything in your life just stopped?" This was the way that this question was raised by Kris Jenkins, a three-hundred-and-sixty-pound Jets defensive tackle, after he tore, six plays into his tenth NFL season, both his meniscus and his anterior cruciate ligament. "So fast, but in slow motion? Like all your senses shut down? Like you're watching yourself?"

I offer you a second way of approaching the moment where everything in your life just stops, this one from the actor Robert Duvall: "I exist very nicely between the words 'action' and 'cut.'"

And even a third way: "It doesn't present as pain," I once heard an oncological surgeon say of cancer.

28

I FIND MYSELF thinking exclusively about Quintana. I need her with me.

Behind the house on Franklin Avenue in Hollywood in which we lived from the day we left Sara Mankiewicz's Minton plates until the day we moved into the beach house, a period of some four years, there was a clay tennis court, weeds growing through the cracked clay. I remember watching her weed it, kneeling on fat baby knees, the ragged stuffed animal she addressed as "Bunny Rabbit" at her side.

Daddy's gone to get a rabbit skin to wrap his baby bunny in.

In a few weeks she will have been dead five years.

Five years since the doctor said that the patient had been unable to get enough oxygen through the vent for at least an hour now.

Five years since Gerry and I left her in the ICU overlooking the river at New York Cornell.

I can now afford to think about her.

I no longer cry when I hear her name.

I no longer imagine the transporter being called to take her to the morgue after we left the ICU.

Yet I still need her with me.

In lieu of her presence I leaf through the books on a table in my office, each one a book she gave me.

One is called *Baby Animals and Their Mothers*, and is just that, black-and-white photographs of baby animals and their mothers: mostly comforting favorites (not unlike Bunny Rabbit), lambs and ewes, foals and mares, but also less common baby animals and their mothers: hedgehogs, koala bears, llamas. Stuck in the pages of *Baby Animals and Their Mothers* I find a French postcard showing a baby polar bear and its mother. "*Câlin sur la banquise*," the caption reads in French, and then, in English: "Cuddling on the ice floe."

"Just a few things I found on my travels that reminded me of you," the note on the card reads, in printing less careful than it once was but still recognizable.

Still hers.

Beneath *Baby Animals and Their Mothers* is Jean-Dominique Bauby's *The Diving Bell and the Butterfly*, an account, by a former editor in chief of French *Elle*, of what it had felt like to have a cerebrovascular accident on a date he knew to have been the eighth of December and next wake at the end of January, unable to speak, able to move only by blinking one eyelid: the condition known as "locked-in syndrome." (Did anyone use the word "syncope"? Did anyone use the words "pre-syncope symptoms"? Can we find any clues here? Any clue to Jean-Dominique Bauby's situation? Any clue to my own?) For reasons that I did not at the time entirely understand and have not since wanted to explore, *The Diving Bell and the Butterfly* had been when it was published extremely meaningful to Quintana, so markedly so that I never told her that I did not much like it, or for that matter even entirely believe it.

Only later, when she was for most purposes locked into her own condition, confined to a wheelchair and afflicted by the detritus of a bleed into her brain and the subsequent neurosurgery, did I begin to see its point.

Beginning to see its point was when I stopped wanting to explore the reasons why it might have been so markedly meaningful to Quintana.

Just let me be in the ground.

Just let me be in the ground and go to sleep.

I return *The Diving Bell and the Butterfly* to the table in my office.

I align it with *Baby Animals and Their Mothers.*

Câlin sur la banquise.

This business of the ice floes is familiar to me. I did not need *Baby Animals and Their Mothers* to bring the image of the ice floes alive. In the first year of Quintana's hospitalizations I had watched ice floes from her hospital windows: ice floes on the East River from her windows at Beth Israel North, ice floes on the Hudson from her windows at Columbia Presbyterian. I think now of those ice floes and imagine having seen, floating past on one or another slab of breaking ice, a baby polar bear and its mother, heading for the Hell Gate Bridge.

I imagine having shown the baby polar bear and its mother to Quintana.

Câlin sur la banquise.

Just let me be in the ground.

I resolve to forget the ice floes.

I have thought enough about the ice floes.

Thinking about the ice floes is like thinking about the transporter being called to take her to the morgue.

I walk into Central Park and sit for a while on a bench to which is attached a brass plaque indicating that a memorial contribution has been made to the Central Park Conservancy. There are now in the park many such brass plaques, many such benches. "*Quintana Roo Dunne Michael 1966–2005*," the plaque on this bench reads. "*In summertime and wintertime.*" A friend had made the contribution, and asked me to write out what I wanted the plaque to read. The same friend had come to visit Quintana when she was doing therapy in the neuro-rehab unit at UCLA, and after she saw Quintana had a cafeteria lunch with me in the hospital patio. It did not occur to either of us on the day we had the cafeteria lunch in the hospital patio at UCLA that Quintana's recovery would end at this bench.

So we still thought of that year.

Quintana's "recovery."

We had no idea then how rare recovery can be.

No idea that "recovery," like "adoption," remains one of those concepts that sounds more plausible than it turns out to be.

Câlin sur la banquise.

The wheelchair.

The detritus of the bleed, the neurosurgery.

In summertime and wintertime.

I wonder if in those revised circumstances she remembered *The Diving Bell and the Butterfly*, what it meant to her then.

She did not want to talk about those revised circumstances.

She wanted to believe that if she did not "dwell" on them she would wake one morning and find them corrected.

"Like when someone dies," she once said by way of explaining her approach, "don't dwell on it."

29

Stop all the clocks, cut off the telephone,
Prevent the dog from barking with a juicy bone,
Silence the pianos and with muffled drum
Bring out the coffin, let the mourners come.

Let aeroplanes circle moaning overhead
Scribbling on the sky the message He Is Dead,
Put crêpe bows round the white necks of the public doves,
Let the traffic policemen wear black cotton gloves.

He was my North, my South, my East and West,
My working week and my Sunday rest,
My noon, my midnight, my talk, my song;
I thought that love would last for ever: I was wrong.

The stars are not wanted now; put out every one,
Pack up the moon and dismantle the sun,
Pour away the ocean and sweep up the wood;
For nothing now can ever come to any good.

So go W. H. Auden's "Funeral Blues," sixteen lines that, during the days and weeks immediately after John died, spoke directly to the anger—the unreasoning fury, the blind rage—that I found myself feeling. I later showed "Funeral Blues" to Quintana. I told her that I was thinking of reading it at the memorial service she and I were then planning for John. She implored me not to do so. She said she liked nothing about the poem. She said it was "wrong." She was vehement on this point. At the time I thought she was upset by the tone of the poem, its raw rhythms, the harshness with which it rejects the world, the sense it gives off of a speaker about to explode. I now think of her vehemence differently. I now think she saw "Funeral Blues" as dwelling on it.

On the afternoon she herself died, August 26, 2005, her husband and I left the ICU overlooking the river at New York Cornell and walked through Central Park. The leaves on the trees were already losing their intensity, still weeks from dropping but ready to drop, not exactly faded but fading. At the time she entered the hospital, late in May or early in June, the blue nights had been just making their appearance. I had first noticed them not long after she was admitted to the ICU, which happened to be in the Greenberg Pavilion. In the lobby of the Greenberg Pavilion there hung portraits of its major benefactors, the most prominent of whom had played founding roles in the insurance conglomerate AIG and so had figured in news stories about the AIG bailout. During the first weeks I had reason to visit the ICU in the Greenberg Pavilion I was startled by the familiarity of these faces in the portraits, and, in the early evening, when I came downstairs from the ICU, would pause to study them. Then I would walk out into the increasingly intense blue of that time of day in that early summer season.

This routine seemed for a while to bring luck.

It was a period when the doctors in the ICU did not seem uniformly discouraging.

It was a period when improvement seemed possible.

There was even mention of a step-down unit, although the step-down unit never exactly materialized.

Then one night, leaving the ICU and pausing as usual by the AIG portraits, I realized: there would be no step-down unit.

The light outside had already changed.

The light outside was no longer blue.

She had so far since entering this ICU undergone five surgical interventions. She had remained ventilated and sedated throughout. The original surgical incision had never been closed. I had asked her surgeon how long he could continue doing this. He had mentioned a surgeon at Cornell who had done eighteen such interventions on a single patient.

"And that patient lived," the surgeon had said.

In what condition, I had asked.

"Your daughter wasn't in great condition when she arrived here," the surgeon had said.

So that was where we were. The light outside was already

darkening. The summer was already ending and she was still upstairs in the ICU overlooking the river and the surgeon was saying she wasn't in great condition when they put her there.

In other words she was dying.

I now knew she was dying.

There was now no way to avoid knowing it. There would now be no way to believe the doctors when they tried not to seem discouraging. There would now be no way to pretend to myself that the spirit of the AIG founders would pull this one out. She would die. She would not necessarily die that night, she would not necessarily die the next day, but we were now on track to the day she would die.

August 26 was the day she would die.

August 26 was the day Gerry and I would leave the ICU overlooking the river and walk into Central Park.

I see as I write this that there is no uniformity in the way I refer to Gerry. Sometimes I call him "Gerry," sometimes I call him "her husband." She liked the sound of that. *Her husband. My husband.*

She would say it again and again.

When she could still speak.

Which, as the days continued to shorten and the track to narrow, was by no means every day.

You notice we're doing hand compression.

Because the patient could no longer get enough oxygen through the vent.

For at least an hour now.

In an underpass beneath one of the bridges in Central Park that day someone was playing a saxophone. I do not remember what song he was playing but I remember that it was torchy and I remember stopping under the bridge, turning aside, eyes on the fading leaves, unable to hold back tears.

"The power of cheap music," Gerry said, or maybe I only thought it.

Gerry. Her husband.

The day she cut the peach-colored cake from Payard.

The day she wore the shoes with the bright-red soles.

The day the plumeria tattoo showed through her veil.

In fact I was not even crying for the saxophone.

I was crying for the tiles, the Minton tiles in the arcade south of Bethesda Fountain, Sara Mankiewicz's pattern, Quintana's christening. I was crying for Connie Wald walking her dog through Boulder City and across Hoover Dam. I was crying for Diana holding the champagne flute and smoking the cigarette in Sara Mankiewicz's living room. I was crying for Diana who had talked to Blake Watson so that I could bring the beautiful baby girl he had delivered home from the nursery at St. John's Hospital in Santa Monica.

Diana who would die in the ICU at Cedars in Los Angeles.

Dominique who would die in the ICU at Cedars in Los Angeles.

The beautiful baby girl who would die in the ICU in the Greenberg Pavilion at New York Cornell.

You notice we're doing hand compression.

Because the patient can no longer get enough oxygen through the vent.

For at least an hour now.

Like when someone dies, don't dwell on it.

30

SIX WEEKS AFTER she died we had a service for her, at the Dominican Church of St. Vincent Ferrer on Lexington Avenue. Gregorian chant was sung. A movement from Schubert's Piano Sonata in B-flat was played. Her cousin Griffin read a few paragraphs John had written about her in *Quintana & Friends*: "Quintana will be eleven this week. She approaches adolescence with what I can only describe as panache, but then watching her journey from infancy has always been like watching Sandy Koufax pitch or Bill Russell play basketball." Her cousin Kelley read a poem she had written as a child in Malibu about the Santa Ana winds:

Gardens are dead
Animals not fed
Flowers don't smell
Dry is the well
People's careers slide right down
Brain in the pan turns around
People mumble as leaves crumble
Fire ashes tumble.

Susan Traylor, her best friend since they met at nursery school in Malibu, read a letter from her. Calvin Trillin spoke about her. Gerry read a Galway Kinnell poem that she had liked, Patti Smith sang her a lullaby that she had written for her own son. I read the poems by Wallace Stevens and T. S. Eliot, "Domination of Black" and "New Hampshire," with which I had put her to sleep when she was a baby. "Do the peacocks," she would say once she could talk. "Do the peacocks," or "do the apple trees."

"Domination of Black" had peacocks in it.

"New Hampshire" had apple trees in it.

I think of "Domination of Black" every time I see the peacocks at St. John the Divine.

I did the peacocks that day at St. Vincent Ferrer.

I did the apple trees.

The following day her husband and my brother and his family and Griffin and his father and I went up to St. John the Divine and placed her ashes in a marble wall in St. Ansgar's Chapel along with those of my mother and John.

My mother's name was already on the marble wall at St. John the Divine.

EDUENE JERRETT DIDION
MAY 30 1910—MAY 15 2001

John's name was already on it.

JOHN GREGORY DUNNE
MAY 25 1932—DECEMBER 30 2003

There had been two spaces remaining, the names not yet engraved.

Now there was one.

During the month or so after placing first my mother's and then John's ashes in the wall at St. John the Divine I had the same dream, repeated again and again. In the dream it was always six in the afternoon, the hour at which the evensong bells are rung and the cathedral doors are closed and locked.

In the dream I hear the six o'clock bells.

In the dream I see the cathedral darkening, the doors locking.

You can imagine the dream from there.

When I left the cathedral after placing her ashes in the marble wall I avoided thinking about the dream.

I promised myself that I would maintain momentum.

"Maintain momentum" was the imperative that echoed all the way downtown.

In fact I had no idea what would happen if I lost it.

In fact I had no idea what it was.

I assumed, incorrectly, that it had something to do with movement, traveling, checking in and out of hotels, going to and from the airport.

I tried this.

A week after placing the ashes in the wall at St. John the

Divine, I flew to Boston and back to New York and then to Dallas and back to New York and then to Minneapolis and back to New York, doing promotion for *The Year of Magical Thinking*. The following week, again doing promotion and still under the misapprehension that momentum was about traveling, I flew to Washington and back and then to San Francisco and Los Angeles and Denver and Seattle and Chicago and Toronto and finally to Palm Springs, where I was to spend Thanksgiving with my brother and his family. From various points on this itinerary, over the course of which I began to grasp that just going to and from the airport might be insufficient, that some further effort might be required, I spoke by telephone to Scott Rudin, and agreed that I should write and he should produce and David Hare should direct a one-character play, intended for Broadway, based on *The Year of Magical Thinking*.

The three of us, Scott, David, and I, met for the first time on this project a month after Christmas.

A week before Easter, in a tiny theater on West Forty-second Street, we watched the first readings of the play.

A year later it opened, starring Vanessa Redgrave in its single role, at the Booth Theater on West Forty-fifth Street.

As ways of maintaining momentum go this one turned out to be better than most: I remember liking the entire process a good deal. I liked the quiet afternoons backstage with the stage managers and electricians, I liked the way the ushers gathered for instructions downstairs just before the half-hour call. I liked the presence of Shubert security outside, I liked the weight of the stage door as I opened it against the wind through Shubert Alley, I liked the secret passages to and from the stage. I liked that Amanda, who ran the stage door at night, kept on her desk a tin of the cookies she baked. I liked that Lauri, who managed the Booth for the Shubert Organization and was doing graduate work in medieval literature, became our ultimate authority on a few lines in the play that involved Gawain. I liked the fried chicken and cornbread and potato salad and greens we brought in from Piece o' Chicken, a kitchen storefront near Ninth Avenue. I liked the matzo-ball soup we brought in from the Hotel Edison coffee shop. I liked the place to sit we set up backstage, the little improvised table with the checked tablecloth and the electrified candle and the menu that read "Café Didion."

I liked watching the performance from a balcony above the lights.

I liked being up there alone with the lights and the play.

I liked it all, but most of all I liked the fact that although the play was entirely focused on Quintana there were, five evenings and two afternoons a week, these ninety full minutes, the run time of the play, during which she did not need to be dead.

During which the question remained open.

During which the denouement had yet to play out.

During which the last scene played did not necessarily need to be played in the ICU overlooking the East River.

During which the bells would not necessarily sound and the doors would not necessarily be locked at six.

During which the last dialogue heard did not necessarily need to concern the vent.

Like when someone dies, don't dwell on it.

31

ON THE EVENING late in August when the play closed Vanessa took the yellow roses provided for her curtain calls and laid them on the stage, beneath the photograph of John and Quintana on the deck in Malibu that was the closing drop of the set Bob Crowley had designed for the production.

The theater cleared.

I was gratified to see how slowly it cleared, as if the audience shared my wish not to leave John and Quintana alone.

We stood in the wings and drank champagne.

Before I left that evening someone pointed out the yellow roses Vanessa had laid on the stage floor and asked if I wanted to take them.

I did not want to take the yellow roses.

I did not want the yellow roses touched.

I wanted the yellow roses right there, where Vanessa had left them, with John and Quintana on the stage of the Booth, lying there on the stage all night, lit only by the ghost light, still there on the stage right down to the inevitable instant of the morning's eight-A.M. load-out. "*Performance 144 + 23 Previews + 1 Actors Fund*," the stage manager's performance notes read for that night. "*Magical evening. Lovely final show. Call from the director pre-show. Roses at the call. Champagne toast. Guests included Griffin Dunne and daughter Hannah and Marian Seldes. Café Didion served up its final Piece o' Chicken and sides.*" By that evening when the play closed it seemed clear that I had in fact maintained momentum, but it also seemed clear that maintaining momentum had been at a certain cost. This cost had always been predictable but I only that night began to put it into words. One phrase that came to mind that night was "pushing yourself." Another was "beyond endurance."

32

"I FELL PREY to water intoxication or low sodium, which is characterized by hallucination, memory loss, and corporeal ineptness; a veritable cornucopia of psychoses. I could hear voices, see four different images on the television at one time, read a book in which each word cd separate to fill the page. I'd ask people on the phone who they thought they were talking to cause i certainly didn't know. & I fell constantly. On top of this phantasmagoric experience, I had a stroke." So wrote the playwright Ntozake Shange, in *In the Fullness of Time: 32 Women on Life After 50*, about the maladies that struck her from the blue in her fifties. "The stroke put an end to nanoseconds of images & left a body with diminished vision, no strength, immobile legs, slurred speech, and no recollection of how to read."

She learned to remember how to read.

She learned to remember how to write.

She learned to remember how to walk, how to talk.

She became the person Quintana dreamed of becoming, the person who, by *not dwelling on it*, wakes one morning and finds her revised circumstances corrected. "I am not dead, I am older," she tells us from this improved perspective. "But I can still memorize a stanza or two. What I have memorized is my child's face at different points in her life."

33

ILL HEALTH, which is another way of describing what it can cost to maintain momentum, overtakes us when we can imagine no reason to expect it. I can tell you to the hour when it overtook me—a Thursday morning, August 2, 2007—when I woke with what seemed to be an earache and a reddened area on my face that I mistook for a staph infection.

I remember thinking of this as trying, time-consuming, the waste of a morning I could not afford.

Because I had what I mistook for an earache I would need that morning to see an otolaryngologist.

Because I had what I mistook for a staph infection I would need that morning to see a dermatologist.

Before noon I had been diagnosed: not an earache, not a staph infection, but herpes zoster, shingles, an inflammation of the nervous system, an adult recurrence, generally thought to have been triggered or heightened by stress, of the virus responsible for childhood chickenpox.

"Shingles": it sounded minor, even mildly comical, something about which a great-aunt might complain, or an elderly neighbor; an amusing story tomorrow.

Tomorrow. When I will be fine. Restored. Well.

Telling the amusing story.

You'll never guess what it turned out to be. "Shingles," imagine.

Nothing to worry about then, I remember saying to the doctor who made the diagnosis.

Zoster can be a pretty nasty virus, the doctor said, guarded.

Still in the mode for maintaining momentum, and still oblivious to the extent to which maintaining momentum was precisely what had led me to the doctor's office, I did not ask in what ways zoster could be a pretty nasty virus.

Instead I went home, smoothed some translucent foundation over what had now been established as not a staph infection, took one of the antiviral tablets the doctor had given me, and left for West Forty-fifth Street. I left for West Forty-fifth Street not because I felt any better (in fact I felt worse) but because going to the theater had been my plan for the day, going to the theater was that day's momentum: get to the Booth in time for the 3:30 understudy rehearsal, walk across West Forty-fifth Street during the break and pick up fried chicken and greens to eat backstage, stay for the performance and have a drink afterwards with Vanessa and whoever else was around. "*Direct, engaging, well-tempered*," the stage manager's performance notes for the evening read. "*Ms. Redgrave nervous preshow. Vortex very clear. Rapt audience. Cell phone at very top of show. In attendance: Joan Didion (piece o' chicken at the café, show, and ladies' cocktail hour). Hot humid day; stage temp: comfortable.*"

I have no memory of Ms. Redgrave nervous preshow.

I have no memory of the ladies' cocktail hour. I am told that it featured daiquiris, blended backstage by Vanessa's dresser, and that I had one.

I remember only that the hot humid day with the comfortable stage temperature was followed, for me, by a week of 103-degree fever, three weeks of acute pain in the nerves on the left side of my head and face (including, inconveniently, those nerves that trigger headaches, earaches, and toothaches), and after that by a condition the neurologist described as "postviral ataxia" but I could describe only as "not knowing where my body starts and stops."

I can only think that this may have been what Ntozake Shange meant by "corporeal ineptness."

I no longer had any balance.

I dropped whatever I tried to pick up.

I could not tie my shoes, I could not button a sweater or clip my hair off my face, the simplest acts of fastening and unfastening were now beyond me.

I could no longer catch a ball.

I mention the ball only because (I do not in fact normally catch balls during the course of the day) the single accurate description I would hear or read of these symptoms I was just then beginning to experience was that provided by a professional tennis player, James Blake, who, after a season of considerable stress—he had fractured a vertebra in his neck before the French Open and by the time he was healing his father was dying—woke one morning in his early twenties with similar symptoms. "Instantly, I realized just how many things were wrong," he later wrote, in *Breaking Back: How I Lost Everything and Won Back My Life*, about his initial attempt to return to what had been his life. "Not only was my balance off, but my vision was messed up as well—I had a hard time tracking the ball from Brian's and Evan's rackets to my own. I could see them hit it, I'd sort of lose it for a moment, then suddenly it would register much closer to me. This was especially disconcerting because neither Brian nor Evan hit anywhere near as hard as the average tour player."

He tries to run right for a shot, and finds that his coordination has gone wherever his vision went.

He tries to volley, just hit a few balls, and finds that the balls now hit him.

He asks the neurotologist to whom he has been referred at Yale–New Haven how long he should expect these symptoms to last.

"At least three months," the neurotologist says. "Or it could take four years."

This is not what the professional tennis player wants to hear, nor is it what I want to hear.

Still.

I maintain faith (another word for momentum) that my own symptoms, which have continued to recur in slightly altered incarnations and have so far lasted closer to four years than to three months, will improve, lessen, even resolve.

I do what I can to encourage this resolution, I follow instructions.

I regularly report to Sixtieth and Madison for physical therapy.

I keep the freezer stocked with Maison du Chocolat vanilla ice cream.

I collect encouraging news, even focus on it.

For example:

James Blake has since returned to the tour. I fix on this fact.

Meanwhile, like Ntozake Shange, I memorize my child's face.

34

I FIND MYSELF STUDYING, in a copy of *The New York Review of Books*, a Magnum photograph of Sophia Loren taken during a Christian Dior fashion show in Paris in 1968. In this photograph Sophia Loren is sitting on a gilt chair, wearing a silk turban and smoking a cigarette, achingly polished, forever soignée as she watches "the bride," the traditional end of the show. It occurs to me that this Magnum photograph would have been taken not long after Sophia Loren herself had been "the bride," in fact twice the bride, married in France to Carlo Ponti for the second time after the annulment of their original Mexican marriage, the marriage for which he had been charged with bigamy and threatened with excommunication in Italy.

A "scandal" of the time.

It has become hard to remember how reliably "scandal" once came our way.

Elizabeth Taylor and Richard Burton, a scandal.

Ingrid Bergman and Roberto Rossellini, a scandal.

Sophia Loren and Carlo Ponti, a scandal.

I continue studying the photograph.

I imagine the object of this particular scandal leaving Dior and going to lunch in the courtyard of the Plaza Athénée.

I imagine her sitting with Carlo Ponti in the courtyard, eating an éclair with a fork, the vines that line the courtyard blowing slightly, ivy, *lierre*, sunlight glowing pink through the red canvas canopies over the windows. I imagine the sound of the little birds that flock in the *lierre*, a twittering, a constant presence and an occasional—when, say, a metal shutter is opened, or when, say, Sophia Loren rises from her table to cross the courtyard—swelling of birdsong.

I imagine her leaving the Plaza Athénée, photographers flashing around her as she slides into a waiting car on the Avenue Montaigne.

The cigarette, the silk turban.

It strikes me that she looks in this photograph not unlike the women in the photographs Nick took at Quintana's christening.

Quintana's christening was in 1966, this Christian Dior show was two years later, 1968: 1966 and 1968 were a world removed from each other in the political and cultural life of the United States but they were for women who presented themselves a certain way the same time. It was a way of looking, it was a way of being. It was a period. What became of that way of looking, that way of being, that time, that period? What became of the women smoking cigarettes in their Chanel suits and their David Webb bracelets, what became of Diana holding the champagne flute and one of Sara Mankiewicz's Minton plates? What became of Sara Mankiewicz's Minton plates? What became of the clay tennis court at the house on Franklin Avenue in Hollywood, the court I watched Quintana weed on her fat baby knees? What gave Quintana the idea that weeding a court on which no one ever played—even the net was down, punched through during years of neglect, dragging in the weeds and the dust that got scuffed off the clay—was a necessary task, her assignment, her duty? Was weeding the unused tennis court at the house on Franklin Avenue something like equipping the projection room in the doll's house in Malibu? Was weeding the unused tennis court something like writing a novel? Was it one more way of assuming an adult role? Why did she so need to assume an adult role? Whatever became of those fat baby knees, whatever became of Bunny Rabbit?

As it happens I know what became of Bunny Rabbit.

She left Bunny Rabbit in a suite at the Royal Hawaiian Hotel in Honolulu.

I learned this halfway across the Pacific, when she was sitting next to me in the darkened upstairs cabin on the evening Pan Am flight back to Los Angeles.

There was still a Pan Am then.

There was still a TWA then.

There was still a Pan Am and there was still a TWA and Bendel's was still on West Fifty-seventh Street and it still had Holly's Harp chiffons and lettuce edges and sizes zero and two.

Sitting next to me on that evening flight back to Los Angeles my child mourned Bunny Rabbit's cruel fate: Bunny Rabbit was lost, Bunny Rabbit was left behind, Bunny Rabbit had been abandoned. Yet by the time we taxied into the gate at LAX she had successfully translated Bunny Rabbit's cruel fate into Bunny Rabbit's good luck: the Royal Hawaiian, the suite, the room-service breakfasts. Where did the morning went. The white sand, the swimming pool. Walking to the reef. Swimming off the raft. Bunny Rabbit was even now, we could be certain, swimming off the raft.

Swim off the raft, walk to the reef.

Imagine a five-year-old walking to the reef.

Like when someone dies, don't dwell on it.

How could I not still need that child with me?

I feel impelled to locate, by way of establishing at least one survivor of the period, a recent photograph of Sophia Loren.

I type her name into Google Images.

I find such a photograph: Sophia Loren arriving at some kind of publicity event, one of those red-carpet arrivals during which the PR people hover close, alerting the photographers to the approach of the celebrity. As I check the caption on the photograph I notice in passing that Sophia Loren was born in 1934, the same year in which I myself was born. I am spellbound: Sophia Loren, too, is seventy-five years old. Sophia Loren is seventy-five years old and no one on that red carpet, to my knowledge, is yet suggesting that she is making an inadequate adjustment to aging. This entirely meaningless discovery floods me with restored hope, a revived sense of the possible.

35

WHEN WE LOSE that sense of the possible we lose it fast. One day we are absorbed by dressing well, following the news, keeping up, coping, what we might call *staying alive*; the next day we are not. One day we are turning the pages of whatever has arrived in the day's mail with real enthusiasm—maybe it is *Vogue*, maybe it is *Foreign Affairs*, whatever it is we are intensely interested, pleased to have this handbook to *keeping up*, this key to *staying alive*—yet the next day we are walking uptown on Madison past Barney's and Armani or on Park past the Council on Foreign Relations and we are not even glancing at their windows. One day we are looking at the Magnum photograph of Sophia Loren at the Christian Dior show in Paris in 1968 and thinking yes, it could be me, I could wear that dress, I was in Paris that year; a blink of the eye later we are in one or another doctor's office being told what has already gone wrong, why we will never again wear the red suede sandals with the four-inch heels, never again wear the gold hoop earrings, the enameled beads, never now wear the dress Sophia Loren is wearing. The sun damage inflicted when we swam off the raft in our twenties against all advice is only now surfacing (we were told not to burn, we were told what would happen, we were told to wear sunscreen, we ignored all warnings): melanoma, squamous cell, long hours now spent watching the dermatologist carve out the carcinomas with the names we do not want to hear.

Long hours now spent getting the intravenous infusions of the medication that promises to replace the bone lost to aging.

Long hours now spent getting the intravenous infusions and wondering why the Vitamin D we thought we were accumulating by not wearing sunscreen failed to realize its bone-building potential.

Long hours now spent waiting for the scans, waiting for the EEGs, sitting in frigid waiting rooms turning the pages of *The Wall Street Journal* and *AARP The Magazine* and *Neurology Today* and the alumnae magazines of the Columbia and Cornell medical schools.

Sitting in frigid waiting rooms once again producing the insurance cards, once again explaining why, the provider's preference notwithstanding, the Writers Guild-Industry Health Plan needs to be the primary and Medicare the secondary, not, despite my age—my age is now an issue in every waiting room—vice versa.

Sitting in frigid waiting rooms once again filling out the New York–Presbyterian questionnaires.

Sitting in frigid waiting rooms once again listing the medications and the symptoms and the descriptions and dates of previous hospitalizations: just make up the dates, just take a guess and stand by it, for some reason "1982" always comes to mind, *well, fine, "1982" it is, "1982" will have to do*, there can be no way to get the answer to this question right.

Sitting in frigid waiting rooms trying to think of the name and telephone number of the person I want notified in case of emergency.

Whole days now spent on this one question, this question with no possible answer: *who do I want notified in case of emergency?*

I think it over. I do not want even to consider "in case of emergency."

Emergency, I continue to believe, is what happens to someone else.

I say that I continue to believe this even as I know that I do not.

I mean, think back: what about that business with the folding metal chair in the rehearsal room on West Forty-second Street? What exactly was I afraid of there? What did I fear in that rehearsal room if not an "emergency"? Or what about walking home after an early dinner on Third Avenue and waking up in a pool of blood on my own bedroom floor? Might not waking up in a pool of blood on my own bedroom floor qualify as an "emergency"?

All right. Accepted. "In case of emergency" could apply.

Who to notify. I try harder.

Still, no name comes to mind.

I could give the name of my brother, but my brother lives three thousand miles from what might be defined in New York as an emergency. I could give Griffin's name, but Griffin is shooting a picture. Griffin is on location. Griffin is sitting in the dining room of one or another Hilton Inn—a few too many people at the table, a little too much noise—and Griffin is not picking up his cell. I could give the name of whichever close friend in New York comes first to mind, but the close friend in New York who comes first to mind is actually, on reflection, not even in New York, out of town, out of the country, away, certainly unreachable in the best case, possibly unwilling in the worst.

As I consider the word "unwilling" my lagging cognition kicks in.

The familiar phrase "need to know" surfaces.

The phrase "need to know" has been the problem all along.

Only one person needs to know.

She is of course the one person who needs to know.

Let me just be in the ground.

Let me just be in the ground and go to sleep.

I imagine telling her.

I am able to imagine telling her because I still see her.

Hello, Mommies.

The same way I still see her weeding the clay court on Franklin Avenue.

The same way I still see her sitting on the bare floor crooning back to the eight-track.

Do you wanna dance. I wanna dance.

The same way I still see the stephanotis in her braid, the same way I still see the plumeria tattoo through her veil. The same way I still see the bright-red soles on her shoes as she kneels at the altar. The same way I still see her, in the darkened upstairs cabin on the evening Pan Am from Honolulu to LAX, inventing the unforeseen uptick in Bunny Rabbit's fortunes.

I know that I can no longer reach her.

I know that, should I try to reach her—should I take her hand as if she were again sitting next to me in the upstairs cabin on the evening Pan Am from Honolulu to LAX, should I lull her to sleep against my shoulder, should I sing her the song about Daddy gone to get the rabbit skin to wrap his baby bunny in—she will fade from my touch.

Vanish.

Pass into nothingness: the Keats line that frightened her.

Fade as the blue nights fade, go as the brightness goes.
Go back into the blue.
I myself placed her ashes in the wall.
I myself saw the cathedral doors locked at six.
I know what it is I am now experiencing.
I know what the frailty is, I know what the fear is.
The fear is not for what is lost.
What is lost is already in the wall.
What is lost is already behind the locked doors.
The fear is for what is still to be lost.
You may see nothing still to be lost.
Yet there is no day in her life on which I do not see her.

SOUTH AND WEST

From a Notebook

For John and Quintana

and for Earl

NOTES ON THE SOUTH

John and I were living on Franklin Avenue in Los Angeles. I had wanted to revisit the South, so we flew there for a month in 1970. The idea was to start in New Orleans and from there we had no plan. We went wherever the day took us. I seem to remember that John drove. I had not been back since 1942–43, when my father was stationed in Durham, North Carolina, but it did not seem to have changed that much. At the time, I had thought it might be a piece.

New Orleans

. . . the purple dream
Of the America we have not been,
The tropic empire, seeking the warm sea,
The last foray of aristocracy . . .
—STEPHEN VINCENT BENÉT, *John Brown's Body*

Would that I could represent to you the dangerous nature of the ground, its oozing, spongy, and miry disposition . . .
—JOHN JAMES AUDUBON, *The Birds of America*, 1830

IN NEW ORLEANS in June the air is heavy with sex and death, not violent death but death by decay, overripeness, rotting, death by drowning, suffocation, fever of unknown etiology. The place is physically dark, dark like the negative of a photograph, dark like an X-ray: the atmosphere absorbs its own light, never reflects light but sucks it in until random objects glow with a morbid luminescence. The crypts above ground dominate certain vistas. In the hypnotic liquidity of the atmosphere all motion slows into choreography, all people on the street move as if suspended in a precarious emulsion, and there seems only a technical distinction between the quick and the dead.

One afternoon on St. Charles Avenue I saw a woman die, fall forward over the wheel of her car. "Dead," pronounced an old woman who stood with me on the sidewalk a few inches from where the car had veered into a tree. After the police ambulance came I followed the old woman through the aqueous light of the Pontchartrain Hotel garage and into the coffee shop. The death had seemed serious but casual, as if it had taken place in a pre-Columbian city where death was expected, and did not in the long run count for much.

"Whose fault is it," the old woman was saying to the waitress in the coffee shop, her voice trailing off.

"It's nobody's fault, Miss Clarice."

"They can't help it, no."

"They can't help at all." I had thought they were talking about the death but they were talking about the weather. "Richard used to work at the Bureau and he told me, they can't help what comes in on the radar." The waitress paused, as if for emphasis. "They simply cannot be held to account."

"They just can't," the old woman said.

"It comes in on the radar."

The words hung in the air. I swallowed a piece of ice.

"And we get it," the old woman said after a while.

It was a fatalism I would come to recognize as endemic to the particular tone of New Orleans life. Bananas would rot, and harbor tarantulas. Weather would come in on the radar, and be bad. Children would take fever and die, domestic arguments would end in knifings, the construction of highways would lead to graft and cracked pavement where the vines would shoot back. Affairs of state would turn on sexual jealousy, in New Orleans as if in Port-au-Prince, and all the king's men would turn on the king. The temporality of the place is operatic, childlike, the fatalism that of a culture dominated by wilderness. "All we know," said the mother of Carl Austin Weiss of the son who had just shot and killed Huey Long in a corridor of the Louisiana State Capitol Building in Baton Rouge, "is that he took living seriously."

As it happens I was taught to cook by someone from Louisiana, where an avid preoccupation with recipes and food among men was not unfamiliar to me. We lived together for some years, and I think we most fully understood each other when once I tried to kill him with a kitchen knife. I remember spending whole days cooking with N., perhaps the most pleasant days we spent together. He taught me to fry chicken and to make a brown rice stuffing for fowl and to chop endive with garlic and lemon juice and to lace everything I did with Tabasco and Worcestershire and black pepper. The first present he ever gave me was a garlic press, and also the second, because I broke the first. One day on the Eastern Shore we spent hours making shrimp bisque and then had an argument about how much salt it needed, and because he had been drinking Sazeracs for several hours he poured salt in to make his point. It was like brine, but we pretended it was fine. Throwing the chicken on the floor, or the artichoke. Buying crab boil. Discussing endlessly the possibilities of an artichoke-and-oyster casserole. After I married he still called me up occasionally for recipes.

> I guess you think this is a better machine than that Wop affair. I guess you think you have redwood flagstones in your backyard. I guess you think your mother used to be County Cookie Chairman. I guess you think I take up a lot of room in a small bed. I guess you think Schrafft's has chocolate leaves. I guess you think Mr. Earl "Elbow" Reum has more personality than I. I guess you think there are no lesbians in Nevada. I guess you think you know how to wash sweaters by hand. I guess you think you get picked on by Mary Jane and that people serve you bad whiskey. I guess you think you haven't got pernicious anemia. Take those vitamins. I guess you think southerners are somewhat anachronistic.

—is a message that man left me when I was twenty-two.

The first time I was ever in the South was in late 1942, early 1943. My father was stationed in Durham, North Carolina, and my mother and brother and I took a series of slow and overcrowded trains to meet him there. At home in California I had cried at night, I had lost weight, I had wanted my father. I had imagined the Second World War as a punishment specifically designed to deprive me of my father, had counted up my errors and, with an egocentricity which then approached autism and which afflicts me still in dreams and fevers and marriage, found myself guilty.

Of the trip I recall mainly that a sailor who had just been torpedoed on the *Wasp* in the Pacific gave me a silver-and-turquoise ring, and that we missed our connection in New Orleans and could get no room and sat up one night on a covered verandah of the St. Charles Hotel, my brother and I in matching seersucker sunsuits and my mother in a navy-blue-and-white-checked silk dress dusty from the train. She covered us with the mink coat she had bought before her marriage and wore until 1956. We were taking trains instead of driving because a few weeks before in California she had lent the car to an acquaintance who drove it into a lettuce truck outside Salinas, a fact of which I am certain because it remains a source of rancor, in my father's dialogue, to this day. I last heard it mentioned a week ago. My mother made no response, only laid out another hand of solitaire.

In Durham we had one room with kitchen privileges in the house of a lay minister whose children ate apple butter on thick slabs of bread all day long and referred to their father in front of us as "Reverend Caudill." In the evenings Reverend Caudill would bring home five or six quarts of peach ice cream, and he and his wife and children would sit on the front porch spooning peach ice cream from the cartons while we lay in our room watching our mother read and waiting for Thursday.

Thursday was the day we could take the bus to Duke University, which had been taken over by the military, and spend the afternoon with my father. He would buy us a Coca-Cola in the student union and walk us around the campus and take snapshots of us, which I now have, and look at from time to time: two small children and a woman who resembles me, sitting by the lagoon, standing by the wishing well, the snapshots always lightstruck or badly focused and, in any case, now faded. Thirty years later I am certain that my father must also have been with us on weekends, but I can only suggest that his presence in the small house, his tension and his aggressive privacy and his preference for shooting craps over eating peach ice cream, must have seemed to me so potentially disruptive as to efface all memory of weekends.

On the days of the week which were not Thursday I played with a set of paper dolls lent me by Mrs. Caudill, the dolls bearing the faces of Vivien Leigh, Olivia de Havilland, Ann Rutherford, and Butterfly McQueen as they appeared in *Gone With the Wind*, and I also learned from the neighborhood children to eat raw potatoes dipped in the soft dust from beneath the house. I know now that eating pica is common in the undernourished South, just as I know now why the driver of the bus on the first Thursday we went out to Duke refused to leave the curb until we had moved from the back seat to the front, but I did not know it then. I did not even know then that my mother found our sojourn of some months in Durham less than ideal.

I could never precisely name what impelled me to spend time in the South during the summer of 1970. There was no reportorial imperative to any of the places I went at the time I went: nothing "happened" anywhere I was, no celebrated murders, trials, integration orders, confrontations, not even any celebrated acts of God.

I had only some dim and unformed sense, a sense which struck me now and then, and which I could not explain coherently, that for some years the South and particularly the Gulf Coast had been for America what people were still saying California was, and what California seemed to me not to be: the future, the secret source of malevolent and benevolent energy, the psychic center. I did not much want to talk about this.

I had only the most ephemeral "picture" in my mind. If I talked about it I could mention only Clay Shaw, and Garrison, and a pilot I had once met who flew between the Gulf and unnamed Caribbean and Central American airstrips for several years on small planes with manifests that showed only "tropical flowers," could mention only some apprehension of paranoia and febrile conspiracy and baroque manipulation and peach ice cream and an unpleasant evening I had spent in 1962 on the Eastern Shore of Maryland. In short I could only sound deranged. And so instead of talking about it I flew south one day in the summer of 1970, rented a car, and drove for a month or so around Louisiana and Mississippi and Alabama, saw no spokesmen, covered no events, did nothing at all but try to find out, as usual, what was making the picture in my mind.

In New Orleans, the old people sitting in front of houses and hotels on St. Charles Avenue, barely rocking. In the Quarter I saw them again (along with desolate long-haired children), sitting on balconies, an ironing board behind them, gently rocking, sometimes not rocking at all but only staring. In New Orleans they have mastered the art of the motionless.

In the evening I visited in the Garden District. "Olly olly oxen free" echoing in the soft twilight, around the magnolias and the trees with fluffy pods of pink. What I saw that night was a world so rich and complex and I was almost disoriented, a world complete unto itself, a world of smooth surfaces broken occasionally by a flash of eccentricity so deep that it numbed any attempt at interpretation.

"I guess nobody knows more about the South than the people in this room right now," my host allowed several times before dinner. We were at his house in the Garden District with the requisite bound volumes of the *Sewanee* and the *Southern Review* and the requisite Degas portrait of his great-great-grandmother, and he was talking about his wife and their friend, an architect of good Mobile family who specialized in the restoration and building of New Orleans Greek Revival houses.

And of course he was talking about himself. "Ben C.," the others called him, their voices fondly inflected. "You just *stop* that, Ben C.," as he bullied the two women, his sister and his wife working together on a Junior League project, a guidebook to New Orleans. Already Ben C. had demanded to know what "athletics" my husband played, and why I had been allowed, in the course of doing some reporting a few years before, to "spend time consorting with a lot of marijuana-smoking hippie trash."

"Who allowed you?" he repeated.

I said that I did not know quite what he meant.

Ben C. only stared at me.

"I mean, who wouldn't have allowed me?"

"You *do* have a husband?" he said finally. "This man I've thought was your husband for several years, he *is* your husband?"

The evening, it developed, had started off wrong for Ben C. It seemed that he had called some of his cousins to come for dinner, and they had made excuses, and he had found that "inexcusable." It further seemed that the excuse made by one cousin, who it would turn out was a well-known southern writer, was a previous engagement with the director of a Head Start program, and Ben C. had found that particularly inexcusable.

"What am I meant to conclude?" he demanded rhetorically of his wife. "Am I meant to conclude he's certifiable?"

"Maybe you're meant to conclude he didn't care to come to dinner," she said, and then, as if to cover her irreverence, she sighed. "I only hope he doesn't get too mixed up with the Negroes. You know what happened to George Washington Cable."

I tried to remember what had happened to George Washington Cable.

"He ended up having to go *north*, is what happened."

I said that I wanted only to know what people in the South were thinking and doing.

He continued to gaze at me. He had the smooth, rounded face of well-off New Orleans, that absence of angularity which characterizes the local genetic pool. I tried to think who had incurred his wrath by going up north and whining.

"I would just guess that we know a little more about the subject," Ben C. said finally, his voice rising, "than one Mr. Willie Morris."

We ate trout with shallots and mushrooms. We drank some white wine, we drank some more bourbon. We passed the evening. I never learned why the spectre of one Mr. Willie Morris had materialized in that living room in the Garden District, nor did I ask.

Ben C.'s wife and sister, Mrs. Benjamin C. Toledano and Mrs. Beauregard Redmond, soon to be Mrs. Toledano Redmond, had many suggestions for understanding the South. I must walk Bourbon or Royal to Chartres, I must walk Chartres to Esplanade. I must have coffee and doughnuts at the French Market. I should not miss St. Louis Cathedral, the Presbytère, the Cabildo. We should have lunch at Galatoire's: trout amandine or trout Marguery. We should obtain a copy of *The Great Days of the Garden District.* We should visit Asphodel, Rosedown, Oakley Plantation. Stanton Hall in Natchez. The Grand Hotel in Point Clear. We should have dinner at Manale's, tour Coliseum Square Park. I should appreciate the grace, the beauty of their way of life. These graceful preoccupations seemed to be regarded by the women in a spirit at once dedicated and merely tolerant, as if they lived their lives on several quite contradictory levels.

One afternoon we took the ferry to Algiers and drove an hour or so down the river, in Plaquemines Parish. This is peculiar country. Algiers is a doubtful emulsion of white frame bungalows and jerry-built apartment complexes, the Parc Fontaine Apts. and so forth, and the drive on down the river takes you through a landscape more metaphorical than any I have seen outside the Sonoran Desert.

Here and there one is conscious of the levee, off to the left. Corn and tomatoes grow aimlessly, as if naturalized. I am too accustomed to agriculture as agribusiness, the rich vistas of the California valleys where all the resources of Standard Oil and the University of California have been brought to bear on glossy constant productivity. No Hunting of Quadrupeds, a sign read in Belle Chasse. What could that mean? Can you hunt reptiles? Bipeds? There are dead dogs by the road, and a sinking graveyard in a grove of live oak.

Getting close to Port Sulphur we began to see sulphur works, the tanks glowing oddly in the peculiar light. We ran over three snakes in the hour's drive, one of them a thick black moccasin already dead, twisted across the one lane. There were run-down antiques places, and tomato stands, and a beauty shop called Feminine Fluff. The snakes, the rotting undergrowth, sulphurous light: the images are so specifically those of the nightmare world that when we stopped for gas, or directions, I had to steel myself, deaden every nerve, in order to step from the car onto the crushed oyster shells in front of the gas station. When we got back to the hotel I stood in the shower for almost half an hour trying to wash myself clean of the afternoon, but then I started thinking about where the water came from, what dark places it had pooled in.

When I think now about New Orleans I remember mainly its dense obsessiveness, its vertiginous preoccupation with race, class, heritage, style, and the absence of style. As it happens, these particular preoccupations all involve distinctions which the frontier ethic teaches western children to deny and to leave deliberately unmentioned, but in New Orleans such distinctions are the basis of much conversation, and lend that conversation its peculiar childlike cruelty and innocence. In New Orleans they also talk about parties, and about food, their voices rising and falling, never still, as if talking about anything at all could keep the wilderness at bay. In New Orleans the wilderness is sensed as very near, not the redemptive wilderness of the western imagination but something rank and old and malevolent, the idea of wilderness not as an escape from civilization and its discontents but as a mortal threat to a community precarious and colonial in its deepest aspect. The effect is lively and avaricious and intensely self-absorbed, a tone not uncommon in colonial cities, and the principal reason I find such cities invigorating.

New Orleans to Biloxi, Mississippi

ON THE CHEF Menteur Highway out of New Orleans there is the sense of swamp reclaimed to no point. Dismal subdivisions evoke the romance of Evangeline on their billboards. Shacks along the road sell plaster statues of the Virgin Mary. The gas stations advertise Free Flag Decals. Lake Pontchartrain can be seen now and then on the left, and the rusted hulks of boats at marine repair places.

The rest of it is swamp. Crude signs point down dirt roads, and along the road are shacks, or "camps," for fishing. Postboxes are supported on twisted rigid chains, as if the inhabitants are as conscious as the traveler of the presence of snakes. The light is odd, more peculiar still than the light in New Orleans, light entirely absorbed by what it strikes.

We stopped at a trinket shack called the Beachcomber. A boy was filling the Pepsi machine outside. Towels hung limply on a display clothesline: "Put Your (picture of a HEART) in Dixie or Get Your (picture of an ASS) OUT!" Inside were boxes of shells and dried devilfish. "They get 'em from Mexico," the boy said.

Across the Mississippi line we took a side road through the pine forest toward what the sign said would be E. Ansley Estates. Rain was beginning to fall, and as we passed a pond a dozen or so boys were climbing out of the water and into two cars. One felt the rain had spoiled their day, and they would be at loose ends, restless. The cliché of the lonely road in the South took on a certain meaning here. The road was scattered occasionally with armadillo shells. The rain continued. The boys and their cars disappeared. We did not find E. Ansley Estates, or any settlement at all.

Signs for fireworks, signs for a reptile farm ahead. The rain let up and we stopped at the reptile farm. The Reptile House was a small shack out in back of the main roadside building, across a dirt yard where chickens ran loose. The place was dirty, littered with peanut shells and empty six-pack cartons marked Dad's Root Beer and Suncrest Orange Drink. There were a few capuchin monkeys, and a couple of big lethargic boas in packing cases, and a Holbrook's king snake and a couple of rattlers.

A cage marked COPPERHEAD appeared to be empty. There was a family in the Reptile House when we were there, a boy about nine and a father and a woman in slacks with her hair piled high and lacquered.

We stood, the five of us, and looked restlessly out into the driving rain, trapped together in the Reptile House. The dust outside was turning to deep mud. Alligators thrashed in a muddy pool a few yards away. A little farther a sign said Snake Pit.

"I never would've stopped if I'd known it was outside," the woman said.

"Known what was outside?" her husband said.

"The Snake Pit, of course. What do you *think* is outside?"

The man drummed his fingers on top of a packing case. The boa inside slid deeper into its coil. To make conversation I asked the man if they had visited a far building marked Reptile House.

"There aren't no reptiles upstairs there," he said, and then, as if I might doubt it: "She told us, there aren't no reptiles upstairs. She said not to go in."

"Maybe there are some reptiles downstairs?" I suggested.

"I don't know about that," he said. "I just wouldn't go in."

"Of course *you* wouldn't," the woman said mildly. She was still staring at the Snake Pit.

I was leaning on the empty copperhead box listening to the rain hiss when an uneasy feeling came over me that the hissing came from inside the box. I looked again and there it was, a copperhead, almost hidden by its shed skins.

We gave up on one another, and on the possibility of the rain's stopping, and ran through the mud back to the main house. I slipped and fell in the mud and had an instant of irrational panic that there were snakes in the mud and all around me.

In the trinket shop the woman and I each paid a dime to use the restroom. With another dime I got a cup of cold coffee from a machine and tried to stop being chilled. The woman bought her son a china potty with a little child disappearing down the drain and the inscription "Goodbye Sweet World." I bought a cheap beach towel printed with a Confederate flag. It is ragged and gray now and sits in my linen closet in California amid thick and delicately colored Fieldcrest beach towels, and my child prefers it to the good ones.

Pass Christian to Gulfport

AT PASS CHRISTIAN in the summer of 1970 the debris of the 1969 hurricane had become the natural look of the landscape. The big houses along the water were abandoned, the schools and churches were wiped out, the windows of places hung askew. The devastation along the Gulf had an inevitability about it: the coast was reverting to its natural state. There were For Sale signs all over, but one could not imagine buyers. I remembered people talking about Pass Christian as a summer place, and indeed the houses had once been pretty and white and the American flags unfaded, but even in the good years there must have been an uneasiness there. They sat on those screened porches and waited for something to happen. The place must have always failed at being a resort, if the special quality of a resort is defined as security: there is here that ominous white/dark light so characteristic of the entire Gulf.

The city hall in Pass Christian faces away from the Gulf, and when you happen upon it from the front it looks like a façade from a studio back lot, abandoned a long time ago. Through the shattered windows one sees the dark glare of the Gulf. You want to close your eyes.

Long Beach seemed poorer, or harder hit, or both. There were none of those big white houses with the screened porches here. There were trailers, and a twisted pool ladder that marked the place where a swimming pool had been before the hurricane. Mass was being held in the school gym. On the beach there was an occasional woman with children. The women wore two-piece bathing suits, shorts and halters, not bikinis. All along the coast there were cars parked and tables set up to sell colored discs that whir in the air, apparently indefinitely. On the cars are hand-lettered signs that read SPACE STATION. You can see discs shimmering in the light from a long way off.

At Gulfport, the county seat of Harrison County, a tanker, broken clean in half during the hurricane, lay rusting offshore. The heat was relentless, the streets downtown broad and devoid of trees. *The Losers* was playing at the Sand Theatre in Gulfport, and would be playing at The Avenue in Biloxi. We went into a café downtown to get something to eat. CAFÉ is all the sign said. The menu had red beans and rice, and the only sounds in the place in the afternoon stillness were the whirring of the air conditioner and the click of a pinball machine. Everyone in the place seemed to have been there a long time, and to know everyone else. After a while a man got up from his beer and walked to the door. "Off to the infirmary," he said over his shoulder.

Between Gulfport and Biloxi, the shingles were ripped from the houses facing the Gulf. Live oak trees were twisted and broken. A long way in the distance one could see the Biloxi Lighthouse, a white tower glowing peculiarly in the strange afternoon light.

I had never expected to come to the Gulf Coast married.

Biloxi

Everything seems to go to seed along the Gulf: walls stain, windows rust. Curtains mildew. Wood warps. Air conditioners cease to function. In our room at the Edgewater Gulf Hotel, where the Mississippi Broadcasters' Convention was taking place, the air conditioner in the window violently shook and rattled every time it was turned on. The Edgewater Gulf is an enormous white hotel which looks like a giant laundry, and has the appearance of being on the verge of condemnation. The swimming pool is large and unkempt, and the water smells of fish. Behind the hotel is a new shopping center built around an air-conditioned mall, and I kept escaping there, back into midstream America.

In the elevator at the Edgewater Gulf:

"Walter, I believe you've grown the most of any town in the state of Mississippi."

"Well, the figures are in question."

"Didn't quite total as high as the chamber of commerce thought they would?"

"No, well—"

"Same in Tupelo. In Tupelo they demanded a recount."

"Well, frankly, I don't think we've got all those people . . . they see the cars, they think they live here, but they come in from around, spend a dollar a day—"

"Dollar, top."

The two men faced the front of the elevator as they spoke, not each other. The dialogue was grave. The possibility of "growth" in small Mississippi towns is ever yearned for, and ever denied. The Mississippi Broadcasters' was, everyone assured me, "the best damn convention in the state of Mississippi."

One evening after dinner we drove around Biloxi, and stopped to watch a Pony League game being played under bright lights. A handful of men in short-sleeved shirts and women in faded cotton blouses and Capri pants sat in the bleachers, watching the children play, Holiday Inn versus Burger Chef. Below the bleachers some children played barefoot in the dust, and a police car was parked, its motor idling, its doors open. There was no one in the car. The game broke up finally, to no one's satisfaction.

There are railroad tracks running through all the towns in Mississippi, or so it seems, and at every crossing is a sign that reads MISSISSIPPI LAW/STOP. The tracks are raised and the wild carrot grows around them.

After the Pony League game broke up we went to get a beer in a bar a few blocks away, and there were some of the other people from the bleachers, and no children in evidence. It was apparently just a way to pass a few hours on a summer evening. They had already seen *The Losers*, say, and it was hot in the house, and supper was finished at sundown.

Another way to pass the time that evening (but I believe it was an almost imperceptibly more middle-class pastime) was at the Kiwanis Fishing Rodeo, where the biggest fish caught that day were displayed in trays of ice. In the sawdust under the awning a small girl sat, stringing the pop tops from beer cans into a necklace.

One morning at 10:30 A.M. during the Mississippi Broadcasters' Convention there was, in the ballroom of the Edgewater Gulf, an event designated on the program as the Ladies' Brunch. The Billy Fane Trio played, and Bob McRaney, Sr., of WROB West Point, presided. "The Billy Fane Trio is becoming something of an institution as regards our convention," he said, and then he introduced another act: "We have an act this morning that . . . I think . . . unless you've been an Indian on a reservation and not many of us have . . . you'll find rather novel and unusual to say the least. Out in Colorado . . . or out somewhere in the West there . . . there's a very quaint little village named Taos. And we have a young man this morning who has perfected a Taos Hoop Dance . . . It's Allen Thomas, from Franklinton, Louisiana, . . . with Martin Belcher on the Indian drums."

"You'll love this act," someone at my table said. "We saw it at the high school up on 49."

"I wish I could play organ like that," someone else said when the Billy Fane Trio was playing.

"Don't you, though?"

"You-all ought to come visit with us," a third woman said.

They were all young women, the oldest among them perhaps thirty. "I'd play organ for you."

"We'll never get up there," the first woman said. "I never been anyplace I wanted to go."

A drawing was held for door prizes, the first prize being a room paneled in Masonite. The women genuinely wanted the Masonite room, and they also wanted the carving set, the playing cards, the pair of Miss America shoes, the lighted cosmetic mirror, and the woodcut of Christ. They recalled among them who had won door prizes in years past, and their wistful envy of each winner suffused the room. Little girls in sandals and sundresses played at the edge of the ballroom, waiting for their mothers, who were now, during the drawing, as children themselves.

The isolation of these people from the currents of American life in 1970 was startling and bewildering to behold. All their information was fifth-hand, and mythicized in the handing down. Does it matter where Taos is, after all, if Taos is not in Mississippi?

At the Mississippi Broadcasters' awards banquet, there were many jokes and parables. Here is a joke: "Can you tell me what you'd get if you crossed a violin with a rooster? The answer is, if you looked out in your chicken yard you might see someone fiddling around with your rooster." This seemed to me an interesting joke, in that no element of it was amusing, yet everyone roared, and at tables all around me it was repeated for those who had missed the punch line.

And here is a parable I heard that night: "There was a bee buzzing in a clover field, and a cow came along and swallowed the bee, and the bee buzzed around and it was warm and sleepy and the bee went to sleep, and when the bee woke up, the cow was gone." As I recall, this parable illustrated some point about broadcasting good tidings rather than bad, and it seemed to make the point very clearly to the audience, but it continued to elude me.

Someone at the rostrum mentioned repeatedly that we were "entering the space age in the new decade," but we seemed very far from that, and in any case had we not already entered the space age? I had the feeling that I had been too long on the Gulf Coast, that my own sources of information were distant and removed, that like the women at the Ladies' Brunch I might never get anywhere I wanted to go. One of the awards that night was for the Best Program Series by a Female.

The luncheon was honoring Congressman William Colmer (D-Miss.), who had been thirty-eight years in the House and was chairman of the House Rules Committee. He was receiving the Broadcasters' Man of the Year award, and had come with his AA, his mother, and his secretary. In accepting his award Rep. Colmer murmured something about "bad apples in every lot," and, about the interest of the rest of the nation in the state of Mississippi, "like havin' an obstetrician in New Jersey when the baby's bein' born in Mississippi."

"We get a lot of bad publicity down here," said someone accepting a Distinguished Public Service award. The solidarity engendered by outside disapproval, a note struck constantly. It seemed to have reached a point where all Mississippians were bonded together in a way simply not true of the residents of any other state. They could be comfortable only with each other. Any differences they might have, class or economic or even in a real way racial, seemed outweighed by what they shared.

Charles L. Sullivan, introduced as "lieutenant governor of the state of Mississippi and a member of the Clarksdale Baptist Church," rose to speak. "I have come to think we are living in the era of the demonstrators—unruly, unwashed, uninformed, and sometimes un-American people—disrupting private and public life in this country." He complained of the press, "for whom two loud 'Ah Hate Mississippis' would be sufficient. This adult generation accomplished more than any generation in the history of civilization—it started the exploration of God's limitless space. I simply will not hear them cry Pig for a situation they themselves began. Ah don't believe the right to disagree is the right to destroy the University at Jackson or Kent State or [the 'even' was implicit] Berkeley. If it is true, as they say, that they have despaired of the democratic process, then I and my fellow demonstrators shall absolutely insist that if our system is to be changed it shall be changed in the ballot box and not in the streets." He finally ended on the rote ending to southern speeches: "We can live together in the dignity and freedom which their Creator surely intended."

With many of the Highway Patrol as honored guests there was an undertone to this lunch and throughout his speech, since it was the Highway Patrol who had done the shooting at Jackson.

Random notes from the weekend: The black station manager from Gulfport standing in line talking to Stan Torgerson from Meridian about black programming, Torgerson saying he programs Top 40, no deep blues or soul, and he owns a record store too "so I know goddamn well what they buy." Bob Evans from WNAG Grenada, trying to explain the class structure of Mississippi towns in terms of five families, with the banker always number one because he makes the loans. A black girl, a student at Jackson State, presented a list of demands at an afternoon meeting and everyone explained to me that she did it "very courteously." A tribute to coverage during Hurricane Camille, "Broadcasting working in symphonic harmony with the weather bureau and the civil defense authorities." After that crisis "celebrities from all over the U.S. came down, Bob Hope, the Golddiggers, Bobby Goldsboro. Bob Hope coming down, that really made people see that the country cared." Mrs. McGrath from Jackson leaning close to tell me Jackson State was a setup.

The Gulf Coast resorts live to a certain extent on illegal gambling, places back up in the pinewoods known to all visitors. The Mafia is strong on the Coast.

The Ladies at the Brunch, on the subject of TV:

"I keep it on for my stories."

"Need to have it for the stories."

"I hear the radio only in the kitchen."

How about driving, I asked. The pretty young woman looked at me as if truly bewildered.

"Drive where?" she asked.

I did not know why we were going to Meridian instead of Mobile as planned, but it seemed, after a few days, imperative to leave the Gulf and the steaming air.

On the Road from Biloxi to Meridian

THERE WAS OCCASIONAL rain and an overcast sky and the raw piney woods. On an AM station out of Biloxi, 1400 on the dial, I listened to Richard Brannan tell a parable about "a sailing trip to the Bahama Islands." The radio was out, but finally they got a fix and headed for port. "Everybody gets happy when the right direction is found," he said. "I mention this because there is another ship in danger of losing its way . . . the old ship of state." Then they played "America the Beautiful" with an angel choir. It was a Sunday. Here and all over were the trailer-sales lots with the signs that said REPOSSESSIONS, the trailers bearing plates from all over the South.

In McHenry, Mississippi, a gas station and a few shacks and a dirt road leading back into the pines, three barefoot children played in the dust by the gas station. A little girl with long unkempt blond hair and a dirty periwinkle-blue dress that hung below her knees carried around an empty Sprite bottle. The older of the two boys got the Coke machine open and they all squabbled gently over their choices. A pickup pulled in with the back piled high with broken furniture and dirty mattresses: it sometimes seemed to me that mattresses were on the move all over the South. A middle-aged blond woman was pumping gas. "One of the boys is off today, so they got me working," she said. We drove on, past cattle, a Church of God, a Jax (Fabacher) beer sign, and the Wiggin Lumber Co. Mfrs. Southern Yellow Pine Lumber.

A somnolence so dense it seemed to inhibit breathing hung over Hattiesburg, Mississippi, at two or three o'clock of that Sunday afternoon. There was no place to get lunch, no place to get gas. On the wide leafy streets the white houses were set back. Sometimes I would see a face at a window. I saw no one on the streets.

Outside Hattiesburg we stopped at a CAFÉ–GAS–TRUCK STOP to get a sandwich. A blond girl with a pellagra face stood sullenly behind the cash register, and a couple of men sat in a booth. Behind the counter was a woman in a pink Dacron housedress. No flicker of expression crossed her classic mountain face, and her movements were so slow as to be hypnotic. She made a kind of ballet of scooping ice into a glass. Behind her a soft-ice-cream machine oozed and plopped, and every now and then ice cubes would fall in the ice machine. Neither she nor the girl nor the two men spoke during the time we were there. The jukebox played "Sweet Caroline." They all watched me eat a grilled-cheese sandwich. When we went back out into the blazing heat one of the men followed us and watched as we drove away.

In Laurel, pop. 29,000: FREE FLAG DECALS, as everywhere. PUMP YOUR OWN GAS SAVE 5¢. It's Fun. Shacks on the backstreets. A black woman sitting on her front porch on the backseat from a car.

Cannibalized rusting automobiles everywhere, in ditches, the kudzu taking over. White wild flowers, red dirt. The pines here are getting lower, bushier. Polled Herefords. In a time when we have come to associate untouched land with parkland, a luxury, Mississippi seemed rich in appearance. One forgets that this is pre-industrial, not parkland purchased at great cost in an industrial society. There is very little of this hill land under the least cultivation. A patch of corn here, but nothing else.

A few signs in Enterprise, Mississippi: SEVEN HAMBURGERS FOR $1. FOOTLONG BARBECUE 30¢. People sitting on the porches.

Basic City, Mississippi, a town not on the map. You go in on a road and there, at the confluence of two railroad tracks, is a quite beautiful white frame house with a green lawn and gazebo. Lacy white flowers. The eccentricity of its location renders the viewer speechless. Across one set of tracks is a sign: PRIVATE DOGWOOD SPRINGS M.E. SKELTON'S FAMILY, OWNER. BASIC CITY MISS. Back on the road, the road into Meridian, 11, is the BASIC COURT CAFÉ AIR COND. When I left Basic City a train was moaning, the Meridian & Bigbee line. One is conscious of trains in the South. It is a true earlier time.

Swimming at the Howard Johnson's in Meridian

THE HOWARD JOHNSON'S in Meridian is just off Interstate 20, the intersection of Interstate 20—running east and west—and Interstate 59—running north and south from New Orleans to New York. Population 58,000, and beyond the grass and the cyclone fence the big rigs hurtle between Birmingham and Jackson and New Orleans. Sitting by the pool at six o'clock I felt the euphoria of Interstate America: I could be in San Bernardino, or Phoenix, or outside Indianapolis. Children splash in the pool. A three-year-old veers perilously toward the deep end, and her mother calls her back. The mother and her three children are from Georgia, and are staying at the Howard Johnson's while they try to find a new house in Meridian.

"I don't never want to go back to Georgia," the little boy says. "I want this to be my home." "This *will* be your home," the mother says. "Soon as Daddy and I find a house." "I mean this," the little boy says. "This motel."

Another woman appeared and called an older child, a boy twelve or thirteen, in for supper. "We're going to get supper now," she said. "Hell," the boy muttered, and stalked after her wrapped in a Confederate-flag beach towel. The sky darkened, thunder clapped, the three-year-old cried, and we all went inside to the air-conditioned chill. In a half hour or so the rain stopped, and at midnight I could hear the older children splashing in the lighted pool.

Meridian Notes

On the far side of the parking lot at the Howard Johnson's in Meridian is a raw field with a mudhole and a tiny duck house, with ducks. The ducks shake the muddy water from their white feathers.

In Weidmann's Restaurant, paintings are hung for sale: we sat beneath one with a calling card taped beneath it. "Mrs. Walter Albert Green," the card was engraved, and then, in a neat hand, "Dalewood Lake 'Oil' York, Ala. Price $35.00." There was also a painting appalling in its apprehension of human silences, called "In Between," by James A. Harris, $150. During the few days that I was in Meridian the painting and James A. Harris and his life in Meridian began to haunt me, and I tried to call him, but never reached him. He was at the air force base.

Gibson's Discount, ubiquitous. Mercedes-Benz Agency and "Citroën Service," certainly not so. Coca-Cola signs and the Mid-South Business College and Townsend's College of Cosmetology and the Hotel Lamar shut down. I tried to make an appointment with the director of Townsend's Academy of Cosmetology but he said he wasn't interested in any magazines at the present time. We had misunderstood each other, or we had not. I had an appointment with the director, Mrs. Lewis, of the Mid-South Business College, but when I arrived the doors were locked. I stood a while in the cool corridors of the Lamar Building and went downstairs and drank a Coca-Cola and came back, but the doors were still locked. We had misunderstood one another, or we had not.

An Afternoon in Meridian with Stan Torgerson

WHEN I CALLED Stan Torgerson for lunch at his radio station, WQIC, and asked him the best place to lunch, he said Weidmann's, "but it wouldn't win any Holiday Magazine awards." In fact it had, and was not a bad restaurant, but everyone in Mississippi begins on the defensive. "I'll be the biggest man in a green shirt to come through the door," he advised me. He was, at lunch, wary at first. He said he didn't think I knew what I was doing. I agreed. He refused a drink, saying he wasn't in New York City. Stan Torgerson came out of the cold North (Minnesota, I think) and headed to Memphis, where he went into broadcasting. He worked in Miami, and then, for a year, in San Diego, living in La Jolla. He felt ill at ease in La Jolla—his neighbors kept to themselves, had their own interests—and he wanted to get back south. His son had won a football scholarship to Ole Miss. He was worried about his children and drugs in California. "Excuse me," he said, "but I just haven't reached the point where I think pot is a way of life."

When the black radio station in Meridian came up for sale he bought it. He also broadcasts the Ole Miss games, something he began doing when he was in Memphis. "That's right," he said, "I own the ethnic station, WQIC. In its thirteenth year of serving the black community here." He programs gospel and soul, and reaches 180,000 blacks in several Mississippi and Alabama counties, "the thirty-second-largest black market in the country, sixty miles in all directions and forty-three percent of that area is black. We serve a major black market, program soul music and gospel music, but what does that mean? A month ago in *Billboard* there was a survey pointing out that the Top 40–format stations are playing basically soul. Jackson 5 with 'ABC,' 'Turn Back the Hands of Time,' that's Top 40 but it's soul. Once in a while we throw in some blue-eyed soul, like Dusty Springfield with 'Son of a Preacher Man.' We don't play rock because our people don't dig it. We don't play your underground groups like the Jefferson Airplane . . . We have goodly reason to believe that ten to fifteen percent of our audience is white; some of the phone calls we get in the afternoon for dedications, they're definitely white voices. We get thirty-six percent of the audience."

He said I was probably wondering why he came back to Mississippi. "I came because I dearly love this state. I had a son—he'll be a senior this fall—playing football at the University of Mississippi."

He pointed out that Meridian was timber country, hill country. Pulpwood is the backbone of the agricultural product. He pointed out how progressive Meridian was: its three new hospitals. "In most southern cities there is a much stronger tendency to old-line money . . . Southern retailers stayed in business privately, home-owned, until very recently. In most cases the retailer has just begun to feel the competition from the chains. There's the greatest business opportunity in the country right here in the South . . . We don't have a McDonald's in a city of almost fifty thousand people, don't have any of these franchises here yet. You give me one corner of one intersection in Jackson, Mississippi, or you give me the whole ball of wax right here in Meridian, I'd take the whole ball of wax and I'd put a McDonald's on one corner, a Burger Chef on the other, a Shoney's Po' Boy 'cross the street . . ."

His voice kept on, weaving ever higher flights of economic possibility. "There is and *must* be," he said, a "continued turning to the South by industry. The climate is certainly one reason. Another is that the South *wants* industry, and is willing to give a tax advantage to get it. Another, of course, is that there is a relatively low level of unionism in the South. Lockheed assembles tail sections here and ships them to California for assembly . . .

"Atlanta is the magic city for the young around here, across the whole social spectrum . . . The great migration out in the past ten years has been black, they get these glowing letters, and of course they've got relatively liberal welfare programs in some of the northern states . . . No doubt, too, there appears to be greater opportunity in the North."

More on the progressive nature of Meridian: "Our radio station has probably got as fine a list of blue-chip clients as any in town, black or not. We've got all four banks, and anyone in retailing who's interested in doing business with the black—the black's dollar is very important. The minimum wage was probably the most important thing to happen along these lines, and then food stamps were a good deal, I would say they added millions of dollars to our economy.

"We are in a transitional phase. There's a tremendous push to education on the part of young blacks. The schools here are completely integrated. Of course neither you nor I can change the older black, the forty-year-old, his life patterns are settled.

"Ole Miss has its standards to keep up. As more and more blacks get an educational advantage, you'll see blacks at Ole Miss. There's a feeling among some black leaders that because these kids have not had advantages they should get some kind of educational break, but basically what has to happen is the standards have to stay up and the people come up to meet them."

We were driving through town at night, and Stan Torgerson interrupted himself to point out the post office. "There's the post office, the courthouse where the famous Philadelphia trials were held, the trials for the so-called Philadelphia deaths."

"If there were elm trees hanging over the street it would be very midwestern," Stan observed as we drove through the residential district. He pointed out his $29,500 house, a two-story frame, "twenty-eight hundred square feet, with magnolia, dogwood, and pecan trees." He pointed out Poplar Drive, the "Park Avenue of Meridian, Mississippi, all the houses built by the old-line families."

Fervently, he kept reverting to the wholesomeness of life in Meridian. His daughter, who would be a high school senior in the fall, had "her sports, her outdoor activities, her swimming. It's a quiet, pacific type of living, which is one of the reasons I wanted to come back down here. The kids are taught to say 'sir' and 'ma'am.' I know it's very fashionable to poke fun at the South, but I'll pit our slum area any day against the slum areas where the Cubans and Puerto Ricans live in Miami, Florida, and Miami'll lose."

Meridian is the largest city between Jackson and Birmingham, and there is a naval base there which means a great deal to the community. At apartment buildings largely inhabited by the navy there are cars with plates from all over the country.

Some random social observations from Stan Torgerson included: most of the local children go to college within the state, at Ole Miss or Mississippi or Southern Mississippi; the other country club, built with federal money, has a membership which includes "assistant managers of stores and some navy people"; most of the subdivisions in Meridian feature "custom houses." Torgerson paused dramatically, to emphasize the versatility of the new blood in town: "A fabric store."

I asked if some children did not leave, and he allowed that some did. "Nothing here for the kid with an engineering degree. And of course the girls go where they marry. Southern girls are notoriously husband hunting, but I guess that's the same anywhere." It occurred to me almost constantly in the South that had I lived there I would have been an eccentric and full of anger, and I wondered what form the anger would have taken. Would I have taken up causes, or would I have simply knifed somebody?

Torgerson was wound up now, and I could not stop his peroration. "There's been a great metamorphosis in recent years in the South, the Volkswagen dealership for example comparable in size to anything you'll find anywhere.

"The KKK which used to be a major factor in this community isn't a factor anymore, both the membership and the influence have diminished, and I cannot think of any place where the black is denied entrance, with the possible exception of private clubs. We don't have any antagonistic-type black leaders working against racial harmony. Since the advent of black pride, black power, there is a little tendency to be self-segregating. On our station, we have a program we call *Adventures in Black History*, to point out the contributions black people have made—a black minister does it. I have blacks working in the WQIC Soul Shop, and there's a black druggist here, a man eminently qualified, who is a local boy who went north and came back, received his training at the University of Illinois. We have a certain degree of black business, including this gas station here, which is owned by a black. The key is racial harmony, and education, and we'll try to provide our people with both, 'cause we're gonna live together a long time. Every major retailer hires black clerks, Sears has a couple of black department heads, there's a black business college here, and a black and white Career Training Institute.

"Of course we have transplants, too, new ideas, like any other hybrid we're generally stronger. We're not nearly as inbred as we used to be. We've been withdrawn in this part of the South for many, many years, but we've become more aggressive, and as people come in they've helped us become more aggressive—we don't wear crinolines anymore, no we don't.

"And about our politics, well, George Wallace got a lot of votes in Indiana, let's face it. I'm not saying I'm going to have a black minister come home to dinner tonight, 'cause I'm not. But things are changing. I had a man the other day, owns an appliance store, he never believed you could send a black repairman into somebody's house. Now he can't find a white . . . He asks me if I know a black man who makes a good appearance. That's progress . . .

"Of course, there's a tremendous lack of skilled blacks, and the problem is training and education. It's no longer a matter of lack of opportunity, it's a matter of lack of skills. We're still two generations from full equality, but so are they in Chicago, in Detroit, and have you ever been in Harlem?"

Glazed by the two hours in which this man in the green shirt had laid Meridian out before us as an entrepreneur's dream, a Shoney's Po' Boy on every corner and progress everywhere, even at the country club, I dropped him off and drove through the still-deserted streets of the downtown. A few black women were on the streets, and they carried umbrellas against the sun. It was almost five o'clock. In the middle of 22nd Avenue, the main street of Meridian, there was a man holding a shotgun. He had on a pink shirt and a golfing cap, and in one ear there was a hearing aid. He raised the shotgun and shot toward the roof of a building several times.

I stopped the car and watched him a while, then approached him. "What are you shooting at?" I asked.

"*Pi-ea*gins," he said cheerfully.

In this one demented afternoon Mississippi lost much of its power to astonish me.

Because I had fallen and hurt a rib in New Orleans, and the rib pained me in the steaming heat and when I swam or turned in bed, I decided to see a doctor in Meridian. I was unsure how long it would be before I was again in a town big enough to have an emergency clinic, and here there were, Stan Torgerson had told me repeatedly, four hospitals, and I even knew the name of one, the Rush Foundation Hospital, and so I went there. One of the younger Rush doctors looked at my rib and sent me for an X-ray. I do not know if it was Dr. Vaughn Rush or Dr. Lowry Rush, who are brothers, or Dr. Gus Rush, who is a cousin. Before the doctor came in a nurse took my history, and she seemed not to believe a word I said. While I waited in my white smock I began to see it through her eyes: A woman walks into a clinic, a stranger to Meridian. She has long straight hair, which is not seen in the South among respectable women past the age of fourteen, and she complains of an injured rib. She gives her address as Los Angeles, but says the rib was injured in a hotel room in New Orleans. She says she is just "traveling through" Meridian. This is not a story to inspire confidence, and I knew it as I told it, which made meeting her eyes difficult.

Dr. Rush himself was willing to let this story go at face value, more or less.

"Just traveling on vacation," he said.

"Actually I'm a writer," I said. "I like going places I've never been."

"Traveling alone?" He pressed at my rib.

"With my husband."

This did not sound exactly right, either, because I was not wearing my wedding ring. There was a long pause.

"I went to school up north," he said. "I liked it a lot up there. I thought once I wouldn't mind living up there."

"But you came back here."

"But . . ." he said, "I came back here."

One evening in Meridian we went to the movies: *Loving* was playing with George Segal and Eva Marie Saint. The audience, what there was of it, gazed at the screen as if the movie were Czech. As it happened I had seen Eva Marie Saint a few weeks before, at dinner at someone's house in Malibu, and the distance between Malibu and this movie house in Meridian seemed limitless. How had I gotten from there to here: there, as always, was the question.

NOTE: Thinking about southern girls I had known in New York, the astonishing way their life in the South remained more vivid to them than anything that was happening to them in the city. Esther Nicol, when told I had been a Tri Delt at Berkeley, sniffed and said that at Ole Miss the Tri Delt house was "mostly Mississippi girls." To Esther, who was from Memphis, this meant something real. Again, remembering having lunch with a girl from Nashville who was working at Condé Nast. She would have to leave in a month, she told me, because home in Nashville the season was beginning and her grandmother was giving a party.

NOTE: On being asked for identification when I ordered a drink in the rural South. Before I came south I had not been taken for seventeen in considerable years, but several times in that month I had to prove I was eighteen. It is assumed that grown women will have their hair done, is all I could think.

NOTE: Remembering that in Durham in 1942 there was something, or was said to be something, called Push Day, when blacks would push whites on the streets. People avoided going downtown shopping on Push Day, which was either Tuesday or Wednesday. And there was that time in Durham, when Mother and my brother, Jimmy, and I got on a bus to go out to Duke and the driver would not start because we were sitting in the back of the bus.

On the Road from Meridian to Tuscaloosa, Alabama

SIGNS: WELCOME TO ALABAMA! TAKE A FUN BREAK! 782,000 ALABAMA BAPTISTS WELCOME YOU!

Dixie Gas stations, all over, with Confederate flags and grillwork.

Boys working on the road between Cuba and Demopolis. Making measurements with fishing poles. Sumter County, Alabama, around in here, is 80 percent black. We crossed the Demopolis Rooster Bridge over the Tombigbee River, another still, brown river. I think I never saw water that appeared to be running in any part of the South. A sense of water moccasins.

In Demopolis around lunchtime the temperature was 96 degrees and all movement seemed liquid. An Alabama state trooper drove slowly around town. I put a penny in a weighing machine on the main street. My weight was ninety-six, and my fortune was "You are inclined to let your heart rule your head."

In the drugstore a young girl was talking to the woman at the counter. "I'm gonna run off and get married," the girl said. "Who to?" the woman asked. The girl crumpled her straw paper. "I'm gonna get married," she said stubbornly, "I don't care who."

To get out of the sun I sat a while in the Demopolis library and contemplated a newspaper photograph of the Demopolis police force (nine of them) pouring out 214 gallons of confiscated moonshine. The moonshine had been confiscated after a four-hour chase and tracking with a bloodhound. The driver of the moonshine car, Clarence Bunyan Barrett of Cedartown, Georgia, was fined $435 and released.

At the desk a small birdlike woman about seventy was chatting with the librarian.

"*The Nashville Sound* in yet?"

"Still on order," the librarian said.

"How 'bout *The World of Fashion*?"

"Still out."

"Put me down on the waiting list for *The World of Fashion*."

The French Lieutenant's Woman was moving briskly that

summer in the Demopolis library. The temperature at two was 98 degrees.

Greene County rolls gently, trees and grass, a light clear green. Pasture. The land looks rich, and many people from Birmingham, etc. (rich people) maintain places here to hunt.

The southern myth: a small bungalow named Grayfield, lots and lots of small one-story houses with two-by-four pillars.

Eutaw, Alabama, is a town the train goes through. Children were bicycling in town, barely moving in the leafy still air. There were tiger lilies everywhere, wild or naturalized. We listened to country music on the radio. There was a funeral taking place at the Eutaw Baptist Church at 4 P.M. on June 16, and the mourners made a frieze outside the church with a group of children on a penny hike. The coin spinning on the sidewalk and the children kneeling to see, with the adults in black around them. In Eutaw there was a white swimming pool and a black swimming pool, and an apartment house, the Colonial Apts., where the sign read APPLY JIMMY'S GRILL.

In the Eutaw City Hall I asked a clerk where the Chamber of Commerce was, but she could not, or would not, tell me. On a corner was a locked-up Teen Center, with posters inside that read GO TIDE and FREAK-OUT. There was one poster of a peace symbol. Children represent a mysterious subculture in small southern towns.

At 5 P.M. on a Tuesday afternoon we drove down a side road into Ralph, Alabama. A sign told us that the ZIP was 35480, the pop. 50, and that the town included:

Bethel (Baptist)
Shiloh (Baptist)
Wesley Chapel
Post Office
School.

Ralph was also a Prize Winner for Cotton Improvement. Tiger lilies and no people, anywhere.

Off US 82-W, near Tuscaloosa, is Lake Lurleen. Bear Bryant Volkswagen in Tuscaloosa. Rebel Oil. Bumper stickers: "Yahweh vs. Evolution / Don't Make a Monkey Out of Yourself." Tiger Lilies. Red Tide, Crimson Tide, Go Tide, Roll Tide.

At the Ramada Inn in Tuscaloosa I sat outside by the swimming pool about five o'clock one afternoon and read Sally Kempton's piece in *Esquire* about her father and other men she had known. There was no sun. The air was as liquid as the pool. Everything seemed to be made of concrete, and damp. A couple of men in short-sleeved nylon shirts sat at another metal table and drank beer from cans. Later we tried to find somewhere open to eat. I called a place on University Boulevard, and the owner said to turn left at the Skyline Drive-in. On the way we got lost and stopped in a gas station to ask directions. The attendant had no idea where University Boulevard was (the University of Alabama is on University Boulevard) but could give us directions to the Skyline.

Birmingham

WHEN I CALLED a friend in Birmingham to ask who I should see around the countryside, what was going on, and he asked me what I wanted to know and I explained, he said, "You want to see who's sitting around the Greyhound bus station and who's sitting around in a Packard car, is that right?" I said that was right.

The country way in which he gave me names: "There's ole Rankin Fife, Speaker of the state House of Representatives, he pretty much runs Winfield. Over to Boligee there's David Johnston, he's got a big farm. There's a union leader, the Haneys, they live outside Guin, and he's a farmer and a preacher and a union leader. There's the Hill family, they run the bank. There's Boyd Aman in Boligee, number one hunter and fisherman—I reckon you could find him at the general store. And if you get in any trouble up there, you be sure to call me."

The sense of sports being the opiate of the people. In all the small towns the high school gymnasium was not only the most resplendent part of the high school but often the most solid structure in the town, redbrick, immense, a monument to the hopes of the citizenry. Athletes who were signing "letters of intent" were a theme in the local news.

At dinner one night in Birmingham there were, besides us, five people. Two of the men had gone to Princeton and the third was, when he was traveling on business, a habitué of Elaine's in New York and the Beverly Hills Hotel in California. They talked with raucous good humor about "seein' those X-rated movies" when their wives were out of town. This was a manner of speaking, a rococo denial of their own sophistication, which I found dizzying to contemplate.

"You could almost say that all the virtues and all the limitations of the South are a function of low population," someone said at lunch in Birmingham. "Cities, well, cities *are* melting pots. What we've had here was an almost feudal situation." We had been in places in Mississippi and Alabama where there had been virtually no ethnic infusion.

"Leave 'em to their stamps," someone said at dinner about the white tenants on his father's place.

Southern houses and buildings once had space and windows and deep porches. This was perhaps the most beautiful and comfortable ordinary architecture in the United States, but it is no longer built, because of air-conditioning.

NOTE: The curious ambivalence of the constant talk about wanting industry. Is not wanting industry the death wish, or is wanting it?

Talking about "a gentleman of the old school," there was the familiarity with generations of eccentric behavior, scandals and arrangements, high extramarital drama played out against the Legion parade.

It is said that the dead center of Birmingham society is the southeast corner of the locker room at the Mountain Brook country club. At Mountain Brook everyone goes to St. Luke's Episcopal Church or Briarwood Presbyterian, and it is hard to make the connection between this Birmingham and that of Bull Connor, and Birmingham Sunday.

Lunch with Hugh Bailey at the club, up high enough to see the smoke haze. "We got a pollution count in Birmingham now, which I guess you could say is a sign of progress." On that day the *Birmingham Post-Herald* (June 18) reported the downtown pollution count at 205, or over the U.S. Public Health Service's critical level, and the number of respiratory deaths in Jefferson County that week at six. There did not seem to be much pollution in Mountain Brook.

In Birmingham at dinner they were talking about catching rattlesnakes. "You take a hose, and go out in the fields, and take a few drops of gasoline down the hose into a hole—any hole—and that makes the rattlesnakes kind of drunk, and they come out for some air."

At every social level, the whole quality of maleness, the concentration on hunting and fishing. Leave the women to their cooking, their canning, their "prettifying."

A sign in a trailer camp in Walker County, Alabama: YOUR VOTE AND SUPPORT APPRECIATED/WALLACE FOR

GOVERNOR. The thought that the reason Wallace has never troubled me is that he is a totally explicable phenomenon.

Most southerners are political realists: they understand and accept the realities of working politics in a way we never did in California. Graft as a way of life is accepted, even on the surface. "You get somebody makes eight hundred dollars a month as state finance director, he's only got four years to make his stake."

Inscriptions on gravestones:

THE ANGELS CALLED HIM

DYING IS BUT GOING HOME

MOORE

ELLIE	JESSIE T.
1888–19	1887–1952

SANDLIN

RAND	IDA M.
1871–1952	1873–19

JENNIE B., *wife of J. R. Jones.*
She was a kind and affectionate wife,
a fond aunt, and a friend to all.

In so many family plots there was someone recently dead—dead after World War II—who remembered the Civil War. This was in a graveyard in a harsh red-dirt hill town, plastic flowers on the plots, overlooking the bright lights of the ballpark.

At the St. Francis Motel in Birmingham I went swimming, which occasioned great notice in the bar. "Hey, look, there's somebody with a bikini on."

Winfield

MAYBE THE RURAL SOUTH is the last place in America where one is still aware of trains and what they can mean, their awesome possibilities.

I put my clothes in the laundromat and walked on down the dirt at the side of the road to the beauty shop. A girl with long straight blond hair gave me a manicure. Her name was Debby.

"I got one more year at Winfield High," Debby said, "then I'm getting out."

I asked her where she would get out to.

"Birmingham," she said.

I asked what she would do in Birmingham.

"Well, if I keep on working while I'm in school, I'll have enough hours for my cosmetologist's license. You need three thousand, I got twelve hundred already. Then I'll go to modeling school." Debby reflected a moment. "I hope I will."

An electric fan hummed in the small shop. The smell of hair conditioners, shampoos, warm and sticky. The only other person there was the daughter of the proprietress. I asked her if she was still in school. She giggled as if she did not believe anyone could ask such a silly question.

"I been *married* three years," she said.

"You don't look old enough," I said.

"I'm *twenty*."

She lives in a trailer with her husband, Scott, who operates a power saw. Trailers got hot, we all agreed. They cool down at night, Debby suggested. "Oh, sure," the twenty-year-old said, "it cools down at night." Her mother, who owned the beauty shop, was home "doing her bookwork." She was in charge, and bossing Debby slightly. "You didn't get her *name*? She couldn't come any other *time*?"

They revert to the theme of the heat. The trailer does cool down at night, they agreed.

"Last night it was cool," the twenty-year-old said.

"I didn't think so," Debby said.

"I don't mean when we went to *bed*, I mean late. I woke up, it was almost cool. 'Course I'd had the *conditioning* on in the trailer all day."

Debby looked impassively out the open door. "So hot, Daddy had to come out from the bedroom to sleep on the couch."

"Cooler in than out."

Debby dried my hands. "I guess," she said idly.

At the little concrete pool between the motel and the creek, two teenage girls in two-piece bathing suits were lying in the sun on the stained pavement. They had come in a pickup truck and a transistor radio on the seat of the pickup played softly. There was algae in the pool, and a cigarette butt. "ABC," the Jackson 5.

I bought a large paper cup full of cracked ice in the drugstore (Hollis Pharmacy) for a nickel and walked back down the road to the laundromat eating it. Nothing had changed in the laundromat in the hour or so I had been gone: the same women, most with rollers in their hair, sat and stared and folded frayed flower-printed towels and sheets. There were two men in the laundromat, a repairman and an officious young man, straw-haired and rednecked, who seemed to be the owner. He regarded the women with contempt and the women regarded him in sullen impassivity.

"Hot 'nough for you?" a middle-aged woman said to me. I said it was. There was no hostility toward or even curiosity about me in the laundromat: by virtue of spending a summer afternoon in this steaming bleak structure I had moved into a realm where all women are sisters in misery. "Use this one," the woman said a while later, pointing out a dryer to me. "This one's dried her clothes and mine both, and she just put in one dime." The woman glanced furtively at the repairman as she spoke, and at the owner, as if fearful that they might fix the machine, deprive us of our jackpot.

On weekday afternoons in towns like Winfield one sees mainly women, moving like somnambulists through the days of their lives. The men work out at plants somewhere, or on farms, or in lumber. When I left the laundromat there was a boy in a bike helmet working on the road. Bike helmets had come to seem a normal mode of dress. *How the West Was Won* was playing at the movie house.

In the Angelyn Restaurant in Winfield at lunchtime a number of men, among the few I saw in town in the daytime, sat around and watched *General Hospital* on the television.

Guin

A TRAVELER in the rural South in the summertime is always eating dinner, dispiritedly, in the barely waning heat of the day. One is a few hundred miles and a culture removed from any place that serves past 7:30 or 8 P.M. We ate dinner one night at a motel on the road between Winfield and Guin. The sun still blazed on the pavement outside, and was filtered only slightly by the aqueous blue-green Pliofilm shades on the windows inside. The food seemed to have been deep-fried for the lunch business and kept lukewarm on a steam table. Eating is an ordeal, as in an institution, something to be endured in the interests of survival. There are no drinks to soften the harshness of it. Ice is begrudged. I remember in one such place asking for iced coffee. The waitress asked me how to make it. "Same way as iced tea," I said. She looked at me without expression. "In a cup?" she asked.

The waitress in the place in Guin trailed me to the cash register. She was holding a matchbook I had left on the table. "I was looking at your matchbook," she said. "Where's it from?" I said it was from Biloxi. "Biloxi, *Mississippi*?" she said, and studied the matchbook as if it were a souvenir from Nepal. I said yes. She tucked the matchbook in her pocket and turned away.

On the outskirts of Guin the sign says GU-WIN/CITY LIMIT. At the Wit's Inn in Guin, an MYF (I think) coffeehouse, there were a couple of kids with guitars entertaining. They were billed as Kent and Phil, and their last engagement had been at Tuscaloosa. They sang "Abraham, Martin and John" and "Bridge over Troubled Water," and the children in the place joined in when asked, in clear sweet voices.

Some of the boys were wearing Guin baseball uniforms and one beautiful boy about sixteen was wearing a tie-dyed shirt and pants. Kids would drink Cokes and then drift out to the street and talk to somebody idling by in a car and then drift back in. The night was warm and there was fresh corn growing high along the road just past town. It seemed a good and hopeful place to live, and yet the pretty girls, if they stayed around Guin, would end up in the laundromat in Winfield, or in a trailer with the air-conditioning on all night.

When the program ended about ten kids all stood around in the street, making idle connections. A half an hour later the only people seen on the streets of Guin were twelve-year-olds wearing baseball uniforms. We drove between Guin and Hamilton on the George C. Wallace White Way, four lanes to nowhere, brightly lit. In Hamilton the street lights were turned off. We were getting Fort Worth and San Antonio on the car radio, gospel stations, "Rock of Ages" and "Lonesome Valley." Drove into a drive-in to see the end of *The Road Hustlers*, starring Jim Davis, Andy Devine, and Scott Brady. *The Losers* was the next bill at the drive-in. We followed *The Losers* all over the South. Outside Guin the night shift was working at the 3M plant.

Grenada, Mississippi

DRIVING OVER FROM Oxford to Grenada to have dinner one night with Bob Evans, Jr., and his wife, I noticed the shadows on the kudzu vine, the vine consuming trees, poles, everything in its range. The kudzu makes much of Mississippi seem an ominously topiary landscape. And the graveyards everywhere, with plastic sweet peas on the graves of infants. Death is still natural and ever present in the South, as it is no more in those urbanized parts of the country where graveyards are burial parks and relegated to unused or unusable land far from sight.

On Highway 7, Buck Brown & Son filling station. The rifles slung across the back cab windows of pickups. The Yalobusha Country Club just south of Water Valley. In Water Valley, blacks hanging around the main street, the highway, leaning on cars, talking across the street, the highway. In Coffeeville, Miss., at 6 P.M., there was a golden light and a child swinging in it, swinging from a big tree, over a big lawn, back and forth in front of a big airy house. To be a white middle-class child in a small southern town must be on certain levels the most golden way for a child to live in the United States.

On Margin Street in Grenada, as we drove in, a girl in a yellow bridesmaid's dress and a tulle headpiece, her husband in a cutaway, walked home from a wedding carrying their daughter, a baby two or three.

At the Evanses' house, there was a framed Christmas card from The President and Mrs. Nixon, and what appeared to be a framed slave deed. We had drinks, and after a while we took our drinks, our road glasses, and went for a drive through town. Mrs. Evans had grown up in Grenada, had been married once before, and now she and her second husband—who was from Tupelo—lived in her mother's old house. "Look at all those people standing around in front of that motel," she said once on the drive. "That's a cathouse," her husband told her. We went out to a lake, and then to dinner at the Holiday Inn, this being another of those towns where the Holiday Inn was the best place to eat. We brought our drinks and a bottle in with us, because there was no liquor served, only setups. I am unsure whether the bottle was legal. The legality or illegality of liquor in the South seems a complication to outsiders, but is scarcely considered by the residents. At dinner some people were watching us, and later came over to say hello to the Evanses. They introduced us as friends from California. "We were wondering where you were from," one of them said.

On our drive we passed a five-year-old in baseball pajamas playing catch with a black maid in a white uniform, the ball going back and forth, back and forth, suspended in amber.

The Evanses had a little baby, their child, and a sixteen-year-old daughter, her child. "She only comes out of her room when it's time to eat or time to go out," he said about her.

About the bottle at dinner: actually we brought three bottles, Scotch, bourbon, and vodka, and it was not legal to bring them inside in this dry county, because Mrs. Evans had them in a large handbag she carried exactly for this purpose.

About the cathouse: the notion that an accepted element in the social order is a whorehouse goes hand in hand with the woman on a pedestal.

Oxford

IN THE STUDENT union at Ole Miss they were watching *General Hospital* on the TV, just as they had been in the Angelyn Restaurant in Winfield.

In the student union there was an official calendar for May, on which was printed "May 28—Vacation—Raise Hell." Below this someone had scribbled, "An appropriate preoccupation for an Ole Miss student." The self-image of the Southern Blood as Cavalier very apparent here.

In the university bookstore, which appeared to be the one place in Oxford to buy a book (with the exception of a drugstore on the square which had several racks of paperbacks), the only books available other than assigned texts were a handful of popular bestsellers and a few (by no means all) novels by William Faulkner.

At the swimming pool at the Holiday Inn, the musical dialogue:

"Get that penny, it's down there yonder."

"Hurt my toe."

"I hurt *my* toe climbing a plum tree."

"*How'd* you hurt your toe?"

"Climbed a plum tree."

"Why."

"Get a plum."

"Hey, Bruiser, drop my sneaks down?"

"OK, Goose."

In the parking lot at the Holiday Inn one afternoon a police car was parked, its door open, the police radio breaking the still afternoon air the whole time I was sitting by the pool. Later when I was swimming a little girl pointed out to me that by staying underwater one could hear, by some electronic freak, a radio playing. I submerged and heard news of the Conservative victory in Great Britain, and "Mrs. Robinson."

When I was driving in the afternoon alone on the Ole Miss campus the wind came up, sudden and violent, and the sky darkened and there was thunder but no rain. I was afraid of a tornado. The suddenness and unpredictability of this shocked me. The weather around here must shape ideas of who and what one is, as it does everywhere.

On the same afternoon I saw a black girl on the campus: she was wearing an Afro and a clinging jersey, and she was quite beautiful, with a NY-LA coastal arrogance. I could not think what she was doing at Ole Miss, or what she thought about it.

At dinner in the Holiday Inn, overhearing an academic foursome: two teachers, the wife of one of them, and a younger woman, perhaps a graduate student or a teaching assistant. They were talking about how the SAEs and the Sigma Nus and the Sigma Chis used to "control politics." The break in this situation had come when Archie Manning, who was I believe a Sigma Nu, had run for something and either lost, or just barely won, which went to prove. There had been "a little article in the *Mississippian* about this," about the way the Greeks used to run things, and, said one of the men, "it said they did no more, but it upset my wife and daughter. Why did that have to be?"

The others added that the piece had been "trivial," "not very well done," but they did not address themselves to their colleague's plaintive question.

At one point during dinner the younger woman stated in a spirit of reckless defiance, "I don't care what the student union looks like, I couldn't care less." At another point she said that she believed the FBI had her "staked out," because she had two friends who used drugs. She did not and would not use drugs herself, she added: "My mind's expanded enough."

When I think about Oxford now I think about Archie Manning, the Sigma Nu, and all the bumper stickers that read ARCHIE and ARCHIE'S ARMY, with a Rebel flag, and about the immense and beautifully landscaped fraternity and sorority houses that surround the campus, and about boys and girls who in 1970 come out of the pinewoods to sing "White Star of Sigma Nu" at dances after football games. I had telephoned someone I knew in the English Department at Berkeley to ask if he knew anyone on any faculty in any department at any college in Mississippi to whom I should talk, anyone noted in any field he knew about, but he did not, and could only suggest that I call up Miss Eudora Welty, in Jackson.

As a matter of fact I had intended to, if ever I got near

Jackson, but I was afraid to get too near Jackson because planes left from Jackson for New York and California, and I knew I would not last ten minutes in Jackson without telephoning Delta or National and getting out. All that month I hummed in my mind "Leavin' on a Jet Plane," Peter, Paul and Mary, and every night in our motel room we got out the maps and figured out how many hours' driving time to Jackson, to New Orleans, to Baton Rouge, to the closest place the planes left from.

We drove out on Old Taylor Road at night to look for Rowan Oak, William Faulkner's house. There were fireflies, and heat lightning, and the thick vines all around, and we could not see the house until the next day. It was large and private, secluded, set back from the road. I read a book about Faulkner in Oxford, interviews with his fellow citizens in Oxford, and I was deeply affected by their hostility to him and by the manner in which he had managed to ignore it. I thought if I took a rubbing from his gravestone, a memento from this place, I would know every time I looked at it that the opinion of others counted for not much one way or another.

So we went out to the graveyard, the Oxford cemetery, to look for the grave. Under a live oak tree a black kid sat in a parked two-tone salmon Buick, the door open. He was sitting on the floorboard with his feet outside, and while I was there several cars with Ole Miss and Archie's Army stickers came winding up the cemetery road, and boys would get out, and they would have some dealing with the black kid and drive away. He seemed to be dealing marijuana, and his car had a Wayne State sticker. Other than that there was nobody, just rabbits and the squirrels and the hum of bees and the heat, dizzying heat, heat so intense I thought of fainting. For several hours we looked for the grave, found the Faulkner plot and a number of other Faulkner/Falkner graves, but we never found William Faulkner's grave, not in that whole graveyard full of Oxford citizens and infant sons.

The way in which all the reporting tricks I had ever known atrophied in the South. There were things I should do, I knew it: but I never did them. I never made an appointment with the bridal consultant of the biggest department store in any town

I was in. I never made the Miss Mississippi Hospitality Contest Semi-Finals, although they were being held in little towns not far from where we were, wherever we were. I neglected to call the people whose names I had, and hung around drugstores instead. I was underwater in some real sense, the whole month.

I kept talking to Mrs. Frances Kirby by telephone in Jackson. Mrs. Kirby was in charge of the Miss Hospitality contests, in Bay Springs, Cleveland, Clinton, Greenwood, Gulfport, Indianola, Leland, Lewisville. I was within a few miles of Cleveland on the day that contest would be held, and I called the sponsors, the chamber of commerce, and they said to come on "up at the country club" and watch, but I never even did that.

A Sunday Lunch in Clarksdale

ONE DAY WE DROVE from Oxford over to Clarksdale, to have Sunday lunch with Marshall Bouldin and his wife, Mel. Lunch was served promptly at noon, a few minutes after our arrival. There was fried chicken and gravy, white rice, fresh green peas, and a peach pie for dessert. The heat was so intense that the ice was already melted in the Waterford water goblets before we sat down at the table. Grace was said. The children were allowed to speak on topics of interest, but not to interrupt. I have never eaten so long or heavy a meal. I was in a place where "Sunday" still existed as it did in my grandmother's house, a leadening pause in the week, a day of boredom so extreme as to be exhausting. It was the kind of Sunday to make one ache for Monday morning.

After lunch we sat in the living room of the small house in town the Bouldins were using while their plantation house was being remodeled. Marshall Bouldin talked, and here are some of the things he said:

"The money and the power in the South have traditionally been in the hands of the people who plant. The Delta, because of that, is rich. There are rich people in the Delta. You don't get governors from the Delta, but you do get the money and the power to elect them. Governors come from the hills, and from Hattiesburg. There's a lieutenant governor now from Clarksdale, but that's unusual. There are fewer blacks in the hill sections. The Delta, which is more affluent, has a higher black population. The third part of Mississippi, besides the hills and the Delta, is the coastal area, which is really an isolated phenomenon.

"I'm so glad to see what has happened in Mississippi. The thinking has come so far in just these twenty years. The hill country is certainly more reactionary. The Delta's still conservative, yes, but people here have money, and people who have money can be exposed to new ideas.

"Mainly we plant cotton here, soybeans are replacing truck crops. We tried cattle, but the soil here is too rich for cattle, the flat land ends at Vicksburg. The Delta is maybe fifty miles wide, and was all overflow land until after the Civil War when the levees were built. Around 1870, then, people began to move in, they had this rich land, all river silt. What size is the average Delta farm? Well, fourteen thousand acres would be a large one, and two hundred to three hundred acres would be a small one, the average is said to be seven hundred seventy, but that would be small for cotton or beans.

"Thirty years ago my dad and my Mel's dad led the ideal planter's life. Now it's more of a business, it's not the same. It was a series of small towns then, there were great social functions, and you went from town to town for your social functions, and this held the country together.

"What you have here is the last of the feudal system. It's an area where you have plenty of servants. We're fortunate to have Charles and Frances here, they were on my dad's place. What you had around here until very lately was mainly the tenant system. Each black family was responsible for the ten or fifteen acres around his cabin. The owner supervised and provided food, and provided anything else the family needed, and these were sizable families, but they'd say, 'Mr. Marshall, take care of me,' and we would. That's part of the change here. Mel's brother is not on the tenant system.

"My dad never put anyone off. And Mel, your dad never did either. Some planters, they abused the tenant system. There was one planter around here, on payday he used to make them smile, he'd hand out silver dollars when he got the smile, but that was just some, and maybe it was condoned but it was never approved of. Mel's daddy kept *books*, and settled with every tenant. The community knew who these people were who took advantage, and frowned on them. Of course, nobody put them in jail, which is maybe what we should've done.

"Automation changed things, the cotton picker meant we didn't need so many. We never put anybody off the land, they just gradually left for Detroit or they moved into town. A few planters told people to get off, but on the whole there was not much dispossessing of the black man.

"The big change, I do think, was when television came. The kids could see the way other people lived, other lives. It has been the greatest educational system in the county.

"My dad's main job was just talking to John, seeing if he needed anything (John was the overseer or foreman). Mel's brother, on the other hand, he runs—I don't want to say it's a factory, but it turns out cotton. He has about three thousand acres in three pieces. In 1950 I farmed like my daddy farmed, on a horse. Now you need to have a manager on each place, in his pickup. You need to have a personal radio, to be able to reach a man you've got in town and tell him to get that part out here in fifteen minutes. You used to be able to have a good time farming. When you got the cotton picked in the fall you read books, went hunting, sat around the fire and socialized. Now, they're working on the machinery all winter. Maybe if you can get the repair work done in January, you can take a month or six weeks off in February, but that's it." He paused, and looked at his wife. "Isn't that right, Mel?"

Mel shrugged. "It's still the good life," she said.

"The black population is still high here," he went on. "In the schools right now it's 80 percent black and 20 percent white, now that we're integrated. We have tortured and tortured over what to do with our children, and our tentative decision for now is to send them to private schools, even though that is against our ideals. I can't sacrifice my child to my ideal. They had to force the black to integrate. Basically I know that the people who are pushing it are right, but they seem so precipitous. They say we had to integrate on February 2. Now, why couldn't they have waited 'til September? It hardened attitudes, is what it did. There are people in this community who might have been showing signs of opening up their minds, and then a parent finds out that as of next week his kid is going to be over in Higgins High—that door is closed, and when it's going to open again nobody knows.

"They say around here it takes three generations to make a gentleman, and yet if I was about a sixteen-year-old black boy I'll be damned if I'd want to wait three generations. All over this area we still have these large maternal families, families with no daddy, nobody to say if you're going to reap the benefits, you've got to put in the work.

"I'm a middle-of-the-roader, and like the majority, we're trying to do the easiest thing that will get us all by happily.

There are five or six houses in Clarksdale right now where this conversation could take place. That may not seem like many but when I was growing up there were none.

"The best thing we can do is raise our children differently, and add four people to the community who can come home from this little Episcopal school and think differently. When the integration orders were flying around Mississippi last year it was hard to think what to do, and it still is."

Charles and Frances came out from the kitchen, to say goodbye. They were on their way to church. Marshall Bouldin beamed as he introduced them. "Charles and Frances were on my daddy's place, isn't that right, Frances?" Frances bobbed her head. "That's right, surely is," she said. "Mr. Marshall and us, we were little itty-bittys together."

There was news of a tornado somewhere near the Delta, although not in Coahoma County, and a telephone call to inform Marshall Bouldin that "a black man died on the place last night."

We drove out to the plantation, where the house was being remodeled. He pointed out the tenant cabins standing empty. "When I was little we farmed it all with mules," he said. "When I went off to college we had four-row equipment. Now we have six-row equipment." He pointed out the tractors, which cost $15,000 apiece, and added that there were $60,000 worth of tractors alone in the shed. He pointed out what had been his father's payoff office, and one tenant cabin which was occupied. "This is one of the tenant cabins still occupied by my old fishing buddy, Ernie." Ernie calls the Bouldins Miss Mel and Mister Marshall.

"That's cotton," he said, "far back as the cypress break." I asked what was beyond the cypress break. "Some more of our place."

Mel Bouldin, for a southern woman of her age and class, had done an extraordinary thing: she had gone to medical school after the birth of her children, and now practiced ob-gyn in Memphis, in partnership with three men. She flew to Memphis from "the place" in a private plane. "I can't stand to sit around the country club and *talk*," she said by way of explanation.

She was, at the time we visited her, taking a year off her practice to supervise the reconstruction of the house. The house was to be "a boys' house, everything rough and ready." "I love boys," she kept saying. In certain ways she seemed to have been affected by the great leap she had taken out of her time and place: in order to be her own woman she had found it necessary to vehemently reject many of the things which traditionally give women pleasure, cooking ("'Course I hate to cook, I'd walk a mile and a half to avoid it"), any vanity about her own appearance, any interest in having her house reflect her own tastes. Her mother's house reflected her mother: Mel's house would reflect "the boys," and her greatest delight was in secret stairways and hideaways she was having built into the walls for the children.

At lunch, or just before, the seven-year-old had been asked to perform, and did so with pleasure, playing "Joy to the World" on the piano, a peculiar melody on this steaming June day in the Delta. Everyone held hands during the blessing at table. The four boys were dressed in matching blue mandarin shirts. The family had just come from church services, at the Presbyterian church. When I called the day before from Oxford and Marshall Bouldin suggested we come to lunch, he had said, "Come after church." The idea of "church" as a Sunday morning donnée has not existed for a couple of generations in the Protestant societies I know, but it exists in the South.

On our drive, we passed Delta Road, where there live "nothing but blacks, or if there were any whites, I wouldn't want to meet them."

Out behind the house, the immense Sears, Roebuck swimming tank, raised five or six feet above the lawn. "Keeps the snakes and frogs out," Mel said.

Clarksdale calls itself "The Golden Buckle on the Cotton Belt." At parties in the Delta they say to one another: "How yo' cotton coming?" And then: "Yeah? What's wrong?"

On Silk Stocking Row in Clarksdale there live a few planters, a lawyer, and the cotton broker. Many of the planters live in town. There is one plantation around Clarksdale owned by an English syndicate.

Down the Delta to Greenville

OUTSIDE THE BOLIVAR COUNTY Courthouse in Rosedale, an old policeman, his collar loosened around his thick neck, sat in his car with the motor idling in the Sunday twilight.

Outside Rosedale, on the sign for a RR crossing, the letters KKK had been painted.

All the billboards were for cotton and soybean insecticides and fertilizers.

In Benoit, the town where *Baby Doll* was shot, people hanging around with that remarkable "vacant" look which people in the South always mention before you do and then become defensive about. ("Ever look on a subway in Detroit, Michigan?")

The endless green of the Delta, the flatness, the haze in the mornings. The algae-covered ditches alive with mosquitoes.

In Greenville, the presence of the levee, a high wall at the end of every street downtown. We ate dinner out on the pier at a place that had good gumbo, and I was glad to be on the river (actually we were on a slough), glad to be in a place with good food, glad to be, I suppose, so very close to the place where the National and Delta flights left for California.

We went to have dinner with Hodding Carter III and his wife, Peggy, and with Lew Powell, the city editor of the paper, and his girl. Hodding picked us up and there was the ubiquitous glass on the dashboard, the road glass, in this instance a martini.

We went to dinner at Boyt's, a roadhouse in the next crossroads over. On Boyt's menu: "Italian or Wop Salad."

Hodding Carter III: "The blacks who leave the Delta say they'd come back if there were just something here—this is a place with a strong pull."

He spoke about New Orleans as the place you cop out to, "you go down there with the eleven-and-a-half-month debutante season." His wife came from New Orleans, went to Miss McGehee's and to Sophie Newcomb, and now, he implied, she lives on the frontier.

It would be a while, he thought, before automation came to southern agriculture. Its arrival in California was "speeded up by labor problems." He saw an industrial New South as a kind of pipe dream, the difficulty being an unskilled labor force. "They talk about cheap labor in the South, but cheap labor is a myth for a national company, for any company with labor contracts. So that's no advantage, and another disadvantage here for industry, we've got social problems you don't have in the North."

"The FBI" as a leitmotif in the South. I had heard it in Biloxi, in Oxford, in Grenada, in Greenville.

The time warp: the Civil War was yesterday, but 1960 is spoken of as if it were about three hundred years ago.

Downriver and Home

THE NAMES of plantations going south on 61: Baconia, Lydia, and Evanna. On the billboards: PESTICIDE DYANAP. A plantation south of Onward: Reality Plantation. The Yazoo County Bookmobile, a cropduster releasing sprays of yellow haze. A Greyhound bus with CHICAGO emblazoned over the window hurtling north on 61 through Warren County.

Outside Vicksburg is a shopping center, with a mall named Battlefield Village. In Port Gibson there is a Presbyterian church with, instead of a cross on top of the steeple, a gold finger, pointing heavenward. The kudzu.

Fayette had the aspect of a set from *Porgy and Bess*, in that there were only blacks to be seen on the street and behind windows. The only white I saw as we drove through was wearing a blue work shirt and had a Zapata mustache.

"The Interstate" as a phrase, and a concept. The great pulsing links between there and everywhere else.

On the window of a coffee shop in South McComb, SUPPORT YOUR CITIZEN'S COUNCIL and STATES RIGHTS—RACIAL INTEGRITY, which pretty much laid it right where it was. (Actually I think the restaurant—Boyt's—with Wop Salad on the menu was in McComb, not in Greenville.)

We stopped at Walker Percy's in Covington, Louisiana. We sat out in back by the bayou and drank gin and tonics and when a light rain began to fall, a kind of mist, Walker never paid any mind but just kept talking, and walking up to the house to get fresh drinks. It was a thunderstorm, with odd light, and there were occasional water-skiers on the black bayou water. "The South," he said, "owes a debt to the North . . . tore the Union apart once . . . and now only the South can save the North." He said he had not wanted to see us in New Orleans, at Ben C.'s, because at Ben C.'s he was always saying things he would not ordinarily say, playing a role. Greenville, he said, was a different kind of town. He had spent some time in Los Angeles once but could not face it. "It was the weather," his wife said mildly. "The weather was bad." "It wasn't the weather," he said, and he knew exactly what it was.

Crossing the Pontchartrain bridge, the gray water, the gray causeway, the gray skyline becoming apparent in the far distance just about the time you lose sight of the shore behind you. The sight of New Orleans coming up like a mirage from about the midway point on the Lake Pontchartrain Causeway.

Sycamores and pit vipers. From Audubon, 1830:

> Deep morasses, overshadowed by millions of gigantic dark cypresses, spreading their sturdy moss-covered branches . . . Would that I could represent to you the dangerous nature of the ground, its oozing, spongy, and miry disposition . . .

A senseless disagreement on the causeway, ugly words and then silence. We spent a silent night in an airport motel and took the 9:15 National flight to San Francisco. I never wrote the piece.

CALIFORNIA NOTES

I had told Jann Wenner of Rolling Stone *that I would cover the Patty Hearst trial, and this pushed me into examining my thoughts about California. Some of my notes from the time follow here. I never wrote the piece about the Hearst trial, but I went to San Francisco in 1976 while it was going on and tried to report it. And I got quite involved in uncovering my own mixed emotions. This didn't lead to my writing the piece, but eventually it led to—years later—*Where I Was From *(2003).*

When I was there for the trial, I stayed at the Mark. And from the Mark, you could look into the Hearst apartment. So I would sit in my room and imagine Patty Hearst listening to Carousel. *I had read that she would sit in her room and listen to it. I thought the trial had some meaning for me—because I was from California. This didn't turn out to be true.*

THE FIRST TIME I was ever on an airplane was in 1955, and flights had names. This one was *The Golden Gate*, American Airlines. Serving Transcontinental Travelers Between San Francisco and New York. A week before, twenty-one years old, I had been moping around Berkeley in my sneakers and green raincoat, and now I was a Transcontinental Traveler, Lunching Aloft on Beltsville Roast Turkey with Dressing and Giblet Sauce. I believed in Dark Cottons. I believed in Small Hats and White Gloves. I believed that Transcontinental Travelers did not wear white shoes in the City. The next summer I went back on *The New Yorker*, United Airlines, and had a Martini-on-the-Rocks and Stuffed Celery au Roquefort over the Rockies.

The image of the Golden Gate is very strong in my mind. As unifying images go, this one is particularly vivid.

At the *Sacramento Union* I learned that Eldorado County and Eldorado City are so spelled but that regular usage of El Dorado is two words; to UPPERCASE Camellia Week, the Central Valley, Sacramento Irrigation District, Liberator bombers and Superfortresses, the Follies Bergere [*sic*], the Central Valley Project, and "such nicknames as Death Row, Krauts or Jerries for Germans, Doughboys, Leathernecks, Devildogs."

Arden School class prophecy:

In Carnegie Hall we find Shirley Long
Up on the stage singing a song.
Acting in pictures is Arthur Raney's job,
And he is often followed by a great mob.
As a model Yavette Smith has achieved fame,
Using "Bubbles" as her nickname . . .
We find Janet Haight working hard as a missionary,
Smart she is and uses a dictionary . . .
We find Joan Didion as a White House resident
Now being the first woman president.

Looking through the evidence I find what seems to me now (or rather seemed to me then) an entirely spurious aura of social success and achievement. I seem to have gotten my name in the paper rather a lot. I seem to have belonged to what were in context the "right" clubs. I seem to have been rewarded, out of all proportion to my generally undistinguished academic record, with an incommensurate number of prizes and scholarships (merit scholarships only: I did not qualify for need) and recommendations and special attention and very probably the envy and admiration of at least certain of my peers. Curiously, I only remember failing, failures and slights and refusals.

I seem to have gone to dances and been photographed in pretty dresses, and also as a pom-pom girl. I seem to have been a bridesmaid rather a lot. I seem always to have been "the editor" or "the president."

I believed that I would always go to teas.

This is not about Patricia Hearst. It is about me and the peculiar vacuum in which I grew up, a vacuum in which the Hearsts could be quite literally king of the hill.

I have never known deprivation.

"How High the Moon," Les Paul and Mary Ford. *High Noon.*

I have lived most of my life under misapprehensions of one kind or another. Until I was in college I believed that my father was "poor," that we had no money, that pennies mattered. I recall being surprised the first time my small brother ordered a dime rather than a nickel ice cream cone and no one seemed to mind.

My grandmother, who was in fact poor, spent money: the Lilly Daché and Mr. John hats, the vicuña coats, the hand-milled soap and the $60-an-ounce perfume were to her the necessities of life. When I was about to be sixteen she asked me what I wanted for my birthday and I made up a list (an Ultra-Violet lipstick, some other things), meaning for her to pick one item and surprise me: she bought the list. She gave me my first grown-up dress, a silk jersey dress printed with pale blue flowers and jersey petals around the neckline. It came from the Bon Marché in Sacramento, and I knew what it cost ($60) because I had seen it advertised in the paper. I see myself making many of the same choices for my daughter.

At the center of this story there is a terrible secret, a kernel of cyanide, and the secret is that the story doesn't matter, doesn't make any difference, doesn't figure. The snow still falls in the Sierra. The Pacific still trembles in its bowl. The great tectonic plates strain against each other while we sleep and wake. Rattlers in the dry grass. Sharks beneath the Golden Gate. In the South they are convinced that they have bloodied their place with history. In the West we do not believe that anything we do can bloody the land, or change it, or touch it.

How could it have come to this?

I am trying to place myself in history.

I have been looking all my life for history and have yet to find it.

The resolutely "colorful," anecdotal quality of San Francisco history. "Characters" abound. It puts one off.

In the South they are convinced that they are capable of having bloodied their land with history. In the West we lack this conviction.

Beautiful country burn again.

The sense of not being up to the landscape.

There in the Ceremonial Courtroom a secular mass was being offered.

I see now that the life I was raised to admire was infinitely romantic. The clothes chosen for me had a strong element of the Pre-Raphaelite, the medieval. Muted greens and ivories. Dusty roses. (Other people wore powder blue, red, white, navy, forest green, and Black Watch plaid. I thought of them as "conventional," but I envied them secretly. I was doomed to unconventionality.) Our houses were also darker than other people's, and we favored, as a definite preference, copper and brass that had darkened and greened. We also let our silver darken carefully in all the engraved places, "to bring out the pattern." To this day I am disturbed by highly polished silver. It looks "too new."

This predilection for "the old" carried into all areas of our domestic life: dried flowers were seen to have a more lasting charm than fresh, prints should be faded, a wallpaper should be streaked by the sun before it looks right. As decorative touches went, our highest moment was the acquisition of a house (we, the family, moved into it in 1951 at 22nd and T in Sacramento) in which the curtains had not been changed since 1907. Our favorite curtains in this house were gold silk organza on a high window on the stairwell. They hung almost two stories, billowed iridescently with every breath of air, and crumbled at the touch. To our extreme disapproval, Genevieve Didion, our grandmother, replaced these curtains when she moved into the house in the late 1950s. I think of those curtains still, and so does my mother (domestic design).

Oriental leanings. The little ebony chests, the dishes. Maybeck houses. Mists. The individual raised to mystic level, mysticism with no religious basis.

When I read Gertrude Atherton* I recognize the territory of the subtext. The assemblies unattended, the plantations abandoned—in the novels as in the dreamtime—because of high and noble convictions about slavery. Maybe they had convictions, maybe they did not, but they had also worked out the life of the farm. In the novels as well as the autobiography of Mrs. Atherton we see a provincial caste system at its most malign. The pride in "perfect taste," in "simple frocks."

In the autobiography, page 72, note Mrs. Atherton cutting snakes in two with an axe.

When I read Gertrude Atherton I think not only of myself but of Patricia Hearst, listening to *Carousel* in her room on California Street.

The details of the Atherton life appear in the Atherton fiction, or the details of the fiction appear in the autobiography: it is difficult to say which is the correct construction. The beds of Parma violets at the Atherton house dissolve effortlessly into the beds of Parma violets at Maria Ballinger-Groome Abbott's house in Atherton's *The Sisters-in-Law*. Gertrude's mother had her three-day "blues," as did one of the characters in *Sleeping Fires*. Were there Parma violets at the Atherton house? Did Gertrude's mother have three-day blues?

*Gertrude Atherton (1857–1948) was born in San Francisco and became a prolific and at times controversial writer of novels, short stories, essays, and articles on subjects that included feminism, politics, and war. Many of her novels are set in California.

When I contrast the houses in which I was raised, in California, to admire, with the houses my husband was raised, in Connecticut, to admire, I am astonished that we should have ever built a house together.

Climbing Mount Tamalpais in Marin County, a mystical ideal. I never did it, but I did walk across the Golden Gate Bridge, wearing my first pair of high-heeled shoes, bronze kid De Liso Debs pumps with three-inch heels. Crossing the Gate was, like climbing Tamalpais, an ideal.

Corte Madera. Head cheese. Eating apricots and plums on the rocks at Stinson Beach.

Until I read Gertrude Atherton I had never seen the phrase "South of Market" used exactly the way my grandmother, my mother, and I had always used it. Edmund G. "Pat" Brown was South of Market.

My father and brother call it "Cal" (i.e., the University of California at Berkeley). They were fraternity men, my father a Chi Phi, my brother a Phi Gamma Delta. As a matter of fact I belonged to a house too, Delta Delta Delta, but I lived in that house for only two of the four years I spent at Berkeley.

There used to be a point I liked on the Malibu Canyon road between the San Fernando Valley and the Pacific Ocean, a point from which one could see what was always called "the Fox sky." Twentieth Century–Fox had a ranch back in the hills there, not a working ranch but several thousand acres on which westerns were shot, and "the Fox sky" was simply that: the Fox sky, the giant Fox sky scrim, the Big Country backdrop.

By the time I started going to Hawaii, the Royal Hawaiian was no longer the "best" hotel in Honolulu, nor was Honolulu the "smart" place to vacation in Hawaii, but Honolulu and the Royal Hawaiian had a glamour for California children who grew up as I did. Little girls in Sacramento were brought raffia grass skirts by returning godmothers. They were taught "Aloha 'Oe" at Girl Scout meetings, and to believe that their clumsiness would be resolved via mastery of the hula. For dances, later, they wanted leis, and if not leis, bracelets of tiny orchids, "flown in" from Honolulu. I recall "flown in" as a common phrase of my adolescence in Sacramento, just "flown in," the point of origin being unspoken, and implicit. The "luau," locally construed as a barbecue with leis, was a favored entertainment. The "lanai" replaced the sunporch in local domestic architecture. The romance of all things Hawaiian colored my California childhood, and the Royal Hawaiian seemed to stand on Waikiki as tangible evidence that this California childhood had in fact occurred.

I have had on my desk since 1974 a photograph that I cut from a magazine just after Patricia Campbell Hearst was kidnapped from her Berkeley apartment. This photograph appeared quite often around that time, always credited to Wide World, and it shows Patricia Hearst and her father and one of her sisters at a party at the Burlingame Country Club. In this photograph it is six or seven months before the kidnapping, and the three Hearsts are smiling for the camera, Patricia, Anne, and Randolph.

The father is casual but festive—light coat, dark shirt, no tie; the daughters flank him in long flowered dresses. They are all wearing leis, father and daughters alike, leis quite clearly "flown in" for the evening. Randolph Hearst wears two leis, one of maile leaves and the other of orchids strung in the tight design the lei-makers call "Maunaloa." The daughters each wear pikake leis, the rarest and most expensive kind of leis, strand after strand of tiny Arabian jasmine buds strung like ivory beads.

Sometimes I have wanted to know what my grandmother's sister, May Daly, screamed the day they took her to the hospital, for it concerned me, she had fixed on me, sixteen, as the source of the terror she sensed, but I have refrained from asking. In the long run it is better not to know. Similarly, I do not know whether my brother and I said certain things to each other at three or four one Christmas morning or whether I dreamed it, and have not asked.

We are hoping to spend part of every summer together, at Lake Tahoe. We are hoping to reinvent our lives, or I am.

The San Francisco Social Register. When did San Francisco become a city with a Social Register? How did this come about? The social ambitiousness of San Francisco, the way it has always admired titles, even bogus titles.

All my life I have been reading these names and I have never known who they were or are. Who, for example, is Lita Vietor?

C. Vann Woodward: "Every self-conscious group of any size fabricates myths about its past: about its origins, its mission, its righteousness, its benevolence, its general superiority." This has not been exactly true in San Francisco.

SOME WOMEN:

Gertrude Atherton
Julia Morgan
Lillie Coit
Jessica Peixotto
Dolly Fritz MacMasters Cope
Lita Vietor
Phoebe Apperson Hearst
Patricia Campbell Hearst
Jessie Benton Frémont

Part of it is simply what looks right to the eye, sounds right to the ear. I am at home in the West. The hills of the coastal ranges look "right" to me, the particular flat expanse of the Central Valley comforts my eye. The place names have the ring of real places to me. I can pronounce the names of the rivers, and recognize the common trees and snakes. I am easy here in a way that I am not easy in other places.

CHRONOLOGY

NOTE ON THE TEXTS

NOTES

INDEX

Chronology

1934–36 Born December 5, 1934, at Mercy General Hospital in Sacramento, California, the first of two children of Eduene Jerrett and Frank Reese Didion, who married on January 1. Mother, twenty-four, worked as an assistant city librarian. Father, twenty-six, is an insurance salesman, prone to drink and dread. He often drives to Nevada to shoot craps. The family shares a house on Highland Avenue in Sacramento with Didion's maternal grandparents. She is a fifth-generation Californian: her great-great-great-grandfather on her father's side, Matthew Kilgore, left Ohio for Sacramento in 1855, and on her mother's side her great-great-great-grandmother, Nancy Hardin Cornwall, came west from Arkansas in 1846.

1937–46 In November 1937, father joins the National Guard. Brother Jim is born in December 1939; the following year, the family moves into a home of their own at 2211 U Street. Mother gives her a Big Five tablet so she can "amuse [her]self"; she begins to visit the public library's Ella K. McClatchy branch. On December 7, 1941, Japanese bombers attack Pearl Harbor, in Hawaii, and the United States enters World War II. Father is sent by the Army Air Corps to Fort Lewis in Tacoma, Washington, then to Duke University in Durham, North Carolina, and finally to Peterson Field in Colorado Springs. The family travels to accompany him. In Colorado Springs, suffers her first migraine; she is eight years old. Learns from an issue of *Vogue* about the magazine's Prix de Paris essay contest for college seniors; her mother says she "could win when I got old enough." In late 1943, the family returns to Sacramento after father is reassigned to Detroit. Attends the Arden School in Sacramento.

1947–48 Reads Ernest Hemingway's *A Farewell to Arms* and retypes the first paragraph to get inside the language and see what makes it work. At her eighth-grade graduation in June 1948, delivers a speech on California heritage. "They who came to California," she declares, "were not the self-satisfied, happy and content people, but the adventurous, the restless, and the daring. They were different even from those who settled in other western states." Family moves to Walnut Avenue in Sacramento, and father buys land for development. That summer, on a family vacation, walks into the Pacific, wanting "to know what it would feel like"; back home, she is fascinated by Sacramento's river culture. In the fall, begins freshman year at C.K. McClatchy Senior High School.

1949–52 Becomes a member of the Mañana Society, a sorority sponsored by the Sacramento school district to promote civic and cultural values; her initiation takes place in the Governor's Mansion, where her friend Nina Warren's father, Earl—later chief justice of the United States Supreme Court—is in his second term as chief executive. An indifferent student, she enjoys acting, both in school productions and at a local repertory house. Reads *Moby-Dick* and *An American Tragedy*, and the work of Henry James. The family moves into a "big dark Victorian" three-bedroom house at 500 Hawthorn Street. In 1950, she learns to drive in an Army jeep her father has bought for her and takes friends to Lake Tahoe on weekend trips. Becomes a member of the Student Council and the Press Club and works on the school newspaper, *The Prospector*, and the yearbook. Takes an after-school job with the society page of *The Sacramento Union*. In April 1952, is rejected by Stanford University, her college of choice. Takes classes at Sacramento Junior College in the fall.

1953 Begins at the University of California at Berkeley in the spring, pledging Delta (Tri-Delt) and living in the sorority house on Warring Street. Among her sorority sisters is Barbara Brown, daughter of future California governor Edmund Gerald (Pat) Brown, Sr. Joins staff of student newspaper *The Daily Californian* her first semester. Coedits a special fashion edition with friend Peggy LaViolette; attempts to interview poet W. H. Auden for the paper but, as she later recalls, "was so absolutely terrified that I couldn't think of any questions." Father is sent to Letterman Army Hospital at the Presidio in San Francisco for observation and treatment of drinking and emotional withdrawal. Visits him on weekends with her mother; they have lunch and watch pickup baseball games.

1954 Leaving sorority life, moves into a house at 2520 Ridge Road, which she shares with three other undergraduate women. In the fall is admitted to Mark Schorer's sought-after creative writing workshop, for which she writes short stories. ("He gave me a sense of what writing was about, what it was for," she later remembers.)

1955 Takes a literature class with Schorer. Is selected by *Mademoiselle* magazine to participate in their summer guest editor program, becoming guest editor in fiction. (Prior participants include Sylvia Plath, who was managing guest editor in 1953.) Arrives in Manhattan in May, staying at the Barbizon Hotel for Women; others in her cohort include Gael Greene and Janet Burroway. On June 14, interviews Jean Stafford for the magazine. Returns to Sacramento by train in July, visiting Boston, Quebec, and Chicago en route. Takes a job for the rest of the summer at *The Sacramento Union*, composing wedding notices. Turns down offer to become society editor. In August, her Stafford piece comes out, her first publication in a national venue. Studies Henry James in a class taught by Henry Nash Smith, who praises her "truly remarkable abilities as a critic." Enters the Prix de Paris writing competition, administered by *Vogue*.

1956–58 Becomes editor of *The Occident*, the UC Berkeley student literary magazine, and publishes her first short story, "Sunset," there. Makes the second round of the Prix de Paris competition, and submits a profile of California residential architect William Wilson Wurster as her final contest entry; on May 15, 1956, is awarded first prize. Choosing a $1,000 cash prize over a two-week trip to Paris, she is also offered a job at *Vogue* in New York for $45 a week. Over the summer, travels from Sacramento to Berkeley each week to complete a Milton course required for graduation. In the fall, moves to New York, where she lives on East 79th Street. At first, writes only promotional copy, on a schedule that allows her to submit to other magazines. Rents a third-floor walkup at 1215 Park Avenue for $130 a month. Meets Noel Parmentel and becomes involved with him; he becomes her guide to literary New York. Learns concision from editor Allene Talmey, who edits her captions with a ruthless efficiency. Begins working on a novel, at first titled *Harvest Home* and then *In the Night Season*, which will eventually be published as *Run River*. In 1958, Parmentel introduces her to John Gregory Dunne, soon to be a writer at *Time*.

1959–62 In the summer of 1959, gives notice at *Vogue* to become college editor at *Mademoiselle*, but decides to stay after *Vogue* editor Jessica Daves offers a new job as feature associate, writing articles at a higher salary. On November 1, begins writing the "People Are Talking About" column, contributing unsigned pieces to the magazine. Continues to freelance for other publications, including *Mademoiselle*, and begins an association with the *National Review*, writing book and film reviews. In the evenings works on her novel, hanging its pages on her living room wall. Publishes her first signed piece in *Vogue* in June 1961, "Jealousy: Is It a Curable Illness?" Moves to 41 East 75th Street. Breaks up with Parmentel and becomes involved with Dunne. Submits pages of the novel as a partial manuscript; a dozen publishers turn it down. At Parmentel's instigation, submits to Ivan Obolensky, who offers an advance of $1,000 but insists she change the title to *Run River*. The money allows her to take a two-month leave from *Vogue* to complete the book. In June 1962, she flies to California; votes for Joe Shell over Richard M. Nixon in the Republican gubernatorial primary because Nixon is insufficiently conservative.

1963 *Run River* is published on April 26. Reviews are brief and mixed, and sales are disappointing. Dunne grows increasingly dissatisfied at *Time*, where, by order of top editors—who support United States military efforts—he has been told to sanitize reports from Vietnam. In the fall, he and Didion become engaged.

1964 Marries Dunne on January 30 at the mission church at San Juan Bautista. Back in New York, begins to write a film column for *Vogue*, but feels overwhelmed by the city. Her anxiety becomes debilitating; as she describes the episode in her 1967 essay "Goodbye to All That," it is hard to leave the house. In April, decides with Dunne to leave New York for Los Angeles on a temporary basis—six or seven months. In June, they rent the Hardin Gatehouse, a four-bedroom home on two acres at 5500 Palos Verdes Drive South, on the Palos Verdes Peninsula in Portuguese Bend. Rent is $500 a month. Aided by Dunne's brother Dominick, a producer, they meet with television executives hoping to write scripts, and sell a story idea to the anthology series *Chrysler Theatre* for $1,000. *Vogue* cancels her film column; she writes short stories, publishing "Coming Home" in *The Saturday Evening Post* on July 11. With Dunne, proposes a film treatment of his project *Show Me a Hero* to agents at William Morris; attends screenings and reads screenplays. Supports Barry Goldwater in the 1964 presidential election, won in a landslide by Lyndon Baines Johnson.

1965 Travels to Mexico for *The Saturday Evening Post*, where John Wayne is working on *The Sons of Katie Elder*. The resulting piece, "John Wayne: A Love Story," offers a template to which she will return, framing her reporting through a personal, even autobiographical, lens. On August 11, Marquette Frye, a twenty-one-year-old African American man, is stopped in the South Los Angeles community of Watts by California Highway Patrol officer Lee Minikus. An altercation ensues, triggering the Watts Riots, which cause 34 deaths and more than 1,000 injuries before they end on August 16. "For days," Didion will write in her 1967 essay "Los Angeles Notebook," "one could drive the Harbor Freeway and see the city on fire, just as we had always known it would be in the end."

1966 Meets Blake Watson, a physician at St. John's Hospital in Santa Monica, who facilitates the private adoption of a baby girl, born on March 3. Didion and Dunne name her Quintana Roo, after the Mexican state on the Yucatan Peninsula. They bring the child home on March 6, cancelling a planned trip to Saigon for *The Saturday Evening Post* after realizing that they cannot take a baby to a war. On May 1, they are evicted from their house in Portuguese Bend and take up temporary residence at 155 Fifth Anita Drive in West Los Angeles, home of Sara Mankiewicz, widow of screenwriter

Herman J. Mankiewicz. Six days later, Didion publishes her most ambitious piece of early journalism, "Some Dreamers of the Golden Dream"—originally titled "How Can I Tell Them There's Nothing Left?" —in *The Saturday Evening Post.* In June, Quintana is christened in Brentwood, at St. Martin of Tours Catholic Church. The couple meets Henry Robbins, an editor at Farrar, Straus & Giroux, who will be influential in both of their careers. Leaving Quintana with her grandparents in Sacramento, they travel to the Central Valley town of Delano to report on César Chávez and the National Farm Workers' strike against grape growers for *The Saturday Evening Post.* In August, they visit Hawaii, the subject of Didion's "Letter from Paradise, 21° 19' N., 157° 52' W." Back in Los Angeles, they move into a crumbling mansion at 7406 Franklin Avenue in Hollywood, at a rent of $400 a month.

1967 On January 14, the Human Be-In takes place at the Polo Fields in San Francisco's Golden Gate Park; more than 20,000 people come to hear Timothy Leary, Allen Ginsberg, Gary Snyder, and bands including the Grateful Dead, Jefferson Airplane, and Big Brother and the Holding Company. The event is widely regarded as introducing the hippie movement to the national consciousness. Didion meets Paul Hawken, a Haight-Ashbury insider who offers her access to the community. She travels to the Bay Area in the spring and summer, staying in Berkeley. On June 3, she publishes her first of more than twenty "Points West" columns in *The Saturday Evening Post*, alternating with Dunne. On July 12, she signs a two-book deal with Henry Robbins for a nonfiction book about "the LSD life in California" and a novel called *Maria Talking* (later published as *Play It As It Lays*). The contract stipulates an advance of $6,000 per title. "Slouching Towards Bethlehem," gathering her impressions of Haight-Ashbury life, appears as the *Post*'s cover story on September 23. Decides she can't expand the essay and instead begins to gather and revise pieces for a collection of her previously published nonfiction.

1968 In the spring, visits California First Lady Nancy Reagan in Sacramento for *The Saturday Evening Post*; the resulting story, "Pretty Nancy," is the first of many she will write about the Reagans. On April 4, the Reverend Martin Luther King, Jr., is shot and killed in Memphis, Tennessee. *Slouching Towards Bethlehem* is published on May 10; Dan Wakefield in *The New York Times*, among many laudatory reviewers, calls it "a rich display of some of the best prose written today in this country." *Time* sends Julian Wasser to photograph Didion; the ensuing sessions, which feature her smoking, with her Corvette Stingray, become the first iconic images of her. On June 5, Senator Robert F. Kennedy is shot in the kitchen of the Ambassador Hotel on Wilshire Boulevard after winning the California Democratic presidential primary; he dies the following day. Didion checks herself into the outpatient psychiatric clinic at St. John's Hospital for vertigo, nausea, and extreme alienation; this, she will later write in "The White Album," "does not now seem to me an inappropriate response to the summer of 1968." In August, Richard M. Nixon is nominated as the Republican candidate for president at the party's convention in Miami Beach. Three weeks later, amidst a police riot against student protesters in Chicago, Vice President Hubert H. Humphrey is nominated by the Democrats. In November, Nixon wins the presidency. Didion, Dunne, and Dunne's brother Dominick acquire the rights to James Mills's 1966 novel *The Panic in Needle Park*, with the couple attached as screenwriters. Didion is named one of the *Los Angeles Times*'s Women of the Year.

1969 Publishes "The Revolution Game," her final piece in *The Saturday Evening Post*, on January 25; the magazine suspends publication in February. On August 9, while swimming in her sister-in-law's Beverly Hills pool, learns of the killings of actress Sharon Tate, hairdresser Jay Sebring, and three others at Tate's Benedict Canyon home. "There were twenty dead, no, twelve, ten, eighteen," she will write of the rumors that swirled through the community. "Black masses were imagined, and bad trips blamed." The next night, supermarket executive Leno LaBianca and his wife Rosemary are murdered in their house at 3301 Waverly Drive. The killers, who won't be arrested until December, are members of the Manson Family, a loose tribe of outcasts, led by a charismatic ex-convict named Charles Manson, who have hung around the countercultural fringes of the entertainment industry since 1968. On November 14, finishes a draft of her second novel, *Play It As It Lays.* She is offered a column by *Life* magazine. Her first piece, written from Hawaii (where she has gone with her family) and later collected in *The White Album* under the title "In the Islands," causes a stir for its revelation that she and Dunne are "on this island in the middle of the Pacific in lieu of filing for divorce."

1970 In January, preproduction begins on *The Panic in Needle Park,* with Dominick Dunne producing and Jerry Schatzberg directing, starring Al Pacino and Kitty Winn. *Play It As It Lays* is published on July 27 to rapturous reviews. It furthers Didion's investigation into fragmentation and narrative breakdown, operating as a series of vignettes separated by white space, like cinematic jump cuts, to tell the story of Maria Wyeth, an actress recovering from a breakdown as she unravels in late 1960s Los Angeles. That summer, she meets Linda Kasabian, a participant in the Tate-LaBianca murders who has chosen to cooperate with prosecuting attorneys in return for a promise of immunity. The *Los Angeles Times* reports in August that Didion is writing a book about her, but the project rapidly unravels. Accompanied by Dunne, spends a month traveling in the South to research a piece for *Life.* Although the article is never finished, the notes will be published in 2017 as part of *South and West.* In October, filming of *The Panic in Needle Park* begins, after six weeks of rehearsal, in Manhattan; shooting wraps on December 22.

1971–72 In January 1971, *Play It As It Lays* is nominated for a National Book Award. Moves with Dunne to 33428 Pacific Coast Highway in Malibu; they hire Harrison Ford, then a carpenter and contractor, to handle renovations. In May, *The Panic in Needle Park* premieres at Cannes. Reviews are mixed, but Kitty Winn is named Best Actress of the Festival. The film cements Didion and Dunne's place at the center of the Hollywood intelligentsia. They are offered projects: a remake of *Tender Is the Night,* a sequel to *The Graduate.* They ultimately settle on an adaptation of *Play It As It Lays,* directed by Frank Perry and produced by Dominick Dunne. It comes out October 19, 1972, starring Tuesday Weld as Maria; she is nominated for a Golden Globe. Didion is diagnosed with multiple sclerosis, the cause of her temporary blindness years before.

1973 In the spring, Henry Robbins is made editor-in-chief of Farrar, Straus & Giroux and offers Didion a $60,000 advance for her next essay collection. Not long afterward, he has a heart attack; he leaves FSG to become executive editor at Simon & Schuster. Didion wants him to remain her editor, offering to return the first half of her advance. Meets Robert Silvers, editor of *The New York Review of Books*, and writes her first piece for him ("Hollywood: Having Fun," published on March 22). During the summer, with Dunne, attends the Cartagena Film Festival in Colombia. From Cartagena, they travel to Bogotá, then back to Los Angeles, stopping to refuel in Panama. The trip inspires her essay "In Bogotá" and her novel *A Book of Common Prayer*, the first of many works on the subject of Latin America and its relationship to the United States. In the fall, begins working with Dunne on *Rainbow Road*, a screenplay loosely adapting *A Star Is Born* (1937/1954) for the rock era; they spend three weeks on the road with rock bands, including Led Zeppelin and Uriah Heep. Dunne envisions James Taylor and Carly Simon in the leading roles.

1974 In May, receives a $210,000 combined advance for her next novel (*A Book of Common Prayer*) and essay collection (*The White Album*), Henry Robbins at Simon & Schuster outbidding others in an auction arranged by her agent, Lois Wallace. In August, with Dunne, submits the third and final draft of *Rainbow Road*, in which Barbra Streisand has taken an interest; they withdraw from the project, receiving $125,000 and 10 percent of future grosses. Other writers will later revise their screenplay, which is retitled *A Star Is Born*.

1975–76 Spends a month at UC Berkeley in the spring of 1975 as a Regents' Lecturer, teaching a class and working on *A Book of Common Prayer*. On April 20, while she is at Berkeley, Saigon falls to the Viet Cong and the People's Army of Vietnam. Three weeks later, delivers a talk titled "Why I Write" to a standing-room-only crowd: "I write entirely to find out what I'm thinking, what I'm looking at, what I see and what it means. What I want and what I fear." On September 18, heiress turned Symbionese Liberation Army revolutionary Patricia Hearst is arrested in San Francisco; *Rolling Stone* editor Jann Wenner asks Didion to cover her trial. After briefly attending the trial, however, she backs away from Hearst as subject, writing about her only in a 1982 essay, "Girl of the Golden West." (She will later publish fourteen pages of her *Rolling Stone* notes in *South and West.*) On December 8, 1976, *A Star Is Born* comes out, to lackluster reviews.

1977–78 *A Book of Common Prayer*—Didion's third novel, set in the fictional Latin American country of Boca Grande —is published on March 1, 1977. She takes eleven-year-old Quintana with her on a national book tour. Dunne publishes his novel *True Confessions*, which becomes a New York Times best seller. They visit London in November; the following July, they move from Malibu to 202 Chadbourne Avenue in Brentwood Park, the family's last address in Los Angeles. Three months later, the Agoura fire jumps the Pacific Coast Highway and burns to within 125 feet of their former Malibu property.

1979–80 Didion's second essay collection, *The White Album*, is published on June 19, 1979; it gathers and extends the nonfiction she has published since *Slouching Towards Bethlehem*, and is widely and glowingly reviewed. ("Essentially," Jerzy Kozinski writes in the *Los Angeles Times*, "*The White Album* is about our American mythologies, both private and collective, and realities both private and collective. Joan Didion is once again our quintessential essayist.") On July 31, Henry Robbins dies of a heart attack on a platform of the Union Square subway station in Manhattan. He is fifty-one years old. In an October *Nation* article titled "Joan Didion: Only Disconnect," Barbara Grizzuti Harrison questions Didion's increasingly high reputation and mocks her style, describing her as "neurasthenic Cher." In June 1980, reviews V. S. Naipaul's recent work in *The New York Review of Books*, whose editor, Robert Silvers, encourages her to write more overtly about politics.

1981–83 With Dunne, works on a screen adaptation of his novel *True Confessions.* Directed by Ulu Grosbard and starring Robert De Niro and Robert Duvall, the film premieres at the Venice Film Festival in September 1981 to considerable acclaim. On June 15, 1982, the couple travels to El Salvador, where they spend just under two weeks; in mid-July, she sends her first report on the trip to *The New York Review of Books.* On October 30, Dominick Dunne's daughter Dominique is strangled by her boyfriend. She dies on November 4. The same day, *The New York Review of Books* publishes the first of three installments of *Salvador.* It is released in book form in March 1983.

1984 *Democracy*, Didion's fourth novel, is published by Simon & Schuster on April 1. A metafiction of sorts, the novel is narrated by a character named Joan Didion, who seems to be reporting on the narrative rather than creating it. Writing in *The New York Times*, Mary McCarthy praises the book's "technical mastery and on-target social observation" but criticizes its "knowingness" and "depthlessness."

1985–86 In November 1985, reads from her work at Bennington College in Vermont, where Quintana is a sophomore, and speaks at a PEN writers' conference in New York. Spends time in Miami the following spring, researching her next book.

1987–88 Publishes *Miami*, her fourth book of nonfiction, on October 1, 1987. The book connects the politics of the 1960s with those of the 1980s—the Kennedy assassination to the Iran-Contra scandal. Dunne learns he is "a candidate for a catastrophic cardiovascular event" and undergoes an angiogram and an angioplasty. He views this new lease on life as a chance to change things up and pushes for the couple to move to New York. In early 1988, they sell their house in Brentwood Park and buy an apartment at 30 East 71st Street in Manhattan. Didion begins to write the "Letter from Los Angeles" for *The New Yorker* and continues to write about politics for *The New York Review of Books.* (Many of these pieces will be collected in her third book of essays, *After Henry.*) During the summer of 1988, she covers the Jesse Jackson campaign and the Democratic Convention in Atlanta.

1989–91 On April 19, 1989, a twenty-eight-year-old woman named Trisha Meili is raped and beaten while jogging in Central Park, and five young men of color are arrested and charged. Didion's account, published in the January 17, 1991, issue of *The New York Review of Books* under the title "Sentimental Journeys," is a ruthless dissection of this constructed narrative. "It is precisely in this conflation of victim and city, this confusion of personal woe with public distress," she writes, "that the crime's 'story' would be found." On December 25, 1990, Dunne faints at Honolulu International Airport. Back in New York, he has open-heart surgery to insert a plastic valve. The couple continues to write scripts, beginning a project based on the life and death of anchorwoman Jessica Savitch. It will eventually be released as *Up Close & Personal*, with Robert Redford and Michelle Pfeiffer. In early 1991, tries to get out of her Simon & Schuster contract, but the company refuses to let her go. Later in the year, participates in a celebrity ad campaign for the Gap; is photographed by Annie Leibovitz with Quintana, wearing matching black turtlenecks. Donates her papers to the Bancroft Library at UC Berkeley.

1992–93 On May 1, 1992, third collection of essays, *After Henry*, is published. The title is an homage to Henry Robbins. The book gathers twelve pieces, including "Sentimental Journeys" and "Girl of the Golden West." Several pieces deal with presidential politics, signaling a new direction, one she will explore throughout the decade. Supports Jerry Brown for president, although she does not register to vote. In July, covers the Democratic National Convention at Madison Square Garden in New York. In December, Frank Reese Didion dies in Monterey at eighty-four. In March 1993, addresses the Charter Day ceremony at the University of California, Berkeley.

1994–98 In June 1994, O.J. Simpson is arrested for murdering his wife, Nicole, and Ronald Goldman after a slow-speed police chase. His trial, which extends into the following year, captivates the nation. Dunne covers it for *The New York Review of Books*. In March 1996, *Up Close & Personal* is released, the last script by Didion and Dunne to be produced. On August 27, Didion's fifth novel, *The Last Thing He Wanted*, is published. Registers to vote to support President Bill Clinton's reelection. In January 1997, Dominick Dunne's ex-wife Lenny dies at sixty-four. In 1998, reports on Clinton's impeachment for *The New York Review of Books*. In October, Quintana is contacted by her birth sister, and meets her biological family for the first time.

1999–2000 Contributes essays on religion in American political life to *The New York Review of Books*, and a profile of Martha Stewart to *The New Yorker*.

2001 On May 15, Eduene Jerrett Didion dies in California, two weeks before her ninety-first birthday. "The preceding afternoon," her daughter writes, "I had talked to her on the telephone from New York and she had hung up midsentence, a way of saying goodbye so characteristic of her . . . that it did not occur to me until morning, when my brother called, that in this one last instance she had been just too frail to keep the connection." On September 11, two hijacked airliners hit the World Trade Center towers in lower Manhattan, destroying them. Another strikes the Pentagon, and a fourth crashes in a field in Pennsylvania, after a passenger revolt. The same day, *Political Fictions*, Didion's fourth book of essays, is published. It collects her political writing from the previous decade and zeroes in on what has become a key theme: that public life is a matter of narrative rather than policy. This represents not just a degradation of the discourse but also another way that "we tell ourselves stories in order to live."

2002 On November 13, gives the Robert B. Silvers Lecture at the New York Public Library; published in *The New York Review of Books* the following January as "Fixed Opinions, or The Hinge of History" and in book form in May as *Fixed Ideas: America Since 9.11*, it argues that the Bush administration has used the events of 9/11 "to stake new ground in old domestic wars."

2003 In June, Dunne has a pacemaker installed, but his health continues to fail. On July 26, Quintana marries Gerry Michael, a Manhattan bartender, in a ceremony at New York's Cathedral of Saint John the Divine. On September 23, publishes *Where I Was From*, her long-anticipated California book, in which she takes apart the myths—the narratives—on which she was raised. "Actually," she will later tell an interviewer, "I started that book several years before my mother and father died. I was unable to get very far with it. Once my mother and father died, I immediately picked it up again after twenty years, and I realized that it had been impossible to write while my mother and father were alive because I didn't want to present a version of California that they would not recognize." On Christmas Day, Quintana is taken to Beth Israel North Hospital in Manhattan. She is admitted to the ICU and diagnosed with pneumonia in both lungs and septic shock. She is put in an induced coma. On December 30, after visiting her at the hospital, Dunne suffers a heart attack and dies. "*Life changes fast*," his wife will write. "*. . . Life changes in the instant. . . . You sit down to dinner and life as you know it ends.*" He is seventy-one.

2004 On January 22, Quintana is released from the hospital. Three days later, she is admitted to Columbia-Presbyterian Hospital in Manhattan with pulmonary embolisms. On March 23, a memorial service for Dunne is held at the Cathedral of Saint John the Divine. Speakers include his wife, daughter, and brother, as well as Calvin Trillin and Susanna Moore. On March 25, Quintana collapses at Los Angeles International Airport and undergoes emergency neurosurgery at UCLA Medical Center in Westwood. Didion flies to California, staying at the Beverly Wilshire Hotel. On April 30, Quintana is transferred to the Rusk Institute at New York University Hospital. She remains there until July. In October, Didion begins to write *The Year of Magical Thinking*, a memoir of her season of grief. She finishes the manuscript at the end of the year.

2005 Writes on "The Case of Teresa Schiavo" for *The New York Review of Books* of June 9. On August 26, Quintana dies of acute pancreatitis at New York–Presbyterian/ Weill Cornell Medical Center. On October 11, *The Year of Magical Thinking* is published, and, despite her loss, Didion embarks on a national tour. Following *Where I Was From*, the book cements a new role for her as memoirist, excavating personal narratives as well as public ones. It sells more than 200,000 copies in hardcover, the biggest numbers of her career. In

October, producer Scott Rudin approaches her about developing the memoir as a play. On November 16, *The Year of Magical Thinking* receives the National Book Award for nonfiction.

2006–7 In January, Didion agrees to the stage adaptation of *The Year of Magical Thinking*, and meets with Rudin and director David Hare. In the spring, Vanessa Redgrave agrees to portray Didion. In the fall, writes a lengthy takedown of Dick Cheney; it appears as the cover story of *The New York Review of Books* on October 5. On March 29, 2007, *The Year of Magical Thinking* premieres at the Booth Theatre on Broadway for a limited run of 144 performances. The play—a one-woman show—diverges from, and expands upon, the book by engaging with Quintana in more detail, functioning as a bridge between the memoir and *Blue Nights*. In an interview, Didion calls the process one of "maintaining movement. And also maintaining a version of things that I could live with. That was very strong with the play. Because as I said in *Blue Nights*, watching that play on 45th Street at night was one moment during the day when Quintana did not necessarily die." In November, she is honored for Distinguished Service to American Letters at the National Book Awards.

2008–10 Reads from her work at Dartmouth College in October 2008 and meets with students. The next year, on August 26, Dominick Dunne dies of bladder cancer at the age of eighty-three.

2011 In the spring, receives an honorary Doctor of Letters from Yale University. On November 4, her memoir *Blue Nights* is published; the book addresses her own aging, as well as her daughter's life and death. "I hadn't dealt with Quintana," she will tell an interviewer. "I had dealt with her to some extent in the play, but the play had, from my point of view, a whole other way of preserving myself, at a distance. Yet, part of the point is that you never work it out."

2012–16 Cancels a planned trip to California after fracturing a kneecap, but is able to travel to Hartford on June 28, 2012, to speak at the Mark Twain House and Museum. On July 3, 2013, is awarded the National Humanities Medal at the White House, by President Barack

Obama. In January 2015 appears in an advertising campaign for the designer Céline, wearing a black pullover and oversized dark glasses.

2017 On March 7, publishes *South and West*, a book of nonfiction gathering material from two early, unfinished pieces: her journey through the South in 1970 and her notes on Patty Hearst for *Rolling Stone*. The book occasions a number of wide-ranging career retrospectives. On October 11, Netflix releases the documentary *Joan Didion: The Center Will Not Hold*, directed by her nephew, Griffin Dunne, the son of Dominick and Lenny.

2018–19 An adaptation of her novel *The Last Thing He Wanted* begins filming in June 2018. Directed by Dee Rees and starring Anne Hathaway and Ben Affleck, it is scheduled for release the following fall.

2021 In January, *Let Me Tell You What I Mean*, a collection of twelve pieces written from 1968 to 2000, is published by Knopf with a foreword by *New Yorker* writer Hilton Als. On December 23, dies of complications from Parkinson's disease at her home in Manhattan. Her remains are interred at the Cathedral Church of Saint John the Divine in New York City, along with those of her husband, John Gregory Dunne, and daughter, Quintana Roo Dunne Michael.

Note on the Texts

This volume gathers all of Joan Didion's books published from 2001 to 2017: *Political Fictions* (2001), *Fixed Ideas: America Since 9.11* (2003), *Where I Was From* (2003), *The Year of Magical Thinking* (2005), *The Year of Magical Thinking: The Play* (2007), *Blue Nights* (2011), and *South and West: From a Notebook* (2017). Most of these works have appeared in new printings and some of them in new editions since their original publication, both in the United States and elsewhere, but Didion is not known to have corrected or revised them, and the texts included here have been taken from first printings.

Political Fictions collects Didion's writings on American politics for *The New York Review of Books*, from 1988 to 2000. Robert Silvers of the *Review* wondered early in 1988 if she might want to report on the upcoming presidential race; not having been asked before to cover what she called "a 'serious' story," she was flattered and agreed. While all of the book originally appeared in the magazine—the dates of first publication appearing under each section title—Didion revised several of her magazine titles and at some points revised her original texts. "The West Wing of Oz" appeared in the *Review* in three parts, as "Shooters, Inc.," "'Something Horrible' in El Salvador," and "The Lion King"; "Eyes on the Prize" appeared as "Eye on the Prize"; "Newt Gingrich, Speaker" as "The Teachings of Speaker Gingrich"; "Political Pornography" as "The Deferential Spirit"; and "Vichy Washington" as "Uncovered Washington." Didion had earlier included two of her *Review* political pieces, "Insider Baseball" and "Shooters, Inc.," in her collection *After Henry*, published by Simon & Schuster in 1992.

Political Fictions was published by Alfred A. Knopf in New York on September 11, 2001. In the wake of the 9/11 terrorist attacks, its de facto release date was delayed to September 18. Didion did not revise her work for a Vintage paperback printing that appeared the following year, or on later occasions, as when the essay "Clinton Agonistes" appeared in *Vintage Didion*, a selection of her writings published by Vintage Books in 2004, or when the entirety of *Political Fictions* was included in the nonfiction omnibus *We Tell Ourselves Stories in Order to Live*, published by Knopf in 2006. The text of *Political Fictions* in the present volume is that of the Knopf first printing of September 2001; in two instances, on pages 142 and 190 herein, errors in the given dates of original publication have been corrected.

Fixed Ideas: America Since 9.11. Didion first presented "Fixed Ideas" as the inaugural Robert B. Silvers lecture at the New York Public Library, on November 13, 2002. It appeared in magazine and then in book form shortly thereafter: in *The New York Review of Books* on January 16, 2003 (as "Fixed Opinions, or The Hinge of History"), and under the New York Review Books imprint on April 1 of the same year, retitled *Fixed Ideas: America Since 9.11* and bearing a new preface by Frank Rich but otherwise in identical form. The lecture has since been published only once, in *Vintage Didion* in 2004, where it bears the magazine title "Fixed Opinions"; Didion's preferred title is uncertain, but she is more likely to have decided on one when her lecture was first published as a book. The text of *Fixed Ideas* in the present volume is that of the New York Review Books first printing of April 2003.

Where I Was From. By her own later account, *Where I Was From* began as an outgrowth of Didion's attempt to write about the trial of Patty Hearst in 1976. Her report on Hearst, commissioned by *Rolling Stone* editor Jann Wenner, was never finished; but the trial "pushed me into examining my thoughts about California," a subject to which she continued to return.

Didion published two California-themed pieces in 1993. "Trouble in Lakewood," which appeared in *The New Yorker* on July 26 of that year, was revised and expanded in *Where I Was From* and printed without a separate title. The same is true of "Golden Land," published in *The New York Review of Books* on October 21. None of the remainder of *Where I Was From* is known to have appeared in print before it was published in book form, by Alfred A. Knopf on September 23, 2003. The book has subsequently appeared in numerous printings, and it was included in its entirety in *We Tell Ourselves Stories in Order to Live* in 2006, without evidence of authorial revision. The text of *Where I Was From* in the present volume is that of the Knopf first printing of September 2003.

The Year of Magical Thinking. Didion's husband John Gregory Dunne died on December 30, 2003. The following fall she began *The Year of Magical Thinking*, a memoir of her grief. The book "just flew out," as she later put it, and was finished in eighty-eight days: "It was like sitting down and crying. I didn't even have the sense that I was writing it. I'm usually very conscious of the rhythm of sentences and how that's working. I didn't even give that any thought." Published by Alfred A. Knopf on October 24, 2005, the book has appeared in multiple printings in the United States, the United Kingdom, and elsewhere, but Didion made no subsequent alterations. The text of

The Year of Magical Thinking in the present volume is that of the Knopf first printing of October 2005.

The Year of Magical Thinking: The Play. The idea to adapt *The Year of Magical Thinking* for the stage was producer Scott Rudin's rather than Didion's. He approached her about the possibility around October 2005, when her memoir was published. She declined at first but changed her mind within a few weeks, deciding that "maybe it was time to do something totally new" and that "it might be interesting to do a play." She met with Rudin and with director David Hare several times beginning around January 2006, and by March or April of that year they began workshop readings from Didion's initial script in a New York theater. Around December, having cast Vanessa Redgrave as Joan Didion and working with her in London, Hare and Didion cut their script by about a third.

The Year of Magical Thinking: The Play opened at the Booth Theatre in New York on March 29, 2007, after 23 previews, and ultimately ran for 144 performances through August 25. Redgrave later reprised her role at the National Theatre in London. The text of the play was published by Vintage Books on May 15, 2007, and then in 2008 in London, by HarperCollins, with an added introduction by Hare. The text of *The Year of Magical Thinking: The Play* in the present volume is that of the Vintage first printing of May 2007.

Blue Nights. Didion began *Blue Nights* after her work on the stage adaptation of *The Year of Magical Thinking* was done, deciding vaguely that she "wanted to write about children, attitudes towards having children," and then returning to the subject of her own child Quintana, who died just before *The Year of Magical Thinking* appeared in print. Early on, the evocative phrase "blue nights" was useful to her as a starting point; the book in some sense "unfolded from the title," she later told Hari Kunzru. It was also unusually difficult for her to complete: at one point she imagined she would have to return her advance to her publisher but was convinced by her agent Lynn Nesbit to set her work aside rather than abandon it, so she then "pushed on." *Blue Nights* was eventually published by Alfred A. Knopf on November 21, 2011. No subsequent printing of the book is known to have been altered by the author. The text of *Blue Nights* in the present volume is that of the November 2011 Knopf first printing.

South and West: From a Notebook gathers two extended excerpts from Didion's notebooks of the 1970s, after a foreword by Nathaniel Rich. "Notes on the South" documents a trip she made through Louisiana, Mississippi, and Alabama in June 1970. She hoped these notes might form the beginning of an essay or book, but she did not pursue the project or attempt to publish what she had written. In similar fashion, she wrote her "California Notes" as part of an abortive effort to report on the trial of Patty Hearst, in 1976. She published "California Notes" on its own only much later, in the May 26, 2016, issue of the *New York Review of Books*, where it is introduced by two brief paragraphs dated March 23, 2016. Other than some differences in paragraphing, italicization, and capitalization, and the omission of this "March 23, 2016" date, the text of "California Notes" is identical in *South and West*, first published by Alfred A. Knopf on March 7, 2017. Didion is not known to have sought to correct or revise her work in subsequent printings of *South and West*. The text of *South and West: From a Notebook* in the present volume is that of the March 2017 Knopf first printing.

This volume presents the texts of the original printings chosen for inclusion here, but it does not attempt to reproduce features of their design and layout. The texts are presented without change, except for the correction of typographical errors and of two dates, as noted above. Spelling, punctuation, and capitalization are often expressive features and they are not altered, even when inconsistent or irregular. The following is a list of errors corrected, cited by page and line number: 69.12, Vaclev; 85.1, Mosley; 111.5–6, Gingrich,; 142.2, September 22; 176.24, millenialistic; 190.2, October 5; 214.29, headline; 287.5, woman; 379.12, Good Will; 598.2–3, 26 2003; 629.20, time. Those; 668.27, December 5 1934; 679.28 (and *passim*), *Colin*.

Notes

In the notes below, the reference numbers denote page and line of this volume (the line count includes chapter headings but not blank lines). Quotations from Shakespeare are keyed to *The Riverside Shakespeare*, ed. G. Blakemore Evans (Boston: Houghton Mifflin, 1974), and biblical quotations to the King James Version. For further information about Didion's life and works, and references to other studies, see Tracy Daugherty, *The Last Love Song: A Biography of Joan Didion* (New York: St. Martin's Press, 2015); Sharon Felton, ed., *The Critical Response to Joan Didion* (Westport, Conn.: Greenwood Publishing, 1993); Ellen G. Friedman, ed., *Joan Didion: Essays & Conversations* (Princeton, NJ: Ontario Review Press, 1984); Scott F. Parker, ed., *Conversations with Joan Didion* (Jackson: University Press of Mississippi, 2018); Mark Royden Winchell, *Joan Didion* (Boston: Twayne, 1980); Kathleen M. Vandenberg, *Joan Didion: Substance and Style* (Albany: SUNY Press, 2021).

POLITICAL FICTIONS

6.18 Malcolm Forbes's] Forbes (1919–1990) was the wealthy publisher of *Forbes*, a business magazine.

13.22–23 Richard Hofstadter . . . American politics] Hofstadter's essay "The Paranoid Style in American Politics" was first published in *Harper's* in November 1964 and collected in *The Paranoid Style in American Politics, and Other Essays* in 1965.

15.25 Tom Hayden] Hayden (1939–2016), an antiwar and civil rights activist, was a California state assemblyman from 1982 to 1992 and later served in the California senate.

21.2 "the best and the brightest"] See *The Best and the Brightest* (1972) by David Halberstam (1934–2007), an account of the failed Vietnam policies of Kennedy administration experts.

21.28 Michael Deaver] Deaver (1938–2007) served as deputy chief of staff at the White House during Ronald Reagan's first term, with responsibility for Reagan's schedule, and played a similar role during his 1976 and 1980 presidential campaigns.

22.4 David Frost] Frost (1939–2013), a British television journalist, was known for his interviews with major public figures.

22.33 Baker] James Baker III (b. 1930), who served as chairman of George H. W. Bush's 1988 presidential campaign and later as secretary of state and White House chief of staff.

23.30 Happy Warrior-ish] Ultimately drawn from William Wordsworth's poem "Character of the Happy Warrior" (1807), the phrase has been applied to American politicians including Alfred E. Smith (1873–1944), the 1928 Democratic presidential nominee, and Hubert Humphrey (1911–1978), vice president from 1965 to 1969 and the 1968 Democratic presidential nominee.

27.26–27 "Coming to America,"] A popular song by Neil Diamond (b. 1941) from his 1980 album *The Jazz Singer*, used as a theme song by the 1988 Dukakis presidential campaign.

27.34–35 pioneered by Theodore H. White] See White's *The Making of the President 1960* (1961) and its sequels covering the elections of 1964, 1968, and 1972.

33.14–17 Tom Brokaw . . . Mary Alice Williams] Brokaw (b. 1940), Chancellor (1927–1996), and Williams (b. 1949) were television news journalists.

35.10 Robert Flaherty] Flaherty (1884–1951) produced and directed the pioneering documentary *Nanook of the North* (1922).

35.12 Piri Thomas . . . 1961] Thomas (1928–2011), later acclaimed as the author of *Down These Mean Streets* (1967), was a community organizer working to combat gang violence in 1961.

36.14 Robert S. Strauss] Strauss (1918–2014), a former chairman of the Democratic National Committee, was reported to have made this remark in a March 28, 1988, *New York Times* article by R. W. Apple Jr., "Jackson Triumph Changes Outlook of Top Democrats."

36.35–39 "How moving it is . . . column] See "The Jackson Reality," *New York Times*, March 31, 1988.

46.1 Tom Enders] Enders (1931–1996) served as assistant secretary of state for inter-American affairs from June 1981 to June 1983. In testimony before a Senate committee in 1992, he denied that a massacre of civilians at El Mozote had taken place.

52.28 Congressman Bonker] Don Bonker (1937–2023), a Washington Democratic congressman from 1975 to 1989.

53.15 *REFTEL*] Reference telegram.

58.9 José Napoleón Duarte] Duarte (1925–1990) was president of El Salvador from 1984 to 1989.

62.24–25 Robert Service's . . . McGee."] Service (1874–1958) published "The Cremation of Sam McGee," a popular recitation piece about the remains of a Yukon prospector, in *Songs of a Sourdough* (1907).

64.38–65.1 to be young . . . very heaven.] See William Wordsworth's posthumously published *Prelude* (1850), book XI.

66.15–18 During a transition . . . no notes.] As recounted in an April 1997 interview with White House staff secretary Richard Darman quoted in Douglas Brinkley's *The Unfinished Presidency: Jimmy Carter's Journey Beyond the White House* (1999).

69.12–13 Václav Havel . . . history.'] From "A Word About Words," Havel's speech in acceptance of the Peace Prize of the German Booksellers' Association, delivered in his absence on October 15, 1989.

74.28 ADR] Additional dialogue replacement, in which an actor's lines are recorded over.

76.26–29 "Elliott . . . Whittlesey"] Conservative activists, writers, and public officials. Abrams (b. 1948) was an assistant secretary of state in the Reagan administration, from 1981 to 1989; George Gilder (b. 1939) the author of *Wealth and Poverty* (1981), an explanation of supply-side economics; Josh Gilder (b. 1954) a speechwriter for President Reagan; Ledeen (b. 1941) a historian and foreign policy analyst, the author of *Perilous Statecraft: An Insider's Account of the Iran-Contra Affair* (1988) and other books; Joshua Muravchik (b. 1947) a foreign policy analyst, the author of *Exporting Democracy: Fulfilling America's Destiny* (1991) and *The Imperative of American Leadership: A Challenge to Neo-Isolationism* (1996); Norquist (b. 1956) a supporter of anti-Soviet guerrilla forces and the founder, in 1985, of Americans for Tax Reform; Reilly (b. 1946) a commentator on foreign policy and special assistant to President Reagan from 1983 to 1985; Sobran (1946–2010) a writer for *The National Review*; and Whittlesey (1939–2018) director of the White House office of public liaison from 1983 to 1985 and an ambassador to Switzerland.

79.18 Shultz] George Shultz (1920–2021), secretary of state from July 1982 to January 1989.

81.1–2 Third Way . . . Peruvian] General Juan Velasco Alvarado (1910–1977), president of Peru from 1968 to 1975, attempted to steer a middle course or "third way," neither capitalist nor communist, in economic and international policy.

83.22–23 Ron Brown . . . so to speak."] Brown (1941–1996), who became head of the Democratic National Committee in 1989, made these remarks at a regional meeting of the DNC in April 1992.

85.3–4 Kathleen Brown . . . Schroeder] Brown (b. 1945) was treasurer of California from 1991 to 1995, during which time she ran unsuccessfully for the California governorship; Roberts (b. 1936) was governor of Oregon and Kelly (b. 1944) the mayor of the District of Columbia during the same years. Schroeder (1940–2023) served in the House from 1973 to 1997 as a Colorado Democrat, and ran for president in 1988.

85.35 Pamela Harriman's] Harriman (1920–1997), a wealthy supporter of the Democratic Party, hosted dinners with power brokers in her Georgetown home; in 1993, President Clinton appointed her as U.S. ambassador to France, a position in which she served until her death.

86.5 Elaine's] An Upper East Side restaurant noted for its clientele of writers and actors. It opened in 1963 and closed soon after the death of its proprietor, Elaine Kaufman (1929–2010).

90.6 CINC] Commander-in-chief.

92.31 Willie Horton] Horton (b. 1951), in prison in Massachusetts for a 1974 murder, was released on weekend furlough in 1986 as part of a state rehabilitation program and did not return, subsequently committing violent crimes in Maryland. George H. W. Bush pointed to his case repeatedly, in speeches and advertisements, during his 1988 presidential campaign against Michael Dukakis, who was governor of Massachusetts at the time.

94.15 Eleanor Clift] A journalist and pundit, Clift (b. 1940) reported on presidential campaigns for *Newsweek*.

117.16 Bill Emerson] Emerson (1938–1996), a Missouri Republican, served in the House from 1981 to 1996.

118.13 Gordon Wood] Gingrich publicly praised Wood's Pulitzer Prize–winning history, *The Radicalism of the American Revolution* (1992).

120.38–121.2 Fred Barnes . . . American civilization."] See Barnes's "Rebel with a Cause," *Daily News* (New York), January 22, 1995.

122.28–29 His Democratic opponent in 1994] Gingrich defeated Ben L. Jones (b. 1941), a congressman whose seat was lost to redistricting and a former actor on the TV comedy *The Dukes of Hazzard* (1979–85).

123.6 Alvin Toffler] Toffler (1928–2016) was a noted futurist, the author of *Future Shock* (1970), *The Third Wave* (1980), and *Powershift* (1990), among other books.

124.31 Tom Swift . . . Jules Verne] Swift is the title character of several series of juvenile adventure and science fiction novels, the first of which began with *Tom Swift and His Motor Cycle* in 1910; conceived by publisher Edward Stratemeyer (1862–1932), the novels were written by various hands and published under a variety of pseudonyms. Verne (1828–1905), a French writer in a number of genres, is most often remembered for his speculative fiction, including the novels *Journey to the Center of the Earth* (1864) and *Twenty Thousand Leagues Under the Sea* (1870).

128.8 an Erewhon] A utopia described in the satirical novel *Erewhon: or, Over the Range* (1872) by Samuel Butler (1835–1902).

128.11 Whitewater] Popular name for controversies in the 1990s surrounding the Clintons' investments in the Whitewater Development Corporation, a failed Arkansas real estate venture.

139.18–19 the crash of the Hasenfus plane] On October 5, 1986, Eugene Hasenfus (b. 1941) survived the crash of a cargo plane shot down over Nicaragua. In the wake of his subsequent capture by Sandinista authorities, the role of the Reagan administration in the illegal supply of weapons to the Nicaraguan opposition was revealed.

139.30 the Tower Commission] A presidential commission, chaired by Texas senator John Tower, charged with investigating the Iran-Contra affair; its report was published on February 27, 1987.

141.9 Rosebud moments] "Rosebud" is the revelatory dying word of Charles Kane, the protagonist of Orson Welles's movie *Citizen Kane* (1941).

145.18 Paula Jones . . . John Huang] Jones (b. 1966) sued President Clinton for sexual harassment in 1994 and in 1998 received an $850,000 settlement. Huang (b. 1945), a leading fundraiser for the Democratic National Committee, pled guilty to a conspiracy charge for his role in accepting illegal campaign contributions from an Indonesian conglomerate.

146.1–6 "offered and assessment . . . strategists."] See Gwen Ifill, "Clinton Delivers a Mainstream Message with a Southern Accent," *New York Times*, December 27, 1991.

147.30 Vernon Jordan] Jordan (1935–2021), a lawyer and civil rights leader, was a friend and advisor to President Clinton and served on his transition team.

152.26 Ron Perelman] Perelman (b. 1943), an investor and businessman, offered Lewinsky a job at Revlon Corporation, which he acquired in 1985, at Jordan's suggestion.

154.10 *Kinder-Kirche*] From the nineteenth-century German phrase *Kinder, Küche, Kirche* (Children, Kitchen, Church), supposed to delimit women's appropriate social roles.

159.9–11 an Ahab . . . highest truth"] See Melville's 1851 novel, *Moby-Dick; or The Whale*.

160.14–15 *George* magazine] A monthly magazine covering politics and popular culture, cofounded by John F. Kennedy Jr. in 1995; it ceased publication in 2001.

162.12 Vincent Foster's] Foster (1945–1993) committed suicide six months into his tenure as deputy White House counsel in the Clinton administration; the circumstances of his death became the subject of several conspiracy theories.

164.11 Richard Mellon Scaife] Scaife (1932–2014), a billionaire heir and owner of the Pittsburgh *Tribune-Review*, was a major contributor to conservative political groups.

164.23–24 Bob Barr] Barr (b. 1948), a Republican congressman from Georgia from 1995 to 2003, served as a House manager of the 1999 impeachment trial of President Clinton.

164.29–30 Rudyard Kipling's "If."] Kipling's poem, first collected in *Rewards and Fairies* (1910), describes skills and experiences that will qualify the speaker's son to "be a Man."

164.35–165.8 The words of Henry V . . . Sensenbrenner."] Novak (1933–2017), the author of *The Spirit of Democratic Capitalism* (1982), and Hyde (1924–2007), a Republican congressman from 1975 until his death, adapted Shakespeare's *Henry V*, IV.iii.41–45. James E. Rogan (b. 1957), Asa Hutchinson (b. 1950), Charles Canaday (b. 1954), Chris Cannon (b. 1950), Bill McCollum (b. 1944), Lindsey Graham (b. 1955), George Gekas (1930–2021), Steve Chabot (b. 1953), Ed Bryant (b. 1948), Steve Buyer (b. 1958), Bob Barr (b. 1948), and Jim Sensenbrenner (b. 1943) served as House managers for the impeachment trial of President Clinton.

165.14 Sean Wilentz] Wilentz (b. 1951), a historian, testified before the House judiciary committee in December 1998 against President Clinton's impeachment.

165.24–25 Maxine Waters . . . Barney Frank] Waters (b. 1938), who is Black, has been a California Democratic congresswoman since 1991. Frank (b. 1940), who came out as gay in 1987, was a Democratic congressman from Massachusetts from 1981 to 2013.

165.35–36 Dan Oliver] Oliver (b. 1939), a former executive editor at the *National Review*, served under Presidents Reagan and Bush as general counsel of the Department of Education (1981–83), general counsel of the Department of Agriculture (1983–86), and chairman of the Federal Trade Commission (1986–90).

168.35 Troopergate] The political controversy surrounding allegations, first published in an article by David Brock ("His Cheatin' Heart," *American Spectator*, December 1993), that Bill Clinton, as Arkansas governor, had used state troopers on duty to help arrange his adulterous sexual liaisons.

169.32 Kathleen Willey] In March 1998, Willey (b. 1946) alleged that she was sexually assaulted by President Clinton while working as a White House volunteer in 1993.

174.30 Travelgate] Popular name for the controversy surrounding the firing, in May 1993, of seven staffers at the White House travel office. The Clinton administration attributed these dismissals to alleged mismanagement and fraud in previous administrations; its critics noted that the positions were given to political allies, who stood to profit from them.

180.36–39 Kenneth Starr . . . career prosecutors."] Starr was quoted in the August 1998 inaugural issue of *Brill's Content*, founded by Steven Brill (b. 1950).

181.15 Fawn Hall] Hall (b. 1959), who was Oliver North's secretary during the Iran-Contra affair, received immunity from prosecution in exchange for her testimony against him.

182.3 Dolly Kyle Browning, Juanita Broaddrick] Deposed in 1998 as part of Paula Jones's sexual harassment case against President Clinton, Browning (b. 1946) claimed to have had a long-standing sexual relationship with Clinton. On the same occasion, Broaddrick (b. 1942) denied rumors that Clinton had sexually assaulted her in 1978, but later recanted her denial.

184.8 Filegate] Popular name for the controversy surrounding the receipt, by the White House Office of Personnel Security, of FBI background reports on officials from previous administrations; it was alleged that these files were improperly obtained for political purposes.

188.11 Peck's Bad Boy] The mischievous title character, Henry "Hennery" Peck, of a series of novels by George Wilbur Peck (1840–1916) beginning with *Peck's Bad Boy and His Pa* (1883) and concluding with *Peck's Bad Boy in an Airship* (1908). These novels were adapted into a number of movies, including *The Bad Boy and the Groceryman* (1905), *Peck's Bad Boy* (1908, 1921, 1934), and *Peck's Bad Boy with the Circus* (1938).

192.17–20 Alcoholics Anonymous . . . we have."] See "Religion and Public Life," *Brookings Review*, Spring 1999.

192.35 Daniel Ellsberg] Ellsberg (1931–2023), a military analyst, was charged with espionage and theft for his role in the 1971 publication of the Pentagon Papers, a secret report on U.S. policy in Vietnam, but charges against him were dismissed in 1973, in part because members of the Nixon administration and their agents committed numerous crimes in order to discredit and gather evidence against him.

197.2 *Cassie Bernall*] Bernall (1981–1999), killed in a school shooting at Columbine High School in Columbine, Colorado, was reported to have affirmed her belief in God immediately prior to her death, and was hailed in evangelical circles as a Christian martyr.

197.5 *Armey*] Dick Armey (b. 1940), a Republican congressman from Texas beginning in 1985 and, from 1995 to 2003, House majority leader.

197.32 Whittaker Chambers's *Witness*] Chambers's autobiography *Witness* (1952) recounts his transformation over the course of the 1920s, 1930s, and 1940s from Communist Party member and spy for the Soviet Union to outspoken anticommunist.

199.28 Patricia Bozell] Bozell (1927–2008) cofounded the Catholic journal *Triumph* in 1966 and in 1982 began working as a freelance editor at Regnery Publishing.

213.24 Lynne Cheney] Cheney (b. 1941) served as chairman of the National Endowment for the Humanities from 1986 to 1993 and in 2001 became U.S. second lady.

215.19 ABRAHAM H. FOXMAN] Foxman (b. 1940), a lawyer, was director of the Anti-Defamation League from 1987 to 2015.

218.28 the Scopes trial] 1925 legal case, prosecuted amid national publicity and debate, in which the state of Tennessee charged high school teacher John T. Scopes (1900–1970) with violating a prohibition against the teaching of evolution in the public schools.

FIXED IDEAS

225.21 an essay about New York . . . 1967] See "Goodbye to All That," collected in *Slouching Towards Bethlehem* (1968).

228.15–22 "It seemed bizarre . . . country's resolve."] See Fish's "Condemnation Without Absolutes," *New York Times*, October 15, 2001.

228.38–229.11 Christopher Hitchens . . . a fifth column."] Hitchens (1949–2011), Kagan (1932–2021), and Sullivan (b. 1963) are quoted in Richard Bernstein, "Counterpoint to Unity: Dissent," *New York Times*, October 6, 2003.

241.30–31 meeting in Prague . . . Mohamed Atta] Atta (1968–2001), an Egyptian terrorist who piloted one of the planes involved in the September 11, 2001, attack on the United States, was alleged shortly thereafter to have met with an Iraqi intelligence agent in Prague prior to the attack. These allegations were repeated by Bush administration officials, including Vice President Cheney, as they made their case for invading Iraq, but have since been retracted and discounted.

WHERE I WAS FROM

252.30 Shreve's] Shreve & Co., a San Francisco jeweler established in 1852.

253.7 the false armistice] On November 7, 1918, four days before the real armistice that ended World War I, a mistaken report that an armistice had been signed was circulated and celebrated around the world.

253.19 Grange picnic] The Grange, founded in 1867, is a national community organization; its local chapters, often in rural areas, host potluck suppers and agricultural fairs.

258.17–18 the co-author of *Mutiny on the Bounty*] Charles Nordhoff (1887–1947) and James Norman Hall (1887–1951) published their novel *Mutiny on the Bounty* in 1932.

265.19 hegira] Exodus or arduous journey.

273.18–19 a Millet painting] First exhibited in 1863, *Man with a Hoe* by Jean-François Millet (1814–1875) is now in the Getty Museum in Los Angeles.

281.2 *chapaderos*] Chaps or *chaparajos*, leather belt–and–leggings worn by cowboys.

287.36–37 *for a thousand . . . yesterday*] Psalms 90:4.

287.39–288.2 Kevin Starr . . . heroic imperatives."] See *Americans and the California Dream, 1850–1915* (1973).

288.2–4 Thomas Starr King . . . the soul."] See King's "Selections from a Lecture-Sermon after Visiting Yosemite Valley," presented in San Francisco on July 29, 1860, and collected in *The California Scrap-book* (1869), compiled by Oscar T. Shuck.

288.7–11 "Some of Mr. Bierstadt's . . . remain there."] See "Letter from 'Mark Twain,'" *Alta California*, August 4, 1867.

288.16–19 John C. Frémont . . . golden horn)."] From Frémont's *Geographical Memoir upon Upper California* (1848).

289.3–4 *Beautiful country . . . Sur Rivers.*] See Jeffers's "Apology for Bad Dreams," first published in the May 1926 *New Masses.*

289.9–17 Muir . . . a few centuries."] See chapter two ("In Camp on the North Fork of the Merced") of Muir's *My First Summer in the Sierra* (1911).

289.17–23 Jeffers . . . ought to be stopped."] See the final line of Jeffers's poem "Orca," first published in *Poetry* in October 1947.

289.29–32 Jeffers . . . *the mountains.*] See Jeffers's poems "Apology for Bad Dreams" and "Shine, Perishing Republic," the latter collected in *Roan Stallion, Tamar, and Other Poems* (1925).

300.5 the bulldog] The early edition of a daily newspaper.

300.13 Joseph LeConte] LeConte (1823–1901) was the first professor of natural history at the University of California and a cofounder in 1892 of the Sierra Club.

302.11 Frank Borman] Borman (1928–2023) commanded the December 1968 Apollo 8 mission to orbit the moon and was later an airline executive.

302.21–27 the traditional tableaux . . . *happy heart!*] See George Sterling's *The Triumph of Bohemia: A Forest Play*, first performed at Bohemian Grove on July 29, 1907.

314.20 a May Company] A Southern California department store chain, established with the acquisition of A. Hamburger & Sons in 1923 and ultimately absorbed by Macy's in 2005.

314.39 Cimarron] Title of two Western movies, the first made in 1931 and the second in 1960, and of the 1930 novel by Edna Ferber (1885–1968) on which they were based. All depict the Oklahoma land rush of 1889.

316.31 the 1992 Rodney King verdicts] On April 29, 1992, a jury acquitted four white Los Angeles police officers of charges of excessive force after their videotaped beating of Black motorist Rodney King (1965–2012) on March 3 of the previous year. The Los Angeles riots, in which sixty-three people were killed, followed in the wake of these verdicts.

324.2–3 Tailhook, Packwood, Anita Hill] The Tailhook scandal involved allegations that U.S. Navy and Marine Corps aviators sexually assaulted or harassed dozens of women and several men at a raucous Las Vegas conference of the aviators' Tailhook Association in 1991. Bob Packwood (b. 1932), a Republican senator from Oregon beginning in 1969, resigned from office in 1995 in the wake of multiple accusations of sexual harassment against him. Hill (b. 1956) testified during the 1991 confirmation hearings of Supreme Court justice Clarence Thomas that Thomas had sexually harassed her when she was his assistant in the early 1980s.

331.2–3 the Lynds'] Robert Staughton Lynd (1892–1970) and Helen Merrell Lynd (1896–1982), husband-and-wife sociologists.

331.13 the Comstock Lode] A large silver ore deposit in what is now Virginia City, Nevada, named after miner Henry Comstock (1820–1870); its existence was revealed in 1859, prompting a rush of prospectors and extensive mining operations.

336.5 the Snark missile] The SM-62 Snark, a ground-launched intercontinental ballistic missile deployed by the U.S. Air Force from 1958 to 1961.

343.14 the American] A California river, running from the Sierra Nevada mountains to the Sacramento River.

343.16 Antioch] A small city in Contra Costa County, California.

346.18 a piece] See "On the Last Frontier with VX and GB," *Life*, February 20, 1970.

347.22 "*Tadpole*."] A romantic comedy featuring Bebe Neuwirth and Sigourney Weaver and directed by Gary Winick, released in August 2002.

357.16 Henry Kaiser] Kaiser (1882–1967) led one of the principal firms responsible for the construction of the Hoover Dam and other major dams, and around 1939 founded another that operated the Kaiser Shipyard in Richmond, California; he was later involved in the automobile and healthcare industries.

358.12 gunite] Sprayed concrete.

359.5 Pickfair] Popular name for the Beverly Hills estate of actors Mary Pickford (1892–1979) and Douglas Fairbanks (1883–1939), which they renovated and expanded in the 1920s.

359.30 Francis Fergusson] Fergusson (1904–1986) was the author of *The Idea of a Theater* (1949).

361.30 when Pat Brown was governor] Brown (1905–1996) was California governor from 1959 to 1967.

371.3 Ripple] An inexpensive brand of fortified and carbonated wine, produced by E. & J. Gallo from 1960 to 1984.

372.17 AFDC] Aid to Families with Dependent Children, a federal welfare program begun in 1935 and replaced in 1997 by the Temporary Assistance for Needy Families program.

THE YEAR OF MAGICAL THINKING

409.32–33 an HBO documentary] *Last Letters Home: Voices of American Troops from the Battlefields of Iraq* (2004), written and directed by Bill Couturié.

411.17–18 *Up Close & Personal*] A 1996 romantic drama starring Michelle Pfeiffer and Robert Redford and directed by John Avnet, for which Didion and Dunne provided the screenplay.

413.8 *Full fathom . . . his eyes.*] See Ariel's song in *The Tempest*, I.ii.397, 399.

415.35 *Sophie's Choice*] A 1997 novel by William Styron (1925–2006).

416.7 *Mrs. Miniver*] A 1942 drama featuring Greer Garson (1904–1994) as the title character, a courageous British housewife who struggles to protect her family amid the terrors and dislocations of war.

416.21 Anthea Sylbert's] Sylbert (b. 1939) began her film career as a costume designer, receiving Academy Award nominations for *Chinatown* (1974) and *Julia* (1977), and was later a producer.

418.13 a famous 1944 study] See "Symptomatology and the Management of Acute Grief," *The American Journal of Psychiatry*, September 1944.

420.4 Christopher Dickey] Dickey (1951–2020) was the author of the memoir *Summer of Deliverance* (1998), the novels *Innocent Blood* (1997) and *The Sleeper* (2004), and several books of nonfiction reporting.

426.1–5 *and what i want* . . . Cummings] From Cummings's untitled poem beginning "Buffalo Bill's / defunct," first published in *The Dial* in January 1920.

427.21–25 Susanna Moore . . . say it."] Moore (b. 1945), the author of novels *My Old Sweetheart* (1982), *The Whiteness of Bones* (1989), *Sleeping Beauties* (1993), and *In the Cut* (1995), reads from T. S. Eliot's "East Coker," the second poem in his *Four Quartets* (1943).

428.2–3 "For a thousand . . . past"] Psalms 90:4.

428.4 "*In paradisum deducant angeli.*"] *May the angels lead you into paradise*, from the traditional Latin mass, often sung.

445.10 Otto Preminger] Didion and Dunne did uncredited work on the screenplay for Preminger's film *Such Good Friends* (1971).

445.17 Barry Farrell] Farrell (1935–1984) was Didion's fellow columnist at *Life* during the early 1970s; he also wrote for *Harper's* and *Time*.

445.21–22 Katherine Ross . . . Conrad Hall] Ross (b. 1940) appeared in *The Graduate* (1967), *Butch Cassidy and the Sundance Kid* (1969), and *The Stepford*

Wives (1975), among other films; she was married to Hall (1926–2003), a noted cinematographer, from 1969 to 1973.

445.26 Jean and Brian Moore] Jean Russell, a former Canadian TV commentator, and Brian Moore (1921–1999), a Belfast-born novelist and screenwriter, lived near Didion in Malibu.

445.37 Lee Grant's] Grant (b. around 1926) starred in the daytime drama *Peyton Place* (1965–66) and films including *Valley of the Dolls* (1967), *In the Heat of the Night* (1967), and *Shampoo* (1975).

446.16 Earl McGrath] McGrath (1931–2016) was a record company and film executive, screenwriter, and art dealer.

449.6 "a motherless child"] From the traditional spiritual "Sometimes I Feel Like a Motherless Child," performed by numerous artists beginning, possibly, with the Fisk Jubilee Singers in the 1870s.

459.13 an OAG guide] *The Official Aviation Guide of the Airways*, an airline reference series published beginning in 1929.

460.15 splits] Half bottles or glasses, usually of champagne or wine.

465.19 a Lasix] Furosemide, a diuretic.

468.7 Dorothy Draper] Draper (1889–1969), an interior decorator, pioneered elements of what has since been called the Hollywood Regency style.

468.13 Maine Chance] A health and beauty spa in Mount Vernon, Maine, established by Elizabeth Arden (1881–1966) in 1934 and closed after a fire in 1970.

468.32 D & C] Dilation and curettage, a procedure performed for a variety of medical purposes, including abortion.

469.32 *té de limón* grass] Lemongrass tea, *Cymbopogon citratus.*

470.15–16 the news of My Lai] On March 16, 1968, U.S. troops massacred over five hundred civilians in My Lai, South Vietnam. News of the massacre was first reported by Seymour Hersh (b. 1937) for the Dispatch News Service on November 12, 1969, *Life* having refused to print it.

473.29 Connie Wald's] Wald (1916–2012), the widow in 1962 of screenwriter and producer Jerry Wald, was a celebrated Hollywood hostess. "I don't think I've ever met anyone with a more developed gift for drawing people together and making them happy," Didion said of her in 2007.

476.8 Sidney Korshak's] Korshak (1907–1996), a labor lawyer who represented a variety of Chicago organized crime figures, had a legendary reputation as a Hollywood "fixer."

476.15 ruana] A type of poncho from the Andean regions of Colombia and Venezuela.

483.8 appointment-in-Samarra aspect] A sense that one cannot escape one's fate. The phrase comes from a Middle Eastern tale, variously retold, about a Baghdad merchant who flees to Samarra to avoid Death, only to find Death waiting there for him.

483.18–19 Tony Richardson's] Richardson (1928–1991) was an English theater and film director, winner of an Academy Award for *Tom Jones* (1963); he moved to Los Angeles in 1974.

487.12 Dorothy] In the film *The Wizard of Oz* (1939) and the L. Frank Baum novel *The Wonderful Wizard of Oz* (1900) on which it is based, the protagonist Dorothy is transported to the fantastic land of Oz after a cyclone touches down on the Kansas farm where she lives.

490.12–13 Donald H. ("Rummy") Rumsfeld] Rumsfeld (1932–2021) served as U.S. defense secretary from 1975 to 1977 and again from 2001 to 2006, in the second instance planning the invasion of Afghanistan in 2001 and the invasion of Iraq in 2003.

490.15–16 Lancelot L. ("Lon") Farrar, Jr.] Farrar (1932–2010) was the author of *Divide and Conquer: German Efforts to Conclude a Separate Peace* (1978) and *Arrogance and Anxiety: The Ambivalence of German Power, 1848–1914* (1981).

490.29 the Nassoons] A Princeton undergraduate a cappella group, formally established in 1941.

491.12–13 "Shine, Little Glow Worm,"] From the 1902 operetta *Lysistrata* by Paul Linke (1866–1946), subsequently adapted by many performers, including the Mills Brothers, who had a hit with the song in 1952.

492.19 Nick and Lenny's daughter Dominique] Dominique Dunne (1959–1982), an actress, the youngest child of writer and producer Dominick Dunne (1925–2009) and Ellen Griffin Dunne (1932–1997), was strangled to death by an ex-boyfriend on October 30, 1982.

493.7 Carolyn Lelyveld] Lelyveld (1940–2004) led several day care centers and established programs for children with cancer and AIDS.

495.27 *True Confessions*] Dunne's 1977 noir novel, adapted for film under the same title in 1981, with a screenplay by Dunne and Didion.

502.24 *kona* storms] Seasonal cyclones arriving from the leeward side of the Hawaiian Islands, usually the west or southwest.

514.2 Louis Farrakhan] Farrakhan (b. 1933) leads the Black nationalist Nation of Islam; he organized the October 1995 Million Man March on Washington, D.C.

515.6 USIA] The United States Information Agency, founded in 1953 to "understand, inform, and influence foreign publics" and merged in 1999 into the State Department.

515.12 I. A. Richards] Richards (1893–1979), an English literary critic who encouraged the close reading of poetry, was the author, among other works, of *The Meaning of Meaning* (1923) and *Practical Criticism* (1929).

518.23–24 daubes and albóndigas] French slow-cooked stews and Mexican meatballs.

518.26–27 *These fragments . . . ruins*] From the last verse paragraph of "The Waste Land" (1922) by T. S. Eliot (1888–1965).

520.4 "Our worst . . . called it.] Keller (1880–1968) is reported to have said, in a June 1955 interview, "self pity is our worst enemy and if we yield to it, we can never do anything wise in the world."

520.4–9 *I never saw . . . sorry for itself.*] See Lawrence's poem "Self-Pity," first collected in *Pansies* (1929).

521.6–15 "I think I am . . . cul de sacs."] See Lewis's memoir *A Grief Observed* (1961), initially published under the pseudonym N. W. Clerk.

522.31–33 Gerard Manley Hopkins . . . *mourn for.*] See Hopkins's poem "Spring and Fall," written in 1880 and first published after his death, in *Poems of Gerard Manley Hopkins* (1918).

523.6–7 *Time is the school* . . . Schwartz] From Schwartz's poem "For Rhoda," first collected in *In Dreams Begin Responsibilities* (1938) and later retitled "Calmly We Walk through This April Day."

525.37–526.2 Sherwin Nuland . . . lost campaign] From Nuland's *How We Die: Reflections on Life's Final Chapter* (1994).

554.10 "*Mon cher pamplemousse,*"] *My dear grapefruit.*

574.10–18 *Black wing . . . light-in-leaves*] From T. S. Eliot's "New Hampshire," the first section of "Words for Music," originally published in the Spring 1934 *Virginia Quarterly Review.* "Words for Music" was later retitled "Landscapes."

585.3 *page 188*] See page 517 in the present volume.

BLUE NIGHTS

592.8 stephanotis] *Stephanotis floribunda* or Madagascar jasmine, a popular flower at weddings.

592.19 Payard] An Upper East Side pâtisserie, founded by François Payard (b. 1966) in 1997.

601.14 Kenneth and Kathleen Tynan] Kenneth Tynan (1927–1980) was an iconoclastic English theater critic, and his wife Kathleen (*née* Halton, 1937–1995) a novelist and screenwriter.

602.12 *The Border*] Richardson directed Jack Nicholson, Harvey Keitel, and Valerie Perrine in *The Border*, which premiered in 1982; filming locations included Texas and Guatemala.

602.15 an HBO project] Didion and Dunne adapted Ernest Hemingway's 1927 short story "Hills Like White Elephants" for the 1990 TV movie *Women and Men: Stories of Seduction.*

602.17 a play together] *The Year of Magical Thinking*, which opened at the Booth Theatre on March 29, 2007.

603.1–2 Fiona Lewis . . . "Girls Just Want to Have Fun,"] Lewis (b. 1946) is a British actress and Asseyev (b. 1943) an American film producer and writer. Written by Robert Hazard (1948–2008) in 1979, "Girls Just Want to Have Fun" was a major pop hit for Cyndi Lauper (b. 1953) in 1983.

603.4–10 lines from W. H. Auden . . . *will go far*] From Auden's "Many Happy Returns," written in 1942.

608.35–38 a line . . . out of date."] In John Russell's 1961 translation, the line reads: "The tropics are not so much exotic as out of date" (chapter nine, "Guanabara").

609.1 had invaded Panama] The United States invaded Panama on December 20, 1989, deposing General Manuel Noriega (1934–2017), leader of its military government.

615.34–35 Angel Clare's role in *Tess of the d'Urbervilles*] Clare is the husband of the title character in Thomas Hardy's 1891 novel.

616.8 Holly's Harp] A Hollywood boutique offering ready-made and couture clothing by Holly Harp (1939–1995), opened in 1968 and closed in 1986, and the name of Harp's design label.

623.5 Morty Hall . . . Diana Lynn] Lynn (1926–1971) was a film and television actress who played many roles in the 1940s and 1950s; her husband Mortimer Hall (1924–2012) held various positions at the *New York Post*, which his family owned.

623.13 Howard and Lou Erskine] Howard Erskine (1926–2011) was a television and theatrical producer, and his wife Lou (b. Etta Lou Propst, 1921) a stage and television actress who appeared as Lucy Prentis.

625.13–15 "Let's just say . . . Evans would later write] See Evans's memoir *The Kid Stays in the Picture* (1994).

630.15 *Le Cercle Sportif*] A Saigon athletic and social club established around 1902 for the French colonial elite and later frequented by visiting Americans.

630.19 the book he had contracted to write] *Delano: The Story of the California Grape Strike*, first published in 1967.

632.25 David Webb] Webb (1925–1975) opened a Manhattan store featuring his designs in 1948; he was known especially for his enameled animal bracelets.

634.33 Sammy Glick in *What Makes Sammy Run*] The unsympathetic, backstabbing title character in Schulberg's 1941 novel rises from modest circumstances to become a leading screenwriter.

639.7 Muffet Hemingway's] Joan "Muffet" Hemingway (b. 1950), actress and eldest granddaughter of Ernest Hemingway.

640.8 *Nicholas and Alexandra*] A 1971 historical epic directed by Franklin J. Schaffner (1920–1989).

641.28–29 *A Star Is Born*] A 1976 drama starring Barbra Streisand (b. 1942) and Kris Kristofferson (b. 1936) for which Didion and Dunne wrote the screenplay, along with director Frank Pierson (1925–2012).

642.21 Katharine Graham] Graham (1917–2001) was publisher of *The Washington Post* from 1963 to 1991.

653.14 Michael Crichton] Crichton (1942–2008), the best-selling author of more than two dozen novels and director of *Westworld* (1973) and *Coma* (1978), published *Rising Sun*, a detective novel addressing the subject of Japanese–American relations, in 1992.

663.6 Pearl River] A Chinese American department store, founded in 1971 and in 1998 located on Canal Street in Chinatown.

663.7 Da Silvano] An Italian restaurant in Greenwich Village popular among celebrities, opened in 1975 and closed in 2016.

675.34 *Driving Miss Daisy*] 1989 comedy-drama in which Jessica Tandy (1909–1994) plays the title character, an increasingly infirm, wealthy widow.

682.13 the AIG bailout] In September 2008, the U.S. Treasury and the Federal Reserve extended assistance of over $180 billion to prevent the bankruptcy of this keystone insurer, considered "too big to fail."

689.24–25 *Marian Seldes*] Seldes (1928–2014) was a noted Broadway actress, a winner of a 1967 Tony Award for her performance in Edward Albee's *A Delicate Balance* (1966).

694.25 *lierre*] French: ivy.

697.10 Barney's] The luxurious nine-story flagship store, open from 1993 to 2020, of the Barneys New York department store chain, founded in 1923.

SOUTH AND WEST

708.14–20 all the kings men . . . seriously."] See Robert Penn Warren's novel *All the King's Men* (1946), which is based on the life of Louisiana governor and senator Huey P. Long (1893–1935). Mrs. C. P. Weiss Sr. was quoted in an Associated Press wire story datelined September 9, 1935.

709.6 Earl "Elbow" Reum] Reum (1931–2010) was a magician and motivational speaker for young people.

711.9 Clay Shaw, and Garrison] Shaw (1913–1974), a New Orleans businessman, was arrested by New Orleans district attorney Jim Garrison (1921–1992) on charges that he had conspired to assassinate President Kennedy; he was found not guilty in March 1969.

712.5 "Ben C.,"] Benjamin Casanas Toledano (1932–2021), an attorney who ran as a Republican in the 1970 New Orleans mayoral race and the 1972 Louisiana senate race.

712.34–35 George Washington Cable] Cable (1844–1925), author of *The Grandissimes: A Story of Creole Life* (1880) and other fiction, moved from New Orleans to Northampton, Massachusetts, in 1885, after the publication of his controversial essays "The Freedman's Case in Equity" and "The Silent South."

713.7 Willie Morris] In his 1967 memoir *North Toward Home*, Morris (1934–1999), a New York magazine editor, recalls his southern upbringing.

715.4 the romance of Evangeline] *Evangeline, a Tale of Acadie* (1847), by Henry Wadsworth Longfellow (1807–1882), dramatizes the forced expulsion by the British of ethnic French Acadians from Canada's Maritime provinces between 1755 and 1764, during the French and Indian War. Some of these Acadians settled in Louisiana, where they became "Cajuns."

718.36 *The Losers*] A 1970 thriller directed by Jack Starrett (1936–1989), in which a group of Hells Angels is sent to Cambodia by the CIA, on a rescue mission.

724.3–4 the shooting at Jackson] Two students at Jackson State College in Jackson, Mississippi, were killed by police during campus protests on May 15, 1970, and a dozen were wounded.

724.19 the Golddiggers, Bobby Goldsboro] The Golddiggers, an all-female song-and-dance troupe, was formed as part of *The Dean Martin Show* in 1968; Goldsboro (b. 1941) was known for his 1968 easy listening hit "Honey."

726.6 "Sweet Caroline."] Popular song by Neil Diamond (b. 1941), released in 1969.

731.19–20 the famous Philadelphia trials . . . deaths."] Civil rights activists James Chaney, Andrew Goodman, and Michael Schwerner were kidnapped and murdered in Philadelphia, Mississippi, in June 1964. Of the eighteen men tried in Meridian, Mississippi, for conspiracy to commit these murders, including the deputy sheriff of Neshoba County and the Imperial Wizard of the White Knights of the Ku Klux Klan, seven were convicted on October 20, 1967. An eighth, Edgar Ray Killen, was retried and found guilty in 2005.

738.2–4 Sally Kempton's . . . had known] See "Cutting Loose," *Esquire*, July 1970.

739.27 Elaine's] See note 86.5.

740.19 Bull Connor, and Birmingham Sunday] Connor (1897–1973) came to national attention in 1963 for the brutality of his response, as Birmingham's public safety commissioner, to civil rights demonstrations. On September 15,

1963, a Sunday, the 16th Street Baptist Church in Birmingham was bombed by white supremacists, killing four young girls.

745.24 MYF] Methodist Youth Fellowship.

745.27–28 "Abraham, Martin . . . Troubled Water,"] Recent popular songs, the former written by Dick Holler (b. 1934) in 1968 and soon recorded by several artists, and the latter released by Paul Simon (b. 1941) and Art Garfunkel (b. 1941) at the beginning of 1970.

750.12 Archie Manning] Manning (b. 1949) was starting quarterback at Ole Miss from 1968 to 1970 and went on, after Didion's visit, to have a celebrated career in the National Football League.

750.38 Eudora Welty] Welty (1909–2001) was an acclaimed short story writer and novelist whose recently published novel *Losing Battles* (1970) was a surprise best seller.

753.3 Marshall Bouldin] Bouldin (1923–2012) was a noted portrait artist, known for his paintings of William Faulkner and Richard Nixon's daughters.

758.10 *Baby Doll*] 1956 comedy about a feud in rural Mississippi, directed by Elia Kazan (1909–2003).

758.23 Hodding Carter III] Carter (1935–2023) reported on the civil rights movement for his father's newspaper, the *Greenville Delta Democrat-Times*, and published *The South Strikes Back* in 1959; after Didion's visit, he served as an assistant secretary of state in the administration of President Carter and worked as a television journalist.

760.12 *Porgy and Bess*] A 1935 opera by George Gershwin (1898–1937) with libretto by DuBose Heyward (1885–1940) and Ira Gershwin (1896–1983), noted for its pioneering all-Black cast.

760.15 a Zapata mustache] Mexican revolutionary Emiliano Zapata Salazar (1879–1919) is often remembered for his thick mustache with downward-curving ends.

760.23 Walker Percy's] Percy (1916–1990) wrote the novels *The Moviegoer* (1961), *The Last Gentleman* (1966), *Love in the Ruins* (1971), *Lancelot* (1977), *The Second Coming* (1980), and *The Thanatos Syndrome* (1987).

765.11 Carousel] 1945 Broadway musical with music by Richard Rodgers (1902–1979) and lyrics by Oscar Hammerstein II (1895–1960).

770.11 Maybeck houses] Bernard Maybeck (1862–1957), an architect associated with the arts and crafts movement, designed many buildings in the San Francisco Bay Area, beginning with a house for poet Charles Keeler in Berkeley in 1895.

771.8 De Liso Debs] The New York footwear firm Palter DeLiso introduced DeLiso Debs, a peep-toe slingback pump, in 1938.

773.1–3 C. Vann Woodward . . . superiority."] See "The Search for Southern Identity," *Virginia Quarterly Review*, Summer 1958.

773.6–14 Gertrude Atherton . . . Jessie Benton Frémont] A list of prominent, pioneering women of California. On Atherton (1857–1948), see Didion's footnote on page 770 of the present volume. Morgan (1872–1957) was the first licensed female architect in the state and the designer of La Cuesta Encantada, William Randolph Hearst's castle at San Simeon. Coit (1843–1929) was a patron and booster of San Francisco's volunteer firefighters; a donation from her estate enabled the construction of Coit Tower. Peixotto (1864–1941) was the first female full professor at Berkeley and led its department of social economics. Cope (1935–1976) was an heiress and real estate developer, the owner among many other properties of the Huntington Hotel on San Francisco's Nob Hill. Vietor (1927–1984) was a California philanthropist, civic leader, and socialite; in the early 1980s she served in the administration of San Francisco mayor Dianne Feinstein as deputy chief protocol officer. Phoebe Apperson Hearst (1842–1919), wife of mining magnate George Hearst, was a benefactor of the University of California and other institutions; her great-granddaughter Patricia Hearst (b. 1954) was kidnapped by members of the radical Symbionese Liberation Army in 1974 and robbed a bank with the group, her thirty-five-year prison sentence for this crime later commuted by President Carter. Frémont (1824–1902) played an unprecedented public role in the 1856 campaign of her husband, John Charles Frémont; she was the author of *A Year of American Travel: Narrative of Personal Experience* (1878) and the short story collection *The Will and the Way* (1891), among other books.

Index

This book is set in 10 point ITC Galliard, a face designed for digital composition by Matthew Carter and based on the sixteenth-century face Granjon. The paper is acid-free lightweight opaque that will not turn yellow or brittle with age. The binding is sewn, which allows the book to open easily and lie flat. The binding board is covered in Brillianta, a woven rayon cloth made by Van Heek–Scholco Textielfabrieken, Holland.

Composition by Gopa & Ted2, Inc.

Printing by Sheridan, Grand Rapids, MI.

Binding by Dekker Bookbinding, Wyoming, MI.

Designed by Bruce Campbell.